THE NEW YORK TIMES ON THE
SUPREME COURT, 1857–2008

THE NEW YORK TIMES ON THE
SUPREME COURT, 1857–2008

KENNETH JOST

CQ PRESS

A Division of SAGE

Washington, D.C.

CQ Press

2300 N Street, NW, Suite 800

Washington, DC 20037

Phone: 202-729-1900; toll-free, 1-866-4CQ-PRESS (1-866-427-7737)

Web: www.cqpress.com

Text Credits:

Pages 107–108: "John Marshall, Our 'Greatest Dissenter,'" by Edmond Cahn, originally
appeared in *The New York Times Magazine,* August 21, 1955. Copyright © 1955 by
Edmond Cahn. Reprinted by permission of the Edmond Cahn Estate.

Pages 374–375: "Miranda's Value in the Trenches," by Scott Turow, originally appeared
in *The New York Times,* op-ed page, June 28, 2000. Copyright © 2000 by Scott Turow.
Reprinted by permission of Brandt & Hochman Literary Agents, Inc.

Cover and interior design: Matthew Simmons, www.myselfincluded.com

Composition: Circle Graphics

∞ The paper used in this publication exceeds the requirements of the American National
Standard for Information Sciences—Permanence of Paper for Printed Library Materials,
ANSI Z39.48-1992.

Printed and bound in the United States of America

12   11   10   09   08   1   2   3   4   5

ISBN: 978-0-87289-922-3

OTHER TITLES FROM

TIMESREFERENCE FROM CQ PRESS

2008

The New York Times on the Presidency, 1853–2008

2009

The New York Times on Critical Elections, 1860–2008

The New York Times on Emerging Democracies, 1980–2009

2010

The New York Times on Booms and Busts, 1851–2010

CONTENTS

About TimesReference from CQ Press   ix

About the Author   xi

Preface   xiii

Prologue: The Supreme Court and
the "War on Terror"   1

PART ONE: THE SUPREME COURT AND THE FEDERAL SYSTEM

Chapter 1: The Court and Congress   7

Chapter 2: The Court and the President   51

Chapter 3: The Court and Judicial Power   103

Chapter 4: The Court and the States   129

PART TWO: THE SUPREME COURT AND THE INDIVIDUAL

Chapter 5: Freedom of Ideas   173

Chapter 6: The Rights of Political Participation   223

Chapter 7: Equal Protection of the Law   253

Chapter 8: Liberty, Property, and Due Process   295

Chapter 9: Crime and Punishment   349

Chapter 10: The Roberts Court   403

Index   435

ABOUT TimesReference FROM CQ Press

The books in the TimesReference from CQ Press series present unique documentary histories on a range of topics. The lens through which the histories are viewed is the original reporting of *The New York Times* and its many generations of legendary reporters.

Each book consists of documents selected from *The New York Times* newspaper accompanied by original narrative written by a scholar or content expert that provides context and analysis. The documents are primarily news articles, but also include editorials, op-ed essays, letters to the editor, columns, and news analyses. Some are presented full text; others, because of length, have been excerpted. Ellipses indicate omitted text. Using the headline and date as search criteria, readers can find the full text of all articles in *The Times'* online archive at nytimes.com, which includes all of *The Times'* articles since the newspaper began publication in 1851.

The Internet age has revolutionized the way news is delivered, which means that there is no longer only one version of a story. Today, breaking news articles that appear on *The Times'* Web site are written to provide up-to-the-minute coverage of events and therefore may differ from articles published in the print edition. Content could also differ between early and late editions of a day's printed paper. As such, there may be discrepancies between articles included in these volumes and versions found elsewhere.

The books are illustrated with photographs and other types of images. While most of these appeared in the print or online edition of the paper, not all were created by *The Times,* which, like many newspapers, relies on wire services for photographs. There are also images and editorial features in these books that did not appear in *The Times;* they were created or selected by CQ Press to enhance the documentary history being told. For example, in The New York Times on the Supreme Court, we added a chronology of President Franklin D. Roosevelt's Court-packing plan, as well as tables outlining the Court's decisions on such issues as school integration, abortion, and the death penalty.

Readers will note that many articles are introduced by several levels of headlines—especially in pieces from the paper's early years. This was done to emphasize the importance of the article. For very important stories, banner headlines stretch across the front page's many columns; every attempt has been made to include these with the relevant articles. Over the years, *The Times* added datelines and bylines at the beginning of articles.

Typographical and punctuation errors are the bane of every publisher's existence. Because all of the documents included in this book were re-typeset, CQ Press approached these problems in several different ways. Archaic spellings from the paper's early days appear as they did in the original documents (for example, "employe" rather than "employee"). CQ Press corrected minor typographical errors that appeared in the original articles to assist readers' comprehension. In some cases, factual or other errors have been marked [*sic*]; where the meaning would be distorted, corrections have been made in brackets where possible.

ABOUT THE AUTHOR

Kenneth Jost is the Supreme Court editor for CQ Press and an associate editor of *CQ Researcher*. He is an honors graduate of Harvard College and Georgetown University Law Center, where he teaches media law as an adjunct professor. Jost has covered legal affairs as a reporter, editor, or columnist since 1970 and has contributed to a variety of legal publications. He is the author of the *Supreme Court Yearbook* and editor of *The Supreme Court A to Z*.

PREFACE

Gun rights *versus* gun control.

Demonstrators on both sides of the gun wars gathered in front of the Supreme Court plaza on June 26, 2008, to await a historic ruling. The United States' highest court was about to define—for the first time in more than 200 years—the meaning of the Second Amendment's declaration that "the right of the people to keep and bear Arms, shall not be infringed."

Gun control advocates argued the amendment did nothing more than protect states' rights to maintain what the opening clause calls "a well regulated Militia." Gun rights advocates passionately believed the amendment guaranteed an individual right to own and possess firearms. They said many gun control laws violated the rights of law-abiding citizens to use guns for hunting, recreation, and self-defense.

The Supreme Court agreed to decide the question in a case challenging a District of Columbia law that essentially banned private ownership of handguns within the nation's capital. The nine justices heard arguments in the case in mid-March. Now, they were set to announce the decision on the final day of the 2007–2008 term.

The Court session opened at the stroke of ten o'clock. The gun ban decision was the last of three rulings announced. Speaking for a five-justice majority, Justice Antonin Scalia explained the Court's conclusion to a hushed courtroom audience: the Second Amendment protects an individual right to own and use guns in the home for self-defense. The District of Columbia law was unconstitutional because it violated that right.

In turn, Justice John Paul Stevens spoke for four dissenters, stating that the ruling misinterpreted the text and the history of the Second Amendment. He also considered it an unwise departure from judicial restraint. "This Court should stay out of this political thicket," he said.

Together, Scalia and Stevens spoke for twenty-five minutes. The justices' opinions in the case ran much longer, coming in at 154 pages total. The task of reading those opinions and explaining them to Americans fell initially to some thirty reporters who cover the Court regularly for major news organizations.

None of those reporters was more respected within journalistic circles than Linda Greenhouse, who had covered the Supreme Court for *The New York Times* for nearly thirty years. Greenhouse's 1,384-word story appeared under a banner headline: "JUSTICES, RULING 5-4, ENDORSE PERSONAL RIGHT TO OWN GUN." (See page 345.) The story was a model of legal reportage: informative but concise, carefully balanced, and free of legal jargon. The ruling, Greenhouse wrote, "appeared certain to usher in a new round of litigation over gun rights throughout the country."

The Times' coverage of the Supreme Court had not always been so thorough since the newspaper's founding in 1851. To take one example, the newspaper's story on the Court's historic Dred Scott decision on March 7, 1857, was less than completely informative. Bearing a one-column notation "IMPORTANT FROM WASHINGTON," the story accurately reported the Court's holdings that blacks could never be citizens of the United States and that Congress had no power to prohibit slavery in the unincorporated territories. The story included no discussion, however, of the potential impact of the ruling—which quickly became a flashpoint between pro- and antislavery forces and helped make the Civil War inevitable. Still, *The Times'* uncredited correspondent included the colorful detail that the courtroom audience included "gentlemen of eminent legal ability, and a due proportion of ladies." (See page 258.)

The New York Times on the Supreme Court chronicles the history and role of the Supreme Court in a unique way. It uses articles gleaned from 158 years of *New York Times* reporting as historical documents to show the ways in which the Court's decisions were reported and understood at the time the rulings were handed down.

Having covered the Supreme Court as a reporter, editor, or columnist for more than thirty years, I relished the chance to spend several months digging through *The Times'* archives. The newspaper's coverage of events and materials that had become quite familiar to me provided new information and new insights. Simply put, the stories, essays, and editorials are fascinating—sometimes surprising, occasionally amusing, and always interesting.

Like CQ Press's other Supreme Court titles—including my one-volume encyclopedia, *The Supreme Court A to Z*—this book strives for objective, nonpartisan exposition and analysis. The design follows the organization of CQ Press's comprehensive *Guide to the Supreme Court,* now in its fourth edition in the capable hands of David Savage, the longtime Supreme Court correspondent for the *Los Angeles Times.*

Part One covers the Supreme Court's role in the federal system established by the U.S. Constitution more than two centuries ago. Chapters 1 and 2 examine the Supreme Court's rulings on the powers of the legislative and executive branches of the national government. Chapter 3 explains the impact of the Court's decisions on its own power and the powers of the federal judiciary generally. Chapter 4 then turns to the Court's rulings on the role and powers of the states.

In Part Two, the focus is on the impact of the Supreme Court on the individual: how the justices' decisions on individual rights and liberties affect Americans in their day-to-day lives. Chapter 5, "Freedom of Ideas," covers the rights protected by the First Amendment: freedom of speech, freedom of the press, and freedom of religion. Chapter 6, "The Rights of Political Participation," examines rulings on the right to vote, the right to equal representation, and the rights of candidates and individuals to spend money in political campaigns.

The next two chapters turn to the Supreme Court's rulings on two important clauses of the post–Civil War Fourteenth Amendment. Chapter 7, "Equal Protection of the Law," chronicles the role the Court has (or has not) played in protecting equal rights for Americans from the days of slavery and Reconstruction through the modern civil rights era. Chapter 8, "Liberty, Property, and Due Process," examines the Court's use of the Due Process Clause to recognize individual rights in a variety of areas, including property rights, reproductive freedom, and gay rights. The gun rights decision also appears in this chapter; it remains to be seen whether—and how—the Court will use the Due Process Clause to apply the Second Amendment to state and local governments.

Chapter Nine, "Crime and Punishment," details the Supreme Court's rulings on criminal justice. It focuses on the controversial decisions of the 1960s enforcing constitutional rights for suspects and criminal defendants and the rulings in the decades since narrowing some of those decisions and going beyond them in some other instances.

Each of these chapters opens by telling the story of one important Supreme Court case that illustrates the chapter's major themes. This vignette is followed by a section entitled "Early Developments" that explains the constitutional underpinnings in the area, relates the Court's first significant rulings, and traces developments up to the beginnings of the Court's modern jurisprudence in the late nineteenth or early twentieth century. The remaining sections in each chapter cover individual topics up to the present day. Subheadings throughout each chapter help guide readers to specific topics, while case data in the margins provide readers with details of justices' votes and direct them to discussion of specific cases. Some chapters include special features to summarize events or Court rulings over time, such as a detailed chronology of the controversy over President Franklin D. Roosevelt's "Court-packing" plan (Chapter 3) or tables on major rulings on school desegregation (Chapter 7), abortion (Chapter 8), and capital punishment (Chapter 9).

Chapter 10, "The Roberts Court," gives an overview of the current Court along with biographical sketches of the justices, including Chief Justice John G. Roberts Jr., now starting his fourth term. Each biography incorporates the profile that *The Times* published when the justice's nomination was announced along with my own brief overview of the justice's career since taking the bench.

The Supreme Court's role in American life has changed dramatically since its opening session on February 1, 1790, with only three of the six justices present. The Court had few cases during its first decade. Even so, Chief Justice John Jay described the work as "intolerable." Justices spent most of their time not in the nation's capital, but "riding circuit"—traveling from place to place, hearing cases individually or as part of three-judge "circuit courts."

Today, the nine justices are in session in Washington, D.C., for nine months every year: from the first Monday in October until, typically, the last week in June. Each year, the Court receives more than 8,000 petitions for certiorari, the legal term for review of a lower court decision. From those petitions, the justices in recent years have been selecting around seventy cases to hear and decide. The work is demanding, but—aided by law clerks and computerized legal research resources—none of the current justices has described it as intolerable.

The Court's early decisions helped define the powers of the three branches of the national government—legislative, executive, and judicial—and the powers of the national government vis-à-vis the states. In many ways, however, the Court's rulings had only limited impact on most people's lives. One reason was an 1833 decision that the Bill of Rights applied only to the federal government, not to the states.

Today, the Court's decisions profoundly affect each and every American in myriad ways, large and small. The Court's influence has grown because of its role in interpreting the vast expansion of federal legislation and its decisions enforcing almost all of the provisions of the Bill of Rights against the states. As a result, the Court now defines free speech rights for high school students and shapes rules for equal treatment in the workplace. The Court has given parents the right to control their children's schooling, women a qualified right to choose to have an abortion, and critically ill or injured patients the right to refuse life-sustaining treatment. The Court has required states to draw legislative districts equally and to follow elaborate procedures in imposing the death penalty. In 2000 the Court even helped decide a closely contested presidential election.

The New York Times has also changed dramatically since its founding on September 18, 1851. The narrow columns, small type, and stilted language of the nineteenth century have been replaced in the twenty-first century with wider columns, bigger type, and more accessible writing—not to mention color photographs.

Through the nineteenth century, *The Times* was one of many New York newspapers, although not one of the more profitable or influential. The newspaper has grown in size and stature since its acquisition by Adolph Ochs in 1896. Under the continuing control of members of the Ochs-Sulzberger family, it has grown into a nationally and internationally recognized newspaper of record with, as Ochs's slogan continues to promise, "All the news that's fit to print."

The Times' coverage of the Supreme Court has also profoundly changed, as illustrated by some of the articles reprinted here. Many of the articles from the nineteenth and early twentieth centuries fall short in explaining the legal reasoning of a decision or the background of the case. *The Times* devoted only two paragraphs to the now infamous 1896 decision in *Plessy v. Ferguson* upholding legally mandated racial segregation—and misspelled Plessy's name besides. (See page 263.) Today, *The Times* devotes much more space to Supreme Court coverage, and stories on individual decisions provide much greater detail as to legal procedure and reasoning and their likely impact. It is difficult to imagine any of the newspaper's recent Supreme Court correspondents giving such slight attention to a landmark decision as *Plessy* received.

The Times' editorial positions have also changed. In the 1880s the newspaper applauded the Supreme Court decisions limiting the federal government's role in enforcing civil rights for African Americans. In 1916 the *Times* opposed the confirmation of Justice Louis D. Brandeis, saying that his "radical" views qualified him for legislative but not judicial service. Today, *The Times* vigorously supports civil rights not only for African Americans and other racial and ethnic minorities, but also for women, gays, and other historically disadvantaged groups. The newspaper opposed as too conservative the confirmation of, among others, three members of the current Court: Chief Justice Roberts and Associate Justices Clarence Thomas and Samuel A. Alito Jr.

For me, reading or re-reading *The Times'* coverage from the past five decades has been a personal journey of sorts. As a teenager, I developed what proved to be a lasting interest in law and journalism from reading Anthony Lewis's marvelous book *Gideon's Trumpet,* the account of the Supreme Court decision that guaranteed indigent criminal defendants the right to an appointed attorney. Lewis covered the Court for *The Times* for six years and won a Pulitzer Prize in 1963 for his reporting.

Lewis, who went on to be a *Times* columnist for more than three decades, can rightly be credited with setting the newspaper on a path to consistently distinguished reporting on the Court. Readers will find in the following pages Lewis's stories on such decisions as *Gideon v. Wainwright* (1963) and the landmark libel law ruling *New York Times Co. v. Sullivan* (1964).

Three reporters still living and working today have helped continue the tradition Lewis established: Fred P. Graham, Linda Greenhouse, and Stuart Taylor Jr. (Warren Weaver Jr., who covered the Court in the mid-1970s, died in 1989.) Graham succeeded Lewis and reported on the Court until 1972, when he joined CBS News; he is now senior editor for truTV (formerly CourtTV). Greenhouse succeeded Weaver in 1978 and covered the Court until her retirement in July 2008, except for a maternity leave in the mid-1980s. Taylor had the beat during Greenhouse's absence; he went on to become a senior writer with *American Lawyer* and is currently a senior writer for *National Journal* and a contributing editor for *Newsweek.*

Many readers will be curious about the qualifications these reporters brought to the Supreme Court beat. Graham and Taylor both graduated from law school and practiced law before joining *The Times*. Lewis and Greenhouse studied law during one-year sabbaticals from the newspaper—Lewis as a Nieman fellow at Harvard University, Greenhouse in a master of law program for journalists at Yale Law School.

My coverage of the Supreme Court began while working the local and state court beat at the *Tennessean* in my hometown of Nashville in the 1970s. In the 1980s, I was editor of the *Los Angeles Daily Journal,* a legal affairs newspaper. For the past twenty years, I have been writing about the Court and legal affairs generally for Congressional Quarterly and for CQ Press, now a division of SAGE. I earned a law degree from Georgetown University Law Center while taking a break from journalism to work on Capitol Hill for then-Rep. Al Gore.

Throughout my career, *The Times'* coverage of the Supreme Court has been indispensable to my understanding of the high court's decisions and procedures. I am glad to be able to count Graham, Greenhouse, and Taylor as friends and colleagues; and I was pleased to meet Lewis in person for the first time while writing this book. My thanks to each of them and to the many other distinguished *Times* journalists for their fine work represented in the following pages.

At CQ Press, my thanks to president John A. Jenkins, an accomplished writer and author on the Supreme Court himself, for nominating me for this undertaking; to Andrea Pedolsky, for superintending the project; and to Doug Goldenberg-Hart, for helping shape it. Thanks also to development editor Andrew Boney and manuscript editor Jennifer Campi for attentive and insightful editing. Very special thanks also go to Mike Kotlarczyk, Jim Harper, and Jeremy McLaughlin, research interns who mined *The Times'* archives for the most informative and insightful stories and editorials while completing their final year of law school at Georgetown. I wish the very best to each of them in their careers as members of the bar.

On a strictly personal note, let me dedicate this book to two exceptional children, Nicole Jost and Andrew (AJ) Jost. My hope for them—and for all Americans—is that they live to see made more nearly real the promise carved in granite above the entrance to the Supreme Court building: "Equal Justice Under Law."

Kenneth Jost
October 2008

THE SUPREME COURT AND THE "WAR ON TERROR"

PROLOGUE

Within a month after the September 11, 2001, attacks on the United States, U.S. intelligence agents gave the government of Bosnia evidence of a suspected "sleeper cell" of the terrorist organization al Qaeda. Evidence against six native Algerians, including intercepted telephone calls between one of them and an al Qaeda operative in Afghanistan, suggested that they might have been plotting an attack on the U.S. embassy in Sarajevo.

Bosnian authorities arrested the men, all Muslims. But after a three-month investigation by Bosnian police, aided by FBI agents and U.S. embassy security personnel, Bosnia's supreme court ordered the men released for lack of evidence. Instead of freeing the men, however, Bosnian authorities turned them over early on the morning of January 18, 2002, to U.S. military police to be flown more than 5,000 miles away to a U.S. prison at the Guantánamo Bay Naval Base in Cuba.

The six men were among hundreds of suspected "enemy combatants" captured in the post-9/11 war in Afghanistan or rounded up in other countries and taken over time to the U.S. naval base under an executive order signed by President George W. Bush on November 13, 2001. Bush's legal advisers had concluded that Guantánamo, more than 500 miles from the nearest U.S. landfall, could be used to detain the suspected terrorists outside the jurisdiction of any U.S. courts.

Bush's advisers were wrong. Two-and-a-half years after the first of the suspected terrorists arrived at Guantánamo, the Supreme Court ruled in June 2004 that federal courts had the power to determine whether they were being held legally. The administration responded by getting Congress to pass a law giving the detainees truncated hearings before special military tribunals or "commissions." In June 2006, however, the Supreme Court ruled that the military commissions did not satisfy standards required by the Uniform Code of Military Justice or the Geneva Conventions, the international treaties governing the treatment of wartime captives.

The Supreme Court's rulings cheered human rights advocates in the United States and abroad, who viewed the administration's policies as violations of constitutional rights as well as international law. The administration and its conservative supporters countered that the Court was intruding on the president's powers as commander in chief and giving enemy captives legal protections unprecedented in time of war.

The administration was surprised by the Court's rulings, but perhaps it should not have been. Back in the 1800s, the French visitor Alexis de Tocqueville wrote that there is no significant political dispute in America that does not sooner or later end up in American courts. In fact, the Supreme Court had closely examined presidential actions in previous conflicts—from Abraham Lincoln's suspension of habeas corpus in the Civil War to Franklin D. Roosevelt's internment of Japanese Americans during World War II. In the late twentieth century, the Court had become more attentive to protecting individual liberties and more jealous of its own role in policing the separation of powers between the legislative, executive, and judicial branches of the national government. (See Part One, "The Supreme Court and the Federal System"; Part Two, "The Supreme Court and the Individual.")

For the president, Congress, and the Court alike, the post-9/11 "war on terror" posed a multitude of new and difficult challenges. At home, Americans shaken by the fearful images of hijacked aircraft toppling the World Trade Center towers and crashing into the Pentagon demanded fail-safe protections against future terrorist attacks. But they also worried about living in a surveillance state with diminished individual freedoms. Abroad, the United States worked to enlist support for a war against extremist Islamic groups. But the government also strove to give reassurances of friendship to the world's Muslims and the governments of Muslim-populated countries.

Legally, the government faced vexing difficulties on how to handle the hundreds of people captured in a war fought by an enemy that owed no allegiance to any state, respected no national border, and had no timetable for victory or surrender. The Geneva Conventions limit interrogation of prisoners of war, but the United States desperately wanted intelligence about al Qaeda's operations, its plans, even the whereabouts of the group's leader, Osama bin Laden. Al Qaeda had not signed the Geneva Conventions and its members did not fight openly and in uniform as the laws of war require. Yet the treaties included provisions—in so-called Common Article 3—setting minimum standards for treatment of any combatants captured in unconventional wars as well.

Bush maintained that his constitutional status as commander in chief gave him broad discretion on these questions. He claimed the power to detain U.S. citizens as enemy combatants, holding them largely incommunicado, for an indefinite period and to try them in military tribunals instead of civilian courts. He claimed the power to hold foreigners as enemy combatants outside U.S. borders similarly for indefinite periods and with limited access to visitors, lawyers, or international representatives. He claimed the power to do all this with only limited oversight by federal courts.

One by one, legal challenges filed by detainees reached the Supreme Court; and in case after case, the Court rejected the administration's policies. In 2004 the Court ruled that Yaser Hamdi, a U.S. citizen held since he was turned over to U.S. forces in November 2001 by the pro-American Northern Front in Afghanistan, was entitled to some hearing before a "neutral decisionmaker." "We have long since made clear that a state of war is not a blank check for the President when it comes to the rights of the Nation's citizens," Justice Sandra Day O'Connor wrote in the main opinion in *Hamdi v. Rumsfeld.*

On the same day, the Court held, 6-3, that the Guantánamo detainees could go to federal courts with petitions for a writ of habeas corpus—the centuries-old procedure for prisoners to ask courts to rule on the legality of their incarceration. "Application of the habeas statute to persons detained at the base is consistent with the historical reach of the writ of habeas corpus," Justice John Paul Stevens wrote in *Rasul v. Bush* (2004).

In passing the Detainee Treatment Act a year later, Congress tried to cut off habeas corpus petitions by the Guantánamo detainees while providing hearings before military tribunals to determine their status as enemy combatants. The Court considered both aspects of the law in a case brought by Salim Ahmed Hamdan, a Yemeni Muslim who had served for more than four years as bin Laden's bodyguard and driver.

The Court's 5-3 decision in *Hamdan v. Rumsfeld* (2006) ruled Congress had not eliminated jurisdiction over pending habeas corpus cases, only future petitions. For the majority, Stevens also found the hearing procedures before the military tribunals inadequate, saying they departed without reason from the more formal requirements of regular courts-martial set out in the Uniform Code of Military Justice as passed by Congress.

Congress and Bush responded only a few months later by passing and signing into law the Military Commissions Act of 2006, which more explicitly barred federal courts from hearing any habeas corpus petitions by Guantánamo detainees. The act provided instead that detainees could challenge their detention before military panels—called Combatant Status Review Tribunals—with limited review of the proceedings by the U.S. Court of Appeals for the District of Columbia Circuit.

The Supreme Court agreed to rule on the constitutionality of the new law after the D.C. Circuit upheld it in a split decision in February 2007. The appeals court had ruled in two consolidated appeals by Guantánamo detainees: *Boumediene v. Bush*, brought on behalf of the Algerians arrested in Bosnia, and *Al Odah v. United States*, brought on behalf of groups of Kuwaiti and Yemeni nationals. The majority on the three-judge panel agreed with the government that aliens held at Guantánamo, outside U.S. territory, had no right to challenge their detention through habeas corpus.

The Court that heard arguments in the case in early December 2007 was—as it had been for years—closely divided along ideological lines. Chief Justice John G. Roberts Jr., appointed by Bush two years earlier, had assumed leadership of a conservative bloc that also included veteran justices Antonin Scalia and Clarence Thomas and a second Bush appointee, Samuel A. Alito Jr. Four justices typically took liberal positions in the Court's most contentious issues: Stevens, David H. Souter, Ruth Bader Ginsburg, and Stephen G. Breyer. In many cases, the pivotal vote belonged to Justice Anthony M. Kennedy, a moderate conservative nominated by President Ronald Reagan in 1987. (See Chapter 10, "The Roberts Court.")

Six months after the arguments, the Court ruled the new law unconstitutional in a dramatic 5-4 decision. "We hold that petitioners may invoke the fundamental procedural protections of habeas corpus," Kennedy wrote for himself and the four liberal justices in *Boumediene v. Bush* (2008).

Habeas corpus applied because the United States exercised de facto sovereignty over Guantánamo, Kennedy wrote in the June 12 ruling. But the procedures under the Military Commissions Act were not an adequate substitute for habeas corpus, he continued, because the law gave detainees no right to bring new evidence into court to challenge the military tribunals' rulings.

In the first of two dissenting opinions for the four conservatives, Roberts said that the majority had found inadequate "the most generous set of procedural protections ever afforded aliens detained by this country as enemy combatants." Scalia was blunter in a dissent that was also joined by the other three conservatives. The Court's ruling would have "disastrous consequences," Scalia argued, by making it harder for the military to detain suspected enemy combatants. "The Nation will live to regret what the Court has done today," he concluded.

In her account in *The New York Times*, the Pulitzer Prize-winning Supreme Court correspondent Linda Greenhouse wrote that the ruling "left some important questions unanswered." She forecast "months or years of continued litigation" ahead.

JUNE 13, 2008
JUSTICES, 5-4, BACK DETAINEE APPEALS FOR GUANTÁNAMO

By LINDA GREENHOUSE

WASHINGTON—The Supreme Court on Thursday delivered its third consecutive rebuff to the Bush administration's handling of the detainees at Guantánamo Bay, ruling 5 to 4 that the prisoners there have a constitutional right to go to federal court to challenge their continued detention.

The court declared unconstitutional a provision of the Military Commissions Act of 2006 that, at the administration's behest, stripped the federal courts of jurisdiction to hear habeas corpus petitions from the detainees seeking to challenge their designation as enemy combatants.

Writing for the majority, Justice Anthony M. Kennedy said the truncated review procedure provided by a previous law, the Detainee Treatment Act of 2005, "falls short of being a constitutionally adequate substitute" because it failed to offer "the fundamental procedural protections of habeas corpus."

Justice Kennedy declared: "The laws and Constitution are designed to survive, and remain in force, in extraordinary times."

The decision left some important questions unanswered. These include "the extent of the showing required of the government" at a habeas corpus hearing in order to justify a prisoner's continued detention, as Justice Kennedy put it, as well as the handling of classified evidence and the degree of due process to which the detainees are entitled.

Months or years of continued litigation may lie ahead, unless the Bush administration, or the administration that follows it, reverses course and closes the prison at Guantánamo Bay, which now holds 270 detainees. . . .

There are some 200 habeas corpus petitions awaiting action in the District Court, including those filed by the

37 detainees whose appeals were before the Supreme Court in the case decided on Thursday, Boumediene v. Bush, No. 06-1195.

Despite the open questions, the decision, which was joined by Justices John Paul Stevens, David H. Souter, Ruth Bader Ginsburg, and Stephen G. Breyer, was categorical in its rejection of the administration's basic arguments. Indeed, the court repudiated the fundamental legal basis for the administration's strategy, adopted in the immediate aftermath of the attacks of Sept. 11, 2001, of housing prisoners captured in Afghanistan and elsewhere at the United States naval base in Cuba, where Justice Department lawyers advised the White House that domestic law would never reach.

In a concurring opinion on Thursday, Justice Souter said the ruling was "no bolt out of the blue," but rather should have been anticipated by anyone who read the court's decision in Rasul v. Bush in 2004. That decision, part of the initial round of Supreme Court review of the administration's Guantánamo policies, held that because the long-term lease with Cuba gave the United States unilateral control over the property, the base came within the statutory jurisdiction of the federal courts to hear habeas corpus petitions.

Congress responded the next year, in the Detainee Treatment Act, by amending the statute to remove jurisdiction, and it did so again in the Military Commissions Act to make clear that it wanted the removal to apply to cases already in the pipeline. The decision on Thursday went beyond the statutory issue to decide, for the first time, the underlying constitutional question.

President Bush, appearing with Prime Minister Silvio Berlusconi of Italy at a news conference in Rome, said he was unhappy with the decision. "We'll abide by the court's decision—that doesn't mean I have to agree with it," the president said, adding that "it was a deeply divided court, and I strongly agree with those who dissented."

The dissenting opinions, one by Chief Justice John G. Roberts Jr. and the other by Justice Scalia, were vigorous. Each signed the other's, and the other two dissenters, Justices Clarence Thomas and Samuel A. Alito Jr., signed both.

Of the two dissenting opinions, Justice Antonin Scalia's was the more apocalyptic, predicting "devastating" and "disastrous consequences" from the decision. "It will almost certainly cause more Americans to be killed," he said. "The nation will live to regret what the court has done today." He said the decision was based not on principle, "but rather an inflated notion of judicial supremacy."

Chief Justice Roberts, in somewhat milder tones, said the decision represented "overreaching" that was "particularly egregious" and left the court open to "charges of judicial activism." The decision, he said, "is not really about the detainees at all, but about control of federal policy regarding enemy combatants." The public will "lose a bit more control over the conduct of this nation's foreign policy to unelected, politically unaccountable judges," he added. . . .

Mr. Bush, in his statement in Rome, said the administration would decide whether to ask Congress to weigh in once more. Success at such an effort would appear unlikely, given that the Supreme Court decision was praised not only by the Democratic leadership, but also by the ranking Republican on the Senate Judiciary Committee, Arlen Specter of Pennsylvania. Senator Specter had voted for the jurisdiction-stripping measure, but then filed a brief at the court arguing that the law was unconstitutional. . . .

Steven Lee Myers contributed reporting from Rome.

• • • • • • • • • • • •

The ruling did spur prompt action by the two federal district court judges in Washington overseeing the habeas cases. In a hearing on July 8, just twenty-six days after the decision, Judge Thomas F. Hogan told government attorneys and the more than 120 lawyers representing detainees in the bulk of the cases that he would do all he could to speed decisions in the cases. Two days later, Judge Richard Leon signaled the same approach for the twelve cases before him. These cases, Leon said, "will be resolved this year."

PART ONE
THE SUPREME COURT AND THE FEDERAL SYSTEM

THE COURT AND CONGRESS

CHAPTER 1

President Franklin D. Roosevelt entered office in March 1933 with the country in the midst of the Great Depression. He took his decisive electoral victory as a mandate for bold action to kick-start the nation's economy and lift its spirits. A solidly Democratic Congress obliged him, passing a host of economic relief measures in FDR's first one hundred days.

The Supreme Court that Roosevelt inherited, however, included a majority of justices with strongly held legal views against the use of congressional power over the national economy. As legal challenges reached the justices, the Court struck down major parts of FDR's New Deal program one by one on grounds that the measures went beyond Congress's constitutional powers.

In the worst single day for Roosevelt at the Court, the justices dealt the popular president three blows on May 27, 1935—so-called Black Monday. Unanimously, the Court struck down two laws passed by Congress: the National Industrial Recovery Act, the centerpiece of FDR's economic recovery program, and a mortgage relief measure for farmers. The justices also barred Roosevelt from removing members of independent regulatory agencies, such as the Federal Trade Commission.

Roosevelt publicly denounced the rulings and—after his landslide re-election in 1936—proposed a plan to add as many as six new members to the Court, ostensibly to help the aging justices do their work. Roosevelt had to withdraw his "Court-packing"

THE GALLOPING SNAIL

The Granger Collection, New York

President Franklin D. Roosevelt is shown in this March 1933 cartoon urging a slow Congress to pass his New Deal programs in his first 100 days in office. The measures, enacted to address the nation's economic crisis, faced an uphill battle with the Supreme Court. The Court ruled a number of the laws unconstitutional, illustrating its fundamental role as a check against congressional power.

plan in the face of strong criticism that he was undermining the independence of the judiciary. Nevertheless, the Court almost simultaneously began taking a broader view of Congress's powers—a view more in line with the president's—in a great ideological shift sometimes called the Revolution of 1937. Over the next few years, the Court consistently upheld New Deal legislation, discarding virtually all of previous eras' legal doctrines limiting Congress's powers over economic affairs.

Roosevelt's battle with the Supreme Court underscores the Court's great power to sit in judgment over the political branches of the federal government: Congress (legislative branch) and the president (executive branch). To rewrite the common constitutional aphorism, the president and Congress propose, but the justices dispose. Yet the justices do not exercise that power in a political vacuum. Over time, the president can reshape the Court—subject to Senate confirmation—as vacancies arise. Even in the short term, the justices are more mindful of changes in political thinking and public attitudes than textbooks sometimes suggest.

The Court's power over Congress stems in part from the unexceptional role of interpreting the laws that Congress passes—applying sometimes ambiguous statutes to specific circumstances. Ever since 1803 the Court has also claimed the power to invalidate laws passed by Congress as unconstitutional. That power is nowhere specified in the Constitution, but two centuries later it is all but universally accepted as essential to the constitutional system.

The Court exercised the power only twice before the Civil War, far more often since. By one count, the Court had declared at least 163 acts of Congress unconstitutional in whole or in part through 2008. Congress finds no safe harbor from any legal ideology: the liberal Warren Court struck down twenty-one laws passed by Congress, the conservative Burger and Rehnquist courts more than thirty each.

Broadly speaking, the Court since the mid-twentieth century has been inclined to uphold Congress's powers over economic affairs and to look more closely at laws that may infringe on individual rights protected by the Bill of Rights or intrude on the prerogatives of the president, the courts, or the states. Some laws ruled unconstitutional were controversial, such as the campaign spending limits in the post-Watergate Federal Election Campaign Act Amendments of 1974 that were struck down as violating the First Amendment. Other measures, however, were passed with overwhelming support in Congress, like the 1990 Gun-Free School Zones Act, which the Rehnquist Court struck down as going beyond Congress's power to regulate interstate commerce.

The early indications from the Roberts Court were somewhat favorable for Congress. In its first two terms, the Roberts Court never explicitly invalidated a congressional statute as unconstitutional, although Chief Justice John G. Roberts Jr. led a 5-4 decision in 2007 that, on constitutional grounds, substantially narrowed a major campaign finance law passed by Congress five years earlier. In 2008, however, the Court struck down two congressional enactments, both by 5-4 votes. A predominantly liberal majority in *Boumediene v. Bush* ruled unconstitutional provisions of the Military Commissions Act of 2006 that sought to deny suspected enemy combatants held at Guantánamo Bay, Cuba, the right to use habeas corpus to challenge their detentions. Two weeks later, a predominantly conservative majority in *Davis v. Federal Election Commission* ruled unconstitutional a provision of the 2002 campaign finance law aimed at leveling the playing field for congressional candidates facing wealthy opponents who financed their campaigns from their own pockets.

EARLY DEVELOPMENTS

The Constitution opens in Article I by vesting in Congress "all legislative Powers herein granted" and follows in section 8 with a laundry list of "enumerated powers." Among the most important are the powers "to lay and collect Taxes," "regulate Commerce with foreign Nations, and among the several States," "declare War," and maintain and provide the rules and regulations for an army and navy. The section concludes by additionally authorizing Congress "to make all Laws which shall be necessary and proper" to carry out those powers "and all other Powers" vested in the national government.

The Marshall Court

Under Chief Justice John Marshall, the Supreme Court played a vital role in breathing life into these provisions to Congress's benefit. In one of his most important opinions, *McCulloch v. Maryland* (1819), Marshall upheld the decision by Congress to charter the private Bank of the United States by interpreting the Necessary and Proper Clause as giving Congress broad discretion to perform its "high duties." As Marshall wrote:

Let the end be legitimate, let it be within the scope of the Constitution, and all means which are appropriate, which are plainly adapted to that end, which are not prohibited, but consist with the letter and spirit of the Constitution, are constitutional.

Five years later, Marshall again supported a broad conception of congressional authority in a decision, *Gibbons v. Ogden* (1824), supporting a federally granted charter to operate a steamboat between New Jersey and New York against a monopoly granted to another steamboat operator by the state of New York. Congress's power to regulate commerce encompassed navigation, Marshall reasoned, and took precedence over any conflicting state law. "In every such case," he concluded, "the act of Congress . . . is supreme; and the law of the state . . . must yield to it."

Despite this backing of congressional legislation, Marshall earlier had laid the groundwork for the Supreme Court's authority to declare acts of Congress void as contrary to the Constitution. The law at issue in *Marbury v. Madison* (1803)—the Judiciary Act of 1789—purported to give the Court original jurisdiction in any proper case to issue a writ of mandamus, a judicial order directing an official to perform a ministerial duty. But the Constitution provides that, with a few specific exceptions, the Supreme Court exercises appellate jurisdiction only. "If a law be in opposition to the constitution . . . ," Marshall explained, "the court must determine which of these conflicting rules governs the case. This is of the very essence of judicial duty." (For more background, see page 106.)

The Court exercised its power to invalidate an act of Congress only one more time before the Civil War, in the infamous case of *Scott v. Sandford* (1857). The case called on the Court to rule on the legal status of Dred Scott, who claimed emancipation from slavery after being taken from the slave state of Missouri to the free state of Illinois and to the Wisconsin Territory. The Missouri Compromise, passed by Congress in 1820, barred slavery in the territories. Congress had repealed that law in the Kansas-Nebraska Act of 1854, but the Court reached out to rule on the constitutionality of the former law anyway. Taking a narrow view of Congress's authority over the territories, Chief Justice Roger B. Taney declared the Missouri Compromise unconstitutional. (For more background, see page 257.)

"SELF-INFLICTED WOUNDS"

In a law school lecture in 1928, the future chief justice Charles Evans Hughes famously described the Dred Scott decision as one of the Court's three "self-inflicted wounds." The ruling's main holding—that African Americans have no rights under the Constitution—was overturned by the post–Civil War Fourteenth Amendment. And the Court in subsequent decisions upheld Congress's power to make laws regulating territories, though subject to constitutional restrictions such as the right to jury trial.

The other two decisions on Hughes's list also came in constitutional challenges to acts of Congress. In the first, *Hepburn v. Griswold* (1870), the Court found no constitutional basis for the Legal Tender Act of 1862, which allowed the Union government to issue paper money—"greenbacks"—not tied to gold or silver in order to finance the Civil War. In the other, the Court in *Pollock v. Farmers' Loan & Trust Co.* (1895) struck down a federal income tax that Congress had passed the year before as part of a trade law, the Wilson-Gorman Tariff Act. Like the Dred Scott decision, both rulings have been overturned—the first by the Court itself and the second by constitutional amendment.

Congress passed the first Legal Tender Act in February 1862, early in the Civil War. The Constitution gives Congress the power "to coin money" and regulate its

---

McCulloch v. Maryland

Decided: March 6, 1819

Vote: 6 (J. Marshall, Washington, W. Johnson, Livingston, Duvall, Story)

0

Opinion of the Court: J. Marshall

Did not participate: Todd

Pollock v. Farmers' Loan & Trust Co. (II) (Income Tax Cases)

Decided: May 20, 1895

Vote: 5 (Fuller, Field, Gray, Brewer, Shiras)

4 (Harlan I, Brown, H. Jackson, E. White)

Opinion of the Court: Fuller

Dissenting opinions (4): Harlan I; Brown; H. Jackson; E. White

value, but makes no mention of printing currency. In *Hepburn*, a creditor refused to accept paper money as payment for a debt contracted before passage of the act. In defending the act, the government argued that the wartime law was a "necessary and proper" exercise of Congress's powers to declare war, regulate commerce, and borrow money.

In a 4-3 opinion, Chief Justice Salmon P. Chase disagreed. The issuance of paper money, he said, was not "an appropriate and plainly adapted means" for executing Congress's war-making powers. Without an express power as authority, a law impairing the obligation of contracts was "inconsistent with the spirit of the Constitution," he said.

The decision, announced on February 7, 1870, stopped short of holding the legal tender laws unconstitutional. By limiting their application to post-enactment debts, however, the rulings threatened financial chaos. But on the very same day, President Ulysses S. Grant sent the Senate nominees for two vacancies on the Court: William Strong and Joseph P. Bradley. The two newly confirmed justices joined in an announcement on April 1 that the Court would hear two other pending legal tender cases and reconsider the *Hepburn* decision.

A year later, the Court reversed itself in a 5-4 decision in the two cases *Knox v. Lee* and *Parker v. Davis*, known collectively as the *Second Legal Tender Cases* (1871). Writing for the majority, Strong said that on the crucial question of Congress's authority to pass the legal tender laws, the Constitution required the Court to defer. "The degree of the necessity for any congressional enactment, or the relative degree of its appropriateness," Strong wrote, "is for consideration in Congress, not here." Six decades later, the Court cited the ruling in the *Gold Clause Cases* (1933) in upholding the government's decision to allow repayment of private bonds in paper currency instead of gold.

MAY 2, 1871
CONSTITUTIONALITY OF THE LEGAL-TENDER ACTS AFFIRMED— IMPORTANT DECISION GIVEN YESTERDAY.

WASHINGTON, D.C., May 1.—There was a large number of the members of the Bar present at the Supreme Court Chambers today, including Solicitor-General Bristow and Senators Trumbull and Cole, as it was known the Court would announce many opinions prepared during the week's recess, previous to adjourning until 16th of October next. All the Judges were on the Bench, with the exception of Mr. Justice Nelson, who is absent from the city. The Chief Justice retired at about 2 o'clock. None of the opinions were announced by him. At 3 o'clock Mr. Justice Clifford read a brief paper in the legal-tender cases of Knox *vs.* Lee and Parker *vs.* Davis, as follows:

In these two cases two questions were heretofore directed to be argued, namely: First—Is the act of Congress known as the Legal-tender act constitutional as to contracts made before its passage?

Second—Is it valid as applicable to transactions since its passage? These questions have been considered by the Court, and both have been decided in the affirmative. The decree of the Supreme Judicial Court of Massachusetts in the case of Parker *vs.* Davis is therefore affirmed, and the judgment of the Circuit Court of the United States of the Western District of Texas is also affirmed. The Chief-Justice, with Associate Justices Nelson, Clifford and Field, dissent from the majority of the Court upon both propositions and the result, holding that the act of Congress, so far as applicable to contracts made before the passage, is repugnant to the Constitution and void, and also that it is repugnant to the Constitution and void, so far as applicable to contracts made since its passage. The opinion of the Court, and the reasons for dissent will be read before the close of the adjourned term. . . .

. . . .

The income tax case that Hughes counted among the Court's "self-inflicted wounds" arose after Congress in 1894 acceded to demands from Populists and other reformers to pass the nation's first peacetime general tax on incomes. The measure imposed a 2 percent levy on all corporate and individual income, with a $4,000 exemption for individuals. Charles Pollock, a stockholder in Farmers' Loan & Trust Company, challenged the act in a suit seeking to block the bank from paying the levy. He contended that it violated the constitutional ban on "direct" taxes unless apportioned on the basis of population (Art. I, sec. 9, cl. 4). In addition, he argued that because of the exemption the act violated the requirement that all taxes be "uniform throughout the United States" (Art. I, sec. 8, cl. 1).

In prior decisions, the Court had defined "direct" taxes narrowly to encompass only head taxes and taxes on land (1796) and had upheld a Civil War–era income tax as an indirect levy (1881). But in *Pollock v. Farmers' Loan & Trust Co.* (1895), a pair of decisions bearing the same name and written by Chief Justice Melville W. Fuller, the Court swept aside those precedents in ruling the income tax unconstitutional. In the first of the cases—heard by only eight justices because Justice Howell E. Jackson was ill—the Court ruled on April 8, 1895, that the tax on income from land was equivalent to a tax on land itself and therefore unconstitutional.

The justices divided evenly on the other issues and granted Pollock's request for reargument—before a full bench. Only six weeks later, the Court issued a 5-4 decision holding the entire income tax unconstitutional. Fuller reaffirmed that a tax on rental income amounted to a prohibited direct tax on land and went on to say that a tax on the income from personal property was likewise a prohibited direct tax.

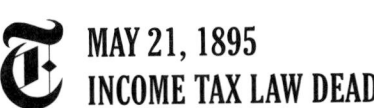

MAY 21, 1895
INCOME TAX LAW DEAD

The Supreme Court Holds It Unconstitutional.

A DIVIDED COURT AGAIN

This Time the Majority Stands Against the Law.

FOUR JUSTICES FILE THEIR PROTEST

Justice Jackson Upholds the Law, but Justice Shiras's Views Have Undergone a Change.

EFFECT ON THE FUTURE REVENUES

The Authorities Take Prompt Measures to Refund the Tax Already Collected.

WASHINGTON, May 20.—"We adhere to the opinion already announced that taxes on real estate, being indisputably direct taxes, taxes on the rents or incomes of real estate are equally direct taxes.

"We are of opinion that taxes on personal property or on the income of personal property are likewise direct taxes.

"The tax imposed by sections 27 to 37, inclusive, of the act of 1894, so far as it falls on the income of real and of personal property, being a direct tax within the meaning of the Constitution, and therefore unconstitutional and void because not apportioned according to representation, all those sections constituting one entire scheme of taxation are necessarily invalid.

"The decrees hereinbefore entered in this court will be vacated; the decrees below will be reversed, and the cases remanded with instructions to grant the relief prayed."

Thus reads the death sentence of the income tax law, pronounced this afternoon by the United States Supreme Court. It came at the close of a carefully prepared opinion by Chief Justice Fuller. Every vestige of the law is effaced from the statutes by this decision.

The law was declared to be unconstitutional by the votes of Chief Justice Fuller and Justices Field, Gray, Brewer, and Shiras. The opposite view was taken by Justices Harlan, Brown, Jackson, and White. The vote of Justice Jackson did not determine the outcome. It was Justice Shiras who changed his position and brought about the annulment of the law.

While the judgment of the court is that of but five members of the tribunal, it has the same effect as if the vote had been unanimous. There is no possibility of a reversal of the decision rendered to-day.

The display of feeling by the dissenting Justices was sufficiently strong to make the scene in the Supreme Court Chamber of extraordinary interest. Justice Harlan made an impassioned appeal from the verdict of the court, which, he said, could not be regarded as otherwise than as a disaster to the country. Justice Jackson denounced the decision as a public calamity. Justice Brown held to the doctrine of stare decisis, maintaining that a century of error may be pregnant with less evil to the State than a newly-discovered truth. Justice White followed the lines of his former argument in favor of the constitutionality of the law.

A stranger to the ways of the court, who listened to the dissenting opinions, might easily have gained the impression that the relations between the Chief Justice and some of his associates had been seriously disturbed. Justice Harlan almost at the beginning of his opinion began to gesture and to address his remarks forcibly to the members of the bar. Warming up, he finally turned deliberately to the Chief Justice, who sits next to him, and gesticulated almost in his very face. Justice Harlan's opinion throughout had a caustic tone almost of sarcasm.

commodate all who desired to witness the scenes attendant upon the delivery of the opinions. Soon after 11 o'clock all the seats in that portion of the chamber devoted to the public were occupied. The bar itself was filled before the Judges entered. Attorney General Olney, accompanied by his Chief Assistants, took [a] seat directly facing that of the Chief Justice. At his right sat James C. Carter of New-York, who had assisted him in defending the law. Senators Hawley, Squire, and Mitchell of Oregon, Representatives Grosvenor and Hare, ex-Representatives Butterworth and Kasson, Controller of the Treasury Bowler, and other prominent men occupied desirable seats. There was the usual number of handsomely-dressed women in the throng.

The silence was impressive as the Justices filed into the chamber from the robing room, and took their places. Chief Justice Fuller carried in his hand a roll of manuscript. The Court Crier had hardly finished his announcement when the Chief Justice, bending over his desk so that his long white locks almost touched it, read the titles of the cases on which the fate of the law depended, and proceeded to give the judgment of the court. He read rapidly, in a low but clear voice. While he was thus occupied, Justice White wrote industriously, and Justice Harlan

> **Lawyers who have practiced for years before the Supreme Court say they never before listened to such revolutionary statements from the bench.**

The effect of the decision has already been to put a stop to the work of collecting the income tax. The Commissioner of Internal Revenue, within an hour from the time the judgment of the court was known, caused telegrams to be sent to all Collectors of internal revenue, instructing them to forward to Washington all returns and data bearing on the excised law. Thus far about $80,000 of the income tax has been collected. This amount, the Commissioner said, would be returned to the persons who paid it as soon as the necessary papers were received by him. The Commissioner added that between $15,000,000 and $18,000,000 had been lost to the Treasury by the overturning of the law. The loss of this sum will not, in his opinion, cripple the Government to the extent that an extra session of Congress will be necessitated.

As on previous occasions of great moment the Supreme Court Chamber to-day proved to be much too small to ac-

gave evidence of nervousness by fidgeting in his chair, finally leaving the chamber for a short time. Justice Jackson looked to be much stronger than when he last occupied a seat on the bench.

Justice Shiras, whose attitude toward the income tax had undergone such a radical change, betrayed no signs of discomfort while the Chief Justice was giving the reasons for killing the law. Justices Field, Gray, and Brewer sat at ease.

There is much adverse comment to-night on the remarks made by Justice Harlan in the course of his opinion in favor of the constitutionality of the law. Lawyers who have practiced for years before the Supreme Court say they never before listened to such revolutionary statements from the bench. The most rampant Populist could not have used more vehement expressions or shown greater contempt for the views of the majority than Justice Harlan did in the long harangue to which he treated the court and spectators. It was little less than a stump speech crowded with inflammatory statements and thinly disguised sneers.

"That opinion, if such a presentation is to be dignified by that name, will do infinite harm to the court," said a prominent Ohio lawyer, who listened attentively to all the opinions.

"Mr. Harlan's utterances will be taken advantage of by irresponsible people who hate the rich for no other reason than that they are rich, and will be paraded as the opinion of a friend of the poor and oppressed. It is well known that Justice Harlan has Presidential ambitions. Perhaps his remarkable outpouring to-day was inspired by the idea that it would strike a responsive chord in the country. I am convinced that his reputation will suffer through his ill-considered remarks. The country has already shown that it is not in sympathy with the Populistic views to which he gave expression."

EDITORIAL
MAY 21, 1895
DEMOCRATIC DOCTRINE DESTROYS THE POPULIST INCOME TAX.

. . . We have seen the end of attempts to tax incomes. Although the court concedes that even a tax upon the income of real estate and personal property would be constitutional if apportioned among the States, an income tax thus imposed would be spurned with contempt by the Socialists law. It gives us great satisfaction to note this determination on its part. We advise the Secretary of the Treasury also to order the returns filed under the act to be at once returned to those who made them. They are now waste paper, but they are in the most delicate sense confidential. The whole

> **Certainly neither the Democratic nor the Republican Party will ever attempt to revive the corpse that the Supreme Court buried yesterday.**

and Populists who were responsible for the tax of 1894. Equitable incidence of taxation is no part of their scheme, and certainly neither the Democratic nor the Republican Party will ever attempt to revive the corpse that the Supreme Court buried yesterday. The Treasury is preparing to refund the taxes already paid in without delay and without suits at income-tax law having been declared unconstitutional, it is questionable whether any penalty could now be imposed upon an Internal Revenue Collector who divulged the secrets of the returns. At any rate, they are safe nowhere but in the hands of those to whose business they relate, and into their hands they should be recommitted. . . .

• • • • • • • • • • •

The second *Pollock* ruling provoked a firestorm of criticism and efforts to overturn it in Congress. Those efforts culminated in ratification of the Sixteenth Amendment in 1913, giving Congress "the power to lay and collect taxes on incomes, from whatever source derived, without apportionment among the several States, and without regard to any census or enumeration." Congress that year passed an income tax, which the Court upheld three years later in *Stanton v. Baltic Mining Co.* (1916).

The greenback and income tax decisions were among more than two dozen the Court issued striking down acts of Congress as unconstitutional from the end of the Civil War until Chief Justice Fuller's death in 1910. Several decisions issued under Fuller's predecessor, Morrison R. Waite, struck down Reconstruction-era civil rights statutes, setting back the integration of African Americans into political and civic life. (See pages 227 and 260.) Some rulings by both the Waite and Fuller courts found violations of the Fourth, Fifth, or Sixth Amendments in criminal laws—for example, a law barring jury trials in the District of Columbia.

The Court during this period also issued several decisions taking a narrow view of Congress's power to regulate interstate commerce. In an early decision, the Court in 1870 struck down a federal ban on naphtha (coal tar) on the ground that Congress had no "police power" to protect public safety. In another, more controversial decision, the Court in the *Employers' Liability Cases* (1908) struck down a law making railroads liable for injuries to their employees. By a 5-4 vote, the Court held the act invalid because it extended to intrastate as well as interstate commerce.

CONGRESSIONAL POWERS

The Supreme Court helped define the scope of congressional power as it encountered cases where Congress's Article I powers over regulation of commerce, taxing and spending, and external relations, as well as its prerogatives over its internal affairs, bumped into the powers, prerogatives, and protections afforded by the Constitution to other branches, the states, and individual citizens.

COMMERCE POWER

The commerce power provides the constitutional authority for a vast number of laws passed by Congress from the New Deal era through the present regulating virtually every aspect of the national economy. The Supreme Court's narrow view of the commerce power thwarted some of Congress's attempts to regulate economic affairs in the early twentieth century—a period known as the "Lochner era" after a controversial 1905 decision striking down a New York law limiting hours for bakery workers. The Court's abrupt shift after 1937 gave Congress almost complete discretion in economic matters. In the 1990s, the Rehnquist Court invoked state sovereignty principles to limit the Commerce Clause's reach somewhat. But in Chief Justice William H. Rehnquist's final term, the Court in 2005 more broadly held that Congress's commerce power extended as far as making it a federal crime for a chronically ill patient to grow marijuana inside her home for her own use to ease the pain from her condition.

THE "LOCHNER ERA"

Congress passed one of its first major pieces of economic regulation in 1890: the Sherman Antitrust Act, which prohibited monopolies and any "combination" or "conspiracy" in restraint of interstate or foreign trade. In its first major decision on the act, the Supreme Court narrowly ruled that the law covered only "commerce," not manufacturing. The 8-1 ruling in *United States v. E. C. Knight Co.* (1895) blocked the government's attempt to break up the American Sugar Refinery Company, which controlled more than 90 percent of the nation's sugar-refining capacity. In later antitrust cases, the Court supported government enforcement efforts by finding that corporate combinations amounted to illegal restraints of trade. The literalist distinction between commerce and manufacturing was to surface again, however, in a major New Deal–era case striking down a law aimed at stabilizing the ailing coal industry.

The Court in the early twentieth century also began upholding some federal laws premised on a federal police power to protect public health, safety, or morals. In *Champion v. Ames* (1903), the justices voted 5-4 to uphold an 1895 law prohibiting the interstate trafficking of lottery tickets. Congress's authority over interstate commerce was "complete in itself," Justice John Marshall Harlan wrote for the majority, and included the power to ban "an evil" that was "offensive to the entire nation." For the dissenters, Chief Justice Fuller argued the law intruded on states' prerogatives.

Eight years later, the Court in 1911 fortified the newly recognized police power by upholding the government's seizure of adulterated food under the Pure Food and Drug Act of 1906. Unanimously, the Court—now led by Chief Justice Edward D. White—rejected the accused egg supplier's argument that the tainted food was no longer in interstate commerce. In 1913 the Court upheld the

Mann Act of 1910, prohibiting the transportation of women across state lines "for the purpose of prostitution or debauchery, or any other immoral purpose."

The Court drew the line, however, when the government relied on the federal police power to defend the constitutionality of the Child Labor Act of 1916. The act, passed to popular applause after a decade-long campaign, prohibited the interstate shipment of goods produced in factories that employed children under the age of sixteen for more than eight hours a day or six days a week. A North Carolina man, Ronald Dagenhart, challenged the law in an effort to prevent a Charlotte textile mill from discharging his children.

The Court's 5-4 decision in *Hammer v. Dagenhart* (1918) found the law unconstitutional because it interfered with the states' authority to regulate working conditions. For the majority, Justice William R. Day said that if Congress could use its commerce power to prohibit goods produced by child labor, "all freedom of commerce would be eliminated." For the dissenters, Justice Oliver Wendell Holmes Jr. cited the antitrust law decisions and police power rulings to uphold Congress's authority to pass the law.

Public reaction to the decision was swift and negative, prompting immediate efforts to pass a new law to meet the Court's objection. Yet after Congress invoked its taxing power to try to ban child labor, the Court in 1922 struck that law down as well in *Bailey v. Drexel Furniture Co.* (See page 30.)

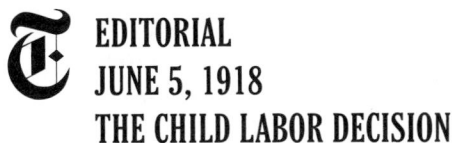

EDITORIAL
JUNE 5, 1918
THE CHILD LABOR DECISION.

The child labor law decision recites that there is a law on the subject in every State. Therefore it is to be presumed that every State has regulated the subject in the manner it prefers. Certainly if any State has not regulated the subject to its satisfaction there is nothing to prevent its doing so. The objection to Federal regulation is partly that such regulation is unnecessary and confusing, but chiefly that it is contrary to our political institutions, which after wide variance of opinion that it would not be right for intolerant opinion on those subjects to impose its will upon others equally entitled to their opinions. There never could have been a United States without local control of local matters, and there is a national danger in forcing Federal regulation upon States in advance of public opinion in each of them.

For those whose motives in opposing child labor are genuine—based on considerations of humanity, not

> **There never could have been a United States without local control of local matters, and there is a national danger in forcing Federal regulation upon States in advance of public opinion in each of them.**

all are worth preserving. The critics of the Supreme Court who politely remark that the decision "increases their contempt for the court" are more zealous than judicious. There is a reason why we have not a national divorce law, although there are some considerations in favor of it. There are similar considerations in favor of a national prohibition law. Also there are similar considerations against it that there are against a national child labor law.

When there are forty-eight varieties, more or less, of temperance laws and child labor laws there is proved to be such a merely on dislike of competition in the labor market— the decision opens the way rather than closes it. They can continue their movement in the States separately. Or they can produce a model statute, and seek to have it adopted by as many States as possible. There is no opposition to genuine reform regarding child labor in upholding the decision as supporting national interests. There is a real national danger in the antagonism sought to be created between State and national interests, and in seeking crosscuts to reforms of any sort in violation of constitutional safeguards of

State or national rights. When sentiment is unanimous there is no difficulty in getting action. Witness the ease with which the Director General wiped out intrastate rates in conflict with interstate rates declared to be reasonable by Federal authority. But when sentiment is diverse in such high degree as upon prohibition and child labor and many social reforms the tedious method of securing unity of sentiment in advance of unity of legislation is preferable.

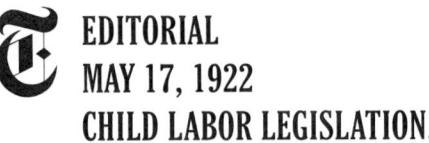

EDITORIAL
MAY 17, 1922
CHILD LABOR LEGISLATION.

The Supreme Court's annulment of the Federal tax on profits made by the employment of children is not to be mistaken for a sentence of children to labor. There is no taint of exploitation of children in the decision of a Chief Justice whose Administration as President was marked by the establishment of the Children's Bureau under a woman Chief of Department. The Supreme Court merely declares invalid unsound legislation, and refers the subject of child labor to the States, where it properly belongs. The real question was preventing conflict between State and Federal regulation of the same subject.

The case reached the Supreme Court on appeal from a State which has its own child labor laws, and whose regulations carry a note that rulings under it "do not in any way affect the national Child Labor law." The decision is that the national Child Labor law in no way affects any State child labor laws. The Federal inspectors told employers of children that their compliance with the North Carolina law in no way exempted them from regulation under the Federal law. Thus there was a conflict. The Supreme Court says that if this were allowed the constitutional division between the powers of the States and the nation would be wiped out. The Court praised the motive of the legislation, but condemned the seeking of a good object in unconstitutional ways.

There is nothing either sectional or partisan in child labor legislation. Federal laws have been passed by votes of both parties. Forty-five States have established minimum age laws. Forty-two States have regulated night labor by children. Thirty-four States, with intent to prevent child labor, enacted minimum educational standards or compulsory school attendance laws. No doubt Federal regulation would be more uniform, but it would not necessarily be better. In any case, our political Constitution should not be subordinated to partisan uses, even if they should be popular. This has occurred twice regarding child labor. It may be supposed that the subject will now be allowed to rest in the control of the States. They are nearer to the children than is the nation.

It will be a further gain if Congress should heed the hint not to load general legislation on revenue bills. A formidable list might be made of such indirect legislation under threat of stopping Government functions. As a result of the Court's decision, backward States should now be impelled to extend their child labor laws. On child labor day it was stated that each year a million children leave school too soon, in order to go to work. The Federal law now annulled covered only 15 per cent. of the children, and left many occupations uncontrolled. Farm hands, domestic servants, street trades, tenement workers and many others were not protected. Here is a field for the States, and public opinion should quicken their efficiency, while supporting the Court in its province, which is to keep both nation and States within their due spheres of influence.

• • • • • • • • • • • •

One year after *Drexel Furniture,* the Court found another limitation on Congress's power over economic affairs by ruling that a minimum wage for female workers in the District of Columbia violated employers' freedom of contract. Two decades earlier, the Court had invoked freedom of contract in a controversial decision, *Lochner v. New York* (1905), by striking down a state law that limited bakery workers to ten-hour workdays. Although the *Lochner* case has given a name to the Court's generally conservative era from the 1890s until 1937, the Court retreated from the decision itself only three years later, in *Muller v. Oregon* (1908), by upholding an Oregon law limiting hours for women employed in laundries and factories.

In *Adkins v. Children's Hospital* (1923), Justice George Sutherland brushed aside the *Muller* decision, saying that the rationale for special protective legislation for women had been weakened by passage of the Nineteenth Amendment, giving women the right to vote. Instead, Sutherland concluded that a federal law setting a minimum wage for women and children in the nation's capital amounted to "a naked, arbitrary exercise of power" not permitted under the Constitution. Congress had relied on its power over the District of Columbia in passing the law, but the reasoning in the 5-3 decision could equally be applied to a law passed under Congress's commerce power.

THE COURT AND THE NEW DEAL

Chief Justice William Howard Taft was a dissenter in *Adkins*, but through the 1920s he steered a conservative Court in a consistently conservative direction on economic issues. Taft resigned on February 3, 1930, and died only one month later. The new chief justice, Charles Evans Hughes, had been Taft's close friend, but he did not hold to conservative views as strongly as Taft had. Still, the bloc of four stalwart conservatives on economic issues—Willis Van Devanter, James C. McReynolds, Sutherland, and Pierce Butler—presaged difficulties for President Roosevelt as he took office in March 1933 and began shaping bold federal action to get the nation's economy moving again.

The centerpiece of FDR's New Deal program was the National Industrial Recovery Act (NIRA), passed by Congress under its commerce power in Roosevelt's third full month in office. The act created an executive agency, the National Recovery Administration (NRA), with the power to promulgate codes of fair competition written by individual industries and trade groups. The act also guaranteed workers the right to organize and bargain collectively. Some business groups and leaders supported the act, but legal challenges arose as the codes were put into operation.

The first of the challenges to reach the Supreme Court resulted from a regulation that sought to stabilize oil prices by prohibiting the interstate shipment of "hot oil," or petroleum produced in excess of limits set by individual states. The Panama Refining Company and other Texas oil producers challenged the NIRA as an unconstitutional delegation of legislative power to the president and an unconstitutional use of Congress's power over interstate commerce. The Court's 8-1 decision in *Panama Refining Co. v. Ryan*, issued on January 7, 1935, agreed with the oil producers on the first ground without ruling on the commerce power issue.

Four months later, the Court went further and ruled the law unconstitutional on both grounds in *Schechter Poultry Corp. v. United States* (1935). The "sick chicken case" began when the government indicted Schechter Poultry, a family-owned kosher poultry business in Brooklyn, for violating the live poultry code provisions on wages, hours, and fair trade requirements. Among the infractions was one count of selling a butcher a chicken unfit for human consumption. The courtroom was filled—with standees permitted in the rear—during two days of arguments on May 1 and 2 as Solicitor General Stanley Reed defended the law in the face of strongly skeptical questions from the justices.

Hughes spoke for a unanimous court in the May 27 decision, rejecting the administration's arguments point by point. He opened by stating that the economic emergency did not "create or enlarge constitutional power." Citing *Panama Refining,* he said that Congress's "sweeping delegation of legislative power" went beyond constitutional limits.

Moreover, Hughes explained, the Schechters' business was not in interstate commerce at all. "So far as the poultry here in question is concerned, the flow in interstate commerce had ceased," Hughes wrote. "The poultry had come to a permanent rest within the state." On that basis, he distinguished other rulings recognizing congressional authority over a "stream of commerce." He went on to reject the government's fallback position that the Schechters' business in any event had an effect on interstate commerce. "Where the effect of intrastate transactions upon interstate commerce is merely indirect," Hughes wrote, "such transactions remain within the domain of state power."

Schechter Poultry Corp. v. United States

Decided: May 27, 1935

Vote: 9 (Hughes, Van Devanter, McReynolds, Brandeis, Sutherland, Butler, Stone, O. Roberts, Cardozo)

0

Opinion of the Court: Hughes

Concurring opinion: Cardozo (Stone)

MAY 28, 1935
COURT IS UNANIMOUS

President Cannot Have 'Roving Commission' to Make Laws by Code.

NO INTRASTATE WAGE PACT

Indirect Effect of an Activity on Interstate Commerce Is Held to Be Insufficient.

PARLEY AT WHITE HOUSE

AAA Officials Also Plunge Into Study of Effect of Opinion on Farm Legislation.

By ARTHUR KROCK.

Special to The New York Times

WASHINGTON, May 27.—By a unanimous decision in the Schechter poultry case the Supreme Court today held unconstitutional the National Industrial Recovery Act, due to expire by limitation on June 16, and, by voiding the 750 codes which are the heart of the National Recovery Administration and denying the right of Congress or its agents to fix wages and hours in intrastate trade activities, demolished the chief administrative recovery weapon of the New Deal.

Immediate cessation of NRA code enforcement was announced by Chairman Richberg of the National Industrial Recovery Board following a conference at the White House in which President Roosevelt, Attorney General Cummings, Solicitor General Reed and Mr. Richberg participated. Mr. Richberg coupled with his announcement a plea to employers not to scrap the achievements in the field of fair practice and la-

HOUR AND WAGE RULES COLLAPSE.

Justice Cardozo pointed out that the attempted regulation of wages and hours was "the bone and sinew of the codes," and that therefore by the decision of the court they "collapse utterly." Since industry directly affecting interstate commerce is too small a group on which to base the NRA recovery plan, the theory and practice of NRA were killed by the decision, even though Congress should re-write the law.

Realizing this, Congressional leaders at once took steps to substitute for the fallen code system such interstate trade regulations as those contained in the Black Thirty-Hour Bill and the Guffey coal legislation, and such labor wage-bargaining as is provided in the Wagner bill.

Government attorneys had been optimistic about the

> " Congress cannot give to the President . . . 'a roving commission' to make laws in the form of codes or otherwise. "

bor relations which had flowed from the Recovery Act.

The court, speaking through the Chief Justice, who read the passages vehemently, once more declared that Congress cannot give to the President or to private persons what Justice Cardozo, in a separate assenting opinion, called "a roving commission" to make laws in the form of codes or otherwise. Congress must specify standards and list objectives and provide a definite range of action.

But even when Congress has done that, said the court, its delegation of authority cannot apply to those engaged in intrastate industry, which was defined as any not "directly" affecting the current or flow of interstate commerce. The court specifically included mining, agriculture and manufacture.

Schechter case and to them the decision was a bombshell. Donald R. Richberg and Solicitor General Reed, who had defended NIRA, left the court room with downcast faces. The Attorney General in his office stopped chewing a ham sandwich. The argument between the House and Senate over the time extension of NIRA and the terms thereof was temporarily laid aside. At the headquarters of Triple-A, which is administering some of the codes, the opinions were studied to determine whether they foreshadow the doom of that recovery experiment also.

Conferences were held at the Department of Justice, and then the Attorney General, the Solicitor General and Mr. Richberg were summoned to a late afternoon conference at the White House—the first of many—to ascertain what could be salvaged in the brief time remaining between today and June 16.

Regret was heard on all sides that the administration had taken the advice of those, among whom Professor Felix Frankfurter is prominently mentioned, who counseled delay in testing the constitutionality of NIRA until it was too late to reform ranks before the June doomsday. The once-despised "chicken-killing" case had taken rank with McCulloch v. Maryland. General satisfaction was expressed that at last, in a grave matter, the court had been united in its opinion.

FOES IN CONGRESS REJOICE.

The many foes of NRA in Congress rejoiced. Senator Borah welcomed the new proclamation of the Constitution and Senator King "thanked God for the Supreme Court." Republicans pointed happily to what they called the vindication of Herbert Hoover's recent attacks on the recovery methods of the New Deal. At NRA headquarters officials and employes sat in gloom, wondering what is to become of them, and Washington landlords and restaurateurs, who have prospered from the influx of government workers, sadly examined their scales of prices. . . .

On May 27, 1935, the Supreme Court struck down the National Industrial Recovery Act, a key piece of President Franklin D. Roosevelt's New Deal legislation. Here, Donald R. Richberg, chairman of the National Industrial Recovery Board, leaves the Capitol after hearing the decision in *Schechter Poultry Corp. v. United States* (1935).

Source: Times Wide World Photo

• • • • • • • • • • •

With the act due to expire in June and becoming increasingly unpopular, the ruling was more important for its implication than for its direct effect. The narrow definition of interstate commerce—endorsed by all the justices—threatened any national legislation dealing with economic affairs, especially wages, hours, and working conditions. A few days after the decision, Roosevelt bitterly complained that the ruling returned the nation to a "horse-and-buggy definition of interstate commerce." But he tried to meet the Court's concerns when he asked Congress to write a relief measure specific to one of the nation's most depressed industries: coal.

As passed by Congress, the Bituminous Coal Conservation Act of 1935, commonly known as the Guffey Act, included detailed recitals on the industry's effects on interstate commerce plus more detailed procedures for a newly created commission to use in writing the industry code. The act also included a tax on coal producers, to be rebated to companies that complied with the code. Even so, a year later the Court struck down that law too—though on a 5-4 instead of unanimous vote.

Writing for the majority in *Carter v. Carter Coal Co.* (1936), Sutherland dealt most extensively with the commerce power issue. Reviving the distinction from the early antitrust case, *United States v. E. C. Knight Co.* (1896), he said that mining constituted production, not commerce. On that basis, the commerce power could be invoked only if intrastate mining operations had direct effects on interstate commerce, but Sutherland determined the labor-related provisions of the measure dealt only with indirect effects. "Working conditions are obviously local conditions," he wrote. "Such effect as they may have upon commerce, however extensive it may be, is secondary and indirect."

In all, the Court ruled six New Deal measures unconstitutional in little over a year, including the Railroad Retirement Protection Act of 1934, which was struck down in 1935 in part on the commerce power issue. The Court also found that law to be an unconstitutional taking of property, in violation of the Fifth Amendment—a ground the Court also cited in the "Black Monday" decision striking down the Frazier-Lemke farm mortgage relief act. Like the coal act, the Agricultural Adjustment Act was ruled to be an improper use of Congress's taxing power. In addition, the Municipal Bankruptcy Act of 1934—allowing municipalities to file for bankruptcy protection—was held in 1936 to be an improper exercise of Congress's power "to establish . . . uniform Laws on the subject of Bankruptcies throughout the United States."

MAY 19, 1936
COURT'S NEW DEAL SCORE
Special to The New York Times

WASHINGTON, May 18.—The defeat of the Guffey Act in the Supreme Court today leaves the score against the government in New Deal cases at 8 to 2. Out of ten New Deal lawsuits decided by the court, the government has won only in the TVA and gold clause cases. The record is as follows:

FOR ·

Case.	Court Vote.	Time Required.
TVA	8 to 1	59 days
Gold Clause	5 to 4	41 days

AGAINST ·

Hot Oil	8 to 1	28 days
Railroad Pensions	5 to 4	54 days
NRA	9 to 0	25 days
Farm Mortgage Moratorium	9 to 0	29 days
AAA	6 to 3	29 days
Rice Millers	9 to 0	27 days
Securities Act of 1933	6 to 3	26 days
Guffey Act	6 to 3	67 days

In the Guffey decision, which related to wages and hours, Chief Justice Hughes agreed with the three dissenters that the price-fixing regulations were legal, that all sections of the act were separable and that sections not invalidated should remain in force.

Before the court met today the Chief Justice had supported three New Deal laws and opposed six. The records of the other justices on New Deal legislation, including today's decisions:

Justice.	For.	Ag'nst.
Van Devanter	1	9
McReynolds	0	10
Brandeis	6	4
Sutherland	1	9
Butler	1	9
Stone	6	4
Roberts	2	8
Cardozo	7	3

This calculation shows that the liberal group, consisting of Justices Brandeis, Stone and Cardozo, has been far ahead in supporting New Deal legislation. Justice McReynolds of the conservatives has invariably held against New Deal laws.

· · · · · · · · · · · ·

THE REVOLUTION OF 1937

Over the span of the next six years, Roosevelt won the Court's approval of modified laws covering many of the same subjects as those the Court had struck down. More important, the Court discarded virtually all limitations on Congress's commerce power. The shift was signaled in a decision announced on March

29, 1937, in the midst of the fierce controversy over FDR's "Court-packing" plan. (See pages 62 and 114.) It came in a ruling not on a law passed by Congress but on a state minimum wage statute.

By a 5-4 vote, the Court in *West Coast Hotel Co. v. Parrish* (1937) upheld a Washington State law creating an "Industrial Welfare Commission" to set minimum wages for women and minors. A year earlier, the Court had struck down a similar New York law, by a 5-4 vote, but Justice Owen J. Roberts switched sides in the new decision. For the majority, Hughes said that protection of women was "a legitimate end of the exercise of state power" and the legislature "had the right" to adopt a minimum wage law as "an important aid" in carrying out the policy. The freedom of contract embraced in *Lochner* and relied on in *Adkins* was inapplicable given the unequal bargaining power between "unconscionable employers" and underpaid workers. As for the contrary decision one year earlier, Hughes explained that the constitutional issue had not been raised in that case, so the Court had not considered it.

The ruling marked the end of the Lochner era. Two weeks later, in another opinion by Hughes, the Court similarly rejected a freedom-of-contract challenge against a law passed by Congress. The National Labor Relations Act of 1935—commonly known as the Wagner Act—guaranteed workers the right to organize, bargain collectively, and strike or take other "concerted action" in their behalf. The act created the National Labor Relations Board and empowered it to punish employers (or employees or unions) for specified "unfair labor practices." After the NLRB ordered Jones & Laughlin Steel Corporation to reinstate ten workers fired for their union activities, the company challenged the constitutionality of the law.

Besides rejecting the freedom of contract argument, the decision in *NLRB v. Jones & Laughlin Steel Corp.* (1937) also cast off the two grounds used in *Carter Coal* to narrow Congress's commerce power. The distinction between manufacturing and commerce was not "determinative," Hughes explained, and the difference between direct and indirect effects could not be considered "in an intellectual vacuum." Given Jones & Laughlin's "far-flung activities," he said, the effect of its labor law violations would not be "indirect or remote," but "immediate" and possibly "catastrophic."

"We have often said that interstate commerce itself is a practical conception," Hughes concluded. "It is equally true that interferences with that commerce must be appraised by a judgment that does not ignore actual experience."

NLRB v. Jones & Laughlin Steel Corp.

Decided: April 12, 1937

Vote: 5 (Hughes, Brandeis, Stone, O. Roberts, Cardozo)

4 (Van Devanter, McReynolds, Sutherland, Butler)

Opinion of the Court: Hughes

Dissenting opinion: Sutherland (Van Devanter, McReynolds, Butler)

APRIL 13, 1937
FIVE CASES DECIDED

Three Apply Commerce Clause to Manufactures First Time

FOUR ARE 5-to-4 RULINGS

Sutherland, Van Devanter, McReynolds and Butler Dissent to Congress's New Power

ASSOCIATED PRESS LOSES

Government Wins Unanimous Victory in Bus Action—Curb on Sit-Downs Expected

By ARTHUR KROCK

Special to The New York Times

WASHINGTON, April 12.—For the first time in American history, industries organized on a national scale, though their products are locally manufactured, were held by the Supreme Court today to come specifically within the regulatory powers of the Congress. The court modernized the commerce clause of the Constitution to this degree when it upheld the National Labor Relations (Wagner) Act in four cases by a vote of 5 to 4, upholding a fifth unanimously.

The effect of the momentous decisions was electric, particularly since far narrower rulings had been expected

The effect of the momentous decisions was electric, particularly since far narrower rulings had been expected.

in the manufacturing cases. Organized labor, affirmed in the right of union organization, affiliation and collective bargaining with large industry, moved to consolidate its victory.

The political community fell to instant argument over the question whether now the President's judiciary bill should be withdrawn. Another group, noting a passage written by the Chief Justice in one of the decisions, began to plan a Wagner act companion in behalf of the employers.

There was a general feeling that, since the decisions today removed the factor of uncertainty about the Wagner act as a justification of the sit-down strike, the country might reasonably expect organized labor to abandon that device.

LOOK TO SECURITY ACT RULING

Government officials, concluding that the industrial powers of Congress are now widely established, expressed the hope that its taxing powers would be equally broadened by the new Supreme Court majority in the forthcoming decision on the Security Act. The President indirectly revealed his jubilation in a telephone message to Speaker Bankhead, congratulating him on his birthday, and adding: "It's been a pretty good day for all of us."

The five cases came to the Supreme Court on appeals from rulings of the National Labor Relations Board, set up by the Wagner act. All grew out of the discharge of employes who had been active in labor organization.

The Supreme Court, following the reasoning in the railway labor case decided two weeks ago, was unanimous in holding that the Washington, Virginia & Maryland Coach Company, having conceded that it is engaged in interstate business, must obey the Wagner act.

Four members of the court—Justices Sutherland, Van Devanter, McReynolds and Butler—reserving decision as to whether The Associated Press conducts an interstate business, dissented from the application to its staff of the Wagner act by the Chief Justice and Justices Brandeis, Stone, Cardozo and Roberts on the ground that this application invades the unrestricted freedom of the press as guaranteed in the First Amendment and threatens the objectivity of the news report.

THREE MANUFACTURING CASES

But the more important cases, and those in which the commerce clause was broadened as never before, affected three manufacturers: the Jones & Laughlin Steel Corporation, the Fruehauf Trailer Company and the Friedman-Harry Marks Clothing Company, Inc. These had all relied on many previous decisions of the court excluding matters in local manufacture from Federal regulation, and the four dissenters agreed with them. All were overruled by the majority, Justice Roberts again joining the four justices who had dissented in the New York minimum wage case to make the new "liberal" majority of the Supreme Court.

The court room was crowded, expectant of the decisions as it had been on several previous Mondays. This time the throng was not disappointed, nor was it disappointed by the matter of the decisions, transcendently important as guides to future Federal legislation dealing with industrial conditions of national economic and social concern. Government lawyers, hailing the outcome, said that the court had put a twentieth century dress on Marshall's dictum in the famous case of Gibbons v. Ogden, reversing the line it has taken in recent years. . . .

EDITORIAL
APRIL 13, 1937
THE WAGNER ACT

. . . It is entirely plain that . . . the new majority of the court has made legal history. We live under a Federal system, with some powers resident in the National Government and some powers reserved to the State governments, and it is wholly natural that over a long period of years

the Supreme Court should have been called upon time and again to decide just where "intrastate" activities end and where "interstate" activities begin. Of this question the majority of the court said yesterday, as it has said before, that the distinction between "what is national and what is

> "It is entirely plain that . . . the new majority of the court has made legal history.

local" is vital to the maintenance of our whole Federal system. But the majority also said that the cardinal principle of judicial construction of the acts of Congress should be "to save and not to destroy"; that, as between two possible interpretations of a statute, "our plain" duty is to adopt that which will save "the act," and that in so far as the Wagner act deals with situations actually "affecting" interstate commerce it may be construed as within the sphere of constitutional authority. In reaching this opinion, the majority of the court plainly ranged itself on the side of the "broad constructionists" of Congressional power under the Constitution. . . .

• • • • • • • • • • • •

A year after the Court handed down its decision in *Jones & Laughlin,* Congress passed the Fair Labor Standards Act of 1938, which established a minimum wage for employers engaged in interstate commerce, required time-and-a-half pay for overtime, and prohibited most employment of minors. As enforcement, the law prohibited the shipment in interstate commerce of goods produced in violation of the standards.

By the time a challenge reached the Court, Roosevelt had appointed five justices, all New Deal supporters, to replace three conservatives and two liberals. The Roosevelt Court had no problems—and no dissents—in upholding the law. "The motive and purpose of a regulation of interstate commerce are matters for the legislative judgment," Justice Harlan Fiske Stone wrote in *United States v. Darby Lumber Co.* (1941). Under the Constitution, courts "are given no control." The decision explicitly overruled the 1923 *Dagenhart* case, calling it "a departure" from previous Commerce Clause principles.

The next year, the Court went even further by holding that Congress's commerce power extended to a farmer's production of wheat intended for use on his farm to feed chickens. Even if the wheat never entered the market, Justice Robert H. Jackson explained in *Wickard v. Filburn* (1942), "it supplies a need of the man who grew it which would otherwise be reflected by purchases in the open market. Home-grown wheat in this sense competes with wheat in commerce."

Wickard v. Filburn

Decided: November 9, 1942
Vote: 9 (Stone, O. Roberts, Black, Reed, Frankfurter, Douglas, Murphy, Byrnes, R. Jackson)
      0
Opinion of the Court: R. Jackson

OBITUARY
AUGUST 28, 1948
CHIEF JUSTICE CHARLES EVANS HUGHES HAD LONG AND NOTABLE CAREER IN SERVICE OF HIS COUNTRY

FOUGHT CORRUPTION IN STATE POLITICS
Hughes' Program as Governor Forced Major Correctives on the Old Legislature
LOST PRESIDENCY IN 1916
But He Added to Honors Later as Secretary of State and Chief Justice of U.S.

. . . Considered a conservative when appointed by President Hoover in 1930, Mr. Hughes blossomed forth as a liberal when a liberal construction of the basic law of the land was essential to a nation struggling in the throes of social and economic revolution. This did not mean he gave blanket approval to all New Deal measures tested in the highest tribunal of the land—he voted against validity of the National Recovery Act, the first Agricultural Adjustment Act and the "hot oil" law—but it did mean an approach of scrupulous fairness to each new proposal.

His basic liberal viewpoint did come to light in his votes to uphold social security legislation, the second AAA, the second Guffey Coal Law and the Wagner Labor Relations Act. It also came to light in his dealings with his fellow justices on the court and the suasion he was credited with exerting on them with regard to legal issues he believed a liberal construction of the Constitution made correct. No more important example of this influence he used can be found than in the case of the Wagner Act.

"COURT PACKING" FIGHT

This case came before the court shortly after it had handed down a series of adverse decisions on major New Deal reforms. Roosevelt Administration forces were complaining about the "nine old men" who were blocking the nation's forward progress. In Congress, the New Dealers were pushing for a court enlargement bill. The nation rocked under the impact of the "court-packing controversy."

Mr. Hughes took the stump against the court reorganization bill, but that alone would not have sufficed to defeat it. The turning point came in the vote on the Wagner Act in which Mr. Hughes and four associates provided the five-to-four margin by which this charter for labor was upheld.

It was often said without denial that the Chief Justice resorted to "judicial statesmanship" to swing at least one of his colleagues to his views on this matter. At all events, court enlargement was at last a dead issue. The integrity of the court was preserved. . . .

• • • • • • • • • • • •

AN EXPANSIVE POWER CHECKED?

The expansive definition of Congress's commerce power prevailed for the next half century, all but unchecked by the Supreme Court. Besides enabling Congress to regulate the nation's workplaces, the broadened commerce power became a linchpin of the federal government's efforts to combat racial discrimination. In an early case, *Morgan v. Virginia* (1946), the Court ruled, 8-1, that a state law requiring racial segregation on interstate buses amounted to an impermissible burden on interstate commerce. In the 1960s, the Court gave short shrift to arguments that the public accommodations provisions of the Civil Rights Act of 1964 could not apply to intrastate businesses. Racial discrimination in local businesses "might have a substantial and harmful effect" on interstate commerce, the Court reasoned in *Heart of Atlanta Motel v. United States* (1964), the first in the series of cases upholding the law. (See page 261.)

Beginning in 1976, however, the Court began using state sovereignty principles to limit the reach of Congress's commerce power, at least as applied to state governments. The 5-4 majority in *National League of Cities v. Usery* (1976) invalidated the decision by Congress two years earlier to extend the wage and hour provisions of the Fair Labor Standards Act to state employees. But the decision was short-lived: nine years later, one of the justices switched sides to produce a new majority overruling the decision in *Garcia v. San Antonio Metropolitan Transit Authority* (1985).

In the 1990s, the Court twice held that Congress could not require state governments to administer federal statutes. The rulings struck down one law requiring state governments to take custody of radioactive waste from nuclear power plants and another requiring local law enforcement agencies to conduct background checks on gun purchases. (See page 159.)

The Court in the 1990s also issued two rulings that more directly narrowed Congress's commerce power in order to invalidate federal statutes. The rulings—both written by Chief Justice William H. Rehnquist—ruled unconstitutional two seemingly popular federal laws on the ground that they relied on an overly expansive definition of interstate commerce to reach areas of local responsibility.

The first ruling, *United States v. Lopez* (1995), struck down the Gun-Free School Zones Act of 1990, which made it a federal crime to

United States v. Lopez

Decided: April 26, 1995

Vote: 5 (Rehnquist, O'Connor, Scalia, Kennedy, Thomas)

4 (Stevens, Souter, Ginsburg, Breyer)

Opinion of the Court: Rehnquist

Concurring opinions (2): Kennedy (O'Connor); Thomas

Dissenting opinions (3): Stevens; Souter; Breyer (Stevens, Souter, Ginsburg)

knowingly possess a firearm within a school zone. Rehnquist reasoned that the law had nothing to do with commerce or any sort of economic enterprise, was not part of a larger regulatory scheme, and did not require the government to prove a connection to interstate commerce in any individual case. Upholding the law on that basis, he said, "would bid fair to convert congressional authority under the Commerce Clause to a general police power of the sort retained by the States." *The New York Times'* Linda Greenhouse called the ruling "a stunning decision."

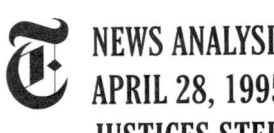

NEWS ANALYSIS
APRIL 28, 1995
JUSTICES STEP IN AS FEDERALISM'S REFEREE
By LINDA GREENHOUSE

Unlike President Clinton, Chief Justice William H. Rehnquist does not hold news conferences. But if he did, it would not occur to anyone to ask him whether he was still relevant.

The Supreme Court's stunning decision of Wednesday that Congress lacked the authority to bar gun possession in or near schools was a forceful reminder not only of the Court's raw power—nine people, divided 5 to 4, invalidated a law that two houses of Congress and the President of the United States approved five years ago—but also of its inevitable role in shaping the country's ongoing political dialogue.

Had Chief Justice Rehnquist's majority opinion in United States v. Lopez landed in a vacuum, it would have been an important constitutional development but scarcely one

become clear, perhaps years from now as its principles are tested in other contexts.

One indication of how far the new majority intends to go could come quickly. The Justices heard arguments two months ago in a case that has received much less attention but that poses a closely related question about the Federal Government's law-enforcement authority under its constitutional power to regulate interstate commerce. A decision could come any week.

This second case, United States v. Robertson, raises the question whether the Federal racketeering law can be applied to a business-related crime that occurs essentially within the borders of a single state.

 A forceful reminder not only of the Court's raw power . . . but also of its inevitable role in shaping the country's ongoing political dialogue.

to provoke statements on the Senate floor or the kind of urgent scrutiny the decision received all over Washington.

But this is a season in which questions of federalism are unusually high on the agenda—not only the efforts of state officials to shed unwanted Federal mandates, a prominent topic during the opening weeks of the new Congress, but also the new interest, prompted by the Oklahoma City bombing and the Clinton Administration's proposed responses, in the appropriate division of law-enforcement authority between the Federal and state governments.

The Court's rediscovery of limits on Federal power under a constitutional provision, the commerce clause, that it had not interpreted in such a way in nearly 60 years is bound to affect the federalism debate in ways that may not be apparent until the full dimensions of the ruling itself

The Federal law, the Racketeer Influenced and Corrupt Organizations Act, or RICO, makes it a crime to invest racketeering proceeds in a business "the activities of which affect interstate or foreign commerce." A Federal appeals court, ruling that the operations of a small Alaska gold mine did not affect interstate commerce, overturned the conviction of a former Federal prosecutor for investing narcotics proceeds in the mine.

By the same token, the Supreme Court ruled on Wednesday that the Gun-Free School Zones Act was not within the power of Congress to regulate interstate commerce because the possession of guns near schools was not sufficiently related to commerce. If the Justices agree with the lower court in the Alaska case, they will be taking that analysis a considerable step further, because the gold mine was self-evidently a commercial operation in a way that schools are not.

Furthermore, Miguel A. Estrada, an assistant solicitor general, argued to the Court in the Government's appeal, people and supplies moved into and out of Alaska as part of the gold mine's operations.

"Is there any business enterprise in America that wouldn't be covered" by the Government's broad theory of the commerce power, a skeptical Justice Sandra Day O'Connor asked Mr. Estrada. No, he replied: "In our economy in this day and age, I can't think of anything that is likely to happen in the real world" that would not be related to interstate commerce.

It was just such a broad interpretation of interstate commerce that the Court's majority, including Justice O'Connor, rejected on Wednesday in the Lopez decision. If the Justices also reject the broad definition when it concerns an actual business, and not only a nonprofit customary function of state government like public education, it will be clear that the Lopez case applies beyond a rather anomalous Federal law.

The Court would then be repudiating one of the fundamental principles underlying the modern understanding of the commerce clause: that the power of the Federal Government grows necessarily, almost organically, as the increasingly complex and interrelated national economy makes the concept of local boundaries essentially obsolete.

In place of that longstanding view, the Court would be reinserting itself into a role it explicitly renounced in a landmark decision 10 years ago: that of guardian of the Federal-state balance.

In that 1985 decision, Garcia v. San Antonio Transit, the Court said restrictions on the scope of Congressional authority to regulate interstate commerce must come not from "judicially created limitations" but from the political process itself. Because states themselves participate in Federal decision-making through their representation in Congress, the Court said, "the political process ensures that laws that unduly burden the States will not be promulgated."

Like the Lopez ruling 10 years later, the Garcia decision left a deeply divided Court. Justices O'Connor and Rehnquist, two of the four dissenters, pledged in their opinion in the Garcia case that "this Court will in time again assume its constitutional responsibility."

Developments not only within the Court but also outside it may have strengthened the Garcia dissenters' hand. To the alarm of much of the Federal judiciary, Congress has demonstrated a nearly insatiable appetite for showing its concern about various problems, from household violence to drive-by shootings, by adding them to the growing list of Federal crimes and, in the process, placing them on the dockets of Federal judges.

The Judicial Conference of the United States, the Federal judiciary's policy-making arm, which Chief Justice Rehnquist heads, has opposed several of these bills and urged Congress to reconsider its approach.

Judge Maryanne Trump Barry of the Federal District Court in Newark, head of the Judicial Conference's criminal law committee, told the House Judiciary Committee last year that the Federal courts were not equipped to take over proceedings for what have historically been state and local offenses. Noting that there were more trial judges on the California state courts than in all the Federal district courts combined, Judge Barry said that "scarce judicial resources needed by the Federal courts to try major crimes" would be "diluted" if various proposals then under consideration in the 1994 crime bill became law. Many did.

While Congressional Republicans generally applauded the Court's solicitude toward the states in Wednesday's decision, they may find that a Supreme Court that reassumes a role as activist policeman of the Federal-state boundary is not always to their liking. The Federal limits on state-court damage awards, now being debated in the Senate as part of the Republican-sponsored civil justice measure, may well not match the Court's view of appropriate Federal action even if the states welcome them. Relevance, in other words, may be a double-edged sword.

* * * * * * * * * * * *

Five years later, Rehnquist followed the same reasoning in a decision striking down a provision of the Violence Against Women Act of 1994 that allowed victims of "gender-motivated" violence to bring a damage suit in federal court against their assailants. Gender-motivated crimes "are not, in any sense of the phrase, economic activity" and also could not be regulated by Congress on the basis of their "aggregate effect" on the national economy, Rehnquist wrote in *United States v. Morrison* (2000). "If Congress may regulate gender-motivated violence," he explained, "it would be able to regulate murder or any other type of violence."

Both rulings were by 5-4 votes, with strong dissents from the bloc of four liberal justices. Without overruling the decisions, however, the Court in 2005 returned to a broader conception of Congress's commerce power in an unusual context: medical marijuana. The case, *Gonzales v. Raich* (2005), arose after California in 1996 passed the Compassionate Use Act to allow patients with some chronic diseases to obtain a doctor's prescription to use marijuana to ease pain or other symptoms. The federal Controlled Substances Act banned possession of marijuana, however, and the Food and Drug Administration had refused to permit an exception for medical use.

Drug Enforcement Administration agents raided the home of one patient, Diane Monson, in 2000 and confiscated the plants that she had been growing to provide marijuana to relieve her chronic back spasms. She and others, including cancer patient Angel Raich, then sued to block federal enforcement. The federal appeals court in California agreed. Arguments before the Supreme Court focused on the old decision in *Wickard v. Filburn*. If Congress could regulate home-grown wheat, Solicitor General Paul Clement argued, it could also regulate home-grown pot—even when used for medical purposes pursuant to a state law.

By a 6-3 vote, the Court agreed. Marijuana cultivation was a "quintessentially economic activity," Justice John Paul Stevens wrote. "Congress had a rational basis for believing that failure to regulate the intrastate manufacture and possession of marijuana would leave a gaping hole in the [federal drug law]," he continued. A nationwide exemption for locally cultivated marijuana, he said, could have "a substantial impact on the interstate market for this extraordinarily popular substance." Stevens cited *Wickard v. Filburn* as a decision "of particular relevance" and distinguished *Lopez* and *Morrison* by noting that those rulings had struck down laws regulating noneconomic activities. Rehnquist was one of the three dissenters.

United States v. Morrison

Decided: May 15, 2000
Vote: 5 (Rehnquist, O'Connor, Scalia, Kennedy, Thomas)
    4 (Stevens, Souter, Ginsburg, Breyer)
Opinion of the Court: Rehnquist
Concurring opinion: Thomas
Dissenting opinions (2): Souter (Stevens, Ginsburg, Breyer); Breyer (Stevens, Souter, Ginsburg)

Gonzales v. Raich

Decided: June 6, 2005
Vote: 6 (Stevens, Scalia, Kennedy, Souter, Ginsburg, Breyer)
    3 (Rehnquist, O'Connor, Thomas)
Opinion of the Court: Stevens
Concurring opinion: Scalia
Dissenting opinions (2): O'Connor (Rehnquist, Thomas); Thomas

JUNE 7, 2005
JUSTICES SAY U.S. MAY PROHIBIT THE USE OF MEDICAL MARIJUANA

By LINDA GREENHOUSE

WASHINGTON, June 6—The Supreme Court on Monday upheld the power of Congress to prohibit and prosecute the possession and use of marijuana for medical purposes, even in the 11 states that permit it.

The 6-to-3 decision, a firm reassertion of federal authority, revealed a deep fissure within the coalition that over the past decade has provided the majority for a series of decisions curbing Congressional power and elevating the role of the states within the federal system. Two members of that coalition, Justices Anthony M. Kennedy and Antonin Scalia, voted this time to uphold federal authority.

The decision overturned a 2003 ruling by a federal appeals court that shielded California's Compassionate Use Act,

the medical-marijuana initiative adopted by the state's voters nine years ago, from the reach of federal drug enforcement.

The appeals court had held that Congress lacked constitutional authority to regulate the noncommercial cultivation and use of marijuana that did not cross state lines.

But "the regulation is squarely within Congress's commerce power," Justice John Paul Stevens said for the majority on Monday. He added that the court's precedents interpreting Congress's authority under the Commerce Clause of the Constitution had clearly established "Congress's power to regulate purely local activities that are part of an economic 'class of activities' that have a substantial effect on interstate commerce."

The decision, Gonzales v. Raich, No. 03-1454, was not necessarily the last word on medical marijuana, either from the courts or from other branches of government. Under the terms of the opinion, the United States Court of Appeals for the Ninth Circuit, in San Francisco, will now consider other challenges to the application of federal drug law.

These include an argument made by the two women who brought the case that it is a violation of their constitutional right to due process to deprive them of what they say is the only drug that eases their suffering from a variety of painful conditions.

Because the two patients, Angel McClary Raich and Diane Monson, prevailed in the Ninth Circuit on their Commerce Clause argument, the appeals court did not address the other issues they raised.

Advocates for medical marijuana, meanwhile, emphasized on Monday that the state laws remained in effect, meaning that state officials would not prosecute patients who used medical marijuana, and that the prospect of fed-

The House of Representatives is due to vote next week on an appropriations amendment that would prohibit the Justice Department from spending money to enforce federal drug laws against patients using marijuana for medical purposes. While the amendment failed last year, 19 Republicans voted for it. It was not brought to a vote in the Senate.

Mrs. Raich, one of the plaintiffs, speaking along with her husband and lawyers in a telephone news conference, said she would continue to use the marijuana that was prescribed by her doctor and is grown for her by friends. "I don't have a choice but to continue because if I stopped I would die," she said. She suffers from a wasting syndrome, among other ailments, and said that only marijuana gave her the appetite to eat enough to maintain her weight.

The women brought the case after federal agents arrived at Ms. Monson's home in 2002 and, after a three-hour standoff, seized and destroyed her six plants. The two

> The 6-to-3 decision, a firm reassertion of federal authority, revealed a deep fissure within the coalition that over the past decade has provided the majority for a series of decisions curbing Congressional power and elevating the role of the states.

eral enforcement was fairly remote. Allen Hopper, a lawyer with the Drug Law Reform Project of the American Civil Liberties Union, noted that the federal government handles only about 1 percent of marijuana prosecutions.

Justice Stevens, noting that "perhaps even more important than these legal avenues is the democratic process," suggested that the executive branch might reclassify marijuana for medical purposes or that Congress might take up the matter.

The first option appeared quite unlikely, given the response by John P. Walters, the Bush administration's "drug czar," the director of national drug control policy. "To date, science and research have not determined that smoking a crude plant is safe or effective," his official statement said, adding, "We have a responsibility as a civilized society to ensure that the medicine Americans receive from their doctors is effective, safe and free from the pro-drug politics that are being promoted in America under the guise of medicine."

women sued for a declaration that the federal Controlled Substances Act did not apply to their situation.

The opinion by Justice Stevens was joined by his allies in many recent battles over federalism, Justices David H. Souter, Ruth Bader Ginsburg and Stephen G. Breyer, and by Justice Kennedy, who did not provide an explanation for his vote.

Justice Scalia, by contrast, explained himself at length. He did not sign the majority opinion, instead offering a separate concurring opinion that was no less definite in its support for federal authority.

"Where necessary to make a regulation of interstate commerce effective, Congress may regulate even those intrastate activities that do not themselves substantially affect interstate commerce," Justice Scalia said. He cited opinions from the early 1940's, after the Supreme Court rallied to support the New Deal and gave Congress a degree of power over national affairs that was not seriously challenged until the Rehnquist Court began invalidating federal laws in the mid-1990's.

Chief Justice Rehnquist was one of the dissenters on Monday. He and Justice Clarence Thomas joined a dissenting opinion by Justice Sandra Day O'Connor; Justice Thomas also wrote a separate dissenting opinion.

As a prime mover of the court's federalism revolution, Justice O'Connor did not hide her dismay. The court's opinion provided a roadmap to "removing meaningful limits on the Commerce Clause" and "threatens to sweep all of productive human activity into federal regulatory reach," she said.

Justice O'Connor said that while she did not support the medical marijuana initiative as public policy, it represented the kind of innovation and "experiment" that came within the latitude the Constitution allows the states.

"The states' core police powers have always included authority to define criminal law and to protect the health, safety and welfare of their citizens," she said, adding that "whatever the wisdom of California's experiment with medical marijuana, the federalism principles that have driven our Commerce Clause cases require that room for experiment be protected in this case."

Justice Thomas said that "if Congress can regulate this under the Commerce Clause, then it can regulate virtually anything, and the federal government is no longer one of limited and enumerated powers."

The sharpest dispute was over the meaning of two of the core decisions of the Rehnquist Court's approach to federalism. Both struck down federal laws, the Gun-Free School Zones Act and the Violence Against Women Act, on the ground that they exceeded Congressional authority, and both were decided by five-member majorities that included Justices Kennedy and Scalia.

While Justice O'Connor declared that the marijuana decision was "irreconcilable" with the earlier ones, Justice Scalia disagreed. Neither of the earlier decisions "involved the power of Congress to exert control over intrastate activities in connection with a more comprehensive scheme of regulation" comparable to federal drug laws, he said.

Besides California, states allowing use of marijuana for medical purposes are Alaska, Arizona, Colorado, Hawaii, Maine, Montana, Nevada, Oregon, Washington and Vermont.

• • • • • • • • • • • •

Fiscal Powers

Congress's power over the national economy flows not only from the Commerce Clause, but also from the Tax Clause and the Spending Clause, which stipulates that no money can be drawn from the Treasury "but in Consequence of Appropriations made by Law" (Art. I, sec. 9, cl. 7). The powers to tax and spend also give Congress indirect leverage over noneconomic activities. The Supreme Court's few major rulings limiting these powers have not survived. Instead, the modern Court has upheld Congress's authority to adopt tax provisions even if enacted for a regulatory purpose. It has also upheld Congress's power to attach strings to federal spending that effectively impose federal mandates in areas, such as education and law enforcement, traditionally within state and local responsibility.

TAXING POWER

The Tax Clause limited Congress to "direct" and "excise" taxes, but the scope of the restrictions did not matter much until the national government's first fiscal crisis during the Civil War. The wartime income tax passed in 1862 was unanimously upheld by the Supreme Court as an indirect tax in 1881—nine years after the law had expired. The issue came before the Court again after Congress in 1894 passed a new income tax to make up for the loss of revenue from the depression of 1893.

The Court's decision, in *Pollock v. Farmers' Loan & Trust Co.* (1895), to strike down the act as an impermissible direct tax represented a legal reversal and a political debacle. "Some of the judges of the Court seem to have no adequate idea of the dividing line between judicial and legislative power," the editor of the generally conservative *American Law Review* wrote. In a series of cases, the Court retreated—most tellingly, in a 1911 decision upholding a corporate income tax as an excise tax, "measured by income," on the privilege of doing business.

Two years later, the states completed ratification of the Sixteenth Amendment, explicitly authorizing a federal levy on income from any source. Congress passed a general income tax the same year. In upholding the levy in 1916, the Court implicitly repudiated the *Pollock* decision, saying that income taxes had traditionally—and correctly—been viewed as indirect, not direct, taxes.

Earlier, the Court had also drawn back from questioning Congress's authority to use its taxing power for a nonrevenue purpose. Unanimously, the Court in *McCray v. United States* (1904) upheld a ten cents per pound tax on colored oleomargarine that was evidently aimed at making the product uncompetitive with real butter. The Court had no authority, then Associate Justice Edward D. White wrote, to "restrain the exercise of a lawful power on the assumption that a wrongful purpose or motive has caused the power to be exerted." In 1919, the Court somewhat similarly upheld a federal narcotics registration tax; four dissenters, though, argued the measure intruded on the states' police powers.

Bailey v. Drexel Furniture Co.

Decided: May 15, 1922

Vote: 8 (Taft, McKenna, Holmes, Day, Van Devanter, Pitney, McReynolds, Brandeis)

1 (Clarke)

Opinion of the Court: Taft

Dissenting without opinion: Clarke

When Congress tried to use the taxing power to ban child labor, however, the Court refused to go along. Congress passed the Child Labor Tax Law of 1919 the year after the Court had struck down a direct ban on child labor as beyond Congress's commerce power. The tax law imposed a ten percent levy on the net profits of any company that employed children under a specific age. With only one dissent, the Court in *Bailey v. Drexel Furniture Co.* (1922) ruled the measure unconstitutional. The tax, Chief Justice Taft wrote, was "a mere penalty with the characteristics of regulation and punishment."

The Court returned to a more deferential approach in a decision, *Sonzinsky v. United States* (1937), upholding a $200 tax on firearms dealers imposed by the National Firearms Act of 1934. In a terse, eight-paragraph opinion, Justice Stone said the courts had no authority to inquire into Congress's "hidden motive" for approving a tax. "An Act of Congress which on its face purports to be an exercise of the taxing power," he wrote, "is not any the less so because the tax is burdensome or tends to restrict or suppress the thing taxed." The Court adopted similar reasoning in approving taxes on marijuana and gambling in the 1950s, as in *United States v. Kahriger* (1953).

MARCH 10, 1953
U.S. GAMBLING LAW WINS IN HIGH COURT

Tribunal, 6-3, Reverses Lower Bench on Registration and Purchase of Tax Stamp

By LUTHER A. HUSTON

Special to The New York Times

WASHINGTON, March 9—The Supreme Court ruled today that the law enacted by Congress in 1951 to require the registration of gamblers and the purchase of a $50 tax stamp was constitutional.

The 6-to-3 opinion of the high court overturned a ruling by Judge George A. Welsh in the United States District Court in Philadelphia that the statute was unconstitutional as a police measure enacted under the guise of a tax bill. The Department of Justice appealed Judge Welsh's ruling to the Supreme Court.

In the case before the high court the constitutionality of the tax imposed by the Revenue Act of 1951 on persons engaged in accepting wagers was attacked on two grounds:

1. That Congress had infringed on the police power reserved to the states in attempting to penalize illegal intrastate gambling through the regulatory features of the law.

2. That the registration provisions of the law violated the privilege of self-incrimination, contrary to the guarantees of the Fifth Amendment.

FOLLOWED SENATE INQUIRY

The law requires that gamblers give their names and places of business and the names of their employes and associates. Information thus obtained is available to the local police in their efforts to enforce anti-gambling laws. The law was passed as an outgrowth of the Senate Crime Investigating Committee's disclosures of gambling and racketeering.

Joseph Kahriger, the defendant, was arrested for failure to register and pay the occupational tax required. His case was the first to come before the Supreme Court.

"The substance of respondent's position with respect to the Tenth Amendment," said Justice Stanley F. Reed in the majority opinion, "is that Congress has chosen to tax a specified business which is not within its power to regulate. The precedents are many upholding taxes similar to

The Treasury Department gave out figures showing that for the first eight months of the 1952 fiscal year the gambling tax was in operation it had yielded $973,197. For the full fiscal year the narcotic tax yielded $914,910 and the firearms tax $28,911.

Justice Robert H. Jackson agreed with the majority but said in a separate concurrence:

"If the minority agreed upon an opinion which did not impair legitimate use of the taxing power I probably would join it.

"If Congress may tax one citizen to the point of discouragement for making an honest living, it is hard to say that it may not do the same to another just because he

> If Congress may tax one citizen to the point of discouragement for making an honest living, it is hard to say that it may not do the same to another just because he makes a sinister living.

this wagering tax as a proper exercise of the Federal taxing power.

"It is conceded that a Federal excise tax does not cease to be valid merely because it discourages or deters the activities taxed. Nor is the tax invalid because the revenue obtained is negligible.

A REVENUE PRODUCER

"The instant tax has a regulatory effect. But regardless of its regulatory effect, the wagering tax produces revenue. As such it surpasses both the narcotics and firearms taxes which we have found valid."

The Tenth Amendment to the Constitution says:

"The powers not delegated to the United States by the Constitution, nor prohibited by it to the States, are reserved to the States respectively, or to the people."

makes a sinister living. If the law-abiding must tell all to the tax collector, it is difficult to excuse one because his business is law-breaking."

Justice Felix Frankfurter, in a dissenting opinion, said that he would have affirmed Judge Welsh's ruling. He held that the wagering tax was "an inadmissible intrusion into a domain of legislation reserved for the states."

"It is a wholly different thing," Justice Frankfurter maintained, "to hold that Congress, which cannot constitutionally grapple directly with gambling in the states, may compel self-incriminating disclosures for the enforcement of gambling laws, merely because it does so under the guise of a revenue measure, obviously not passed for revenue purposes."

Justices Hugo L. Black and William O. Douglas also dissented on the ground that the law required a gambler, by registering, to confess an illegal activity and thus be a witness against himself, in violation of his Constitutional rights.

. . . .

SPENDING POWER

The Spending Clause gives Congress control over the federal purse strings, and Congress has come to enjoy broad discretion in how to spend money under its first enumerated power "to provide for the common Defence and general Welfare" (Art. I, sec. 8, cl. 1). Just how much discretion should be permitted has been a matter of some debate. Among the framers of the Constitution, James

Madison understood the General Welfare Clause to authorize spending only to carry out the other enumerated powers, whereas Alexander Hamilton argued that the clause conferred a power independent of those enumerated, and that view eventually prevailed.

In its first interpretation of the General Welfare Clause, the Supreme Court in 1935 limited the scope of the clause somewhat as the justices struck down the Agricultural Adjustment Act (AAA) of 1933, the centerpiece of President Roosevelt's farm relief program. The statute established an excise tax on the processors of seven food commodities, with the proceeds to be used to pay benefits to farmers who reduced their production of those commodities. By a 6-3 vote, the Court in *United States v. Butler* (1936) ruled the act unconstitutional.

For the majority, Justice Roberts accepted that Congress had broad discretion in exercising its taxing power, but concluded that the tax on processors was actually "an expropriation of money from one group for the benefit of another" as part of a regulatory device. The tax could not pass muster as a regulatory levy, Roberts explained, because agricultural production was an intrastate matter beyond Congress's commerce power. Turning to the benefits scheme, Roberts also found it unconstitutional. Although he agreed that spending under the General Welfare Clause was not limited to Congress's enumerated powers, he found the payments unconstitutional because they were aimed at the impermissible purpose of regulating agricultural production. Both the tax and the appropriations, he concluded, were "means to an unconstitutional end."

A little more than a year later, the Court on May 24, 1937, effectively reduced *Butler* to a dead letter when it upheld two New Deal programs that, like the 1933 AAA, used federal tax provisions to fund benefit plans. The Social Security Act of 1935 taxed employers based on their total payroll, but gave them a tax credit if they contributed to a federally approved state unemployment compensation system. The act's old-age benefit provisions taxed employers to create a trust fund to be used to pay retired workers. The Alabama-based Charles C. Steward Machine Company challenged the unemployment compensation scheme, while George Davis, a stockholder in the Edison Illumination Company, sued the government to prevent the company from having to pay the old-age benefits tax.

In *Steward Machine Co. v. Davis* (1937), the Court voted 5-4 to uphold the act's unemployment compensation provisions. Justice Benjamin N. Cardozo easily found the tax on employment to be within Congress's Commerce Clause power. He distinguished the agricultural production case by stressing that under the Social Security Act, the employers' tax went into general revenues. And he said that given the "extreme" crisis of the Depression—with as many as sixteen million people unemployed—there was no argument that the jobless benefits were "for any purpose narrower than the promotion of the general welfare."

Cardozo also wrote the 7-2 ruling in *Helvering v. Davis* (1937), upholding the act's old-age benefits provision. The ruling explicitly adopted the Hamiltonian view of an independent spending power under the General Welfare Clause and bowed to Congress in how to use it. "The discretion belongs to Congress," Cardozo wrote, "unless the choice is clearly wrong, a display of arbitrary power, not an exercise of judgment." He went on to stress that Congress was not tied to a "static" concept of general welfare. "What is critical or urgent changes with the times," he wrote.

The rulings left the *Butler* decision on the books, but Congress got around it in the AAA of 1938 by directly establishing crop production quotas, which the Court upheld a year later. The broad conception of Congress's spending power then became the basis for the vast number

United States v. Butler

Decided: January 6, 1936

Vote: 6 (Hughes, Van Devanter, McReynolds, Sutherland, Butler, O. Roberts)

3 (Brandeis, Stone, Cardozo)

Opinion of the Court: O. Roberts

Dissenting opinion: Stone (Brandeis, Cardozo)

Helvering v. Davis

Decided: May 24, 1937

Vote: 7 (Hughes, Van Devanter, Brandeis, Sutherland, Stone, O. Roberts, Cardozo)

2 (McReynolds, Butler)

Opinion of the Court: Cardozo

Dissenting without opinion: McReynolds, Butler

of federal laws enacted since the end of World War II—and upheld by the Court—regulating state and local governments with strings attached to federal aid.

As early as 1947, the Court described the technique of placing conditions on federal aid to the states—"assumedly for the general welfare"—as "not unusual." In that ruling, *Oklahoma v. Civil Service Commission,* the Court upheld the requirement that state employees administering federally funded programs must comply with the Hatch Act's restrictions on partisan political activities. The 5-2 decision upheld the government's withholding of $10,800 in highway construction funds, representing two years' salary of a state highway commissioner who had served simultaneously as his state's Democratic Party chairman.

Four decades later, the Court upheld a broader example of federal aid string-tying: a provision cutting a state's highway aid funds by five percent unless the state established twenty-one as the minimum legal age for drinking. South Dakota challenged the law, arguing that the states' unanimous compliance with its terms proved its coercive effects. Chief Justice Rehnquist, ordinarily solicitous of states' prerogatives, brushed the argument aside. "We cannot conclude," he wrote in *South Dakota v. Dole* (1987), "that a conditional grant of federal money of this sort is unconstitutional simply by reason of its success in achieving the congressional objective." Two dissenting justices argued only that the act interfered with the post-Prohibition Twenty-first Amendment, which gives states exclusive authority to regulate alcoholic beverages.

South Dakota v. Dole

Decided: June 23, 1987

Vote: 7 (Rehnquist, B. White, T. Marshall, Blackmun, Powell, Stevens, Scalia)
2 (Brennan, O'Connor)

Opinion of the Court: Rehnquist

Dissenting opinions (2): Brennan; O'Connor

JUNE 24, 1987
JUSTICES BACK USE OF AID TO GET STATES TO RAISE DRINKING AGE

By STUART TAYLOR JR.

The Supreme Court, by a vote of 7 to 2, today upheld a Federal law aimed at encouraging states to raise the legal drinking age to 21 years by withholding some highway grants from those that fail to do so. . . .

The drinking-age decision essentially leaves the status quo intact by removing doubt about the validity of the 1984 Federal law. Twenty-three states, including New York and Connecticut, have raised their drinking ages since it was passed. The ruling was widely expected.

Chief Justice William H. Rehnquist's majority opinion rejected arguments by South Dakota and several state and local government groups that the law violated constitutional principles of federalism and the broad powers of the states under the 21st Amendment to regulate sales of alcoholic beverages. He called the law a "relatively mild encouragement to the states to enact higher minimum drinking ages than they would otherwise choose."

JUSTICES DISAGREE

Justices Sandra Day O'Connor and William J. Brennan Jr. dissented separately. Justice O'Connor said the law was "an attempt to regulate the sale of liquor" that encroached on the powers of states under the 21st Amendment, which repealed Prohibition and authorized states to regulate sales of alcoholic beverages.

A major goal of the 1984 law was to reduce highway deaths by preventing teen-agers from drinking and driving, and especially to remove the incentives to cross state lines to buy liquor.

It provided for withholding part of Federal highway funds otherwise due to states that allow people under 21 to drink. Five percent of a state's highway funds can be withheld for the current fiscal year, and the figure will rise to 10 percent for the next fiscal year. The total cost for a state that does not have a 21-year-old drinking age could come to many millions of dollars.

As of last March, six states and the Commonwealth of Puerto Rico had legal drinking ages for some or all alcoholic beverages of 18 or 19, according to a General Accounting Office study. Those states are South Dakota, Wyoming, Montana, Louisiana, Colorado and Ohio. Under South Dakota law, 19- and 20-year-olds are permitted to buy low-alcohol beer.

All other states had adopted 21-year-old drinking-age laws. Nineteen of them, including New Jersey, had adopted such laws before 1984, and were essentially unaffected by the new Federal law.

DECISION WAS EXPECTED

Critics of the law said today that they were disappointed but not surprised by the decision today, which followed a long line of Supreme Court rulings that the Federal Government has broad powers to attach conditions to grants of money to state and local governments and others.

Chief Justice Rehnquist said in his opinion that the Court did not have to decide whether the 21st Amendment would bar Congress from legislating directly a national minimum drinking age. He said past decisions had already established that "the constitutional limitations on Congress when exercising its spending power

are less exacting than those on its authority to regulate directly."

He said in his opinion the 1984 law's purpose of reducing drunken driving was "directly related to one of the main purposes for which highway funds are expended: safe interstate travel."

Justice O'Connor, in her dissent, said the vast majority of highway deaths involving drinking were caused by people over the age of 21. "Establishment of a minimum drinking age of 21 is not sufficiently related to interstate highway construction to justify so conditioning funds appropriated for that purpose," she said.

South Dakota had argued in its appeal (South Dakota v. Dole, No. 86-260) that its law fostered "temperance and safety" by giving 19- and 20-year-olds access to "legal drinking, as opposed to surreptitious drinking that will inevitably occur."...

* * * * * * * * * * * *

The Court also gave Congress an important spending power victory by striking down a law—passed by Congress itself—giving the president the authority to veto individual appropriations in the federal budget or some targeted tax breaks. The Line Item Veto Act, passed in 1996, was an effort by a Republican-controlled Congress to tame government spending by giving the president the right to strike out specific items in a funding measure without vetoing the entire bill. President Bill Clinton, a Democrat, signed the bill into law and then invited a test case by vetoing, among other items, a provision waiving the government's right to recoup about $2.6 billion from the state of New York collected from health-care providers.

New York City challenged the line-item veto as unconstitutional, and the Supreme Court agreed in a 6-3 decision, *Clinton v. City of New York* (1998). Justice Stevens said the act violated the Presentment Clause, which provides that before a bill can become law, it must be passed by the House of Representatives and Senate and then "presented" to the president for signing (Art. I, sec. 7, cls. 2 and 3). The laws left on the books after Clinton's vetoes, Stevens wrote, were "truncated versions" of the bills passed by Congress. Whatever the policy arguments, he said, "Congress cannot alter the procedures set out in Article I, section 7, without amending the Constitution."

JUNE 26, 1998
JUSTICES, 6-3, BAR VETO OF LINE ITEMS IN BILLS
SPENDING AT ISSUE
By ROBERT PEAR

The Supreme Court ruled today that the Constitution prohibited the President from rewriting legislation by vetoing single items of spending or specific tax breaks approved by Congress.

In a 6-to-3 decision, the Court rejected a decades-old effort to strengthen the hand of the President in struggles with Congress.

The Court quoted George Washington, who presided over the Constitutional Convention and later wrote that a President must "approve all the parts of a bill, or reject it in toto," but cannot modify the text of legislation presented to him by Congress.

The Court's reasoning today was exceptionally simple. "The President has amended two acts of Congress by repealing a portion of each," said the majority opinion, by Justice John Paul Stevens. "Repeal of statutes, no less than enactment, must conform with Article I" of the Constitution, which established "a single finely wrought and exhaustively considered procedure" for enacting laws.

In 1996, Congress tried to change that procedure, and reduce the budget deficit, by allowing the President to cancel individual items of Federal spending and tax breaks. But the Court said today that such line item vetoes were unconstitutional.

"Failure of political will does not justify unconstitutional remedies," Justice Kennedy declared. "Abdication of responsibility is not part of the constitutional design."

The Line Item Veto Act was passed as part of the Republicans' "Contract With America." Sixty-nine senators and more than 290 House members voted for it.

Presidents since Ulysses S. Grant have sought the line item veto, and Ronald Reagan popularized the idea.

Justice Kennedy said that the device "compromises the political liberty of our citizens" by concentrating power in the hands of the President. "Liberty is always at stake when one or more of the branches seek to transgress the separation of powers," he said.

The dissenters—Justices Antonin Scalia, Stephen G. Breyer and Sandra Day O'Connor—would have upheld the line item veto. Justice Scalia said that "there is not a dime's worth of difference" between allowing the President to cancel

> " Failure of political will does not justify unconstitutional remedies.
> —Justice Anthony M. Kennedy, *Clinton v. City of New York* "

"The Line Item Veto Act authorizes the President himself to effect the repeal of laws, for his own policy reasons, without observing the procedures set out in Article I," Justice Stevens said.

President Clinton, traveling in China, said he was "deeply disappointed" with the ruling. "The decision is a defeat for all Americans," Mr. Clinton said. "It deprives the President of a valuable tool for eliminating waste in the Federal budget and for enlivening the public debate over how to make the best use of public funds."

Mr. Clinton has used the line item veto to rewrite 11 laws, eliminating 82 items, including money for New York City hospitals and a tax break for Idaho potato growers.

Today's decision came in lawsuits filed by New York City, the Greater New York Hospital Association, two unions of health care workers, the Snake River Potato Growers and one of its officers.

In an opinion concurring with Justice Stevens, Justice Anthony M. Kennedy chided Congress for surrendering power to the President.

a particular project, through the line item veto, and allowing him to spend money on a particular item at his discretion.

In addition to Justice Kennedy, Chief Justice William H. Rehnquist and Justices David H. Souter, Clarence Thomas and Ruth Bader Ginsburg joined the majority opinion by Justice Stevens in the case, Clinton v. City of New York, No. 97-1374.

Two champions of the line item veto, Senators John McCain of Arizona and Daniel R. Coats of Indiana, both Republicans, said they would keep fighting for it.

They have proposed an alternative, under which each item in an omnibus appropriations bill would be submitted to the President as a separate piece of legislation for him to sign or veto.

Under this arrangement, the President would receive thousands of bills each year.

Justice Stevens said the Line Item Veto Act "gives the President the unilateral power to change the text of duly enacted statutes."

In exercising the power, President Clinton has infuriated members of Congress, including many who supported the device in principle. Conservative Republicans joined Democrats in complaining that Mr. Clinton had killed worthy projects in their home states. In February, Congress overturned the vetoes of 38 military construction projects worth $287 million.

The amount of money saved by Mr. Clinton's line item vetoes is difficult to calculate, but members of Congress said it was less than 1 percent of the total Federal budget of $1.6 trillion.

Senator Robert C. Byrd, Democrat of West Virginia, the foremost opponent of the line item veto, was ecstatic today.

"This is a great day for the United States of America, a great day for the Constitution of the United States," Mr. Byrd said. "Today we feel that the liberties of the American people have been assured. God save this honorable Court!"

In a dissenting opinion, Justice Breyer said the line item veto was an acceptable "experiment" that did not "threaten the liberties of individual citizens."

Mr. Byrd, who has served in the Senate for nearly 40 years, disagreed.

The Senator quoted Sir William Blackstone, the 18th century English jurist, who wrote: "In all tyrannical governments, the supreme magistracy, or the right of both making and enforcing the laws, is vested in one and the same man, or one and the same body of men. And wherever these two powers are united together, there can be no public liberty."

Mr. Byrd led six members of Congress in challenging the constitutionality of the line item veto last year, before Mr. Clinton had used the device. In June 1997, the Supreme Court ruled that there was no genuine "case or controversy" because the lawmakers had not suffered any "personal, concrete injury."

Today, by contrast, the Court said that the New York hospitals and the Idaho potato growers had suffered an "actual injury." Justice Stevens said that the line item veto, by creating a potential liability of at least $2.6 billion for New York, could harm the city's financial strength and borrowing power.

Senator Daniel Patrick Moynihan, Democrat of New York, rejoiced at the decision. "In the history of Congress," Mr. Moynihan said, "we have never had an issue of such importance for the powers of the executive and legislative branches. Liberty has prevailed."

As a result of the ruling, New York can keep all the Federal money it received for the care of poor people under Medicaid, and Idaho potato growers can keep the tax break they received from Congress. Under the Line Item Veto Act, the President could cancel tax breaks that benefited fewer than 101 people.

People affected by other line item vetoes, including banks and insurance companies and military contractors, will also benefit, even though they did not challenge President Clinton's actions in court.

"Everybody who was a victim should be standing in line at the Treasury or some other agency to get their money or to file for a tax refund if they've already paid taxes," said Alan B. Morrison, a lawyer who filed a brief for three House Democrats opposed to the line item veto.

One of those Democrats, Representative David E. Skaggs of Colorado, said, "The Supreme Court has saved Congress from itself."

More than 40 governors have some form of line item veto, but the power is usually granted by state constitutions, not just by state laws.

Justice Stevens said the Court was expressing "no opinion about the wisdom of the procedures authorized by the Line Item Veto Act." But, he said, if Congress wants to establish such procedures, it must amend the Federal Constitution.

. . . .

NATIONAL DEFENSE AND FOREIGN AFFAIRS

The Constitution divides powers over national defense and foreign affairs between the president and Congress. Congress's enumerated powers include the power "to declare war," but the president is "Commander in Chief" of the armed forces (Art. II, sec. 2, cl. 1). The president has the power to make treaties, but only with "the Advice and Consent of the Senate" (Art. II, sec. 2, cl. 2). The Supreme Court has generally upheld Congress's authority to pass wartime legislation even if the measures tested constitutional limits. The Court has also generally upheld the president's exercise of presidential powers and—up until the war on terrorism cases—steered clear of refereeing wartime disputes between the two branches. (See page 84.)

NATIONAL DEFENSE

Congress has formally declared war only five times: the War of 1812, the Mexican War, the Spanish American War, World War I, and World War II. No formal declaration was made in other conflicts, including the Civil War, the Korean War, and the Vietnam War. Congress did approve formal authorizations for the president to use military force in the Gulf War (1991) and the Iraq War (2003–).

In its one clear ruling on the issue, the Court upheld President Abraham Lincoln's exercise of war-making powers at the start of the Civil War without a formal declaration from Congress. But the Court's narrow majority relied in part on Congress's later ratification of Lincoln's actions.

With Congress in recess, Lincoln had ordered a blockade of Southern ports in April 1861; Congress passed measures in July and August authorizing the closing of Southern ports and ratifying Lincoln's other actions as if Congress had authorized them beforehand. Owners of several vessels seized as "prizes" before the congressional action sued later for compensation. The Court's decision in the *Prize Cases* (1863) rejected the owners' plea by a 5-4 vote.

The president cannot initiate war, Justice Robert C. Grier wrote, but the chief executive is "bound to accept the challenge without waiting for special legislative authority." Even if Lincoln had overstepped his authority, Grier said, Congress's later action "operated perfectly to cure the defect." The four dissenters argued, however, that under the Constitution, only Congress, not the president, has "the power to declare war or recognize its existence."

MARCH 11, 1863
DECISION IN THE NEW-ALMADEN CASE—PRIZE CASES—
CLOSE OF THE TERM.

WASHINGTON, Tuesday, March 10.

The previous announcement that the Supreme Court of the United States would, to-day, pronounce its decisions in the great Almaden case and the prize cases, attracted to the Court-room an unusually large number of distinguished lawyers from different parts of the country. The Almaden case has been argued by Messrs. Peachy, of California; O'Conor, of New-York; Reverdy Johnson, of Maryland, for the claimants, and by Judge J. J. Black, of Pennsylvania, and B. R. Curtis, formerly Associate Justice of the Supreme Court of the United States. Associate Justice Clifford occupied about three hours in the reading of the decision. All the facts in the case were particularly cited, and the documents involved critically examined. The result reached by the Court is in substance:

First—That no grant could be made of these quicksilver mines in Santa Clara County, California, excepting under the Colonization law, and none of the conditions were complied with. The proposition of the claimant could not stand, as it was founded on an erroneous assumption of the dispatch of the Mexican Minister of Relations, and therefore the claim for two square leagues of land cannot be sustained.

Second—The decision of the United States Commissioner cannot be rejected.

Third—Nothing like forfeiture is now proposed, because the title had never been acquired, for the claimant did not pursue the necessary steps to obtain it. There was no registry or survey, no boundary fixed, no stakes set, &c., and in addition the claimant failed to show that the Alcalde had a right to confirm the title.

Fourth—The parties most interested knew the bill was invalid, and the Government of Mexico must have known the claim was unfounded. This position was maintained by an examination of papers connected with the case. Justice Wayne, Catron and Grier dissented from this opinion, believing there was no fraud.

The counsel in the several prize cases heretofore argued were Messrs. Lord and Edwards, of New-York, and Carlisle, of Washington, for the claimants, and Representative Sedgwick and Mr. Evarts, of New-York; Mr. Dana, District Attorney of Massachusetts; and Mr. Eames, for the United States. Justice Grier, in delivering the opinion of the Court, in the prize cases, of which the following is a brief abstract, said there were certain principles of law which were applicable to all of them. That a blockade *de facto* actually existed by the President's Proclamation of the 19th of April, 1861, is an admitted fact, and that the President, as Chief Executive of the Government and Commander-in-Chief of the Army and Navy, was the proper person to make such ratification, is not questioned. To justify the capture of prizes, a war must exist *de facto*, and the parties to be affected must have knowledge of the use of this mode of coercion. Under the Law of Nations, to prosecute a war it was not necessary that both parties should be sovereign nations. Insurrection against a Government

attack upon Fort Sumter, and a knowledge of a Government of the seceded States became known in Europe, England issued a proclamation of neutrality. This was similarly followed by other nations. After such an official recognition by foreign States they are estopped from denying the existence of a war and complaining of our treatment toward them as neutrals. They cannot deny the existence of a civil war and thus cripple the army of the Government by sophistical definitions. The law of nations is the common consent as well as the common sense of the world. Congress had approved and ratified the acts of the President as if they were legally done previous to their legalization. Authorities were here cited from Chief-Justice Story.

His Honor Justice Grier, remarked:

"We are of the opinion that the President had a right *jure belli*, to proclaim a blockade which neutrals were bound to observe. The destruction of property is a consequence of war. Money, wealth, the product of agriculture, are said to be the sinews of war. The law of nations autho-

> " A civil war is never publicly proclaimed. Its actual existence is a fact. The true test of its existence is stated when the whole course of justice is interrupted by revolt or rebellion; when the Courts cannot be kept open, and hostilities are conducted as if foreigners were invading the land. "

may or may not culminate in civil war, which is never solemnly declared, because it may occur by accident. After dwelling some time on this point, he said, the laws of war have their foundation in reason. Parties to a civil war exercised the practices and usages of nations at war, such as the exchange of prisoners, &c. These parties at the time must be two separate bodies, and in arms, as in this case. A civil war is never publicly proclaimed. Its actual existence is a fact. The true test of its existence is stated when the whole course of justice is interrupted by revolt or rebellion; when the Courts cannot be kept open, and hostilities are conducted as if foreigners were invading the land, Congress cannot declare war against the State. According to the Constitution, the President is bound by oath to take care that the laws are executed, and he can call out the militia to aid him in so doing, and to suppress insurrection against the Government and repel foreign invasion. He has no power to initiate and declare war, but he is bound to accept it. War, whether foreign or domestic, may exist without a declaration, as laid down by most writers on the law of nations. As soon as the

rize the cutting of these sinews by capturing property on the high seas. Under our very peculiar Constitution, citizens not only owe allegiance to the United States, but the States in which we live, hence the people acted as States in rising in hostility against the United States, and their right to do so is being decided by the wager of battle. The boundary between the belligerents is marked by bayonets. South of the line is the enemy's territory. The proclamation of the blockade is according to the law of nations. The cargo must share the rate of the vessel in case of violation."

Associate Justice Nelson delivered a dissenting opinion. After stating the circumstances of the case of the British ship *Hiawatha*, which was delayed for want of a tag at City Point after the fifteen days' notice given by the proclamation of the blockade, he said that the vessel had no intention of breaking the blockade, and from the facts in the case the seizure was not warranted. Another ground of objection was the vessel was entitled to warning according to the terms of the Proclamation. According to the Proclamation neutral ships were entitled to warning, and could be legally seized only on the second attempt to enter or leave a port. After discussing these points Mr. Nelson said as a law cannot be lawfully commenced without an act of Congress, it is equivalent to a most solemn declaration. The right of making war belongs to the supreme or sovereign power of a State, regulated by the fundamental laws of a nation. By our Constitution this power is lodged in Congress, and no power short of the Executive. It might be asked what would become of the peace and integrity of the country if the power could not be exercised until the meeting of Congress. The framers of the Constitution fully understood this question. He then quoted the laws authorizing the President to call out the militia, and using so much of the land and naval forces as may be necessary to suppress the insurrection, or to repel foreign invasion. There is ample provision in such cases during the recess of Congress. This is an exercise of the power under the municipal law of the country, and not under the law of nations. In further argument he said: Congress passed a law confirming all the President's acts after the 4th of March, 1861, as far as possible. It had been argued that this legislation brought into effect *ex post facto* civil war; but admitting the full weight of this, it affords no grounds of justification. These acts were constitutionally valid. No subsequent ratification can make them valid. After the most careful consideration of this question, there can be no civil war between this Government and the States until it is recognized by act of Congress of July 13, 1861. The President does not possess power under the Constitution to declare war or recognize its existence under the Constitution. Changing the condition of the country from peace to war belongs to Congress, and, consequently, no other power can set on foot a blockade under the law of nations. Hence, the captures under it prior to July 13, 1861, are illegal and void, and hence the decrees of condemnation should be reversed. Chief Justice Taney and Associates Clifford and Catron, joined Judge Nelson in this dissenting opinion. . . .

* * * * * * * * * * *

A century after the Civil War, some opponents of the Vietnam War argued strenuously that the war was unconstitutional because it was never formally declared by Congress. The Court stayed out of the dispute by refusing to review lower court decisions on the ground that the challenges raised political questions not resolvable by the courts. As the war wound down, Congress in 1973 passed the War Powers Act to limit presidential war-making powers. The resolution, enacted over President Richard M. Nixon's veto, requires the president to notify Congress before introducing U.S. armed forces into conflict abroad and requires congressional approval for a commitment after sixty days. Later presidents have contended the measure is unconstitutional; the Court has never ruled on the issue.

NEWS ANALYSIS
NOVEMBER 12, 1967
THE COURT AND WAR
By FRED P. GRAHAM

WASHINGTON—The legality of the United States Vietnam policy has been debated in Congress, the legal journals and the United Nations, but it has never been mentioned before the tribunal that is supposed to settle America's legal issues—the Supreme Court.

Until recently, nobody had criticized the Court for this, but last week the Court was taken to task by an unlikely critic—sober, straightlaced Justice Potter Stewart.

Justice Stewart's complaint was that the Supreme Court had been neither hawk nor dove, but chicken.

> "Justice Stewart's complaint was that the Supreme Court had been neither hawk nor dove, but chicken."

He dissented Monday when the majority declined to review the appeal of three soldiers who had attempted unsuccessfully in the lower courts to bar the Army from sending them to Vietnam.

SUIT DISMISSED

They claimed that the war was illegal and that they might be held guilty as war criminals if they participated in it. But the lower courts dismissed the suit on the grounds that these were political and military questions that had no place in a court of law.

"These are large and deeply troubling questions," Justice Stewart said in his dissent. "We cannot make these problems go away simply by refusing to hear the case of three obscure Army privates. I think the Court should squarely face them."

He and Justice William O. Douglas, who had protested in a previous dissent that the Supreme Court should not close its eyes to legal problems simply because they are linked to the war, ticked off the list of legal problems that have been argued in other forums but frozen out of the courts.

Is the war a "war" in the constitutional sense that it must be declared by Congress? If it is not, where did the President get the authority to send troops into combat? If he is right in saying that Congress's Gulf of Tonkin resolution authorized him in advance to fight in Vietnam, was it an improper delegation of Congress's power to declare war? Is the war required or prohibited by any U.S. treaties?

Both Justices made it clear that they were not prejudging these questions, but they thought that the Supreme Court should at least decide if men who are called upon to fight can raise them in court.

With only two Justices having declared themselves in favor of taking a look (Justice Thurgood Marshall's views

War Record

The Supreme Court has a record, reaching as far back as the Civil War, of permitting highly questionable acts by the Executive during wartime. Occasionally it has declared those, or similar acts, illegal—but only after the war had ended.

Not until the Civil War was over, for example, did the Court declare that President Lincoln had overstepped his Constitutional authority in suspending habeas corpus by trying civilians in military courts.

It similarly waited until peace came before declaring unconstitutional the martial law imposed on Hawaii during World War II.

are unknown because he did not take part in the week's decision), it seems unlikely that the present Court will ever touch such a case. The votes of four Justices are necessary to grant review of an appeal.

This does not, as columnist David Lawrence wrote last week, indicate that there are no serious questions about the legality of the war. Nor does it mean that the Supreme Court cannot legally review the acts of the Commander in Chief. Technically, its power of judicial review extends to all Federal constitutional questions.

Rather, it stems from a longstanding judicial reluctance to lock horns with the President in wartime over the legality of his wartime actions.

This tradition underscores the regrettable fact that wars are exercises of power, not law. In the jargon of the courts, questions about the conduct of wars tend not to be "justiciable"—susceptible to resolution in the courts—and nobody seriously expects the Supreme Court to resolve them.

· · · · · · · · · · · ·

The federal government conscripted men into the army during the Civil War, but the constitutionality of a draft law was not tested in court until World War I. Opponents of the war challenged the draft law immediately after Congress passed it on May 17, 1917. Among other arguments, they contended the law amounted to involuntary servitude in violation of the anti-slavery Thirteenth Amendment.

The Supreme Court relied on Congress's enumerated power "to raise and support armies" in rejecting the challenge in a unanimous decision officially cited as *Arver v. United States* (1918) and commonly known as the *Selective Draft Law Cases.* "As the mind cannot conceive an army without the men to compose it," Chief Justice White wrote, "on the face of the Constitution the objection that it does not give power to provide for such men would seem to be too frivolous for further notice." The involuntary servitude argument, White said, was "refuted by its mere statement." He similarly brushed aside arguments that the law gave state officials too broad discretion in administering the draft or that it violated either the Establishment or the Free Exercise Clause by exempting some but not all religious opponents of the war.

**Arver v. United States
(Selective Draft Law Cases)**

Decided: January 7, 1918

Vote: 9 (E. White, McKenna, Holmes, Day, Van Devanter, Pitney, McReynolds, Brandeis, Clarke)

0

Opinion of the Court: E. White

JANUARY 8, 1918
DRAFT LAW UPHELD BY SUPREME COURT

Right to Compel Military Service in Time of Need Held to be Fundamental.

DECISION ON SEVEN CASES

Conspiracy Appeals, Including Those of Berkman and Goldman, to be Adjudicated Later.

Special to The New York Times

WASHINGTON, Jan. 7.—The United States Supreme Court today passed upon seven cases arising under the selective draft law, and decided all, excepting those involving the charge of conspiracy, adversely to the men drafted or subject to draft. The constitutionality of the Draft act was sustained against every contention. Several times in the opinion, which was written by the Chief Justice, argu-

1917. Jones petitioned for a writ of habeas corpus after he had been put into jail. The others rested their resistance to the act on the assertion that it was unconstitutional, and contended that the Constitution did not give Congress the power to compel military service by a selective draft.

The decision, therefore, turned on the construction to be placed on the language of Article I., Section 8, of the

> " It may not be doubted that the very conception of a just Government and its duty to the citizen includes the reciprocal obligation of the citizen to render military service in case of need and the right to compel it.
>
> —Chief Justice Edward D. White, *Arver v. United States* "

ments made for the drafted men were characterized as "absolutely without merit."

The conspiracy cases, in which Emma Goldman and Alexander Berkman were defendants in the United States District Court for the Southern District of New York (Manhattan), and Charles E. Ruthenberg, Alfred Wagenknecht, and Charles Baker defendants in the District Court for the Northern District of Ohio, were held for further consideration.

The cases decided involved the failure of Joseph F. Arver, Alfred F. Grahl, Otto and Walter Wangerin, Morris Becker, and Louis Kramer, all of Minnesota; Albert Jones of Georgia, and Meyer Graubard of Kansas to present themselves for registration under the draft law, enacted May 18,

Constitution, which provides that Congress has power "to declare war * * * to raise and support armies * * * to make rules for the government and regulation of the land and naval forces * * * to make all laws which shall be necessary and proper for carrying into execution the foregoing powers. * * *"

POWER OF CONGRESS.

Regarding the contention that Congress has no power to exact enforced military duty by the citizen the decision says:

"This but challenges the existence of all power, for governmental power which has no sanction to it and which can only be exercised provided the citizen consents is in no substantial sense such a power. It is argued, however, that, although this is abstractly true, it is not concretely so because, as compelled military service is repugnant to a free Government and in conflict with all the great guarantees of the Constitution as to individual liberty, it must be assumed that the authority to raise armies was intended to be limited to the right to call an army into existence, counting alone upon the willingness of the citizen to do his duty in time of public need—that is, in time of war. But the premise of this proposition is so devoid of foundation that it leaves not even a shadow of ground upon which to base the conclusion.

"It may not be doubted that the very conception of a just Government and its duty to the citizen includes the reciprocal obligation of the citizen to render military service in case of need and the right to compel it. To do more than state the proposition is absolutely unnecessary in view of the practical illustration afforded by the almost universal legislation to that effect now in force.". . .

• • • • • • • • • • • •

In later decisions, the Court said Congress's power to classify and conscript manpower for military service is "beyond question." The Court in 1981 also deferred to Congress's decision to exempt women from the draft. The 7-2 decision in *Rostker v. Goldberg* rejected a sex discrimination challenge brought by several men. "Congress acted well within its constitutional authority when it authorized the registration of men, and not women, under the Military Selective Service Act," then Associate Justice Rehnquist wrote.

The Court has been more tentative in ruling on wartime economic measures, though it has never invalidated such a law while a war was going on. The Court's rulings in the *Legal Tender Cases* first struck down but then upheld the Civil War law authorizing paper money; later, the Court upheld the Civil War income tax. The Court in 1921 struck down a World War I statute controlling food prices as too vague, but did so without squarely ruling on Congress's authority to pass the law. The Court's decision in *Yakus v. United States* (1944) upheld the Emergency Price Control Act of 1942, which created the Office of Price Administration to set maximum prices on commodities and rents. The 6-3 ruling rejected an argument that the law delegated too much power to the agency; the Court noted that the defendants convicted of violating the law had not challenged Congress's authority to pass it.

FOREIGN AFFAIRS

The Supremacy Clause makes treaties—just like the Constitution and laws passed by Congress—"the supreme Law of the Land" (Art. VI, cl. 2). But this lawmaking power originates with the president, not Congress. The only treaty power explicitly given Congress under the Constitution is the Senate's power of "advice and consent" to approve treaties, by a two-thirds vote, as negotiated by the executive.

Ever since 1795, however, the Senate has claimed the power to amend and modify treaties, and the Supreme Court twice has endorsed the authority. The Senate "must agree" to a treaty before it becomes law, the Court wrote in *Haver v. Yaker* (1870), and is "not required to adopt or reject as a whole, but may modify or amend it." The ruling prevented the Swiss heirs of a Kentucky man from claiming inheritance rights under a treaty that the Senate did not ratify until after the man's death. In 1901 the Court implicitly upheld the Senate's power to amend a treaty in discussing a proposed amendment that actually failed to win two-thirds approval. In a concurrence, one of the justices specified that the Senate could make its approval conditional upon adoption of amendments to the treaty.

The Court has said that Congress has the authority to abrogate a treaty, yet it has also suggested in passing comments that the president alone can abrogate a treaty. The justices avoided ruling on the question when some senators challenged President Jimmy Carter's abrogation of the mutual defense treaty with Taiwan after recognizing the Chinese government in Beijing. The summary 6-3 decision in *Goldwater v. Carter* (1979) ordered the case dismissed without a ruling. Four justices deemed the issue a nonjusticiable political question, while a fifth said the case was not "ripe" because Congress itself had not acted to challenge Carter's action. In a dissent, Justice Byron R. White argued the case should have been set for full argument; White said the president's authority to abrogate a treaty was "a substantial issue that we should address only after briefing and oral argument."

DECEMBER 14, 1979
HIGH COURT BACKS CARTER ON ENDING OF TAIWAN PACT

By LINDA GREENHOUSE
Special to The New York Times

WASHINGTON, Dec. 13—The Supreme Court today ordered a lower court to dismiss a challenge by 24 members of Congress to President Carter's termination of the defense treaty with Taiwan. The action cleared the way for expiration of the treaty on Jan. 1, the date that President Carter announced a year ago when he declared United States recognition of the Peking regime as "the sole legal Government of China."

Six Justices agreed with the dismissal of the suit and a seventh, Associate Justice William J. Brennan, voted to affirm last month's Court of Appeals opinion that upheld the President's authority. Only two Justices, Harry A. Blackmun and Byron R. White, voted to hear oral argument in the case, the course urged by Senator Barry Goldwater and the other legislators who brought the original lawsuit.

Paul D. Kamenar, a lawyer for the members of Congress, said the Court's action in summarily disposing of the case without argument was "indefensible."

"I am ashamed for the Court," he said.

At the Justice Department, Kenneth S. Geller, a Deputy Solicitor General, called the Court's action "a substantial victory for the executive branch's prerogatives in the foreign affairs field." The department had urged the Court to deny the Goldwater petition for review of the Court of Appeals decision. The Justices went further, ordering dismissal of the suit itself.

TWO DIFFERENT RATIONALES

The six who voted for dismissal pursued two different rationales. Associate Justice William H. Rehnquist, in a four-page statement joined by Chief Justice Warren E. Burger and Associate Justices Potter Stewart and John Paul Stevens, said the question presented by the suit was "political" and therefore not appropriate for resolution by the Federal courts.

This was the argument made unsuccessfully by the Government in the lower courts. The Justice Department said at the Court of Appeals that the dispute should be resolved through the "give-and-take accommodation of the political process," because judicial intervention in treaty matters "would create a serious potential for disruption of lengthy and complex diplomatic negotiations."

The Court of Appeals rejected that argument, however, and went on to decide the merits of the case in the President's favor.

In his statement today, Justice Rehnquist said the case was "nonjusticiable because it involves that authority of the President in the conduct of our country's foreign relations and the extent to which the Senate or the Congress is authorized to negate the action of the President."

In a fifth vote for dismissal, Associate Justice Lewis F. Powell said the "political question" analysis was mistaken. Rather, he said, the suit should be dismissed as "not ripe for judicial review," because Congress itself, as opposed to the 24 members who brought the suit, had never taken "appropriate formal action" to challenge the President's termination authority.

If such action had been taken, Justice Powell wrote, "the resulting uncertainty could have serious consequences for our country." In that event, he said, "it would be the duty of this Court to resolve the issue."

The sixth Justice for dismissal, Thurgood Marshall, said only that he "concurs in the result." He did not elaborate.

Justice Brennan, who voted to affirm the Court of Appeals opinion "insofar as it rests upon the President's well-established authority to recognize, and withdraw recognition from, foreign governments," said that the Rehnquist group "profoundly misapprehends the political question principle."

"The issue of decision-making authority," he wrote, "must be resolved as a matter of constitutional law, not political discretion; accordingly, it falls within the competence of the courts."

. . . .

Missouri v. Holland

Decided: April 19, 1920

Vote: 7 (E. White, McKenna, Holmes, Day, McReynolds, Brandeis, Clarke)

2 (Van Devanter, Pitney)

Opinion of the Court: Holmes

Dissenting without opinion:
Van Devanter, Pitney

In an 1899 ruling, the Court said that a treaty cannot "authorize what the Constitution forbids," but it has never found a treaty provision unconstitutional. Indeed, the Court once appeared to suggest that a treaty could give Congress authority it otherwise lacked. The 7-2 decision in *Missouri v. Holland* (1920) rejected Missouri's effort to challenge federal regulation of the hunting of migratory birds. Congress adopted the regulations in the Migratory Bird Treaty Act of 1918 to implement a pact negotiated between the United States and Great Britain (for Canada) two years earlier. Although similar regulations that Congress passed before the treaty had been ruled unconstitutional by lower federal courts, the Supreme Court said the treaty eliminated any doubts about the new law. "If the treaty is valid," Justice Holmes wrote, "there can be no dispute about the validity of the statute under Article 1, Section 8, as a necessary and proper means to execute the powers of the Government."

APRIL 20, 1920
MIGRATORY BIRD LAW UPHELD

Supreme Court Sustains Act to Carry Out Treaty with Britain.

WASHINGTON, April 19.—The migratory bird act of 1918, designed to carry out provisions of a treaty between this country and Great Britain for the protection of migratory birds, was held constitutional today by the Supreme Court.

Justice Holmes, in rendering the majority opinion, declared that "a national interest of very nearly the first magnitude" was involved, and that, except for the treaty and the statute, there soon might be no birds for any power to deal with.

"We see nothing in the Constitution that compels the Government to sit by while a food supply is cut off and the protectors of our forests and our crops are destroyed," Justice Holmes said.

. . . .

The Court clarified the decision somewhat in a later ruling that found unconstitutional a provision in an executive agreement between the United States and Great Britain permitting military dependents overseas to be prosecuted in U.S. military courts instead of civilian courts. "No agreement with a foreign nation can confer power on the Congress, or on any other branch of Government, which is free from the restraints of the Constitution," Justice Hugo L. Black wrote in *Reid v. Covert* (1957). The ruling in *Missouri v. Holland,* Black explained, dealt only with the issue of state versus national authority under the Tenth Amendment. (For more on executive agreements, see page 98.)

Congressional Affairs

The Constitution makes no specific mention of a congressional power of investigation, but the Supreme Court has said that the power is "inherent in the legislative process." The Court has ruled that investigations must have a legislative purpose, however, and has exercised judicial review in some cases to protect witnesses' rights. The Constitution does specify Congress's authority over its internal affairs, including each chamber's power to prescribe rules of procedure. The Court has found few occasions to interfere with Congress's exercise of these prerogatives.

INVESTIGATIVE POWERS

Congress first claimed a power of investigation in 1792, when the House of Representatives conducted an inquiry into an Indian attack on an army road-building party the year before that left six hundred men dead. Since the late twentieth century, televised congressional hearings like those on the Vietnam War or the Nixon administration's Watergate scandals have commanded national attention, helping shape public opinion whether or not they result in legislation.

The Supreme Court recognized the congressional power of investigation as early as 1820 with a decision upholding Congress's power to summarily punish a nonmember for contempt. Neither the House or the Senate has exercised that power since 1932. Instead, contempt of Congress is now treated—as first authorized under an 1857 statute—as a criminal offense to be prosecuted by the executive branch.

The Court first asserted the right to review congressional contempt citations in 1881, when it heard a challenge by a witness, Hallett Kilbourn, who had refused to produce papers sought by a House committee investigating the failure of the banking firm of Jay Cooke & Company. After the House ordered Kilbourn jailed for contempt, he filed a habeas corpus petition naming as defendants several House officers, including Sergeant at Arms John Thompson. In *Kilbourn v. Thompson* (1881), the Court ruled the investigation an improper inquiry into a bankruptcy case pending in the courts. Congress could not exercise its contempt power, Justice Samuel F. Miller wrote, "beyond the power of any court or any other tribunal whatever to inquire into the grounds on which the order was made."

Kilbourn established a three-part rule: congressional investigations must not invade areas reserved to the executive or the judiciary, must deal with subjects within Congress's legislative powers, and must suggest in their resolutions a congressional intent to legislate on the subject. In later cases, the Court relaxed those requirements somewhat, dropping the need to specify a legislative intent and affirming Congress's right to delve into affairs considered by a witness to be private. The "power of inquiry—with process to enforce it—is an essential and appropriate auxiliary to the legislative function," the Court declared in *McGrain v. Daugherty* (1927). The decision upheld the Senate's right to subpoena Mally (Mal) S. Daugherty, brother of Attorney General Harry M. Daugherty, as part of an investigation into the attorney general's failure while in office to prosecute the primary instigators of the Teapot Dome oil-lease scandal.

McGrain v. Daugherty

Decided: January 17, 1927

Vote: 8 (Taft, Holmes, Van Devanter, McReynolds, Brandeis, Sutherland, Butler, Sanford)

0

Opinion of the Court: Van Devanter

Did not participate: Stone

JANUARY 18, 1927
CONGRESS CAN FORCE WITNESS TO TESTIFY, HIGH COURT DECIDES

Sweeping Opinion Says Senate Has Right to Punish Mal Daugherty for Contempt.

OTHER CASES ARE AFFECTED

Reed Will Proceed Against Insull and Crowe for Silence on Primary Funds.

SINCLAIR ALREADY CITED

Supreme Bench Unanimously Holds Power Over Witnesses Is a Needed Legislative Aid.

Special to The New York Times

WASHINGTON, Jan. 17.—Congress, in the exercise of its legislative functions, has the right to compel attendance of witnesses at hearings and recusant or recalcitrant witnesses may be haled before it for citation for contempt, the Supreme Court held today, in a decision in the Mal S. Daugherty case. This decision is regarded as one of the most sweeping ever handed down by the tribunal.

Under today's decree Mal S. Daugherty, brother of Harry M. Daugherty, who was Attorney General in the Harding Cabinet, may and probably will be called before the Senate to answer questions he failed to answer during the investigation by the Brookhart committee of the Daugherty administration of the Department of Justice.

The court's assertion of the right of Congress to require witnesses to attend its committees in response to subpoenas is said to affect the case of Harry F. Sinclair, who refused to testify in the Senate oil investigation and on that account awaits trial on a charge of contempt.

M. Daugherty as Attorney General, did not participate in consideration of the case.

Whatever disposition the Senate may make of the case of Mal Daugherty or those who refused to testify before the Reed committee was regarded as unimportant in contrast with the broad principle laid down by the court that the right of "inquiry" is part of the power to legislate, and this power, even if "abusively and oppressively exerted," cannot be denied.

Leaders of both branches of Congress hailed the Supreme Court decision as fully confirming the inquisitorial powers of both bodies, as the court emphasized that its decision as to the power of the Senate in dealing with witnesses applied with equal force to the House of Representatives.

Senator Wheeler, author of the resolution under which former Attorney General Daugherty's administration was investigated, said tonight that Mal Daugherty would be called before the Senate to answer charges of contempt and to receive punishment.

> This decision is regarded as one of the most sweeping ever handed down by the tribunal.

It also affects Samuel Insull, public utility executive of Illinois; Robert E. Crowe, State's Attorney of Illinois; E. H. Wright, a colored political leader of Chicago, and Thomas F. Cunningham of Philadelphia, who refused to give certain information to the Senate campaign fund investigating committee.

Senator Reed of Missouri, Chairman of the Campaign Fund Committee, gave notice in the Senate today that in view of the court's decision in the Mal Daugherty case he would cite the witness who had proved recalcitrant before his committee for such action as the Senate deemed appropriate.

BROAD PRINCIPLE LAID DOWN.

Today's opinion, handed down by Associate Justice Van Devanter, was concurred in by eight of nine members of the court. Associate Justice Stone, who succeeded H.

The Senator had not yet decided whether Mr. Daugherty would be questioned and would not do so until he had conferred with Emory S. Buckner, Federal Attorney at New York, as Mr. Wheeler does not wish to bring out testimony from Mal Daugherty which might embarrass or interrupt a new trial of Harry M. Daugherty and Thomas F. Miller, former Alien Property Custodian, on charges growing out of the American Metals case. Senator Wheeler will inform the Senate in a few days of the action of the Supreme Court and will ask for a resolution to bring Mal Daugherty before the Senate.

LOWER COURT IS REVERSED.

Senator Wheeler charged that Harry M. Daugherty as Attorney General had been guilty of various acts of misfeasance and nonfeasance. As head of the Midland National Bank of Washington Court House, Ohio, Mal Daugherty refused twice to appear before the Brookhart committee. The first subpoena directed him to bring the deposit ledgers of his bank and other documents, all of which, according to testimony in the Daugherty-Miller trial, were later destroyed.

No explanation was made of the failure of Mal Daugherty to comply with the Senate subpoenas. Daugherty's recalcitrancy was reported to the Senate on April 26, 1924, which adopted a resolution for his arrest.

Two days later Mr. Daugherty was taken into custody by a Deputy Sergeant at Arms of the Senate on a warrant. He sued for a writ of habeas corpus in the Federal District Court at Cincinnati and was released on $5,000 bond. On Aug. 19, 1924, appeal was taken from the lower court, whose ruling was reversed today.

SENATE DISCUSSES DECISION.

News of the decision reached the Senate a few minutes after Justice Van Devanter began to read the opinion.

"The Supreme Court reverses the findings of the District Court, so that the Senate is at liberty to proceed as it deems proper—and, of course, within the law—against Mr. Daugherty," Senator Reed of Missouri told the Senate.

"I say that for the information of the Senate and only desire to add that the decision is of vast importance to both House and Senate in that it firmly establishes the right of either of these bodies, when engaged in an investigation which has relation to the legislative powers of Congress, and the right of either body to punish for contempt witnesses who refuse to answer proper questions.". . .

• • • • • • • • • • • •

Despite the broad berth for congressional investigations, the Court has continued to exercise the power of judicial review to protect witnesses' rights, most notably during the anti-subversion investigations of the early Cold War era. In the most important ruling, *Watkins v. United States* (1957), the Court threw out a contempt of Congress citation against John Watkins, a union official who had refused in 1954 to answer questions from the House Special Committee to Investigate Un-American Activities about other individuals' association with the Communist Party. "There is no congressional power to expose for the sake of exposure," Chief Justice Earl Warren wrote in the 6-1 decision. Communist infiltration of labor unions was a proper subject for congressional inquiry, Warren said, but the committee had not made its topic clear when Watkins asked the panel to explain why the questions were pertinent.

Earlier, the Court in 1955 had upheld a witness's right to plead the Fifth Amendment privilege against self-incrimination in refusing to answer questions from a congressional committee. By the time the case reached the high court, Congress had already responded to the tactic by passing the Immunity Act of 1954, which created a procedure for compelling a witness to testify by granting immunity from prosecution. The Court upheld the act in a 1956 case. "Once the reason for the privilege ceases, the privilege ceases," Justice Felix Frankfurter wrote in *Ullmann v. United States*.

Watkins v. United States

Decided: June 17, 1957

Vote: 6 (Warren, Black, Frankfurter, Douglas, Harlan II, Brennan)
            1 (Clark)

Opinion of the Court: Warren

Concurring opinion: Frankfurter

Dissenting opinion: Clark

Did not participate: Burton, Whittaker

INTERNAL AFFAIRS

The Constitution specifies that each chamber of Congress "shall be the Judge of the . . . Qualifications of its own Members" (Art. I, sec. 5, cl. 1). The Supreme Court ruled that power entailed the right to investigate election disputes in a pair of cases arising from the 1926 election of Republican William S. Vare to a Senate seat from Pennsylvania. The ruling in *Reed v. County Commissioners of Delaware County, Pa.* (1928) upheld a Senate committee's suit to compel local officials to produce ballot boxes from the election. In *Barry v. United States ex rel. Cunningham* (1929), the Court held that a Vare campaign contributor could be arrested for refusing to answer questions about his donations.

The Court has also upheld each chamber's power to punish or, with a two-thirds vote, expel a member. The Court ruled that the House overstepped its bounds in 1967, however, when it refused to seat Adam Clayton Powell Jr., a controversial African American Democratic congressman from New York, following his re-election to a twelfth term in 1966. The House action denied Powell his seat pending an investigation, which eventually led to a House vote on March 1, 1967, to exclude Powell from Congress. He then won election to the seat in a special election and again in a regular election in 1968 while also pursuing a constitutional challenge to the original exclusion.

Powell v. McCormack

> **Decided:** June 16, 1969
>
> **Vote:** 7 (Warren, Black, Douglas, Harlan II, Brennan, B. White, T. Marshall)
>
> 1 (Stewart)
>
> **Opinion of the Court:** Warren
>
> **Concurring opinion:** Douglas
>
> **Dissenting opinion:** Stewart

By a 7-1 vote, the Court held in *Powell v. McCormack* (1969) that the House had gone beyond its power to investigate the constitutionally prescribed qualifications for membership: age, citizenship, and residency in the House district. "The Constitution leaves the House without authority to exclude any person, duly elected by his constituents, who meets all the requirements for membership expressly prescribed in the Constitution," Chief Justice Warren wrote.

JUNE 17, 1969
HIGH COURT FINDS POWELL'S BARRING BY HOUSE ILLEGAL

BURGER REVERSED

7-1 Opinion, Written by Warren, Points to the Constitution

By FRED P. GRAHAM

Special to The New York Times

WASHINGTON, June 16—The Supreme Court ruled today that the House of Representatives had violated the Constitution when it excluded Representative Adam Clayton Powell from the 90th Congress.

In the historic 7-to-1 ruling, the Court upheld the Harlem Democrat's claim that a house of Congress cannot refuse to seat a duly elected member who meets the requirements of age, residency and American citizenship set out in the Constitution.

The House voted on March 1, 1967, to exclude Representative Powell on the ground that he had misused public funds and was contemptuous of the New York courts and committees of Congress. He sat out the 90th Congress and was readmitted last January after his constituents had elected him to represent them in the 91st Congress.

OTHER QUESTIONS REMAIN

The decision today did not involve a $25,000 fine levied against Representative Powell by the House or the question of his loss of 22 years' seniority and the chairmanship of the Education and Labor Committee. The Court returned the question of whether he should receive back pay to a lower court.

Chief Justice Earl Warren, announcing what may be his last major decision before he retires later this month, wrote the opinion, which asserted for the first time the Court's power to rule on the legality of an action of Congress in excluding a member.

In holding that "it is the responsibility of this Court to act as the ultimate interpreter of the Constitution," he reversed an opinion by the man who is scheduled to succeed him, Judge Warren E. Burger.

In his present capacity as a judge on the Court of Appeals for the District of Columbia, the recently confirmed Chief Justice-designate wrote an opinion dismissing Representative Powell's suit for reinstatement. The Burger opinion, which was one of three that reached the same conclusion, said that the courts should not rule on a political issue so fraught with dangers of conflicts between Congress and the courts.

CONFRONTATION UNCERTAIN

"Our system of government requires that Federal courts on occasion interpret the Constitution in a manner at variance with the construction given the document by another branch," Chief Justice Warren said today. "The alleged conflict that such an adjudication may cause cannot justify the courts' avoiding their constitutional responsibility."

Whether today's decision will, in fact, precipitate a confrontation between Congress and the Supreme Court over the separation of powers was not immediately evident. Few members of the House had had time to read the Chief Justice's 62-page opinion.

However, the Court sweetened the pill and lessened the prospects of a direct clash by means of two statements in the opinion—a declaration that the decision affected only Congress' power to exclude members and not its authority to expel them, and a ruling that Representative Powell's claim for lost wages must be pressed against employes of the House and not against its key members.

Representative Powell and 13 of his constituents in New York's 18th Congressional District initially brought the suit against the elected leaders of the House and some of its employes, asking for a declaratory judgment that they had acted unconstitutionally in excluding him.

The main thrust of his suit was for a vindication of his rights and for recovery of the $55,000 in pay that was lost.

Representative Powell won a clear statement today that his exclusion was illegal, but he won little else of immediate value. The High Court referred the case back to the Federal District Court here to rule on the "propriety" of his claim for a court order to force the House officials to pay his salary.

Mr. Powell is expected to ask Congress to restore his seniority and to revoke his fine, as well as to pay his $55,000 in back salary. In view of Congress's present attitude toward the Court, it would not be surprising if he

court reserved any opinion as to whether the House might legally expel a member after he is seated for malfeasances similar to those charged against Representative Powell, but it said that a member might not be excluded if he is over 25 years old and is an American citizen and a resident of the state from which he was elected. The House had never denied that Representative Powell met these qualifications.

Chief Justice Warren conceded that the House had in the past excluded properly elected members because they were polygamists, Socialists and Confederates, but he noted that Congress had also refused to bar controversial members on the ground that it lacked the power.

"Unquestionably," today's opinion stated, "Congress has an interest in preserving its institutional integrity, but in most cases that interest can be sufficiently safeguarded by the exercise of its power to punish its members for disorderly behavior and, in extreme cases, to expel a member with the concurrence of two-thirds.

"In short, both the intention of the framers, to the ex-

> " Throughout the litigation the House's attorneys insisted that the matter was no business of the courts. "

were rebuffed. Then he would probably go back to Federal District Court for an order to obtain his pay. He might also bring a new suit to bar collection of the fine and to regain his lost seniority.

ARTICLE I CITED

Throughout the litigation the House's attorneys insisted that the matter was no business of the courts.

They cited Article I, Section 5 of the Constitution, which declares that "each house shall be the judge of the elections, returns and qualifications of its own members . . ." and that "each house may determine the rules of its proceedings, punish its members for disorderly behavior, and, with the concurrence of two-thirds, expel a member." The vote against Representative Powell was 307 to 116, a margin of more than two-thirds.

The court opinion stressed that during the debate John W. McCormack, the Speaker of the House, had ruled that the action against Mr. Powell was an exclusion. The

tent it can be determined, and an examination of the basic principles of our democratic system persuade us that the Constitution does not vest in the Congress a discretionary power to deny membership by a majority vote."

The House's attorneys had also argued that the suit was forbidden by Article I, Section 6, Clause 1, which says that members of Congress "shall not be questioned in any other place" because of their votes. On that ground, the Court agreed in this case to dismiss the suit against the Congressman defendants, while upholding the suit against W. Pat Jennings, the Clerk of the House; Zeake W. Johnson Jr., the Sergeant-at-Arms, and William M. Miller, the Doorkeeper.

The Court also ruled against the House's claims that the case had become moot because Representative Powell was now back in his seat. It was on this point that the lone dissenter, Justice Potter Stewart, disagreed with the majority.

The House retained Bruce Bromley, a prominent New York lawyer, to prepare and argue its case, on the ground that separation-of-powers questions might be raised by having the Solicitor General's office represent the Legislative Branch.

Arthur Kinoy of New York and Herbert O. Reid of Washington, argued for Representative Powell.

HARLEM LEADERS HAIL RULING

Several Harlem leaders said yesterday that they hoped Congress would restore Representative Adam Clayton Powell to his committee chairmanship.

State Senator Basil Paterson, Harlem Democrat, said: "Now that the Supreme Court has established the fact that Congress illegally expelled Congressman Powell, I hope it will now obey the law and restore him to the chairmanship of the House Education and Labor Committee. He was never voted out as chairman but lost his chairmanship only as a result of the motion to unseat him."

Roy Wilkins, executive director of the National Association for the Advancement of Colored People, called the decision a "welcome indication of the faith of those who regard the Court as a bulwark of civil rights and liberties."

The Rev. A. Kendall Smith, pastor of the Beulah Baptist Church, 125 West 130th Street, expressed hope that "this law-and-order Congress will respect the law and ruling of the Supreme Court and will return to Mr. Powell all that is rightfully his legally."

Livingston Wingate, director of the New York branch of the National Urban League warned: "If they don't give him back his chairmanship, the Democrats have forfeited the black vote forever."

* * * * * * * * * * * * *

U.S. Term Limits v. Thornton

Decided: May 22, 1995

Vote: 5 (Stevens, Kennedy, Souter, Ginsburg, Breyer)

4 (Rehnquist, O'Connor, Scalia, Thomas)

Opinion of the Court: Stevens

Concurring opinion: Kennedy

Dissenting opinion: Thomas (Rehnquist, O'Connor, Scalia)

The Court relied on the *Powell* decision when it ruled in 1995 that states have no power to prescribe term limits for members of Congress except through a constitutional amendment. The 5-4 ruling in *U.S. Term Limits v. Thornton* (1995) effectively ended a movement that had gained approval of limiting the tenure of members of Congress in twenty-three states. For the majority, Justice Stevens said the tenure limitation would amount to a new qualification for members of Congress.

The Constitution also specifies that each chamber "may determine the Rules of its Proceedings" (Art. I, sec. 5, cl. 2). The Court has ruled that a House or Senate rule must give way if it conflicts with private rights. In 1949, for example, the Court overturned the perjury conviction of a witness in a House committee's anti-Communist investigation because there was no showing that a quorum was present during the witness's testimony. More typically, however, the Court has upheld each chamber's control over its rules. In the most recent instance, the Court in *Nixon v. United States* (1993) upheld the Senate's use of a fact-finding committee instead of the full Senate to conduct impeachment proceedings against a federal judge.

THE COURT AND THE PRESIDENT

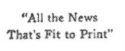

CHAPTER 2

The New York Times

LATE CITY EDITION

"All the News That's Fit to Print"

Weather: Mild, rain early today; partly cloudy tonight, tomorrow. Temp. range: today 66-76; Wed. 60-68. Highest Temp.-Hum. Index yesterday: 66. Details on Page 66.

VOL.CXXIII..No.42,551   © 1974 The New York Times Company   NEW YORK, THURSDAY, JULY 25, 1974   15 CENTS

NIXON MUST SURRENDER TAPES, SUPREME COURT RULES, 8 TO 0; HE PLEDGES FULL COMPLIANCE

House Committee Begins Debate on Impeachment

Presidents can attempt to influence the ideological balance of the Supreme Court through their power to nominate justices, but history has shown that they have little control over judicial appointees once confirmed. The Court's decision in *United States v. Nixon* (1974), written by Nixon appointee Chief Justice Warren E. Burger, clearly illustrates the high court's central role as a check on presidential power.

Two days after the June 17, 1972, arrest of five men for breaking into the Democratic National Committee headquarters at the Watergate office building in Washington, D.C., President Richard M. Nixon's press secretary Ron Ziegler dismissed the case as a "third-rate burglary attempt." Over the next two years, the Watergate break-in became the subject of a select Senate committee investigation, criminal investigations directed in turn by two special prosecutors, and impeachment proceedings against Nixon in the House of Representatives.

Throughout the investigations, Nixon claimed executive privilege to limit the information that he would release concerning his actions and conversations about the break-in and any White House involvement. The demands for information became more insistent after a former White House aide disclosed to the Senate Watergate committee in summer 1973 that Nixon had secretly tape-recorded all of his Oval Office conversations.

In April 1974, U.S. District Court judge John Sirica issued a subpoena for the tapes as requested by special prosecutor Leon Jaworski. Nixon moved to quash the subpoena, but the federal court in Washington refused. When Nixon appealed, Jaworski asked the Supreme Court to hear the case on an expedited basis.

With the fate of Nixon's presidency in the balance, the Supreme Court agreed and scheduled the case for argument in a special session on July 8. The nearly three hours of argument featured dramatic debate over the powers of the presidency and the power of the courts to review the president's exercise of those powers.

United States v. Nixon

 Decided: July 24, 1974

 Vote: 8 (Burger, Douglas, Brennan,
      Stewart, B. White,
      T. Marshall, Blackmun,
      Powell)

     0

 Opinion of the Court: Burger

 Did not participate: Rehnquist

Only sixteen days later, the court handed down its verdict in a unanimous opinion written by Chief Justice Warren E. Burger, one of Nixon's appointees. While the Court recognized an executive privilege to protect the confidentiality of presidential conversations, Burger said that the privilege had to yield to the need for "demonstrably relevant" evidence in a criminal trial. Sustaining the privilege, the chief justice wrote in *United States v. Nixon* (1974), "would cut deeply into the guarantee of the due process of law and gravely impair the basic function of the courts."

JULY 25, 1974
NIXON MUST SURRENDER TAPES, SUPREME COURT RULES, 8 TO 0;
HE PLEDGES FULL COMPLIANCE

OPINION BY BURGER

Name of President Is Left in Indictment as Co-Conspirator

By WARREN WEAVER Jr.

Special to The New York Times

WASHINGTON, July 24—The Supreme Court ruled today, 8 to 0, that President Nixon must provide potential evidence for the criminal trial of his former subordinates, rejecting flatly the President's contention that he had absolute authority to withhold such material.

of the republic, that the judicial branch decides what the law is and the executive branch is bound by that determination.

Not since its refusal in 1952 to permit President Truman to seize the nation's steel mills, had the Supreme Court dealt so serious a blow to a President who read

> Not since its refusal in 1952 to permit President Truman to seize the nation's steel mills, had the Supreme Court dealt so serious a blow to a President who read broader powers into his constitutional mandate than the Court was willing to recognize.

Eight hours later in California, the President announced through his attorney that he would accept the high court ruling and comply fully. Until today, White House spokesmen had strongly indicated that Mr. Nixon might choose to defy the Justices.

64 CONVERSATIONS CITED

As a result of the historic Court decision, announced by Chief Justice Warren E. Burger in a tense, packed chamber, the President will surrender tape recordings and other data involving 64 White House conversations for use in the Watergate cover-up trial, and possibly in impeachment proceedings as well.

In a broader perspective, the Supreme Court reaffirmed with today's ruling its position, carved out in the early days

broader powers into his constitutional mandate than the Court was willing to recognize.

POSSIBLE VOTE EFFECT

As an immediate consequence, today's one-sided decision appeared likely to sway some undecided Republicans on the House Judiciary Committee to vote in support of articles of impeachment.

Over a somewhat longer range, the ruling was expected to increase the number of Republicans and conservative Democrats in the House who were willing to vote against the President if the impeachment issue reaches the floor, as is now expected, late in August or early in September.

The special Watergate prosecutor, Leon Jaworski, had sought the data on the conversations as evidence to use in the September trial of six former Nixon aides accused of conspiring to conceal the 1972 burglary of Democratic national headquarters in the Watergate complex here.

Today's ruling was made with three of President Nixon's appointees joining in the vote against him. The fourth, Associate Justice William H. Rehnquist, had disqualified himself. The high court took the following actions:

- Told the President to comply "forthwith" with Judge Sirica's order to turn over the tape recordings and other documents for screening and subsequent submission to Mr. Jaworski of all portions that provide relevant and admissible evidence for the cover-up trial.
- Left standing the Watergate grand jury action naming President Nixon as an unindicted co-conspirator in the cover-up. The Justices ruled that the question whether the jury could name him was irrelevant and that they should not have agreed to review Judge Sirica's refusal to strike the President's name from the indictment.
- Denied a motion by James D. St. Clair, the President's chief defense counsel, that the Justices examine the records of the Watergate grand jury to determine whether there was enough evidence to warrant the naming of Mr. Nixon as a co-conspirator.

Reading a condensed version of his 31-page opinion, Chief Justice Burger rejected every legal defense that the White House had attempted to erect in defense of the President's refusal to deliver the tape recordings to Judge Sirica.

The Court concluded unanimously, the Chief Justice said, that the President did not have an absolute constitutional right to keep his records confidential and that the interests of fairness in administering criminal justice outweighed the qualified privilege Mr. Nixon did enjoy.

"The allowance of the privilege to withhold evidence that is demonstrably relevant in a criminal trial would cut deeply into the guarantee of due process of law and gravely impair the basic function of the courts," Mr. Burger declared.

COURT EFFECT FEARED

"Without access to specific facts, a criminal prosecution may be totally frustrated," he continued, adding, "The President's broad interest in confidentiality of communications will not be vitiated by disclosure of a limited number of conversations preliminarily shown to have some bearing on the pending criminal cases."

The tapes, transcripts or memorandums that President Nixon was ordered to deliver to Judge Sirica will be screened by the District Court for any information considered relevant to the conspiracy trial of six former Nixon aides who are charged with covering up the Watergate burglary. The evidence will then be passed on by the court to the special prosecutor.

Mr. Jaworski expressed hope after the Court session that any evidence involved would be available in time for the scheduled trial opening on Sept. 9.

It appeared unlikely, however, that any material on the tapes would become available for the purposes of impeachment before the full House votes on charges against Mr. Nixon that the Judiciary Committee is expected to adopt within the next few days.

The Supreme Court cautioned in its decision that Judge Sirica's screening must involve "scrupulous protection against any release or publication of material not found by the court, at that stage, probably admissible in evidence and relevant to the issues of the trial for which it is sought."

Justice Burger also cautioned Judge Sirica to "discharge his responsibility to see to it that, until released to the special prosecutor, no in camera [privately examined secret] material is revealed to anyone."

Once relevant excerpts of the White House tapes have been delivered to Mr. Jaworski, it is up to him to decide what information, if any, should be forwarded to the House Judiciary Committee for impeachment purposes, and whether any such transmittal should be delayed because of the cover-up trial.

Some Judiciary Committee members were arguing that the impeachment proceedings be held up to take into consideration whatever evidence the new tapes may provide, but that would clearly require a postponement of six weeks to two months.

The Supreme Court decision did not recognize the interrelation between the Watergate trial evidence, officially before the Justices, and its possible applicability to impeachment, a connection that Mr. St. Clair had repeatedly urged it to weigh.

Voting against the White House position, in addition to Chief Justice Burger, were two other appointees of the President: Associate Justices Harry A. Blackmun and Lewis F. Powell Jr. The fourth Nixon appointee, Justice Rehnquist, declined to sit on the case, apparently because of his prior service in the Justice Department under Attorney General John N. Mitchell, one of the defendants in the cover-up trial.

Also concurring in the unanimous decision were Associate Justices William O. Douglas, William J. Brennan Jr., Potter Stewart, Byron R. White and Thurgood Marshall.

PRESSURE FOR UNANIMITY

Some Supreme Court observers had predicted that there would be strong pressure for a unanimous ruling by the Justices, in an institutional effort to discourage President Nixon from refusing to obey the Court.

For the second time in three weeks, the Court chamber was packed with lawyers, newsmen and spectators, many of whom had waited in line on the marble steps for hours. The palpable suspense was ended almost immediately, as Chief Justice Burger began announcing the ruling.

Observers had predicted that the Chief Justice would write the opinion in this politically sensitive case only if the decision was unanimous, and that the only unanimous decision possible, based on the July 8 arguments before the Court, would involve a ruling against the President.

For 17 minutes, Mr. Burger read carefully and unemotionally from the opinion. Only occasionally did he nod to emphasize a point, such as his assertion that "it is 'emphatically the province and the duty' of this Court 'to say what the law is' with respect to the claim of privilege presented in this case."

The Justices had obviously reacted negatively to Mr. St. Clair's argument that the high court had no authority to review a unilateral decision by the President that certain material was legally privileged.

NAME STAYS ON INDICTMENT

As a result of the Justices' decision that they should not have considered reviewing the unindicted co-conspirator question, Mr. Nixon's name will remain on the indictment, pursuant to Judge Sirica's refusal to expunge it.

The court held that Judge Sirica's ruling upholding the subpoena of the material was appealable because, otherwise, it could be reviewed only by citing the President for contempt and appealing that order, a method the Justices called "peculiarly inappropriate" under the circumstances.

Also rejected unanimously was Mr. St. Clair's contention that Mr. Jaworski did not have legal standing to sue the President. The special prosecutor's guarantees of independence upon his appointment, the Court ruled, made this "the kind of controversy courts traditionally resolve."

Chief Justice Burger pointedly denied the White House contention that the President, not the courts, had the ultimate right to make some legal determinations.

"The judicial power of the United States vested in the Federal courts by the Constitution can no more be shared with the executive branch than the chief executive, for example, can share with the judiciary the veto power, or the Congress share with the judiciary the power to override a Presidential veto."

The Court summed up its holding that Mr. Nixon does not have independent authority to decide which evidence he should withhold from the criminal justice system this way:

"To read the powers of the President as providing an absolute privilege as against a subpoena essential to enforcement of criminal statutes on no more than a generalized claim of the public interest in confidentiality of nonmilitary and nondiplomatic discussions would upset the constitutional balance of 'a workable government' and gravely impair the role of the courts."

It is standard Supreme Court procedure for the Justice who wrote the majority opinion in any case to deliver a brief synopsis of it from the bench, at the call of the Chief Justice. Mr. Burger's presentation today was much longer than is normal for less prominent cases.

Mr. Jaworski sat at one of the counsel tables with two of his assistants. Mr. St. Clair was not present, having flown to California over the weekend to confer with the President. He was represented by three White House staff attorneys.

• • • • • • • • • • •

Nixon's release of the tapes twelve days after the Court's decision—on August 5—sealed his fate. The transcripts showed that Nixon had approved a plan aimed at shielding the White House from the FBI's investigation of the break-in. With three articles of impeachment already voted by the House Judiciary Committee, Nixon announced his resignation on August 9.

The Supreme Court's decisive role in the events confirmed its central place in the constitutional system. An unelected court had made clear that a president—even one re-elected in a landslide less than two years earlier—was not above the law. Nixon's case is not the only such ruling. Two decades earlier, the Supreme Court had ruled that a wartime president—Harry S. Truman—had no unilateral authority to seize the nation's steel mills to maintain production essential to the war effort. And two decades after Nixon, the Court ruled that a sitting president—Bill Clinton—had no legal immunity from a private citizen's civil lawsuit for monetary damages for alleged actions before he took office.

Yet the Supreme Court has also supported the vast increase in the powers of the presidency over the nation's history, especially after the United States assumed a global leadership role in the twentieth century. The Court has generally taken a broad view of the president's executive power. It has steered clear of refereeing disputes between the president and Congress—typically to the president's advantage. And the Court has sometimes kept its own power in check to avoid or deflect a confrontation with the executive.

The post-9/11 terrorism cases presented difficult questions of presidential power for the Court. President George W. Bush claimed powers as commander in chief to detain foreigners and even U.S. citizens as enemy combatants to be tried in military tribunals, with only limited judicial review, instead of in civilian courts. The Supreme Court rejected Bush's policies in a pair of narrow but dramatic decisions in 2004, another ruling in 2006, and still another in 2008.

The rulings left the president discretion to refashion procedures, however. In that sense, the Court's decisions—as in many other constitutional confrontations—were not final rulings, but only interim steps in a continuing dialogue between all three branches in shaping the law that the president is constitutionally commanded to faithfully execute.

EARLY DEVELOPMENTS

Article II of the Constitution vests the president with "the executive Power"—a term that is not defined. The article's section 2 specifies some of those powers: The president is "Commander in Chief" of the army and navy and of state militias "when called into the actual Service of the United States." The president has the power, with the Senate's concurrence, to "make Treaties" and to "appoint" ambassadors, judges of the Supreme Court, and other "Officers of the United States"— except for "inferior Officers" whose appointments may be vested by Congress in courts or the heads of executive departments. And in section 3, the president is given the power—and the responsibility— to "take Care that the Laws be faithfully executed."

The president also shares legislative power with Congress. The Presentment Clause specifies that a bill passed by the House and Senate must be "presented" to the president, who can sign it, allow it to become law after ten days without signing it, or return it to Congress with "Objections." The bill can still become law if the president's veto—a term not found in the Constitution—is over-ridden by a two-thirds majority vote in each chamber of Congress (Art. I, sec. 7, cl. 2).

The spare language regarding presidential powers left many questions for future chief executives to work out—either in cooperation or confrontation with the other branches. In one of the most important developments, the First Congress—in what is sometimes called "the decision of 1789"— effectively ratified the president's power to remove as well as appoint executive branch officers.

As passed by Congress, the bill creating an executive department for foreign affairs included the wording "whenever the principal officer shall be removed by the president of the United States." The measure's sponsors made clear they intended the language not as a grant of power from Congress but as recognition of a power inherent in the presidency. The Supreme Court endorsed that understanding in a 1926 decision striking down a law that sought to limit the president's removal power.

President George Washington and Congress reached a more ambiguous agreement in the first major test of the president's foreign policy powers. In April 1793, Washington unilaterally proclaimed that the United States was neutral in the war between Britain and revolutionary France. The action sparked a pseudonymous debate between the Federalist Alexander Hamilton, supporting Washington's authority to issue the proclamation, and the Republican James Madison, who argued for congressional control of foreign policy except in areas specified by the Constitution. The debate was mooted somewhat in June 1794, when Congress itself passed a neutrality proclamation.

Under the commander-in-chief powers, early presidents also took the initiative in committing U.S. forces overseas without formal declarations of war—although with congressional approval. President John Adams responded to French attacks on U.S. shipping by launching a two-year naval war (1798–1800), but only after Congress had voted to rescind the 1778 Treaty of Alliance with France and to authorize attacks on French vessels. Presidents Thomas Jefferson and James Madison similarly fought the First and Second Barbary Wars (1801–1805, 1815) with congressional authorizations but no formal declarations of war. The Supreme Court never had to rule on the issue and, through history, has never opposed the president's deployment of forces abroad.

Earlier, Congress in 1798 had passed a law explicitly authorizing the president to call out the militia of any state in case of invasion or "imminent danger of invasion" from a foreign nation or Indian tribe. The Court in 1827 upheld the law as a proper delegation of authority to the president. "Authority to decide whether the exigency has arisen, belongs exclusively to the President, and . . . his decision is conclusive upon all other persons," the Court wrote in *Martin v. Mott*. The ruling upheld a fine imposed in a court-martial on a New York militiaman who had refused service during the War of 1812.

THE CIVIL WAR

Prize Cases

    Decided: March 10, 1863

    Vote: 5 (Wayne, Grier, Swayne, Miller, Davis)

           4 (Taney, Catron, Nelson, Clifford)

    Opinion of the Court: Grier

    Dissenting opinion: Nelson (Taney, Catron, Clifford)

The Civil War resulted in the Court's first direct reviews of presidential actions taken as commander in chief without obtaining prior authorization from Congress. One ruling helped fortify presidential powers by upholding Lincoln's decision in April 1861—with Congress in recess—to blockade Southern ports. "The President is not only authorized but bound to resist force, by force," the Court wrote in the *Prize Cases* (1863). That was true, the Court explained, "whether the hostile party be a foreign invader, or States organized in rebellion." Dissenting justices in the 5-4 decision argued that no civil war existed until Congress acted in July to ratify Lincoln's actions.

Two other cases produced rulings against Lincoln's policies for trying rebel supporters in military instead of civilian courts. Neither of the rulings, however, had a direct effect on wartime actions. In the federal court case of *Ex parte Merryman* (1861), Chief Justice Roger B. Taney, sitting as circuit justice in Maryland, ordered federal military officials to justify their detention of John Merryman, a Southern sympathizer detained for his part in burning bridges near Baltimore. (Through the nineteenth century, Supreme Court justices were required to "ride circuit"—that is, travel within a designated federal circuit and preside over trials or appeals.) The military commander refused, citing Lincoln's unilateral suspension of the writ of habeas corpus. Taney wrote an opinion excoriating Lincoln for taking on both legislative and judicial powers. Lincoln ignored the ruling, though Merryman was eventually transferred to civilian authorities and tried for treason.

MAY 28, 1861
REPORTS FROM BALTIMORE.

BALTIMORE, Monday, May 27.

In the case of John Merryman, a writ of *habeas corpus* has been issued by Judge Taney, made returnable this morning in the United States District Court. Gen. Cadwallader declined surrendering the prisoner till he heard from Washington. An attachment has been issued for Gen. Cadwallader, returnable to-morrow morning. Merryman is still at Fort McHenry. . . .

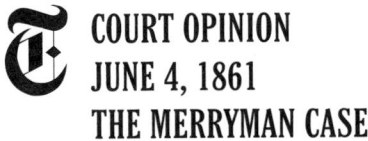

COURT OPINION
JUNE 4, 1861
THE MERRYMAN CASE.

Decision of Chief Justice Taney.

. . . And even if the privilege of the writ of *habeas corpus* was suspended by act of Congress, and a party not subject to the rules and articles of war, was afterwards arrested and imprisoned by regular judicial process—he could not be detained in prison or brought to trial before a military tribunal, for the article in the Amendments to the Constitution, immediately following the one above referred to—that is the 6th article—provides that "In all criminal prosecutions the accused shall enjoy the right to a speedy and public trial by an impartial Jury of the State and district wherein the crime shall have been committed, which district shall have been previously ascertained by law, and to be informed of the nature and cause of the accusation; to be confronted with the witnesses against him; to have compulsory process for obtaining witnesses in his favor, and to have the assistance of counsel for his defence."

tive arm. But in exercising power he acts in subordination to judicial authority, assisting it to execute its process and enforce its judgments.

With such provisions in the Constitution, expressed in language too clear to be misunderstood by any one, I can see no ground whatever for supposing that the President, in any emergency or in any state of things, can authorize the suspension of the privilege of the writ of *habeas corpus,* or arrest a citizen, except in aid of the judicial power. He certainly does not faithfully execute the laws if he takes upon himself legislative power by suspending the writ of *habeas corpus,* and the judicial power also, by arresting and imprisoning a person without due process of law. Nor can any argument be drawn from the nature of sovereignty, or the necessities of government, for self-defence in times of tumult and danger. . . .

> "With such provisions in the Constitution, expressed in language too clear to be misunderstood by any one, I can see no ground whatever for supposing that the President, in any emergency or in any state of things, can authorize the suspension of the privilege of the writ of *habeas corpus.*
> —Chief Justice Roger B. Taney, *Ex parte Merryman*"

And the only power, therefore, which the President possesses, where the "life, liberty or property" of a private citizen is concerned, is the power and duty prescribed in the third section of the second article, which requires "that he shall take care that the laws be faithfully executed." He is not authorized to execute them himself, or through agents or officers, civil or military, appointed by himself, but he is to take care that they be faithfully carried into execution, as they are expounded and adjudged by the coordinate branch of the Government to which that duty is assigned by the Constitution. It is thus made his duty to come in aid of the judicial authority, if it shall be resisted by a force too strong to be overcome without the assistance of the Execu-

And these great and fundamental laws which Congress itself could not suspend, have been disregarded and suspended, like the writ of *habeas corpus,* by a military order, supported by force of arms. Such is the case now before me, and I can only say that if the authority which the Constitution has confided to the Judiciary Department, and judicial offices may thus upon any pretext and under any circumstances, be usurped by the military power at its discretion, the people of the United States are no longer living under a Government of laws, but every citizen holds life, liberty and property at the will and pleasure of the army officer in whose military district he may happen to be found. . . .

In a second decision, *Ex parte Milligan* (1866), the full Court ruled after the war had ended that the president had no power to require military trials for civilians in areas where regular courts continued to function. The Court ordered the release of Lambdin P. Milligan and four other Southern sympathizers who had been tried by a military commission in Indiana on charges of conspiring to release and arm Confederate prisoners of war. "Martial law can never exist where the courts are open, and in the proper and unobstructed exercise of their jurisdiction," wrote Justice David Davis, a Lincoln appointee.

DECEMBER 18, 1866
WASHINGTON.

Special Dispatches to the New-York Times.

WASHINGTON, Monday, Dec. 17.

MILITARY TRIALS OF CIVILIANS IN LOYAL STATES.

It will be recollected that the Supreme Court of the United States, at its former term, announced its decisions in the case ex parte of Lambdin P. Milligan, declaring the illegality of his trial for alleged conspiracy, before a Military Commission in Indiana, and, in effect, ordering his discharge from prison, he having been convicted and condemned to the punishment of death. To-day Associate Justice Davis read an elaborate opinion in this case, in which reference was made to the importance of observing the Constitutional guarantees for the protection of the citizen in his person and property. The experience of our past history showed the wisdom of the framers of the Constitution, in constructing it to be alike efficient in war as in peace, as was shown in the civil contest through which we have just passed. The powers of

of appeal to the civil tribunals under the Act of March, 1863. Although the privilege of the writ of *habeas corpus* had been suspended, his right under the Constitution and laws still remained. He was a citizen of Indiana, and had never been in the land or naval service, or in the active militia. It was true a conspiracy existed in Indiana, when the defendant was accused of participating [in it], but according to the act of March, 1863, provision was clearly made for the trial of such classes of offences before a Civil Court. The Circuit Court of Indiana was open and unobstructed, and business therein continued to be transacted. The Court under the law could have punished such crimes, and there was no fear of an interruption of process. There were troops in Indiana, but the State was not the scene of war. The troops were employed in the event of invasion, or sent to operate where military necessity might require. No matter how guilty Milligan was,

> The powers of the Constitution should not be strained to suit emergencies, for on its maintenance in all its integrity depended our liberties and free Government, not only in the present but for all time to come.

the Constitution should not be strained to suit emergencies, for on its maintenance in all its integrity depended our liberties and free Government, not only in the present but for all time to come. The case being before the United States Supreme Court, on certificate of division of opinion of the two Judges of the United States Circuit Court for Indiana, the former maintains that the matter was properly before it. The fact that the Bench were divided could not operate to the prejudice of the complainant, nor deprive him of his right

there existed no authority to try him before a Military Commission, he not being in the military or naval service; nor did Congress attempt by its legislation to confer such power. Therefore the Court should order his release from military custody, and remand him to the civil tribunal.

To this all the members of the Court gave an affirmative answer, and also to the second question, namely: Ought the Court to issue a writ of *habeas corpus,* and order his release? And they say no to the third question: Had the military commission the legal right to try him? The opinion reviews the subject of martial law, and condemns its exercise in cases where the civil Courts are open, and process is unobstructed.

Chief-Justice Chase, for himself and Associates Wayne, Swayne and Miller, read a dissenting opinion relative to the third point, namely, military tribunals, taking the ground that they may be ordered by Congressional authority in cases where the civil Courts are obstructed, and in districts where military operations are in process. Fortunately, in Indiana the Judges were loyal, together with the great mass of the people; but it might happen that a disloyal Judiciary might impede the course of justice. Hence there should be the means of affording protection by the military power. The guilt of the defendant had nothing to do with the present decision, which has reference to the legality of the military Commission which tried the case of Milligan. The dissenting

Judges agreed with the majority of the Court that Congress did not confer it in this case the power to try the accused by such a Commission, but had made provision for the determination of the question before the civil Courts. It will be recollected that the cases of Bowles and Horsey were analogous to that of Milligan, and that the parties were released from prison consequent upon the decision of the Supreme Court. The counsel in these cases were Judge McDonald, Gen. Garfield and Dudley D. Field for the petitioners; and for the other side, Attorney General Speed, Mr. Stanbery and Gen. Butler. No notes were permitted to be taken by reporters in the Court, but the above, it is believed, give the general points of the decision. The court-room was crowded with members of the Bar, including a number from various States, and members of both Houses of Congress. It is understood that the opinions delivered to-day are to be printed in pamphlet form for public information. . . .

• • • • • • • • • • • •

LABOR CONFLICTS AND DOMESTIC LAW ENFORCEMENT POWERS

Three decades later, the Court strengthened the president's domestic law enforcement powers in a ruling that backed President Grover Cleveland's use of federal troops in a major labor conflict: the strike against the Pullman railroad car company in 1894. Pullman workers went on strike to protest a wage reduction order, and members of the American Railway Union carried out a secondary boycott by refusing to service Pullman sleeping cars attached to trains. The strike paralyzed rail traffic west of Chicago. With violence threatening, Cleveland dispatched troops to preserve order and directed the U.S. attorney in Chicago to obtain an injunction preventing the railway union and its president, Eugene V. Debs, from continuing the boycott.

Debs and his associates ignored the court order, were convicted of contempt of court, and sentenced to prison. They petitioned the Supreme Court for a writ of habeas corpus, but the Court unanimously upheld the president's actions. "The strong arm of the national government may be put forth to brush away all obstructions to the freedom of interstate commerce or the transportation of the mails," Justice David J. Brewer wrote in *In re Debs* (1895). "If the emergency arises, the army of the nation, and all its militia, are at the service of the nation to compel obedience to its laws."

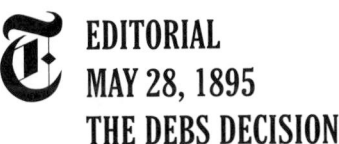

EDITORIAL
MAY 28, 1895
THE DEBS DECISION.

The Supreme Court has decided unanimously that the action of the inferior court by which Eugene V. Debs was sentenced to imprisonment was within the Constitution and legal. This is a very important decision in many ways.

It is the first instance in which the Supreme Court has been called upon to consider, first, the full scope of the powers of Congress with reference to the vast transportation system of the country by virtue of its relations to the Postal Service and to inter-State commerce, and, second, the procedure by injunction and sentence for contempt of court in disobeying an injunction. As to the latter especially, the conduct of the court of the Illinois Circuit has been sharply criticised, not only in the press, but by a portion of the bar. Both questions are fully met and definitely determined by the Supreme Court. Considering the membership of the court as to parties and as to sectional distribution, the unanimous decision of the Justices is of the highest importance.

The court holds that the "relations of the General Government to inter-State commerce and the transportation of mails" are "those of direct supervision, control, and management." And while the General Government is "properly styled a Government of enumerated powers, yet within the limits of such enumeration it has all the attributes of sovereignty, and in the exercise of those enumerated powers acts directly upon the citizen, and not through the intermediate agency of the State." The court adds:

"The entire strength of the Nation may be used to enforce in any part of the land the full and free exercise of all national powers and the security of all rights intrusted by the Constitution to its care. The strong arm of the National Government may be put forth to brush away all obstructions to the freedom of inter-State commerce or the transportation of the mails. If the emergency arises, the army of the Nation and all its militia are at the service of the Nation to compel obedience to its laws."

So much for the powers of the United States Government. As to the method by which they were sustained and exercised through the courts, the Supreme Court is equally emphatic. It cannot be "doubted that the Government has such an interest in the subject matter as enables it to appear as a plaintiff." "That the bill filed in this case disclosed special facts calling for the exercise of the powers of the court is not open to question." "If ever there was a special exigency presented, one which demanded that the court should do all that courts can do, it is apparent on the face of this bill, and we need not turn to the public history of the day, which only reaffirms with emphasis all its allegations."

At the time of the Debs conspiracy and practical insurrection in Chicago, we called attention explicitly to the very great scope of the powers then exercised and for the exercise of which there was no distinct precedent. We expressed the opinion that the action of the lower court and that of the Federal Executive would be sustained by the Supreme Court. We had not ventured to think that the decision of the Supreme Court would be at once so complete and unqualified and be unanimous. That it is so marks a radical change, not in the legal powers of the General Government, but in its exercise of those powers with absolute and undisputed authority. Henceforth whenever the General Government, acting under a Constitutional law, applies for and receives an order of a United States court to enjoin resistance to that law, the whole power of the Nation is made available to enforce that order.

• • • • • • • • • • •

PRESIDENTIAL POWERS

During the history of the Republic, the Supreme Court has had occasion to rule on nearly every aspect of presidential power laid out in Article II of the Constitution. Presidential powers include appointment powers, executive powers, powers as the commander in chief of the armed forces, and the power to conduct foreign affairs.

PRESIDENTS AND JUSTICES

Of all a president's appointments, none has longer lasting impact than nominations to the Supreme Court. Every president to serve at least one full term, except Jimmy Carter (1977–1981), has made at least one appointment to the Court. In filling vacancies, most presidents have tried to shape the Court according to their own legal and political views. Several of those who made more than one appointment have succeeded at least to an extent, but with lifetime tenure justices are beyond

Presidents' power to appoint justices to the Supreme Court gives them the opportunity to influence American legal doctrine for years, if not decades, after they have left office. Nominated by Lyndon Johnson as the first African American justice, Thurgood Marshall served as a consistent liberal voice on the Court for more than twenty years.

Source: The New York Times

a president's control or influence once in office. Several presidents have been surprised and disappointed by decisions made by justices they appointed.

As the first president, George Washington named all of the members of the first Supreme Court, and his appointees generally shared his views on the need for a strong national government. His Federalist successor, John Adams, made perhaps the most consequential Supreme Court appointment in history—that of John Marshall, who as chief justice from 1801 to 1835 forged the Court into a powerful instrument in support of a powerful national government.

President Andrew Jackson selected Taney, his secretary of the Treasury, as Marshall's successor; along with Jackson's other four appointees, Taney moved the Court in a direction more favorable to the states in clashes over federal powers. Taney and three of the others served through the beginning of the Civil War—their legacy tarnished by the decision in the Dred Scott case, which inflamed instead of resolving the bitter sectional dispute over slavery. (See page 257.)

Like Jackson, President Abraham Lincoln appointed five justices, including Taney's successor as chief justice, Salmon P. Chase. Lincoln's appointees moved the Court toward the nationalist, pro-business orientation it would maintain into the early twentieth century. But some of the justices proved to be less supportive of a federal role in enforcing civil rights for African Americans than Lincoln likely would have been.

The twentieth century's first two Republican presidents named justices with markedly different records in cases challenging government regulation of the economy. Theodore Roosevelt's three appointees generally upheld state or federal legislation dealing with economic matters, though one—Oliver Wendell Holmes Jr.—disappointed the trust-busting Roosevelt in a major antitrust case. By contrast, four of William Howard Taft's five appointees shared his opposition to government interference in the economy. Later, President Warren G. Harding named Taft as chief justice and consulted him in naming three other stalwart conservatives to the court in the 1920s.

Presidents must win Senate confirmation of their Supreme Court nominees. Through the nineteenth century, twenty-two presidential nominations to the Court failed, most of them because of partisan politics. Political and legal ideology began to play a more prominent role in twentieth-century nominations and confirmation battles, including eight failed nominations.

In one of the first fights of that century, President Woodrow Wilson's nomination of Louis D. Brandeis won Senate approval in 1916 on a 47-22 vote after overcoming criticism—tinged with anti-Semitism—of Brandeis's legal advocacy on behalf of consumers and workers. Brandeis, the first Jewish justice, served as a strong liberal until he retired in 1939. Paradoxically, Wilson had earlier appointed James C. McReynolds, an anti-Semite who openly shunned Brandeis and the Court's second Jewish justice, Benjamin N. Cardozo. McReynolds would become one of the four conservative justices famously nicknamed "the four horsemen" for voting to block some of President Franklin D. Roosevelt's New Deal economic recovery programs.

FDR responded to the string of Supreme Court setbacks in 1937 by asking Congress to pass a law allowing him to name an additional justice for every member over the age of seventy—six in all. Roosevelt's "Court-packing" plan failed, but he was able to make nine appointments over the next six years. Eight of his nominees had records as New Deal supporters before joining the Court; the ninth, Harlan Fiske Stone, originally named to the Court by President Herbert Hoover in 1930, had compiled a moderate record before FDR elevated him to chief justice in 1941. (For more on the "Court-packing plan," see pages 112–114.)

President Harry S. Truman picked people he knew well in making his four appointments to the Court; all four, including Chief Justice Frederick (Fred) M. Vinson, had moderately conservative records. Truman's successor, Dwight D. Eisenhower, repaid a campaign debt by naming California's progressive Republican governor, Earl Warren, as chief justice in 1953 after Vinson's death. Three years later, Eisenhower appointed a well-regarded New Jersey judge, William J. Brennan Jr. His campaign advisers hoped that selecting a Catholic from the Northeast would gain him votes from Catholics in large cities.

Warren and Brennan became the architects of the Court's liberal rulings on criminal law and other issues in the 1960s. Eisenhower is reputed to have said that he made two mistakes while president—and both were serving on the Supreme Court. But he also named two moderate conservatives with long tenures: John Marshall Harlan, the grandson and namesake of the first Justice Harlan (1877–1911), and Potter Stewart.

Democrats John F. Kennedy and Lyndon B. Johnson both looked to personal connections and political ideology in their Supreme Court appointments. Byron R. White had campaigned for Kennedy before serving as deputy attorney general; Arthur J. Goldberg was Kennedy's secretary of labor. Johnson prevailed on Goldberg to accept appointment as ambassador to the United Nations in 1965, paving the way for him to name a longtime friend and supporter, Abe Fortas, to the Court. Johnson made history with his next appointment in 1967 by appointing Thurgood Marshall, the architect of the successful campaign to abolish racial segregation in public schools, as the first African American justice. Johnson's attempt to elevate Fortas to chief justice fell victim to presidential campaign politics in 1968, however, and Fortas was forced to resign one year later because of allegations of financial misconduct.

JUNE 14, 1967
MARSHALL NAMED FOR HIGH COURT, ITS FIRST NEGRO

Johnson Calls Nominee 'Best Qualified,' and Rights Leaders Are Jubilant—
Southerners Silent on Confirmation

By ROY REED

Special to The New York Times

WASHINGTON, June 13—President Johnson named Solicitor General Thurgood Marshall to the Supreme Court today.

Mr. Marshall, the great-grandson of a slave, will be the first Negro to serve on the Court if the Senate confirms him.

He is the best-known Negro lawyer of the century because of his battles against segregation. Southerners in the Senate once delayed his appointment to the Federal judiciary for several months. But judging from initial reaction in the Senate today, his confirmation to the Court seems likely.

Non-Southern Senators applauded the appointment and Southerners accepted it, at least for the moment, in silence.

HAILED BY NEGRO LEADERS

Negro leaders were jubilant. Floyd B. McKissick, the militant chairman of the Congress of Racial Equality, said the appointment had stirred "pride in the breast of every black American."

'A PLACE IN HISTORY'

Mr. Marshall stood by with his hands in his pockets, his usually mobile face solemn, as the President told of his nomination.

"I believe he has already earned his place in history," Mr. Johnson said. "But I think it will be greatly enhanced by his service on the Court."

Mr. Johnson declared that Mr. Marshall had earned the appointment by his "distinguished record" in the law. He added:

"He is best qualified by training and by very valuable service to the country. I believe it is the right thing to do, the right time to do it, the right man and the right place."

Mr. Marshall's official selection was chiefly the work of two Texans—Lyndon Johnson and his Attorney General, Ramsey Clark, the son of the retiring Justice.

Attorney General Clark recommended Mr. Marshall, who as solicitor general has been the Number 3 man in the Justice Department, with enthusiasm matching the President's.

> **Blinking in the sun, Mr. Johnson stepped in front of the microphones and matter-of-factly announced what may be the most dramatic appointment of his Presidency.**

Mr. Marshall, 58 years old, is to succeed Associate Justice Tom C. Clark, who retired yesterday.

It had been expected for years that Mr. Marshall would eventually become the first Negro justice, but recent speculation had given him no special edge over other prospective nominees at this time.

The President, as is his custom, gave no advance hint of his selection. Reporters were unexpectedly called into the White House Rose Garden outside his office shortly before noon.

Blinking in the sun, Mr. Johnson stepped in front of the microphones and matter-of-factly announced what may be the most dramatic appointment of his Presidency.

"Thurgood Marshall will bring to the Supreme Court a wealth of legal experience rarely equalled in the history of the Court," Mr. Clark said in a statement today.

"It was my strong recommendation to the President that Thurgood Marshall be appointed to the Supreme Court," he said. "I have no doubt that his future contributions will add even more prominence to his already well-established place in American history."

Mr. Marshall, reportedly acting on White House instructions, said he would have little to say about his nomination until the Senate acts. He described his appointment as "not something you'd expect but something you hope for."

Mr. Marshall was the towering figure of the legal phase of the Negro's fight for equality in this century. He tried and won dozens of lawsuits striking down discriminatory laws, including the suit that led to the Supreme Court's 1954 decision outlawing school segregation.

That case and other school suits—he was involved in such notable battles as the desegregation of the schools of Little Rock and New Orleans—once cast considerable doubt on his chances of sitting on the Supreme Court. Powerful Southerners in the Senate saw him as one of the nation's baleful influences.

But in recent years he has become identified with a more moderate element of Negro leadership, in large part because younger men have emerged as more militant. And he has now proved his acceptability to the Senate twice, winning its confirmation first as a Federal judge and then as Solicitor General.

TIES TO MODERATE NEGROES

His appointment to the Supreme Court reaffirms Mr. Johnson's ties to the moderate, established Negro leadership at a time when young Negroes are growing increasingly militant.

At the same time, it gives the Johnson Administration one more claim to the loyalty of Negroes in general, along with such legislation as the Civil Rights Act of 1964 and the Voting Rights Act of 1965.

Mr. Johnson said in a news conference after his announcement that he had received "very little pressure of any kind" on the Court appointment. He was asked if he had been advised to appoint a more conservative justice. "No," he replied.

He said he had consulted the American Bar Association and the association had found Mr. Marshall "highly acceptable."

Senator James O. Eastland of Mississippi, chairman of the Senate Judiciary Committee, which must pass on the nomination, had no comment on the appointment.

Senator Everett McKinley Dirksen, the minority leader and the ranking Republican on the Judiciary Committee, predicted confirmation "without undue difficulty or delay."

"He's a good lawyer," Senator Dirksen said, "and the fact of color should make no difference."

Mr. Marshall will be President Johnson's second appointment to the Supreme Court. The first was Abe Fortas. . . .

• • • • • • • • • • •

Two Republican presidents, Nixon and Ronald Reagan, had greater success than Kennedy or Johnson in reshaping the Court. In campaigning for the presidency in 1968, Nixon promised to appoint to the Court "strict constructionists" who would be more sympathetic to police and less supportive of defendants' rights. He named a new chief justice, Burger, who led a tenuous conservative majority in limiting some of the Warren Court's liberal rulings on criminal procedure. Nixon also named Burger's close friend, Harry A. Blackmun, in 1970 after the Senate rejected the president's first two nominees for the vacancy, Clement F. Haynsworth Jr. and G. Harrold Carswell. Blackmun evolved from a moderate judge to become the Court's strongest liberal by the time of his retirement in 1994. Nixon's other two appointees were the moderate conservative Lewis F. Powell Jr. and the conservative future chief justice, William H. Rehnquist.

EDITORIAL
APRIL 9, 1970
THE CARSWELL DECISION

The Senate's rejection, by the astonishing vote of 51 to 45, of the nomination of Judge G. Harrold Carswell to the Supreme Court is a triumph of constitutional responsibility over political partisanship.

The Senate has now discharged its clear-cut if painful duty to protect the stature and authority of one of the most vital of American institutions of government. It has reminded the President of the wisdom of a Constitution designed to reduce the risk of unwise or arbitrary use of executive power. At the same time, it has answered those who decry the American political system as one that is unresponsive to the need—and the demand—for integrity and justice.

The rebuke to the Administration, especially difficult for those Republican and Southern Senators whose conscience forced them to their credit to vote against Judge Carswell, will surely alert the President and his advisers to the savage toll exacted by the insensitivity of their political strategies as illustrated in the Carswell case.

The telephone campaign, mounted by a member of Judge Carswell's court and condoned by a high official of the Justice Department, to persuade Federal District judges to endorse the nomination of their superior on the Circuit Court was symbolic of such insensitivity. It represented an extraordinary debasement of the Federal judi-

ciary through an unwonted and unwarranted incursion into politics on the bench.

The dismal experience of the past weeks must emphasize to the President the urgency of turning quickly to the nomination of a first-rate jurist. The suggestion by a White House spokesman that Mr. Nixon might not act until after the November elections gratuitously introduced a new element of politics and also ignores the severe pressure of the mounting workload on each of the eight sitting justices.

Mr. Nixon should not find it difficult to name a candidate whose record inspires confidence across party lines. The President is entitled to select a Southerner and a conservative whose philosophies of the law are compatible with his own. The one irrevocable requirement is that the candidate's qualifications, ability and character are such that he will add to rather than diminish the quality of the nation's highest tribunal.

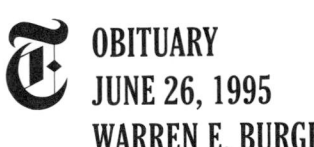

OBITUARY
JUNE 26, 1995
WARREN E. BURGER IS DEAD AT 87
Was Chief Justice for 17 Years
By LINDA GREENHOUSE

... An energetic court administrator, Chief Justice Burger was in some respects a transitional figure despite his tenure, the longest for a Chief Justice in this century. He presided over a Court that, while it grew steadily more conservative with subsequent appointments, nonetheless remained strongly influenced by the legacy of his liberal

to find "strict constructionists" and "practitioners of judicial restraint" who would turn back the activist tide that the Court had built under Chief Justice Warren, its leader since 1953.

The nomination on May 21, 1969, immediately made Mr. Burger, a white-haired, 61-year-old Federal appeals court

> **The Supreme Court in the Burger years was in its way as activist as the [Warren] Court that preceded it.**

predecessor, Chief Justice Earl Warren. The constitutional right to abortion and the validity of busing as a remedy for school segregation were both established during Chief Justice Burger's tenure, and with his support.

The country knew Chief Justice Burger as a symbol before it knew much about him as a man or a judge.

He was President Richard M. Nixon's first Supreme Court nominee, and Mr. Nixon had campaigned on a pledge

judge, a lightning rod for those who welcomed as well as those who feared the end of an era of judicial activism.

It was a central contradiction of Mr. Burger's tenure as Chief Justice that long after he became one of the most visible and, in many ways, innovative Chief Justices in history he remained, for many people, the symbol of retrenchment that Mr. Nixon had presented to the public on nominating him.

In fact, the Supreme Court in the Burger years was in its way as activist as the Court that preceded it, creating new constitutional doctrine in areas like the right to privacy, due process and sexual equality that the Warren Court had only hinted at.

"All in all," one Supreme Court scholar, A. E. Dick Howard, wrote in the Wilson Quarterly in 1981, "the Court is today more of a center for the resolution of social issues than it has ever been before." . . .

• • • • • • • • • • •

Reagan made history in 1981 by appointing Sandra Day O'Connor, an Arizona judge and former legislator, as the Court's first female justice. Five years later, he elevated Rehnquist to chief justice and appointed another conservative—Antonin Scalia—as associate justice. Reagan and his conservative backers suffered a stinging defeat in 1987, however, when the Senate rejected his nomination of the prominent conservative Robert Bork. Reagan's eventual nominee was Anthony M. Kennedy, a moderate conservative who—along with O'Connor and David H. Souter, President George H. W. Bush's first Supreme Court appointee—disappointed conservatives by voting in 1992 to reaffirm the *Roe v. Wade* abortion rights ruling. (See page 323.)

JULY 8, 1981
REAGAN NOMINATING WOMAN, AN ARIZONA APPEALS JUDGE, TO SERVE ON SUPREME COURT

REACTION IS MIXED

Senate Seems Favorable but Opposition Arises on Abortion Stands

By STEVEN R. WEISMAN

WASHINGTON, July 7—President Reagan announced today that he would nominate Sandra Day O'Connor, a 51-year-old judge on the Arizona Court of Appeals, to the United States Supreme Court. If confirmed, she would become the first woman to serve on the Court.

"She is truly a 'person for all seasons,' " Mr. Reagan said this morning, "possessing those unique qualities of temperament, fairness, intellectual capacity and devotion to the public good which have characterized the 101 'brethren' who have preceded her."

White House and Justice Department officials expressed confidence that Judge O'Connor's views were compatible with those espoused over the years by Mr. Reagan, who has been highly critical of some past Supreme Court decisions on the rights of defendants, busing, abortion and other matters.

SOME QUICK OPPOSITION

From the initial reaction in the Senate, it appeared her nomination would be approved. However, her record of favoring the proposed Federal equal rights amendment and having sided once against antiabortion interests while

she was a legislator provoked immediate opposition to her confirmation by the National Right to Life Committee, Moral Majority and other groups opposed to abortion.

At a brief news conference in Phoenix, Judge O'Connor declined to explain her views, saying that she intended to leave such matters to her confirmation hearings before the Senate Judiciary Committee.

Mr. Reagan, himself an opponent of abortions, said in response to a question that he was "completely satisfied" with her position on that issue.

NO RADICAL SHIFT EXPECTED

White House officials were hopeful that Judge O'Connor's appointment could be historic not only because she is a woman but also because her presence on the Court, as a replacement for Associate Justice Potter Stewart, who was often a swing vote between ideological camps on the Court, could shift the Court's balance to the right.

However, an examination of the Court's voting patterns suggests no radical shift is likely even if she does vote with the more conservative Justices.

It is the additional hope of Mr. Reagan's aides to make the Court even more conservative in the years ahead, when more vacancies are possible.

Judge O'Connor was appointed to Arizona's second-highest court in 1979 by Gov. Bruce Babbitt, a Democrat, after five years as an elected Superior Court judge in Maricopa County, Ariz. Before becoming a judge, she served in the Arizona State Senate for six years.

With the selection, Mr. Reagan fulfilled a campaign promise last year to pick a woman for the Court at one of his earliest opportunities. Associate Justice Stewart announced his retirement last month after 23 years on the Court.

In a brief statement before television cameras at the White House, Mr. Reagan urged the Senate's "swift bipartisan confirmation so that, as soon as possible, she may take her seat on the Court and her place in history."

Reagan Administration officials had said earlier that Mr. Reagan placed a high priority on finding a woman with conservative views for the Court. It seemed likely, however, that Judge O'Connor's past positions on issues linked to feminists would serve as a focus for any confirmation battle.

While a member of the Arizona Senate, Judge O'Connor at first advocated passage of the equal rights proposal, and then, for reasons that are unclear, supported a different version that was regarded by some as less sweeping. She is also on record as opposing a measure that would have outlawed abortions in some state facilities.

PERSONALLY OPPOSED TO ABORTIONS

White House officials asserted that Judge O'Connor had assured President Reagan in an Oval Office interview last Wednesday that she was personally opposed to abortions. They quoted her as saying that she opposed the anti-abortion measure only because it was not germane to the legislation to which it was attached and the Arizona Constitution forbids nongermane amendments. But those officials also said that she felt the legality of abortions was a legitimate matter for the legislative branch to decide.

Abortion foes, however, also cited votes in which, they said, Mrs. O'Connor supported a 1970 bill to legalize abortion and a 1973 bill permitting Arizona state agencies to participate in family planning.

In response, the White House said that there was no record of the 1970 vote and that, contrary to what the anti-abortion groups say, the 1973 bill was not pro-abortion and made no mention of abortion. The White House also noted that Mrs. O'Connor had sponsored a 1973 bill, which passed, giving hospitals, physicians and other medical personnel the right not to participate in abortion procedures.

POSITION ON RIGHTS PROPOSAL

As for the proposed equal rights amendment, a senior White House official maintained that Judge O'Connor's one-time support had lessened and that she now had "more problems" with the proposal. He pointed out that Mr. Reagan himself had once supported the proposal before changing his position. Feminist groups characterized Judge O'Connor as a supporter of the amendment, however.

Tonight an enthusiastic Mr. Reagan said in Chicago that his appointment made it "a happy day for me and I hope for my country." Speaking before a Republican fund-raising dinner, he praised Judge O'Connor's "long and brilliant record as a legislator and jurist" and said she had impressed him "as a thoughtful and capable woman whose judicial temperament is highly appropriate for the Court." He added that her principles adhered to those in the Republican Party platform.

IMPRESSION ON REAGAN

Michael K. Deaver, the deputy White House chief of staff, told reporters in Chicago that Mr. Reagan was impressed with "her kind of moderate approach" in the sense that "she had not been an activist" on the rights amendment or abortion issue and had taken "a moderate position" on both. . . .

● ● ● ● ● ● ● ● ● ● ● ●

George H. W. Bush chose as his other Supreme Court appointee Clarence Thomas, an African American conservative, to succeed Marshall in 1992. Thomas narrowly won Senate confirmation only after close questioning of his legal views and a fierce fight over allegations of sexual harassment—still unresolved—made by a former employee.

President Clinton turned to two federal judges with reputations as moderate liberals to fill Supreme Court vacancies in his first two years in office: Ruth Bader Ginsburg to succeed White and Stephen G. Breyer to succeed Blackmun. Under Rehnquist's leadership, however, the Court continued to move to the right in a number of areas, including church-state issues, civil rights, and federalism.

In the 2000 presidential campaign, George W. Bush said he would look for Supreme Court nominees in the mold of conservatives Scalia and Thomas. No vacancy arose during Bush's first term, and the Court remained closely divided between conservative and liberal blocs, with O'Connor and Kennedy often casting the decisive votes. In his second term, Bush was faced almost simultaneously with two vacancies: O'Connor announced her retirement in June 2005 and Rehnquist died in September after a yearlong bout with thyroid cancer.

Bush consulted closely with leading conservative figures before choosing two federal judges who came of age as lawyers in the Reagan administration: John G. Roberts Jr. and Samuel A. Alito Jr. Both faced opposition from liberal groups and some Democratic senators. Roberts won Senate confirmation, 78-22, in September 2005—in time to preside as chief justice at the opening of the new term in October. With the stakes of filling O'Connor's seat so high, opponents mounted a strong campaign to defeat Alito, but he won confirmation, 58-42. In their first three terms, both Roberts and Alito cast conservative votes—tilting the Court's balance in the 2006–2007 term in major cases on abortion rights, campaign finance, and school integration.

EXECUTIVE POWERS

The Supreme Court has helped maintain presidential power by generally supporting the president's authority to appoint and remove executive branch officers and to exercise discretion in executing laws as passed by Congress. But the Court has also limited presidential power by recognizing Congress's authority to curb the president's removal power in some instances. In addition, the Court has recognized Congress's primacy over the budget by limiting the president's power to refuse to spend funds specifically appropriated for a designated purpose.

REMOVAL POWER

Despite Congress's recognition of the president's removal power in 1789, presidents and Congresses clashed over the issue through the nineteenth century. In the most significant fight, the post–Civil War Congress passed the Tenure of Office Act of 1867 requiring the president to obtain Senate approval before removing any officer confirmed by the Senate. President Andrew Johnson's refusal to comply with the law in removing the secretary of war was one of the grounds cited in the unsuccessful attempt to impeach him in 1868. The law was repealed in 1877 without any judicial test of its constitutionality.

The Supreme Court finally issued a direct ruling on the president's removal power in 1926 in a case involving an 1876 law making the removal of postmasters subject to Senate consent. Despite the law, President Woodrow Wilson in 1920 fired Oregon postmaster Frank Myers without the Senate's consent. A test of the law reached the Court after both Wilson and Myers had died.

In a 6-3 decision, *Myers v. United States* (1926), the Court ruled the law unconstitutional. Chief Justice (and former president) Taft said that requiring Senate approval to remove department or bureau heads "might make impossible that unity and coordination in executive administration essential to effective action." The dissenting justices—Holmes, McReynolds, and Brandeis—viewed the law as a legitimate limitation on a power granted by Congress. "Power to remove an inferior administrative officer appointed for a fixed term," Brandeis wrote in his opinion, "cannot conceivably be deemed an essential of government."

Myers v. United States

Decided: October 25, 1926

Vote: 6 (Taft, Van Devanter, Sutherland, Butler, Sanford, Stone)

3 (Holmes, McReynolds, Brandeis)

Opinion of the Court: Taft

Dissenting opinions (3): Holmes; McReynolds; Brandeis

OCTOBER 26, 1926
PRESIDENT'S OUSTER POWER WITHOUT SENATE CONSENT UPHELD BY SUPREME COURT

HISTORIC POINT SETTLED

Decision Ends Dispute Which Started in the First Congress.

BENCH DIVIDES BY 6 TO 3

Taft Gives Majority Ruling Against Oregon Postmaster Removed by Wilson.

FIRM DISSENT IS ENTERED

'Revolutionary,' Says McReynolds—Holmes and Brandeis See Executive Power Widened.

Special to The New York Times.

WASHINGTON, Oct. 25.—In a decision on a constitutional question of great moment that has been in controversy since the foundation of the Government and regarded by lawyers as one of the most important judicial interpretations in many years, the United States Supreme Court today through Chief Justice Taft upheld the President in the exclusive power to remove executive officers from their positions.

The majority decision and the dissenting opinions comprise a formidable document of more than 50,000 words, of which the prevailing opinion is stated in some 24,000 words, and the dissenting opinion of Justice McReynolds in more than 20,000. The dissenting opinions of Justices Holmes and Brandeis are considerably shorter.

The decision was returned in the famous Myers postmastership case arising in Oregon and was determined by a vote of 6 to 3. The Court ruled that the President—in this instance the late President Wilson—had authority to dismiss Myers irrespective of the act of 1876, which provided for removal of the first three classes of postmasters "by and with the advice and consent of the Senate."

The decision rendered the act of 1876 void and likewise invalidated other statutes which tended to curtail the power of the President to order removals from office.

Three members of the Court—Associate Justices McReynolds, Holmes and Brandeis—dissented from the conclusions of the majority. Justice McReynolds criticized the majority opinion as "revolutionary." He declared the effect of the decision would be to vest the President with authority to make removals which formerly could be effected only for malfeasance in office.

In announcing his dissent from the bench he departed from his text to say that "we now have a foolish or unwise Controller General," and he indicated plainly that, in his opinion, that official, in the light of today's judgment, would not long remain at his post despite the language of the budget act giving him a fifteen-year tenure.

MYERS SUED FOR BACK PAY.

The Myers case came to the high court on appeal from a judgment of the Court of Claims. Frank S. Myers, Postmaster at Portland, was ordered removed by executive order dated Feb. 3, 1920. He asserted the illegality of the order, refused to submit and was summarily ejected. He sued in the Court of Claims for back salary, lost his case there and then took an appeal to the Supreme Court.

The importance attached to the issues involved was evidenced by the action of the Chief Justice in naming Senator George Wharton Pepper of Pennsylvania to make an argument as a "friend of the court." Mr. Pepper contended that removals from office could not be made without the consent of the Senate, basing his argument on constitutional and statutory grounds.

James M. Beck, then Solicitor General of the United States, upheld the executive prerogative to remove, and the Court's decision was regarded as a notable court victory for Mr. Beck.

Today's decision is not expected to affect the vast army of general employes of the United States. It is held to apply practically only to those whose nominations are transmitted to the Senate by the President.

Suggestion was made in the dissenting opinions of Justices McReynolds and Brandeis that today's decision ran counter to that of the Supreme Court in the case of Marbury vs. Madison in the early days of the Republic and in direct conflict with many laws of Congress.

In the majority opinion, which was concurred in by Associate Justices Butler, Sanford, Stone, Van Devanter and Sutherland, as well as the Chief Justice, it was held that the power of removal was inherent in the Executive and that it was necessary for effective administration of his office.

Justice McReynolds's dissent, which was almost as elaborate as the 24,000-word opinion of the majority, was one of the most vigorous in tone heard in the Supreme Court in some years.

DECISION A LANDMARK, SAYS BECK.

Mr. Beck tonight declared today's decision "as a landmark in constitutional law." He said:

"I naturally am much gratified at the result. The decision of the court ends a controversy which has continued from the beginning of the Government. Almost the first question that the first Congress of the United States discussed was the question that is now decided. In the intervening 135 years the question has constantly arisen in the courts. The question was of such delicacy that courts naturally avoided a decision until it became imperatively necessary.

"It has now been decided, and the decision is in accord with that reached in the first Congress of the United States, when, by a majority in the House and a tie vote in the Senate, it was decided in favor of the Presidential prerogative. Any other decision would have disturbed the equilibrium of our Government, and would have made Congress almost omnipotent, for it is obvious, from the practical standpoint, that if the President could not remove any official of the Government without the consent of the Senate, the executive power of the President would be, in a practical sense, reduced to a shadow.

"One thing is clear, that this notable decision is likely to be a landmark in constitutional law for many years to come, and both majority and minority opinions are worthy of the best traditions of that great tribunal and of the magnitude of the question that has now been authoritatively settled." . . .

• • • • • • • • • • • •

Humphrey's Executor v. United States
Decided: May 27, 1935
Vote: 9 (Hughes, Van Devanter, McReynolds, Brandeis, Sutherland, Butler, Stone, O. Roberts, Cardozo)
   0
Opinion of the Court: Sutherland
Concurring without opinion: McReynolds

Taft's opinion in *Myers* included broad language that appeared to extend the president's removal power even to members of independent regulatory agencies. Nine years later, however, the Court squarely upheld Congress's power to give tenure protections to the members of bodies such as the Federal Trade Commission (FTC), which by the 1930s were on the way to becoming a powerful "fourth branch" of the federal government. The issue in *Humphrey's Executor v. United States* (1935) was Franklin Roosevelt's decision to replace William E. Humphrey, a conservative who had been appointed and reappointed to the FTC by Roosevelt's two Republican predecessors, with a more moderate Republican.

Humphrey noted that he had been appointed for a seven-year term and argued that, under the law establishing the FTC, he could be removed by the president only for cause, such as inefficiency, neglect of duty, or malfeasance. Humphrey sued for his salary, but died during the court proceedings. In ruling for his executor, the Supreme Court said that Congress had the authority to create "quasi-legislative or quasi-judicial agencies" that would act "independently of executive control." That authority, Justice George Sutherland wrote, "includes . . . power to fix the period during which they shall continue in office, and to forbid their removal except for cause in the meantime." The unanimous decision was announced on May 27, 1935—the day called "Black Monday" because of two other rulings striking down major parts of FDR's New Deal legislative program. (See page 17.)

MAY 28, 1935
PRESIDENT CURBED IN REMOVAL POWER

Supreme Court Overrules Dismissal of W. E. Humphrey as Trade Commissioner.

CERTAIN OFFICERS EXEMPT

Those of Legislative or Judicial Agency Are Not Subject to Ouster 'at Mere Will.'

Special to The New York Times.

WASHINGTON, May 27.—President Roosevelt's action in demanding removal of the late William E. Humphrey from the Federal Trade Commission was held illegal by the Supreme Court today.

In an opinion by Justice Sutherland, the court unanimously declared that the President exceeded his powers in dismissing Mr. Humphrey, not for the statutory "inefficiency, neglect of duty or malfeasance in office," but upon other grounds, which actually were, Mr. Roosevelt then stated, that he did not think that his mind and Mr. Humphrey's were linked either on the policies or administering of the commission.

The court decided that the term of Trade Commissioners was fixed by law, that they must not be removed except upon statutory reasons, and that to hold that the commissioners must continue in office "at the mere will of the President, might be to thwart in large measure the very ends which Congress sought to realize by definitely fixing a term of office."

WILSON CASE HELD NOT TO APPLY.

This case, which has attracted intense interest because Mr. Humphrey was a Republican of the old high protective tariff school, was argued some weeks ago. William J. Donovan, former assistant to the Attorney General, appeared for Samuel F. Rathbun, executor of the Humphrey estate.

The government, in this argument, pointed to the case of Myers, an Oregon postmaster, whose removal by Woodrow Wilson was upheld by the Supreme Court, but Justice Sutherland held today that Myers was "merely a unit in the Executive Department," always subject to Presidential pleasure.

While the President may discharge postmasters and certain other executive employes, he lacks constitutional power to dismiss officials of a legislative or judiciary agency except for causes established by Congress for their removal, the court held.

"We think it plain under the Constitution," the opinion continued, "that illimitable power of removal is not possessed by the President in respect of officers of the character of those just named."

CASE A SUIT FOR SALARY.

Representing one of the bitterest clashes ever occurring between a President and a government official, the Humphrey case was actually a suit by Mr. Rathbun to collect salary due the former commissioner from Oct. 8, 1933, when the President sought to remove him, down to the day of his death Feb. 14, 1934. Through his opinion, Justice Sutherland answered "yes" to two questions asked by the Court of Claims regarding the Presidential power.

Nominated by President Hoover on Dec. 10, 1931, to succeed himself as a member of the commission, Mr. Humphrey was confirmed by the Senate and started to serve his term set until Sept. 25, 1938. But on July 25, 1933, Mr. Roosevelt asked for his resignation on the ground that "the aims and purposes of the administration with respect to the work of the commission can be carried out most effectively with personnel of my own selection," but, as Justice Sutherland noted, disclaiming reflection upon Mr. Humphrey personally or upon his services.

Some correspondence ensued, Mr. Humphrey meanwhile consulting his friends. On Aug. 31, the President wrote:

"You will, I know, realize that I do not feel that your mind and my mind can go along together on either the policies or the administering of the Federal Trade Commission and frankly I think it is best for the people of the country that I should have a full confidence."

HUMPHREY REFUSED TO RESIGN.

Mr. Humphrey declined to resign. On Oct. 7, the President wrote him a formal two-line notice of removal, but Mr. Humphrey insisted he was still a member of the commission entitled to salary at the rate of $10,000 annually.

He instituted suit which eventuated in these two questions certified to the Supreme Court by the Court of Claims:

(1) Do the provisions of Section 1 of the Federal Trade Commission Act stating that "any commissioner may be removed by the President for inefficiency, neglect of duty, or malfeasance in office," restrict the power of the President to remove a commissioner except upon one or more of the causes named?

If the foregoing question is answered in the affirmative, then—

(2) If the power of the President to remove a commissioner is restricted or limited as shown by the foregoing interrogatory and the answer made thereto is yes, is such a restriction or limitation valid under the Constitution of the United States?

CASE OF APPRAISER RECALLED.

Dealing with the first question, Justice Sutherland took up the case of an appraiser of merchandise named Shurtleff, whom a President once removed without assigning any cause. The Court of Claims dismissed Shurtleff's petition to recover salary, upholding the President's power to remove for causes other than those stated, and the Supreme Court refused Shurtleff's plea.

But Mr. Sutherland pointed out that Shurtleff's term of office was not fixed by Congressional act and that to agree to the appraiser's contention would really mean his right to hold office for life.

The situation in the Humphrey case, he continued, was "plainly and wholly different," as the Trade Commission law fixed a term of office.

"The fixing of a definite term, subject to removal for cause, unless there be some countervailing provision or circumstance indicating the contrary, which here we are unable to find, is enough to establish the legislative intent that the term is not to be curtailed in the absence of such cause," the court continued, "but if the intention of Congress that no removal should be made during the specified term, except for one or more of the enumerated causes were not clear upon the face of the statute, as we think it is, it would be made clear by a consideration of the character of the commission and the legislative history which accompanied and preceded the passage of the act.

CONGRESSIONAL INTENT.

"The language of the act, the legislative report and the general purposes of the legislation, as reflected by the debates, all combine to demonstrate the Congressional intent to create a body of experts who shall gain experience by length of service—a body which shall be independent of executive authority except in its selection, and free to exercise its judgment without the leave or hindrance of any other official or any department of the government. To the accomplishment of these purposes it is clear that Congress was of opinion that length and certainty of tenure would vitally contribute, and to hold that, nevertheless, the members of the commission continue in office at the mere will of the President, might be to thwart in large measure the very ends which Congress sought to realize by definitely fixing a term of office.

"We conclude that the intent of the act is to limit the Executive power of removal to the causes enumerated, the existence of none of which is claimed here."

POSTMASTER "MERELY A UNIT."

Of the Myers case, Justice Sutherland said:

"The office of a postmaster is so essentially unlike the office now involved that the decision in the Myers case cannot be accepted as controlling our decision here. A postmaster is an executive officer, restricted to the performance of executive functions. He is charged with no duty at all related to either the legislative or judicial power. The actual decision in the Myers case finds support in the theory that such an officer is merely one of the units in the executive department and, hence, inherently subject to the exclusive and illimitable power of removal by the Chief Executive, whose subordinate and aid he is."

The opinion emphasized the necessity of keeping the Federal Trade Commission, Interstate Commerce Commission and Court of Claims free from any outside persuasion which would exist if their members were subject to removal at random.

Justice McReynolds, agreeing with his associates, noted his opinion in the Myers case, in which he dissented from the idea that the postmaster could be removed.

Five decades later, the Court held that Congress could also create an executive branch office—independent counsel—beyond both the president's appointment and removal powers. Congress first created the office as part of the Ethics in Government Act of 1978 in imitation of the "special prosecutor" that had overseen the Watergate cover-up cases. The independent counsel—charged with investigating allegations of wrongdoing by high executive branch or political party officials—was to be appointed by a special three-judge panel and subject to removal, only for cause, by the attorney general.

Theodore B. Olson, assistant attorney general for the Office of Legal Counsel and later U.S. solicitor general, became the subject of an independent counsel investigation into accusations that he testified falsely to a congressional committee in 1985. He and two other Justice Department officials challenged subpoenas issued by independent counsel Alexia Morrison, who appealed to the Supreme Court after the federal appeals court in Washington ruled the act unconstitutional.

By a 7-1 vote, the court in *Morrison v. Olson* (1988) ruled that the independent counsel was an "inferior officer" whose appointment, under the Appointments Clause, could be vested by Congress in the courts. Chief Justice Rehnquist cited the office's limited power and duration in classifying it as "inferior" while stressing the attorney general's power to remove the independent counsel as preserving a measure of executive branch control. Rehnquist also said the law did not violate general separation of power principles. Congress had not acted to increase its own powers, Rehnquist explained, and the judiciary had no role in overseeing the office after the appointment was made.

In a strong dissent, Justice Scalia warned of possible abuse by unaccountable independent counsels. By the late 1990s, lawmakers in both parties had come to agree that investigations of both Republican and Democratic administrations had run amok. Congress let the law expire in 1999.

Morrison v. Olson

Decided: June 29, 1988

Vote: 7 (Rehnquist, Brennan, B. White, T. Marshall, Blackmun, Stevens, O'Connor)

1 (Scalia)

Opinion of the Court: Rehnquist

Dissenting opinion: Scalia

Did not participate: Kennedy

JUNE 30, 1988
SUPREME COURT VOTE UPHOLDS LAW ON SPECIAL PROSECUTORS

7-1 RULING IS REBUFF TO REAGAN

SCALIA IN DISSENT

By STUART TAYLOR JR.

Special to The New York Times

In one of its most important interpretations of the doctrine of separation of powers, the Supreme Court today upheld the Federal law that provides for independent prosecutors to investigate suspected crimes by high-ranking officials.

The Court's 7-to-1 ruling was a stunning rebuff to the Reagan Administration, which has been awash in investigations of its officials and former officials. The law provides for judges to appoint special prosecutors in such cases, insulated from Presidential control. The Administration argued that this was an unconstitutional encroachment on the power of the President.

The decision was one of nine rulings the Court handed down on an unusually busy day, the last full opinions of its 1987–1988 term. The special prosecutor decision upholds a measure of Congressional power to curb what many political conservatives believe to be the absolute constitutional authority of the executive branch to appoint, control and remove Federal prosecutors.

ISSUE OF PRESIDENT'S POWERS

The Court showed no sympathy for the sweeping view of the President's inherent constitutional powers that was urged upon it by political conservatives, who have pressed for judicial invalidation of the special prosecutor law and of an array of other Congressional restraints on the executive branch.

Chief Justice William H. Rehnquist, who wrote the opinion for the Court, rejected the various arguments for invalidating the law, concluding that the law does not violate any specific constitutional provision and "does not violate the separation-of-powers principle by impermissibly interfering with the functions of the executive branch." The special prosecutor law had been denounced by many conservative legal thinkers, and supported by many liberals. Nevertheless, Chief Justice Rehnquist, perhaps the best known conservative legal theorist in the recent history of the Court, confounded expectations that he would support the Administration on the issue.

Justice Antonin Scalia, in a passionate 38-page dissent, said the Court had subverted the Constitution's separation of powers in what he called "one of the most important opinions the Court has issued in many years."

SCALIA DISSENTS FROM BENCH

Summarizing his dissent aloud from the bench, which is rarely done, he said in a nine-minute statement that "what is at issue in this case is purely executive power, quintessentially executive power to prosecute," and that the law had an "intimidating effect" on Presidential advisers in disputes with Congress.

The decision takes away a key argument from defense lawyers representing several former Administration officials who are being investigated or have been prosecuted by independent counsels, as the special prosecutors are formally called. Among them are two former close Reagan aides, Michael K. Deaver and Lyn Nofziger, who are appealing criminal convictions obtained by special prosecutors.

The decision also removes a potential impediment to Lawrence E. Walsh, the special prosecutor investigating the Iran-contra affair, who has obtained indictments of Oliver L. North; John M. Poindexter, a former National Security Adviser, and three others.

Mr. Walsh said today that the law "provides a workable solution to a difficult problem," adding, "we are gratified" by the decision. The decision was also praised by many members of Congress and by the American Bar Association, which had filed a brief supporting the law.

President Reagan would not comment today, saying, "I can't comment on individual cases." Marlin Fitzwater, the White House spokesman, said that despite Mr. Reagan's doubts about the law, the decision "will have no practical effect on the Administration's implementation of the Independent Counsel Act or the ongoing investigations."

SPECIAL PROSECUTOR LAW UPHELD

The decision today overturned a 2-to-1 ruling on Jan. 22 by the Federal appeals court here, which had held the special prosecutor law to be an unconstitutional transfer of executive authority to the courts by Congress, and had assailed the law as unfair to officials covered by it.

Chief Justice Rehnquist's opinion was joined by Justices William J. Brennan Jr., Byron R. White, Thurgood Marshall, Harry A. Blackmun, John Paul Stevens and Sandra Day O'Connor. Justice Anthony M. Kennedy had disqualified himself in the case, without stating his reasons.

The President elevated Mr. Rehnquist from Associate Justice to Chief Justice in 1986. He also appointed Justice O'Connor, Justice Scalia and, most recently, Justice Kennedy.

The Watergate-inspired special prosecutor law was first passed in 1978, as part of the Ethics in Government Act, to insulate investigations and prosecutions of high-level executive branch officials from Presidential control. It was reenacted with minor amendments in 1982, with the name being changed to "independent counsel," and again last year.

HOW THE LAW OPERATES

The law requires the Attorney General first to conduct a preliminary investigation of allegations that any of certain enumerated high-ranking executive branch officials may have committed a crime, and then to ask a special three-judge Federal appellate court here to appoint an independent counsel to complete the investigation and conduct any prosecutions unless the allegations prove insubstantial.

The law provides that the Attorney General may remove a special prosecutor from office "only for good cause," and subject to judicial review.

The decision today upheld an appeal from the Jan. 22 appellate ruling by Alexia Morrison, one of several special prosecutors who are currently operating.

It means she can resume her investigation of Theodore B. Olson, a former Justice Department official, and two other former officials to determine whether they misled Congress in 1983 in a dispute over alleged political manipulation of the toxic waste cleanup program by Administration officials.

Ms. Morrison said she was "delighted not just by the opinion but by the near-unanimity."

The power balance between the executive and legislative branches has figured in several major Supreme Court decisions in recent years. In 1983, the Court supported executive authority by ruling that Congress may not overrule executive regulations through a "legislative veto" mechanism, although it may do so by passing new legislation. In 1986, the Court held that Congress could not set up a mechanism for automatic budget cuts that gave final authority to an official who was removable by Congress itself.

Today, while it did not make broad pronouncements about the separation of powers, Chief Justice Rehnquist's opinion clarified the limits of those earlier rulings.

COURT MESSAGE DISCERNED

"The clear message of these decisions taken together is that the Court is willing to allow Congress some leeway in putting limitations on executive power but that it is wholly unwilling to permit Congress to participate in administering the laws itself or through its agents," said Alan B. Morrison, a Washington lawyer who filed a brief as a friend of the Court supporting the special prosecutor law. He was also on the winning side in the 1983 and 1986 decisions.

In particular, Chief Justice Rehnquist's reasoning seemed to rule out any adoption by the Court of suggestions by Attorney General Edwin Meese 3d and some other conservatives that it is unconstitutional for Congress to insulate regulatory agencies like the Federal Trade Commission from Presidential control.

In the case decided today, Chief Justice Rehnquist rejected the challenges to the special prosecutor law by the Administration and others point by point.

First, he said, appointment of special prosecutors by the courts was valid under the Constitution's provision that "the Congress may vest the appointment of such inferior officers, as they think proper" in courts of law. He rejected arguments that special prosecutors' powers were so broad that they were not "inferior officers" and that the appointments clause was not intended to allow judges to appoint prosecutors.

Second, Chief Justice Rehnquist said the limited powers given by the law to the special three-judge court to choose a special prosecutor when requested by the Attorney General, and to exercise limited supervision, did not involve judges in matters inconsistent with their duties under Article III of the Constitution.

Third, he said the law's limitation of the Attorney General's power to remove special prosecutors, and other provisions, did not violate the constitutional principle of separation of powers.

The law did not amount to "Congressional usurpation of executive branch functions," Chief Justice Rehnquist said, because it gave Congress no control over special prosecutors.

He added that while special prosecutors are independent to some degree, the law "gives the executive branch sufficient control over the independent counsel to insure that the President is able to perform his constitutionally assigned duties." . . .

. . . .

LAW ENFORCEMENT

As part of the president's powers, the Court has generally supported a broad view of executive discretion in enforcing and carrying out laws passed by Congress. In 1915, for example, the Court upheld Taft's decision while president to withdraw 3 million acres of public lands containing oil deposits from private exploration despite a law generally permitting private acquisition of such lands. "The President was in a position to know when the public interest required particular portions of the people's lands to be withdrawn from public entry or relocation," the Court wrote in *United States v. Midwest Oil Co.*

In earlier cases, the Court similarly upheld presidential actions in carrying out duties specifically delegated by Congress. In *Field v. Clark* (1892), for example, the Court upheld the McKinley Tariff Act of 1890 against a claim that it improperly delegated to the president authority to impose duties on imported goods if the country of origin imposed unreasonable duties on U.S. goods. "It is often desirable, if not essential," Justice Joseph R. Lamar wrote, "to invest the president with large discretion in matters arising out of the execution of statutes relating to trade and commerce with other nations."

In three rulings in the 1930s, however, the Court ruled that Congress had gone too far in delegating power to the president without setting standards for exercising that power. The rulings struck down two major parts of FDR's economic recovery program, including the centerpiece: the National Industrial Recovery Act (NIRA) of 1933. In the first of the decisions, *Panama Refining Co. v. United States* (1935), the Court invalidated the president's authority under a section of the NIRA to prohibit interstate shipment of oil produced in excess of state limits (so-called hot oil). Chief Justice Charles Evans Hughes said the provision was invalid because, with "no criterion to govern the President's course," it gave the president "an unlimited authority to determine the policy."

Four months later—on "Black Monday," May 27, 1935—the Court more broadly ruled the entire NIRA unconstitutional as an excessive delegation of power to the president. Hughes again wrote for the Court in *Schechter Poultry Corp. v. United States* (1935), describing the president's authority under the act to write detailed industry-by-industry codes of production and labor policy as a "sweeping delegation of legislative power." Justice Benjamin N. Cardozo, the lone dissenter in *Panama Refining*, joined to make this ruling unanimous. In a concurring opinion, he described the act as "delegation run riot." A year later, the Court in *Carter v. Carter Coal Co.* (1936) cited excessive delegation as one of several grounds to strike down the Bituminous Coal Conservation Act of 1935.

None of the three rulings has been overturned, but they have lost force. Congress has responded by taking more care in specifying some criteria or policies when delegating power to the president. For its part, the Court has been more receptive to presidential power generally since the late 1930s. Indeed, the most important delegation ruling since the 1930s struck down Congress's attempt to exercise a "legislative veto" to retain control over executive branch actions.

Congress inserted legislative veto provisions in hundreds of laws in the 1970s. The provisions made it possible for one chamber of Congress—or even a single congressional committee—to block regulations by executive branch agencies or decisions in individual cases. In one instance, Congress included a provision in an immigration law permitting either chamber to veto a decision by the attorney general to suspend deportation of a deportable alien.

Jagdish Rai Chadha, an East Indian born in Kenya, challenged the provision after the House voted in December 1975 to override the attorney general's decision to suspend Chadha's deportation for overstaying a student visa. By a 7-2 vote in *INS v. Chadha* (1983), the Court ruled legislative veto provisions unconstitutional. "Congress made a deliberate choice to delegate to the Executive Branch, and specifically to the Attorney General, the authority to allow deportable aliens to remain in this country in certain specified circumstances," Chief Justice Burger wrote. "Congress must abide by its delegation of authority until that delegation is legislatively altered or revoked."

INS v. Chadha

Decided: June 23, 1983

Vote: 7 (Burger, Brennan, T. Marshall, Blackmun, Powell, Stevens, O'Connor)

  2 (B. White, Rehnquist)

Opinion of the Court: Burger

Opinion concurring in judgment: Powell

Dissenting opinions (2): B. White; Rehnquist (B. White)

JUNE 24, 1983
SUPREME COURT, 7-2, RESTRICTS CONGRESS'S RIGHT TO OVERRULE ACTIONS BY EXECUTIVE BRANCH

By LINDA GREENHOUSE

Special to The New York Times

The Supreme Court today swept aside a 50-year-old practice used by Congress to delegate authority to the President and then block his action under the law when it disagreed.

The Court, by a historic 7-to-2 vote, struck down this so-called legislative veto, saying that it exceeded constitutional limits designed to preserve the separation of powers.

Legislative veto provisions, which spell out and often restrict the President's authority under the law, have been written into about 200 statutes.

The ruling may profoundly alter the balance of power between the White House and Congress. It presumably strips Congress, for example, of the unilateral power it gained under the War Powers Resolution of 1973 to require the President to withdraw American troops from foreign hostilities.

FROM HOOVER PRESIDENCY

The legislative veto procedure dates to 1932, when Congress added it to an appropriations bill to give President Hoover authority to reorganize the Government.

Under a legislative veto, either or both houses can, by a simple majority, block specific actions that the President or a Federal agency takes to carry out authority that Congress has delegated.

As a result of today's ruling, Congress will be able to disapprove executive branch action only if a bill to that effect passes both houses and receives the President's signature. If the President vetoes the legislation, Congress may block the President's action only by overriding his veto by a two-thirds vote.

The initial Congressional reaction was that the ruling would create "conflict and chaos" on Capitol Hill. There were differing views today as to whether it would give the President or Congress the upper hand over the long run.

IMMIGRATION CASE BEFORE COURT

The decision, written by Chief Justice Warren E. Burger, came in a relatively minor immigration case, one of several legislative veto cases before the Court. The Justices had wrestled with the case for nearly two years, hearing argument in February 1982 and again last October.

The legislative veto has been a subject of debate for years among politicians, political scientists and legal scholars, many of whom awaited the Court's decision today with intense interest. While the breadth of the ruling was something of a surprise, the particular result, which upheld a 1980 ruling by the United States Court of Appeals for the Ninth Circuit in California, was not.

The Court ruled that the House of Representatives exceeded its constitutional powers when, exercising a legislative veto provision in the Immigration and Nation-

ality Act, it blocked the Attorney General's decision to suspend deportation for a Kenyan student who had overstayed his visa.

A LEGISLATIVE ACT

Chief Justice Burger said that the action by the House was, in effect, legislation. The Constitution, he said, permits the enactment of legislation only "in accord with a single, finely wrought and exhaustively considered procedure," namely, "passage by a majority of both houses and presentment to the President" for his signature or veto.

That procedure, the Chief Justice said, can be "clumsy" and "inefficient." But, he continued, "with all the obvious flaws of delay, untidiness, and potential for abuse, we have not yet found a better way to preserve freedom than by making the exercise of power subject to the carefully crafted restraints spelled out in the Constitution."

The Court's theory encompasses legislative vetoes requiring action by both houses as well as the one-house immigration veto. It will take further litigation, however, to establish on a case-by-case basis which of the approximately 200 laws with legislative veto provisions are unconstitutional in their entirety and which, like the immigration law, will survive without the unconstitutional veto provision.

ATTORNEY GENERAL 'GRATIFIED'

Attorney General William French Smith said he was "gratified" by the decision and praised the Court for having "reaffirmed in a strong and compelling opinion the vital and important role under our Constitution of the principle of separation of powers."

The Justice Department had joined the Kenyan student, Jagdish Rai Chadha, in challenging the constitutionality of the immigration veto. Mr. Chadha's case was brought by Public Citizen, a nonprofit organization loosely affiliated with Ralph Nader.

Alan B. Morrison, Public Citizen's director of litigation, said the outcome was also a victory for consumers and that "special interest lobbies will no longer be able to gut laws protecting consumers, workers and the environment" by pressing Congress to veto administrative regulations.

Last year, in another Public Citizen lawsuit, the Federal appeals court here struck down a two-house veto that prevented the Federal Trade Commission from requiring usedcar dealers to disclose major defects to their customers.

The Senate and House appealed that ruling to the Supreme Court, which presumably will now affirm it.

Five members of the Court joined the Chief Justice's broadly worded opinion today. The seventh member of the majority, Associate Justice Lewis F. Powell Jr., said he would have preferred to decide the case on the narrower ground that the House of Representatives had usurped a judicial function in overruling an immigration decision.

Observing that the majority's approach "apparently will invalidate every use of the legislative veto," Justice Powell said: "The breadth of this holding gives one pause."

'MODERN ADMINISTRATIVE STATE'

In a dissenting opinion, Associate Justice Byron R. White said that the legislative veto was an essential part of "the modern administrative state" that "has become a central means by which Congress secures the accountability of executive and independent agencies."

Associate Justice William H. Rehnquist dissented without addressing the broader constitutional issue, saying only that Congress would never have given the Attorney General the right to suspend deportations if it could not have kept for itself the power to veto individual suspensions.

The Associate Justices who joined the majority opinion were William J. Brennan Jr., Thurgood Marshall, Harry A. Blackmun, John Paul Stevens, and Sandra Day O'Connor.

RARE MOMENTS OF DRAMA

The announcement of the decision, a few minutes after 10 o'clock this morning, produced some rare moments of drama in the courtroom. Chief Justice Burger's practice is simply to announce the result in cases in which he has written the opinion, unlike the other eight Justices, who briefly explain their decisions and the rationale.

As usual, the Chief Justice announced this morning only that in the case of Immigration and Naturalization Service v. Chadha, the Court had affirmed the judgment of the United States Court of Appeals for the Ninth Circuit. He then said that Justice White would read a dissenting opinion.

Justice White said it had been many years since he had read an oral dissent aloud. "But this is probably the most important case the Court has handed down in many years," he said, calling the decision a "destructive action" that was "clearly wrong and unnecessarily broad."

There was a moment of silence. Then Chief Justice Burger began to talk, apparently without notes. "We all agree on one thing," he said, "that this is a very difficult and important case."

He talked about the framers of the Constitution—the "draftsmen in Philadelphia," he called them—and said that "the Constitution is a document designed to assign and delegate and separate the powers of government, and to limit them."

The courtroom was half empty, and it was unlikely that many of the tourists present knew what an unusual event they had happened upon. The majority opinion was grounded in the explicit constitutional text and on what Chief Justice Burger called "the profound conviction of the Framers that the powers conferred on Congress were the powers to be most carefully circumscribed."

He said that the provisions of Article I, requiring that every bill pass both houses and "be presented to the President" before becoming law, "are integral parts of the constitutional design for the separation of powers."

"The hydraulic pressure inherent within each of the separate branches to exceed the outer limits of its power, even to accomplish desirable objectives," he said, "must be resisted." In this case, the Chief Justice continued, the House of Representatives took action that "was essentially legislative in purpose and effect."

The decision, I.N.S. v. Chadha, No. 80-1832, is no longer as important to Mr. Chadha himself as it appeared to be when he first went into Federal court in 1977. He married an American citizen in 1980, a fact that probably would have freed him from the prospect of deportation even if he had lost his case.

• • • • • • • • • • •

In an important case favoring Congress, however, the Court made clear that Congress's power of the purse includes the ability to limit the president's discretion to withhold appropriate federal funds. President Nixon clashed repeatedly with a Congress controlled by the opposition Democratic Party over budget issues. He claimed the right to "impound" funds appropriated by Congress in order to reduce federal spending. The issue reached the Court in a case challenging the refusal by the Environmental Protection Agency—acting at Nixon's direction—to allot only $2 billion out of $5 billion that Congress had appropriated to help municipalities improve sewers and sewage treatment works. In a unanimous decision, *Train v. City of New York* (1975), the Court said that the agency had to disburse all the money. "The legislation was intended to provide firm commitment of substantial sums within a relatively limited period of time in an effort to achieve an early solution of what was deemed an urgent problem," the Court wrote.

Two decades later, the Court also bolstered Congress's power of the purse by invalidating a law—passed by a budget-minded Congress—to give the president the power to veto individual items in spending measures. The 6-3 decision in *Clinton v. City of New York* (1998) said that the Line Item Veto Act of 1996 effectively gave the president the power to amend an act of Congress by repealing part of it. But, as Justice John Paul Stevens explained, "There is no provision in the Constitution that authorizes the President to enact, to amend, or to repeal statutes." (See page 34.)

PRIVILEGE AND IMMUNITY

The Constitution makes no mention of executive privilege or executive immunity, but both are important elements of presidential power that gained acceptance over time largely without formal approval by the Supreme Court. When the Court was confronted in the late twentieth century with cases squarely testing the limits of the doctrines, it dealt damaging blows to two presidents—Nixon and Clinton—by rejecting Nixon's claim of privilege in the Watergate case and Clinton's claim of immunity in a private civil lawsuit.

Executive Privilege

Starting with George Washington, presidents from time to time have claimed the right to withhold information, documents, or testimony from Congress in the interest of protecting confidentiality among advisers or secrecy in dealings with foreign countries. Precedents for the practice are ambiguous. Some experts have concluded that until the mid-twentieth century Congress generally succeeded in obtaining most of the information it sought. The Supreme Court expressly recognized Congress's right to examine executive branch decision making in *McGrain v. Daugherty* (1927), which upheld the Senate's inquiry into the failure of President Warren G. Harding's attorney general to prosecute major figures in the Teapot Dome scandal.

The phrase "executive privilege" appears to have been coined by Justice Stanley F. Reed in a 1958 decision while sitting on the U.S. Court of Claims after his retirement from the high court. Four years earlier, President Eisenhower had laid out the basis for the claimed privilege in justifying his refusal to allow executive branch officials to testify before the Senate Permanent Subcommittee on Investigations headed by Sen. Joseph R. McCarthy, R-Wis. Both Presidents Kennedy and Johnson claimed executive privilege on occasion while also assuring Congress that it would be asserted only with specific approval by the president.

Nixon invoked the privilege repeatedly in clashes with the Democratic-controlled Congress, as did other administration officials—in some instances without Nixon's specific autho-

Train v. City of New York

Decided: February 18, 1975

Vote: 9 (Burger, Douglas, Brennan, Stewart, B. White, T. Marshall, Blackmun, Powell, Rehnquist)

0

Opinion of the Court: B. White

Concurring opinion: Douglas

Clinton v. City of New York

Decided: June 25, 1998

Vote: 6 (Rehnquist, Stevens, Kennedy, Souter, Thomas, Ginsburg)

3 (O'Connor, Scalia, Breyer)

Opinion of the Court: Stevens

Concurring opinion: Kennedy

Dissenting opinions (2): Scalia (O'Connor, Breyer); Breyer (O'Connor, Scalia)

rization. Both the Senate Watergate Committee and the special Watergate prosecutor subpoenaed Nixon personally for tapes of his Oval Office conversations and then challenged his claim of privilege in refusing to produce them. The federal appeals court in Washington rejected the committee's effort to enforce its subpoena, but the Supreme Court sided with the special prosecutor in ordering Nixon to turn over the tapes for use in the criminal trials of former Nixon aides charged with covering up White House involvement in the Watergate break-in.

In his opinion for the Court in *United States v. Nixon* (1974), Chief Justice Burger said that a "presumptive privilege for presidential communications" was "fundamental to the operation of government and inextricably rooted in the separation of powers under the Constitution." But the president's "weighty" interest in confidentiality, he continued, was outweighed by the need for evidence for a particular criminal case. "The generalized assertion of privilege must yield," Burger concluded, "to the demonstrated, specific need for evidence in a pending criminal trial."

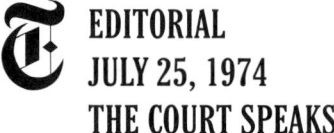

EDITORIAL
JULY 25, 1974
THE COURT SPEAKS

In a unanimous and firmly-worded opinion, the Supreme Court has reaffirmed the supremacy of law over Presidential pretensions and restated its own authority as the ultimate arbiter of the law. The opinion written by Chief Justice Warren Burger left Mr. Nixon no lawful alternative except to surrender the tapes and documents to United States District Judge John Sirica for his inspection and for possible use in the forthcoming Watergate trial.

If this nation was to remain the Republic established by the authors of the Constitution, the Court could only have ruled as it did yesterday. A decision in Mr. Nixon's favor would have meant that he or any future President could operate outside the law and conceal evidence of wrongdoing from the courts. That was the true meaning of the argument of Mr. Nixon's defense counsel that the separation of powers precludes review by the courts of a Presidential claim of privilege.

The Court had no difficulty apprehending the implications of that argument. It dealt with it by quoting the magisterial language of Chief Justice John Marshall in *Marbury v. Madison* in 1803: "It is emphatically the province and duty of the judicial department to say what the law is." . . .

The Court, naturally enough, had difficulty in conceiving that conversations with a President would normally be inhibited by the fear of those present that what they said might some day be subpoenaed for use in a criminal trial. That is a concern that might be expected in the office of a Mafia chieftain but not in the Oval Office of the White House. For that reason, the Court readily disposed of Mr. St. Clair's far-fetched contention that making Presidential materials available to a trial Judge in a criminal case would gravely impair the ability of future Presidents to receive free and frank advice.

On the contrary, the Chief Justice declared: "The allowance of the privilege to withhold evidence that is demonstrably relevant in a criminal trial would cut deeply into the guarantee of due process of law and gravely impair the basic function of the courts." . . .

By its decision, the Court has brought the Nixon White House back within the limits of the law. It has served notice that even the most powerful office in the Government cannot be used as a sanctuary for miscreants nor its legitimate privileges deployed to withhold evidence of wrongdoing. In the continuing struggle to restrain the abuses of the powerful modern Presidency, this decision is sure to be a landmark for the long future of the Republic.

• • • • • • • • • • • •

Three years later, the Court also rejected Nixon's attempt after his resignation to overturn the 1974 act of Congress that placed the records, tapes, and papers of his presidency in federal custody. Previously, presidential papers had been treated as the president's personal property. The 7-2 decision in *Nixon v. Administrator, General Services Administration* (1977) said that Nixon could be treated as "a legitimate class of one" for purposes of constitutional interpretation and found that the law did not violate general separation of powers principles or Nixon's personal privacy. A year later, Congress passed the Presidential Records Act of 1978 to make papers of all future presidents public property.

Presidential Immunity

The Watergate grand jury named Nixon as an "unindicted co-conspirator" in the break-in at the Democratic National Committee headquarters and the cover-up. The House Judiciary Committee subsequently accused Nixon of abuse of office, obstruction of office, and contempt of Congress in the three articles of impeachment that it approved in the days after the Supreme Court's decision in the Oval Office tapes case. Nixon's resignation in August 1974 ended the impeachment proceeding. President Gerald R. Ford's decision to pardon Nixon soon thereafter eliminated the possibility of a criminal trial and left unresolved the question whether a sitting president could be prosecuted for crimes in office.

Nixon did prevail at the Supreme Court in a case that established the president's absolute immunity from civil liability for official conduct while in the White House or after leaving office. A. Ernest Fitzgerald sued Nixon and other executive branch officials, blaming them for the loss of his air force job after having revealed cost overruns to Congress. Only three presidents had ever been sued while in office—all for conduct unrelated to their office. But in *Nixon v. Fitzgerald* (1982), the Court found that absolute immunity from civil suit was "a functionally mandated incident of the president's unique office, rooted in the constitutional tradition of the separation of powers and supported by our history." Leaving a president vulnerable to lawsuits while in office or after, Justice Powell wrote, "could distract a President from his public duties."

Nixon v. Administrator, General Services Administration

Decided: June 28, 1977
Vote: 7 (Brennan, Stewart, B. White, T. Marshall, Blackmun, Powell, Stevens)
2 (Burger, Rehnquist)
Opinion of the Court: Brennan
Concurring opinion: Stevens
Opinions concurring in judgment (3): B. White; Blackmun; Powell
Dissenting opinions (2): Burger; Rehnquist

Nixon v. Fitzgerald

Decided: June 24, 1982
Vote: 5 (Burger, Powell, Rehnquist, Stevens, O'Connor)
4 (Brennan, B. White, T. Marshall, Blackmun)
Opinion of the Court: Powell
Concurring opinion: Burger
Dissenting opinions (2): B. White (Brennan, T. Marshall, Blackmun); Blackmun (Brennan, T. Marshall)

JUNE 25, 1982
HIGH COURT HOLDS PRESIDENT IMMUNE FROM DAMAGE SUITS
5-4 RULING ON NIXON CASE
Companion Decision Upholds 'Qualified' Protection for White House Advisers
By LINDA GREENHOUSE

The Supreme Court ruled 5 to 4 today that no President may be sued for damages for any official action he takes while in office.

Overturning a lower court ruling in a suit against former President Richard M. Nixon, the Court declared that "absolute Presidential immunity" is a "functionally mandated incident of the President's unique office, rooted in the constitutional tradition of the separation of powers and supported by our history."

In a companion ruling, the Court refused, 8 to 1, to accord the same absolute immunity to top Presidential advisers. But the Justices effectively rewrote the law of "qualified immunity" that applies to most Federal and state officials, making it substantially more likely that courts will dismiss suits against such officials before trial.

COURT BITTERLY DIVIDED

Because officials covered by "qualified immunity" are sued much more often than the President, the companion ruling has more practical significance than the ruling on Presidential immunity.

But it was the decision on Presidential immunity that left the Court bitterly divided after almost seven months of grappling with the case. The ruling was on a damage suit by a former Air Force budget analyst, A. Ernest Fitzgerald, who charged that he had lost his job as a result of a White House conspiracy to deprive him of his civil rights. He was dismissed after exposing cost overruns in the C5-A transport plane.

The rulings concerned only immunity from civil suits for damages, not from criminal prosecutions or from other types of judicial action. The majority made clear that it was not casting any doubt on the Court's 1974 ruling that required President Nixon to turn over the Watergate tapes. Today's ruling was based largely on what Associate Justice Lewis G. Powell Jr. called the "public interest" in permitting a President to act as he sees fit without fear of being sued.

Associate Justice Lewis F. Powell Jr. wrote the majority opinion, joined by Chief Justice Warren E. Burger and Associate Justices William H. Rehnquist, John Paul Stevens and Sandra Day O'Connor.

Associate Justice Byron R. White's dissenting opinion, which labeled the majority ruling "tragic" and "bizarre," was joined by Associate Justices William J. Brennan Jr., Thurgood Marshall and Harry A. Blackmun.

The Supreme Court has accorded absolute immunity from civil suits to judges and prosecutors, and Justice Powell said that, like those officials, "a President must concern himself with matters likely to arouse the most intense feelings."

COMPELLING CONCERN ON PRESIDENT

"Yet, as our decisions have recognized," he continued, "it is in precisely such cases that there exists the greatest public interest in providing an official the maximum ability to deal fearlessly and impartially with the duties of his office. This concern is compeling where the officeholder must make the most sensitive and far-reaching decisions entrusted to any official under our constitutional system."

The majority rejected the argument that the scope of a President's immunity should be limited to particular functions, concluding that absolute immunity extends to all "acts within the 'outer perimeter' of his official responsibility." Mr. Fitzgerald had argued that whatever immunity a President might enjoy should not extend to discharging civil servants.

Mr. Fitzgerald recently settled a separate suit against the Federal Government, winning back his job and $200,000 in legal fees.

Earlier, he and Mr. Nixon had entered into an agreement to avoid a trial of his damage suit no matter how the Supreme Court ruled on the immunity issue. Mr. Nixon paid him $142,000 and would have paid him $28,000 more had the Supreme Court upheld the ruling of the United States Court of Appeals for the District of Columbia that the President did not have absolute immunity. . . .

* * * * * * * * * * * *

Clinton v. Jones

> **Decided:** May 27, 1997
>
> **Vote:** 9 (Rehnquist, Stevens, O'Connor, Scalia, Kennedy, Souter, Thomas, Ginsburg, Breyer)
>
> 0
>
> **Opinion of the Court:** Stevens
>
> **Opinion concurring in judgment:** Breyer

In *Clinton v. Jones* (1997), however, the Court found that a sitting president does not enjoy immunity from civil suit for private conduct before taking office. Paula Jones, a former Arkansas state employee, claimed in her 1994 sexual harassment suit that Clinton had made an indecent advance to her in 1991, while he was the state's governor. Clinton's attorneys cited *Nixon v. Fitzgerald* in asking that discovery in the case be deferred until after he left office. A trial judge agreed, but the U.S. Circuit Court of Appeals in St. Louis ruled that discovery should proceed.

In a unanimous decision, the Supreme Court agreed. "We have never suggested that the President, or any other official, has an immunity that extends beyond the scope of any action taken in an official capacity," Justice Stevens wrote. He said there was "no possibility" the outcome of the case could curtail the president's power, as the judge presiding would presumably take steps to accommodate the president's "busy schedule."

All of the justices except Breyer joined Stevens's opinion. In an opinion concurring in the judgment, Breyer worried that a civil lawsuit could be "a distraction" for a president while in office.

MAY 28, 1997
SUPREME COURT, 9-0, REJECTS CLINTON REQUEST TO PUT OFF SUIT ON SEXUAL HARASSMENT

By LINDA GREENHOUSE

Ruling for the first time that a sitting President can be sued for actions outside the scope of his official duties, the Supreme Court today decisively rejected President Clinton's request to delay proceedings in a sexual harassment suit brought by a former Arkansas state employee, Paula Corbin Jones.

The 9-to-0 decision does not mean that the lawsuit, filed in 1994 over an encounter that allegedly took place in 1991, will now go to trial promptly, or even that it will necessarily go to trial at all. President Clinton's lawyers have other legal avenues to pursue beyond the immunity claim the Court rejected today. Settlement of the case also remains an option.

Judge Susan Webber Wright of Federal District Court in Little Rock, Ark., said a scheduling order, including a trial date, would be set after the Supreme Court officially remands the case to the court, in about a month, and soon after Mr. Clinton has filed his answer to the complaint within the 20 days set forth in the Federal Rules of Civil Procedure. Usually, a trial would be set for 10 to 12 months later, but that varies.

With surprising unanimity, given the differing views among the lower court judges who dealt with the case and the variety of possible outcomes, the Court ruled that neither the Constitution nor public policy justified giving the President what he wanted: a delay of pretrial proceedings and the trial itself until after Mr. Clinton has left office.

"The Federal District Court has jurisdiction to decide this case," Justice John Paul Stevens said in his opinion for the Court. "Like every other citizen who properly invokes that jurisdiction," he said, Ms. Jones "has a right to an orderly disposition of her claims."

Ms. Jones is seeking $700,000 in damages for an unwanted sexual overture she maintains that Mr. Clinton, then the Governor of Arkansas, made to her in a Little Rock hotel room in 1991, when she was a state employee. Her suit, filed in 1994, two days before a three-year statute of limitations expired, claims that Mr. Clinton used the powers of his office to violate her civil rights.

While rejecting Mr. Clinton's arguments for delaying the case, Justice Stevens said today that "the high respect that is owed to the office of the Chief Executive" should "inform the conduct of the entire proceeding" and lead the trial court to accommodate the President's schedule as much as possible. He said the President's testimony could be taken at the White House and that he need not attend the trial itself, "though he could elect to do so."

Whatever its eventual practical or political effect, the decision is guaranteed a place in constitutional history, joining a tiny pantheon of cases in which the Court has confronted, and rejected, claims that the essential nature of the Presidency requires the judiciary to yield to the President's own view of the prerogatives of his office. In his opinion, Justice Stevens cited two landmark rulings, the 1952 decision in which the Court ruled unconstitutional President Harry S. Truman's seizure of the steel industry and the 1974 decision ordering President Richard M. Nixon to surrender the Watergate tapes.

"If the judiciary may severely burden the executive branch by reviewing the legality of the President's official conduct, and if it may direct appropriate process to the President himself," Justice Stevens said, "it must follow that the Federal courts have power to determine the legality of his unofficial conduct."

Justice Stephen G. Breyer, while agreeing with the outcome of the case, did not sign the majority opinion. In a separate opinion, he said he was more "skeptical" than the other Justices that courts could manage cases like this one without impinging unduly on the President's handling of his official duties, or that the ruling would not inspire other private plaintiffs to sue sitting Presidents over earlier events.

Only three sitting Presidents have been defendants in civil lawsuits involving incidents before they took office. Suits against Theodore Roosevelt and Truman were dismissed, and a suit against John F. Kennedy involving a car accident during his 1960 campaign was settled. None of the cases reached the High Court.

The only arguably relevant precedent for the Court to consider in this case was a 1982 ruling, Nixon v. Fitzgerald, which held that a President has absolute immunity from civil lawsuits over actions taken in his official capacity. The rationale for that decision was to permit the President to carry out his duties without the fear of future lawsuits.

"This reasoning provides no support for an immunity for unofficial conduct," Justice Stevens said today.

Mr. Clinton's lawyers had argued that the Court in the Fitzgerald case had also acknowledged a more general concern, not only that a President might be chilled by the fear of future lawsuits but also that the nation should not have to pay the price of the drain on a President's attention from attending to litigation.

That concern "finds little support in either history or the relatively narrow compass of the issues raised in this particular case," Justice Stevens said. If the trial court "properly managed" this case, he added, "it appears to us highly unlikely to occupy any substantial amount" of the President's time.

Justice Stevens also rejected what he called Mr. Clinton's "strongest argument," that the text and structure of the Constitution, particularly the unique responsibilities of the President and the concept of the separation of powers, limited the ability of the Federal courts to interfere with the executive branch by requiring a sitting President to stand trial.

That argument failed, Justice Stevens said, "by presuming that interactions between the judicial branch and the executive, even quite burdensome interactions, neces-sarily rise to the level of constitutionally forbidden impairment of the executive's ability to perform its constitutionally mandated functions."

The tone of the opinion, Clinton v. Jones, No. 95-1853, was measured and sober, in marked contrast to the appellate court decision that it upheld. Writing for a 2-to-1 majority in the January 1996 opinion, Judge Pasco M. Bowman of the United States Court of Appeals for the Eighth Circuit essentially characterized the President's argument as a request to be put beyond the reaches of the law. "We start with the truism" that the Constitution "did not create a monarchy," Judge Bowman said in ruling against a delay of the trial.

By contrast, Justice Stevens said pointedly that Mr. Clinton "does not contend that the occupant of the office of the President is 'above the law' " in arguing "merely for a postponement of the judicial proceedings that will determine whether he violated any law."

In 1994, Judge Wright ruled that while Mr. Clinton was entitled to a delay of the trial, pretrial depositions could proceed.

Justice Stevens said today that Judge Wright's decision to delay the trial was an abuse of judicial discretion because it took "no account whatever" of Ms. Jones's interests in proceeding with the case.

· · · · · · · · · · · ·

Breyer's concerns were somewhat prophetic. In a deposition in Jones's suit, Clinton denied under oath any recollection of having had a sexual relationship with White House intern Monica Lewinsky. He repeated the same false testimony before a federal grand jury convened by independent counsel Kenneth Starr. The House of Representatives charged Clinton with perjury and obstruction of justice in two articles of impeachment in December 1998. With his Senate impeachment trial pending, Clinton settled Jones's civil suit for $850,000 on January 12, 1999. One month to the day later, the impeachment trial ended in the Senate with Clinton's acquittal on both counts.

War Powers

The president's power as commander in chief was seen as purely military in nature until the Civil War. In confronting the national emergency of secession, Abraham Lincoln justified extraordinary actions—such as the use of military tribunals—by combining his power as commander in chief with the president's general duty to take care that the laws be faithfully executed. The Supreme Court allowed Woodrow Wilson and Franklin D. Roosevelt to exercise similarly broad powers during World War I and World War II. But the Court drew the line when Harry Truman tried to seize the nation's steel mills during the undeclared Korean War and again when George W. Bush instituted irregular procedures for dealing with suspected enemy combatants in the war on terror.

WORLD WAR I

Acting under broadly phrased delegations of power from Congress, Wilson exercised extraordinary powers over the national economy during World War I. In August 1917—four months after the United States entered the war—Congress passed the Lever Food and Fuel Control Act, giving the president authority to control the production and distribution of food and the marketing of fuel. One section made it a criminal offense to "exact excessive prices for any necessaries." After the war had ended, the Supreme Court ruled in *United States v. L. Cohen Grocery Co.* (1921) that the statute was "void for repugnancy to the Constitution" because the broad phrasing provided no "ascertainable standard of guilt."

WORLD WAR II

Congress passed another broad price control act in late January 1942, less than two months after the United States entered World War II. The Emergency Price Control Act included standards for writing and publishing administrative regulations and provisions for challenging regulations before a special court. Citing those details, the Court upheld the act in a 6-3 decision, *Yakus v. United States* (1944).

After the Japanese attack on Pearl Harbor, President Franklin D. Roosevelt issued Executive Order 9066, which greatly restricted the movement of Japanese Americans on the West Coast and was upheld by the Supreme Court in *Hirabayashi v. United States* (1943). Roosevelt's subsequent order to relocate more than 100,000 Japanese Americans to internment camps, such as the one pictured above, was ruled constitutional by the Court in *Korematsu v. United States* (1944).

Source: United Press International

For the majority, Chief Justice Stone contrasted the act's provisions to the standardless delegation of powers in the National Industrial Recovery Act, which the Court had struck down in 1935.

Roosevelt also won three Supreme Court tests of actions he took to protect the country from sabotage, including the controversial internment of Japanese Americans relocated from the West Coast. In the years since, each of the rulings has attracted much criticism for short-circuiting important constitutional safeguards.

In *Ex parte Quirin* (1942), the Court upheld Roosevelt's use of a military tribunal to try eight German saboteurs captured after entering the United States clandestinely from a German submarine. The secret tribunal sentenced all eight to death on July 2, 1942. Despite a provision in Roosevelt's proclamation barring review in U.S. courts, the Supreme Court heard arguments on July 29 and 30, 1942, on habeas corpus petitions filed by seven of the Germans. With the public clamoring for executions, the Court issued an unsigned, three-paragraph opinion only one day later finding the tribunals had been "lawfully constituted."

JULY 5, 1942
NAZI SABOTEURS FACE STERN ARMY JUSTICE
Order for a Military Trial Comes as National Anger at Invasion Rises
By LEWIS WOOD

WASHINGTON, July 4—The sensational capture on our shores of eight self-confessed Nazi saboteurs drives home the realization of the constant peril from these secret enemies armed with weapons of destruction. The fact that these desperate men planned attacks against such great enterprises as the Aluminum Company plants, the Hell Gate Bridge, and the New York City water supply system, startlingly emphasizes the ever-present menace of which we become really aware only through such incidents as those of Long Island and Florida.

Yet the rapid and effective action of the G-men in seizing the Germans almost as they landed on the sandy

ing note at a moment when indignant Americans everywhere were demanding this extreme punishment for the audacious criminals. Americans wanted to hear the roar of rifles in the hands of a firing squad, and the government has apparently agreed that this is the proper course.

Living up to expectations, the foreign agents had been assigned to strike at industrial plants, transportation systems and the services providing cities with water, heat, light and such needs of living for many thousands of Americans. These are the targets of sabotage in wartime, particularly the factories, when a nation rises to enormous war production such as ours.

 Americans wanted to hear the roar of rifles in the hands of a firing squad, and the government has apparently agreed that this is the proper course.

beaches gave a feeling of comfort and security. Men and women felt satisfaction and confidence that the government was infinitely better prepared to cope with spies and saboteurs than during the last war.

ANSWERS PUBLIC DEMAND

Expectation, too, that the Administration would seek the death penalty for the Hitler spies before the military commission chosen by the President sounded a hearten-

As far back as 1939, the year when Hitler terrorized Europe by his onslaughts, the G-men undertook what is now providing the most extensive protective program in history. . . .

PLANT PRODUCTION SET-UP

Aware of the physical weakness of defense factories, the FBI surveyed about 2,400 plants before the Army and Navy later assumed the protective work. With minute care, government detectives studied details such as placing and guarding of gates; location of protective fences; type, availability and quality of fire-fighting equipment; flood-lighting, and adequacy of measures to safeguard blueprints, drawings and secret parts.

Up to the days when the eight Germans were taken into custody, there has been only one really important example of sabotage, and this was the case of Michael William Etzel, the youth who damaged bombers in the Martin plant at Baltimore. Rigid scrutiny revealed that over a period of eighty-three days thirty-four separate destructive acts had been committed on twenty-four of the big airships, and eventually Etzel was arrested and is now serving fifteen years in prison.

Divided from sabotage by only a thin line is espionage, and several striking cases of this kind have come to light in recent years. In one of these Karl Allen Drummond, a 21-year-old inspector in a California airplane plant, stole highly confidential blueprints and offered to sell them for $2,000 to the Japanese consul at Los Angeles. Convicted of violation of the espionage act, Drummond was sentenced to serve two years.

CLOSE INVESTIGATIONS

All through the last 12 months and intensively since Pearl Harbor, government agencies have closely investigated every incident where sabotage was implied, even though not proved. The G-men, the Army counter-intelligence, and the Navy's secret service have gone into every clue and have submitted exhaustive reports.

Although actual sabotage has not yet been demonstrated in some of these cases, the investigative work is not yet completed. As a matter of fact it may take years to prove that Axis powers are responsible. . . .

CASE OF THE SEA CAPTAINS

Just as in the first World War, sabotage here has been largely directed by the diplomats stationed at Washington and the consuls scattered throughout the United States. The Italian merchant ship captains who damaged their craft at Newark, Los Angeles, Jacksonville and elsewhere flatly said they smashed machinery with hammers and cut wiring entirely on order of their official government representatives.

With the sabotage incidents of the last war still fresh in memory after a quarter century, a mounting sense of outrage has been evident since the arrival of the Nazi saboteurs in this country. The people insist that there must be no delay or pussyfooting in dealing with the present criminals and all others who come after them.

· · · · · · · · · · · ·

Six of the eight German saboteurs were executed on August 8; Roosevelt commuted the sentences of the two who had confessed and assisted in capturing the others. In a full opinion issued in October, Chief Justice Stone said that constitutional requirements for a jury trial and other procedural rights did not apply to enemy belligerents and that the offenses charged constituted violations of the law of war triable by military commissions.

Two months after the Japanese attacked Pearl Harbor, Roosevelt issued Executive Order 9066 on February 19, 1942, placing Japanese Americans living on the West Coast under rigid nighttime curfew laws and restricting their movements. Congress passed a resolution a month later ratifying the action. Roosevelt later ordered the removal of all persons of Japanese ancestry from the coastal region. Under Roosevelt's order, more than 100,000 Japanese Americans were relocated to internment camps, some for periods as long as four years.

In *Hirabayashi v. United States* (1943), the Court unanimously upheld the curfew order as "within the boundaries of the war power." Chief Justice Stone emphasized Congress's ratification of Roosevelt's order and said the Court was not considering whether the president could have issued the order on his own. Stone deferred to "military authorities" in assessing the danger of disloyalty among Japanese Americans and the need for the curfew, saying the circumstances afforded "a rational basis" for the decision. "Whether we would have made it," he added, "is irrelevant."

Hirabayashi v. United States

Decided: June 21, 1943

Vote: 9 (Stone, O. Roberts, Black, Reed, Frankfurter, Douglas, Murphy, R. Jackson, W. Rutledge)

0

Opinion of the Court: Stone

Concurring opinions (3): Douglas; Murphy; W. Rutledge

Korematsu v. United States

Decided: December 18, 1944

Vote: 6 (Stone, Black, Reed,
Frankfurter, Douglas,
W. Rutledge)

3 (O. Roberts, Murphy,
R. Jackson)

Opinion of the Court: Black

Concurring opinion: Frankfurter

Dissenting opinions (3): O. Roberts;
Murphy; R. Jackson

Eighteen months later, the Court in *Korematsu v. United States* (1944) upheld the exclusion of Japanese Americans from their West Coast homes—but this time three justices dissented. For the majority, Justice Hugo L. Black again deferred to the judgment by "military leaders" on the need for the exclusion order. "There was evidence of disloyalty on the part of some, the military authorities considered that the need for action was great, and time was short," he wrote. "We cannot—by availing ourselves of the calm perspective of hindsight—now say that at that time these actions were unjustified."

In a separate decision on the same day, however, the Court unanimously ruled that the government had no power to detain a Japanese American girl, Mitsuye Endo, after it conceded her loyalty to the United States. The ruling in *Ex parte Endo* (1944) ended the internment program. Within forty-eight hours, the government announced that, with a few exceptions, all the Japanese Americans were free to go home. While the Supreme Court has never repudiated *Hirabayashi* or *Korematsu,* Congress in 1988 passed and President Ronald Reagan signed a law apologizing for the wartime internments and promising the estimated 60,000 surviving internees compensation of $20,000 each.

DECEMBER 19, 1944
SUPREME COURT UPHOLDS RETURN OF LOYAL JAPANESE TO WEST COAST

By LEWIS WOOD

Special to The New York Times

WASHINGTON, Dec. 18—... The Supreme Court rulings came only twenty-four hours after the Army announcement that exclusion of Japanese-Americans from the West Coast would be ended Jan. 2. They came also at about the time Secretary Ickes declared in a statement that he did not foresee a "hasty mass movement" of evacuees back to the West Coast.

Justice Hugo L. Black wrote the majority opinion on the evacuation question, which involved the 1942 order of Maj. Gen. John L. De Witt as applied to Fred Toyosaburo Korematsu.

Upholding the order as "of the time it was made and when (Korematsu) violated it," he deplored compulsory exclusion, but said that Korematsu was excluded because we were at war with Japan, adding:

"When under conditions of modern warfare our shores are threatened by hostile forces, the power to protect must be commensurate with the threatened danger.

"We are unable to conclude that it was beyond the war powers of Congress and of the Executive to exclude those of Japanese ancestry from the West Coast area at the time they did."

Justices Owen J. Roberts, Frank Murphy and Robert H. Jackson all entered dissents on the ground that the majority finding violated the Constitution.

The unanimous opinion regarding confinement in war relocation centers was written by Justice William O. Douglas in the case of 22-year-old Mitsuye Endo, held at Topaz, Utah. Without going into constitutional issues, Mr. Douglas held that, as Miss Endo's detention was not related to espionage or sabotage, she must be released. He noted that she was a concededly loyal citizen and stated:

"Loyalty is a matter of the heart and mind, not of race, creed or color."

'HARDSHIPS ARE PART OF WAR'

As in the case of Miss Endo, no question has been raised concerning the loyalty of Korematsu, native American. Accused of remaining in a military zone after his exclusion was ordered, he was convicted and sentenced to serve five years, but was placed on probation.

In upholding the exclusion order, Justice Black said that the court was "not unmindful of the hardships" which it imposed on a large group of American citizens.

"But," he stated, "hardships are part of war, and war is an aggregation of hardships. All citizens alike, both in and out of uniform, feel the impact of war in greater or lesser measure."

Pressing public necessity may sometimes justify the existence of restrictions on a racial group, but "racial antagonism never can," Justice Black remarked.

He pointed out that in the Hirabayashi case of several months ago the Supreme Court had held that a curfew applied properly to the program controlling Japanese-Americans.

"We upheld the curfew order as an exercise of the power of the Government to take steps necessary to prevent espionage and sabotage in an area threatened by Japanese attack," he said.

STEPS TO PREVENT SABOTAGE

"In the light of the principles we announced in the Hirabayashi case, we are unable to conclude that it was beyond the war power of Congress and the Executive to exclude those of Japanese ancestry from the West Coast area at the time they did. True, exclusion from the area in which one's home is located is a far greater deprivation than constant confinement to the home from 8 P.M. to 6 A.M., the curfew hours.

"Nothing short of apprehension by the proper military authorities of the gravest imminent danger to the public safety can constitutionally justify either. But exclusion from a threatened area, no less than curfew, has a definite and close relationship to the prevention of espionage and sabotage."

Justice Black declared that it was wrong to "cast this case into outlines of racial prejudice," for, he contended, Korematsu was not excluded "because of hostility to him or his race," but because of the war circumstances. He pointed out that while many persons of Japanese origin were loyal to the United States, 5,000 refused to swear allegiance and several thousands sought repatriation to Japan.

In one of the dissents, Justice Jackson said the majority seemed to be "distorting the Constitution to approve all that the military may deem expedient." He asserted that he could not determine on the evidence whether General De Witt's orders were reasonable cautions. . . .

. . . .

KOREAN WAR

The Supreme Court's first direct repudiation of a president's claim of wartime powers came in 1952 after Truman ordered the seizure of the nation's steel mills to avert a threatened strike. In issuing Executive Order 10340 on April 8, 1952, Truman claimed the same authority that Roosevelt had exercised to mobilize the economy during World War II. In 1947, however, Congress had passed— over Truman's veto—the Labor-Management Relations Act, commonly known as the Taft-Hartley Act, which included provisions for averting strikes but denied any such power to the president acting alone.

Steel companies challenged Truman's order, naming Commerce Secretary Charles Sawyer as defendant. Two lower courts blocked the seizure, and the Supreme Court agreed in a 6-3 decision, *Youngstown Sheet and Tube Co. v. Sawyer* (1952). In the relatively short majority opinion, Justice Black said Truman's order could not be sustained as an exercise of his power as commander in chief or under the "take care" clause. Instead, Black said, the order amounted to impermissible presidential lawmaking. "The President's order does not direct that a congressional policy be executed in a manner prescribed by Congress," Black wrote. "It directs that a presidential policy be executed in a manner prescribed by the President."

A longer concurring opinion by Justice Robert H. Jackson has proved to be more influential than Black's in evaluating presidential powers. Jackson's three-part test views the president's power at its greatest when the president acts "pursuant to an express or implied authorization from Congress" and at "its lowest ebb" when—as in this case—the actions are "incompatible with the express or implied will of Con-

Youngstown Sheet and Tube Co. v. Sawyer

Decided: June 2, 1952

Vote: 6 (Black, Frankfurter, Douglas, R. Jackson, Burton, Clark)

3 (Vinson, Reed, Minton)

Opinion of the Court: Black

Concurring opinions (4): Frankfurter; Douglas; R. Jackson; Burton

Opinion concurring in judgment: Clark

Dissenting opinion: Vinson (Reed, Minton)

gress." In between, Jackson said, lies "a zone of twilight" where the president may have "independent powers." In those cases, Jackson said, "congressional inertia, indifference or quiescence" may invite independent presidential action, and the legality "is likely to depend on the imperatives of events and contemporary imponderables rather than on abstract theories of law."

JUNE 3, 1952
SUPREME COURT VOIDS STEEL SEIZURE, 6 TO 3; HOLDS TRUMAN USURPED POWERS OF CONGRESS; WORKERS AGAIN STRIKE AS MILLS ARE RETURNED

BLACK GIVES RULING

President Cannot Make Law in Good or Bad Times, Majority Says

VINSON IS DISSENTER

Rejects Idea Executive Is 'Messenger Boy' in Crisis—Steel Curbed

By JOSEPH A. LOFTUS

Special to The New York Times.

WASHINGTON, June 2—The Supreme Court of the United States ruled, 6 to 3, today that President Truman's seizure of the steel industry to avert a strike violated the Constitution by usurping the legislative powers reserved to Congress.

The President bowed promptly by directing Secretary of Commerce Charles Sawyer to release the properties to their private owners, and the United Steelworkers of America, C. I. O., went on strike.

Dissenting were: Chief Justice Fred M. Vinson and Justices Stanley F. Reed and Sherman Minton.

FOUNDING FATHERS' ACTION CITED

The court ruled in effect that when the President seized the steel mills he seized the lawmaking power, because only Congress could authorize the taking of private property for public use.

> The founders of this nation entrusted the lawmaking power to the Congress alone in both good and bad times.
>
> —Justice Hugo L. Black, *Youngstown Sheet & Tube Co. v. Sawyer*

As a result of the walkout the Government ordered a halt in deliveries of steel from retail warehouses to consumer goods producers in an effort to conserve steel for defense needs.

Authorities said the action was directed at preventing a drain on warehouses by buyers who usually got their steel at the mills. Manufacturers who ordinarily receive steel from warehouses will continue to do so, they added. No order was issued against steel exports.

The Supreme Court justices who voted to uphold District Judge David A. Pine's order dispossessing the Government were: Hugo L. Black, Felix Frankfurter, William O. Douglas, Robert H. Jackson, Harold H. Burton and Tom C. Clark.

"The Constitution did not subject this law-making power of Congress to Presidential or military supervision or control," said the opinion of the court, written by Justice Black.

"The founders of this nation entrusted the lawmaking power to the Congress alone in both good and bad times," it added. "It would do no good to recall the historical events, the fears of power and the hopes for freedom that lay behind their choice. Such a review would but confirm our holding that this seizure order cannot stand."

Chief Justice Vinson, writing a vigorous dissent, declared that the President's action to keep steel flowing was warranted by the world emergency.

"History bears out the genius of the founding fathers, who created a Government subject to law but not left subject to inertia when vigor and initiative are required," the Chief Justice wrote.

VINSON CRITICIZES MAJORITY

"As the district judge stated, this is no time for 'timorous' judicial action," he declared. "But neither is this a time for timorous executive action."

Chief Justice Vinson said the majority of the court, not the minority, was seeking to amend the Constitution. He declared:

"The broad Executive power granted by Article II to an officer on duty 365 days a year cannot, it is said, be invoked to avert disaster.

"Instead, the President must confine himself to sending a message to Congress recommending action. Under this messenger-boy concept of the office, the President cannot even act to preserve legislative programs from destruction so that Congress will have something left to act upon."

The court, contrary to a widely held expectation among lawyers, grasped the Constitutional issue firmly and interpreted it without equivocal language. It might have disposed of the case without reaching the ultimate question; indeed, it is the practice of the judiciary to do so whenever possible.

The court acted with unusual speed. Legal controversies often take years in their course through the three levels of the Federal judiciary. This decision came less than eight weeks after the President seized the steel mills.

The seizure took effect on April 9. The district court granted the steel companies' injunction against seizure on April 29. The Circuit Court of Appeals stayed the injunction the next day. The Supreme Court accepted the case the same week and heard oral argument on May 12.

In the three-week interval since argument was heard, the justices wrote more than 50,000 words in opinions in the steel case alone. Each of the six justices in the majority wrote concurring opinions. Only Justices Reed and Minton refrained from writing.

The history-making case hereafter will be known to law students and lawyers as Youngstown Co. v. Sawyer.

OPINIONS TAKE 2½ HOURS

Delivery of the opinions took two hours and thirty-five minutes. The court convened at noon and Chief Justice Vinson announced that, contrary to custom, the admissions of attorneys to practice before the Supreme Court would be deferred until later. Usually that is the first order of business. . . .

. . . .

VIETNAM WAR

Presidential power was fiercely debated during the Vietnam War, but the full Supreme Court never ruled on the issues. In several cases, the Court declined to review lower court rulings that found the constitutionality of the congressionally undeclared war to be a political question not for the courts to decide. In one of those cases, however, two of the justices took their colleagues to task for not facing the issue. "We cannot make these issues go away simply by refusing to hear the case of three obscure Army privates," Justice Potter F. Stewart wrote in the November 6, 1967, order declining to hear the case of Mora v. McNamara.

As the war wound down, Congress in 1973 passed over Nixon's veto the War Powers Act requiring the president to notify Congress within forty-eight hours of committing U.S. forces overseas and requiring congressional approval for commitments after sixty days. In vetoing the measure, Nixon called it both dangerous and unconstitutional. The act, he said, "would attempt to take away . . . authorities which the President has properly exercised under the Constitution for 200 years." The Supreme Court has never ruled on the constitutionality of the law.

WAR ON TERROR

One week after the September 11, 2001, attacks on the United States, President Bush signed into law a bill passed by Congress that authorized him "to use all necessary and appropriate force against those nations, organizations, or persons" that were responsible for the attacks or that "harbored such organizations or persons." Bush invoked the Authorization to Use Military Force in October to launch air strikes against and later to invade Afghanistan in order to topple the Islamist government for its role in sheltering the al Qaeda organization responsible for the attacks.

With the ground war advancing, Bush on November 13 issued Military Order No. 1, providing for the detention and trials before specially constituted "military commissions" of members of al Qaeda or anyone else who had plotted terrorist attacks against the United States or harbored anyone who had. The secretary of defense was given broad discretion in forming the tribunals and in deciding where to hold the detainees—"outside or within the United States." The tribunals themselves were authorized to consider any "probative" evidence, to withhold classified evidence from the detainees, to close proceedings, and to decide cases by a two-thirds majority—all procedures that departed from regular courts-martial.

Thousands of prisoners captured in the Afghanistan war and many other suspected terrorists rounded up in other countries were brought to the U.S. naval station at Guantánamo Bay, Cuba, beginning in January 2002. The government also used naval brigs within the United States to hold two U.S. citizens designated as enemy combatants. Yasir Hamdi, who was born in the United States to Saudi parents, had been handed over to U.S. forces in Afghanistan in November 2001. Jose Padilla, a convert to Islam, had been arrested on May 8, 2002, as he deplaned at Chicago's O'Hare Airport and was charged with plotting to set off a radioactive "dirty bomb" in the United States.

Denied access to lawyers or any opportunity for hearings, Hamdi and Padilla both filed habeas corpus petitions challenging their detentions. Many of the Guantánamo detainees similarly filed habeas corpus petitions seeking hearings to contest the basis for their confinement. The administration argued that the president had authority as commander in chief to order the detainees held without hearings and—in the case of the Guantánamo detainees—that federal courts had no jurisdiction because the base lay outside the United States.

In June 2004, the Supreme Court rejected both positions. In *Hamdi v. Rumsfeld,* five justices agreed that the congressional authorization to use force gave the president the power to detain suspected enemy combatants. But an overlapping majority of six justices said that the citizen detainees must be given—as Justice Sandra Day O'Connor wrote in the main opinion—"a meaningful opportunity to contest the factual basis for the detention before a neutral decisionmaker." Two justices—John Paul Stevens and Antonin Scalia—went further and said Hamdi was entitled to trial in a civilian court. (Padilla's case was dismissed for procedural reasons, but he later gained the benefit of the ruling.) Only Clarence Thomas agreed with the administration that no hearing was required.

Hamdi v. Rumsfeld

Decided: June 28, 2004

Vote: 6 (Rehnquist, O'Connor,
            Kennedy, Souter, Ginsburg,
            Breyer)
         3 (Stevens, Scalia, Thomas)

Judgment of the Court: O'Connor
            (Rehnquist, Kennedy, Breyer)

Opinion concurring in part and
    dissenting in part: Souter
    (Ginsburg)

Dissenting opinions (2): Scalia
    (Stevens); Thomas

JUNE 29, 2004
JUSTICES AFFIRM LEGAL RIGHTS OF 'ENEMY COMBATANTS'

ACCESS TO COURTS

Ruling Applies to Those Held Either in U.S. or at Guantánamo

By LINDA GREENHOUSE

Declaring that "a state of war is not a blank check for the president," the Supreme Court ruled on Monday that those deemed enemy combatants by the Bush administration, both in the United States and at Guantánamo Bay, Cuba, must be given the ability to challenge their detention before a judge or other "neutral decision-maker."

> ## A state of war is not a blank check for the president.
> —Justice Sandra Day O'Connor, *Hamdi v. Rumsfeld*

Although divided in its rationale, the court was decisive in rejecting the administration's core legal argument that the executive branch has the last word in imposing open-ended detention on citizens and noncitizens alike. The justices' language was occasionally passionate, reflecting their awareness of the historic nature of this confrontation between executive and judicial authority.

Eight justices, all but Justice Clarence Thomas, said the two-year-long detention of an American citizen, Yaser Esam Hamdi, had either been invalid from the beginning or had become so, for constitutional or statutory reasons. The controlling opinion, by Justice Sandra Day O'Connor, said that Mr. Hamdi's detention was permissible if designation as an enemy combatant proved to be correct, but that his inability so far to appear before a judge, challenge the government's evidence, and tell his side of the story had deprived him of his constitutional right to due process.

The opinion said that a citizen held as an enemy combatant was entitled to "notice of the factual basis for his classification" and a "fair opportunity to rebut the government's factual assertions before a neutral decision-maker." Writing for herself, Chief Justice William H. Rehnquist, and Justices Anthony M. Kennedy and Stephen G. Breyer, Justice O'Connor said, "These essential constitutional promises may not be eroded."

She added that "we necessarily reject the government's assertion that separation of powers principles mandate a heavily circumscribed role for the courts in such circumstances." She said that the administration's position that the courts could not examine individual detainees' cases "serves only to condense power into a single branch of government."

Mr. Hamdi, picked up on the battlefield in Afghanistan, has sought to contest his designation as an enemy combatant. The federal appeals court that heard his case ruled last year that a nine-paragraph statement filed by a Pentagon official, Michael Mobbs, was a sufficient basis for Mr. Hamdi's continued detention and that no further inquiry into his case was required.

In a second case Monday, concerning the hundreds of noncitizens confined at the United States naval base at Guantánamo Bay, the court ruled 6 to 3 that federal judges have jurisdiction to consider petitions for writs of habeas corpus from detainees who argue that they are being unlawfully held.

The administration's position on the Guantánamo detainees was that under a World War II-era Supreme Court precedent, no federal court had jurisdiction to hear their cases because the base is outside the sovereign territory of the United States. But for a variety of reasons, the precedents the administration relied on did not govern the analysis, Justice John Paul Stevens said for the majority. A main factor was the nature of Guantánamo Bay, "territory over which the United States exercises exclusive jurisdiction and control" under a 101-year-old lease, Justice Stevens said.

The majority's analysis suggested, in fact, that federal courts might have jurisdiction to hear claims of illegal detention from those held in other foreign locations as well. While Justice Stevens was not explicit on this point, his suggestion was enough to provoke Justice Antonin Scalia to complain in dissent that "the court boldly extends the scope of the habeas statute to the four corners of the earth." Chief Justice Rehnquist and Justice Thomas joined the dissent.

The Supreme Court also dealt with a third case Monday, that of Jose Padilla, an American citizen picked up at O'Hare International Airport in Chicago on suspicion of planning to detonate a radioactive device. This case ended with what was essentially a nonruling. Mr. Padilla's habeas corpus petition was brought in the wrong court, the Supreme Court said by a 5 to 4 majority. His lawyers said they would act promptly to refile the case, which is now considerably strengthened by the court's analysis in the Hamdi case.

The decisions in the Hamdi and Padilla cases came two months to the day after those cases were argued. Just hours after the arguments concluded on April 28, CBS television broadcast the first images of the mistreatment of Iraqi prisoners at the Abu Ghraib prison.

While the Supreme Court cases all involved detentions resulting from the war against the Taliban in Afghanistan and had no connection to Iraq, there was much speculation in the intervening weeks about what impact the revelations from Abu Ghraib might have on the court.

Not surprisingly, no justice made a direct reference to those events. But it was difficult to read some of the passages in a vacuum. For example, Justice Stevens, dissenting from the court's refusal to reach the merits of the Padilla case, noted that Mr. Padilla had been held without charges or access to a lawyer for two years, and then said:

"Executive detention of subversive citizens, like detention of enemy soldiers to keep them off the battlefield, may sometimes be justified to prevent persons from launching or becoming missiles of destruction. It may not, however, be justified by the naked interest in using unlawful procedures to extract information. Incommunicado detention for months on end is such a procedure. Whether the information so procured is more or less reliable than that acquired by more extreme forms of torture is of no consequence. For if this nation is to remain true to the ideals symbolized by its flag, it must not wield the tools of tyrants even to resist an assault by the forces of tyranny."

Justice Breyer and Justices David H. Souter and Ruth Bader Ginsburg joined that dissent.

In her opinion in the Hamdi case, Justice O'Connor said that "indefinite detention for the purpose of interrogation is not authorized." She also said: "History and common sense teach us that an unchecked system of detention carries the potential to become a means for oppression and abuse of others."

All three decisions left important questions unanswered. In the Guantánamo case, Rasul v. Bush, No. 03-334, while it is clear that the detainees there can now bring habeas corpus petitions in federal court, the justices said little about the range of claims they could present or about how judges are to weigh those claims against the government's arguments about the need for continued detention.

Barbara Olshansky, deputy legal director of the Center for Constitutional Rights, a New York legal organization representing the Guantánamo detainees, said in an interview that lawyers would move quickly to test the scope of the court's ruling. The case the Supreme Court decided was brought in the name of 16 British, Australian, and Kuwaiti detainees, two of whom have been released by the government and sent home to England. Ms. Olshansky said the case may now be expanded into a class-action suit on behalf of many others.

Justice O'Connor's opinion in the Hamdi case, Hamdi v. Rumsfeld, No. 03-6696, offered a more detailed blueprint for what might happen next.

As a matter of constitutional due process, Justice O'Connor said, the lower courts must now balance Mr. Hamdi's interest in liberty against the "weighty and sensitive governmental interests in ensuring that those who have in fact fought with the enemy during a war do not return to battle against the United States."

"Striking the proper constitutional balance here is of great importance to the nation during this period of ongoing combat," she said, adding: "But it is equally vital that our calculus not give short shrift to the values that this country holds dear or to the privilege that is American citizenship."

On Mr. Hamdi's side, she said, was "the most elemental of liberty interests—the interest in being free from physical detention by one's own government."

Justice O'Connor said the Federal District Court [in Norfolk, Va.] that first handled Mr. Hamdi's petition for habeas corpus had been too demanding on the government, requesting many records, while the United States Court of Appeals for the Fourth Circuit had been too quick to set aside the district court's order and dismiss Mr. Hamdi's petition.

Suggesting that the proper path lay somewhere in between, Justice O'Connor said that "enemy combatant proceedings may be tailored to alleviate their uncommon potential to burden the executive at a time of ongoing military conflict." She said that the normal rules that curbed the use of hearsay evidence might be bent and that there could be a "presumption in favor of the government's evidence" as long as a detainee had "a fair opportunity for rebuttal."

The administration had argued that if any kind of hearing was found necessary, the government's submission should be accepted according to a low standard of proof known as the "some evidence" standard, which is used in administrative proceedings to provide that as long as there is "some evidence" in the record, the government wins. This standard was "inadequate" and "ill suited" to evaluate the basis for detaining a citizen, Justice O'Connor said. She added: "Plainly, the 'process' Hamdi has received is not that to which he is entitled under the Due Process Clause."

It was not clear from the opinion whether the court would insist in all circumstances that a detainee's case be evaluated by a federal judge. "There remains the possibility that the standards we have articulated could be met by an appropriately authorized and properly constituted military tribunal," Justice O'Connor said.

Four other justices who found fault with the administration's position took very different lines of attack. Justices Souter and Ginsburg said that in their view, Mr. Hamdi's detention lacked a legal basis as a matter of statutory authority. There was consequently no need to delve into constitutional issues, the two said in an opinion by Justice Souter.

This opinion relied on a 1971 federal law, the Non-Detention Act, which provides: "No citizen shall be imprisoned or otherwise detained by the United States except pursuant to an Act of Congress." There has been no act of Congress to justify the detention of Mr. Hamdi, they said.

Justice O'Connor had found statutory justification in the Authorization for Use of Military Force, which Congress passed in the days following the terrorist attacks of Sept. 11, 2001, to authorize "all necessary and appropriate force" to pursue and prevent international terrorism. While only three other justices joined her opinion, Justice Thomas expressed a similar view of the statutory authorization in what was otherwise a dissenting opinion, thus giving a majority of five votes on the statutory question.

But Justices Souter and Ginsburg said the use-of-force law said nothing about detaining citizens. "If the government raises nothing further than the record now shows, the Non-Detention Act entitles Hamdi to be released," Justice Souter said, adding: "On the record in front of us, the government has not made out a case on any theory."

At another point, Justice Souter referred to the court's 1952 decision that overturned President Harry S. Truman's seizure of the steel mills. "It is instructive to recall Justice Jackson's observation that the president is not commander in chief of the country, only of the military," he said.

* * * * * * * * * * * *

Separately, the Court ruled, 6-3, in *Rasul v. Bush* (2004) that federal courts did have jurisdiction to hear habeas corpus petitions by the Guantánamo detainees. Stevens emphasized that the terms of the U.S. agreement with Cuba gave the United States "complete jurisdiction and control" over the base. With other questions put to the side, Stevens said the immediate question was only "whether the federal courts have jurisdiction to determine the legality of the Executive's potentially indefinite detention of individuals who claim to be wholly innocent of wrongdoing." The answer to that question, he said, was "in the affirmative."

At Bush's request, Congress responded in 2005 by passing the Detainee Treatment Act. The law was aimed at repealing federal courts' jurisdiction over the detainees' habeas corpus cases and providing a statutory basis for the military tribunals to hear the cases at Guantánamo. Even so, the Court's 5-3 ruling in *Hamdan v. Rumsfeld* (2006) found that courts still had jurisdiction over the pending habeas corpus cases. More significantly, the Court held that the military commissions were defective because they did not comply with either the Uniform Code of Military Justice (UCMJ) or the Geneva Conventions.

For the majority, Stevens said that the president had failed to show the need for the tribunals to depart from the UCMJ's regular court-martial procedures—in particular, the right of the accused to be present at all proceedings. He said the tribunals also failed to satisfy a requirement in "Common Article 3" of the Geneva Conventions: that any enemy captives be tried by "a regularly constituted court." "In undertaking to try Hamdan and subject him to criminal punishment," Stevens concluded, "the Executive is bound to comply with the Rule of Law that prevails in this jurisdiction."

Hamdan v. Rumsfeld

Decided: June 29, 2006
Vote: 5 (Stevens, Kennedy, Souter, Ginsburg, Breyer)
3 (Scalia, Thomas, Alito)
Opinion of the Court: Stevens
Concurring opinions (3): Stevens (Souter, Ginsburg, Breyer); Breyer (Kennedy, Souter, Ginsburg); Kennedy (Souter, Ginsburg, Breyer)
Dissenting opinions (3): Scalia (Thomas, Alito); Thomas (Scalia, Alito); Alito (Scalia, Thomas)
Did not participate: J. Roberts

In a dissenting opinion, Thomas said the ruling "openly flouts our well established duty to respect the Executive's judgment in matters of military operations and foreign affairs." Scalia and one of Bush's appointees, Alito, also dissented. Chief Justice Roberts was recused because he had participated in the case while on the federal appeals court in Washington—in which he had sided with the administration.

JUNE 30, 2006
JUSTICES, 5-3, BROADLY REJECT BUSH PLAN TO TRY DETAINEES

GUANTÁNAMO CASE

Military Panels Found to Lack Authority—New Law Possible

By LINDA GREENHOUSE

WASHINGTON, June 29—The Supreme Court on Thursday repudiated the Bush administration's plan to put Guantánamo detainees on trial before military commissions, ruling broadly that the commissions were unauthorized by federal statute and violated international law.

"The executive is bound to comply with the rule of law that prevails in this jurisdiction," Justice John Paul Stevens, writing for the 5-to-3 majority, said at the end of a 73-page opinion that in sober tones shredded each of the administration's arguments, including the assertion that Congress had stripped the court of jurisdiction to decide the case.

A principal flaw the court found in the commissions was that the president had established them without Congressional authorization.

The ruling marked the most significant setback yet for the administration's broad expansions of presidential power.

The courtroom was, surprisingly, not full, but among those in attendance there was no doubt they were witnessing a historic event, a defining moment in the ever-shifting balance of power among branches of government that ranked with the court's order to President Richard M. Nixon in 1974 to turn over the Watergate tapes, or with the court's rejection of President Harry S. Truman's seizing of the nation's steel mills, a 1952 landmark decision from which Justice Anthony M. Kennedy quoted at length.

Senator Arlen Specter, Republican of Pennsylvania and chairman of the Judiciary Committee, introduced a bill

 The decision was such a sweeping and categorical defeat for the administration that it left human rights lawyers who have pressed this and other cases on behalf of Guantánamo detainees almost speechless with surprise and delight.

The decision was such a sweeping and categorical defeat for the administration that it left human rights lawyers who have pressed this and other cases on behalf of Guantánamo detainees almost speechless with surprise and delight, using words like "fantastic," "amazing" and "remarkable."

Michael Ratner, president of the Center for Constitutional Rights, a public interest law firm in New York that represents hundreds of detainees, said, "It doesn't get any better."

President Bush said he planned to work with Congress to "find a way forward," and there were signs of bipartisan interest on Capitol Hill in devising legislation that would authorize revamped commissions intended to withstand judicial scrutiny.

immediately and said his committee would hold a hearing on July 11, as soon as Congress returned from the July 4 recess. Mr. Specter said the administration had resisted his effort to propose similar legislation as early as 2002.

Two Republican senators, Lindsey Graham of South Carolina and Jon Kyl of Arizona, said in a joint statement that they were "disappointed" but that "we believe the problems cited by the court can and should be fixed."

"Working together, Congress and the administration can draft a fair, suitable and constitutionally permissible tribunal statute," they added.

Both overseas and in the United States, critics of the administration's detention policies praised the decision and urged Mr. Bush to take it as an occasion to shut down the Guantánamo prison camp in Cuba.

"The ruling destroys one of the key pillars of the Guantánamo system," said Gerald Staberock, a director of the International Commission of Jurists in Geneva. "Guantánamo was built on the idea that prisoners there have limited rights. There is no longer that legal black hole."

The majority opinion by Justice Stevens and a concurring opinion by Justice Kennedy, who also signed most of Justice Stevens's opinion, indicated that finding a legislative solution would not necessarily be easy. In an important part of the ruling, the court held that a provision of the Geneva Conventions known as Common Article 3 applies to the Guantánamo detainees and is enforceable in federal court for their protection.

The provision requires humane treatment of captured combatants and prohibits trials except by "a regularly constituted court affording all the judicial guarantees which are recognized as indispensable by civilized people."

The opinion made it clear that while this provision does not necessarily require the full range of protections of a civilian court or a military court-martial, it does require observance of protections for defendants that are missing from the rules the administration has issued for military commissions. The flaws the court cited were the failure to guarantee the defendant the right to attend the trial and the prosecution's ability under the rules to introduce hearsay evidence, unsworn testimony, and evidence obtained through coercion.

Justice Stevens said the historical origin of military commissions was in their use as a "tribunal of necessity" under wartime conditions. "Exigency lent the commission its legitimacy," he said, "but did not further justify the wholesale jettisoning of procedural protections."

The majority opinion was joined by Justices David H. Souter, Ruth Bader Ginsburg and Stephen G. Breyer, who wrote a concurring opinion focusing on the role of Congress. "The court's conclusion ultimately rests upon a single ground: Congress has not issued the executive a blank check," Justice Breyer said.

The dissenters were Justices Clarence Thomas, Antonin Scalia and Samuel A. Alito Jr. Each wrote a dissenting opinion.

Justice Scalia focused on the jurisdictional issue, arguing that Congress had stripped the court of jurisdiction to proceed with this case, Hamdan v. Rumsfeld, No. 05-184, when it passed the Detainee Treatment Act last December and provided that "no court, justice, or judge" had jurisdiction to hear habeas corpus petitions filed by detainees at Guantánamo Bay.

The question was whether that withdrawal of jurisdiction applied to pending cases. The majority held that it did not.

Justice Thomas's dissent addressed the substance of the court's conclusions. In a part of his opinion that Justices Scalia and Alito also signed, he called the decision "untenable" and "dangerous." He said "those justices who today disregard the commander in chief's wartime decisions" had last week been willing to defer to the judgment of the Army Corps of Engineers in a Clean Water Act case. "It goes without saying that there is much more at stake here than storm drains," he said.

Chief Justice John G. Roberts Jr. did not take part in the case. Last July, four days before Mr. Bush nominated him to the Supreme Court, he was one of the members of a three-judge panel of the federal appeals court here that ruled for the administration in the case.

In the courtroom on Thursday, the chief justice sat silently in his center chair as Justice Stevens, sitting to his immediate right as the senior associate justice, read from the majority opinion. It made for a striking tableau on the final day of the first term of the Roberts court: the young chief justice, observing his work of just a year earlier taken apart point by point by the tenacious 86-year-old Justice Stevens, winner of a Bronze Star for his service as a Navy officer in World War II.

The decision came in an appeal brought on behalf of Salim Ahmed Hamdan, a Yemeni who was captured in Afghanistan in November 2001 and taken to Guantánamo in June 2002. According to the government, Mr. Hamdan was a driver and bodyguard for Osama bin Laden. In July 2003, he and five others were to be the first to face trial by military commission. But it was not until the next year that he was formally charged with a crime, conspiracy.

The commission proceeding began but was interrupted when the federal district court here ruled in November 2004 that the commission was invalid. This was the ruling the federal appeals court, with Judge Roberts participating, overturned.

Lt. Cmdr. Charles Swift, Mr. Hamdan's Navy lawyer, told The Associated Press that he had informed his client about the ruling by telephone. "I think he was awe-struck that the court would rule for him, and give a little man like him an equal chance," Commander Swift said. "Where he's from, that is not true."

The decision contained unwelcome implications, from the administration's point of view, for other legal battles, some with equal or greater importance than the fate of the military commissions.

For example, in finding that the federal courts still have jurisdiction to hear cases filed before this year by detainees at Guantánamo Bay, the justices put back on track for decision a dozen cases in the lower courts here that challenge basic rules and procedures governing life for the hundreds of people confined at the United States naval base there.

In ruling that the Congressional "authorization for the use of military force," passed in the days immediately after the Sept. 11 attacks, cannot be interpreted to legitimize the military commissions, the ruling poses a direct challenge to the administration's legal justification for its secret wiretapping program.

Representative Adam Schiff, a California Democrat who has also introduced a bill with procedures for trying the Guantánamo detainees, said the court's refusal to give an open-ended ruling to the force resolution meant that the resolution could not be viewed as authorizing the National Security Agency's domestic wiretapping.

Perhaps most significantly, in ruling that Common Article 3 of the Geneva Conventions applies to the Guantánamo detainees, the court rejected the administration's view that the article does not cover followers of Al Qaeda. The decision potentially opened the door to challenges, by those held by the United States anywhere in the world, to treatment that could be regarded under the provision as inhumane.

Justice Stevens said that because the charge against Mr. Hamdan, conspiracy, was not a violation of the law of war, it could not be the basis for a trial before a military panel.

* * * * * * * * * * *

Bush responded to the *Hamdan* decision by successfully pressing Congress to pass a new law, the Military Commissions Act of 2006, which unambiguously denied federal courts jurisdiction over habeas petitions by any of the Guantánamo detainees. The federal appeals court in Washington upheld the law, ruling in a pair of consolidated cases brought on behalf of more than sixty detainees that aliens held outside the United States have no habeas corpus rights.

In a direct rebuke to both Bush and Congress, the Court ruled the law unconstitutional. The 5-4 decision in *Boumediene v. Bush* (2008) held that the federal habeas statute extended to Guantánamo because the United States exercised "*de facto* sovereignty" over the base. The act amounted to an unconstitutional suspension of habeas corpus, the majority said, because it provided only limited judicial review of the military tribunals' decisions. In a final section, Justice Kennedy found no "prudential" reasons for the courts to refrain from hearing the cases because the government had failed to show any "onerous burdens" in responding to the actions.

In a pair of sharply written dissenting opinions, Roberts and Scalia criticized the decision as judicial overreaching. Roberts said the ruling shifted responsibility for "sensitive foreign policy and national security decisions" from the elected branches of government to the courts. Scalia said the decision gave military commanders "the impossible task" of producing evidence sufficient to satisfy a civilian court to justify the confinement of each detainee. The ruling, he predicted, "will almost certainly cause more Americans to be killed."

Foreign Policy

The Constitution grants the president the power to make treaties, subject to the "advice and consent" of two-thirds of the Senate, and to receive and appoint ambassadors. From those specific powers, presidents have claimed a broad authority to speak and act for the nation in international relations. The Supreme Court has generally supported presidential primacy in foreign affairs. It has given the president extensive discretion to act with or in some cases without authority from Congress. It has limited the courts' role in reviewing presidential actions in foreign affairs. And it has blocked state laws that might interfere with the president's authority in relations with other countries.

The Court has consistently ruled since 1796 that treaties take precedence over conflicting state laws. In recent cases, the Court has gone further to hold that even without a direct conflict, state laws can be pre-empted if they interfere with the president's diplomatic initiatives. In one of the rulings, for example, the Court in *Crosby v. National Foreign Trade Council* (2000) blocked a Massachusetts law imposing economic sanctions on the nation of Myanmar (formerly Burma) because the measure interfered with less severe penalties the president was authorized to impose to try to undermine the country's military dictatorship.

In a separate line of decisions supporting presidential power, the Court has turned aside cases challenging the president's conduct of foreign affairs as presenting political questions beyond the courts' ability to determine. In *Williams v. Suffolk Ins. Co.* (1839), for example, the Court said that the president's decision whether to recognize a foreign government's sovereignty was "conclusive on the judicial department." The case involved an effort by an insurance company to avoid paying for a shipment of goods confiscated by the government of Argentina; the company disputed the United States' position that Britain, not Argentina, exercised sovereignty over the Falkland Islands. In 1918 the Court similarly declined to question the United States' recognition of the post-revolutionary government in Mexico.

In similar vein, the Court in 1901 rejected a New York man's effort to avoid extradition to Cuba by questioning the duration of the U.S. military occupation of the island after the Spanish-American War. "It is not competent for the judiciary to make any declaration upon the question of the length of time during which Cuba may be rightfully occupied and controlled by the United States in order to effect its pacification," Justice John Marshall Harlan wrote in *Neely v. Henkel*.

The president does share foreign affairs powers with Congress. The full Congress has the power to regulate foreign commerce and to define and punish offenses against international law, while the Senate must approve treaties. But the Court has advantaged the president by leaving some aspects of the treaty-making power ambiguous. (See page 42.) The Court has also permitted the president to enter into executive agreements with other countries without congressional action.

The Court's most expansive view of presidential control of foreign affairs came in a 1936 decision upholding criminal convictions of three U.S. companies for violating an arms embargo. President Roosevelt imposed the embargo four days after Congress passed a May 24, 1934, resolution authorizing him to do so if, in his judgment, it would contribute to ending a border war between Bolivia and Paraguay.

In upholding the embargo and the resulting convictions, the Supreme Court relied on Congress's action as well as the president's authority over foreign affairs. The case involved not only a legislative grant of power, Justice George Sutherland wrote in *United States v. Curtiss-Wright Export Corp.* (1936), but also "the very delicate, plenary and exclusive power of the President as the sole organ of the federal government in the field of international relations." That power, Sutherland said, "does not require as a basis for its exercise an act of Congress."

United States v. Curtiss-Wright Export Corp.

Decided: December 21, 1936
Vote: 7 (Hughes, Van Devanter, Brandeis, Sutherland, Butler, O. Roberts, Cardozo)
1 (McReynolds)
Opinion of the Court: Sutherland
Dissenting opinion: McReynolds
Did not participate: Stone

✠ EDITORIAL
DECEMBER 22, 1936
THE COURT ON FOREIGN POLICY

The Supreme Court yesterday upheld as constitutional the granting of broad discretionary powers to the President in matters of foreign policy. The case which prompted this decision arose under a joint resolution of Congress adopted in May, 1934. This resolution gave the President authority to prohibit the sale of arms to Bolivia and Paraguay—two nations then at each other's throats in the Chaco—provided, in his judgment, such an embargo would help to re-establish peace.

The point at issue was whether Congress could properly leave such a decision to the individual judgment of the President. Was its delegation of broad discretionary power valid or invalid? Invalid, in the opinion of the Federal Court of the Southern District of New York, given in a test case brought before it. But this opinion the Supreme Court itself has now overruled, in a seven-to-one decision. The court takes the position that, if embarrassment—"perhaps serious embarrassment"—is to be avoided in matters of foreign policy, the President must be granted "a degree of discretion and freedom from statutory restriction" which would not be admissible were domestic affairs alone involved. The President is the sole organ of the Federal Government in the field of international relations. His power in

almost from the inception of the National Government to the present day. Unfortunately, however, Congress itself has recently pursued a policy which is at cross-purposes with this well-established principle. The joint resolution which gave the President power to act in the war between Bolivia and Paraguay was followed by a much more ambitious act in which Congress prescribed in great detail a foreign policy for the country. This act was the "neutrality resolution" of 1935, renewed in 1936 and now in force, in its amended form, until

> **It would be wise for Congress to untie the knots it has tied and to restore to the Executive greater freedom of action in the field of foreign policy.**

this field is "delicate, plenary and exclusive." In the court's opinion, it is therefore unwise to require Congress to lay down narrowly definite standards by which the President is to be governed in matters of foreign policy.

Certainly, the best interests of the country require a very considerable freedom of action for the President in matters of this kind. And certainly, as the court notes, the principle which justifies such freedom "finds overwhelming support in the unbroken legislative practice" which has prevailed

May 1, 1937. In this act Congress attempted to take the leadership in foreign affairs away from the President. To be sure, it left him certain discretionary powers. But it prescribed many rules which are mandatory, and most of these rules are written in a spirit of political and economic isolation.

When the present act expires, it would be wise for Congress to untie the knots it has tied and to restore to the Executive greater freedom of action in the field of foreign policy.

* * * * * * * * * * * *

The ruling in December 1936 contrasts with the Court's three decisions in the previous two years striking down parts of Roosevelt's domestic economic recovery programs on the ground that Congress had been too general in delegating power to the president. Sutherland said the president's access to confidential information in foreign affairs demonstrated "the unwisdom of requiring Congress . . . to lay down narrowly definite standards by which the President is to be governed."

United States v. Belmont

Decided: April 12, 1937

Vote: 5 (Hughes, Brandeis, Stone,
            O. Roberts, Cardozo)
        4 (Van Devanter, McReynolds,
            Sutherland, Butler)

Opinion of the Court: Hughes

Dissenting opinion: McReynolds (Van
            Devanter, Sutherland, Butler)

Five months later, the Court explicitly confirmed the president's authority to bypass the Senate in concluding some agreements with foreign countries. The ruling in *United States v. Belmont* (1937) upheld an executive agreement that Roosevelt reached with the Soviet Union after extending diplomatic recognition to the Communist government in 1933. "An international compact, as this was, is not always a treaty which requires the participation of the Senate," Sutherland wrote. The ruling, enforcing provisions of the agreement aimed at resolving financial claims between the two countries, allowed the United States to sue a New York businessman to recover funds he received after the Soviets' nationalized his holdings in Russia.

Roosevelt relied on executive agreements for some of his major diplomatic moves before World War II, including the 1942 Lend-Lease Agreement with Britain. In the Cold War period, executive agreements became even more important instruments for presidential diplomacy. Although many agreements were authorized by congressional action, some were not. From time to time, Congress has considered requiring the president to submit executive agreements for approval but has never completed action on such a proposal.

The Court again deferred to the president's power in upholding the executive agreement that President Carter reached with Iran to end the 1979–1981 hostage crisis. As part of the agreement, the United States agreed to release all judicial attachments against property of the Iranian government within the United States. The U.S. engineering firm Dames & Moore contested the agreement in an effort to collect money it was owed for work on a nuclear power plant in Iran.

The 8-1 decision in *Dames & Moore v. Regan* (1981) rejected the company's plea. Justice Rehnquist said that the settlement was necessary to resolve a major foreign policy dispute and that Congress had acquiesced in the president's action. On that basis, he concluded, "we are not prepared to say that the President lacks the power to settle such claims."

Dames & Moore v. Regan

> **Decided:** July 2, 1981
> **Vote:** 8 (Burger, Brennan, Stewart, B. White, T. Marshall, Blackmun, Rehnquist, Stevens)
> 1 (Powell)
> **Opinion of the Court:** Rehnquist
> **Concurring opinion:** Stevens
> **Dissenting opinion:** Powell

JULY 3, 1981
HIGH COURT RULES PACT ON HOSTAGES WITH IRAN IS LEGAL

By LINDA GREENHOUSE
Special to The New York Times

The Supreme Court ruled unanimously today that Presidents Carter and Reagan had the legal authority to carry out the agreement with Iran that ended the hostage crisis.

The Court acted on the final day of its 1980–81 term, only 17 days before more than $2 billion in Iranian assets are due to be transferred out of the country under the terms of the agreement. The ruling, in which all nine Justices took part, upheld the authority of the White House to nullify court orders and to suspend private lawsuits in order to honor the settlement.

Associate Justice William H. Rehnquist emphasized several times in his 31-page opinion for the Court the narrowness of the ruling and its foundation in Congressional enactments and attitudes that have developed over many years, rather than on broad constitutional precepts.

"We do not decide," Justice Rehnquist said, "that the President possesses plenary power to settle claims, even as against foreign governmental entities."

BUSINESS LAWYERS NOT SURPRISED

He continued: "But where, as here, the settlement of claims has been determined to be a necessary incident to the resolution of a major foreign policy dispute between our country and another, and where, as here, we can conclude that Congress acquiesced in the President's action, we are not prepared to say that the President lacks the power to settle such claims."

Lawyers representing some of the companies with court claims against the Iranian assets said the Court's decision did not surprise them.

Justice Rehnquist said that the Court was attempting "to lay down no general 'guideline' covering other situations not involved here." The Court tried to confine its opinion, he said, "only to the very questions necessary to decision of the case."

'ONLY ONE MORE EPISODE'

"We are obviously deciding only one more episode in the neverending tension between the President exercising the executive authority in a world that presents each day some new challenge with which he must deal and the Constitution under which we all live and which, no one disputes, embodies some sort of system of checks and balances," Justice Rehnquist said.

The decision averted what the Federal Government had told the Court would be a major foreign policy embarrassment for the United States. It cleared the way for the once-frozen Iranian assets, now held in banks around the country, to be assembled at the Federal Reserve Bank of New York next week for transfer out of the United States.

A nine-member Iran-United States Claims Tribunal was established under the hostage settlement to arbitrate claims by American companies against Iran. It is now holding organizational sessions in The Hague and will receive

$1 billion of the Iranian assets as an initial fund from which to pay claims. Iran agreed to maintain a minimum balance of $500 million until all awards are paid.

Before the hostage crisis ended on Jan. 20, more than 400 American companies had filed breach-of-contract suits totaling $3 billion to $4 billion against Iran. They obtained court orders of attachment, or liens, against Iranian funds deposited in this country as guarantees that they would be available to satisfy any judgments.

To carry out the hostage agreement, President Carter issued executive orders nullifying these attachments and President Reagan issued orders suspending the private lawsuits. Dozens of the companies challenged the legal and constitutional authority for these actions. . . .

THE COURT AND JUDICIAL POWER

CHAPTER 3

As the editor of the *Vicksburg Times,* William McCardle bitterly opposed the post–Civil War military occupation of Mississippi under the Reconstruction acts of 1867. In a fiery November 1867 editorial, McCardle denounced the leading generals by name as "infamous, cowardly, and abandoned villains" and urged all white Mississippians to boycott elections for representatives to a state constitutional convention. When eight white voters showed up at the polls, McCardle called them "cowards, dogs, and scoundrels" and promised to publish their names if he could identify them.

Maj. Gen. Alvin Gillem, military governor for the state, ordered McCardle arrested and charged him in a military tribunal with libel, inciting insurrection, and impeding Reconstruction. McCardle challenged his arrest by filing a petition for a writ of habeas corpus, as provided by the federal Habeas Corpus Act of 1867. As authority, he cited the Supreme Court's 1866 decision, *Ex parte Milligan,* prohibiting the use of military tribunals against civilians if civilian courts are open and available.

The circuit court denied McCardle relief, and he appealed to the Supreme Court. The justices upheld their jurisdiction to hear the case in February 1868 and scheduled arguments on the merits in March. Congressional Republicans, fearing a possible ruling to strike down the Reconstruction acts altogether, responded by passing a law—over President Andrew Johnson's veto—to repeal the provision of the habeas corpus act permitting an appeal to the high court. Sponsors made clear the purpose was to prevent the Court from ruling on McCardle's case.

THE INGENIOUS QUARTERBACK!

When the Supreme Court was created in 1789, it consisted of six justices. Throughout the country's history, the number of justices has changed seven times, with the most sitting justices—ten—serving during the Lincoln administration. Frustrated by a series of rulings against his New Deal legislation in the 1930s, President Franklin D. Roosevelt proposed a radical plan to increase the number of justices to as many as fifteen. His Court-packing plan proved unpopular, however, and was not enacted by Congress.

The confrontation played out as Chief Justice Salmon P. Chase was presiding over the Senate's impeachment trial of Johnson. Nearly a year later, the Court heard a new round of arguments in March 1869 on the effect of the congressional repeal on McCardle's case. Two senators argued for the government after Attorney General Homer Stansberry stepped out of the case: he had previously advised Johnson that the Reconstruction act was unconstitutional.

MARCH 27, 1869
STATUTORY JURISDICTION—REPEAL—EFFECT ON THE JUDICIAL POWER—THE M'CARDLE CASE.

Ex Parte Wm. H. McCardle.—This was the argument on the question of the effect of the repeal of the act of 1867, in cases of appeal from the Circuit Court, on *habeas corpus.* The facts of the case will be remembered. The appellant, McCardle, filed his petition in the Circuit Court for the Southern District of Mississippi, in November, 1867, for a writ of *habeas corpus,* to be directed to General Ord, or General Gillem, or both, by whom, or by whose orders, the petitioner alleged he was illegally detained in prison. The writ was issued and the body of the appellant was produced in Court, and a full return made, setting forth the cause of imprisonment. No issue was made upon the facts stated in the return, but the appellant moved for his discharge upon the ground of the insufficiency of the return as matter of law. The Circuit Court held the return sufficient, and remanded McCardle to the custody of the military authorities, from which he has been taken by the writ. McCardle then took his appeal from the decision and judgment of the Court, in pursuance of the act in question, giving such a right of appeal. Pending this appeal, and after the cause had been heard and submitted to this Court, Congress, by the act of March, 1868, repealed so much of the act of 1867 as authorized an appeal from the judgment of the Circuit Court to the Supreme Court of the United States, or the exercise of any jurisdiction by this Court on appeals which have been or may hereafter be taken. No decision was thereafter rendered by this Court in the case, and the Court at the present term directed argument to be made on the question of its jurisdiction, subsequently to such repeal. On the part of the Government and the military authorities, it is contended that this Court had no jurisdiction of this proceeding, it being an appeal from the Circuit Court, except under the act of 1867, and that it was so held by the Court on the motion to dismiss made by the authorities. The act conferring the jurisdiction having been repealed, the jurisdiction ceased, and the Court had thereafter no authority to pronounce an opinion or render any judgment in the case. The Constitution of the United States gives to Congress the power to "except" any or all of the cases mentioned in the jurisdictional clause of that instrument, from the appellate jurisdiction of the Supreme Court, and it was clearly the intention of Congress, by this act, to so except all the cases of this kind, whether pending or thereafter to be brought. This Court never had appellate jurisdiction in such cases, until it was authorized by the act of 1867. That act has been repealed; and when an act of Congress is repealed, it must be considered the same as if it had never been passed. This proposition is claimed to be so clear that no argument can be required to sustain it. No Court can do any act in any case without jurisdiction of the subject matter, and any act attempted to be done under such circumstances is simply void. It can make no difference at what period in the progress of a cause the jurisdiction ceases. After it has ceased no judicial act can be performed. In Insurance Co. *vs.* Ritchie, (5 Wall, 554,) the Chief Justice delivering the opinion of the Court says: "It is clear that when the jurisdiction of a cause depends upon the statute; the repeal of the statute takes away the jurisdiction." And, in that case, the repealing statute which was passed during the pending of the cause was held to deprive the Court of all jurisdiction. This is the uniform doctrine of this Court and of all Courts. The causes which were pending in this Court against States were all dismissed by the amendment of the Constitution denying jurisdiction, and no further proceedings were had in those cases. In Norris *vs.* Crocker (13 How., 429,) this Court affirmed and acted on the same principle; and the exhaustive argument of the present Chief Justice, then at the Bar, reported in that case, and the numerous authorities there cited, render any further argument unnecessary.

The opposite view is maintained at length on the part of McCardle, Senators Carpenter and Trumbull and Enuch Totton for the Government, and W. I. Sharkey for appellant.

Only six weeks after hearing the arguments, the justices blinked. In a terse opinion, Chase acknowledged that the Constitution gives Congress the power to make "exceptions" to the Supreme Court's appellate jurisdiction (Art. III, sec. 2, cl. 2). "We are not at liberty to inquire into the motives of the legislature," Chase wrote in *Ex parte McCardle* (1869). "We can only examine into its power under the Constitution, and the power to make exceptions to the appellate jurisdiction of this court is given by express words."

Chase added a significant qualifier, however. He said the repeal did not eliminate any pre-existing Supreme Court jurisdiction—a tacit reference to the Court's power to hear habeas corpus cases under the original Judiciary Act of 1789.

A new case soon reached the Court. Edward M. Yerger filed a habeas corpus petition, this time under the unrepealed 1789 act, challenging his military trial on charges of murdering the army general who was serving as acting mayor of Jackson, Mississippi. The government blinked. Stansberry and Yerger's lawyer reached a compromise to turn Yerger over to civilian authorities for trial, and Congress dropped plans to consider totally abolishing the Court's jurisdiction over habeas corpus cases. Meanwhile, Gillem's successor in Vicksburg had dropped the charges against McCardle.

The Supreme Court's sidestep, avoiding a direct confrontation with Congress, demonstrates not only the reach of the Court's power but also its fragility. Congress has the power of the purse; the executive, the power of the sword. The Supreme Court's power is the power of the gavel: that much, but no more.

Through history, the Court has handed down many decisions that unflinchingly challenged the powers of Congress, the president, or the states—and some number that defied prevailing public opinion. On occasion, Congress, presidents, and the states have responded by challenging the Court's authority. The efforts have included plans to limit the Court's jurisdiction, change the number of justices, overturn rulings by constitutional amendment, or even remove sitting justices through impeachment.

Conscious of the fragility of its power, the Court has preserved its position at times by exercising its powers narrowly—or not at all. In fact, the Supreme Court has developed a series of "prudential" rules to define types of cases that it will not decide. Further, justices ordinarily seek to decide a case on narrow grounds, leaving broader questions to be decided, if at all, in some future case. (See "The Supreme Court's Rules of Restraint," right.)

Seventy years later, as Chief Justice John G. Roberts Jr. ended his first term on the high court, he endorsed that view of judicial restraint in a commencement address at Georgetown University Law Center in May 2006. "If it is not necessary to decide more to dispose of a case," Roberts said, "in my

Ex parte McCardle

Decided: April 12, 1869

Vote: 8 (S.P. Chase, Nelson, Grier, Clifford, Swayne, Miller, Davis, Field)

0

Opinion of the Court: S.P. Chase

THE SUPREME COURT'S RULES OF RESTRAINT

In a concurring opinion in *Ashwander v. Tennessee Valley Authority* (1936), Justice Louis D. Brandeis delineated a set of Court-formulated rules used in avoiding constitutional decisions:

The Court developed, for its own governance in the cases confessedly within its jurisdiction, a series of rules under which it has avoided passing upon a large part of all the constitutional questions pressed upon it for decision. They are:

1. The Court will not pass upon the constitutionality of legislation in a friendly, non-adversary, proceeding. . . .

2. The Court will not "anticipate a question of constitutional law in advance of the necessity of deciding it." . . .

3. The Court will not "formulate a rule of constitutional law broader than is required by the precise facts to which it is to be applied."

4. The Court will not pass upon a constitutional question although properly presented by the record, if there is also present some other ground upon which the case may be disposed of.

5. The Court will not pass upon the validity of a statute upon complaint of one who fails to show that he is injured by its operation. . . .

6. The Court will not pass upon the constitutionality of a statute at the instance of one who has availed himself of its benefits. . . .

7. "When the validity of an act of the Congress is drawn in question, and even if a serious doubt of constitutionality is raised, it is a cardinal principle that this Court will first ascertain whether a construction of the statute is fairly possible by which the question may be avoided." . . .

view it is necessary not to decide more." A year later, however, some critics saw Roberts as the leader of a conservative majority that was flexing its muscles by skirting the Court's own precedents to reach conservative results in such controversial areas as abortion rights, campaign finance, church-state issues, and school integration.

EARLY DEVELOPMENTS

Article III of the Constitution opens by vesting "the judicial Power of the United States" in "one supreme Court" and "in such inferior Courts as the Congress may from time to time ordain and establish." Section 1 goes on to include two important safeguards for judicial independence: lifetime tenure and a prohibition against reduction in pay. Section 2 provides that the judicial power—which is not defined—"shall extend to all Cases" arising under the Constitution or laws or treaties of the United States and to various other categories of cases; among the most important, and specifically mentioned, are cases in which the United States, a state, or citizens of different states are parties.

While the first two articles list some of the specific powers of Congress and the president, Article III includes no enumeration of judicial powers. Delegates to the Constitutional Convention appear to have assumed that the judicial power included the authority to nullify laws contrary to the Constitution. Alexander Hamilton made the point explicitly in *Federalist* No. 16, saying that courts have "the duty . . . to declare all acts contrary to the manifest tenor of the Constitution void." In *Federalist* No. 78, however, Hamilton called the judiciary "the least dangerous" branch of government because it would be "in continual jeopardy of being over-powered, awed, or influenced by its coordinate branches."

The Court's Beginnings

In its first session, Congress passed the Judiciary Act of 1789, establishing the Supreme Court with six justices and creating a nationwide system of federal district courts to handle lesser cases and circuit courts—then composed of a district court judge and two Supreme Court justices—to hear more important cases. The Supreme Court was given "original jurisdiction" over some categories of cases—notably, cases between states or between a state and the United States—and "appellate jurisdiction" in all others. In section 25 of the act, Congress explicitly gave the Supreme Court the power to review final rulings of a state supreme court upholding a state law if the law was challenged as conflicting with the Constitution, a federal law, or a treaty.

The Court created a confrontation with the states in its first major decision, *Chisholm v. Georgia* (1793), by ruling that, under Article III, federal courts could entertain a suit by citizens of one state against another state. The decision produced such a storm of protest that Congress and the states overturned it by ratifying the Eleventh Amendment—the first change to the Constitution after the Bill of Rights. States also resisted the Court's authority under section 25 to declare state laws unconstitutional, but the Court successfully stood its ground on the issue in rulings in the early nineteenth century. (For more information, see page 133.)

Less controversial was the Court's first case testing the constitutionality of a federal law. Virginian Daniel Hylton challenged a federal tax on carriages as an impermissible "direct" tax that, under Article I, had to be levied based on population. The government defended the tax without questioning the Court's authority to review its validity. Unanimously, the Court in *Hylton v. United States* (1796) upheld the law.

The Marshall Court

Seven years later, the Court touched off a major controversy with its first decision invalidating a law passed by Congress. The landmark case of *Marbury v. Madison* (1803) played out against the political conflict over the federal judiciary between the Federalists and Thomas Jefferson's Democratic-Republicans. The case began in the final hours of John Adams's presidency in 1801 with a commission appointing William Marbury, a Federalist, to be a justice of the peace for the District of Columbia. When Jefferson, Adams's successor, refused to deliver the commission, Marbury filed suit in the Supreme Court for a writ of mandamus to order Secretary of State James Madison to deliver the commission, citing the Judiciary Act's section 13 giving the Court original jurisdiction to issue such writs. Jeffersonians were so concerned about the case that Congress repealed the law providing for a June 1802 term of the Supreme Court, delaying consideration of the case for fourteen months.

Chief Justice John Marshall spoke for a unanimous Court on February 24, 1803, in a decision that found Jefferson had no right to withhold Marbury's commission but the Court had no authority to order it issued. Marshall explained that Congress had no authority under the Constitution to give the Supreme Court original jurisdiction to issue writs of mandamus. Although the Federalist Marshall surrendered one judgeship to Jefferson, his political adversary, he established the Court's power to declare acts of Congress unconstitutional. "It is emphatically the province and duty of the judicial department to say what the law is," Marshall wrote, in a sentence repeated in innumerable rulings in the two centuries since.

Marbury v. Madison

Decided: February 24, 1803

Vote: 5 (J. Marshall, Paterson, S. Chase, Washington, Moore)

0

Opinion of the Court: J. Marshall

Did not participate: Cushing

TRIBUTE
AUGUST 21, 1955
JOHN MARSHALL—OUR 'GREATEST DISSENTER'

By EDMOND CAHN

Next Wednesday a ceremony will be held on Philadelphia's new Independence Mall commemorating the 200th anniversary of the birth of John Marshall. The event is one of a number this year in which patriotic Americans of various political faiths are honoring the great jurist. Born on Sept. 24, 1755, in what is now Fauquier County, Virginia, Marshall served as Chief Justice of the United States from 1801 until his death in 1835.

"Stone by stone, he built the foundation of our constitutional structure, and he constructed it sufficiently strong to support everything we have since built upon it."

There were three basic principles in Marshall's constitutional philosophy. He believed that the United States Constitution, as drafted in 1787, provided for a federal government with powers strong enough to solve the problems of a developing nation and flexible enough

> " Stone by stone, he built the foundation of our constitutional structure, and he constructed it sufficiently strong to support everything we have since built upon it.
>
> —Chief Justice Earl Warren on John Marshall "

There may be many conflicting opinions as to who was the nation's greatest President, or Senator, or Congressman. But there is complete agreement that John Marshall stands without rival as our greatest Chief Justice. In a recent address which inaugurated the bicentennial ceremonies, Chief Justice Earl Warren said:

to succeed and endure permanently. He also believed that every governmental action—whether Federal or state—which conflicted with the Constitution was null and void. Finally, he believed that when a legal case or controversy arose presenting a constitutional issue, it was the specific function of the Supreme Court to interpret the Constitution and pronounce a judgment of validity or invalidity which would be binding on everyone, including the President, the Congress, and the state governments.

Marshall's famous decisions establishing these principles (Marbury v. Madison. McCulloch v. Maryland, Cohens v. Virginia, Gibbons v. Ogden) remain today as firm cornerstones of the American fabric of government. While it was Thomas Jefferson and James Madison who supplied us with the keystone of civil liberty, this, too, like the remainder of the structure, rests for support and effectiveness on Marshall's doctrine that the Constitution is the supreme law of the land.

Before Marshall's appointment as Chief Justice in 1801, the Constitution was in many respects no more than a controversial piece of parchment; when, in 1835, he transmitted it to his successor, it had become a vital, operative method of government. Before 1801, the Supreme Court was feeble and ineffectual; when Marshall departed, even his opponents recognized that he had elevated the court to be—what it has been ever since—the most powerful judicial tribunal in the history of civilized government.

When, even in our own time, Congress decides to adopt some advanced plan of social or economic legislation, it is exercising Federal powers that Marshall staked out and made available for use. As the Constitution is great and enduring, so is John Marshall's work. . . .

. . . .

The political dispute over judgeships continued after the *Marbury* decision. Jefferson complained to a House ally in May 1803 about partisan behavior by one of the justices, Samuel Chase. In truth, Chase had violated modern standards of judicial conduct: he campaigned for Adams in 1800 while on the Court, behaved highhandedly in several politically charged cases while riding circuit, and harshly denounced Jefferson's administration to a grand jury in Baltimore earlier in May 1803. Jefferson's complaint started a process that led in March 1804 to Chase's impeachment by the House on eight counts of misconduct. Even with a two-thirds Democratic-Republican majority, however, the Senate acquitted Chase on all eight counts; the vote count was nowhere close to the needed two-thirds majority on any of the charges. Several factors contributed to the outcome, but the result—as Jefferson complained in frustration—was to all but remove impeachment as a political weapon against Supreme Court justices.

Over the next three decades, Marshall built a solid foundation for a powerful Supreme Court. In one important step, he established the practice of deciding cases with a single opinion for the Court—unanimous whenever possible—instead of a confusing series of opinions by individual justices. Besides *Marbury,* his own landmark opinions included *McCulloch v. Maryland* (1819), supporting a broad view of Congress's power, and *Cohens v. Virginia* (1821), affirming the Court's power to overturn decisions by state courts. In his final years in office, Marshall's power waned as his health weakened, and President Andrew Jackson began to name states' rights–minded justices to the Court. As Marshall had clashed with Jefferson at the start of his tenure, he too clashed with Jackson near the end—two of history's several sharp confrontations between presidents and the Court.

Cohens v. Virginia

Decided: March 3 and March 5, 1821
Vote: 6 (J. Marshall, W. Johnson, Livingston, Todd, Duvall, Story)
    0
Opinion of the Court: J. Marshall
Did not participate: Washington

THE PRESIDENT VERSUS THE COURT

Twice in the nation's first century, presidents openly defied rulings from the Supreme Court, and the Court proved powerless to enforce its judgments. Since the Civil War, however, no president has flouted a Supreme Court decision or successfully challenged its standing with the public. Instead—just as President George W. Bush did in the post–9/11 terrorism cases—presidents regularly promise to abide by a final decision of the Supreme Court even if they disagree with it.

Andrew Jackson

Andrew Jackson clashed with the Court in the case of two missionaries convicted of violating a Georgia law that prohibited white people from living in Cherokee Indian territory without the state's permission. The two missionaries, Samuel Worcester and Elizur Butler, supported the Cherokees' resistance to forced relocation from the state. In *Worcester v. Georgia* (1832), the Court ruled the state law void because it interfered with the Cherokees' right to self-government guaranteed by treaty with the United States.

In ordering the missionaries' release, the Court said that the convictions violated federal laws "which authorize the Chief Magistrate to exercise his authority." But Jackson, the former Indian fighter, gave the Court no help. Historians still debate whether his oft-quoted remark— "John Marshall has made his decision; now let him enforce it"—is genuine or apocryphal. Georgia courts ignored the ruling, and Worcester and Butler remained in prison until their release by a new governor in January 1833.

Abraham Lincoln

Less than two months after the outbreak of the Civil War, Abraham Lincoln came into conflict with the Court over his first suspension of habeas corpus in Maryland and other states. John Merryman filed a habeas corpus petition in federal court in Maryland after military authorities arrested him on May 25, 1861, on charges of burning railroad bridges needed to transport Union troops south from Pennsylvania. Sitting as circuit justice, Chief Justice Roger B. Taney ordered that Merryman be brought to court. When the military commander refused, citing Lincoln's suspension of habeas corpus, Taney wrote a stinging opinion declaring the president had no such power.

Taney closed his opinion in *Ex parte Merryman* (1861) by saying that he would order the record of the case sent to the president so that "that high official" could "determine what measures he will take to cause the civil process of the United States to be respected and enforced." Lincoln made no direct response. Merryman was indicted in July and later tried for treason, but Lincoln continued throughout the war to defend the military's authority to detain draft resisters or suspected Southern sympathizers. The measures, Lincoln wrote in 1863, "are constitutional wherever the public safety may require them."

Woodrow Wilson

Later presidents had many occasions to disagree with Supreme Court rulings, but they responded without direct disobedience. When the Court struck down a federal ban on child labor in 1918, for example, Woodrow Wilson worked with Congress to enact a new law designed to comply with the ruling by imposing a federal tax on goods manufactured with use of child labor. In 1922, however, the Court struck down that law as well.

William Howard Taft as Chief Justice

As chief justice during the 1920s, former president William Howard Taft led the Court in gaining additional confidence in its place in the constitutional system. To achieve a visible manifestation of the Court's equal standing with the other two branches, Taft pushed hard for the construction of a separate building to house the Court, which had until then met in a courtroom in the U.S. Capitol. Congress approved the construction in 1929. Taft died in 1930—five years before the justices moved into the completed building at the beginning of the October 1935 term.

The U.S. Supreme Court had no building to call its own for much of
the country's history. The Court moved into its current building in
1935, vacating its chambers in the U.S. Capitol. Above, tourists leave
what *The Times* dubbed the Court's "new marble palace" after the
Court held its first session in its new quarters in October 1935.

Source: Times Wide World Photos

 ## OCTOBER 8, 1935
HIGH COURT MEETS AMID NEW SPLENDOR

Justices Cling to Traditional Customs as They Sit in $10,000,000 Home.

A NEW DEAL CASE DROPPED

Lawyers Admitted—Mooney Motion Made—Audience Fills the Room.

Special to The New York Times

WASHINGTON, Oct. 7.—The Supreme Court today
held its first session in its splendid new ten-million-dollar
home, devoting a 1-hour-and-20-minute session to the admission of 113 lawyers to practice before the bar and the
hearing of motions.

Agreeing to one of these motions, the court swept from
the docket one of the five constitutional tests of the New Deal
sought by various interests. This was the case in which the
Kansas Utilities Company challenged the constitutionality of
Federal loans or grants through the PWA to finance construction of municipal power plants and distributing systems.

The motion to dismiss this suit left on the docket the
Hoosac Mills test of the Agricultural Adjustment Act, the
challenge of the Bankhead Cotton Control Act, the validity of
TVA legislation and the dispute over the government's right
to condemn land for slum clearance and low-cost housing.

Withdrawal of the Kansas case, according to the utility company's attorneys, was due to the fact that another and a stronger case is pending in the District of Columbia Supreme Courts.

USUAL CUSTOMS FOLLOWED.

The opening day of a session expected to be of paramount importance because of the New Deal litigation was devoid of any unusual ceremony, for all the forms and rites which were used in the old building were still followed.

bas-reliefs. The scene was magnificent but it was strange to the court attachés, hundreds of attorneys and spectators and probably to the nine justices, although they did not reveal it.

This unfamiliar atmosphere was prevalent throughout the great building, where spaces seemed vast as compared to the distance from the clerk's office to the court chamber in the Capitol. Lawyers and attendants were lost going from one quarter to another. In the white marble entrance hall one whimsical justice is said to have remarked:

"I wonder if we will look like nine black beetles in the Temple of Karnak."

> *I wonder if we will look like nine black beetles in the Temple of Karnak.*
> *—Unnamed Justice*

Nevertheless the intimacy of the rich little old room in the Capitol where the court sat for seventy-five years was missing in the new, majestic chamber with its huge Sienna marble columns, ornate ceiling, heavy crimson hangings [and]

Scores beyond the capacity of the court room sought admission, but Frank Key Green, the veteran marshal, handled the situation as suavely as if the court had never moved from the old building. . . .

OCTOBER 8, 1935
STILL THE SUPREME COURT.

In its massive new building, occupied for the first time yesterday, the Supreme Court of the United States will find its dignity as well as its convenience better served than in the contracted quarters where it had long sat. The project for a more stately edifice was agitated and maturely considered for many years. Finally Congress voted the money for it, so as

rendered as they were, provoked a considerable amount of loose talk about abridging its authority or limiting its jurisdiction. But that has found little favor with the American people. They have erected the new structure of the Supreme Court on a site near the Capitol, as if to fix it there forever as a coordinate branch of their Government. They expect it to remain

> *They have erected the new structure of the Supreme Court on a site near the Capitol, as if to fix it there forever as a coordinate branch of their Government.*

to give the Supreme Court a separate home of its own, fitting its high repute and its place in the American Government. Nothing exactly like it exists in any other country. Its power is great. So are its responsibilities, which the judges of this highest tribunal in the land have always met with unquestioned integrity. Some of its recent decisions, conscientiously

secure in all its duties and functions so long as the Government itself endures. In its magnificent new court room, as in its cramped former place for legal argument and judicial decision, it will be, of course, the ability and high character and political impartiality of the judges that make the Supreme Court famous and respected and obeyed.

· · · · · · · · · · ·

CHRONOLOGY OF ROOSEVELT'S COURT-PACKING PLAN

FEBRUARY 5, 1937

President Franklin D. Roosevelt sends Congress his proposal—"prepared . . . with deepest secrecy"—to permit an increase in Supreme Court membership from nine to a maximum of fifteen judges; an extra seat would be added for each judge reaching the age of 70 who declined to retire. Passage of the bill "is generally expected."

FEBRUARY 8, 1937

Some of Roosevelt's "friends" in Congress begin pressing for compromise on the judicial reform plan. Talk of compromise comes amid indications that FDR's liberal supporters cannot be counted on.

FEBRUARY 9, 1937

House leaders seeking compromise on judicial reform are expected to push for a bill to permit Supreme Court justices to retire with full pay after ten years of service. Leaders say this strategy "might permit the President to 'remake' the court without the appearance of 'packing' it."

FEBRUARY 11, 1937

Roosevelt moves to head off "incipient Congressional revolt" over his judicial

reform proposal by calling a group of senators to the White House for the purpose of "dissipating any feeling" over lack of prior consultation and presenting his arguments for the plan.

FEBRUARY 23, 1937

House leaders assure Roosevelt that the House will approve his judicial reform plan but say the Senate must act first. A poll in the Senate indicates at least thirty-seven senators "might be counted on" to oppose the plan.

FEBRUARY 24, 1937

A poll shows thirty-five senators opposed to the plan and five others leaning in that direction; forty-two senators are described as favorable to the plan, with seven more leaning in favor. The count suggests opponents are short of votes to block the plan but can delay a vote indefinitely.

FEBRUARY 26, 1937

The Senate passes a Supreme Court justice retirement bill. The first Senate Judiciary Committee hearing on the judicial reform plan is scheduled for March 10, the day after FDR is to deliver a "fireside chat" to the nation.

MARCH 23, 1937

Chief Justice Charles Evans Hughes, in a letter to the Senate, calls the judicial reform plan unnecessary and says it would "impede" the Court's efficiency. His letter "took administration forces by surprise and sent them scurrying to strengthen their defenses."

MAY 13, 1937

The Senate Judiciary Committee holds final hearing on the Court bill amid indications that it will fail in the Senate after a likely unfavorable vote in committee. House Republican leader calls GOP victory in a Pennsylvania special election "an emphatic repudiation" of the Court-packing plan.

MAY 18, 1937

Justice Willis Van Devanter announces he will retire on June 2, giving FDR his first chance for a Supreme Court appointment, four years into his presidency. Shortly after, the Senate Judiciary Committee votes 10-8 to report the president's bill adversely with recommendation to full Senate that "it do not pass."

MAY 21, 1937

Administration leaders actively seek compromise to permit Roosevelt to

FRANKLIN D. ROOSEVELT

After suffering a string of defeats at the hands of the Supreme Court, Franklin D. Roosevelt devised a different tactic in 1937 to try to get around unfavorable rulings. As part of a judicial reorganization plan outlined to Congress on February 5, 1937, Roosevelt proposed creating one new seat on the Court for each justice who remained on the Court after reaching the age of seventy—six in all, at the time. Roosevelt claimed the Court was "handicapped by insufficient personnel" and the presence of

appoint two additional justices. Chief Justice Hughes and Justice James W. McReynolds both deny rumors of planned retirements.

MAY 24, 1937

The Supreme Court gives Roosevelt a "wide-sweeping victory" by upholding the Social Security Act. This ruling "further cut the propulsion from behind the court bill."

JUNE 5, 1937

Roosevelt dispatches administration leaders to Capitol Hill "to work out the best plan to end the controversy." Lawmakers look for an "early settlement" of the dispute to speed work on other parts of the administration's legislative program.

JUNE 18, 1937

Administration supporters decide not to draft a minority report to answer the Judiciary Committee majority's denunciation of the plan.

JULY 2, 1937

Senate leaders introduce a new bill to add one justice a year to the Supreme Court for justices past age 75 who decline to retire.

JULY 6, 1937

Administration forces in the Senate move "with vigor" to push through a compromise version of Roosevelt's Court plan. But Majority Leader Joseph T. Robinson, D-Ark., agrees to adjourn the session at 1 o'clock to permit senators to attend baseball's All Star game.

JULY 8, 1937

The "bitterest Senate session in years" takes place as administration leaders invoke "seldom-used rules" to thwart the threatened filibuster against the compromise Court bill.

JULY 12, 1937

The Senate "crackle[s] . . . with two more blistering attacks" on the compromise Court bill after the weekend recess "failed to relieve any of the heat worked up over the issue."

JULY 14, 1937

Robinson dies; his death "upsets court fight plans."

JULY 17, 1937

Three White House emissaries advance a new compromise Court bill to senators and representatives aboard Robinson's funeral train en route to Little Rock.

JULY 19, 1937

The administration is "determined . . . to fight to the last ditch" to prevent opponents from killing the Court bill by recommitting the measure to the Judiciary Committee.

JULY 20, 1937

Roosevelt is reported to have agreed to shelve his Supreme Court reorganization plan. The report gains "wide credence" despite denial by the White House.

JULY 22, 1937

The Senate votes 70-20 to recommit the Court bill, marking the administration's "surrender" on the plan. The vote instructs the committee to report a bill within ten days dealing with procedural reforms in lower courts, but the Supreme Court section is "dead." The outcome is the "worst defeat suffered by a President since the Senate rejected President Wilson's League of Nations covenant in 1920."

Quotations derived from contemporary New York Times articles.

elderly judges no longer able to perform their duties. But his true purpose was evident: to change the Court's ideological balance by appointing New Deal supporters to the new seats.

The size of the Court had been changed several times before Roosevelt made his proposal, sometimes in order to affect the ideological balance among the justices. (See page 122.) But Roosevelt's proposal—quickly dubbed a "Court-packing" plan—was widely denounced, even by some New Deal supporters, as an attack on judicial integrity and independence. (See "Chronology of Roosevelt's Court-Packing Plan," above.)

As Roosevelt continued to push the plan, Chief Justice Charles Evans Hughes dealt it a fatal blow with a letter in March that rejected the president's ostensible justifications for the measure. "There is no congestion of cases upon our calendar," Hughes wrote to the senator leading the opposition to the plan. "An increase in the number of Justices," he added, "would not promote the efficiency of the Court."

Dramatic changes at the Court further undercut the proposal, beginning with the Court's ruling upholding a state minimum-wage law on March 29—a 5-4 decision reached before Roosevelt announced his proposal. Two weeks later, the Court upheld the National Labor Relations Act, a major New Deal enactment, by the same 5-4 vote. In addition, on May 18 Justice Willis Van Devanter announced that he would retire at the end of the term—thus giving Roosevelt his first Supreme Court appointment. The Senate formally killed the measure on July 22; a month later, Roosevelt signed a watered-down judicial reorganization bill with no changes in Supreme Court membership.

HARRY S. TRUMAN

Roosevelt's successor, Harry S. Truman, sustained a direct defeat when the Court ruled on June 2, 1952, that the president had no authority to seize the nation's steel mills to avert a threatened strike during the Korean War. While the case, *Youngstown Sheet & Tube Co. v. Sawyer,* was pending, Truman had promised to abide by the Court's decision. Although he believed he was right and the Court was wrong, as he later insisted in his memoirs, the president responded to the ruling immediately by directing Commerce Secretary Charles Sawyer to release the properties to the steel companies. Truman asked Congress for legislative authorization to take over the steel mills, but Congress refused. The strike lasted fifty-four days.

RICHARD M. NIXON

The Court's decision in *United States v. Nixon* (1974), the Watergate tapes case, intruded further on presidential prerogatives by rejecting Richard Nixon's effort to guard the confidentiality of his private conversations with his closest aides in the Oval Office. Giving the president "an absolute privilege" against a criminal subpoena on nothing but "a generalized claim" of confidentiality "would upset the constitutional balance of a 'workable government' and gravely impair the role of the courts under Art. III," Chief Justice Warren E. Burger wrote. "No case of the Court," he added, "has extended this high degree of deference to a President's general interest in confidentiality."

BILL CLINTON

Bill Clinton's claim of immunity from civil suit while in office for private conduct suffered the same fate at the Court. Nothing in the Court's precedents or separation of power principles supported Clinton's claim for immunity from judicial process while president, Justice John Paul Stevens explained in *Clinton v. Jones* (1997). "Petitioner errs by presuming that interactions between the Judicial Branch and the Executive, even quite burdensome interactions, necessarily rise to the level of constitutionally forbidden impairment of the Executive's ability to perform its constitutionally mandated functions," he wrote.

George W. Bush

George W. Bush failed in case after case in his attempts to use his powers as commander in chief to circumvent the Court's oversight of the government's handling of suspected enemy combatants detained in the war on terror. In *Hamdi v. Rumsfeld* (2004), the Court said that a U.S. citizen detainee could not be held solely on the president's order but must be afforded notice of charges and an opportunity to be heard before some "impartial adjudicator." The decision in *Rasul v. Bush* (2004) recognized the right of foreigners held at the U.S. naval base at Guantánamo Bay, Cuba, to challenge their detention through habeas corpus. Two years later, the Court insisted, in *Hamdan v. Rumsfeld* (2006), on examining the procedures that Bush had instituted for military tribunals to try the Guantánamo detainees; after the examination, the Court ruled them inadequate under both the Uniform Code of Military Justice and the Geneva Conventions.

The Court dealt Bush another rebuke in his last year as president by striking down his third attempt to block habeas corpus petitions by the Guantánamo detainees. The 5-4 decision in *Boumediene v. Bush* (2008) held that the Military Commissions Act of 2006—passed by Congress at Bush's strong urging—did not provide a constitutionally adequate substitute for habeas corpus. The law allowed the federal appeals court in Washington, D.C., to review military tribunals' decisions, but did not permit detainees to present any new evidence. "The role of an Article III court in the exercise of its habeas corpus function cannot be circumscribed in this manner," the Court said.

Rasul v. Bush

Decided: June 28, 2004

Vote: 6 (Stevens, O'Connor, Kennedy, Souter, Ginsburg, Breyer)

3 (Rehnquist, Scalia, Thomas)

Opinion of the Court: Stevens

Concurring opinion: Kennedy

Dissenting opinion: Scalia (Rehnquist, Thomas)

Boumediene v. Bush

Decided: June 12, 2008

Vote: 5 (Stevens, Kennedy, Souter, Ginsburg, Breyer)

4 (J. Roberts, Scalia, Thomas, Alito)

Opinion of the Court: Kennedy

Concurring opinion: Souter

Dissenting opinions (2): J. Roberts; Scalia

CONGRESS VERSUS THE COURT

Congress has a variety of ways to try to influence the Supreme Court: some direct, some indirect. The Senate has tried on numerous occasions—and succeeded several times—to use the confirmation process to alter the ideological balance on the Court. It has overturned many specific decisions by enacting new statutes and, in four instances, by proposing constitutional amendments later ratified by the states. Other ways of pressuring the Court have been more controversial and less successful, such as attempting to limit the Court's jurisdiction, changing the size of the Court, or trying to impeach a sitting justice.

Confirmation Process

Among the thirty-four failed Supreme Court nominations, Senate opposition to the nominating president or to the nominee's views has been the primary factor in well over half.

All of the failed nominations in the twentieth century had evident effects on the Court's ideological balance. The Senate's 1930 rejection of John J. Parker—a nominee opposed by organized labor and the National Association for the Advancement of Colored People—led to President Herbert Hoover's appointment of Owen J. Roberts, who played a pivotal role in shifting the Court in a liberal direction from 1937 forward. Republican-led opposition to Abe Fortas's nomination as chief justice in 1968 paved the way for President Nixon to appoint the conservative Burger in 1969.

The Democratic-controlled Senate's rejection of Nixon's next two nominees—Clement Haynsworth Jr. and G. Harrold Carswell—led the president to turn to Harry A. Blackmun, who evolved from a moderate conservative into a staunch liberal during his twenty-four years on the

Court. With Democrats again in control, the Senate's rejection of conservative Robert Bork in 1987 forced President Ronald Reagan to settle on a less doctrinaire conservative, Anthony M. Kennedy, for the seat. Kennedy has sided with liberal justices in closely divided rulings on such issues as abortion, capital punishment, school prayer, and President Bush's war on terror policies.

MAY 8, 1930
SENATE REJECTS JUDGE PARKER, 41 TO 39; SPIRITED ATTACK BY JOHNSON PRECEDES FINAL VOTE ON HOOVER'S CHOICE FOR BENCH

NOMINEE'S CAREER ASSAILED

Californian Terms Him 'a Perennial Candidate' in Last Day's Debate.

RESULT IN DOUBT TILL END

Ten Regular Republicans Deserted the Administration on the Roll-Call.

WHITE HOUSE IS SILENT

But the President Is Expected to Make Some Comment on Result Later.

Special to The New York Times

WASHINGTON, May 7.—The Senate today rejected the nomination of Judge John J. Parker to be an Associate Justice of the United States Supreme Court by a vote of 41 to 39. It was the first time in thirty-six years that such a nomination had been rejected.

While no comment was made at the White House today, it is probable the President may later issue a statement discussing the Senate's action.

Following Judge Parker's rejection, President Hoover conferred with Senator Allen of Kansas and Under-Secretary of State Cotton relative to the advisability of making a public statement. It was decided not to do so today, but the President is expected to analyze the situation informally at some later date.

There was no intimation today who would be nominated next, or whether the President would act until the next session of Congress.

The opposition to Judge Parker's confirmation was led by Senators Borah and Norris, while Senators Fess of Ohio and Overman of North Carolina directed the battle for confirmation. . . .

The Senate galleries were packed with distinguished visitors today, and hundreds failed to gain admission. The debate lasted an hour and a half, and, under previous agreement, the vote was taken at 1:30 o'clock. Both sides approached the vote with a show of confidence, although the administration forces were not so hopeful as the opposition.

RESULT IN DOUBT UNTIL END.

A few minutes before the roll-call, members of the House drifted into the Senate chamber and lined its walls three deep. The utmost silence prevailed as the Senators answered their names.

At the outset of the roll-call, the opposition led greatly, and it was not until Senator Swanson voted for confirmation and Senator Steiwer in opposition that the vote was tied. And it ran very close until the end, with Judge Parker rejected by a margin of 2 votes.

There was only one shift in the impartial poll made last night. Senator Steck, Democrat, of Iowa, had declared himself opposed. Today he supported Judge Parker.

These regular Republicans deserted the administration: Senators Capper, Kansas; Couzens and Vandenberg, Michigan; Deneen and Glenn, Illinois; McNary and Steiwer, Oregon; Pine, Oklahoma; Robinson, Indiana; Robsion, Kentucky.

Senator Glass of Virginia rose to the defense of Judge Parker when the Senate began the last day's debate. He pronounced Judge Parker fit. . . . He criticized those who were accusing the opposition to Supreme Court nominations of being Socialistic. . . .

OCTOBER 2, 1968
SENATE BARS MOVE TO END FILIBUSTER BY FORTAS CRITICS

Nomination Appears Doomed as Bid to Invoke Closure Falls Short by 14 Votes

NEXT STEP UNDECIDED

Griffin Warns That Others Want to Talk—Dirksen Sees Early Adjournment

By FRED P. GRAHAM

Special to The New York Times

WASHINGTON, Oct. 1—The Senate refused by a wide margin today to stop the filibuster by opponents of the nomination of Abe Fortas to be Chief Justice of the United States. The action appeared to doom the nomination.

The vote was 45 to 43 in favor of cutting off debate—14 votes short of the two-thirds margin necessary to end the filibuster and clear the way for a confirmation vote.

After the clerk announced the tally, the Senate majority leader, Mike Mansfield, set the nomination aside—for the time being, at least—and brought before the Senate the $71.9-billion defense appropriation bill.

Speaking in a flat, dispassionate voice, Mr. Mansfield lectured his colleagues briefly for what he said was the Senate's failure "to exercise its responsibilities."

NEXT MOVE NOT SET

"The Senate has refused to face squarely the issue of the nomination of Mr. Justice Fortas—refused to allow the Senate to consider the issue on its merits," the Montana Democrat said.

He returned the Fortas nomination to the calendar of executive appointments and said that he would announce his next move on the matter in two or three days.

Because the target date for adjournment is so near, most observers assumed the nomination of the Associate Justice to be Chief Justice was dead.

The Senate minority leader, Everett McKinley Dirksen of Illinois, estimated today that the Congressional session would end in a week or 10 days.

Senator Dirksen said that he was not privy to the Johnson Administration's plans but that he would not expect Mr. Johnson to withdraw the nomination until Justice Fortas asked him to do so. . . .

If today's vote killed the Fortas nomination, it marks the second time in the nation's history that a nomination for Chief Justice has been rejected by the Senate. The first was George Washington's nomination of John Rutledge in 1795.

President Johnson nominated Justice Fortas to succeed Chief Justice Earl Warren, who announced his intention to retire but is remaining at the head of the Supreme Court pending approval of a successor.

Supporters of the Fortas nomination said in speeches before the closure vote that defeat of their position would also mark the first time that a Supreme Court nomination had been denied Senate confirmation because of a filibuster. . . .

Today's vote came after four days of debate in which anti-Fortas speakers concentrated on these issues:

- Questions over whether a vacancy exists in view of Chief Justice Warren's retirement being conditioned upon the confirmation of his successor.
- Charges that Justice Fortas and the Warren court had been too liberal in their ruling on such matters as obscenity, criminal defendants' rights and anti-subversive efforts.
- Assertions that Justice Fortas had violated the separation of powers doctrine by advising President Johnson on the Vietnam war, urban riots and other matters. The nominee's judgment and sense of judicial propriety were also questioned because of these activities and the $15,000 fee.

The shelving of the Fortas nomination appeared to extinguish any chance for the eventual confirmation of Federal Judge Homer Thornberry, who was nominated by President Johnson to fill the Court vacancy that would have been created by the resignation of Justice Warren and the elevation of Justice Fortas.

OCTOBER 24, 1987
BORK'S NOMINATION IS REJECTED, 58-42; REAGAN 'SADDENED'

Both Foes and Allies Ask Less Antagonism as President Picks a New Nominee

By LINDA GREENHOUSE

Special to The New York Times

WASHINGTON, Oct. 23—One of the fiercest battles ever waged over a Supreme Court nominee ended today as the Senate decisively rejected the nomination of Judge Robert H. Bork.

The vote was 58 against confirmation and 42 in favor, the biggest margin by which the Senate has ever rejected a Supreme Court nomination. Judge Bork's was the 27th Supreme Court nomination to fail in the country's history, the sixth in this century, and the first since 1970, when the Senate rejected President Nixon's nomination of G. Harrold Carswell by a vote of 51 to 45. There have been 104 Supreme Court justices in the nation's history.

the vacancy on the court. The White House is not expected to name a new candidate before the middle of next week.

The President has publicly vowed to find a nominee who will upset Judge Bork's opponents "just as much" as Judge Bork himself. Mr. Reagan said today, "My next nominee for the Court will share Judge Bork's belief in judicial restraint—that a judge is bound by the Constitution to interpret laws, not make them."

Meanwhile, senators on both sides of the debate urged the President to adopt a less confrontational tone.

"I would recommend they not send someone as controversial," Senator Strom Thurmond of South Carolina,

> **This has been a great debate, a debate about fundamental principle, about how one interprets the Constitution.**
>
> —Sen. Joseph R. Biden Jr., D-Del.

BORK 'GLAD DEBATE TOOK PLACE'

The vote came two weeks after Judge Bork, in the face of expected defeat, said he would not withdraw his name and wanted the full Senate to vote on his nomination. In a statement issued from his chambers at the Federal courthouse here, where he still serves on the United States Court of Appeals for the District of Columbia Circuit, Judge Bork said he was "glad the debate took place."

"There is now a full and permanent record by which the future may judge not only me but the proper nature of a confirmation proceeding," the 60-year-old judge said.

President Reagan, in a statement released by the White House, said, "I am saddened and disappointed that the Senate has bowed today to a campaign of political pressure."

THE NEXT NOMINEE?

In the final hours of the three-day debate on the Senate floor, senators turned their attention to the next nominee for

the ranking Republican on the Judiciary Committee, said at a news conference after the vote. In his closing remarks on the Senate floor, Senator Thurmond called Judge Bork "a great judge who would have adorned the Supreme Court with honor."

At his news conference, Senator Thurmond added that "as a matter of fairness," the next nominee should be from the South. Justice Lewis F. Powell Jr., whose retirement last June created the vacancy, is from Virginia, and there is now no Southerner on the Court.

Democrats were more pointed in their warnings to the White House.

"If we receive a nominee who thinks like Judge Bork, who acts like Judge Bork, who opposes civil rights and civil liberties like Judge Bork, he will be rejected like Judge Bork, just like that," Senator Edward M. Kennedy of Massachusetts said on the Senate floor. . . .

Although the outcome of the vote today was decided more than two weeks ago when the number of senators on record as opposing confirmation reached a majority, a sense of drama nonetheless arose in the Senate chamber when the moment came, shortly after 2 P.M.

The galleries were filled, both with members of the general public and with leaders of organizations that had played leading roles in lobbying for and against confirmation.

In an ordinary roll-call vote, senators wander through the chamber, chatting with colleagues and voting by a casual hand signal. But for this vote, Senator Byrd asked senators to remain at their seats and vote. As the clerk called each name, senators stood up, intoning "aye" or "no" in solemn voices.

FAMILY IN THE VISITORS' GALLERY

But earlier in the day, the scene was less dramatic than poignant. Then, the chamber was nearly deserted save for a few senators making their final speeches and Judge Bork's wife, Mary Ellen, and two sons, who sat expressionless in the visitors' gallery. They left before the vote began. Mrs. Bork and the judge's children, Charles, Ellen and Robert Jr., had sat with him in his five days of testimony last month before the Judiciary Committee. In his statement today, Judge Bork said that his family's "love and counsel sustained me throughout the extended process we have been through together."

Senator John C. Danforth, a Missouri Republican who was a student of Judge Bork's at Yale Law School, gave a long speech on his behalf this morning, contending that opponents had distorted the nominee's record and defeated him by making the public afraid of him.

The normally soft-spoken Senator continued, his voice rising: "What has happened to Robert Bork is wrong. The man's been trashed in our house. Some of us helped gen-

erate the trashing, others yielded to it, but all of us are accomplices."

Senator Biden replied that Senator Danforth was making "one heck of an indictment of your colleagues" by suggesting that senators had not reached independent decisions on Judge Bork but had "succumbed to raw pressure."

Senator Biden continued: "I have a higher opinion of the ability of my colleagues to do what's right."

'A GREAT DEBATE'

Later, in closing the debate, the Judiciary Committee chairman said: "This has been a great debate, a debate about fundamental principle, about how one interprets the Constitution."

Senator Biden repeated the statement with which he opened Judge Bork's confirmation hearings last month, and which he has made a theme for the entire proceeding. "I believe I have rights because I exist, in spite of my government, not because of my government," he said. "Judge Bork believes that rights flow from the majority, through the Constitution to individuals, a notion I reject."

After the vote, Senator Biden said that although "I enjoy winning," this particular victory was "less enjoyable than others, because we are talking about a man who had to sit home and listen to this, a fine man who just had a view of the Constitution that is out of touch with the 1980's and 1990's."

The debate thus ended with Judge Bork's supporters and opponents holding fundamentally irreconcilable views of what had gone wrong for the nominee. His supporters insisted that he had been misunderstood and mischaracterized, while his opponents maintained that he lost precisely because the senators and their constituents did understand his views, and rejected them.

• • • • • • • • • • •

In many other instances, Senate opponents have tried but failed to defeat a president's nominee. Those justices too have left their mark on the Court's decisions. Among the twentieth-century justices who won ideologically charged confirmation fights were Louis D. Brandeis (47-22), William H. Rehnquist (68-26 as associate justice, 65-33 as chief justice), Clarence Thomas (52-48), and President George W. Bush's two appointees, Chief Justice Roberts (78-22) and Justice Samuel A. Alito Jr. (58-42).

REVERSALS OF RULINGS BY LEGISLATION

Congress can reverse a Supreme Court decision that restricts or invalidates a federal statute by passing a new or revised law. One scholar counted more than 120 such instances in the period 1967–1990.

One of the most important reversals occurred eight decades after the Court's decision. The Court in 1883 ruled unconstitutional the Civil Rights Act of 1875, saying the Thirteenth and Fourteenth amendments gave Congress no power to prohibit private racial discrimination. In passing the Civil Rights Act of 1964, Congress claimed that authority under its power to regulate interstate commerce. The Court upheld the law. (See pages 261 and 267.)

By contrast, it took only a few years in the 1930s for Congress to pass and win Supreme Court approval of revised laws to replace New Deal measures that the Court had struck down. In an even shorter time span, Congress in 1991 passed a bill aimed at reversing several 1989 decisions that somewhat narrowed legal remedies in federal employment discrimination cases.

OCTOBER 31, 1991
SENATE APPROVES CIVIL RIGHTS BILL, 93-5

By ADAM CLYMER

Seeking to still two years of bitter debate over discrimination and quotas, the Senate today passed, 93 to 5, a civil rights bill intended to make it easier to sue in job bias cases.

The House is expected to move quickly to adopt the compromise bill, which was worked out late last week by Senators John C. Danforth and Edward M. Kennedy and the Bush Administration. President Bush, who is expected to sign it quickly, said on Friday that it provided "a new standard against discrimination and for equal opportunity."

his party, continued: "I think everybody is right to claim victory. It is a victory for our country." He said, "The great victory is reconstituting a political consensus in our country that had been threatened."

Mr. Kennedy, a Massachusetts Democrat, said today's action "is all the more satisfying because it involves a welcome restoration of the bipartisan coalition in Congress and between Congress and the Administration." Mr. Kennedy stayed in the background this sum-

> The Supreme Court in the 1989 term cast a shadow over the nation's commitment to civil rights.
>
> —Sen. Christopher J. Dodd, D-Conn.

The overwhelming margin exceeded even the steadily rising expectations that followed last week's compromise. Five very conservative Republicans cast the no votes.

Mr. Danforth, a Missouri Republican who challenged the White House this summer and worked to assemble a veto-proof majority for the bill before last week's deal, told the Senate, "Everybody is claiming victory: Democrats, Republicans, liberals, conservatives."

'A VICTORY FOR OUR COUNTRY'

The Senator, who continually warned that the recent emphasis on race in politics was bad for the nation and for

mer to let Mr. Danforth seek Republican backing while working to maintain solid Democratic support for his efforts.

"Civil rights has always been the unfinished business of America, and it will continue to be our unfinished business for many years to come," Mr. Kennedy said.

Senator Bob Dole of Kansas, the Republican leader who pressed both sides for a compromise and brought the White House to the bargaining table last Thursday, praised President Bush, who he said had always led "the charge for responsible legislation, not the grab-bag approach advocated by the Beltway interest groups and the lawyers' lobby." He called the bill "the only way out of the civil rights quagmire without producing quotas." Supporters of the earlier versions of the bill have insisted all along that they would not lead to quotas.

5 WHO VOTED NO

The five Republicans who voted against the compromise bill were Daniel R. Coats of Indiana, Jesse Helms of North Carolina, Robert C. Smith of New Hampshire, Steve Symms of Idaho and Malcolm Wallop of Wyoming.

Before the bill was passed, a Senate embarrassed by televised hearings into an accusation of sexual harassment against Judge Clarence Thomas, who was later confirmed to the Supreme Court, voted without a roll-call to give its own staff members the extraordinary right to take complaints of job discrimination to a Federal appeals court.

But the two years' work of legislative and political wrestling was concentrated on overturning eight Supreme Court decisions, most of them from 1989.

The most important of them, Wards Cove v. Atonio, made it much harder to prove a civil rights violation where employers use hiring or promotion practices that appear fair, like a strength test or an educational requirement, but that have the effect of discriminating against women, blacks or others protected by civil rights laws.

That case was at the heart of Mr. Bush's earlier complaints that remedial legislation would force employers who wanted to stay out of court to employ racial quotas, a charge he said Friday did not apply to this bill. The bill passed today does not offer a precise and detailed description of how to decide when a business may use such tests or standards.

But it says those practices must be "job related for the position in question and consistent with business necessity," and tells the Supreme Court that its Wards Cove decision "has weakened the scope and effectiveness of Federal civil rights enforcement."

An equally important provision would give victims of intentional job discrimination based on sex, religion or national origin the right to win cash damages under the 1964 Civil Rights Act.

Victims of intentional racial discrimination can already win damages for bias in hiring, using a Reconstruction-era law, and today's bill would reverse the Supreme Court's 1989 deci-

sion in Patterson v. McLean Credit Union, which said that statute did not provide a remedy against harassment on the job.

One key compromise in establishing the ability of women to sue against discrimination, including sexual harassment, is a limitation on damages, depending on the size of the employer's work force. While awards for back pay and past out-of-pocket damages like medical bills would not be limited, other damages would be capped at between $50,000 for small companies and $300,000 for big ones.

Women's and civil rights groups objected to the limits, but Mr. Kennedy insisted they were necessary to get opposing forces on the bill to agree on a compromise. He said he would introduce new legislation soon to repeal the limits.

OTHER PROVISIONS OF BILL

Other important elements of the bill include these:

- The measure prohibits the adjustment of employment tests to score individuals differently because of race, a practice known as "race-norming."
- It overturns one of this year's Supreme Court decisions, Equal Employment Opportunity Commission v. Aramco. That case held that American companies operating overseas were not covered by the 1964 Civil Rights Act. The bill says they are covered and may not discriminate against employees who are American citizens.
- The bill reverses a 1989 Supreme Court decision, Martin v. Wilks, that enabled white firefighters in Birmingham, Ala., to reopen an old consent decree that provided for hiring more black firefighters. It bars reopening old cases if the new plaintiffs knew or should have known of the decree.
- It reverses a 1989 Supreme Court decision, Lorance v. A.T.&T. Technologies, that said challenges to discriminatory procedures had to be made soon after the practices were begun. The bill says they must be made soon after the discriminatory effect becomes clear.

The Court's decisions were often criticized in today's debate. A typical comment came from Senator Christopher J. Dodd, Democrat of Connecticut, who said, "The Supreme Court in the 1989 term cast a shadow over the nation's commitment to civil rights."

Sometimes the Court has refused to go along with congressional efforts to void one of its decisions by legislation. In one notable instance, the Court in 2000 struck down a law that Congress passed in 1968 aimed at circumventing the Miranda rule on police interrogation by providing that any "voluntary" confession was admissible in federal court. (See page 372.)

Reversals of Rulings by Constitutional Amendment

Four times, Congress has proposed and the states have ratified constitutional amendments to reverse Supreme Court decisions. The Eleventh Amendment (1798) overturned the Court's decision permitting federal courts to hear citizen suits against states. The Fourteenth Amendment (1868) overturned the Court's holding in the Dred Scott case that blacks could never become U.S. citizens. The Sixteenth Amendment (1913) overturned the Court's decision barring a federal income tax. The Twenty-sixth Amendment (1971) guaranteed eighteen-year-olds the right to vote in state as well as federal elections, reversing the effect of a Court decision that denied Congress the power to establish the age requirement in state balloting.

Congress in 1924 approved an amendment to overturn the Court's decisions invalidating federal child labor laws, but the amendment fell short of the number of states needed for ratification. The issue became moot in 1941, however, when the Court overturned its previous ruling. Other proposed amendments on such subjects as reapportionment, school prayer, busing, abortion, and flag-burning have failed to win approval in Congress.

Jurisdiction-Stripping

Congress's first attempts to remove part of the Supreme Court's jurisdiction were aimed in the 1820s and 1830s at section 25 of the Judiciary Act of 1789, which gave the Court authority to review state supreme court decisions on federal law issues. Amidst widespread criticism of an 1830 Supreme Court decision limiting the states' sovereignty, the House Judiciary Committee reported a bill to repeal section 25 in 1831. Supporters of the Court managed to repulse the repeal movement.

Congress passed the 1868 measure repealing the Court's authority to hear habeas corpus appeals explicitly to block a potential decision in the McCardle case to invalidate the Reconstruction Act. In fact, Chief Justice Chase wrote a letter less than a month later saying that without the congressional action, the Court "doubtless" would have held McCardle's military imprisonment unconstitutional. The 1869 decision allowing Congress to repeal the Court's jurisdiction over the case remains controversial. In a dissenting opinion in a 1962 case, Justice William O. Douglas wrote that the McCardle opinion might not command majority support today.

Congress considered proposals in the 1950s to repeal the Court's jurisdiction over cases involving internal subversion. The Senate Judiciary Committee considered such a bill in 1958, but it approved a watered-down version that was defeated on the Senate floor.

Changing the Court's Size

Congress changed the size of the Court seven times between 1801 and 1869. Several of the changes were aimed at influencing the Court's outlook by either allowing or preventing appointment of new justices. Only one specific ruling can be said to have been affected by the tinkering: the Court's 5-4 reversal in 1871 of its earlier ruling on the constitutionality of paper money. The decision resulted in part from the expansion of the Court's authorized size from seven to nine members approved two years earlier.

The number of seats has remained at nine ever since. The failure of Roosevelt's "Court-packing" plan has come to be viewed as a precedent against tampering with the number of justices for ideological purposes.

IMPEACHMENT

The Senate's acquittal of Justice Chase after his impeachment in 1804 provided an early precedent against ideologically driven efforts to remove a sitting justice. President Jefferson, who had lodged the initial complaint against Chase, said the acquittal showed that impeachment was "a mere scarecrow."

In modern times, the House twice investigated impeachment charges against Justice Douglas—first in 1953 after Douglas temporarily stayed the execution of convicted spies Julius and Ethel Rosenberg and then again in 1970 on several charges of alleged irregularities lodged by the House minority leader, Gerald R. Ford, R-Mich. The first effort was tabled, the second rejected by a subcommittee that found Douglas had not violated any law or rule of judicial ethics.

DECEMBER 4, 1970
HOUSE PANEL VOTES AGAINST IMPEACHING DOUGLAS

By MARJORIE HUNTER
Special to The New York Times

WASHINGTON, Dec. 3—A special House subcommittee has concluded that there are no grounds for impeachment of Associate Supreme Court Justice William O. Douglas.

The decision, based on findings in a subcommittee staff report, was reached by the three Democrats on the five-member panel, Emanuel Celler of Brooklyn, Byron G. Rogers of Colorado and Jack Brooks of Texas.

One of the two Republican members, Edward Hutchinson of Michigan, announced that he would file a minority view. The other, William M. McCulloch of Ohio, refrained from joining in either the majority or minority view.

The impeachment controversy was touched off last April in a floor speech by the House Republican leader, Gerald R. Ford of Michigan. Suggesting that Justice Douglas may have had ties with gambling and underworld figures, Mr. Ford termed him "unfit" and said, "I would vote to impeach him right now."

Within days, a coalition of 52 Democrats and 52 Republicans joined Mr. Ford in calling for creation of a special committee to consider possible impeachment.

Before the House could act on creation of such a special investigation panel, Mr. Celler and his Judiciary Committee

 Mr. [Gerald] Ford accused Justice Douglas of espousing 'hippie-yippie style revolution,' of writing for pornographic magazines, of links to 'left-wing organizations' and of possible connections with 'gamblers and underworld figures.'

The subcommittee report recommending against impeachment will be presented to the House Judiciary Committee before Congress adjourns later this month. It is generally believed that the Democratic majority on the full committee will accept the subcommittee's findings, thus ending the impeachment investigation, at least for this session.

However, critics are expected to renew their call for creation of a special committee to investigate possible impeachment of the Associate Justice, who has been on the Supreme Court for 31 years.

moved last April to take over the inquiry by establishing the five-man subcommittee.

Mr. Celler, who headed the special panel, declined today to make public the staff findings until the report was considered by his full committee.

"At that time, it will be printed and made public," he said.

Critics of the Celler subcommittee's investigation have complained that the panel did not hold public hearings and did not examine any witnesses under oath.

The subcommittee inquiry was termed a "contrived whitewash" by Representative Louis C. Wyman, Republican of New Hampshire, a leading House critic of Justice Douglas.

In the speech last spring that prompted the impeachment inquiry, Mr. Ford accused Justice Douglas of espousing "hippie-yippie style revolution," of writing for pornographic magazines, of links to "left-wing organiza-tions" and of possible connections with "gamblers and underworld figures."

Before impeachment proceedings can begin, charges must be brought against an official by a simple majority of the House membership. The case is then heard by the Senate, sitting as a jury, and two-thirds of the Senators sitting must vote in favor of impeachment to remove the official from office.

• • • • • • • • • • • •

No formal move to impeach Chief Justice Earl Warren was ever considered despite calls by right-wing groups through the years to remove him because of liberal rulings on civil rights, criminal procedure, and other issues.

THE COURT AND PUBLIC OPINION

The framers of the Constitution intended the Supreme Court to be an independent check on the political branches of the federal government. To that end, they insulated the Court from public opinion by providing for the justices to be appointed rather than elected and to be given lifetime tenure rather than fixed terms. Yet the Court is not expected to completely ignore the popular will or the legitimate roles of the other branches of government.

As a result, the Court at times seems to reflect public opinion and at other times to give it little heed. The public's attitude toward the Court varies as well. Often, large segments of the public have strongly disapproved of certain decisions. But the Court enjoys a reservoir of public support larger than either Congress or the president. Much of the public appears to trust the Court to be above partisan politics, to protect individual liberties without going too far, and to prevent overreaching by Congress, the president, or the states.

EARLY VIEWS OF THE COURT

The Supreme Court's first major decision—the 1793 ruling in *Chisholm v. Georgia* to permit private suits against a state in federal court—produced a strong backlash that resulted in a constitutional amendment—the eleventh—to overrule it only two years later. After Marshall became chief justice in 1801, he strove to nurture public support for the Court's decisions and for the Court as an institution helping to unify the nation. Marshall Court decisions provoked controversy from states' rights advocates, but Marshall was widely revered by the time of his death in 1835.

Under Chief Justice Taney, the Court similarly tried to build public respect for the Court but failed to satisfy public opinion on the overriding issue of the day: slavery. Taney led the Court in giving greater leeway to the states on a variety of issues, partly in the hope of avoiding entanglement with the slavery issue. As a result, many abolitionists came to view the Court as an accomplice of slaveholders and slave states.

Taney hoped the Court's 1857 ruling in the Dred Scott case would settle the slavery issue by barring Congress from prohibiting slavery in the territories. Instead, it provoked a new firestorm of criticism from opponents of slavery—including future president Abraham Lincoln—but failed to deter Southern states from the path to secession.

The sidewalk in front of the Supreme Court plaza has become a dynamic showplace of public opinion surrounding the Court's rulings. Here, hooded demonstrators protest the treatment of detainees at Guantánamo Bay Naval Base as the Court hears arguments in the case of *Boumediene v. Bush* on December 5, 2007.

Source: Doug Mills/The New York Times

THE CIVIL WAR TO THE NEW DEAL

The Court faced two major issues from the end of the Civil War to the New Deal era: race relations and economic regulation. Its decisions upholding racial segregation and supporting business and propertied interests reflected in part the public sentiment of the late nineteenth century. When the Court upheld racial segregation in *Plessy v. Ferguson* (1896), for example, the ruling went largely unnoticed.

By the turn of the century, however, the Court was falling out of step with public opinion on economic issues. Rulings in the 1890s that narrowed federal antitrust laws, upheld use of federal court injunctions against strikes, and struck down a federal income tax gave the Court a reputation among organized labor, farmers, and progressives as a tool of special privilege. In time, these groups succeeded in overturning the income tax ruling by constitutional amendment and winning passage of a broader antitrust law and a statute limiting the use of injunctions in strikes.

Despite criticism, the Court hewed to a conservative course on economic regulation issues through the mid-1930s. President Roosevelt badly misjudged public opinion toward the Court, however, when he proposed his infamous "Court-packing" plan in 1937. Congress received a deluge of mail protesting the plan. In June the Senate Judiciary Committee rejected the plan, calling it an attempt to make the Court "subservient to the pressures of public opinion of the hour." Even so, many observers saw the Court's changed stance toward economic regulation—which began just as the Court-packing plan was pending—as an acknowledgment of sorts that the Court was out of sync with prevailing political sentiment.

THE WARREN COURT

Under Chief Justice Warren, the Supreme Court entered an unprecedented era of liberal judicial activism. In contrast to the pro-business activism of earlier eras, the Warren Court exercised its judicial powers in behalf of underprivileged and underrepresented elements of society.

At the same time, Warren took steps to minimize public criticism of some of the Court's rulings. He wrote a deliberately understated opinion in the landmark school desegregation case, *Brown v. Board of Education* (1954), and lobbied the other justices to make the decision unanimous. In *Baker v. Carr* (1962), Warren put off detailed questions about how federal courts should deal with reapportionment and redistricting. And the Court put its revolution in criminal procedure in effect step by step rather than in one broad stroke.

Nonetheless, the Court came under sustained attack. Its school desegregation decisions provoked massive resistance in the South. The Court's rulings in the early 1960s barring organized prayer in the public schools drew strong criticism from religious elements in the South and elsewhere. Then, with its criminal procedure decisions, the Court became the target of fierce criticism that it was handcuffing the police and letting criminals go free.

The Warren Court "was the object of more heartfelt execration by conservatives than any other Supreme Court in our history," Yale law professor Joseph W. Bishop Jr. wrote in *The New York Times Magazine* in 1969—more even than liberals had directed at the Court in the 1930s.

The Court had been a major issue in the 1968 presidential campaign. On the campaign trail, Richard Nixon accused the Court of "weakening the peace forces as against the criminal forces in this country" and promised to name "strict constructionist" justices reflecting his conservative views. As president, Nixon appointed four justices—including Chief Justice Burger—who helped form a more conservative majority that halted further expansion of the Warren Court's rulings on the exclusionary rule and police interrogation.

THE BURGER COURT

In 1973 the Burger Court produced an activist decision of its own: the abortion rights ruling, *Roe v. Wade.* Over the next two decades, the decision became the focal point of polarized debate. Efforts to overturn the ruling by constitutional amendment failed, but Congress and many state legislatures did pass laws limiting the use of public funds to pay for abortion or attempting to regulate abortion procedures. Abortion became a major issue in several Supreme Court confirmation battles, including the Senate's rejection of Robert Bork in 1987 and narrow approval of Clarence Thomas in 1991. When the Court reaffirmed *Roe v. Wade* in 1992, the pivotal justices—Sandra Day O'Connor, Kennedy, and David H. Souter—justified the decision in part by saying that public respect for the Court might be lowered if it appeared to be reversing itself because of popular pressure.

PUBLIC OPINION AND DECISIONS

The political cartoonist Finley Peter Dunne famously had his fictional Irish bartender Mr. Dooley declare in 1900 that the Supreme Court "follows the election returns." Public opinion may not play such a direct role in the Court's decision making, but many examples illustrate the justices' sensitivity to prevailing sentiment. Given the public support for the internment of Japanese Americans during World War II, for example, the Court's decision upholding the government's policy was hardly surprising. The Court supported laws aimed at communists and subversives in the early years of the Cold War but shifted as the public came to recognize evidence of excesses.

To many observers, the Court's abortion rights ruling is a prime example of ill-advised over-reaching. Public opinion polls since 1973 generally show strong support for a woman's right to choose an abortion along with comparable support for various restrictions on the right. The Court's decisions have mirrored the ambivalence to some extent by upholding abortion regulations even while reaffirming *Roe v. Wade*'s essential holding.

The Court has followed a similar path in other areas. *Brown* has become a universally honored landmark for equal rights, but the Court cut back on school desegregation remedies in the wake of a backlash against its 1971 decision permitting the use of busing for racial balance. The Burger Court mirrored public sentiment in cutting back expansive readings of the Warren Court's criminal procedure decisions. No one, however, questions the Warren Court's ruling in *Gideon v. Wainwright* (1962) to provide lawyers to indigent defendants; and even the once controversial *Miranda* decision, requiring police to inform suspects of their rights, was pronounced by Chief Justice Rehnquist in 2000 to have become "part of our national culture."

The interaction between Supreme Court decision making and public opinion has led some contemporary observers to question the traditional view of the Court as a "countermajoritarian" check on the political branches. New York University law professor Barry Friedman has written of the Court as one participant in a continuing "constitutional dialogue" with Congress, the president, and the public. Jeffrey Rosen, law professor and legal editor of *The New Republic,* described the courts in a book title as *The Most Democratic Branch.* The Supreme Court, Rosen wrote, "has become increasingly adept at representing the views of the center of American politics."

Whether or not the justices are following the polls, public opinion surveys over the last three decades show that the Court has enjoyed greater confidence from the public than either the president or Congress. Since 2000, Gallup surveys have found that most people approve of the way the Court is handling its job, but the percentage has fallen from 62 percent in 2000 to 51 percent in fall 2007. In the latter survey, 43 percent of those polled said the Supreme Court's decisions were "about right," 32 percent said they were "too conservative," and 21 percent said they were "too liberal."

THE COURT AND THE STATES

CHAPTER 4

Probation officers must put in long hours and work at unusual times to monitor criminal offenders. Citing those requirements, probation officers in Maine sued the state government in 1992 for overtime pay under the federal Fair Labor Standards Act, which requires covered employers to pay time-and-a-half for work beyond the normal forty-hour week.

A decade earlier, the Supreme Court had ruled that state governments are subject to the federal wage-and-hours law. The federal judge in Maine agreed with the probation officers' argument and ordered the state to begin paying time-and-a-half for overtime.

The federal law also allows recovery for back pay. The judge was moving on to address that part of the case when the Supreme Court issued a startling decision in 1996: private citizens could not sue state governments for money in federal court—even for violations of federal law.

Applying that ruling, the judge dismissed the probation officers' back-pay claims. Undeterred, the probation officers filed an identical claim in Maine's state court system. But the state invoked the centuries-old doctrine of sovereign immunity to ask that the suit be thrown out. Maine's supreme court agreed.

The probation officers said the state high court ruling meant that the federal law was a "dead letter" for them and asked the U.S. Supreme Court to review the decision. The case reached the justices after a series of Court rulings through the 1990s that had relied on concepts of state sovereignty to limit the power of the federal government vis-à-vis the states.

The Supreme Court has played a powerful role in shaping the balance between state and national governments and the authority vested in each. This was evident in the ruling in *Gonzales v. Raich* (2005). Angel Raich, left, used marijuana legally, for medical reasons, under California law. The Court, however, ruled such use illegal under federal antidrug law, citing Congress's commerce powers.

These new federalism rulings were seen as the work of Chief Justice William H. Rehnquist, who had championed states' rights ever since he joined the Court in 1972. Rehnquist had been in dissent on federalism issues more often than not in the 1970s and 1980s, but found himself with a working majority in the 1990s thanks to the appointment of conservative justices by Presidents Ronald Reagan and George H. W. Bush.

In one decision, the Court voted 5-4 in 1995 to invalidate a federal law, the Gun-Free Schools Zone Act of 1990, which made it a federal crime to possess a handgun near a school. Writing for the majority in *Lopez v. United States,* Rehnquist said the law infringed the states' traditional role in local law enforcement.

Alden v. Maine

Decided: June 23, 1999

Vote: 5 (Rehnquist, O'Connor, Scalia, Kennedy, Thomas)

4 (Stevens, Souter, Ginsburg, Breyer)

Opinion of the Court: Kennedy

Dissenting opinion: Souter (Stevens, Ginsburg, Breyer)

Two years later, the Court threw out—by the same margin—provisions of the Brady Handgun Violence Prevention Act of 1993 requiring local law enforcement agencies to conduct background checks on prospective gun purchasers. The law improperly "commandeered" state governments to enforce a federal law, Justice Antonin Scalia wrote in *Printz v. United States* (1997).

Although the 1996 ruling limiting damage suits against state governments, *Seminole Tribe v. Florida,* had received less attention, the justices showed that they were willing to extend it in their decision in the Maine probation officers' case. By another 5-4 vote, the Court in *Alden v. Maine* (1999) barred private citizens from suing state governments in state as well as federal courts for money damages for violations of federal law. Justice Anthony M. Kennedy said that immunity from suit was a "fundamental aspect" of states' sovereignty before the Constitution and that states did not surrender the protection after ratification.

JUNE 24, 1999
STATES ARE GIVEN NEW LEGAL SHIELD BY SUPREME COURT

By LINDA GREENHOUSE

Thrusting the doctrine of state sovereignty well beyond existing boundaries, the Supreme Court placed sharp new curbs today on the ability of Congress to make Federal law binding on the states.

In three cases, all decided by identical 5-to-4 votes, the Court made states immune from suits by state employees for violations of Federal labor law; by patent owners for infringement of their patents by state universities and agencies; and by people bringing unfair-competition suits over states' activities in the marketplace.

final day of the 1998–99 term, was greater than the sum of its parts. It was the most powerful indication yet of a narrow majority's determination to reconfigure the balance between state and Federal authority in favor of the states.

"Congress has vast power but not all power," Justice Anthony M. Kennedy declared in one decision, a case from Maine holding that state employees cannot sue for violations of Federal labor law.

"When Congress legislates in matters affecting the states," Justice Kennedy added, "it may not treat these

> Congress must accord states the esteem due to them as joint participants in a Federal System.
>
> —Justice Anthony M. Kennedy, *Alden v. Maine*

In the labor case, in particular, the Court had already ruled that a state's sovereign immunity meant that it could not be sued in Federal court. The Court's decision today closed the only other avenue for employees to try to force a state to comply with Federal law: bringing a lawsuit in state court. The ruling, then, leaves enforcement to individual Federal agencies, like the Department of Labor, but Government lawyers argued that the department does not have the resources to sue every time there is a complaint.

While each decision will have similar substantial practical impact, the whole of the Court's actions today, the

sovereign entities as mere prefectures or corporations. Congress must accord states the esteem due to them as joint participants in a Federal system."

The decisions were announced from the bench this morning in a scene of extraordinary drama. After the author of each majority opinion—Justice Kennedy, Justice Antonin Scalia and Chief Justice William H. Rehnquist—summarized his reasoning and conclusion, a different one of the four dissenters spoke in rebuttal. The rhetorical volleys, with Justices David H. Souter, Stephen G. Breyer and John Paul Stevens speaking in dissent, consumed about 45 minutes and held the audience spellbound.

Justice Stevens, using pungent language that did not appear in his written dissent, accused the majority of constructing a doctrine of sovereign immunity "much like a mindless dragon that indiscriminately chews gaping holes in Federal statutes." He said the Court was returning to "the brief period of confusion and crisis when our new nation was governed by the Articles of Confederation."

The other Justices in the five-member majority were Sandra Day O'Connor and Clarence Thomas. Justice Ruth Bader Ginsburg was the fourth dissenter.

When the Court's work was over, two Federal laws had been declared unconstitutional, one 35-year-old precedent was explicitly overturned, and one 15-year-old precedent was effectively dead.

And it was also strikingly apparent that the fault line that runs through the current Court as an all but unbridgeable gulf has to do not with the higher-profile issues of race, religion, abortion or due process, but with federalism. It was clear from the courtroom scene this morning and from the 185 pages of often impassioned prose the Court produced in the three cases that, for these Justices, the question of the proper allocation of authority within the American system is not abstract or theoretical but urgent and fundamental, with the two sides holding irreconcilable visions of what the Constitution's framers had in mind.

With more than a dozen other federalism cases pending, the Court has already accepted two for decision in its next term, and is likely to accept several others. One in particular may be affected by the decisions today, a case from Florida that raises the question of whether state employees may sue a state for violating the Federal law against age discrimination (Kimel v. Florida Board of Regents, No. 98-791, to be argued in October). Other cases awaiting the Court's action involve suits against states for violations of the Equal Pay Act and the Americans With Disabilities Act.

At the heart of the debate on the Court today was the meaning of the 11th Amendment, which stripped the Federal courts of authority to hear suits against one state by a citizen of another. The Court has long since interpreted the amendment as also barring suits in Federal courts by people against their own state. The Court had also viewed Congress as having the power to abrogate the states' immunity from particular types of suits, if it did so explicitly.

Three years ago, in Seminole Tribe v. Florida, the Court overturned one of its precedents by the same 5-to-4 vote as in the decisions today. It ruled that Congress did not have the power to force states to defend themselves in Federal court under laws enacted under Article I of the Constitution, including laws that regulate interstate commerce.

One such law was the Fair Labor Standards Act, a basic Federal labor law that established minimum wages and hours and that Congress had extended in 1974 to cover millions of people employed by states. In an early taste of the current federalism battle, the Supreme Court declared that extension unconstitutional in 1976, only to reverse itself in 1985, in a disputed 5-to-4 ruling called Garcia v. San Antonio Metropolitan Transit Authority. Chief Justice Rehnquist, then an Associate Justice, declared in dissent in the Garcia case that he was not reconciled to the outcome and would work to have the Court reverse itself again.

In 1992, 65 state probation officers and juvenile caseworkers in Maine sued the state in Federal court for violating the Fair Labor Standards Act by not giving them premium pay for overtime. The case was pending when the Supreme Court issued the Seminole Tribe decision, which clearly required the dismissal of the state workers' suit.

Because Congress had also provided that employees could bring Fair Labor Standards Act cases in state court, the workers refiled their case in the Maine courts. But the Maine Supreme Court ruled last year that the state had sovereign immunity in its own courts similar to its 11th Amendment immunity in Federal court, and dismissed the suit. The question in one case the Court decided today, Alden v. Maine, No. 98-436, was whether closing the state courthouse to a suit based on a federally protected right was a proper application of state sovereign immunity.

Also in the early 1990's, the Federal courts had begun to dismiss patent and trademark suits that people were bringing against state agencies, on the ground that Congress had not met the Supreme Court's standards for explicitly abrogating the states' 11th Amendment immunity from suits of this type. In response, Congress passed two laws in 1992, the Trademark Remedy Clarification Act and the Patent Remedy Clarification Act, explicitly permitting these kinds of suits against states in Federal court.

Two years later, the College Savings Bank, based in Princeton, N.J., sued the state of Florida under both the new laws. The College Savings Bank sells a special certificate of deposit tailored for parents saving for college tuition. When Florida entered the same market through a new state agency, the Florida Prepaid Postsecondary Education Expense Board, the College Savings Bank alleged that the state was infringing its patent on its investment method and was engaging in false advertising and unfair competition in violation of the Federal Lanham Act, which protects trademarks.

These lawsuits were also pending when the Supreme Court decided the Seminole Tribe case. As a result, the trademark case was dismissed, on the ground that the trademark law had been enacted as an exercise of Congress's power to regulate commerce. But the United States Court of Appeals for the Federal Circuit refused Florida's request to dismiss the patent suit, reasoning that patent cases were not governed by the Seminole Tribe decision because patents were a type of property. The appeals court held that Congress had the power to prevent the deprivation of property without due process under its power to enforce the due process guarantee of the 14th Amendment, a power the Supreme Court had not limited in the Seminole Tribe case.

Both sides appealed to the Supreme Court. The trademark case was College Savings Bank v. Florida, No. 98-149, and the patent case was Florida v. College Savings Bank, No. 98-531.

In his opinion upholding the Maine Supreme Court's decision that the state was immune from suit in its own courts, Justice Kennedy acknowledged that the 11th Amendment did not provide a direct answer to the question, because it limits only the jurisdiction of the Federal courts. But he said the principle of state immunity "is demarcated not by the text of the amendment alone but by fundamental postulates implicit in the constitutional design."

In fact, Justice Kennedy said, for Congress to be able to authorize suits in a state's own courts "would be even more offensive to state sovereignty than a power to authorize the suits in a Federal forum." He added: "A power to press a state's own courts into Federal service is the power first to turn the state against itself and ultimately to commandeer the entire political machinery of the state against its will and at the behest of individuals."

In his dissenting opinion, Justice Souter said the majority opinion was based on a "demonstrably mistaken" view of history. He said: "There is much irony in the Court's profession that it grounds its opinion on a deeply rooted historical tradition of sovereign immunity, when the Court abandons a principle nearly as inveterate, and much closer to the hearts of the framers: that where there is a right, there must be a remedy."

He said that about 4.7 million state workers were now foreclosed from suing their employer in state or Federal court. The Federal Government can still sue in state court, but Government lawyers told the Justices that the Labor Department was not equipped to do that, with enforcement always having depended on private suits. While the Supreme Court did not overrule the Garcia decision, which upheld the extension of Federal labor law to the states, that was likely to be its practical effect.

Justice Scalia wrote the majority opinion in the College Savings Bank's trademark case. He rejected a theory the Clinton Administration, on the bank's behalf, had offered as a way of getting around the Seminole Tribe obstacle: that because Florida had made itself a player in the commercial marketplace, it had implicitly waived its immunity from suit for its activities in that marketplace.

That argument was based on a 1964 Supreme Court precedent, Parden v. Terminal Railway, which had permitted a suit against Alabama on such a theory. Justice Scalia, calling the Parden decision an "ill-conceived experiment," declared that it was now overruled. He also chided the dissenters for insisting on their position "in a degree of repetitive detail that has despoiled our northern woods."

Dissenting in this case, Justice Breyer said the Court was undercutting the very federalism that it purported to serve, by making it "more difficult for Congress to decentralize governmental decision making and to provide individual citizens, or local communities, with a variety of enforcement powers." He accused the majority of elevating a vision of sovereignty "more akin to the thought of James I than of James Madison."

In the patent case, Chief Justice Rehnquist wrote for the majority that the appeals court had been mistaken to view the patent law as a valid exercise of Congress's authority to enforce the 14th Amendment. He said Congress had failed to find, when it passed the 1992 law, that there was a constitutional problem requiring a solution based on the 14th Amendment. He cited a decision two years ago, in which the Court struck down the Religious Freedom Restoration Act on the ground that Congress had exceeded its 14th Amendment authority.

Dissenting in this case, Justice Stevens slyly accused the majority of the judicial activism its members often deplore. He said the court had endorsed a version of sovereign immunity "defined only by the present majority's perception of constitutional penumbras rather than constitutional text."

The invalidation of the two 1992 laws is likely to have the direct effect of curbing copyright suits against states as well. Briefs had been filed by publishers, the movie industry, and others interested in intellectual property, warning the Court that states would have an unfair advantage over the private sector in biotechnology, publishing and other ventures if they were immune from suit. . . .

· · · · · · · · · · · ·

The states'-rights rulings provoked sharp criticism from the Court's liberal justices. They complained that the decisions were curtailing Congress's power to deal with national problems and allowing state governments to ignore federal laws with relative impunity.

In their opposing opinions, the justices rehearsed debates that the Court had heard over the past two centuries. Under Chief Justice John Marshall, the Court established its authority to review state laws and state court decisions—but only with difficulty. In fact, the Court before Marshall had suffered the indignity of seeing its first major decision—a ruling against state governments—reversed by a constitutional amendment only three years later.

The Supreme Court showed greater sympathy toward the states in the decades leading up to the Civil War and those after. Early in the twentieth century, however, a conservative Court invoked property rights and due process to overturn state economic and social policy laws. Later, liberal Courts decided to enforce provisions of the Bill of Rights against the states. That new approach resulted in the criminal procedure revolution in the 1960s under Chief Justice Earl Warren.

As a lawyer in the Reagan administration in the 1980s, John G. Roberts Jr. criticized many of the Court's decisions under Chief Justices Warren and Warren E. Burger in part for intruding on states' prerogatives. In his 2005 confirmation hearing to become chief justice himself, Roberts emphasized the importance of the division between federal and state powers as fundamental to the constitutional scheme.

During his first three terms, Roberts evinced a concern for states' interests in a variety of settings, including criminal procedure, damage suits, and free speech—but the Rehnquist-led federalism revolution was largely put on hold. In one of the few direct tests of federal power versus state sovereignty, the Court ruled 5-4 in 2006 that a bankruptcy trustee could sue a state entity for funds that a debtor improperly transferred before filing bankruptcy. Roberts was among the dissenters.

EARLY DEVELOPMENTS

The Supremacy Clause makes the Constitution, federal laws, and treaties "the supreme Law of the Land" (Art. VI, cl. 2). It also provides that "Judges in every State shall be bound thereby, any Thing in the Constitution or Laws of any State to the Contrary notwithstanding."

Congress acted immediately after ratification of the Constitution to give practical effect to that provision in the Judiciary Act of 1789. Section 25 of the act empowered the Supreme Court to reexamine any "final judgment or decree" by a state's highest court that ruled against the validity of a federal treaty or statute; sustained the validity of a state law challenged as "repugnant" to the Constitution or federal law; or rejected a "title, right, privilege, or exemption" claimed on the basis of the Constitution or federal law.

EARLY COURT CLASHES AND FEDERAL SUPREMACY

The states' first clash with the Supreme Court arose when the justices interpreted the Constitution itself—specifically, Article III's delineation of federal courts' jurisdiction—to permit federal courts to hear a suit by citizens of one state against another state.

Chisholm v. Georgia

Decided: February 18, 1793

Vote: 4 (Jay, Cushing, Wilson, Blair)
1 (Iredell)

***Seriatim* opinions (5):** Jay; Cushing; Blair; Wilson; Iredell

Chisholm v. Georgia (1793) involved a claim by two South Carolinians, acting as executors of a decedent's estate, for money that was owed by persons whose property had been confiscated by Georgia during the Revolutionary War.

Georgia objected so strongly to the Court's decision to hear the suit that it refused even to appear before the Court. In a 4-1 decision, the Court held that the suit fell within Article III's grant of jurisdiction over "controversies . . . between a State and citizens of another State." Writing for the majority, Chief Justice John Jay called federal jurisdiction "wise," "honest," and "useful" because "it leaves not even the most obscure and friendless citizen without means of obtaining justice from a neighboring state." Only Justice James Iredell dissented.

States protested the decision not only for the principle of state sovereignty but also for the feared financial consequences of liability for property confiscated during the war. On January 8, 1795, the House and the Senate approved a constitutional amendment to overturn the ruling; less than a month later, on February 7, the states completed ratification of what became the Eleventh Amendment, denying federal courts power over any suit against a state by citizens of another state or a foreign country.

Only one year later, the Court ruled on a second clash between federal and state power, once again upholding federal courts' jurisdiction—this time successfully. *Ware v. Hylton* (1796) began with a suit by British creditors against Virginia debtors. The 1783 peace treaty with Britain provided that neither the United States nor Britain would raise legal obstacles to recovery of debts due from its citizens to those of the other nation. With huge sums at stake, however, Virginia passed a law providing that debtors could satisfy their obligations to British subjects by making payments to the state.

Sitting as circuit justice, Iredell upheld the Virginia law and discharged the debts. On appeal, however, the Supreme Court ruled 4-0 for the British creditors in its first decision striking down a state law on federal law grounds. The federal treaty "overrules all state laws upon the subject to all intents and purposes," Justice William Cushing wrote. (Iredell did not participate in the appeal.)

The Court sustained federal authority in two more early clashes with Virginia, both after Marshall's 1803 appointment as chief justice. The first ruling involved a dispute over property owned by Lord Fairfax and left after his death in 1781 to his nephew, Denny Martin, a British subject. Virginia law prohibited aliens from inheriting property; Virginia also claimed that it had confiscated the property and granted portions to other owners, including David Hunter. Some of the contested land was eventually purchased by Marshall's brother and perhaps by Marshall himself—resulting in the chief justice's recusal when the case reached the Court.

Hunter had died by the time the Court initially ruled on the case in 1813. Under the name *Fairfax's Devisee v. Hunter's Lessee,* the Court ruled 3-1 that aliens could inherit land in Virginia despite the contrary state law and that Martin therefore had title to the property. In a forceful opinion, Justice Joseph Story ordered Virginia courts to issue an order to that effect. Instead, the state supreme court ruled that the Judiciary Act's section 25—giving the U.S. Supreme Court jurisdiction over the case—was itself unconstitutional.

Martin v. Hunter's Lessee

Decided: March 20, 1816

Vote: 6 (Washington, W. Johnson, Livingston, Todd, Duvall, Story)

0

Opinion of the Court: Story

Concurring opinion: W. Johnson

Did not participate: J. Marshall

Less than three months later, the Supreme Court responded, again forcefully, in a decision called *Martin v. Hunter's Lessee* (1816). Section 25 "is supported by the letter and spirit of the constitution," Story wrote. "The people had a right," he continued, "to make the powers of the state governments, in given cases, subordinate to those of the nation." Without the Supreme Court's power to override state courts, he concluded, "the public mischiefs" that would result "would be truly deplorable."

Five years later, the Court reaffirmed federal supremacy again in ruling on the convictions of two Virginia men for violating a state law against the sale of out-of-state lottery tickets. P. J. Cohen and M. J. Cohen argued that the state law was inconsistent with the federal law that authorized the District of Columbia's lottery and sale of those tickets. Virginia sought to dismiss the Cohens' appeal for lack of jurisdiction. With Marshall participating, the Court again rejected the state's position. Nothing in the Constitution, Marshall wrote in *Cohens v. Virginia* (1821), left state courts "the power of resisting, or defeating, in the form of law, the legitimate measures of the Union." After upholding the Court's jurisdiction, Marshall nevertheless went on to reject the Cohens' appeal and affirm the convictions.

GEORGIA'S BATTLE WITH THE COURT AND BEYOND

Over the next decade, states backed a series of efforts in Congress to repeal or modify section 25. One proposal called for the Senate to serve as the court of appeals for all cases involving states; another would have required a supermajority of justices to agree in any decision involving the validity of a state law. None of the efforts succeeded. But as Marshall's long tenure neared an end, one state—Georgia—openly defied the Court in a succession of disputes over the state's relations with the Cherokee Nation.

Georgia tried to gain control over the Cherokee and the lands they occupied within the state's borders in the 1820s through a series of increasingly stringent laws. Finally, the Cherokee—acting as an independent nation—filed a request with the Supreme Court, under its original jurisdiction, for an order directing Georgia to stop enforcing the laws. Georgia not only refused to appear before the Court, but also executed an Indian convicted of murder under the contested laws—in direct defiance of the Court's decision to review the conviction. The Court ultimately ruled in *Cherokee Nation v. Georgia* (1831) that it had no original jurisdiction to consider the Cherokee suit.

A second challenge quickly arose after two missionaries sympathetic to the Cherokee were convicted under a Georgia law that required white persons living in Indian territory to obtain a state license. Samuel Worcester and Elizur Butler appealed their convictions to the Supreme Court; Georgia again refused to appear for the February 20, 1832, argument. On March 3, the Court ruled in *Worcester v. Georgia* (1832) that federal jurisdiction over the Cherokee was exclusive and the state therefore had no power to pass laws affecting them.

The ruling overturned Worcester's and Butler's convictions, but the Court put off issuing an order that they be released until the 1833 term. The course was dictated by political realities: Georgians were furious with the decision, and President Andrew Jackson was known to side with the state. By the end of 1832, Marshall was pessimistic enough to write to Story that he feared the Constitution would not last.

Opponents of federal power, however, overplayed their hand. Late in 1832, South Carolina, protesting a new tariff and other federal intrusions, approved the Nullification Ordinance, asserting the right to nullify any federal laws it deemed unconstitutional. The ordinance specifically forbade any appeal from state to federal courts in cases involving the ordinance or any federal law. Jackson responded by describing the nullification theory as treason. In Georgia, a new governor bowed to the changed political climate by pardoning Worcester and Butler early in 1833.

States continued to engage in occasional confrontations over federal judicial review in the years leading up to the Civil War. In one protracted dispute, a state judge in Wisconsin ordered the release of an abolitionist newspaper editor, Sherman Booth, who had been sentenced to one month in prison under the federal Fugitive Slave Act of 1850 for helping a runaway slave escape from a deputy federal marshal. In *Ableman v. Booth* (1859), Chief Justice Roger B. Taney spoke for a unanimous Court in rejecting the Wisconsin courts' power to interfere with federal authority. By then, however, southern states were on the road toward secession and a violent confrontation with the national government that was to end—more than 600,000 lives later—with a lasting affirmation of federal supremacy.

Ableman v. Booth

> **Decided:** March 7, 1859
>
> **Vote:** 9 (Taney, McLean, Wayne, Catron, Daniel, Nelson, Grier, Campbell, Clifford)
>
> 0
>
> **Opinion of the Court:** Taney

EDITORIAL
APRIL 11, 1859
WISCONSIN *VS.* THE SUPREME COURT.

Some years ago the Supreme Court of the State of Wisconsin declared the Fugitive Slave Law of 1851 unconstitutional, and discharged from the custody of the United States Marshal, and from that of the jailor to which he had been committed, one Sherman M. Booth, a citizen of Milwaukee, who was in custody first under a commitment by a Commissioner of the United States Circuit Court, to answer a complaint, and afterwards upon a commitment of the District Court of the United States, after indictment, trial and conviction. Mr. Booth was at that time editor of a newspaper called *The Free Democrat,* from which position he has very recently retired, owing to the finding of an indictment against him for the seduction of a girl of fourteen who was an inmate of his family.

constitutionality of the act under which that process issues can, after such return, be inquired into, either upon a writ of *habeas corpus* from a State tribunal, or upon any other State process. The right of possession of persons or property cannot he inquired into by a State Court by any process which transfers the same from the custody of a United States officer. The Supreme Court, moreover, took occasion to declare unanimously, that the Wisconsin tribunal had erred in its judgment as to the act of 1851, and that said act was constitutional in all its parts.

This decision of the Supreme Court of the United States was not very graciously received by the Legislature of Wisconsin. On the 17th of March ult., that body being in session, passed a series of denunciatory resolutions, in which it char-

> Such questions of jurisdiction between the Supreme Court and State tribunals, are in their nature among the most dangerous which are likely to a rise in the practical working of our Government.

In October, 1855, the United States Supreme Court issued a writ of error commanding the Supreme Court of Wisconsin to send up the record of its proceedings in the case, which writ that Court refused to obey. But the United States Attorney-General managed to obtain certified copies of the proceedings, as also of the written opinions pronounced by the Wisconsin Judges, and thus the case was held to be duly brought before the Supreme Court, which rendered its decision therein on the 7th of last month.

It was held, all the Judges on the Bench concurring, that when a person is in the custody of an officer of the United States, a State may indeed issue a writ of *habeas corpus,* and the officer holding in custody the person in question must make return to the writ, so far as to show that he holds him under a precept of the United States Court, but no further; and that thereupon the power of the State Court is at an end. Neither the formality nor the validity of the process, nor the

acterizes the action of the Court as an "assumption of jurisdiction," "an act of undelegated power," and "without authority, void and of no force." The resolutions in question passed the Wisconsin Senate 13 to 12, and the House of Representatives 47 to 37, reported to have been a strict party vote.

Such questions of jurisdiction between the Supreme Court and State tribunals, are in their nature among the most dangerous which are likely to a rise in the practical working of our Government. In the case referred to, indeed, no serious consequences are to be apprehended; but similar disputes have heretofore been the most disturbing forces our political machinery has been subjected to, and what has already occurred may happen again. The remedy must be looked for in mutual forbearance on the part of the General Government from the exercise of odious and doubtful powers, and on that of the several States by acquiescence where no serious injury can result.

· · · · · · · · · · ·

THE STATES AND THE ECONOMY

One aim of the Constitution was to reduce economic rivalries between the states. Toward that end, it gave Congress the power "to regulate Commerce with foreign Nations, and among the several States" (Art. I, sec. 8, cl. 3). It also prohibited the states, except with the consent of Congress, from imposing "Imposts or Duties" on imports or exports except as needed to execute state inspection laws (Art. I, sec. 10, cl. 2).

The Supreme Court has enforced these provisions to further the framers' aim of a unified national economy but has also left the states some discretion to control economic affairs within their borders. In addition to the Commerce Clause, the Court has interpreted other provisions of the Constitution to limit the states' power over economic matters—most significantly, the Contract Clause, which prohibits the states from passing any "Law impairing the Obligation of Contracts" (Art. I, sec. 10, cl. 1).

CONTRACT CLAUSE

The Marshall Court used the Contract Clause as a principal instrument to establish federal control over state actions. Two early cases illustrate its importance.

In *Fletcher v. Peck* (1810), the Court rejected an effort by the Georgia legislature to nullify corruption-tainted land titles granted by a previous legislature. The legislature in 1795 had granted title to some 35 million acres of land west of the Yazoo River—the area that became the states of Alabama and Mississippi—to four land speculation companies. The legislature revoked the titles after learning that the speculators had promised land to some of the legislators. In a unanimous decision, however, the Court ruled that the land grant amounted to an unbreakable contract. "Once rights had vested under that contract," Marshall wrote, "a repeal of the law cannot devest those rights."

In like vein, the Court blocked an effort by New Hampshire to alter the terms of a royal charter granted to Dartmouth College in 1769. Marshall again wrote for the Court in *Dartmouth College v. Woodward* (1819), holding that the charter amounted to a contract that the legislature could not impair. In a concurring opinion, though, Justice Story suggested that a legislature could amend such a charter without violating the Constitution if it reserved the right to do so when the charter was issued.

Two years after Marshall's death, the Court relaxed its approach somewhat. In an opinion by Chief Justice Taney, the Court rejected an effort by the operators of a toll bridge between Boston and Cambridge to use their legislative charter to prevent the Massachusetts legislature from authorizing a second, competing bridge. The state's power to promote safe, cheap transportation "shall not be construed to have surrendered or diminished," Taney wrote in *Charles River Bridge v. Warren Bridge* (1837), "unless it shall appear by plain words that it was intended to be done." Later, the Taney Court ruled in 1847 that a state could use the power of eminent domain to take—subject to compensation—a privately owned bridge from an owner operating under a state grant.

Charles River Bridge v. Warren Bridge

Decided: February 12, 1837

Vote: 4 (Taney, Baldwin, Wayne, Barbour)

3 (McLean, Story, Thompson)

Opinion of the Court: Taney

Concurring opinion: Baldwin

Dissenting opinions (3): McLean; Story; Thompson

The Court eventually recognized additional restrictions of the scope of the Contract Clause. In *Stone v. Mississippi* (1879), the Court held that a charter to operate a lottery did not prevent the state from enacting a subsequent law under its police power to make lotteries illegal. "The legislature cannot bargain away the police power," Chief Justice Morrison R. Waite wrote.

At the depth of the Depression, a closely divided Court cited the economic emergency in upholding a Minnesota mortgage moratorium law that extended the time for homeowners, farmers, and business owners to avoid foreclosure. A state has an inherent power "to safeguard the vital interests of its people," Chief Justice Charles Evans Hughes wrote in *Home Building and Loan Association v. Blaisdell* (1934).

EDITORIAL
JANUARY 10, 1934
"EMERGENCY" LAWS.

Sometimes an insignificant litigant with a trifling case brings about a judicial decision of the most far-reaching importance. As Hooker said of the law, its care extends to "the least" as well as the greatest. John and Rosala Blaisdell, his wife, of Minnesota, could not pay the interest on a mortgage which they had given. It was foreclosed. But an appeal was taken under a State law granting a two-year extension of time on mortgages of that kind. Upheld by the Supreme Court of Minnesota, this statute was challenged in the Supreme Court of the United States, mainly on the ground that it was in violation of the Federal Constitution, which forbids any State to impair the obligations of a contract. By the opinion of a divided court, 5 to 4, it was held that the "emergency" caused by the depression justified the Minnesota legislation. Thus that particular case is settled, and in the principles laid down in the prevailing

Both judges agree that an emergency creates no new power of government. It does, however, warrant an extension of existing powers. The sole question is how their exercise is to be reconciled with constitutional limitations. Judge Sutherland is for the strictest interpretation. If the Constitution declares that a State must not do a certain thing, we must not allow the thing to be done even if it would greatly minister to the public comfort. Chief Justice Hughes, on the other hand, joined as he was by the four so-called "liberals" of the Court, thinks of the Constitution as a living and flexible organism, able to adapt itself to the changing needs of successive generations. If a destructive hurricane warrants a temporary stretching of governmental power, so may an economic crisis. Emphasis is laid on the fact that such legislation as that in Minnesota had a "proper occasion," was directed toward a "legitimate end," laid down

> " If the Constitution declares that a State must not do a certain thing, we must not allow the thing to be done even if it would greatly minister to the public comfort. "

opinion, written by Chief Justice Hughes, it is believed that a clear indication is given what the attitude of the Supreme Court will be when various acts of Congress under the recovery program come up for adjudication. It is not forgotten that the decision of the Court of Appeals of New York upholding the act of the Legislature which virtually fixed prices for milk was based distinctly on the "emergency" doctrine. From that decision an appeal was allowed to the Supreme Court at Washington.

In such sharp divisions of constitutional interpretation as appear in the decision read by Chief Justice Hughes, and the dissent written by Mr. Justice Sutherland, it is hard for the layman to grasp all the fine distinctions that are made.

conditions which "do not appear to be unreasonable," and was "temporary in operation." It is "limited to the exigency which called it forth."

Lawyers will still ask upon what evidence judges depend in order to establish the existence of an "emergency." They will continue to inquire, and we doubt very much if they will get an answer, what provision or fair implication of the Constitution permits a judicial declaration in favor of emergency powers. For most laymen, as doubtless for John and Rosala of Minnesota, it will seem sufficient that the Supreme Court has spoken. For the present, at any rate, the country will be disposed to say: "Roma dixit causa finita est" ["Rome has spoken, the case is closed"].

• • • • • • • • • • • •

The Contract Clause receded in importance after the liberal transformation of the Court that began in 1937. Yet in 1978, the Court struck down, 5–3, a Minnesota law that retroactively imposed pension-funding obligations on employers that terminated a pension plan or closed an office in the state. The law violated the Contract Clause, Justice Potter Stewart wrote in *Allied Structural Steel Co. v. Spannaus,* "by super-imposing retroactive obligations upon the company substantially beyond the terms of its employment contracts."

COMMERCE CLAUSE

The Marshall Court also established federal primacy in economic matters by ruling that the Commerce Clause prevents states from regulating matters that the federal government has regulated—or that it could regulate. The Taney Court allowed states to exercise concurrent authority if their actions did not conflict with federal regulation, but the principle of federal supremacy in any case of conflicting regulations has held fast. In addition, the so-called dormant Commerce Clause prohibits states from adopting economic regulations that would have the effect of impeding interstate commerce even if there is no actual conflict with federal law.

THE MARSHALL COURT TO THE CIVIL WAR

Marshall's opinion in *Gibbons v. Ogden* (1824), striking down New York's decision to give a monopoly to a steamboat company, broadly construed Congress's power over interstate commerce and then required states to yield to it. "Commerce among the states cannot stop at the external boundary line of each state, but may be introduced into the interior," he wrote.

Five years later, however, Marshall recognized that states retained some power over navigation within their borders as long as Congress had not acted to regulate it. The ruling in *Wilson v. Blackbird Creek Marsh Co.* (1829) rejected an effort by the owners of a federally licensed sloop to avoid paying damages for ramming a privately owned dam; they claimed the dam was an unauthorized obstruction of interstate commerce.

The Taney Court gave the states more room to regulate. In *Mayor of New York v. Miln* (1837), the Court ruled that a state law requiring reports to be filed on all passengers arriving on ships in New York City's port did not intrude on federal authority. Fifteen years later, the Court similarly upheld a Pennsylvania law requiring ships entering the port of Philadelphia to take on a pilot to enter it or to pay a certain fee. The ruling in *Cooley v. Board of Wardens of the Port of Philadelphia* (1852) recognized that Congress had exclusive authority over "subjects . . . in their nature national," but concluded that states could regulate local matters—including "the local necessities of navigation."

THE RISE OF A NATIONAL ECONOMY

In the decades after the Civil War, the Court expanded federal jurisdiction in some instances and state jurisdiction in others—with a common effect of protecting the economic interests of major businesses and industries. The Court in 1876 struck down several state laws that impeded employers' access to cheap labor by requiring owners of ships bringing immigrants into their ports to give a bond for each alien. "This whole subject has been confided to Congress by the Constitution," Justice Samuel F. Miller wrote in *Henderson v. Wickham* (1876).

Gibbons v. Ogden

Decided: March 2, 1824

Vote: 6 (J. Marshall, Washington, W. Johnson, Todd, Duvall, Story)

0

Opinion of the Court: J. Marshall

Concurring opinion: W. Johnson

Did not participate: Thompson

Cooley v. Board of Wardens of the Port of Philadelphia

Decided: March 2, 1852

Vote: 6 (Taney, Catron, Daniel, Nelson, Grier, Curtis)

2 (McLean, Wayne)

Opinion of the Court: Curtis

Concurring in judgment: Daniel

Dissenting opinion: McLean

Did not participate: McKinley

A decade later, Miller wrote for the Court in ruling that states could not regulate railroad rates if the railroad was part of a national network. "This species of regulation is one which must be, if established at all, of a general and national character," Miller wrote in *Wabash, St. Louis & Pacific Railway Co. v. Illinois* (1886).

OCTOBER 26, 1886
AN INTER-STATE COMMERCE CASE—MOTIONS AND ARGUMENTS.

WASHINGTON, Oct. 25.—The Supreme Court rendered its decision to-day in the case of the Wabash, St. Louis and Pacific Railroad Company, plaintiffs in error, vs. the People of the State of Illinois. The specific allegation was that the railroad company charged Elder and McKinney 15 cents per 100 pounds for transporting goods from Peoria to New-York City and on the same day charged Isaac Bailey and F. O. Swannell 25 cents per 100 pounds for the same class of goods from Gilman, Ill., to New-York, Gilman being 86 miles nearer than Peoria to New-York. The discrimination, it was alleged, was in violation of the law of Illinois, which prohibits any charge for the transportation of passengers or freight within the State of Illinois proportionately greater than would be charged for the transportation of passengers or like classes of freight "over a greater distance of the same road." The gist of the decision is contained in the conclusion, as follows: "When it is attempted to apply to transportation through an entire series of States a principle of this kind, and each one of the States or of half dozen States shall attempt to establish its own rates of transportation, its own methods to prevent discrimination in rates, or to permit it, the deleterious influence upon the freedom of commerce among the States and upon the transportation of goods through those States cannot be overestimated. That this species of regulation is one which must be,

if established at all, of a general and national character, and cannot be safely and wisely remitted to local rules and local regulations, we think is clear from what has already been said. And if it be a regulation of commerce, as we think we have demonstrated it is, and as the Illinois court concedes it to be, it must be of that national character, and the regulation can only appropriately be by general rules and principles which demand that it should be done by the Congress of the United States under the commerce clause of the Constitution." The judgment of the Supreme Court of Illinois, which was adverse to the railroad, is reversed and the case is remanded to that court for further proceedings in conformity with the above opinion.

OPINION BY JUSTICE MILLER.

Justice Bradley delivered a dissenting opinion in which the Chief-Justice and Justice Gray concurred. In this opinion it is conceded that Congress might, if it saw fit, regulate the matter under consideration, but not having done so, it is held that the State does not lose its power to regulate the charges of its own railroads in its own territory simply because the goods or persons transported have been brought from or are destined to a point beyond the State borders. . . .

• • • • • • • • • • • •

By contrast, the Court from the late 1880s until the New Deal era narrowed federal jurisdiction by narrowly defining "commerce" so as to exclude "manufacturing," which it held to be exclusively within state jurisdiction. "Commerce succeeds to manufacture, and is not a part of it," the Court wrote in its decision in *United States v. E. C. Knight Co.* (1895), blocking the government's attempt to use the Sherman Antitrust Act of 1890 to break up a sugar monopoly. State control of manufacture, Chief Justice Melville W. Fuller explained, was "essential to the preservation of the autonomy of the states as required by our dual form of government."

In later decisions, however, the Court invoked freedom of contract to block the states from enacting some economic regulations themselves. Thus, the Court struck down a maximum hours law for bakery workers in *Lochner v. New York* (1905) and a state minimum wage law three decades after that in *Morehead v. New York ex rel. Tipaldo* (1936).

Lochner v. New York

Decided: April 17, 1905

Vote: 5 (Fuller, Brewer, Brown, Peckham, McKenna)

4 (Harlan I, E. White, Holmes, Day)

Opinion of the Court: Peckham

Dissenting opinions (2): Harlan I (E. White, Day); Holmes

EDITORIAL
APRIL 19, 1905
"FUSSY LEGISLATION."

After all, and much as some of us in our haste may be tempted to deny it, the Supreme Court of the United States has its uses. It is true that it would be more useful if it were more apt to be unanimous. A large part of the population of these United States is still, when it stops to think about it, dissatisfied with a famous judgment that was rendered by "eight to seven." And it is by no means satisfactory to find so many judgments of our highest tribunal rendered by five to four, leaving it open to any disappointed suitor to maintain that the moral and intellectual weight of the judgment does not coincide with the

presumably procured the passage of the same, relied to nullify its liability for the damage it might do in the raising of its tracks in the upper part of this island, to the easements of light and air which at common law formed part of the property of the neighboring owners in their holdings. This decision was not only in contempt of the statute in question. It was equally in contempt and reversal of a decision of some years' standing of the Court of Appeals of the State of New York that the English doctrine of "ancient lights" had no application to the growing cities and villages of this country.

> The ridiculousness of this legislative prohibition is likely to blind many to the outrageousness of it. It is, in fact, as scandalous an interference as can be conceived with constitutional freedom.

numerical showing. All the same, the Supreme Court does a needful service when it reminds us that this is a Government of law, and that, while the law must evidently, under our Government, in the long run coincide with the verdict of the people of, for, and by whom this Government is, yet little local and temporary gusts of fancy or prejudice are not to be mistaken for the deliberate judgment of the American people. In order to reach and affect the Supreme Court, that body must have evidence of a kind satisfactory to itself and according to its rules that the mind of the American people is made up on the question under consideration.

Last week the court upset a statute of the State of New York upon which the New York Central Railroad, which

This week we have from the same quarter an equally impressive admonition to the Legislature of New York. This time the admonition is that that Legislature must not, at the demand of "labor leaders" or upon any other instigation, presume to interfere with freedom of contract, including specifically the freedom of a journeyman baker to make a contract to work more than ten hours a day, if such an agreement suits both himself and his employer. If organized capital offers the most serious threat against our institutions, the most impudent threats are without question those offered by organized labor. Its impudence may be more apparent than intentional, and may proceed from its ignorance. In the present instance, this ignorance was partaken by the Legislature of the State of New York, as the Supreme Court decides. Or, if not that, legislators affected the ignorance which with the labor leaders was genuine, in order to cater to the demands of those leaders for legislation. It is most gratifying to observe that the Supreme Court does not allow of the sanctity of any contracts which may have been made between the demagogues in the Legislature and the ignoramuses among the labor leaders in bringing to naught their combined machinations.

The crucial example at present of what has been called "fussy legislation" has been furnished by the Legislature of Indiana, in its furtherance of the "crusade" against cigarette smoking. The ridiculousness of this legislative prohibition is likely to blind many to the outrageousness of it. It is, in fact, as scandalous an interference as can be conceived with constitutional freedom. It is to be expected that that view of it will be taken in Indiana, and that a test case will be made and a popular protest entered. Any Indianian, who understood the importance and the magnitude of the question involved may be expected to join in the protest, even to the extent of marching in a procession of defiant lawbreakers smoking cigarettes, even though he personally detests the practice of smoking cigarettes, and even though his own cigarette, which he publicly smokes in token of protest, should make him extremely ill.

. . . .

THE NEW DEAL ERA AND BEYOND

The post–New Deal Court expanded both state and federal authority over economic matters by scrapping the freedom of contract doctrine and discarding the distinction between commerce and manufacturing. In the seventy years since then, states have been relatively free to regulate economic matters unless the state regulation improperly discriminates against businesses in other states or federal laws "pre-empt" the state regulation either explicitly or by implication.

The Court has enforced the prohibition against discriminating against out-of-state businesses—sometimes called the negative or dormant Commerce Clause—in areas ranging from milk and liquor to garbage. As early as 1935, the Court barred New York from setting a minimum price for milk—effectively, raising the price for milk from neighboring Vermont. "Neither the power to tax nor the police power may be used by the state of destination with the aim and effect of establishing an economic barrier against competition with the products of another state or the labor of its residents," Justice Benjamin N. Cardozo wrote in *Baldwin v. G.A.F. Seelig, Inc.* (1935).

Five decades later, the Court similarly struck down a Hawaii law that imposed a 20 percent excise tax on liquor but exempted domestically produced fruit wines (*Bacchus Imports, Ltd. v. Dias*, 1984). More recently, the Court invalidated laws in several wine-producing states—Michigan, New York, and Virginia—that either banned or established special requirements for direct shipments to customers by out-of-state wineries (*Granholm v. Heald*, 2005).

MAY 17, 2005
SUPREME COURT LIFTS BAN ON WINE SHIPPING
By LINDA GREENHOUSE

WASHINGTON, May 16—States must permit in-state and out-of-state wineries to play by the same rules when it comes to shipping their product directly to consumers, the Supreme Court ruled on Monday in a decision that is likely to shift the battleground of the wine wars from the courts back to the state legislatures.

By a 5-to-4 vote, the court overturned state liquor laws in New York and Michigan that gave preferential treatment to in-state wineries. Both states permit in-state wineries to ship directly to consumers, bypassing both retailers and wholesalers.

Michigan prohibited direct shipment by out-of-state wineries while New York nominally permitted it for out-of-state wineries that maintain a New York office, a requirement that no out-of-state winery has met and that the majority on Monday found so financially burdensome for small wineries as to amount to a prohibition.

In his majority opinion, Justice Anthony M. Kennedy said both states were engaging in the kind of protectionism that the Commerce Clause of the Constitution forbids and that the 21st Amendment does not excuse. The 21st Amendment repealed Prohibition and granted the states much leeway in regulating alcohol. But "state regulation of alcohol is limited by the nondiscrimination principle of the Commerce Clause," Justice Kennedy said.

It was this last part of the analysis that prompted four justices to dissent. Justice John Paul Stevens said that while the two states' laws "would be patently invalid" under ordinary Commerce Clause principles, "our Constitution has placed commerce in alcoholic beverages in a special category" and exempted it from those principles.

Justice Clarence Thomas, who wrote a dissenting opinion that was also signed by Justice Stevens, Justice Sandra Day O'Connor and Chief Justice William H. Rehnquist, said that "in holding that the Constitution prohibits Michigan's and New York's laws, the majority turns the amendment's text on its head."

Justice Thomas said that while the majority evidently "believes that its decision serves this nation well," both the 21st Amendment and a pre-Prohibition statute, the Webb-Kenyon Act, which served as a model for the 21st Amendment, "took those policy choices away from judges and returned them to the states."

Now that the Supreme Court has spoken, the issue does return to the states, though in a circumscribed form. The court's insistence on equal treatment leaves states free to decide how to respond: to permit direct shipment by all wineries or to prohibit it for all. The court's decision, Granholm v. Heald, No. 03-1116, did not address this remedial issue.

Hours after the ruling, the head of Michigan's Liquor Control Commission, Nida Samona, said at a telephone news conference that she would urge the state's Legislature to prohibit all direct sales. Ms. Samona said she viewed such a measure as the best way to police sales to minors.

By contrast, Gov. George E. Pataki, while also mentioning a concern about minors' access to wine, indicated his support for changing New York's law to open the state to direct shipment for all wineries. Speaking at a morning news conference, Mr. Pataki called the ruling "a plus for the wineries of New York," adding that "it's something I've thought is the right policy for some time."

In addition to New York and Michigan, six other states permit direct shipment by in-state wineries while restricting it for others. They are Connecticut, Massachusetts, Florida, Ohio, Indiana and Vermont. Thirteen others are known as reciprocity states, which permit direct sales only from wineries in states that in turn permit out-of-state direct shipments.

Under the court's analysis, which lamented "the current patchwork of laws" that Justice Kennedy said was "essentially the product of an ongoing, low-level trade war," those laws are also now invalid. The reciprocity states are California, Colorado, Hawaii, Idaho, Illinois, Idaho, Minnesota, Missouri, New Mexico, Oregon, Washington, Wisconsin and West Virginia.

An additional 15 states currently prohibit all direct-to-consumer wine shipments. They are Alabama, Arkansas, Delaware, Kansas, Kentucky, Maine, Maryland, Mississippi, Montana, New Jersey, Oklahoma, Pennsylvania, South Dakota, Tennessee and Utah.

New York was vigorous in its defense of the law, which was upheld by the federal appeals court in Manhattan in a lawsuit brought by small wineries in Virginia and California along with three New York wine drinkers. The Michigan law, challenged by a California winery and 13 Michigan residents, was overturned by the United States Court of Appeals for the Sixth Circuit, in Cincinnati.

An effort to repeal the New York law, which dates to 1970, failed in 1995 because of a veto by Governor Pataki. On Monday, he said he would support a direct-sale bill that had sufficient safeguards against purchases by minors.

In addition to their 21st Amendment arguments, New York and Michigan defended their laws as necessary to guard against sales to minors as well as tax evasion. The majority rebuffed these arguments, concluding that the states "provide little concrete evidence for the sweeping assertion that they cannot police direct shipments by out-of-state wineries." In any event, Justice Kennedy said, the states' concerns could not justify discrimination.

"Minors are just as likely to order wine from in-state producers as from out-of-state ones," he said.

The majority opinion was joined by Justices Antonin Scalia, David H. Souter, Ruth Bader Ginsburg and Stephen G. Breyer, making for one of the more unusual alignments on the current court. Also unusual was the fact that with the three senior justices—the chief justice and Justices Stevens and O'Connor—in dissent, Justice Scalia was the senior justice in the majority and therefore in the position to give the opinion-writing assignment to Justice Kennedy.

The big loser in the case was the wholesale liquor industry, which is now likely to expend considerable resources to preserve its niche in a market in which direct sales have been growing rapidly.

Direct sales to consumers account for [about $350 million] in annual sales from the more than 3,200 wineries in this country.

• • • • • • • • • • • •

Among several rulings on garbage, *Philadelphia v. New Jersey* (1978) struck down a New Jersey law forbidding the importation of solid or liquid waste originated or collected from another state. The Commerce Clause protects the states "from efforts by one State to isolate itself in the stream of interstate commerce from a problem shared by all," Justice Potter Stewart wrote. In 1994 the Court in *C. A. Carbone Inc. v. Town of Clarkstown* also struck down a local ordinance requiring that all locally generated trash be processed locally, saying it discriminated against out-of-state processors. In 2007, however, the Court upheld a similar ordinance requiring local trash to be processed by a municipally owned facility, in *United Haulers Association, Inc. v. Oneida-Herkimer Solid Waste Management Authority*.

Federal preemption cases reflect no simple or consistent pattern; they turn on the specifics of federal and state laws and regulatory schemes. In an often-cited decision, *Rice v. Santa Fe Elevator Corp.* (1947), the Court described three conditions for finding state laws preempted. First, a federal regulatory scheme could be "so pervasive" that Congress appeared to leave no room for the states to supplement it. Second, the federal scheme could be "so dominant" that it precluded enforcement of state laws. Third, the state policy could produce "a result inconsistent" with the federal objective.

Applying that three-part test, the Court in 1963 allowed California to enact stricter standards for avocados than required under federal law, but in 1977 struck down a California law for labeling package weight of flour that differed from the federal regulation. In more recent decisions, the Court in 2000 struck down Washington State regulations governing oil tankers, but two years later allowed local governments to go beyond federal regulation of tow truck operators.

The Court has struggled to find a consistent approach on preemption issues under the federal law regulating employer-provided pensions and benefits: the Employee Retirement Income Security Act (ERISA) of 1974, which includes a broadly worded provision that it "shall supersede any and all" state laws relating to employee benefit plans. Citing that provision, the Court in 1992 ruled that states cannot require employers to provide disabled former employees the same health insurance offered to current workers. The Court ruled in 2002, however, that ERISA does not prevent states from requiring health maintenance organizations (HMOs) to reimburse covered employees for a second opinion on a requested medical procedure.

The Court has ruled that federal laws can limit state courts from awarding damages in product liability cases. In one major case, *Cipollone v. Liggett Group, Inc.* (1992), the Court ruled that the federal Cigarette Labeling and Advertising Act prohibited smokers and their families from filing state court suits against tobacco companies for failing to warn consumers of the health hazards of smoking. The fractured decision did, however, permit smokers to file suits in state courts based on claims that tobacco companies had deliberately concealed evidence of the health risks or fraudulently denied the dangers of smoking.

Cipollone v. Liggett Group, Inc.

Decided: June 24, 1992

Vote: 7 (Rehnquist, B. White, Blackmun, Stevens, O'Connor, Kennedy, Souter)

2 (Scalia, Thomas)

Opinion of the Court: Stevens

Concurring in judgment: Blackmun (Kennedy, Souter)

Dissenting opinion: Scalia (Thomas)

JUNE 25, 1992
COURT OPENS WAY FOR DAMAGE SUITS OVER CIGARETTES

By LINDA GREENHOUSE

The Supreme Court today opened the door wide to damage suits by smokers against the cigarette industry in a surprisingly broad decision rejecting many of the industry's arguments that such lawsuits were barred by Federal law.

The decision, in its most significant aspects, overturned rulings by a Federal appeals court in a case brought against three cigarette manufacturers by the family of Rose Cipollone, a Little Ferry, N.J., woman who died of lung cancer in 1984 after smoking for 42 years. The vote in most parts of the decision was 7 to 2.

The appeals court, the United States Court of Appeals for the Third Circuit, in Philadelphia, had ruled that smokers could not sue cigarette companies for injuries that stemmed from their smoking after Jan. 1, 1966. On that day, the first Federal law requiring warning labels on cigarette packages and advertising took effect. The appeals court found that the law, as well as a tougher law that Congress passed in 1969, served to pre-empt suits for damages "relating to smoking and health" that challenged the way cigarettes were advertised or promoted.

SORTING OUT TWO LAWS

In its decision today, the Court ruled that the first law, the Federal Cigarette Labeling and Advertising Act, did not pre-empt damage suits at all, because it did nothing more than bar states from setting their own requirements for the contents of cigarette labels.

The 1969 law, the Public Health Cigarette Smoking Act, was more broadly worded and did have some pre-emptive effects, the Court said today in an opinion by Justice John Paul Stevens.

But while the opinion did foreclose some legal claims by individual smokers, principally claims based on the theory that cigarette makers had a legal duty to go beyond the warning-label requirements and to issue more urgent warnings about the dangers of their products, the Court found no bar against suits based on legal theories that could prove particularly damaging to the industry.

Among the lawsuits that will now be permitted are those based on a theory that by concealing facts about smoking and health, or by actually lying about damaging information in their possession, the manufacturers breached a legal duty not to deceive. Also permitted will be lawsuits alleging a conspiracy among cigarette manufacturers to misrepresent or conceal the truth about smoking and health.

Justice Stevens said that in the 1969 law "Congress offered no sign that it wished to insulate cigarette manufacturers from longstanding rules governing fraud."

The decision apparently sent mixed signals to Wall Street, which had been watching the case with intense interest. Most tobacco stocks were off slightly for the day, although Philip Morris Companies closed up 5/8, at $73.75.

Industry spokesmen sought to minimize the scope of the decision, asserting it would neither lead to more lawsuits nor help plaintiffs win. Philip Morris called the decision "a significant victory" because "the court held that smokers can't sue cigarette companies claiming that after 1969 they weren't adequately warned of the risks of smoking."

Charles Wall, vice president and associate general counsel of Philip Morris, said the ruling that lawsuits could be brought charging the tobacco industry with fraudulently concealing the medical dangers of smoking was not a threat.

"The company did not engage in that kind of activity," Mr. Wall said. "I am not concerned about it."

But Matthew Myers, counsel for the American Heart Association and other health organizations, called that aspect of the ruling "the potential Achilles heel" of the tobacco industry. The industry was vulnerable, he said, if it had information on the negative effects of smoking and if the companies intentionally misled the public about that information, as plaintiffs have charged in some recent cases.

SEEING A 'MAJOR VICTORY'

Alan Morrison, litigation director for the Public Citizen group in Washington, said the ruling was "a major victory for the antismoking forces" in permitting suits to be brought for concealing medical information, the legal theory most likely to win a sympathetic hearing for jurors.

Most of the previous suits had been brought under the theory the court barred today: that cigarette companies should have provided more extensive warnings than required by the Federal law. Juries were largely unpersuaded by these "failure to warn" cases anyway. In the more than 300 cases filed since 1954, a plaintiff has yet to collect a cent from suing a tobacco company for health problems.

The Cipollone family's lawsuit, against the Liggett Group Inc., Philip Morris Companies Inc. and the Loews Corporation, the parent company of Lorillard, can now be revived in a new trial. In its 1990 ruling, the Third Circuit had also set aside a $400,000 judgment that the family won based on Mrs. Cipollone's smoking before 1966, ordering a new trial on that part of the case. The pre-1966 liability issue was not before the Supreme Court today.

The lawyer representing the Cipollone family, Marc Z. Edell, told The Associated Press today that at the new trial he would introduce evidence demonstrating that the cigarette companies conspired to mislead the public and falsely advertised.

Laurence H. Tribe, a Harvard law professor who argued the family's appeal in the Supreme Court in January, said today that he expected that the new trial would be successful. He said the majority today had analyzed the pre-emption question in a way that created a favorable climate for plaintiffs, not only in smoking cases but also in suits for damages from other products for which the Federal Government requires warning labels, like some kinds of food and alcohol products as well as items like children's pajamas.

THREE FACTIONS ON COURT

Pre-emption is a complex legal area, and the Court's rulings, even within the current term, have not been particularly consistent. The fact that there was no single majority opinion for the most important aspects of the ruling today underscored the degree to which the Court is divided on the issue.

Justice Stevens wrote for a plurality of four Justices that also included Chief Justice William H. Rehnquist and Justices Byron R. White and Sandra Day O'Connor. This group controlled the outcome of the case by occupying the middle ground between two other groups of Justices. On one side, Justices Antonin Scalia and Clarence Thomas viewed the two Federal laws as pre-empting all aspects of the smokers' lawsuits. On the other side, Justices Harry A. Blackmun, Anthony M. Kennedy and David H. Souter found none of the claims to be pre-empted.

Consequently, when the Stevens four found that a particular claim was not pre-empted, there were seven votes

to support that conclusion. When they found that a claim was barred, there were six votes for that holding.

Three of the nine Justices smoke. Chief Justice Rehnquist smokes cigarettes, Justice Scalia smokes cigarettes and a pipe, and Justice Thomas favors cigars.

The case, Cipollone v. Liggett Group Inc., No. 90-1038, was initially argued last October, before Justice Clarence Thomas joined the Court. After he took his seat, the Court ordered reargument in the case, giving rise to speculation that the Court was deadlocked 4 to 4, with the new Justice holding the balance. That was evidently not the case.

Federal courts have uniformly found pre-emption in smokers' lawsuits, but the cigarette industry was beginning to lose on the question in state courts. Despite having won before the Third Circuit, the industry urged the Supreme Court to hear the Cipollone appeal to resolve the matter.

Some of the claims the Court decided to permit today are among the most worrisome to the industry. For example, earlier this year, a Federal district judge in New Jersey, H. Lee Sarokin, issued a pretrial ruling ordering the industry to release a number of internal documents to the plaintiff in another case, a suit on behalf of a smoker who died in 1982.

In his ruling, Judge Sarokin said that his review of the documents indicated to him that "the tobacco industry may be the king of concealment and disinformation" and that the documents contained evidence of fraud. The industry said the judge had drawn unsupported inferences from the documents.

The legal question for the Court was the meaning of a pre-emption provision that Congress wrote into the 1969 law. The provision said that "no requirement or prohibition based on smoking and health shall be imposed under state law with respect to the advertising or promotion of any cigarettes the packages of which are labeled in conformity with the provisions of this act."

WHEN PRE-EMPTION APPLIES

The question was whether a lawsuit alleging that a cigarette manufacturer had breached a legal duty under state law was in effect an effort to subject the manufacturer to a "requirement or prohibition" of the sort that the 1969 law did not allow.

In his plurality opinion, Justice Stevens said that there was no one answer to this question, and that each claim in the Cipollone lawsuit had to be examined separately to see if it sought to impose a "requirement or prohibition based on smoking and health."

The Court then found pre-emption for allegations that the industry had failed to include more warnings than required by Federal law in its advertisements, as well as for allegations that depictions of vigorous and attractive men and women in cigarette advertisements were a deceptive effort to "neutralize" the required warning labels. Both of these legal theories related directly to smoking and health, the subject of the Federal law, the Court said.

But Justice Stevens said that the other legal theories were based on general principles of state law, like the "duty not to conspire to commit fraud," and consequently could not be seen as state efforts to impose on the cigarette companies any special prohibitions based on smoking and health.

● ● ● ● ● ● ● ● ● ● ● ●

In other liability rulings, the Court in 2000 barred suits against automakers for failing to install air bags before they were required to do so by federal regulation or against railroads for failing to install warning guards not required by federal law. But two years later, the Court did allow a suit against a recreational boat manufacturer for failing to install propeller guards not required by the Federal Boat Safety Act.

In its first major ruling in the area, the Roberts Court disappointed plaintiffs' and consumer groups by ruling that federal law preempts personal injury suits in state courts against the makers of medical devices if the devices are approved by the Food and Drug Administration. The 8-1 decision in *Riegel v. Medtronic, Inc.* (2008) barred a suit by a New York woman for injuries suffered by her late husband after the rupture of a balloon catheter inserted into his coronary artery during an operation in 1996.

STATES AND THE INDIVIDUAL

The original Constitution included only two provisions specifically protecting individual liberties against the state governments, and the Bill of Rights was long held inapplicable to the states. The Fourteenth Amendment's Due Process and Equal Protection Clauses did specifically apply to the states, but the Supreme Court was slow to enforce them meaningfully. In the twentieth century, however, the Court's decisions enforcing the Bill of Rights and the Fourteenth Amendment brought about a series of revolutions requiring states to honor individual rights in regard to free speech, racial justice, criminal law, and personal liberties.

The Constitution prohibits either the federal government or a state from enacting a bill of attainder—punishment without trial—or an ex post facto or retroactive law. In an early case, *Calder v. Bull* (1792), the Court ruled that the Ex Post Facto Clause only prohibited laws that retroactively criminalized previously legal behavior and did not apply to civil cases or cases involving property. In criminal law, the Court has ruled that the clause does not prevent retroactive changes in trial procedure or rules of evidence. In *Stogner v. California* (2003), however, the Court applied the Ex Post Facto Clause to overturn a California law that retroactively changed the statute of limitations for child molestation cases from three years to ten.

The Bill of Attainder Clause was first broadly applied after the Civil War in rulings on laws enacted by the federal government and many states requiring persons who wanted to engage in specific occupations or activities to take "test oaths" to ensure their loyalty to the Union. In *Cummings v. Missouri* (1867), the Court overturned the conviction of a Catholic priest and former Confederate supporter, John Cummings, for practicing as a clergyman after refusing to take a required test oath. The law operated as a bill of attainder, the Court said, because it assumed Cummings's guilt from his refusal to take the oath. In a separate case, the Court also held the federal test oath invalid. In the twentieth century, however, the Court ruled that states could require some public employees to take narrowly drawn loyalty oaths.

THE BILL OF RIGHTS AND THE POST–CIVIL WAR AMENDMENTS

Barron v. Baltimore

    Decided: February 16, 1833

    Vote: 7 (J. Marshall, W. Johnson, Duvall, Story, Thompson, McLean, Baldwin)

         0

    Opinion of the Court: J. Marshall

Before the Civil War, the Court ruled that the Bill of Rights' more detailed safeguards were not binding on the states. The decision in *Barron v. Baltimore* (1833) rejected a Baltimore wharf owner's claim for compensation under the Fifth Amendment's Takings Clause; John Barron said his wharf became unusable after the city dumped debris and gravel into the Baltimore harbor. "The amendments contain no expression indicating an intention to apply them to the state governments," Chief Justice Marshall wrote.

The post–Civil War Fourteenth Amendment set out three specific prohibitions for the states. No state could make a law abridging the "privileges or immunities of citizens of the United States." No state could "deprive any person of life, liberty, or property, without due process of law." And no state could "deny to any person within its jurisdiction the equal protection of the laws."

EDITORIAL
JULY 31, 1865
THE FOURTEENTH AMENDMENT.

The Secretary of State has promulgated the ratification of the Fourteenth Amendment. This official act sets at rest all questions hitherto raised upon the legitimacy or otherwise of the ratification. That is a great point gained. But what is settled by the Fourteenth Amendment? That is the important question.

I. No State can abridge the privileges or immunities of citizens of the United States, *i.e.,* of "persons born or naturalized in the United States, and subject to the jurisdiction thereof." The equal protection of the laws is guaranteed to all, without any exception.

II. The basis of representation is altered. If the negroes of the South are excluded from the franchise, then the Southern States lose the representation based upon the number of colored population.

III. No person who has violated his oath to support the Constitution of the United States can become a Senator or Representative, or a Presidential Elector, or hold any civil or military office under either the State or the Federal Government. But this disability can be annulled by a two-thirds vote of each House of Congress.

IV. The validity of the public debt—including debts incurred for the payment of soldiers' pensions and bounties—is placed beyond question. And all obligations incurred in the aid of rebellion are pronounced illegal and void.

That is the accomplished result. And it must be observed, in regard to political disabilities and the invalidity of the rebel debt, that the provisions of the amendment are general—they are not confined in their operation to the special case of the late rebellion.

Thus stands the Constitution to-day. Even the election of [Horatio] Seymour for President cannot alter the matter. The nullification of reconstruction cannot repeal this constitutional amendment.

And what will be the effect of this amendment in its operation in the South? It takes all its strength from the Democratic platform. That platform nullifies reconstruction, but does any clear-headed man for a moment suppose that Mississippi, or Louisiana, or South Carolina would exclude the negroes from the suffrage, when by so doing they would sacrifice nearly one-half of their power in the United States Congress? The ratification of the Fourteenth Amendment furnishes, therefore, the strongest motive to the Southern States to support the reconstruction measures.

EDITORIAL
JULY 17, 1868
THE FOURTEENTH AMENDMENT.

The Fourteenth Amendment to the Constitution of the United States has been ratified and is now a part of the organic law—to which fact we invite the attention of Democrats, who profess so obsequious an observance of "the Constitution and the laws." On the 15th the President transmitted to Congress a letter from Secretary Seward, announcing the ratification of this amendment by the Legislatures of twenty-three Northern States, including Tennessee; and also by Arkansas, Florida and North Carolina. To these twenty-six States must be added Louisiana, South Carolina and Alabama. Here then are twenty-nine States, so that even if we except Ohio and New-Jersey, whose Legislatures have attempted to undo their work, we have the requisite three-fourths of the States, which, according to the Constitution, makes the amendment a part of our Constitution.

This Amendment was supported by every Republican member of both Houses in the Thirty-ninth Congress, and was opposed by every Democratic member. In the twenty-three State Legislatures at the North the same party-line was drawn. The Democratic Legislatures of Delaware, Maryland and Kentucky rejected the Amendment, and this year, the Democrats having a majority in the Ohio and New-Jersey Legislatures, have repealed the act of ratification, notwithstanding the majorities in these States in its favor in 1866. It was opposed by President Johnson, who sent a telegram to Gov. Parsons, advising the Legislature of Alabama against its ratification. The Amendment was rejected by every Southern State except Tennessee, which latter State by its adoption was restored to the Union. If it had been accepted by the South as the basis of restoration, reconstruction would

have been an accomplished fact two years ago; no military governments would have been imposed upon the South, and all sectional jealousies would have been obliterated.

And why should it not have been accepted? It simply proclaimed that all citizens born or naturalized in the United States were citizens of the United States and of the State in which they resided; it prohibited laws abridging the privileges or immunities of citizens, or denying to any citizen the equal protection of the laws; it did not impose negro suffrage, but in case the franchise should not be given to negroes, it reduced representation accordingly; it temporarily disabled from holding office all those who, after taking an oath, "as a member of Congress, or as an officer of the United States, or as a member of any State Legislature, or as an executive or judicial officer of any State," had afterward engaged in rebellion, leaving this disability to be removed by Congress so soon as expediency required; it declared the validity of our public debt, and it repudiated all obligations incurred by rebellion, and all claims for compensation on account of emancipation.

All these conditions of restoration were explicitly demanded by the people, and were sustained by their votes in the elections of 1866. They were rejected only by the Democratic Party and its Southern allies.

But, in spite of opposition, the amendment has triumphed. The Fortieth Congress made its adoption the principal condition of restoration. If Congress appealed to the negro vote to accomplish this, it was driven to that extremity by the Democrats who opposed it, in the first instance, and who now threaten its abrogation.

· · · · · · · · · · · · ·

Like the antislavery Thirteenth Amendment and the equal-suffrage Fifteenth Amendment, the Fourteenth Amendment was evidently aimed at safeguarding the rights of African Americans. But the Court first interpreted the Fourteenth Amendment in a different context when a group of New Orleans butchers challenged—unsuccessfully—a law granting one company the exclusive right to operate a slaughterhouse in the city. By a 5-4 vote, the Court ruled in the *Slaughterhouse Cases* (1873) that the monopoly did not abridge a "privilege" or "immunity" of U.S. citizenship. "The privileges and immunities relied on . . . are those which belong to citizens of the States as such," Justice Samuel F. Miller wrote, "and are left to the state governments for security and protection."

Slaughterhouse Cases
Decided: April 14, 1873
Vote: 5 (Clifford, Miller, Davis, Strong, Hunt)
4 (S. P. Chase, Swayne, Field, Bradley)
Opinion of the Court: Miller
Dissenting opinions (3): Field (S. P. Chase, Swayne, Bradley); Swayne; Bradley

EDITORIAL
APRIL 16, 1873
THE SCOPE OF THE THIRTEENTH AND FOURTEENTH AMENDMENTS.

The Supreme Court has just rendered its first decision defining the scope of the Thirteenth and Fourteenth Amendments to the Federal Constitution. The opinion is very important, for several reasons. It is calculated to throw the immense moral force of the Court on the side of rational and careful interpretation of the rights of the States and those of the Union. It is calculated to maintain, and to add to, the respect felt for the Court, as being at once scrupulous in its regard for the Constitution, and unambitious of extending its own jurisdiction. It is also a severe and, we might almost hope, a fatal blow to that school of constitutional lawyers who have been engaged, ever since the adoption of the Fourteenth Amendment, in inventing impossible consequences for that addition to the Constitution.

intention of the people in adopting them. The Court reviews this history, to show that the general purpose of the amendments was to protect the rights of the freedmen. To this end slavery was abolished by the Thirteenth Amendment. The servitude so done away with was personal servitude. It was of the kind that would include penal servitude, if that had not been distinctly excluded. It was not and could not be that subordination in matters of business and profit which it is not in the province of the National Constitution to regulate, and which the people did not intend to bring within the jurisdiction of the National Government. Similarly as to the provisions defining citizenship of the United States and of the several States, and securing the privileges and immunities of the

> " In short, the Fourteenth Amendment was not a piece of abstract declaration, meant to establish a general definition of rights for Congress to legislate for, and the Supreme Court to adjudicate on. "

The decision referred to was in the case of certain New-Orleans butchers against the Crescent City Live Stock Landing and Slaughter-house Company. This company was incorporated three years ago by the Legislature of Louisiana. The act of incorporation gave it the exclusive privilege of erecting slaughter-houses and landings for live stock in the City of New-Orleans. On the other hand, the act required the company to provide buildings for slaughtering 500 animals each day, and to admit any person to slaughter animals in their slaughter-houses for certain fixed rates. The butchers claim that this act is contrary to the Thirteenth and Fourteenth Amendments of the United States Constitution, in that it creates an involuntary servitude, in that it abridges the privileges and immunities of citizens of the United States, in that it denies to the plaintiffs the equal protection of the laws, and in that it deprives them of their property without due process of law. The Supreme Court decides against the plaintiffs on all these points.

It holds, substantially, that the amendments must be construed by the light thrown by their history on the

former. By the record of the Supreme Court, the negro was denied the right of citizenship of the United States. He was recognized in some States and rejected in others as a citizen of the State in which he might happen to reside. The Fourteenth Amendment made him a citizen of the United States, and forbade any State to abridge his privileges and immunities as such. It also made him a citizen of the State in which he resides, and required that his rights of property and person shall be respected, and that he shall have equal protection of the laws. These provisions are, of course, general. But they were framed for the freedmen, and had not the condition of that great body of our people required it, the amendment never would have been passed. The Court holds, in substance, that this obvious fact in the history of the amendment must be considered in interpreting it; that the "privileges and immunities" it was intended to protect were the fundamental ones belonging to citizens of the United States as such, and not the specific ones, which vary in the several States; and that while it required each State to recognize the rights of the citizens of any other State as the same as those of its own citizens, it did not intend to deprive any State of the power of defining the rights of its own citizens. In short, the Fourteenth Amendment was not a piece of abstract declaration, meant to establish a general definition of rights for Congress to legislate for, and the Supreme Court to adjudicate on. It was a piece of practical legislation, meant to remove certain obvious evils, and to establish certain results which were the logical outgrowth of the war. . . .

· · · · · · · · · · ·

EQUAL PROTECTION AND DUE PROCESS

A decade later, the Court limited the reach of the Equal Protection Clause by holding that it applied only to state action and not to private action. The 8-1 ruling in the *Civil Rights Cases* (1883) struck down the Civil Rights Act of 1875, which prohibited racial discrimination in public accommodations. Upholding the law, Justice Joseph P. Bradley wrote, "would be to make Congress take the place of the state Legislatures, and to supersede them."

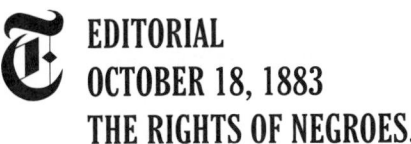

EDITORIAL
OCTOBER 18, 1883
THE RIGHTS OF NEGROES.

It is more than ten years since the late lamented Mr. Sumner conceived the idea that the fourteenth amendment and sundry scattered passages of the Constitution gave to Congress authority to enforce the right of negroes to the same treatment as whites on public conveyances and in inns and places of entertainment. He passed away before he succeeded in convincing or persuading the majority of Republicans in the body of which he was an honored member that his view was correct. But after his death, a bill, the result of the combined efforts of those eminent jurists Senator Howe and Gen. Ben Butler, was passed. While these various measures were under discussion, The Times took occasion frequently to point out that they were each and all impracticable, unwise, and, above all, without authority in the Constitution. As early as December, 1873, we remarked:

> "Law has done all that it can for the negroes, and the sooner they set about securing their future for themselves the better it will be for them and their descendants."

In the following May, pointing out the legal effect of the measure then before Congress as well as the political consequences which must follow its passage, we said:

> "This bill is in fact a distinction against all classes except the negroes and as such it is sure to meet with very general opposition. If it is accepted as a Republican measure the party is sure to suffer from it."

Again, in December, 1874, we called attention to the fact that the granting of the suffrage to the negro had been urged and had been justified by the argument that "with the ballot in his hand the negro would be enabled to defend himself, and that the Federal Government would from that time be less and less called upon to intervene in the affairs of the individual States to protect him in those liberties which it had guaranteed to him." We maintained that this argument had been accepted in good faith, and that the country would not consent that it should be ignored, and that the general Government should attempt to do for the negro by forced construction of the Constitution that which the ballot, properly used, should enable him to do for himself. Of the bill which had then passed under the wing of Gen. Butler we declared:

> "It is clear to us that the Republican Party cannot do better with it than to kill it or to let it die."

The bill was passed. In April, 1875, commenting on a decision of the Supreme Court to the effect that the fourteenth amendment did not confer the right of suffrage upon women, we indicated the error of trying to stretch the amendment to cover much, including "civil rights," which could not be fairly brought under it.

Finally, after eight years, in which the law has been practically a dead letter, the Supreme Court has decided, as it was evident that it must decide, that the act was unconstitutional. But while the law has, in one sense, been inoperative, in another it has been of great influence, and that mischievous. It has kept alive a prejudice against the negroes and against the

> " The judgment of the court is but a final chapter in a history full of wretched blunders, made possible by the sincerest and noblest sentiment of humanity, but in which the cunning and conscienceless schemers of the Butler school have played the larger part. "

"There can be little doubt that the judicial construction of the amendment will be, like the practical and common sense view of it, that it only determines who are citizens, and that all the United States can constitutionally do in securing the privileges and immunities of citizenship is to see that a citizen of Pennsylvania being in New-York enjoys the same rights enjoyed by the citizens of New-York. And this view will leave the civil rights supposed to be secured by the legislation of last Winter exactly where the Supreme Court has left the right of suffrage—with the States; and they ought to be left there."

Republican Party in the South, which without it would have gradually died out. It has furnished demagogues like Butler with the means of misleading the colored race, arousing hostility among the Southern whites, and rendering the Republican Party ridiculous. Unhappily, the decision which kills the law comes too late to remedy the ills which it produced. The principle which it involves is no longer an issue in national politics and can never again be made one. The judgment of the court is but a final chapter in a history full of wretched blunders, made possible by the sincerest and noblest sentiment of humanity, but in which the cunning and conscienceless schemers of the Butler school have played the larger part.

. . . .

The Court breathed some life into the Equal Protection Clause in a decision three years later in favor of Chinese laundrymen who had sued the city of San Francisco for discriminatory enforcement of a newly enacted licensing ordinance. Evidence in *Yick Wo v. Hopkins* (1886) showed that the board of supervisors denied licenses to all 200 Chinese immigrants who applied but granted licenses to all but one of the eighty white applicants. "No reason for it exists except hostility to the race and nationality to which the petitioners belong," the Court wrote. The precedent had little effect until many decades later, however, when it was cited to prevent states and cities from enforcing ostensibly neutral laws in a racially discriminatory manner.

A decade after *Yick Wo,* the Court also applied the Due Process Clause in an unintended context by extending it to economic rights. The majority in *Allgeyer v. Louisiana* (1897) held that due process protected a citizen's right to do business with out-of-state as well as in-state insurance companies. Liberty, Justice Peckham wrote, includes "the right of the citizen . . . to live and work where he will; to earn his livelihood by any lawful calling; to pursue any livelihood or avocation; and for that purpose to enter all contracts which may be proper, necessary, and essential to his carrying out to a successful conclusion the purposes above mentioned."

In the same year, the Court first ruled that the Due Process Clause encompassed one of the provisions of the Bill of Rights: the Fifth Amendment's requirement that "just compensation" be paid when private property is taken for public use. The Chicago, Burlington & Quincy Railroad brought the case to the Court after a jury in Chicago awarded only $1 as compensation for its right-of-way taken by the city in a street widening. "The legislature may prescribe a form of procedure to be observed in the taking of private property for public use, but it is not due process of law if provision be not made for compensation," Justice John Marshall Harlan wrote in *Chicago, Burlington & Quincy R. R. v. Chicago* (1897). Harlan found the compensation adequate, however. One justice dissented, on the ground that the nominal compensation amounted to none at all.

The process of reading Bill of Rights provisions into the Due Process Clause came to be called the "incorporation doctrine." The doctrine was next evident in an almost offhand sentence in *Gitlow v. New York* (1925) that assumed the First Amendment's freedom of speech applied to the states. Other First Amendment provisions were incorporated in the 1930s and 1940s. (See page 180.) The various provisions governing arrests, searches, criminal trials, and punishment in the Fourth, Fifth, Sixth, and Eighth Amendments were made binding on the states beginning in the late 1940s and continuing through the 1960s. (See page 352.)

Meanwhile, the Court had begun to give substance to the Equal Protection Clause with a succession of cases aimed at state laws mandating racial segregation. In the first, *Gaines v. Canada* (1938), the Court ruled that Missouri violated a black resident's rights by offering a graduate education not in the state's own segregated university but in another state's. The obligation to provide an equal education "cannot be cast by one state upon another," Chief Justice Hughes wrote. The landmark ruling in *Brown v. Board of Education* (1954), ordering school integration, produced a strong backlash in several southern states and litigation that continues to the present day. (See page 265.)

The Court has also found that the Equal Protection Clause protects women and aliens from some forms of unequal treatment under state laws. The high court's reapportionment and redistricting rulings stem from findings of inequality in voting rights. But the Court has refused to recognize wealth as a "protected category" for equal protection purposes. Instead, the Court said in *San Antonio School District v. Rodriguez* (1973), educational equity reforms "are matters reserved for the legislative process of the states."

The Right to Privacy

The Court's recognition of a right to privacy also originated in cases striking down state laws. Two rulings in the 1920s invalidated a Nebraska law against teaching modern foreign languages in the schools and an Oregon statute requiring all children to attend public schools. The first extended discussion came in *Griswold v. Connecticut* (1965), in which the Court struck down a law that prohibited married couples from using contraceptives. *Griswold* laid the groundwork for the landmark abortion-rights ruling in *Roe v. Wade* (1973) that invalidated virtually all existing state laws on the subject.

Like the school race issue, abortion continues to be a source of contentious litigation over the constitutionality of state laws. In many areas, the Court has been loosening strictures on the states in the late twentieth and early twenty-first century. *Gonzales v. Carhart* (2007), for example—the Roberts Court's first major abortion ruling—upheld a federal law banning a specific abortion procedure despite a decision only seven years earlier striking down a similar state law. In the same year, however, the Court limited the ability of states or local school boards to adopt racial-balance plans in elementary and secondary education. The ruling in consolidated cases decided under the name *Parents Involved in Community Schools v. Seattle School District No. 1* (2007) found that pupil assignment plans in Seattle and Jefferson County, Kentucky (Louisville), violated white students' rights under the Equal Protection Clause.

STATES AS SOVEREIGNS

The Constitution created a new, potentially powerful national government, but by leaving the states in place as constituent units preserved for them a measure of sovereignty. The Tenth Amendment underscores the states' status by specifying that powers not delegated to the national government nor prohibited to the states are "reserved to the States respectively, or to the people." The Supreme Court's view of the amendment and of the degree of sovereignty retained by the states has swung back and forth over time. Since the 1990s, the pendulum has been swinging toward somewhat greater protections for the states against the powers of the national government.

DUAL FEDERALISM AND THE EARLY COURTS

Despite the states' success in ratifying the Eleventh Amendment to limit federal court jurisdiction to hear private suits against state governments, the Marshall Court went on to fortify the powers of the national government and to limit the ability of the states to interfere with those powers. In *McCulloch v. Maryland* (1819), the Court blocked the state of Maryland from taxing the private, congressionally chartered Bank of the United States. States have no power, Marshall wrote, "to retard, impede, or in any manner control the operations of the constitutional laws enacted by Congress."

The Taney Court was friendlier toward the states. Under Taney, the Court developed the concept of dual federalism, which saw the national government and the state each sovereign within its own sphere and the powers of the national government limited by those reserved to the states. From the end of the Civil War to the New Deal era, the Court went further by relying on Tenth Amendment principles to strike down some federal laws and narrow the scope of others. At the same time, the Court invoked the Due Process Clause in some decisions to limit the states' own powers over economic affairs.

Meanwhile, the Court in one decision had strengthened the states' protection against private suits but weakened the protection somewhat in another ruling that allowed private suits to enjoin state officials from violating federal law. The ruling in *Hans v. Louisiana* (1890) blocked a bondholder from suing his own state in federal court after the state decided to stop payment on the bonds. The Court extended the Eleventh Amendment's prohibition on suits by citizens of another state by invoking the pre-existing principle of sovereign immunity that bars suit against a sovereign without its consent.

In *Ex parte Young* (1908), though, the Court said that principle did not prevent suits against individual state officials. The ruling allowed various railroads to sue Minnesota officials to block enforcement of a rate regulation measure that they claimed was unconstitutionally confiscatory. The suit was not against the state, Justice Peckham explained, but against a state official for "attempting, by the use of the name of the state, to enforce a legislative enactment which is void because unconstitutional."

Ex parte Young

Decided: March 23, 1908

Vote: 8 (Fuller, Brewer, E. White, Peckham, McKenna, Holmes, Day, Moody)

1 (Harlan I)

Opinion of the Court: Peckham

Dissenting opinion: Harlan I

MARCH 24, 1908
FEDERAL LAW UPHELD AGAINST TWO STATES

Supreme Court Deals Blow to Minnesota and North Carolina Railroad Legislation.

JUSTICE HARLAN DISSENTS

Says Opinion Closes the Courts of a State Against Itself and Predicts Pernicious Results.

WASHINGTON, March 23.—The Supreme Court to-day handed down a decision refusing to grant to Attorney General Young of Minnesota a writ of habeas corpus releasing him from the penalty imposed by the United States Circuit Court for the District of Minnesota, on the charge of contempt of court in instituting a proceeding in a State court for the enforcement of the railroad rate law after the Federal court had prohibited such a course. The decision also affirms the decision of Judge Pritchard of the United States Circuit Court for the Western District of North Carolina, discharging from imprisonment James H. Wood, a ticket agent of the Southern Railway at Asheville, after he had been sentenced by the Asheville Police Court to serve a term in the rock pile on the charge of collecting for a ticket on that road a greater price than was permitted by the State railroad law.

In both cases the right of the States to fix rates for railroad transportation was the issue, and both involved conflicts between the Federal and the State courts. The decision in each case was opposed both to the States and to their courts. The opinion of the court in both cases was announced by Justice Peckham, and, with the exception of Justice Harlan, all the other members of the court assented.

Justice Harlan read a dissenting opinion in the Young case, in which he took the view that the suit was practically a proceeding against the State, and therefore not permissible under the Eleventh Amendment to the Constitution. He characterized the opinion as era-making in the history of the court, said it had the effect of closing the courts of a State against the State itself, and predicted that the result would be disastrous.

The two cases were so similar that both practically were decided in one opinion.

COULDN'T QUESTION VALIDITY.

Justice Peckham's opinion was, in part, as follows:

"By reason of the enormous penalties provided in the rate laws, by way of fines against the companies and imprisonment of their agents and employes, the companies were, in effect, prevented from ever questioning the validity of those laws, as the risk of confiscation of property and imprisonment of agents in case the companies failed in their defense was too much to undertake in order to obtain a judicial decision of the question of such validity.

"Such laws are therefore held unconstitutional, as they prevented the companies from resorting to the courts, and therefore deprived them of the equal protection of the laws.

"The laws providing rates for transportation of passengers and freight in the two cases under consideration have been held by the courts below to be so low as to be substantially confiscatory, and should, therefore, not be enforced until after further trials. The courts had jurisdiction to make such an order.

"It has also for many years been held that a suit is not one against the State, although it prevents a State officer from bringing suits for the enforcement of a State enactment, which fixed rates so low as to be confiscatory, and which act was, therefore, a violation of the Constitution of the United States, and this principle is reiterated and again decided in these cases.

"It is no more a suit against the State than is a proceeding which compels an officer of the State to produce a person in his custody charged with a crime against the State before a Federal court or Judge, who thereupon discharges such person on the ground that his imprisonment is in violation of the Federal Constitution.

FEDERAL COURTS' JURISDICTION.

"The jurisdiction of the Federal courts in such cases is only exercised where the State enactment is alleged to be a violation of the Constitution of the United States, and in such case it is proper for those courts to take jurisdiction equally with the State courts, as the Constitution of the United States is by its own provisions the supreme law of the land, anything in any State Constitution or law to the contrary notwithstanding, and there is no usurpation of jurisdiction in such event.

"The same duties rest upon the State courts, and the party had his choice of forum without any invidious distinction against the State courts and in favor of the Federal courts because of his choice of the latter.

"When a Federal court has taken jurisdiction of a case before any proceeding in a State court has been commenced, the former court has authority to decide the case and to enjoin any person from proceeding in a State court until the Federal court has proceeded to judgment. This is also a well-established right of a court of equity, and no new ground is taken in this case."

THE MINNESOTA CASE.

The proceeding in Young's case grew out of an effort by the Minnesota Federal court on May 31 last to restrain Young from executing, or attempting to execute, the rate law. Stockholders of the Northern Pacific Railway Company filed a suit asking for an injunction prohibiting the State officials from carrying the law into effect on the ground that the rate fixed was so low as to make impossible returns to the company on its investment.

The injunction was granted on the ground that the law was confiscatory. Attorney General Young asked the Ramsey County State District Court to direct the issuance of a writ of mandamus commanding the Northern Pacific Company to comply with the rate law. The State court issued the writ, and this brought about a conflict between the Federal and State courts. Mr. Young was summoned before the former, and, failing to make a satisfactory explanation, he was subjected to a fine of $100 for contempt.

Refusing either to pay the fine or to dismiss the case, Mr. Young brought the case to the Supreme Court on a petition for a writ of habeas corpus.

The North Carolina case, that of Sheriff Hunter of Buncombe County against Agent Wood of the Southern Railway, was for a time the cause of very sharp conflict between the courts of the United States and those of North Carolina. Wood was indicted, found guilty, and sentenced to serve a term of thirty days on the rock pile at Asheville on the charge of selling railroad tickets for more than the maximum rate established by the State statute. He appealed to Federal Judge Pritchard, who had granted an injunction against the putting of the State rate law into effect, and the latter issued a writ of habeas corpus ordering his release by Sheriff Hunter.

Considering the North Carolina case to have been disposed of by the action of the court in the Minnesota case, Justice Peckham did not elaborate his views.

JUSTICE HARLAN'S DISSENT.

Justice Harlan closed his dissenting statement in the following words:

"Neither the words nor the policy of the Eleventh Amendment will, under our former decisions, justify any order of a Federal court the necessary effect of which will be to exclude a State from its own courts. Such an order attended by such results cannot, I submit, be sustained consistently with the powers which the States, according to the uniform declarations of this court, possess under the Constitution.

"The wise men who framed the Constitution and who caused the adoption of the Eleventh Amendment would be startled by the suggestion that a State of the Union can be prevented by an order of a subordinate Federal court from being represented by its Attorney General in a suit brought by the State in one of its own courts, and that such an order would be inconsistent with the dignity of the States as involved in their constitutional immunity from the judicial process of the Federal courts, (except in the limited cases in which they may constitutionally be made parties in this court,) and would be attended by most pernicious results."

• • • • • • • • • • • •

Peckham discounted warnings that the *Ex parte Young* ruling would invite "a great flood of litigation." In fact, the ruling became the basis for expansive federal court jurisdiction in the twentieth century over state government institutions such as schools. Later decisions went further by upholding federal courts' power to issue affirmative as well as negative injunctions—orders specifically directing state officials to take actions to cure constitutional violations and to pay for them.

In *Milliken v. Bradley* (1977), for example, the Court upheld an order requiring the state of Michigan to pay some of the costs of a school desegregation plan for the city of Detroit. In another case, *Missouri v. Jenkins* (1990), the Court ruled, 5-4, that a judge could even order a municipality—Kansas City—to raise property taxes to pay its share of a desegregation plan, though the judge could not put the tax increase into effect himself. Further, in several cases—including an earlier proceeding in the Kansas City case—the Court ruled that federal courts may order states to pay attorneys' fees to prevailing parties in civil rights cases.

"COOPERATIVE FEDERALISM" AND THE POST–NEW DEAL COURT

The post–New Deal Court discarded the doctrine of dual federalism in favor of a view of overlapping state and federal authority that came to be called "cooperative federalism." The Tenth Amendment faded in importance as a shield against federal encroachment on the powers of the states. When the Court upheld the federal Fair Labor Standards Act (FLSA) of 1938 in *United States v. Darby Lumber Co.* (1941), Justice Hugo L. Black described the amendment as "a truism that all is retained which has not been surrendered."

The idea of state sovereignty continued to recede for several decades after the end of World War II. In 1947, the Court ruled in *Oklahoma v. Civil Service Commission* (1947) that Congress could attach conditions to federal aid to states—in that case, requiring state employees in federally funded programs to abide by the 1939 Hatch Act's curbs on political activities. Four decades later, the Court in *South Dakota v. Dole* (1987) similarly upheld a highway construction law that called for reducing funding for any state with a minimum drinking age below twenty-one.

The Court wavered but eventually further limited state sovereignty by upholding Congress's decisions to require state and local governments to comply with the FLSA, the federal wage-and-hours law. Initially, Congress extended the act's protections to employees of state schools, hospitals, and institutions; the Court upheld the law in *Maryland v. Wirtz* (1968). But when Congress extended the act in 1974 to all state employees, the Court balked. Writing for a 5-4 majority in *National League of Cities v. Usery* (1976), Justice Rehnquist said the amendments were unconstitutional to the extent that they displaced the states' "freedom to structure integral operations in areas of traditional governmental functions."

Lower courts applying that test grappled with deciding what state agencies or entities were engaged in "traditional" governmental functions. When one of those cases reached the Court, Justice Harry A. Blackmun switched sides and led a new 5-4 majority in overruling *National League of Cities* and requiring all state and local governments to comply with the federal law. In *Garcia v. San Antonio Metropolitan Transit Authority* (1985), Blackmun criticized Rehnquist's test for having led to "inconsistent results," but concluded more broadly that the federal overtime and minimum wage requirements were not "destructive of state sovereignty or violative of any constitutional provision."

Garcia v. San Antonio Metropolitan Transit Authority

Decided: February 19, 1985

Vote: 5 (Brennan, B. White, T. Marshall, Blackmun, Stevens)

4 (Burger, Powell, Rehnquist, O'Connor)

Opinion of the Court: Blackmun

Dissenting opinions (3): Powell (Burger, Rehnquist, O'Connor); Rehnquist; O'Connor (Powell, Rehnquist)

FEBRUARY 20, 1985
JUSTICES ENHANCE FEDERAL POWERS OVER THE STATE

By LINDA GREENHOUSE
Special to The New York Times

WASHINGTON, Feb. 19—Taking the rare step of overruling one of its own recent precedents, the Supreme Court today significantly enhanced the power of the Federal Government to regulate state activities that had been considered immune from Federal control.

The decision, one of the Court's most important rulings on the subject of federalism, created a new framework for analyzing the constitutional balance between Federal and state authority.

The Court ruled, 5 to 4, that Federal minimum wage and hour standards cover employees of publicly owned mass transit systems. In immediate practical terms, the decision is likely to lead to higher wages for transit workers. While nearly all these employees receive more than the minimum wage, they typically work split shifts, with long breaks between the morning and evening rush hours, and would receive increased overtime pay.

EFFECT ON OTHER STATE EMPLOYEES

By extension, the decision also restores most other state employees to protected status under the Fair Labor Standards Act. The 1976 decision, which the Court overruled today, held that the Constitution did not permit Congress to extend wage and hour coverage to state employees because to do so would "directly displace the states' freedom to structure integral operations in areas of traditional governmental functions."

Justice Blackmun appeared to be implying that once the states have lost a battle in Congress, the judiciary should interfere only with extreme reluctance, if at all.

In a bitter dissenting opinion, Associate Justice Lewis F. Powell Jr. accused the majority of abandoning the Court's age-old principle of judicial review and of establishing in its place the doctrine that Federal political officials "are the sole judges of the limits of their own power."

"The states' role in our system of Government is a matter of constitutional law, not of legislative grace," Justice Powell said.

The decision, Garcia v. San Antonio Metropolitan Transit Authority, No. 82-1913, was the latest episode in an unusual chapter of constitutional history. Two other

> ❝ The political process insures that laws that unduly burden the states will not be promulgated.
>
> —Justice Harry A. Blackmun, *Garcia v. San Antonio Metropolitan Transit Authority* ❞

As important as the decision is for state and local employees, the Court went further: it swept away the theoretical underpinnings of what has been known as the "new federalism." This was the belief, for which the 1976 decision served as the rallying cry, that the Constitution gives the states special protections and sets affirmative limits on the Federal Government's power to interfere in state affairs.

RELYING ON POLITICAL PROCESS

With "rare exceptions," Associate Justice Harry A. Blackmun wrote for the majority today, the Constitution imposes no such limits. Rather, he said, the states are protected against Federal intrusions into their sovereignty only to the degree that they can use the "political process" to protect themselves.

It is "the structure of the Federal Government itself" that protects the states, Justice Blackmun continued, and not any "judicially created limitations on Federal power." He said efforts by the Supreme Court and the lower courts to impose other limits on the power of Congress had proven "both impracticable and doctrinally barren."

Citing the presence of state delegations in Congress and the states' role in the Electoral College, Justice Blackmun said: "The political process insures that laws that unduly burden the states will not be promulgated."

dissenters, Associate Justices William H. Rehnquist and Sandra Day O'Connor, each suggested in their own dissenting opinions that the chapter may not be closed, and that today's decision itself may soon be a target for overruling.

Chief Justice Warren E. Burger also dissented. Justice Blackmun's majority opinion was joined by Associate Justices William J. Brennan, Byron R. White, Thurgood Marshall and John Paul Stevens.

BLACKMUN'S PIVOTAL ROLE

The key role was that of Justice Blackmun. He had been a reluctant member of the 5-to-4 majority in the 1976 decision, which was written by Justice Rehnquist. That decision, National League of Cities v. Usery, struck down Congress's extension of the Fair Labor Standards Act to state employees by resurrecting one of the most obscure provisions of the Bill of Rights, the 10th Amendment.

The 10th Amendment provides that powers not granted by the Constitution to the Federal Government "are reserved to the states." The National League of Cities decision found in that amendment an affirmative check on the ability of Congress to exercise its power over interstate commerce in ways that affected the "states as states." It was the first time in 40 years that the Court had invalidated an action taken by Congress under the Commerce Clause power, and the decision appeared to herald a major shift in the Federal-state balance of power.

That promise did not materialize, however, as the Court seemed to pull back from the full implications of the 1976 decision. In 1982, for example, the Court ruled that employees of the state-owned Long Island Rail Road had a federally guaranteed right to strike, despite the 10th Amendment, because running a railroad was not a "traditional" state function. In 1983, a 5-to-4 decision that Justice Blackmun joined held that Congress could cover state employees under the Federal age discrimination law.

A SEVERELY FRAYED DOCTRINE

By the time the Court reached the mass transit case, it was apparent that the National League of Cities doctrine was severely frayed. A Federal District Court in Texas had ruled, based on the 1976 decision, that San Antonio was immune from being required to pay its mass transit workers according to Federal wage and hour scales. Both the transit workers and the Federal Government appealed to the Supreme Court, arguing that mass transit was not a traditional state function and that the 10th Amendment analysis should not apply.

The Court argued the case last March and, after failing to reach a decision by the end of the term, ordered a new argument for last October with an added issue: "Whether or not the principles of the 10th Amendment as set forth in National League of Cities v. Usery should be reconsidered."

It was clear, then, that the result today was a possibility, although few people expected the sweeping terms with which the Court reached the result. Solicitor General Rex E. Lee, arguing for the Federal Government, had urged the Court to uphold National League of Cities as a "fundamental constitutional insight." He said today that he was "surprised and grieving" over the outcome. . . .

The National League of Cities issued a statement saying the Court had "clearly upset any semblance of balance between the interests of Federal policy and our once-proud traditions of local self-government."

Gerald W. McEntee, president of the American Federation of State, County and Municipal Employees, said the decision ended a period of "second-class citizenship" for employees of state and local government.

Justice Blackmun's 28-page opinion did not discuss the 10th Amendment. Rather, he discussed the extent to which the National League of Cities approach had proved "unsound in principle and unworkable in practice."

"We have no license to employ freestanding conceptions of state sovereignty when measuring Congressional authority under the Commerce Clause," Justice Blackmun said. "State sovereign interests are more properly protected by procedural safeguards inherent in the structure of the Federal system than by judicially created limitations on Federal power."

. . . .

THE REHNQUIST COURT AND THE REVIVAL OF STATE SOVEREIGNTY

Rehnquist became chief justice a year later and, with Justice Clarence Thomas's appointment in 1991, gained a somewhat reliable majority for his view on federalism issues. Over the next decade, Rehnquist led a revival of state sovereignty principles that yielded three lines of decisions limiting federal intrusions on state prerogatives.

In the first of the decisions, the Court in *New York v. United States* (1992) struck down part of a nuclear-waste disposal law that required states to take steps to dispose of low-level radioactive waste or to "take title" to and assume liability for the waste themselves. Writing for the 6-3 majority, Justice Sandra Day O'Connor said Congress could enact national regulations, but it had no authority to "commandeer" the states' legislative process.

JUNE 20, 1992
HIGH COURT EASES STATES' OBLIGATION OVER TOXIC WASTE

By LINDA GREENHOUSE

Declaring that the Federal Government "may not conscript state governments as its agents," the Supreme Court today held unconstitutional a central portion of a law aimed at making states take responsibility for the low-level radioactive waste generated within their borders.

The 6-to-3 decision was a victory for New York State, which has been unable to find a politically acceptable site in the state for disposing of contaminated medical and industrial waste. Such wastes have been the focus of a nationwide policy dispute.

New York had sued the Federal Government to invalidate the 1985 law on the ground that it infringed on state sovereignty. The state had been prodded by residents of Allegany County, a rural area about 70 miles south of Rochester that was a probable location for a waste site if New York had met the law's requirement to create one.

LAW IS COMPARED TO 'COERCION'

Gov. Mario M. Cuomo of New York said today that the Court's decision would put more pressure on utilities to help states develop disposal sites or face the possibility

caused by the material. "In this provision, Congress has crossed the line distinguishing encouragement from coercion," Justice O'Connor said.

Justice O'Connor based her decision principally on the 10th Amendment, which provides that powers not expressly given to the Federal Government by the Constitution are "reserved to the states" or to "the people."

There has been considerable ferment on the Court in the last 15 years over the meaning of this inherently obscure constitutional provision, which the Court has interpreted as placing at least some measure of restraint on the Federal Government's ability to interfere with the operation of state governments.

Beyond its substantial practical importance, the case today was closely watched because the Court had appeared poised for a major expansion of state power under the 10th Amendment. The underlying constitutional question was whether the Court would use this case, which it accepted against the Bush Administration's advice, as a vehicle for overturning recent precedents suggesting that the 10th Amendment may not actually mean very much.

> " State governments are neither regional offices nor administrative agencies of the Federal Government.
> —Justice Sandra Day O'Connor, *New York v. United States* "

that low-level radioactive wastes could be stored at their nuclear plants indefinitely. In the decision by Justice Sandra Day O'Connor, the Court today upheld portions of the law that provide financial incentives to states to find places to store the low-level waste, either on their own or in partnership with other states.

But the Court declared unconstitutional the law's central enforcement mechanism, a provision that in effect makes a state the legal owner of all low-level radioactive waste within its borders if it has not met its disposal needs by Jan. 1, 1996.

Under this "take title" provision, the state would assume not only ownership but all legal liability for any harm

But Justice O'Connor cautiously steered clear of confronting those precedents, which she herself has sharply criticized in the past. Instead, finding them not directly relevant, she said it had long been the case that though the Federal Government can try to influence the states to go along with a regulatory program, "Congress may not simply commandeer the legislative processes of the states."

"State governments are neither regional offices nor administrative agencies of the Federal Government," Justice O'Connor said.

Justice O'Connor is the only member of the Court to have served as an elected state official, and her analysis may have reflected her experience as majority leader of the Arizona State Senate. She noted that the Federal Government has the constitutional power to regulate nuclear waste disposal directly, by pre-empting state regulations and imposing a uniform national policy, and that by doing so, the Federal Government would assume political accountability for the policy.

"But where the Federal Government directs the states to regulate," she said, "it may be state officials who will bear the brunt of public disapproval, while the Federal officials who devised the regulatory program may remain insulated from the electoral ramifications of their decision."

The decision, New York v. United States, No. 91-543, was a partial reversal of a ruling last year by the United States Court of Appeals for the Second Circuit. That court, in Manhattan, upheld all provisions of the law, the Low-Level Radioactive Waste Policy Amendments Act of 1985. Justice O'Connor's opinion was joined by Chief Justice William H. Rehnquist and by Justices Antonin Scalia, Anthony M. Kennedy, David H. Souter and Clarence Thomas.

SUPPORT FOR THE LAW

Justices Byron R. White, Harry A. Blackmun and John Paul Stevens dissented from the portion of the opinion that struck down the "take title" provision.

"Hard public policy choices sometimes require strong measures," Justice White said in an opinion that the other two dissenting Justices signed. He called the 1985 law, which the National Governors Association was actively involved in negotiating, "very much the product of cooperative federalism" that "reflected hard-fought agreements among states as refereed by Congress." New York had participated in the process, Justice White said, and "should not now be permitted to complain."

While New York has had more problems than many other states in dealing with its low-level radioactive waste problem, its legal position attracted many allies among the other states. Connecticut, New Jersey, and 15 others filed or joined briefs in New York's behalf.

On the other hand, the only three states that have low-level radioactive waste disposal sites, Washington, South Carolina, and Nevada, entered the case on behalf of the Federal Government to defend the constitutionality of the law. . . .

• • • • • • • • • • •

The Court applied the same principle five years later in a 5-4 decision striking down the provision of the Brady Handgun Violence Prevention Act of 1993 that required state and local law enforcement agencies to conduct background checks on prospective gun purchasers. "The Federal Government may not compel the States to implement, by legislation or executive action, regulatory programs," Justice Antonin Scalia wrote in *Printz v. United States* (1997).

In a second pair of decisions—both by 5-4 votes and both written by Rehnquist—the Court limited Congress's power to use the Commerce Clause to support laws intruding on states' traditional law enforcement powers. *United States v. Lopez* (1995) struck down a law prohibiting carrying a firearm within or near a school. *United States v. Morrison* (2000) struck down a provision in the Violence Against Women Act that authorized federal courts to hear damage suits by victims of "gender-motivated violence" against their assailants.

In both cases, Rehnquist rejected the government's argument that the cumulative effect of either gun crimes or domestic violence had the "substantial" effect on interstate commerce needed to support a federal statute. Under the government's arguments, Rehnquist wrote in *Lopez,* "it is difficult to perceive any limitation on federal power, even in areas such as criminal law enforcement or education where States have historically been sovereign."

APRIL 27, 1995
HIGH COURT KILLS LAW BANNING GUNS IN A SCHOOL ZONE

By LINDA GREENHOUSE

The Supreme Court today dealt a stinging blow to the Federal Government's ability to move into the realm of local law enforcement, ruling in a bitterly divided 5-to-4 decision that Congress acted beyond its constitutional authority five years ago when it made possession of a gun within 1,000 feet of a school a Federal crime.

The decision, with a majority opinion by Chief Justice William H. Rehnquist, was based on the Court's interpretation of the authority of Congress to regulate interstate commerce. While not overturning any precedents, the decision marked a sharp departure from the modern Supreme Court's expansive view of Congressional power to regulate commerce.

Justice Stephen G. Breyer, in a dissenting opinion, said the decision "threatens legal uncertainty in an area of law that, until this case, seemed reasonably well settled."

The Constitution's grant of authority to Congress to regulate interstate commerce has been the basis for the development of the Federal Government in many of its most familiar aspects, particularly since the Supreme Court reversed course in 1937 and began to uphold the regulatory laws at the heart of the New Deal.

The last time the Court overturned a Federal law on the ground that it exceeded the Congressional commerce authority was 1936, when it struck down minimum-wage and maximum-hour requirements in the coal industry.

The ruling today, declaring unconstitutional the Gun-Free School Zones Act of 1990, cast doubt on the ability of Congress to exercise jurisdiction over a range of activities it has recently defined as Federal crimes, including car jacking, drive-by shootings and violent demonstrations at abortion clinics.

Unlike the law the Court struck down today, which made it a crime simply to have a gun in a particular place, most Federal gun laws regulate activities like buying, selling or importing guns, activities that fall within the classic definition of interstate commerce and that the ruling today did not disturb.

But at the least, the decision is likely to encourage a new round of legal challenges to other gun control laws. "Everything will be tested now," one Congressional aide said.

For example, one recently enacted Federal law, the ban on assault weapons, which is already the subject of a Federal court challenge by the National Rifle Association, makes it a crime to possess the weapons as well as to manufacture or import them. Possession of machine guns, undetectable handguns and "cop-killer" bullets are also crimes under various Federal laws that may now be open to legal attack.

The Brady law, which imposes a five-day waiting period for gun purchases and requires state officials to conduct background checks of purchasers, has already been declared unconstitutional in a half-dozen Federal district courts. The basis for those decisions, which the Clinton Administration is appealing, was not the Congressional commerce power but state autonomy under the 10th Amendment, which reserves to the states the powers not explicitly delegated to the Federal Government by the Constitution.

While that is a different rationale than the one the Court employed today, the 10th Amendment and the commerce clause are closely related elements of an ongoing constitutional debate over state power within the Federal system.

The language of federalism rang strongly through Chief Justice Rehnquist's majority opinion, as well as in a concurring opinion filed by Justices Anthony M. Kennedy and Sandra Day O'Connor. Justices Antonin Scalia and Clarence Thomas, who filed his own concurring opinion, were the other members of the majority.

Joining Justice Breyer in dissenting were Justices John Paul Stevens, David H. Souter and Ruth Bader Ginsburg. Justice Breyer took the unusual step of reading from the bench this morning a portion of the dissenting opinion he wrote for himself and the three others. Justices Stevens and Souter filed their own dissenting opinions as well. Justice Stevens called the majority ruling "extraordinary."

In his majority opinion, Chief Justice Rehnquist said the Administration's arguments for upholding the Gun-Free School Zones Act "would bid fair to convert Congressional authority under the commerce clause to a general police power of the sort retained by the states."

The Chief Justice said the law was "a criminal statute that by its terms has nothing to do with 'commerce' or any sort of economic enterprise, however broadly one might define those terms." He rejected the Administration's argument that guns and violence in schools hurt the economy by undermining the educational process and making children less productive workers and citizens.

"If we were to accept the Government's arguments, we are hard-pressed to posit any activity by an individual that Congress is without power to regulate," Chief Justice Rehnquist said. By the same logic, he added, school curriculums and state laws governing divorce and child custody would also come under Federal control.

In his dissenting opinion, Justice Souter accused the majority of having abandoned the principles of judicial restraint. He urged his colleagues to remember the "painful lesson" of the New Deal era, when the Court's activism in striking down Federal laws under the commerce clause brought the Court into disrepute and under sustained political attack.

"It seems fair to ask whether the step taken by the Court today does anything but portend a return to the untenable jurisprudence from which the Court extricated itself almost 60 years ago," Justice Souter said.

One lesson from that period, he said, was that "nothing about the judiciary as an institution made it a superior source of policy on the subject Congress dealt with."

In the dissenting opinion that Justices Souter, Stevens and Ginsburg also joined, Justice Breyer said the decision "threatens legal uncertainty" in legal matters that until now "seemed reasonably well settled." His opinion included a 17-page appendix listing studies and reference works on violence in the schools and on the connection between education and the economy.

"Why could Congress, for commerce clause purposes, not consider schools as roughly analogous to commercial investments from which the nation derives the benefit of an educated work force?" Justice Breyer asked.

One question the majority left unresolved was whether the Gun-Free School Zones Act might have been upheld had Congress, in passing the legislation, included the references and detailed argument that the dissenting Justices provided.

Some passages in Chief Justice Rehnquist's opinion could be read as indicating that a more detailed rationale for the legislation—not by Government lawyers defending it in Court but by those sponsoring and voting for it at the time—could have bolstered the case that education was sufficiently connected with the national economy to come within Congressional authority.

But other part [*sic*] of the opinion appeared to look the other way, both with respect to the question at hand and to the broader issue of structural limits on Federal power over the states. The outer limits of Congressional authority under the commerce clause "always will engender legal uncertainty," he said, adding, "The Constitution mandates this uncertainty by withholding from Congress a plenary police power that would authorize enactment of every type of legislation."

Federal actions like caps on medical malpractice awards, which have been approved by the House of Representatives and are being debated in the Senate, will be open to challenge under today's ruling if they ever become law because this area of law is historically a state preserve with a limited connection to interstate commerce. The pending legislation also includes limits on damage awards for defective products, which would be likely to survive a challenge because products move in interstate commerce.

The decision, United States v. Lopez, No. 93-1260, upheld a 1993 ruling by the United States Court of Appeals for the Fifth Circuit, in New Orleans. That court overturned the conviction of a San Antonio high school student, Alfonso Lopez Jr., for violating the Gun-Free School Zones Act by carrying a concealed .38-caliber pistol and five bullets to school. The appellate court invalidated the law, calling it "a singular incursion by the Federal Government into territory long occupied by the states."

MAY 16, 2000
WOMEN LOSE RIGHT TO SUE ATTACKERS IN FEDERAL COURT
By LINDA GREENHOUSE

Declaring that "the Constitution requires a distinction between what is truly national and what is truly local," the Supreme Court today invalidated a six-year-old provision of federal law that permitted victims of rape, domestic violence and other crimes "motivated by gender" to sue their attackers in federal court.

The 5-to-4 decision, striking down the civil remedy provision of the Violence Against Women Act, was the lat-

est application of the court's newly restrictive view of Congressional power and of the degree of deference that Congress is owed by federal courts. Although one of the most sweeping of the justices' decisions in this area recently, it will almost certainly not be the last.

Chief Justice William H. Rehnquist's majority opinion rejected each of the two sources of constitutional authority that Congress had asserted as the basis for the legislation. The majority concluded that the civil remedy provision was neither a valid regulation of interstate commerce nor a proper means of enforcing the equal protection guarantee of the 14th Amendment.

The decision affirmed a ruling last year by the federal appeals court in Richmond, Va., dismissing a suit brought by a college student against two varsity football players whom she accused of raping her in her dormitory room shortly after the start of her freshman year.

The plaintiff, Christy Brzonkala, withdrew from Virginia Polytechnic Institute and brought her suit after learning that the football players, Antonio Morrison and James Crawford, would not be disciplined by the college. When the defendants then challenged the constitutionality of the Violence Against Women Act, the federal government intervened in the suit to defend the law.

The law's supporters argued that widespread violence against women, and fear of violence, had a negative effect on the nation's economy, measured in the billions of dollars a year, by impairing the productivity and the mobility of female employees and students. To accept that reasoning, the chief justice said today, "would allow Congress to regulate any crime as long as the nationwide, aggregated impact of that crime has substantial effects on employment, production, transit or consumption." But a general police power is something "which the founders denied the national government and reposed in the states," he added.

The Violence Against Women Act also has a criminal provision, making it a federal crime to cross state lines to engage in domestic violence or stalking. The Supreme Court last year refused to hear a challenge to that provision, which was not at issue in the case today but which the chief justice suggested in a footnote was constitutional because of the explicit requirement of interstate conduct. The law also provides federal money to the states for programs to prevent violence and assist victims.

Much of the attention and debate surrounding the law has focused on the civil damages provision at issue today, which the lower courts have applied some 50 times, a number that would probably have been larger had the law not been under a constitutional cloud. While most states have laws permitting people, including victims of sexual assaults, to seek damages against their attackers, Congress acted after dozens of studies showed that women seeking such relief faced considerable obstacles from state judicial systems that regarded sex offenses as unworthy of serious attention.

Senator Joseph R. Biden Jr., the chief Senate sponsor of the Violence Against Women Act, said at a news conference today that "this decision is really all about power: who has the power, the court or Congress?"

Senator Biden, a Democrat from Delaware, said there had been notable improvement in the states since Congress put the issue on its agenda in the early 1990's. He predicted that the decision today "will have a lot less impact on violence against women than on the future role of the United States Congress," adding, "The damage done to the act is not as bad as the damage done to American jurisprudence."

Both Senator Biden and Senator Charles E. Schumer, a New York Democrat who was the law's chief sponsor when he represented Brooklyn in the House of Representatives, said years of hearings before the legislation was passed had been aimed at compiling a record of the scope of the problem, to persuade the Supreme Court that a national solution was warranted.

"Just at a time when the economic and social conditions of the world demand that we be treated as one country and not as 50 states, the Supreme Court seems poised to undo decades and decades of a consensus that the federal government has an active role to play," Senator Schumer said in an interview.

In a dissenting opinion today, Justice David H. Souter included three pages of the findings from various Congressional reports, and predicted that the majority's "new judicially derived federalism" would eventually prove as serious a wrong turn for the court as the decisions of the 1930's that, in rejecting elements of the New Deal, provoked the court-packing crisis of 1937. Referring to that episode's "pedigree of near-tragedy," Justice Souter said that "today's decision can only be seen as a step toward recapturing the prior mistakes."

The justices' 5-to-4 division was familiar from a series of decisions over the last five years that have struck down federal laws or created new state immunities from the application of federal law. Beginning with its ruling in United States v. Lopez in 1995, which overturned a law against carrying a gun near a school and marked the first time since the New Deal that the court had invalidated a law as exceeding the power of Congress to regulate interstate commerce, the court has also struck down part of the Brady gun control law and laws making states liable to suit in federal court for patent and trademark violations. Earlier this year, the court ruled that states could not be sued by their employees for violating the Age Discrimination in Employment Act.

Joining Chief Justice Rehnquist in the majority today, as in all the other decisions, were Justices Sandra Day O'Connor, Antonin Scalia, Anthony M. Kennedy and Clarence Thomas. Justice Thomas wrote a brief concurring opinion to say that the court should have put Congress under an even tighter rein. Justice Stephen G. Breyer wrote a dissenting opinion and also signed Justice Souter's dissent, as did Justices John Paul Stevens and Ruth Bader Ginsburg.

Although the tone of the opinions today, totaling 71 pages, was quite muted, the gulf between the two factions of the court is wide and growing wider. The court has already granted review in three more federalism cases, and the decision today, United States v. Morrison, No. 99-5, is likely to inspire more challenges to the reliance of Congress on its authority to regulate interstate commerce. Federal environmental regulations that restrict the use of private property might present an inviting target for such a challenge, some students of these recent developments believe.

Chief Justice Rehnquist's majority opinion today reiterated that the "economic nature of the regulated activity" was at the heart of any analysis of Congress's exercise of its commerce authority. "Gender-motivated crimes of violence are not, in any sense of the phrase, economic activity," he said.

The opinion stopped short of adopting a categorical rule that Congress can never do what it claimed to do in this law: address the aggregate economic effect of activity that itself may not be inherently economic. But the chief justice noted pointedly that the court had never endorsed such an approach. In any event, he said, the court is and will remain "the ultimate expositor of the constitutional text."

In his dissenting opinion, Justice Souter said that when it came to "supposed conflicts of sovereign political interests implicated by the Commerce Clause," the court should step back and let the political system work out the problem. Noting that 36 states had filed briefs supporting the law, he said it was "not the least irony" of the case that "the states will be forced to enjoy the new federalism whether they want it or not."

Chief Justice Rehnquist said the provision could not be sustained under the 14th Amendment because that amendment prohibits discrimination by states or "state actors" rather than the private individuals whose conduct is the target of this law.

Kathryn J. Rodgers, executive director of the NOW Legal Defense and Education Fund, which represented Ms. Brzonkala (pronounced brahn-KAH-lah), criticized the decision, saying it took "the federal government out of the business of defining civil rights and creating remedies."

Michael E. Rosman, general counsel of the Center for Individual Rights, which challenged the law on behalf of the defendants, said the decision was a welcome reminder that "democratic majorities are limited by the text of the Constitution."

"This was an effort by Congress to aggrandize its authority," Mr. Rosman added, "and the court is now requiring Congress to toe the constitutional line."

- - - - - - - - - - - -

The third line of decisions—in which the Court limited private damage suits against state governments—began with *Seminole Tribe v. Florida* (1996). The ruling struck down a provision in the Indian Gaming Regulatory Act of 1988 that subjected states to damage suits if they did not negotiate in good faith with tribes seeking permission to permit gambling on reservations. The Eleventh Amendment, Rehnquist reasoned, prevented Congress from using its Commerce Clause power to abrogate the states' protection from private damage suits.

Seminole Tribe v. Florida

Decided: March 27, 1996

Vote: 5 (Rehnquist, O'Connor, Scalia, Kennedy, Thomas)

4 (Stevens, Souter, Ginsburg, Breyer)

Opinion of the Court: Rehnquist

Dissenting opinions (2): Stevens; Souter (Ginsburg, Breyer)

MARCH 28, 1996
JUSTICES CURB FEDERAL POWER TO SUBJECT STATES TO LAWSUITS

By LINDA GREENHOUSE

Escalating its profound and divisive debate over the relationship between the states and the Federal Government, the Supreme Court today bolstered state power by sharply curbing the authority of Congress to subject states to suits in Federal court.

The 5-to-4 ruling came in a case challenging the constitutionality of a 1988 law permitting Indian tribes to sue states in Federal court for failing to negotiate in good faith over the operation of gambling casinos on tribal land. In an opinion by Chief Justice William H. Rehnquist, the Court ruled today that this portion of the law, the Indian Gaming Regulatory Act, was an unconstitutional incursion on state sovereignty.

But the significance of today's decision extends far beyond the particular context of the case, raising questions about whether individuals can use the courts to force states to abide by a variety of Federal laws.

With respect to Indian gambling, the decision left unanswered many important questions, which the Justices may soon address in related cases awaiting Court action. But the paradoxical effect may be that even though an Indian tribe was nominally the loser in the case, it will now be easier for tribes to open casinos by getting authorization directly from the Interior Department rather than dealing with the states at all.

And at the broadest level, the decision made it stunningly clear that last term's ruling in United States v. Lopez that Congress lacked authority to ban possession of guns near schools was not an aberrant decision, as some thought then.

It is evident now that the Lopez decision was a signal that the current majority is in the process of revisiting some long-settled assumptions about the structure of the Federal Government and the constitutional allocation of authority between Washington and the states.

The lineup in the two cases was the same: Chief Justice Rehnquist wrote for the majority, joined by Justices Sandra Day O'Connor, Anthony M. Kennedy, Antonin Scalia and Clarence Thomas, while dissenting votes were cast by Justices John Paul Stevens, David H. Souter, Ruth Bader Ginsburg and Stephen G. Breyer.

The subject of the case today was the 11th Amendment, which bars jurisdiction in the Federal courts to hear suits against a state by citizens of another state. An 1890 Supreme Court decision, Hans v. Louisiana, gave the amendment the broader interpretation of generally barring Federal court suits against states without their consent, whether by their own residents or residents of other states.

The significance of Hans v. Louisiana as a precedent had been watered down over the years, as the Court permitted suits against states in Federal court to enforce a variety of Federal laws, most recently, in a 1989 decision, the Federal Superfund environmental law. The Court today overruled that decision, Pennsylvania v. Union Gas, declaring that laws enacted by Congress in the exercise of its authority to regulate interstate commerce were not enforceable against states in Federal court.

Also overruled, by implication, was a series of recent decisions holding that the 11th Amendment required only that Congress make clear its intention to subject the states to suits in Federal court to enforce particular laws. If the Federal law was clear enough, these cases held, the states' 11th Amendment immunity would be abrogated. Chief Justice Rehnquist said today that although Congress had made its intention to subject the states to suit by Indian tribes "absolutely clear," the 11th Amendment barred the suits anyway.

The practical significance of the decision is far from clear. In a dissenting opinion, Justice Stevens cited Federal copyright, bankruptcy and antitrust laws as among those that would "have no remedy" for state violations, an assertion that Chief Justice Rehnquist disputed in his majority opinion.

The full scope of the ruling will have to be filled out in future cases. Some limits on the decision are clear. Suits may still be brought against states to enforce the right to equal protection guaranteed by the 14th Amendment, which Chief Justice Rehnquist noted was adopted "well after" the adoption of the 11th Amendment and which "operated to alter the pre-existing balance between state and Federal power."

Suits may also be brought by the Federal Government against states, and by individuals against state officials for injunctions to prohibit future illegal actions. The principal effect of the decision will be to limit suits to enforce rights granted by Congress within its authority under the Commerce Clause, which encompasses much of modern Federal regulation.

That was the area addressed in the Union Gas case in 1989, in which the Court held that a Federal court could order a state to pay environmental cleanup costs. In declaring today that the Union Gas precedent was overruled, Chief Justice Rehnquist said it was a "deeply fractured" ruling, unsupported by a majority opinion, that had "created confusion among the lower courts" and "deviated sharply from our established federalism jurisprudence."

Regardless of the immediate practical effects, the breadth of the debate was clear from the vigor of the language on both sides.

Justice Stevens and Justice Souter both filed dissenting opinions; Justice Souter's 92-page dissent (compared with 31 pages for the majority opinion) was also signed by Justices Ginsburg and Breyer.

Justice Stevens, disputing the Chief Justice's assertion that the Court was simply restoring a long-dominant view of federalism, called the decision a "sharp break with the past." He referred to "the shocking character of the majority's affront to a co-equal branch of our Government," meaning Congress, and said the decision was "profoundly misguided."

Justice Souter attacked the majority opinion on both broad theoretical grounds and specific legal analysis. He said the majority was endorsing and giving constitutional status to a notion of state sovereignty that was incompatible with the Federal Government that the Constitution had established.

He said the ratification of the Constitution "demonstrated that state governments were subject to a superior regime of law in a judicial system established, not by the state, but by the people through a specific delegation of their sovereign power to a national government that was paramount within its delegated sphere."

He added, "Given the framers' general concern with curbing abuses by state governments, it would be amazing if the scheme of delegated powers embodied in the Constitution had left the national government powerless to render the states judicially accountable for violations of Federal rights." Justice Souter said the Court was making the same mistake it made at "the nadir of its competence" early in this century, when it applied common-law concepts of property rights and contract to overrule Congressional economic regulation.

Chief Justice Rehnquist dismissed Justice Souter's opinion by saying it "disregards our case law in favor of a theory cobbled together from law review articles and its own version of historical events."

The decision, Seminole Tribe v. Florida, No. 94-12, upheld a ruling by the United States Court of Appeals for the 11th Circuit, in Atlanta. That court ruled in 1994 that the 11th Amendment barred a suit by the Seminole Tribe under the Indian Gaming Regulatory Act to force Florida to negotiate the terms of a tribal-state compact to open a casino on Seminole land.

The Indian gaming act set up a complex procedure under which a tribe, if frustrated by a state, can take its request to the Secretary of the Interior. Under the appeals court's analysis, that option remains now that tribes can no longer sue the states.

Gambling in reservation casinos is now a $4-billion a year business, with 200 tribes operating 126 casinos in 24 states. The decision today may enhance the prospects in Congress for an overall review of the situation.

Representative Robert G. Torricelli, Democrat of New Jersey, where the Atlantic City casinos are strongly opposed to gambling on Indian reservations, said today that Congress should hold hearings to assess the decision and "must enact comprehensive reform to redefine the playing field."

It is quite possible the Court has not yet said its final word on the Indian gaming act. The Justices will act soon on a challenge to the law brought by Oklahoma, which is attacking not only the lawsuit provision the Court struck down today but the ultimate authority of the Federal Government under the 10th Amendment to require unwilling states to accept tribal casinos. That further question was not before the Court today. The Court has not yet agreed to hear the Oklahoma case, Oklahoma v. Ponca Tribe, No. 94-1029, but today's majority may not be able to resist the opportunity.

Three years later, the Court followed similar reasoning in two simultaneous rulings blocking suits for patent infringement or false advertising claims against arms of state government. On the same day, *Alden v. Maine* (1999) extended the states' protection to damage suits for federal law violations even in their own courts. Justice Kennedy cited both the Tenth and Eleventh Amendments in describing immunity from private suits as "central to sovereign dignity." He warned that damage suits against state governments could pose a "severe" danger to state budgets and declared them unnecessary because federal agencies could enforce federal laws against the states.

The Court extended the doctrine in two more cases that blocked suits under the federal Age Discrimination in Employment Act of 1967 (*Kimel v. Florida Board of Regents,* 2000) and the Americans with Disabilities Act of 1990 (*Board of Trustees of the University of Alabama v. Garrett,* 2001). In both of those cases, plaintiffs claimed that Congress was using powers granted by the Fourteenth Amendment to enforce antidiscrimination provisions against the states. But the 5-4 majorities in each case said that even if the amendment prohibited discrimination on account of age or disability, Congress had too little evidence of such discrimination by state employers to override the states' immunity.

Nevada Department of
Human Resources v. Hibbs

  Decided: May 27, 2003
  Vote: 6 (Rehnquist, Stevens,
             O'Connor, Souter, Ginsburg,
             Breyer)
             3 (Scalia, Kennedy, Thomas)
  Opinion of the Court: Rehnquist
  Concurring opinions (2): Souter
             (Ginsburg, Breyer); Stevens
  Dissenting opinions (2): Scalia;
             Kennedy (Scalia, Thomas)

With *Kimel* and *Garrett,* the Rehnquist-led federalism drive peaked. In 2003 the Court permitted private damage suits against states in two cases. Rehnquist wrote the majority decision in *Nevada Department of Human Resources v. Hibbs,* which allowed a state employee to sue after he was denied time off under the federal Family and Medical Leave Act of 1993. The law was aimed at combating gender discrimination, Rehnquist said, and the "weighty record" of states' "unconstitutional participation" in the practice justified the law's provision for private damage suits. In *Tennessee v. Lane* (2004), the Court allowed suits against a state for failing to make courthouses accessible to persons with disabilities. Access to courts, Justice John Paul Stevens wrote, was a "fundamental right" enforceable under the Fourteenth Amendment.

One year later, the Court ruled that Congress's power to regulate interstate commerce gave the federal ban on marijuana precedence over a California initiative to permit medical use of the drug by some patients with chronic illnesses. Writing for the 6-3 majority in *Gonzales v. Raich* (2005), Stevens said that a state exemption for personal, intrastate use of marijuana would leave "a gaping hole" in enforcement of the federal law. (See page 27.)

Rehnquist dissented. He died three months later, after a year-long fight against thyroid cancer. His federalism rulings were cited by all observers as one of his major legacies.

OBITUARY
SEPTEMBER 5, 2005
WILLIAM H. REHNQUIST, ARCHITECT OF CONSERVATIVE COURT, DIES AT 80

By LINDA GREENHOUSE

... Including 14 years as an associate justice, Chief Justice Rehnquist's tenure on the court was not only one of the longest in the institution's history but also one of the most consequential. With a steady hand, a focus and commitment that never wavered, and the muscular use of the power of judicial review, he managed to translate many of his long-held views into binding national precedent.

Chief among those views was an enhanced role for the states within the federal system, which the court accomplished under his leadership by overturning dozens of federal laws that sought to project federal authority into what the Supreme Court majority viewed as the domain of the states. . . .

He staked his ground early in the debate over the boundary between state and federal authority. His majority opinion in a 1976 case, National League of Cities v. Usery, invalidated the application of federal minimum wage and hour requirements to employees of state and local governments. Though a narrow majority overturned that decision, over Justice Rehnquist's dissent, nine years later in Garcia v. San Antonio Metropolitan Transit Authority, the 1976 opinion had the important effect of reviving interest in the 10th Amendment. That amendment, previously one of the most obscure provisions of the Bill of Rights, reserves to the states or "to the people" any powers not explicitly given elsewhere in the Constitution to the federal government.

His focus in the Lopez decision was on a different constitutional provision, the Commerce Clause, for more than half a century the source of Congress's nearly unquestioned authority to oversee national affairs.

He said that because the possession of guns near schools "has nothing to do with 'commerce' or any sort of economic enterprise, however broadly one might define those terms," Congress had lacked authority to pass the law under its constitutional power to regulate interstate commerce. The decision was the first time since the New Deal that the court had invalidated an exercise of Congress's commerce authority. . . .

The Lopez case was followed by a string of decisions expanding state immunity from federal regulation and constricting the authority of Congress. Nearly all were decided by 5-to-4 votes. Justices Sandra Day O'Connor, Anthony M. Kennedy, Antonin Scalia and Clarence Thomas

> "With a steady hand, a focus and commitment that never wavered, and the muscular use of the power of judicial review, [Rehnquist] managed to translate many of his long-held views into binding national precedent."

The 1976 decision put federal regulatory authority on the defensive as it had not been for a generation. Chief Justice Rehnquist's majority opinion in United States v. Lopez in 1995 raised the stakes in the debate over federal authority even higher. The decision declared unconstitutional a law, the Gun Free School Zones Act of 1990, that made it a federal crime to carry a gun within 1,000 feet of a school.

were his reliable allies in the Rehnquist Court's federalism revolution.

That revolution appeared to stall during the last term, when the court voted 6 to 3, over the chief justice's dissent, to reassert federal authority by upholding the power of Congress to prohibit the use of marijuana for medical purposes, even in the 11 states that permit it. . . .

PART TWO
THE SUPREME COURT
AND THE INDIVIDUAL

FREEDOM OF **IDEAS**

CHAPTER 5

"All the News That's Fit to Print"

The New York Times

LATE CITY EDITION
Weather: Chance of showers today, tonight. Partly sunny tomorrow. Temp. range: today 74-94; Wed. 72-91. Temp. Hum. Index yesterday 82. Full U.S. report on Page 94.

VOL. CXX...No. 41,431   © 1971 The New York Times Company   NEW YORK, THURSDAY, JULY 1, 1971   15 CENTS

SUPREME COURT, 6-3, UPHOLDS NEWSPAPERS ON PUBLICATION OF THE PENTAGON REPORT; TIMES RESUMES ITS SERIES, HALTED 15 DAYS

Nixon Says Turks Agree To Ban the Opium Poppy

By JOHN HERBERS

PRESIDENT CALLS STEEL AND LABOR TO WHITE HOUSE

He Asks Both Sides to Meet With Him Tuesday Before Contract Talks Start

By PHILIP SHABECOFF

Pentagon Papers: Study Reports Kennedy Made 'Gamble' Into a 'Broad Commitment'

By HEDRICK SMITH

BURGER DISSENTS

First Amendment Rule Held to Block Most Prior Restraints

Decision, concurring opinions, dissents start on Page 17.

By FRED P. GRAHAM

Soviet Starts an Inquiry Into 3 Astronauts' Deaths

By BERNARD GWERTZMAN

U.S. and Diem's Overthrow: Step by Step

CHOU TIES U.N. SEAT TO TAIPEI'S OUSTER

Jim Garrison Is Arrested; U.S. Says He Took Bribes

Pitting calls of national security against demands for freedom of the press, the Supreme Court's landmark decision in *New York Times Co. v. United States* (1971) granted the newspaper the right to continue a series of reports publishing confidential government information on the Vietnam War.

The Supreme Court convened in an extraordinary Saturday session on June 26, 1971, to hear an extraordinary case. The federal government was asking the justices to stop two of the nation's leading newspapers, *The New York Times* and the *Washington Post,* from publishing the contents of a classified Pentagon study of U.S. involvement in the Vietnam War.

The so-called Pentagon Papers had been leaked to the newspapers by Daniel Ellsberg, a one-time Pentagon aide turned anti-war activist. The government asked federal courts to block newspapers from writing about the documents by arguing that the articles would endanger U.S. service members and prisoners of war in Southeast Asia and jeopardize ongoing peace negotiations. Lawyers for the newspapers argued that the government's request amounted to censorship in violation of the First Amendment's guarantee of freedom of the press.

"Congress shall make no law," the amendment declares, "respecting an establishment of religion, or prohibiting the free exercise thereof; or abridging the freedom of speech, or of the press; or the right of the people peaceably to assemble, and to petition the Government, for a redress of grievances."

With those forty-five words, the authors of the Bill of Rights—ratified in 1791—added to the new Constitution important limitations on the powers of the newly established national government. A nation settled by religious dissidents and forged by political radicals wanted to protect freedoms of ideas—freedom of speech and freedom of religion—and the right to translate those ideas into action by assembling peacefully or petitioning the government.

The amendment is written in absolute terms, but its provisions have never been interpreted as absolutes. Congress and state legislatures have enacted any number of laws restricting speech; regulating the press, including print, electronic, and online media; and governing the relationship between church and state. Initially, the Supreme Court treated the amendment as applying only to Congress, but in the twentieth century it held that the prohibitions applied equally to state and local governments.

The broader reach of the First Amendment—and a broader view of its limits on government power—have brought an array of disputes to the Court. The justices have been asked to rule on the speech rights of high school students and commercial advertisers, flag burners and online pornographers. In church-state cases, the Court has had to rule on the constitutionality of prayer in the classroom and government aid to parochial schools. Rulings on these issues in the late twentieth century were often closely divided and intensely controversial.

Overall, free speech and free press advocates have won broader protections from the Supreme Court since the late 1950s. A decade after the onset of the Cold War, the Court under Chief Justice Earl Warren began to limit or strike down anticommunist measures such as loyalty oaths for public employees. In a landmark free speech case, *The New York Times* won a 1964 ruling that makes it difficult for public officials to win libel suits against news organizations or individuals. Seven years later, *The Times* emerged victorious along with the *Post* in the Pentagon Papers case.

JULY 1, 1971
SUPREME COURT, 6-3, UPHOLDS NEWSPAPERS ON PUBLICATION OF THE PENTAGON REPORT; TIMES RESUMES ITS SERIES, HALTED 15 DAYS
BURGER DISSENTS

First Amendment Rule Held to Block Most Prior Restraints

By FRED P. GRAHAM

Special to The New York Times

WASHINGTON, June 30—The Supreme Court freed The New York Times and The Washington Post today to resume immediate publication of articles based on the secret Pentagon papers on the origins of the Vietnam war.

By a vote of 6 to 3 the Court held that any attempt by the Government to block news articles prior to publication bears "a heavy burden of presumption against its constitutionality."

In a historic test of that principle—the first effort by the Government to enjoin publication on the ground of na-

tional security—the Court declared that "the Government has not met that burden."

The brief judgment was read to a hushed courtroom by Chief Justice Warren E. Burger at 2:30 P.M. at a special session called three hours before.

OLD TRADITION OBSERVED

The Chief Justice was one of the dissenters, along with Associate Justices Harry A. Blackmun and John M. Harlan, but because the decision was rendered in an unsigned opinion, the Chief Justice read it in court in accordance with long-standing custom.

In New York Arthur Ochs Sulzberger, president and publisher of The Times, said at a news conference that he had "never really doubted that this day would come and that we'd win." His reaction, he said, was "complete joy and delight."

The case had been expected to produce a landmark ruling on the circumstances under which prior restraint could be imposed upon the press, but because no opinion by a single Justice commanded the support of a majority, only the unsigned decision will serve as precedent.

UNCERTAINTY OVER OUTCOME

Because it came on the 15th day after The Times had been restrained from publishing further articles in its series mined from the 7,000 pages of material—the first such restraint in the name of "national security" in the history of the United States—there was some uncertainty whether the press had scored a strong victory or whether a precedent for some degree of restraint had been set.

the absolutist view that the courts lack the power to suppress any press publication, no matter how grave a threat to security it might pose.

Justices Black and Douglas restated their long-held belief that the First Amendment's guarantee of a free press forbids any judicial restraint. Justice Marshall insisted that because Congress had twice considered and rejected such power for the courts, the Supreme Court would be "enacting" law if it imposed restraint.

The second group, which included William J. Brennan Jr., Potter Stewart and Byron R. White, said that the press could not be muzzled except to prevent direct, immediate and irreparable damage to the nation. They agreed that this material did not pose such a threat.

THE DISSENTERS' VIEWS

The third bloc, composed of the three dissenters, declared that the courts should not refuse to enforce the executive branch's conclusion that material should be kept confidential—so long as a Cabinet-level officer had decided that it should—on a matter affecting foreign relations.

> In revealing the workings of government that led to the Vietnam war, the newspapers nobly did precisely that which the founders hoped and trusted they would do.
> —Justice Hugo L. Black, *New York Times Co. v. United States*

Alexander M. Bickel, the Yale law professor who had argued for the Times in the case, said in a telephone interview that the ruling placed the press in a "stronger position." He maintained that no Federal District Judge would henceforth temporarily restrain a newspaper on the Justice Department's complaint that "this is what they have printed and we don't like it" and that a direct threat of irreparable harm would have to be alleged.

However, the United States Solicitor General, Erwin N. Griswold, turned to another lawyer shortly after the Justices filed from the courtroom and remarked: "Maybe the newspaper will show a little restraint in the future." All nine Justices wrote opinions, in a judicial outpouring that was described by Supreme Court scholars as without precedent. They divided roughly into groups of three each.

The first group, composed of Hugo L. Black, William O. Douglas and Thurgood Marshall, took what is known as

They felt that the "frenzied train of events" in the case before them had not given the courts enough time to determine those questions, so they concluded that the restraints upon publication should have been retained while both cases were sent back to the trial judges for more hearings.

The New York Times's series drawn from the secret Pentagon study was accompanied by supporting documents. Articles were published on June 13, 14 and 15 before they were halted by court order. A similar restraining order was imposed on June 19 against The Washington Post after it began to print articles based on the study.

Justice Black's opinion stated that just such publications as those were intended to be protected by the First Amendment's declaration that "Congress shall make no law . . . abridging the freedom of the press."

Paramount among the responsibilities of a free press, he said, "is the duty to prevent any part of the Government from deceiving the people and sending them off to distant lands to die of foreign fevers and foreign shot and shell.

"In my view, far from deserving condemnation for their courageous reporting, The New York Times, The Washington Post and other newspapers should be commended for serving the purpose that the Founding Fathers saw so clearly," he said. "In revealing the workings of government that led to the Vietnam war, the newspapers nobly did precisely that which the founders hoped and trusted they would do."

Justice Douglas joined the opinion by Justice Black and was joined by him in another opinion. The First Amendment's purpose, Justice Douglas argued, is to prohibit "governmental suppression of embarrassing information." He asserted that the temporary restraints in these cases "constitute a flouting of the principles of the First Amendment."

Justice Marshall's position was based primarily upon the separation-of-powers argument that Congress had never authorized prior restraints and that it refused to do so when bills were introduced in 1917 and 1957.

He concluded that the courts were without power to restrain publications. Justices Brennan, Stewart and White, who also based their conclusions on the separation-of-powers principle, assumed that under extreme circumstances the courts would act without such powers.

Justice Brennan focused on the temporary restraints, which had been issued to freeze the situation so that the material would not be made public before the courts could decide if it should be enjoined. He continued that no restraints should have been imposed because the Government alleged only in general terms that security breaches might occur.

Justices Stewart and White, who also joined each other's opinions, said that though they had read the documents they felt that publication would not be in the national interest.

But Justice Stewart, a former chairman of the Yale Daily News, insisted that "it is the duty of the executive" to protect state secrets through its own security measures and not the duty of the courts to do it by banning news articles.

He implied that if publication of the material would cause "direct, immediate, and irreparable damage to our nation or its people," he would uphold prior restraint, but because that situation was not present here, he said that the papers must be free to publish.

Justice White added that Congress had enacted criminal laws, including the espionage laws, that might apply to these papers. "The newspapers are presumably now on full notice," he said, that the Justice Department may bring prosecutions if the publications violate those laws. He added that he "would have no difficulty in sustaining convictions" under the laws, even if the breaches of security were not sufficient to justify prior restraint.

The Chief Justice and Justices Stewart and Blackmun echoed this caveat in their opinions—meaning that one less than a majority had lent their weight to the warning.

Chief Justice Burger blamed The Times "in large part" for the "frenetic haste" with which the case was handled. He said that The Times had studied the Pentagon archives for three or four months before beginning its series, yet it had breached "the duty of an honorable press" by not asking the Government if any security violations were involved before it began publication.

He said he found it "hardly believable" that The Times would do this, and he concluded that it would not be harmed if the case were sent back for more testimony.

Justice Blackmun, also focusing his criticism on The Times, said there had been inadequate time to determine if the publications could result in "the death of soldiers, the destruction of alliances, the greatly increased difficulty of negotiation with our enemies, the inability of our diplomats to negotiate." He concluded that if the war was prolonged and a delay in the return of United States prisoners result from publication, "then the nation's people will know where the responsibility for these sad consequences rests."

In his own dissenting opinion, Justice Harlan said: "The judiciary must review the initial executive determination to the point of satisfying itself that the subject matter of the dispute does lie within the proper compass of the President's foreign policy relations power.

"The judiciary," he went on, "may properly insist that the determination that disclosure of that subject matter would irreparably impair the national security be made by the head of the executive department concerned—here the Secretary of State or the Secretary of Defense—after actual personal consideration.

"But in my judgment, the judiciary may not properly go beyond these two inquiries and redetermine for itself the probable impact of disclosure on the national security."

The Justice Department initially sought an injunction against The Times on June 15 from Federal District Judge Murray I. Gurfein in New York.

Judge Gurfein, who had issued the original temporary restraining order that was stayed until today, ruled that the material was basically historical matter that might be embarrassing to the Government but did not pose a threat to national security. Federal District Judge Gerhard A. Gesell of the District of Columbia came to the same conclusion in the Government's suit against The Washington Post.

The United States Court of Appeals for the Second Circuit, voting 5 to 3, ordered more secret hearings before Judge Gurfein and The Times appealed. The United States Court of appeals for the District of Columbia upheld Judge Gesell, 7 to 2, holding that no injunction should be imposed. Today the Supreme Court affirmed the Appeals Court here and reversed the Second Circuit.

The Supreme Court also issued a brief order disposing of a few other cases and adjourned until Oct. 4, as it had been scheduled to do Monday.

. . . .

Even with a more conservative Court in the 1980s and 1990s, free speech still appeared to have a favored position—as illustrated by two rulings striking down laws that prohibited desecration of the U.S. flag. Under Chief Justice William H. Rehnquist, however, the Court did shift direction on church-state cases by relaxing restrictions on government aid to parochial schools and other religious organizations.

The Court's direction under Chief Justice John J. Roberts Jr. remains to be seen, but one decision in Roberts's second term gave free speech advocates pause. Roberts wrote the majority opinion in upholding an Alaska high school student's ten-day suspension for displaying a banner—"BONG HiTS 4 JESUS"—that the school's principal interpreted as advocating the use of illegal drugs. The First Amendment does not require schools to allow student speech promoting illegal drug use, Roberts wrote in *Morse v. Frederick* (2007). In dissent, Justice John Paul Stevens replied, "A full and frank discussion of the costs and benefits of the attempt to prohibit the use of marijuana is far wiser than suppression of speech because it is unpopular."

EARLY DEVELOPMENTS

Only seven years after ratification of the First Amendment, Congress sharply limited its protection for freedom of speech and the press. The Sedition Act of 1798 was a blatant effort by President John Adams and his fellow Federalists to cripple Vice President Thomas Jefferson's rival Republican Party (later the Democratic-Republican Party). The act made it a crime, punishable by up to two years in prison, to publish any "false, scandalous, or malicious" criticism of the government, the president, or either chamber of Congress with the intent to defame or excite hatred against any of them, stir up sedition, or aid foreign enemies. Adams's administration prosecuted editors of prominent Republican journals, forcing some of them to fold or suspend operations while their editors were in jail.

Federalists defended the constitutionality of the law by arguing that the First Amendment prohibited "prior restraints" on the press—censorship—but not subsequent punishment for defamatory publications. Jefferson's ally James Madison, one of the main authors of the Bill of Rights, wrote that the Federalist argument made a "mockery" of the free speech protection. The Supreme Court never ruled on the issue. The unpopularity of the law helped Jefferson win the presidency in the 1800 election. He pardoned all those convicted under the law, and Congress allowed the act to expire in 1801.

WAR AND SPEECH

Martial law during the Civil War at times imposed substantial limits on freedom of speech and the press. In the most prominent episode, Maj. Gen. Ambrose E. Burnside in 1863 prosecuted a prominent Northern Democratic war critic, Clement Vallandingham, for advocating resistance to the draft;

he also ordered the closing of a leading "Copperhead" newspaper, the *Chicago Times.* When President Abraham Lincoln learned of the actions, he ordered Burnside to allow the newspaper to resume operations. Later, Lincoln commuted Vallandingham's prison sentence to exile to the Confederacy. The Supreme Court never passed on the constitutionality of any of the antispeech measures.

JUNE 4, 1863
GEN. BURNSIDE'S DEPARTMENT.

The Suppression of the Chicago Times.
THE OFFICE IN POSSESSION OF THE MILITARY.
A Mass Meeting in Front of the Office.

CHICAGO, Wednesday, June 3.

Shortly after 12 o'clock last night Judge Drummond issued a writ directing the military authorities to take no further steps or measures to carry into effect the order of Maj.-Gen. Burnside for the suppression of the Chicago *Times,* until the application for a permanent writ of injunction could be heard in open Court to-day.

At 3½ o'clock this morning, after nearly the whole edition of the Chicago *Times* had been worked off, a file of Federal soldiers broke into the office and took possession of the establishment.

The soldiers remained in possession of the establishment for some time, and then left, after giving notice that if any attempt was made to publish another paper, the military would take permanent possession of the office. . . .

JUNE 5, 1863
GEN. BURNSIDE'S DEPARTMENT.

The Order Suppressing the Chicago Times Revoked.
The New-York World Allowed to Circulate.

CHICAGO, Thursday, June 4.

The *Times* having issued a paper this morning, the military took possession of the office, and remained until evening, when a telegram received by the proprietors from Gen. Burnside, saying that his order suppressing their circulation having been revoked by the President, they were at liberty to continue its publication.

In the United States Court, to-day, the entire session was devoted to hearing arguments of the counsel for the *Times. . . .*

• • • • • • • • • • •

The Court's first detailed examinations of the First Amendment's meaning came in the wake of World War I era laws aimed at suppressing anti-war sentiment. The Espionage Act of 1917 made it a crime, for example, to interfere with the military or obstruct recruitment or enlistment. The Sedition Act of 1918 broadened the law to prohibit saying or publishing anything intended to cause contempt or scorn for the government of the United States, the Constitution, the flag, or the uniform of the armed forces. Nearly 2,000 persons were prosecuted under the acts, and 900 were convicted, including Eugene V. Debs, the Socialist Party's presidential candidate.

In a series of decisions, the Supreme Court in 1919 and 1920 upheld convictions under the two laws, rejecting constitutional challenges and taking a lax view of the evidence needed to sustain a prosecution. In the first of the rulings, *Schenck v. United States* (1919), the Court unanimously upheld the conviction of Carl Schenck, secretary of the Socialist Party, for mailing draftees leaflets opposing the recently enacted Selective Service Act of 1917. Justice Oliver Wendell Holmes Jr.'s opinion is best remembered for his observation that freedom of speech "would not protect a man in falsely shouting fire in a theatre and causing panic."

More substantively, Holmes in *Schenck* set out an influential test— "clear and present danger"—for judging restrictions on speech. "The question in every case," he wrote, "is whether the words used are used in such circumstances and are of such a nature as to create a clear and present danger that they will bring about the substantive evils that Congress has a right to prevent." Holmes added that "many things that might be said in time of peace" would be "such a hindrance" during wartime that "no Court could regard them as a constitutional right."

Schenck v. United States

> **Decided:** March 3, 1919
> **Vote:** 9 (E. White, McKenna, Holmes, Day, Van Devanter, Pitney, McReynolds, Brandeis, Clarke)
> 0
> **Opinion of the Court:** Holmes

A week after the *Schenck* ruling, the Court was again unanimous in upholding Debs's conviction for a speech he delivered in Canton, Ohio, on June 16, 1918. Debs devoted most of the speech to socialism in general, but he told the crowd of some 1,200 supporters, "You need to know that you are fit for something better than slavery and cannon fodder." The government charged and a jury agreed that the speech was intended to interfere with recruiting and to incite insubordination in the armed forces. In *Debs v. United States* (1919), Holmes said the evidence was sufficient to sustain a conviction if opposition to the war was "one purpose" of the speech and its "probable effect."

When the Court upheld convictions in three later cases, however, Holmes dissented, arguing for a stricter application of his "clear and present danger" test. In the most important of the cases, the Court in *Abrams v. United States* (1919) upheld the convictions and twenty-year prison sentences of five Russian-born immigrants for distributing allegedly seditious pamphlets criticizing the U.S. government for sending troops into Russia in 1918. The "plain purpose of the propaganda," the Court wrote, "was to excite . . . disaffection, sedition, riots, and, as they hoped, revolution in this country."

In a dissent joined by Justice Louis D. Brandeis, Holmes saw no evidence of a "present danger" from what he called "a silly leaflet by an unknown man." He went on to argue eloquently for a broader view of free speech. "We should be eternally vigilant," he wrote, "against attempts to check the expression of opinions that we loathe and believe to be fraught with death, unless they so imminently threaten immediate interference with the lawful and pressing purposes of the law that an immediate check is required to save the country."

Holmes and Brandeis dissented again in two cases in 1920 upholding convictions of officers of a German-language newspaper for publishing wartime articles favorable to Germany and of several Socialist Party members for distributing a pamphlet viewed as intended to incite insubordination in the armed forces. Following Holmes's lead, Brandeis argued the articles and pamphlet were unlikely to have hampered the war effort. He went on in *Schaefer v. United States* (1920) to warn that upholding wartime restrictions on speech could carry over into peacetime: "In peace, too, men may differ widely as to what loyalty to our country demands; and an intolerant majority, swept by passion or by fear, may be prone in the future, as it has often been in the past, to stamp as disloyal opinions with which it disagrees."

SPEECH AND THE STATES

The Holmes and Brandeis dissents helped pave the way for the broader view of freedom of speech that developed gradually over the four decades that followed. In its next cases, the Court continued to take a narrow view of First Amendment protection by upholding state laws aimed at political dissent. Some of the laws stemmed from the assassination of President William McKinley in 1901 and prohibited criminal anarchy, defined as the advocacy of the overthrow of government by force. In the aftermath of the communist revolution in Russia, many states passed broader laws aimed at anticapitalist sentiment in the United States. These laws prohibited "criminal syndicalism," which was generally defined as advocating or teaching the use of crime, violence, or sabotage to bring about political change or a change in industrial ownership.

Gitlow v. New York

Decided: June 8, 1925

Vote: 7 (Taft, Van Devanter, McReynolds, Sutherland, Butler, Sanford, Stone)

2 (Holmes, Brandeis)

Opinion of the Court: Sanford

Dissenting opinion: Holmes (Brandeis)

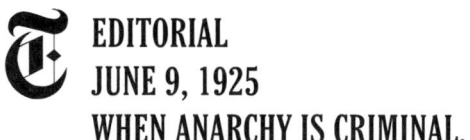

In two important cases in the 1920s, the Supreme Court upheld convictions under such laws. In the first, Benjamin Gitlow, a member of the left wing of the Socialist Party, had been convicted under New York's criminal anarchy law for distributing a pamphlet calling for "class action of the proletariat in any form having as its objective the conquest of the power of the state." In upholding the conviction in *Gitlow v. New York* (1925), Justice Edward T. Sanford dropped Holmes's "clear and present danger" test in favor of what came to be called the "bad tendency" test. The government has the power, Sanford wrote, to punish "those who abuse this freedom [of expression] by utterances inimical to the public welfare, tending to corrupt public morals, incite to crime, or disturb the peace." Justices Holmes and Brandeis dissented.

Despite the result, *Gitlow* expanded First Amendment protections by saying, for the first time, that the provisions applied not only to Congress, but also to the states. "For present purposes we may and do assume that freedom of speech and of the press . . . are among the fundamental personal rights and 'liberties' protected by the due process clause of the Fourteenth Amendment from impairment by the States," Sanford wrote. The statement—so casual that it went unmentioned in *The Times'* story—represented the birth of the so-called incorporation doctrine, the process of applying most of the Bill of Rights provisions to the states. (See table, page 355.)

EDITORIAL
JUNE 9, 1925
WHEN ANARCHY IS CRIMINAL.

Yesterday's decision of the Supreme Court in the Gitlow case is, in its essence, simply a reaffirmation of an old principle of law and government. Any constituted Government is entitled to protect itself against overthrow by violence. It

our highest judicial tribunal has now upheld its right to make criminal, is advocacy of the destruction of the Government by arms. Two dissenting Justices argue that the utterances of Benjamin Gitlow did not involve an "immediate danger"

> Were not Washington and Adams justified in rebelling against the British Government and attempting to overthrow its rule in this country? Certainly they were, but they knew what would happen to them if they were caught in arms as rebels.

can make the use of force against itself a crime. It is not, as the Supreme Court said, a question of an abstract or doctrinaire discussion of what may be the best form of government. What the State of New York made criminal, and what

to the Government of New York. Doubtless this is true. The vaporings of one anarchist, or of 10,000 anarchists, could not make the authorities tremble. But there is such a thing as a moral peril in addition to one merely physical. And the

Supreme Court is of the opinion that an open incitement to violence against the State is a moral peril against which the State may lawfully protect itself by a stringent statute.

This is no denial of free speech. But the free speakers must be ready to face their responsibility to the law for what they say. The Supreme Court does not rule against a political revolution. But the revolutionists must be prepared to undergo the penalty of failure. Were not Washington and Adams justified in rebelling against the British Government and attempting to overthrow its rule in this country? Certainly they were, but they knew what would happen to them if they were caught in arms as rebels.

As Daniel Webster said in his reply to Hayne, the right of revolution is unquestioned, but it must frankly be admitted to be a revolution; and those who engage in it must not whine if they are visited with the punishments made and provided for such acts as theirs. That is one trouble with our theoretic revolutionists of today. They want to eat their cake and have it too. They wish to bear themselves as rebels, yet to be treated as good and worthy citizens. The Supreme Court has decided that this can't be done. Revolutionists retain their old privilege of perishing gloriously in arms, but they can't incite others to perish and hope to get off themselves scot free.

. . . .

Two years after *Gitlow,* the Court similarly upheld the conviction of Anita Whitney, a niece of the late Supreme Court justice Stephen J. Field, under California's criminal syndicalism law for helping establish a state branch of the Communist Labor Party. Writing in *Whitney v. California* (1927), Sanford saw no distinction between Whitney's action and Gitlow's manifesto. For technical reasons, Holmes and Brandeis concurred in the result, but Brandeis wrote a memorable concurring opinion with a stirring defense of free speech. The founders of the nation, he wrote,

> believed that freedom to think as you will and to speak as you think are means indispensable to the discovery and spread of political truth; that without free speech and assembly discussion would be futile; that with them, discussion affords ordinarily adequate protection against the dissemination of noxious doctrine; that the greatest menace to freedom is an inert people; that public discussion is a political duty; and that this should be a fundamental principle of the American government.

In two cases a decade later, the Court created more room for political dissent. In *De Jonge v. Oregon* (1937), the Court unanimously reversed Dirk De Jonge's conviction for conducting a public meeting under Communist Party auspices. "Peaceable assembly for lawful discussion cannot be made a crime," Chief Justice Charles Evans Hughes wrote in the Court's first exposition on the right of assembly. In a second case, the Court reversed the conviction of an African American Communist Party organizer who was sent to Atlanta to distribute a booklet that called for black self-determination in the South. The majority in *Herndon v. Lowry* (1937) rejected Sanford's "bad tendency" test and, strictly applying Holmes's "clear and present danger" test, found the Georgia law "so vague and indeterminate" as to violate the Constitution.

FREE PRESS AND THE STATES

In the meantime, the Court had issued an important free press ruling that years later served as the standard for judging the government's effort to block publication of the Pentagon Papers. The ruling in *Near v. Minnesota* (1931) struck down a 1925 Minnesota law that prohibited, as a public nuisance, publication of any "malicious, scandalous, and defamatory newspaper, or other periodical."

Under the law, the truth of the articles could be used as a defense only if the allegations being challenged were published with good motive and for justifiable ends.

Floyd Olson, the Hennepin County (Minneapolis) attorney, invoked the law in 1927 to shut down the *Saturday Press,* a muckraking weekly, for publishing articles charging that a Jewish gangster controlled gambling, bootlegging, and racketeering in Minneapolis. The articles further charged that the Minneapolis police chief was in collusion with the gangster and that Olson was derelict in failing to stop the vice operations. After the Minnesota Supreme Court upheld an injunction forbidding continued publication of the paper, the manager, Jay Near, asked the U.S. Supreme Court to overturn it. Although Near was openly anti-Semitic in his writings, in oral arguments Justice Brandeis—then the only Jewish justice—clearly sided with the newspaper. "You cannot disclose evil without naming the doers of evil," Brandeis said during an extended colloquy with the state's attorney.

By a 5-4 vote, the Court held the "press gag" law was an unconstitutional prior restraint in violation of the First and Fourteenth Amendments. For the majority, Chief Justice Hughes acknowledged that the law did not operate exactly like the old English licensing laws that required prior approval of publication. But, he said, the practical effect of allowing public authorities to haul a publisher into court and then permitting a court to enjoin publication unless the publisher could prove the truth of any charges and show justifiable ends was much the same. "This is of the essence of censorship," Hughes concluded.

Prior restraints, Hughes continued, could be justified only in limited circumstances. He listed four: publication of crucial war information, such as the number and location of troops or the sailing dates of transport ships; obscene publications; incitements to acts of violence or the overthrow of the government; and protection of private rights. Forty years later, the justices who cast the deciding votes in the Pentagon Papers case found that the government had not met the standard Hughes laid down to justify a prior restraint on publication.

JANUARY 31, 1931
BRANDEIS CRITICIZES MINNESOTA GAG LAW

Justice, During Supreme Court Argument, Holds That It Limits Free Press.

DEFAMATION IS ADMITTED

"You Cannot Disclose Evil Without Naming Doers of Evil,"

He Says, Regarding Newspaper Articles.

Special to The New York Times

WASHINGTON, Jan. 30.—Arguments today on the constitutionality of the so-called Minnesota "gag law" before the Supreme Court today brought forth a comment from Justice Brandeis that "it is difficult to see how one can have free press and the protection it affords a democratic community without the privilege this act seeks to limit."

The case which was argued before the Supreme Court involves the appeal of J. M. Near from a ruling by the high court of Minnesota upholding an injunction issued in 1927 against The Saturday Press, a paper formerly published in Minneapolis by Mr. Near and Howard A. Guilford.

The injunction was issued under a law providing that any person engaged in the business of regularly or custom-arily publishing a periodical which is "malicious, scandalous and defamatory" is guilty of a nuisance and may be enjoined without jury trial.

Weymouth Kirkland, assisted by Howard Ellis and Edward C. Caldwell, the attorneys engaged by The Chicago Tribune, together with Thomas E. Latimer of Minneapolis, represented Mr. Near. The State was represented by James E. Markham, Deputy Attorney General, and William C. Larson and Arthur L. Markve, assistant county attorneys.

DEFAMATION IS ADMITTED.

While Mr. Markham was arguing Justice Brandeis interrupted with his comment.

The justice referred to the record in which appeared the text of The Saturday Press issue on which the case is based.

"In these articles," he said, "the editors state that they seek to expose combinations between criminals and public officials in conducting and profiting from gambling hells. They name the Chief of Police and other officials. They state that they have been threatened with being, to use their own words, 'bumped off.'

"They state that shortly after commencing publication Guilford was set upon by thugs and shot in the abdomen.

"We do not know whether these allegations are true or false, but we do know that just such criminal combinations exist, to the shame of some of our cities.

"What these men did seems like an effort to expose such a combination. Now, is that not a privileged communication, if there ever was one? How else can a community secure protection from that sort of thing if people are not allowed to engage in free discussion in such matters?

"Of course there was defamation. You cannot disclose evil without naming the doers of evil. It is difficult to see how one can have a free press and the protection it affords in the Democratic community without the privilege this act seeks to limit.

"You are dealing here not with a sort of a scandal too often appearing in the press, and which ought not to appear to the interest of any one, but with a matter of prime interest to every American citizen.

"What sort of a matter could be more privileged?"

CANNOT ALWAYS AWAIT THE COURT.

"Assuming it to be true," Mr. Markham interposed.

"No," Justice Brandeis answered, "a newspaper cannot always wait until it gets the judgment of a court. These men set out on a campaign to rid the city of certain evils."

"So they say," Mr. Markham interposed again.

"Yes, of course, so they say," Justice Brandeis admitted. "They went forward with a definite program and certainly they acted with great courage. They invited suit for criminal libel if what they said was not true. Now, if that campaign was not privileged, if that is not one of the things for which the press chiefly exists, then for what does it exist?

"As for such defamatory matter being issued regularly or customarily, how can such a campaign be conducted except by persistence and continued iteration?"

Justice Brandeis's statement was regarded among those in court as a liberal interpretation of a statute relating to the publication by newspapers of "defamatory" statements involving an individual's character.

Mr. Markham contended that the power contemplated in the law was within the police powers of the State, and that it was for the State Supreme Court to construe the provisions of the State Constitution. The law, he argued, did not violate the guarantees of the Federal Constitution because it provided for "due process of law" as commanded by the Fourteenth Amendment. He denied that the issue of "previous restraint" was raised.

Arguing on behalf of Mr. Near, Attorney Kirkland said the Minnesota law did in fact violate the Federal Constitution. He admitted that the matter published had been defamatory.

"So long as men do evil, so long will newspapers publish defamation," he asserted. " 'Boss' Tweed would have invoked such a law as this against the newspapers who exposed the corruption of his régime."

The question of jurisdiction was at issue as well as the appeal itself, Mr. Kirkland said.

It was considered an indication that the court had this in mind when Chief Justice Hughes announced, during the course of Mr. Markham's argument, that he need not argue further whether or not freedom of the press was a privilege or immunity under the Fourteenth Amendment, as prior decisions of the court had so held it.

• • • • • • • • • • •

FREEDOM OF SPEECH

By making nine appointments to the Supreme Court from 1937 to 1943, President Franklin D. Roosevelt wrought what proved to be a lasting transformation in the Court's jurisprudence. The most immediate effect of the "Revolution of 1937" was a new willingness to uphold the power of Congress to regulate economic affairs. (See page 20.) Within a few years, the Court also began to adopt a newfound solicitude toward individual rights—particularly in free speech disputes. Despite various twists and turns, the Court ever since has subjected government restrictions on speech to much more rigorous scrutiny than it had before.

CHANGING TRENDS: THE "REVOLUTION OF 1937"

In one early indication of the new trend, the Court in 1939 upheld the right of labor unions to assemble in public places. The case, *Hague v. CIO,* stemmed from actions by Frank Hague, the powerful mayor of Jersey City, New Jersey, to prevent labor organizing efforts by the Committee for Industrial Organization (which later merged with the American Federation of Labor to form the AFL-CIO). Hague claimed the ban was needed to prevent riots or strikes. In the Court's main opinion, Justice Owen J. Roberts said that although the right to use public streets and parks to discuss public issues was not absolute, "it must not, in the guise of regulation, be abridged or denied."

More dramatic evidence of the changed attitude toward speech issues came in a pair of cases that first upheld and then struck down local school boards' requirement that students salute the U.S. flag. Most Americans viewed the daily flag salute as a valuable ritual for inculcating patriotism in youngsters. To Jehovah's Witnesses, however, the exercise violated the teaching of their faith against worshiping graven images. The issue reached the Supreme Court after lower federal courts ruled in favor of two young people, Lillian and William Gobitas, who were expelled from their school in Minersville, Pennsylvania, for refusing to salute the flag.

In an 8-1 decision in *Minersville School District v. Gobitis* (the family name was misspelled in Court records), the Court in 1940 upheld the school board's requirement. Hailing the flag as the "symbol of our national unity," Justice Felix Frankfurter said state and local authorities had discretion to use "various means to evoke that unifying sentiment without which there can ultimately be no liberties, civil or religious." Only Justice Harlan Fiske Stone dissented. Two years later, however, three of the FDR-appointed justices who had joined in the decision—Hugo Black, William O. Douglas, and Frank Murphy—wrote in another case involving Jehovah's Witnesses that they had changed their views of the issue.

JUNE 4, 1940
COMPULSORY FLAG SALUTE UPHELD BY SUPREME COURT IN SCHOOL CASE

Banner Symbolizes Unity 'Transcending All Differences,' Says Opinion, Denying Right of Religious Exemption

Special to The New York Times

WASHINGTON, June 3—School boards can compel a salute by children to the American flag, "symbol of our national unity," no matter how conscientious the religious beliefs of the children, the Supreme Court ruled in an eight-to-one decision today. Justice Stone alone objected to the ruling in the last session before the Summer recess.

Arguing on the reconciliation of the two "rights" of religious freedom and national unity, Mr. Frankfurter concluded that the courts could not interfere with the convic-

tions of Legislatures that a particular program would best promote in the minds of children "an attachment to the institutions of their country."

In his dissent, Mr. Stone said that the majority decision seemed "no more than the surrender of the constitutional protection of the liberty of small minorities to the popular will."

Leaving the bench, the justices promised a review, at the October term, to four important cases. These included a challenge to the constitutionality of the Wage and

Hour Act, a California court conviction of The Los Angeles Times for contempt; sentences of two Russian-born men for espionage in California, and the power of the National Labor Relations Board to force written agreements between employers and labor unions.

On the other hand, the court declined to grant reviews to the American Medical Association in its protest that as a "learned profession" and not a "trade," it cannot be prosecuted under the anti-trust laws, and to Grover Cleveland Bergdoll, World War draft dodger, seeking release from a military prison.

The Frankfurter decision concerned Lillian and William Gobitis, members of Jehovah's Witnesses, who when 12 and 10 years old in 1935, refused to salute the American flag, as required by the school board of [Minersville], Pa. They asserted that the salute violated their religious tenets. Expelled by the school board they sought an injunction which was granted by the Federal District Court and upheld by the Third Circuit Court of Appeals. The latter tribunal was reversed by the Frankfurter ruling.

"Propagation of belief—even of disbelief in the supernatural—is protected, whether in church or chapel, mosque or synagogue, tabernacle or meeting-house," said Justice Frankfurter.

Later, however, he denied that "freedom to follow conscience" did not have "limits in the life of a society." He added:

"The religious liberty which the Constitution protects has never excluded legislation of general scope not directed against doctrinal loyalties of particular sects. Judicial nullification of legislation cannot be justified by attributing to the framers of the Bill of Rights views for which there is no historic warrant."

The American flag is the "symbol of our national unity, transcending all internal differences, however large," within the framework of the Constitution, Justice Frankfurter stated.

"This court," he added, "has had occasion to say that the flag is the symbol of the nation's power, the emblem of freedom in its truest, best sense. It signifies government

resting on consent of the governed; liberty regulated by law; the protection of the weak against the strong; security against the exercise of arbitrary power, and absolute safety for free institutions against foreign aggression.

"The precise issue then, for us to decide, is whether the Legislatures of the various States and the authorities in a thousand counties and school districts of this country are barred from determining the appropriateness of various means to evoke that unifying sentiment without which there can ultimately be no liberties, civil or religious.

"To stigmatize legislative judgment in providing for the universal gesture of respect for the symbol of our national life in the setting of the common school as a lawless inroad on that freedom of conscience which the Constitution protects, would amount to no less than the pronouncement of pedagogical and psychological dogma in a field where courts possess no marked and certainly no controlling competence.

"The wisdom of training children in patriotic impulses by those compulsions which necessarily pervade so much of the educational process is not for our independent judgment. Even were we convinced of the folly of such a measure, such belief would be no proof of its unconstitutionality."

Justice Stone said that by the school law, Pennsylvania seeks "to coerce these children to express a sentiment which, as they interpret it, they do not entertain, and which violates their deepest religious convictions.

"The law is unique in the history of Anglo-American legislation," he continued. "It does more than suppress freedom of speech and more than prohibit the free exercise of religion which conceivably are forbidden by the First Amendment and are violations of the liberty guaranteed by the Fourteenth.

"History teaches us that there have been but few infringements of personal liberty by the State which have not been justified, as they are here, in the name of righteousness and the public good, and few which have not been directed, as they are now, at helpless political minorities."

. . . .

West Virginia State Board of Education v. Barnette

Decided: June 14, 1943

Vote: 6 (Stone, Black, Douglas, Murphy, R. Jackson, W. Rutledge)

   3 (O. Roberts, Reed, Frankfurter)

Opinion of the Court: R. Jackson

Concurring opinions (2): Black (Douglas); Murphy

Dissenting opinion: Frankfurter

Dissenting without opinion: O. Roberts, Reed

A year later—with Stone elevated to chief justice and two more FDR appointees—the Court reversed the prior decision in a ruling that has become an oft-quoted, free-speech landmark. Writing for the 6-3 majority in *West Virginia State Board of Education v. Barnette* (1943), Justice Robert H. Jackson voiced doubt that the strength of the government depended on the "power of the State to expel a handful of children from school." Writing with the nation at war, Jackson continued:

To believe that patriotism will not flourish if patriotic ceremonies are voluntary and spontaneous instead of a compulsory routine is to make an unflattering estimate of the appeal of our institutions to free minds. . . .

If there is any fixed star in our constitutional constellation, it is that no official, high or petty, can prescribe what shall be orthodox in politics, nationalism, religion, or other matter of opinion, or force citizens to confess by word or at their faith therein.

JUNE 15, 1943
SUPREME COURT ENDS COMPULSION OF FLAG SALUTE

Reverses 1940 Stand in 6-to-3 Decision Upholding Jehovah Sect Under Bill of Rights

GIVEN ON EMBLEM'S DAY

Jackson, for Majority, Forbids 'Coercion'—Frankfurter Sees No Curb on Religious Belief

By LEWIS WOOD

Special to The New York Times

WASHINGTON, June 14—In a reversal of the Gobitis decision of June, 1940, the Supreme Court held by 6 to 3 today that under the Bill of Rights public school children could not be compelled to salute the American flag if this ceremony conflicted with their religious beliefs.

The ruling was handed down while the nation was celebrating Flag Day in commemoration of the 164th anniversary of the Stars and Stripes.

It upheld a challenge by members of the sect of Jehovah's Witnesses to a flag-salute regulation issued by the West Virginia Board of Education.

In the Gobitis case the Witnesses brought a test against similar regulations of the Minersville, Pa., School District, but the Supreme Court then sustained the flag-salute order by 8 to 1.

PROTECTION BY CONSTITUTION

Writing the majority opinion in today's case, Justice Robert H. Jackson said:

"We think the action of the local authorities in compelling the flag salute and pledge transcends constitu-

tional limitations on their power and invades the sphere of intellect and spirit which it is the purpose of the First Amendment to our Constitution to reserve from all official control."

The First Amendment protects freedom of religion, speech and the press, and right of assembly and petition.

Specifically overruling the Minersville and similar decisions, Justice Jackson also said:

"To sustain the compulsory flag salute we are required to say that a Bill of Rights which guards the individual's right to speak his own mind left it open to public authorities to compel him to utter what is not in his mind."

Justices Owen J. Roberts, Stanley F. Reed and Felix Frankfurter all dissented, standing by their attitude in the Gobitis case, in which Harlan F. Stone, then an associate justice, alone opposed the compulsory flag salute.

Justices Hugo L. Black, William O. Douglas and Frank Murphy, who were in the majority in the Gobitis decision, written by Justice Frankfurter, switched in the new test. Justices Jackson and Wiley Rutledge were not members of the court in 1940.

SECT WINS OTHER CASES

Dealing with other controversies involving Jehovah's Witnesses, the Supreme Court today unanimously held invalid a Mississippi statute under which three members of the sect were convicted of sedition for disseminating teachings "tending to create an attitude of stubborn refusal to salute, honor and respect" the flag and the Federal Government.

Justice Roberts wrote this opinion, which was controlled by the West Virginia ruling. Following recent precedents, the jurists also arranged for dismissal of a case in which a Jehovah's Witness was convicted for selling literature in the District of Columbia.

More than ten years ago, Mr. Jackson recalled, Chief Justice Charles Evans Hughes "led this court in holding that the display of a red flag as a symbol of opposition to peaceful and legal means to organized government was protected by the free-speech guarantees of the Constitution."

"Here it is the State that employs a flag as a symbol of adherence to government as presently organized," he went on. "It requires the individual to communicate by word and sign his acceptance of the political ideas it thus bespeaks.

"Objection to this form of communication when coerced is an old one, well known to the framers of the Bill of Rights."

> To sustain the compulsory flag salute we are required to say that a Bill of Rights which guards the individual's right to speak his own mind left it open to public authorities to compel him to utter what is not in his mind.
>
> —Justice Robert H. Jackson,
> *West Virginia State Board of Education v. Barnette*

In the West Virginia case Justice Jackson pointed out that children of the Jehovah's Witnesses, obeying a canon of the sect against worshiping an image, had been expelled from school and threatened with reformatory terms for refusal to salute the flag, while their parents had been prosecuted.

"RIGHTS OF THE INDIVIDUAL"

Asserting that the refusal of the children to participate in the ceremony did not interfere with or deny the rights of others to do so, Mr. Jackson continued:

"Nor is there any question in this case that their behavior is peaceful and orderly. The sole conflict is between authority and rights of the individual.

"The State asserts power to condition access to public education on making a prescribed sign and profession and at the same time to coerce attendance by punishing both parent and child. The latter stand on a right of self-determination in matters that touched individual opinion and personal attitude."

Discussing the meaning of pledges and the flag salutes as symbols of an idea, Mr. Jackson remarked:

"A person gets from a symbol the meaning he puts into it, and what is one man's comfort and inspiration is another's jest and scorn."

"FUTILITY" OF COMPULSION

Justice Jackson also said that there was a doubt whether Abraham Lincoln "would have thought that the strength of government to maintain itself would be impressively vindicated by our confirming power of the State to expel a handful of children from school."

Dwelling upon "the ultimate futility of such attempts to compel coherence," he added:

"To believe that patriotism will not flourish if patriotic ceremonies are voluntary and spontaneous instead of a compulsory routine is to make an unflattering estimate of the appeal of our institutions to free minds.

"If there is any fixed star in our constitutional constellation, it is that no official, high or petty, can prescribe what shall be orthodox in politics, nationalism, religion, or other matter of opinion, or force citizens to confess by word or act their faith therein."

DISSENT BY FRANKFURTER

In a separate dissent, Justice Frankfurter, a Jew, said that "one who belongs to the most vilified and persecuted minority in history is not likely to be insensible to the freedoms guaranteed by our Constitution."

He said that, were his "purely personal attitude relevant," he would whole-heartedly associate himself with "the general libertarian views in the Court's opinion, representing as they do the thought and action of a lifetime."

"But," he contended, "saluting the flag did not curb religious beliefs, and West Virginia had power to make the regulations without violating constitutional rights."

"It is self delusive to believe that the liberal spirit can be enforced by judicial invalidation of illiberal legislation," he stated.

Noting the existence of 250 religious denominations in the United States, he commented:

"Certainly this court cannot be called upon to determine what claims of conscience should be recognized and what should be rejected as satisfying the 'religion' which the Constitution protects.

"I cannot bring my mind to believe that the 'liberty' secured by the Due Process Clause gives this court authority to deny to the State of West Virginia the attainment of that which we all recognize as a legitimate legislative end—namely, the promotion of good citizenship, by employment of the means here chosen."

Mr. Frankfurter pointed out that the flag salute had been five times previously before the Supreme Court, and that every justice—thirteen in all—who had participated "found no constitutional infirmity in what is now condemned."

Justices Roberts and Reed said in four lines that their judgment in the Gobitis decision was still correct. Justices Black and Douglas and Justice Murphy presented special concurrences with Justice Jackson.

With three major cases still on the calendar, the court announced another decision session for next Monday.

*   *   *   *   *   *   *   *   *   *   *   *   *

Communists and Subversives in the Cold War

The Cold War presented the Court with a wide array of free speech issues in the context of various federal and state laws aimed at curbing communist or subversive activity within the United States. The Alien Registration Act of 1940, known as the Smith Act, made it a crime to advocate—or to belong to an organization that advocated—overthrowing the government by force or violence. The Internal Security Act of 1950, informally the McCarran Act, required communist-action and communist-front groups to register with the government and disclose their members and officers; members of such groups were prohibited from holding federal jobs or jobs in defense-related industries. Separately, Congress required labor union officers to certify that they were not members of the Communist Party. In addition, many states passed laws requiring loyalty oaths by public employees, especially teachers.

As with the flag salute issue, the Court initially upheld these laws but later—with a change in membership—issued rulings that narrowed the enforcement of some of the laws and struck others down completely. In 1951, for example, the Court in *Dennis v. United States* upheld on a 6-2 vote the Smith Act convictions of eleven leaders of the Communist Party, including the party's general secretary, Eugene Dennis. In the main opinion, Chief Justice Frederick (Fred) M. Vinson applied a relaxed version of the "clear and present danger" test, citing "the inflammable nature of world conditions." A year later, the Court voted 6-3 in *Adler v. Board of Education* to uphold a New York law barring members of subversive organizations from teaching in public schools. "School authorities have the right and the duty to screen . . . officials, teachers, and employees as to their fitness to maintain the integrity of the schools as a part of ordered society," Justice Sherman Minton wrote.

The Warren Court: Changing Outlooks on Free Speech

President Dwight D. Eisenhower's first three appointments to the Supreme Court—Earl Warren as chief justice and John Marshall Harlan and William J. Brennan Jr. as associate justices—changed the Court's outlook on antisubversive measures. When a new batch of fourteen Smith Act convictions reached the Court in 1957, Harlan—the namesake grandson of the nineteenth-century justice—wrote for a 5-4 majority in holding that the act prohibited advocacy or teaching of the forcible overthrow of the government only when connected to some effort to instigate action to that end. The ruling in *Yates v. United Sates* effectively put an end to most federal prosecutions under the act. On the same day, the Court in *Watkins v. United States* significantly curbed Congress's power to summon members of antisubversive organizations and threaten them with contempt citations for refusing to answer; the Court said that congressional hearings had to be held for a legitimate legislative purpose. "High Court Has Made a New Historic Turn," *The New York Times* declared in a headline.

NEWS ANALYSIS
JUNE 23, 1957
HIGH COURT HAS MADE A NEW HISTORIC TURN

This Shift is Toward a Renewed Concern for Personal Rights
By LUTHER A. HUSTON
Special to The New York Times

WASHINGTON, June 22—The primary function of the Supreme Court is to relate the law to the Constitution.

How it performs that function varies with the personnel of the court at any given time. History is replete with incidents of a court of today discarding a constitutional interpretation of a court of yesterday.

No more notable example can be found than the high court's ruling in the school segregation cases. There the court of 1954 discarded the separate-but-equal doctrine laid down by the court of 1896.

The present court is less disposed than some of its predecessors to stick to "stare decisis," which means, roughly, stand by the decisions of the past. If any description fits the court of today it is that it makes up its own mind, whether on the basis of law or its own ideas of how the law should be applied.

WASHINGTON COMMENT

A comment heard in Washington this week after the high court had acquitted five minor Communist leaders and ordered new trials for nine others and had set aside the conviction of a labor leader for contempt of Congress was that if a few more "Eisenhower radicals" were appointed to the tribunal, it would wreck both the Legislative and Executive branches of the Government.

Eisenhower appointees do not dominate the court as yet. There are nine members and General Eisenhower has appointed only four of them.

It is significant, however, that at least three of the Eisenhower appointees have joined in recent major decisions with Justices who were appointed by President Franklin D. Roosevelt to strike down administrative enforcement pro-

One thing stands out, however, with regard to the present court. More than any of its recent predecessors, it is independent of other branches of the Government. It doesn't care who it slaps down.

By and large, this is a court that believes that the Constitution and the law should be interpreted in the light of changing concepts of political and social problems.

One thing stands out, however, with regard to the present court. More than any of its recent predecessors, it is independent of other branches of the Government. It doesn't care who it slaps down.

cedures of laws enacted during the Truman Administration. The two Truman appointees remaining on the court have been the dissenters.

Of the members of the present court, Justices Hugo L. Black, Felix Frankfurter and William O. Douglas were Roosevelt appointees. President Truman named Justices Harold H. Burton, a Republican, and Tom C. Clark to the court. Eisenhower appointees are Chief Justice Earl Warren, and Justices John M. Harlan, William J. Brennan Jr., a Democrat, and Charles Evans Whittaker.

It is illogical and unsafe to list any Justice at any time in any specific category, like liberal or conservative.

But there is a discernible pattern of judgment in today's court. And it is a pattern that appears to have changed with the Eisenhower appointees.

No one familiar with Chief Justice Warren's political record as Governor of California could have expected him to bring to the high court an arch-conservative viewpoint.

BLOC IN COURT

It has surprised many, however, and dismayed some, that Chief Justice Warren has so often been found in alignment with Justices Black and Douglas, who came to court as avowedly New Deal liberals.

So, if there is a bloc on the court that can be classified as "liberal" it consists of Chief Justice Warren and Justices Black and Douglas, each of whom came to the court with differing personal backgrounds, political experience and educations.

In such recent decisions as the du Pont-General Motors antitrust case and the ruling that the military could not try civilians accompanying the armed forces for capital or infamous crimes committed abroad, another Eisenhower appointee has lined up with this so-called "liberal faction." He is Justice Brennan, who was appointed on his judicial record as a member of the Supreme Court of New Jersey.

There are many who contend that social philosophies, rather than profound legal knowledge or sound judicial experience predominate in the opinions of the court's liberals. That appraisal has not been applied, however, to Justice Harlan, the second man named to the court by President Eisenhower.

It has been said of Justice Harlan that if he can give a liberal application to the law he will do so but in any case he will stick to what he believes to be the law.

NEWEST APPOINTEE

The fourth Eisenhower appointee, Justice Whittaker, has not been on the court long enough to warrant an estimate of where he will fit in any division of the court into categories.

Justice Frankfurter came to the court out of the turbulent days of the Roosevelt New Deal. Perhaps more than any other sitting Justice he is steeped in constitutional lore and equipped with a wide knowledge of Congressional history and administrative law. The safest thing to do with him, however, is not to place him in any particular category but just to classify him as "Mr. Justice Frankfurter."

When Justice Clark was named to the court, he was regarded as something less than a hide-bound conservative. He had served as a Justice Department attorney in the Roosevelt days, and as Attorney General in the Truman administration.

In recent decisions, such as the Watkins and Smith Act cases this week, he has been the sharp dissenter.

It would be inaccurate to draw any conclusion from Justice Clark's position in these cases, however, other than that his background and experience have convinced him that the high court should not lightly invalidate laws designed to make thorny the path of the criminal or strike down procedures of law enforcement agencies unless their injustice to individuals is clearly demonstrable.

'CONSERVATIVE' LISTING

Logic might compel the listing of Justice Burton as the sole "conservative," as the term is generally applied, on the court. He wrote a well-reasoned dissent from the majority decision in the du Pont antitrust case and joined Justice Clark in dissents in other cases where he felt that the majority was overturning established precedents or unnecessarily restricting the operations of Congress or executive agencies.

The court is scheduled to end its present term in a few weeks. Just what has been its contribution to constitutional law undoubtedly will be a subject of discussion in law reviews and bar association meetings—and in Congress—for an indeterminate future. Careful study and painstaking analysis is essential to a final appraisal.

INDIVIDUAL RIGHTS

A permissible generality, however, is that whenever the present court has decided a constitutional issue it has placed political, academic and individual freedoms ahead of corporate or property rights or legislative and executive enactments and procedures.

It has interpreted the Constitution with emphasis on the Bill of Rights wherever those amendments to the national charter could be applied.

This is because the men who sit in judgment are the product of an era that witnessed the emergence of a new and worldwide regard for human freedoms wherever they came in conflict with traditional regard for the rights of property. Some of those who sit on the high court have been leaders in the development of this era.

• • • • • • • • • • •

The Court followed with a series of rulings in the 1960s striking down state loyalty oaths. These culminated in a 1967 decision, *Keyishian v. Board of Regents,* striking down the New York law upheld fifteen years earlier in *Adler.* Writing for the 5-4 majority, Justice Brennan described academic freedom as "a special concern" of the First Amendment and said that curtailing teachers' freedom of association without any proof of specific action to further unlawful aims would have "a stifling effect on the academic mind."

The Court gave even greater protection to political advocacy the next year in a decision that discarded Justice Holmes's "clear and present danger" test in favor of an "incitement" test requiring a closer connection between advocacy and threatened illegal conduct. The ruling in *Brandenburg v. Ohio* (1969) unanimously reversed the conviction of Clarence Brandenburg under Ohio's criminal syndicalism law for his provocative speech at a Ku Klux Klan rally near Cincinnati. "The constitutional guarantees of free speech and free press do not permit a State to forbid or proscribe advocacy of the use of force or of law violation," the Court declared, "except where such advocacy is directed to inciting or producing imminent lawless action and is likely to incite or produce such action." The opinion was unsigned, but it was learned later that it was drafted by Justice Abe Fortas and released only after he had been forced to resign because of ethics scandals.

A year earlier, the Court had been somewhat less protective of so-called symbolic speech—specifically, the burning of a draft card to protest the Vietnam War. The ruling in *United States v. O'Brien* (1968) upheld the conviction of David O'Brien, who along with three other anti-war protesters burned his draft card on the steps of the South Boston courthouse in 1966. In a 7-1 decision, the Court said that the government has the power to punish conduct that combines both "speech" and "nonspeech" elements. The *O'Brien* test allows restrictions on speech if three conditions are met: the regulations must be within the government's constitutional powers; they must further an important or substantial governmental interest unrelated to the suppression of free expression; and any incidental restrictions on First Amendment freedom must be no greater than essential to that interest. Chief Justice Warren said the government's interest in enforcing Selective Service laws met those conditions.

Brandenburg v. Ohio

> **Decided:** June 9, 1969
> **Vote:** 8 (Warren, Black, Douglas, Harlan II, Brennan, Stewart, White, T. Marshall)
> 0
> **Opinion:** *Per curiam*
> **Concurring opinions (2):** Black; Douglas (Black)

Armbands and Assembly: The Court during the Vietnam Era

A different use of symbolic speech to protest the Vietnam War produced a landmark ruling the next year in favor of free speech rights for students. The ruling in *Tinker v. Des Moines Independent Community School District* (1969) invalidated the suspensions of three teenagers for wearing black armbands to school to show their opposition to the war. Students or teachers do not "shed their constitutional rights to freedom of speech or expression at the schoolhouse gate," Justice Fortas wrote for the 7-2 majority. Fortas rejected what he called school officials' "undifferentiated fear" that the protest might cause a disturbance. But the ruling left open the possibility of restricting students' speech if officials have reasonable grounds to anticipate "substantial disruption of or material interference with school activities" or intrusion on the "school affairs or lives" of other students.

Tinker v. Des Moines Independent Community School District

> **Decided:** February 24, 1969
> **Vote:** 7 (Warren, Douglas, Brennan, Stewart, B. White, Fortas, T. Marshall)
> 2 (Black, Harlan II)
> **Opinion of the Court:** Fortas
> **Concurring opinions (2):** Stewart; B. White
> **Dissenting opinions (2):** Black; Harlan II

The Vietnam War era tested the boundaries of what constituted free speech. Mary Beth and John Tinker were suspended from school for wearing black armbands in protest of the war. In 1969 the Supreme Court upheld their right to do so.

Source: The Granger Collection, New York

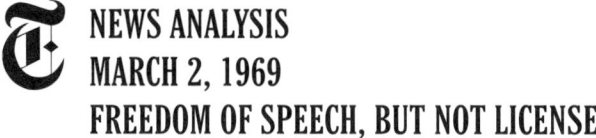

NEWS ANALYSIS
MARCH 2, 1969
FREEDOM OF SPEECH, BUT NOT LICENSE

WASHINGTON—There is less than meets the eye to the Supreme Court's new ruling that public school students have a constitutional right to be heard as well as seen.

On the face of it, the Court seemed to be doing a groovy new thing when it held last Monday that the city fathers of Des Moines, Iowa, violated the free speech rights of seven students (including Paul Tinker, age eight, a second-grader) when they made them remove the black armbands they had put on as a protest against the Vietnam war.

The Court had never before said that students of public schools—or colleges, for that matter—have free speech rights that the courts will enforce against their elders. The ruling drew a strong dissent from Justice Hugo L. Black, who is 83 years old, and some youngsters may have believed that they had scored in a big way.

"If the time has come when pupils of state-supported schools—kindergarten, grammar school or high school—can defy and flout orders of school officials to keep their minds on their own school work, it is the beginning of a new revolutionary era of permissiveness in this country fostered by the judiciary," Justice Black said.

'STUDENT POWER'

It may be that some of Justice Black's predictions will come true, but events are likely to show that the Court's ruling won't usher "student power" into the public schools. The only real alternative to the decision was to say that students have no free speech rights, and the law had almost developed too far to take that position now.

The Supreme Court had ruled as far back as 1943 that public school students were protected by the "freedom of religion" clause of the First Amendment, and that they did not have to salute the flag if it was against their faith.

A string of cases since then have established that public school teachers are also protected by the "free speech" clause of the First Amendment. Many lawyers had assumed that the Supreme Court would eventually extend the free-speech guarantee to students as well.

Lower courts had already done this. Southern school authorities were barred from making Negro students remove their civil rights buttons. A South Carolina college's rule against any and all demonstrations was struck down.

The Supreme Court's new decision will reinforce these actions and will probably pave the way for a few embellish-

ever there is reason to believe it would cause disorder or invade the rights of others—a restrictive standard that will give school personnel power to limit students' speech under many, and perhaps most, circumstances.

Furthermore, free "speech" to students means only non-disruptive talk, plus a narrow class of conduct called "symbolic speech," such as armbands, placards and banners. Last week's decision specifically said that sit-ins, picketing and demonstrations are not protected.

> **Many legal observers believed that students who take the decision as a license to tell off the teacher or sit-in at the principal's office could be in for a surprise.**

ments. Students may get by with more criticism of teachers and school officials, and parents' efforts to purge material they don't like from the reading lists will probably be barred.

But many legal observers believed that students who take the decision as a license to tell off the teacher or sit-in at the principal's office could be in for a surprise. The Justices, according to this view, realized that when they extended the First Amendment's free speech right to children that it would have to be a child-sized First Amendment—and so they trimmed it down to fit the occasion.

RESTRICTIVE STANDARD

An adult usually cannot be penalized by the Government for what he says unless his words create a "clear and present danger" of trouble. But the free speech right extended by the Supreme Court to students permits school authorities to curb students' right of expression when-

The opinion by Justice Abe Fortas made no distinction between students' rights according to age or grade; but obviously the "reasonableness" test means that college students must be granted more freedom of expression than grade school children. None of this applies to private school students, since the First Amendment controls actions of only public officials.

Finally, the student's new right of expression does not help those who choose miniskirts and hippie hair styles as a way of expressing their individualism. Since 1923, when the Arkansas Supreme Court upheld the expulsion of a high school girl who powdered her face in violation of a school rule, students have lost every time they've gone to court over this issue.

So before the school children of the country decide to begin swinging with their new constitutional rights, they would do well to read some of the fine print in the decision and reflect that all nine justices are, after all, "over 30."

—FRED P. GRAHAM

• • • • • • • • • • •

Through the 1960s, the Court also issued a series of freedom of assembly rulings limiting the government's power to use breach of peace or disorderly conduct laws to bar public demonstrations. The Court in 1941 had made clear that local governments could impose reasonable "time, place, and manner" regulations on public parades and demonstrations. But the rulings in a series of civil rights–related cases in the 1960s underscored that peaceful demonstrations could not be blocked selectively or arbitrarily. Between 1963 and 1969, the Court threw out convictions for demonstrating at South Carolina's state Capitol, a Louisiana courthouse, a public library in Louisiana, and a residential neighborhood in Chicago. In the only exception to the trend, the Court sustained on a 5-4 vote trespassing convictions arising from a demonstration at a Florida jail, citing security grounds.

Campaign Finance and Flag Burning as Free Speech

The Court in 1976 created a new First Amendment right when it struck down as a free speech violation provisions of a federal law setting ceilings on campaign spending by candidates for Congress or the presidency. (See page 246.) In other areas, however, the Court since the 1960s has generally applied prior rulings to new circumstances with varying results that often reject First Amendment claims. In the 1980s, for example, the Court issued rulings upholding the right of school officials to punish a high school student for a sexually tinged speech to a student assembly or to censor a high school newspaper published as part of the school's curriculum. In the 1990s, the Court ruled that judges could set limits on protests outside abortion clinics if they blocked access by patients or staff. In 1991 and again in 2000, the Court ruled that local governments can ban nude dancing—though each time in fractured and closely divided decisions.

Texas v. Johnson

 Decided: June 21, 1989

 Vote: 5 (Brennan, T. Marshall,
   Blackmun, Scalia, Kennedy)

   4 (Rehnquist, B. White,
   Stevens, O'Connor)

 Opinion of the Court: Brennan

 Concurring opinion: Kennedy

 Dissenting opinions (2): Rehnquist
   (B. White, O'Connor); Stevens

In its most controversial of recent free speech rulings, however, the Court twice struck down laws prohibiting the burning or other desecration of the American flag. Congress in 1967 had passed a law making it a federal offense to "knowingly cast contempt upon any flag of the United States by publicly mutilating, defacing, defiling, burning or trampling" upon it. Texas and forty-seven other states had similar laws against flag desecration. By a 5-4 vote in *Texas v. Johnson* (1989), the Court reversed the conviction of Gregory Johnson, who had set fire to a flag outside the Republican National Convention in Dallas in 1984 to protest Reagan administration policies. For the majority, Justice Brennan said the government has no power to prohibit expression "simply because society finds the idea itself offensive or disagreeable." He went on, "We do not consecrate the flag by punishing its desecration, for in doing so we dilute the freedom that this cherished emblem represents."

JUNE 22, 1989
JUSTICES, 5-4, BACK PROTESTERS' RIGHT TO BURN THE FLAG

By LINDA GREENHOUSE
Special to The New York Times

In a decision virtually certain to be a First Amendment landmark, the Supreme Court ruled today that no laws could prohibit political protesters from burning the American flag.

The 5-to-4 decision had the effect of declaring unconstitutional the flag desecration laws of 48 states, as well as a similar Federal statute, in cases of peaceful political expression. It left open the possibility that burning a flag to incite a riot could be prosecuted as a crime. Only Alaska and Wyoming do not make flag burning a crime.

In his majority opinion today, Justice William J. Brennan Jr. said, "We do not consecrate the flag by punishing its desecration, for in doing so we dilute the freedom that this cherished emblem represents."

OPINIONS ARE READ ALOUD

The case cut across the usual ideological divisions on the Court and appeared to engage the Justices' deepest emotions. There was a spellbinding session in the courtroom this morning when, in contrast to the usual cursory announcements of the court's rulings, Justice Brennan spent 15 minutes reading much of his majority opinion aloud in a gravelly but firm voice. Justice John Paul Stevens, usually a liberal ally of Justice Brennan's, then read aloud his dissenting opinion. Dissenting Justices rarely read their opinions in the courtroom.

Two of the Court's most conservative Justices, Antonin Scalia and Anthony M. Kennedy, joined Justice Brennan, as did Justices Thurgood Marshall and Harry A.

Blackmun. Chief Justice William H. Rehnquist and Justices Byron R. White and Sandra Day O'Connor were the other dissenters.

'84 PROTEST IN DALLAS

The case began with a protest against the 1984 Republican National Convention in Dallas. In front of the City Hall, a demonstrator doused an American flag with kerosene and set it on fire as several dozen others chanted, "America, the red, white and blue, we spit on you."

The demonstrator, Gregory L. Johnson, was convicted of violating the Texas flag desecration law. The state's Court of Criminal Appeals overturned his conviction on constitutional grounds, and the state appealed to the Supreme Court, arguing that the law served the valid purpose of preserving the flag as a "symbol of nationhood."

'PERSONAL TOLL'

Justice Stevens, a Navy veteran who won the Bronze Star in World War II, concluded his dissenting opinion with a reference to American heroes, including "the soldiers who scaled the bluff at Omaha Beach." He said, "If those ideas are worth fighting for—and our history demonstrates that they are—it cannot be true that the flag that uniquely symbolizes their power is not itself worthy of protection from unnecessary desecration."

It was the concurring opinion by Justice Kennedy, the Court's newest member, that will probably receive the closest scrutiny from those trying to chart the Court's likely future course.

Justice Kennedy, noting that he joined Justice Brennan's opinion "without reservation," observed that the case had taken a "personal toll." He said: "The hard fact

> We do not consecrate the flag by punishing its desecration, for in doing so we dilute the freedom that this cherished emblem represents.
> —Justice William J. Brennan Jr., *Texas v. Johnson*

As much as any decision in recent memory, the case revealed the distinctive views held by individual Justices on the Court's role in interpreting the Constitution. The four separate opinions, two in the majority and two in dissent, were essays on political philosophy and American history as well as jurisprudence.

Chief Justice Rehnquist, noting the widespread legislative prohibitions against flag burning, said, "Surely one of the high purposes of a democratic society is to legislate against conduct that is regarded as evil and profoundly offensive to the majority of people—whether it be murder, embezzlement, pollution or flag burning."

His dissenting opinion, which Justices White and O'Connor also signed, included generous quotations from "The Star-Spangled Banner" and Ralph Waldo Emerson's "Concord Hymn," which describes the "embattled farmers" at the start of the American Revolution, "their flag to April's breeze unfurled." The Chief Justice also included the complete text of John Greenleaf Whittier's Civil War poem "Barbara Frietchie," which includes these lines:

"Shoot, if you must, this old gray head, But spare your country's flag," she said.

is that sometimes we must make decisions we do not like. We make them because they are right, right in the sense that the law and the Constitution, as we see them, compel the result."

In his majority opinion, Texas v. Johnson, No. 88-155, Justice Brennan said Mr. Johnson was prosecuted "for his expression of dissatisfaction with the policies of this country, expression situated at the core of our First Amendment values."

He continued: "If there is a bedrock principle underlying the First Amendment, it is that the Government may not prohibit the expression of an idea simply because society finds the idea itself offensive or disagreeable."

REJOINDER FROM REHNQUIST

Justice Brennan said, "The flag's deservedly cherished place in our community will be strengthened, not weakened, by our holding today." He said the decision was an assertion of "the nation's resilience, not its rigidity," and added:

"The way to preserve the flag's special role is not to punish those who feel differently about these matters. It is to persuade them that they are wrong."

This part of the majority opinion drew a sharp rejoinder from Chief Justice Rehnquist, who called it "a regrettably patronizing civics lecture."

The majority opinion left open the prospect that a state could prosecute flag desecration if the act was simple vandalism without expressive content or if the act of burning a flag was likely to create an immediate, violent response from onlookers. "We do not suggest that the First Amendment forbids a state to prevent imminent lawless action," Justice Brennan said.

PRISON SENTENCE FOR DEMONSTRATOR

The Texas demonstrator, Mr. Johnson, was originally fined $2,000 and sentenced to one year in prison. He was represented at the Supreme Court by the Center for Constitutional Rights, a public-interest law firm in New York that represents liberal causes. William M. Kunstler, who argued the case for Mr. Johnson, said today that the decision "forbids the state from making the American flag a religious icon."

The case drew enormous attention and briefs from many outside groups. Jasper Johns, Robert Rauschenberg and a number of other artists filed an unusual brief on Mr. Johnson's behalf that included color prints of works of theirs that used the American flag as an image.

Response to the decision was, predictably, sharply divided. Patrick B. McGuigan of the Free Congress Center for Law and Democracy, a conservative research group here, called the ruling "an exercise in absurdity" and added, "I never thought I'd say it: John Paul Stevens is right, while Anthony Kennedy and Antonin Scalia are wrong, wrong, wrong."

H. F. Gierke, the National Commander of the American Legion, said his reaction was one of "extreme sadness," adding: "Many a Gold Star mother cherishes that carefully folded, triangular bundle of red, white and blue as the closest link to a fallen hero son."

Arthur J. Kropp, president of People for the American Way, a liberal lobbying group, said the ruling was "a victory for freedom of speech." He added: "As a nation, we are strong enough to withstand the pain of seeing our flag burned. What we could not withstand is seeing the First Amendment cast aside out of a misguided sense of nationalism."

The Federal law that makes flag burning a crime was enacted in 1967 in response to protests against the war in Vietnam that sometimes included burning the flag.

· · · · · · · · · · · ·

Amidst a storm of public protest over the *Texas v. Johnson* ruling, Congress within weeks passed the Flag Protection Act, which allowed the arrest of anyone who "knowingly mutilates, defaces, physically defiles, burns, maintains on the floor or ground, or tramples upon any flag." In *United States v. Eichman* (1990), the Court by the same 5-4 majority ruled that law unconstitutional as well. Over the next fifteen years, critics in Congress proposed constitutional amendments to overturn the decisions. Three times, the House of Representatives approved the proposals by the needed two-thirds majority, but twice supporters fell short of the two-thirds majority in the Senate—by three votes in 1995 and four votes in 2000. When the House again approved the amendment in 2005, the Senate did not take up the resolution.

FREEDOM OF THE PRESS

Free press issues engaged the Supreme Court frequently from the 1960s on, resulting in two early landmark rulings favoring press rights but mixed decisions on a variety of issues after. *The New York Times* was involved in three of the major cases. It won victories in two—including the Pentagon Papers case and an earlier decision limiting libel suits by public officials—but lost a third battle over protecting confidential sources. By the end of the twentieth century, the Court also began confronting how to apply the First Amendment to the Internet. In a potentially seminal decision, the Court called for minimal regulation of cyberspace as it struck down Congress's attempt to prevent children's access to indecency online.

Public Figures, Private Individuals
LIBEL AND *THE TIMES*

The landmark libel law decision, *New York Times Co. v. Sullivan* (1964), stemmed from a libel suit that L. B. Sullivan, an elected city commissioner in Montgomery, Alabama, brought against *The Times* and four civil rights leaders who placed a full-page advertisement in the paper in 1960. The ad described recent confrontations between civil rights demonstrators and police in several southern cities, including Montgomery. Sullivan was not named, but he argued the ad necessarily implicated him and he cited several minor factual errors. A jury awarded him $500,000 against *The Times,* and the Alabama Supreme Court upheld the verdict.

In unanimously reversing the decision and dismissing the suit, the Supreme Court repudiated statements in its earlier decisions that libel was outside constitutional protection. Instead, Justice Brennan wrote, the rules in libel cases had to satisfy First Amendment standards. "We consider this case," he wrote, "against the background of a profound national commitment to the principle that debate on public issues should be uninhibited, robust, and wide-open, and that it may well include vehement, caustic, and sometimes unpleasantly sharp attacks on public officials." For that reason, Brennan concluded, public officials cannot recover damages in a libel suit unless they show that a false statement was published with " 'actual malice'—that is, with knowledge that it was false or with reckless disregard of whether it was false or not."

New York Times Co. v. Sullivan

   Decided: March 9, 1964

   Vote: 9 (Warren, Black, Douglas, Clark, Harlan II, Brennan, Stewart, B. White, Goldberg)

      0

Opinion of the Court: Brennan

Concurring opinion: Black (Douglas)

Opinion concurring in judgment: Goldberg (Douglas)

MARCH 10, 1964
HIGH COURT CURBS PUBLIC OFFICIALS IN LIBEL ACTIONS

It Rules for New York Times and 4 Negro Ministers in Alabama Suit on Ad

DECISION IS UNANIMOUS

Says Malice Must Be Shown—Opinion Likely to Aid Press Freedom in South

By ANTHONY LEWIS

Special to The New York Times

WASHINGTON, March 9—The Supreme Court held today that a public official cannot recover libel damages for criticism of his official performance unless he proves that the statement was made with deliberate malice.

This constitutional landmark for freedom of the press and speech came in a decision throwing out a $500,000 Alabama libel judgment against The New York Times and four Negro ministers.

The Justices were unanimous in reversing the libel award. The Court's opinion, by Justice William J. Brennan Jr., was joined by Chief Justice Earl Warren and Justices Tom C. Clark, John Marshall Harlan, Potter Stewart and Byron R. White.

Justices Hugo L. Black and Arthur J. Goldberg, in separate opinions, said the Court should have gone further and established an absolute privilege for criticism of officials,

even for malicious statements. Justice William O. Douglas joined these opinions.

RELATED TO RACE ISSUE

The case could have an immediate impact on press coverage of race relations in the South.

Including today's case, which is subject to possible further action, The Times faces a total of $5 million in libel suits in Alabama. The Columbia Broadcasting System is being sued there for $1.5 million.

The Times argued that the purpose and effect of these suits was to discourage coverage of the racial situation. That view was supported by friend-of-the-court briefs by The Chicago Tribune, The Washington Post and the American Civil Liberties Union.

THE NEW YORK TIMES, TUESDAY, MARCH 29, 1960

"The growing movement of peaceful mass demonstrations by Negroes is something new in the South, something understandable. . . . Let Congress heed their rising voices, for they will be heard."

—New York Times editorial
Saturday, March 19, 1960

Heed Their Rising Voices

As the whole world knows by now, thousands of Southern Negro students are engaged in widespread non-violent demonstrations in positive affirmation of the right to live in human dignity as guaranteed by the U. S. Constitution and the Bill of Rights. In their efforts to uphold these guarantees, they are being met by an unprecedented wave of terror by those who would deny and negate that document which the whole world looks upon as setting the pattern for modern freedom...

In Orangeburg, South Carolina, when 400 students peacefully sought to buy doughnuts and coffee at lunch counters in the business district, they were forcibly ejected, tear-gassed, soaked to the skin in freezing weather with fire hoses, arrested en masse and herded into an open barbed-wire stockade to stand for hours in the bitter cold.

In Montgomery, Alabama, after students sang "My Country, 'Tis of Thee" on the State Capitol steps, their leaders were expelled from school, and truckloads of police armed with shotguns and tear-gas ringed the Alabama State College Campus. When the entire student body protested to state authorities by refusing to re-register, their dining hall was padlocked in an attempt to starve them into submission.

In Tallahassee, Atlanta, Nashville, Savannah, Greensboro, Memphis, Richmond, Charlotte, and a host of other cities in the South, young American teenagers, in face of the entire weight of official state apparatus and police power, have boldly stepped forth as pro-

tagonists of democracy. Their courage and amazing restraint have inspired millions and given a new dignity to the cause of freedom.

Small wonder that the Southern violators of the Constitution fear this new, non-violent brand of freedom fighter... even as they fear the upswelling right-to-vote movement. Small wonder that they are determined to destroy the one man who, more than any other, symbolizes the new spirit now sweeping the South—the Rev. Dr. Martin Luther King, Jr., world-famous leader of the Montgomery Bus Protest. For it is his doctrine of non-violence which has inspired and guided the students in their widening wave of sit-ins; and it is this same Dr. King who founded and is president of the Southern Christian Leadership Conference—the organization which is spearheading the surging right-to-vote movement. Under Dr. King's direction the Leadership Conference conducts Student Workshops and Seminars in the philosophy and techniques of non-violent resistance.

Again and again the Southern violators have answered Dr. King's peaceful protests with intimidation and violence. They have bombed his home almost killing his wife and child. They have assaulted his person. They have arrested him seven times—for "speeding," "loitering" and similar "offenses." And now they have charged him with "perjury"—a *felony* under which they could imprison him for *ten years.* Obviously, their real purpose is to remove him physically as the leader to whom the students and millions

of others—look for guidance and support, and thereby to intimidate *all* leaders who may rise in the South. Their strategy is to behead this affirmative movement, and thus to demoralize Negro Americans and weaken their will to struggle. The defense of Martin Luther King, spiritual leader of the student sit-in movement, clearly, therefore, is an integral part of the total struggle for freedom in the South.

Decent-minded Americans cannot help but applaud the creative daring of the students and the quiet heroism of Dr. King. But this is one of those moments in the stormy history of Freedom when men and women of good will must do more than applaud the rising-to-glory of others. The America whose good name hangs in the balance before a watchful world, the America whose heritage of Liberty these Southern Upholders of the Constitution are defending, is *our* America as well as theirs...

We must heed their rising voices—yes—but we must add our own.

We must extend ourselves above and beyond moral support and render the material help so urgently needed by those who are taking the risks, facing jail, and even death in a glorious re-affirmation of our Constitution and its Bill of Rights.

We urge you to join hands with our fellow Americans in the South by supporting, with your dollars, this combined appeal for all three needs—the defense of Martin Luther King—the support of the embattled students—and the struggle for the right-to-vote.

Your Help Is Urgently Needed . . . NOW!!

Stella Adler	Dr. Alan Knight Chalmers	Anthony Franciosa	John Killens	L. Joseph Overton	Maureen Stapleton
Raymond Pace Alexander	Richard Coe	Lorraine Hansbury	Eartha Kitt	Clarence Pickett	Frank Silvera
Harry Van Arsdale	Nat King Cole	Rev. Donald Harrington	Rabbi Edward Klein	Shad Polier	Hope Stevens
Harry Belafonte	Cheryl Crawford	Nat Hentoff	Hope Lange	Sidney Poitier	George Tabor
Julie Belafonte	Dorothy Dandridge	James Hicks	John Lewis	A. Philip Randolph	Rev. Gardner C.
Dr. Algernon Black	Ossie Davis	Mary Hinkson	Viveca Lindfors	John Raitt	Taylor
Marc Blitztein	Sammy Davis, Jr.	Van Heflin	Carl Murphy	Elmer Rice	Norman Thomas
William Branch	Ruby Dee	Langston Hughes	Don Murray	Jackie Robinson	Kenneth Tynan
Marlon Brando	Dr. Philip Elliott	Morris Iushewitz	John Murray	Mrs. Eleanor Roosevelt	Charles White
Mrs. Ralph Bunche	Dr. Harry Emerson	Mahalia Jackson	A. J. Muste	Bayard Rustin	Shelley Winters
Diahann Carroll	Fosdick	Mordecai Johnson	Frederick O'Neal	Robert Ryan	Max Youngstein

We in the south who are struggling daily for dignity and freedom warmly endorse this appeal

Rev. Ralph D. Abernathy *(Montgomery, Ala.)*	Rev. Matthew D. McCollom *(Orangeburg, S.C.)*	Rev. Walter L. Hamilton *(Norfolk, Va.)*	Rev. A. L. Davis *(New Orleans, La.)*
Rev. Fred L. Shuttlesworth *(Birmingham, Ala.)*	Rev. William Holmes Borders *(Atlanta, Ga.)*	I. S. Levy *(Columbia, S.C.)* Rev. Martin Luther King, Sr. *(Atlanta, Ga.)*	Mrs. Katie E. Whickham *(New Orleans, La.)*
Rev. Kelley Miller Smith *(Nashville, Tenn.)*	Rev. Douglas Moore *(Durham, N.C.)*	Rev. Henry C. Bunton *(Memphis, Tenn.)*	Rev. W. H. Hall *(Hattiesburg, Miss.)*
Rev. W. A. Dennis *(Chattanooga, Tenn.)*	Rev. Wyatt Tee Walker *(Petersburg, Va.)*	Rev. S.S. Seay, Sr. *(Montgomery, Ala.)*	Rev. J. E. Lowery *(Mobile, Ala.)*
Rev. C. K. Steele *(Tallahassee, Fla.)*		Rev. Samuel W. Williams *(Atlanta, Ga.)*	Rev. T. J. Jemison *(Baton Rouge, La.)*

COMMITTEE TO DEFEND MARTIN LUTHER KING AND THE STRUGGLE FOR FREEDOM IN THE SOUTH

312 West 125th Street, New York 27, N.Y. UNiversity 6-1700

Chairmen: A. Philip Randolph, Dr. Gardner C. Taylor; *Chairmen of Cultural Division:* Harry Belafonte, Sidney Poitier; *Treasurer:* Nat King Cole; *Executive Director:* Bayard Rustin; *Chairmen of Church Division:* Father George B. Ford, Rev. Harry Emerson Fosdick, Rev. Thomas Kilgore, Jr., Rabbi Edward E. Klein; *Chairman of Labor Division:* Morris Iushewitz

Please mail this coupon TODAY!

Committee To Defend Martin Luther King
and
The Struggle For Freedom in The South
312 West 125th Street, New York 27, N.Y.
UNiversity 6-1700

I am enclosing my contribution of $_____
for the work of the Committee.

Name _____
Address _____
City _____ Zone _____ State _____

☐ I want to help   ☐ Please send further information

Please make checks payable to:
Committee to Defend Martin Luther King

The newspaper advertisement at the center of *New York Times Co. v. Sullivan* (1964), originally placed to raise money for Rev. Martin Luther King Jr.'s legal defense, was deemed libelous by Montgomery, Alabama, commissioner L. B. Sullivan. The Supreme Court ruled that public officials cannot collect damages in libel suits unless "actual malice" can be proved, thereby releasing *The Times* and other involved parties from liability.

The Court did not, of course, limit its discussion to the racial context. It said that freedom to comment on official conduct, protected by the free-speech and free-press clauses of the First Amendment, would be endangered by unlimited libel awards.

FEARS 'PALL OF TIMIDITY'

"Whether or not a newspaper can survive a succession of such judgments," Justice Brennan said, "the pall of fear and timidity imposed upon those who would give voice to public criticism is an atmosphere in which the First Amendment freedoms cannot survive."

Even false statements about public officials are given protection by the decision. Justice Brennan said it would put too great a burden on free speech to make a person sued for libel prove the truth of every statement.

No Southern official was named in the ad. Nevertheless four present and former city officials of Montgomery, Ala., and the Governor at the time, John P. Patterson, claimed they had been defamed.

Mr. Patterson sued for $1 million and the other officials each sued for $500,000. In addition to these five suits, which total $3 million, there are pending other libel suits that seek a total of $2 million. These are not related to the ad.

Those suing over the ad cited two paragraphs.

One of the paragraphs mentioned Montgomery. It said that leaders of a Negro college student protest there had been expelled, the campus ringed with police and the college dining hall padlocked to starve the students "into submission."

The second said that "southern violators" had bombed Dr. King's home and, among other things, arrested him seven times.

> " Whether or not a newspaper can survive a succession of such judgments, the pall of fear and timidity imposed upon those who would give voice to public criticism is an atmosphere in which the First Amendment freedoms cannot survive.
> —Justice William J. Brennan Jr., *New York Times Co. v. Sullivan* "

Nor is the decision limited to newspapers or other media of communication. It bars libel or slander suits against anyone for comment on official conduct—as long as they are not malicious.

The Court made no distinction between editorial and advertising matter in protection from libel suits. The fact that an alleged libel appeared in a paid advertisement, Justice Brennan said, is "as immaterial as the fact that newspapers and books are sold."

This case did arise from an advertisement—one published in The Times on March 29, 1960.

SOUGHT TO RAISE FUNDS

The full-page ad, entitled "Heed Their Rising Voices," sought to raise funds for the defense of Dr. Martin Luther King Jr., the Negro leader, and for other civil rights causes. It attacked conditions in many parts of the South in strong terms.

The first suit tried was one brought by L. B. Sullivan, a Montgomery city commissioner with general charge of the police there. He said that the public would connect the alleged illegal activity described in the advertisement with him, and so he would be injured.

GIVEN ALL HE ASKED

Mr. Sullivan did not try to prove any financial loss. Under Alabama law there was no limit on the amount the State Court jury could award as either compensatory or punitive damages. This jury gave Mr. Sullivan all he had asked, $500,000.

The Times was a joint defendant in the case along with four Alabama Negro ministers—Ralph D. Abernathy, Fred L. Shuttlesworth, S. S. Seay Sr. and J. E. Lowery.

Their names had appeared as signers of the ad, although they said that this had been done without their permission. The four ministers were jointly liable with The

Times for the $500,000 judgment. Since they had few assets, The Times would have had to pay most of the award if it had been sustained.

The Alabama courts upheld the judgment. They found the ad "libelous per se" because they held it tended to injure Mr. Sullivan's reputation and was therefore presumptively malicious.

The one defense left was absolute truth. And The Times could not argue this because it had conceded certain errors in the ad. For example, the college dining hall had never been padlocked, and Dr. King had been arrested four times, not seven.

Herbert Wechsler of New York, who argued the case for The Times, made two alternative contentions. He said that the First Amendment barred all libel suits for comment on official conduct—the view taken in the concurring opinions today—or at least ruled out so loose a test of libel as Alabama had applied.

Former Attorney General William P. Rogers and Samuel R. Pierce Jr. of New York argued the case for the ministers. M. Roland Nachman Jr. of Montgomery represented Mr. Sullivan.

Justice Brennan followed the second branch of Mr. Wechsler's argument. He started with the premise of ["]a profound national commitment to the principle that debate on public issues should be uninhibited, robust and wide-open, and that it may well include vehement, caustic and sometimes unpleasantly sharp attacks on government and public officials."

He traced the history of the hated Sedition Act of 1798, which punished "false, scandalous and malicious" statements about Federal officials. History, Justice Brennan said, has produced common agreement that the act was unconstitutional.

The opinion noted that today's case was "the first time" that an ordinary civil libel action had been found by the Supreme Court to conflict with the First Amendment.

Justice Brennan said that the effect of this suit was as repressive as a criminal statute such as the Sedition Act. He noted in passing that the maximum fine for criminal libel in Alabama is only $500.

From the history of the First Amendment Justice Brennan drew the rule that "neither factual error nor defamatory content suffices to remove the constitutional shield from criticism of official conduct."

He held that the Constitution "prohibits a public official from recovering damages for a defamatory falsehood relating to his official conduct unless he proves the statement was made with actual malice—that is, with knowledge that it was false or with reckless disregard of whether it was false or not."

Alabama libel standards were much too loose to meet that test, Justice Brennan concluded, and this judgment must be reversed.

He sent the case back to the Alabama courts for further proceedings consistent with today's opinion.

But he observed that Mr. Sullivan might seek a new trial at which he might try to prove "actual malice" by The Times and the ministers. Justice Brennan therefore went on to discuss the sufficiency of the evidence in this case to meet the test.

At most, he concluded, The Times may have shown "negligency" in failing to discover the misstatements in the ad, not the "recklessness" constitutionally "required for a finding of actual malice."

As for the ministers, he said, there was no showing that they knew of any errors in the ad if they had authorized it at all.

Finally, Justice Brennan said that the evidence was "constitutionally defective in another respect"—it could not support the contention that the ad concerned Mr. Sullivan at all.

If Mr. Sullivan could take these vague words as a reference to him, the opinion said, then any criticism of government in general could be met by individual officials' libel suits.

The latter part of Justice Brennan's opinion, some legal observers thought, was designed to answer one point in Justice Black's concurrence. This was that, because of hostility over the racial issue, a Montgomery jury would have returned a verdict for Mr. Sullivan no matter what rules it was told to apply.

Justice Black said the Court's rules were "stopgap measures." He called for "granting the press an absolute immunity for criticism of the way public officials do their public duty."

Justice Goldberg, taking the same approach in his concurring opinion, said that the right to speak out about public affairs "should not depend upon a probing by the jury of the motivation of the citizen or press."

The Brennan opinion does leave it open to Mr. Sullivan to seek a new trial. But the Court made it plain, lawyers here noted, that it would upset any jury verdict for him based on the kind of evidence produced in the first trial.

One other case arising out of the same advertisement has been tried in Montgomery, and the jury also returned the full $500,000 demanded. That case is pending on a motion for a new trial and along with the others has been awaiting today's decision.

The other libel suits faced by The Times in Alabama arise from a series of articles on conditions in Birmingham. Officials there have sued for $2 million. The writer of the articles—Harrison E. Salisbury—has been charged with 42 counts of criminal libel. . . .

MARCH 10, 1964
DECISION WELCOMED BY TIMES PUBLISHER

Arthur Ochs Sulzberger, president and publisher of The New York Times, issued a statement last night welcoming the Supreme Court decision throwing out a $500,000 Alabama libel judgment against The Times and four Negro ministers.

The statement follows:

"We are, of course, delighted with the decision of the Supreme Court. It clearly illuminates several basic issues regarding freedom of the press and therefore is of fundamental importance not only for newspapers, but other news media as well.

"The opinion of the Court makes freedom of the press more secure than ever before."

• • • • • • • • • • • •

The ruling in *New York Times Co. v. Sullivan* has been hailed as a free press milestone, but criticized for leaving news media all but immune from libel suits by public officials. The Court later extended the same "actual malice" standard to suits by "public figures." In 1974, however, the Court ruled in *Gertz v. Robert Welch Inc.* that states could set a lower requirement for private figures, but barred punitive damages in such cases unless "actual malice" was shown.

PRIVATE INFORMATION MADE PUBLIC

The Court has been somewhat protective but less definitive in limiting invasion of privacy suits against the media. In 1975 it blocked a suit by the father of a rape-murder victim after a television station broadcast her name, which had been obtained from public records (*Cox Broadcasting Corp. v. Cohn*). It extended the ruling in 1989 to block a suit by a rape victim whose name was published after a local sheriff's office mistakenly made the crime report available to reporters. The decision in *The Florida Star v. B.J.F.* stopped short, however, of the position urged by media groups: an absolute constitutional privilege to publish truthful information if lawfully obtained.

New York Times Co. v. United States (1971)

The press victory in the Pentagon Papers case, *New York Times Co. v. United States* (1971), came two weeks after President Richard M. Nixon personally directed the Justice Department to try to block publication of the mammoth study. Daniel Ellsberg, who had worked on the study while at the Defense Department, leaked the study to *The Times* in spring 1971. The newspaper's reporters and editors studied the report for two months before publishing an initial story on June 13. The government asked *The Times* to return its copy of the study and, when the newspaper refused, persuaded a federal judge and then the federal appeals court in New York to issue restraining orders against further publication. Meanwhile, the *Washington Post* had begun publishing stories based on portions of the report. The government went to court against the *Post,* but the federal appeals court in Washington, D.C., refused to enjoin publication.

New York Times Co. v. United States

Decided: June 30, 1971

Vote: 6 (Black, Douglas, Brennan,
Stewart, B. White,
T. Marshall)

3 (Burger, Harlan II, Blackmun)

Opinion: *Per curiam*

Concurring opinions (6): Black
(Douglas); Douglas (Black);
Brennan; Stewart (B. White);
B. White (Stewart); T. Marshall

Dissenting opinions (3): Burger;
Harlan II (Burger, Blackmun);
Blackmun

After hearing arguments on June 26, the Supreme Court ruled for the newspapers only four days later in a 6-3 decision. The unsigned opinion stated simply that the government had failed to meet "the heavy burden of showing justification" to prevent further publications. Each of the nine justices wrote a separate opinion. Two—Black and Douglas—said the government had no power to censor newspapers. Brennan said the government might have that power in a clear-cut emergency, but it could not use "surmise or conjecture" to justify a prior restraint. Potter Stewart said he saw no threat of "direct, immediate, and irreparable damage to the Nation" from publication, while Byron R. White and Thurgood Marshall both relied in part on the lack of congressional authorization for the government's action. In his dissent, Chief Justice Warren E. Burger said both newspapers had been derelict in their duty to report the discovery of the stolen documents to the government. That duty, Burger wrote, "rests on taxi drivers, Justices, and the *New York Times*."

NEWS ANALYSIS
JULY 4, 1971
COURT DECISION:
PRESSES ROLL—BUT THE CONFLICT REMAINS

WASHINGTON—Tersely, for the most part reluctantly, and, for different reasons, angrily, the nine justices of the Supreme Court let the presses roll again last week with more revelations from the now notorious Pentagon study of how the United States went to war in Indochina.

Their decision was the climax of a bizarre legal contest over a bizarre journalistic episode. But it was by no means the end of the affair of the Pentagon papers. Some of the repercussions were clearly evident, but most were still the subject of widespread speculation.

The justices of the highest Court could agree, by a vote of 6 to 3, only on the narrowest possible definition of the case: any prior restraint on free expression comes before the courts with a heavy presumption that it violates the Constitution; the Government thus carries a "heavy burden" of proof that restraint is justified; the Government had not met that burden in its case against The New York Times and other papers under restraint; the papers were thus free to print.

That much took three paragraphs. But there followed, in this unprecedented case of novel and perhaps unique constitutional and journalistic issues, a flood of nine separate opinions running to 11,000 words, with eight of the justices subscribing to at least two opinions and with no opinion attracting the concurrence of more than three men. They wrote about the law, but also about the war, about newspapers, about the Government's system of secrecy, and about the Pentagon papers themselves.

Thus ended one of the most frenzied court battles in history and the first restraint ever imposed on American newspapers by their Government. And thus was resumed the voluminous presentation of hitherto secret records and analyses of how the administrations of Presidents Truman, Eisenhower, Kennedy and Johnson assumed commitments to resist the advance of Communists in Indochina, moved the nation toward massive war against them and ultimately found themselves entrapped in an unsuccessful enterprise—while withholding from the public at virtually every stage the gravity of the judgments they were making.

That such a massive study of decision-making should have been conducted inside the Government well before the end of the war was in sight is itself highly unusual. And that such a study, with many secret documents, should have been made available to the press while the war still goes on makes this case unique.

Little wonder, therefore, that in mid-publication the case of the Pentagon papers also generated a unique outpouring of judicial views.

Six of the justices deeply resented the case—three because they believe that freedom of the press means freedom of the press and that no agency of government has the right to stop the press; and three because they believe the President's right to conduct foreign policy gives him broad power to define the necessary secrets of state and that the lower courts, had they not been "irresponsibly feverish" in this case, were duty bound to decide only whether the attempt at censorship fell within the foreign-policy prerogatives of the executive branch.

Only three justices, therefore, were inclined to grope for a new judicial definition of the circumstances in which they might tolerate a restraint on publication in the interest of "national security." Since they held the balance of power they decided the issue in this case and wrote the only new law that it produced for future generations to accept or discard.

of express and appropriately limited Congressional authorization for prior restraints. . . ."

The common thread in these three opinions—inspired by the argument of Prof. Alexander Bickel of Yale on behalf of The Times—was that prior restraint on a newspaper story was justified only when that story could be shown "inevitably" or "surely" to lead "directly" and "immediately" to some irreparable damage to the nation. The justices held, in effect, that all other pleas that foreign policy may be embarrassed, or inhibited, or complicated, or frustrated in some *contributory*—in contrast to a *primary*—way cannot meet the "heavy burden" of proof that might justify some limitation on the First Amendment.

Justices Hugo L. Black, William O. Douglas and Thurgood Marshall were virtually agreed, however, that no claim to censor had any standing in court against the Bill of Rights—Justices Black and Douglas arguing that the

> **Several of the justices recalled the admonition of Justice Oliver Wendell Holmes that 'great cases like hard cases make bad law.' They might have added that they generate at least as much heat as light.**

In the words of Justice William J. Brennan Jr.: ". . . The First Amendment tolerates absolutely no prior judicial restraints of the press predicated upon surmise or conjecture that untoward consequences may result . . . only governmental allegation and proof that publication must inevitably, directly and immediately cause the occurrence of an event kindred to imperiling the safety of a transport already at sea can support even the issuance of an interim restraining order. . . ."

In the words of Justice Potter Stewart, with Justice Byron R. White concurring: ". . . I am convinced that the Executive is correct [in wishing to keep secret] some of the documents involved. But I cannot say that disclosure of any of them will surely result in direct, immediate, and irreparable damage to our Nation or its people."

And in the words of Justice White, Justice Stewart concurring: ". . . Revelation of these documents will do substantial damage to public interests . . . But I nevertheless agree that the United States has not satisfied the very heavy burden which it must meet to warrant an injunction against publication in these cases, at least in the absence

Constitution forbids it and Justice Marshall arguing that the Court could hardly act the censor when the Congress has twice in this century specifically refused to authorize censorship, even in wartime.

The majority of six was thus formed by three justices ruling on the basis of law and three on the basis of the facts in this case. The three dissenters—Chief Justice Warren E. Burger, Justice John M. Harlan and Justice Harry A. Blackmun—said the Government had not been given the time or deference it deserved to make its case; they would have held up publication pending further litigation.

All the rest was advice, opinion, remonstrance and policy judgment aplenty.

Justices White and Stewart said the Government's mistake in seeking an injunction against publication does not mean it might not have a good case for criminal prosecution after publication, and Mr. Burger and Mr. Blackmun agreed.

Justices Stewart and White did not describe the "damage" they expected from publication of some of the material. But they also said the executive branch had to be more alert in guarding its secrets and should avoid compromising the whole system by practicing secrecy "for its own sake."

Justices Black and Douglas said the press had not only a right but a duty to prevent governmental deception and the dispatch of people "to distant lands to die of foreign fevers and foreign shot and shell." The Times and The Washington Post deserved praise for "revealing the working of government" on the way to war in Vietnam, they said, all the more since "it is all history, not future events," and highly relevant to current debate about Vietnam.

Justices Harlan, Burger and Blackmun reached beyond any actual testimony in the case to find the "seemingly uncontested facts" that the newspapers knowingly received "feloniously acquired" documents. The Chief Justice found it "hardly believable" that The Times did not report its possession of secrets to the Government and attempt to reach "agreement" on what might be published. Justice Blackmun felt himself the object of "pressure and panic and sensationalism," perceived the possibility of damage even in some cursory study of the material and raised at least the possibility that the nation might wish to blame the newspapers for a possible prolongation of the war and further delay in the release of American prisoners.

Several of the justices recalled the admonition of Justice Oliver Wendell Holmes that "great cases like hard cases make bad law." They might have added that they generate at least as much heat as light.

In any event, two weeks after it was ordered to suspend their publication, The Times resumed on Thursday its documented reports on the Pentagon study. Attorney General John N. Mitchell said "all avenues of criminal prosecution" remained open, without saying where they might lead beyond the indictment of Dr. Daniel Ellsberg, one of the 36 authors of the study who has said he passed the materials to the press.

Secretary of State William P. Rogers asked for voluntary restraint in the handling of some of the material and offered to help identify the passages he deemed harmful. The Times replied that it was taking the "interests of the country, including national security" into account in presenting its reports.

What The Times's comment buried in a single phrase was, of course, the essence of the conflict: When do the fundamental interests of the country and its citizens take precedence over the conventional concerns of national security? And when do the demands of national security justify infringement of the guarantees of democracy?

The authors of the Bill of Rights preferred to run the risks of injury flowing from unrestrained expression to the historically known risks of allowing government to silence its citizens.

The effect of the Court's ruling last week, and the uniqueness of the case itself, make it highly unlikely that a comparable conflict will come before the courts again. But there will be other consequences, some of which can only be the subject of conjecture at this point.

The national debate over Vietnam policy and President Nixon's formula for gradual disengagement, which the White House had hoped to contain and eliminate altogether before next year's election campaign, is likely to take some odd turns. Two Senate committees have already laid claim to the Pentagon papers as the basis for a full-fledged investigation next fall on the origins of the war.

The political prospects of Mr. Nixon and some of his potential challengers—especially Senators Hubert H. Humphrey and Edmund S. Muskie who defended the war in 1968—may be significantly affected, if not by the publication of the papers then by the Congressional inquiries and the discussion they inspire.

North Vietnam's tactics at the Paris negotiations—including a new move last week on the issue of prisoners and withdrawal—may be timed to take propaganda advantage of the new debate in the United States and the Administration's response may have to be readjusted accordingly.

Beyond that, both the Congress and the press may come out of this incident with a new degree of skepticism about all public policy declarations. And the executive branch, moving to prevent future security breaches of this magnitude, has already begun a review of the procedures by which it designates and preserves its secrets—with many officials arguing that better security depends paradoxically on better and faster publication of most information.

This strange study of the war, therefore, may shape the war's consequences in ways that neither the justices nor anyone else could foresee.

—MAX FRANKEL

. . . .

CONFIDENTIAL SOURCES AND FREEDOM OF INFORMATION

News organizations failed, however, in another high-profile fight aimed at winning a privilege for journalists to refuse to divulge confidential sources. The issue reached the Supreme Court in cases brought by three reporters seeking to quash—throw out—grand jury subpoenas asking for the identity of sources to whom each had pledged confidentiality. Paul Branzburg of the *Louisville Courier-Journal* had written about drug users, while television newsman Paul Pappas and *New York Times* reporter Earl Caldwell had both written about the Black Panthers. State courts ruled against Branzburg and Pappas, while a federal appeals court backed Caldwell's refusal to appear before the grand jury.

By a 5-4 vote, the Supreme Court in *Branzburg v. Hayes* (1972) refused to recognize a journalist's privilege to protect confidential sources. "The public . . . 'has a right to every man's evidence,' " Justice White wrote, quoting an earlier case. The use of confidential sources is permitted, he acknowledged, but the desire for anonymity by sources who have committed crimes "is hardly deserving of constitutional protection." In a concurring opinion, Justice Lewis F. Powell Jr. suggested judges should conduct a case-by-case balancing before forcing reporters to divulge confidential sources. News organizations responded to the ruling by winning passage of journalist shield laws in many states, but the laws still allowed compelled disclosure of confidential sources if certain standards were met.

Branzburg v. Hayes

> **Decided:** June 29, 1972
> **Vote:** 5 (Burger, B. White, Blackmun, Powell, Rehnquist)
> 4 (Douglas, Brennan, Stewart, T. Marshall)
> **Opinion of the Court:** B. White
> **Concurring opinion:** Powell
> **Dissenting opinions (2):** Douglas; Stewart (Brennan, T. Marshall)

News organizations had a mixed record in efforts to gain legally protected access to governmental proceedings, facilities, or information. In companion cases in 1974, the Court upheld, against a First Amendment challenge, federal and state rules limiting reporters' ability to interview prison inmates. In 1980, however, the Court in *Richmond Newspapers, Inc. v. Commonwealth of Virginia* recognized a First Amendment right of the press and public to attend criminal trials. In the main opinion, Chief Justice Burger noted that an open court "has long been an indispensable attribute of an Anglo-American trial." Justice Brennan wrote a pivotal concurrence, stressing that open trials served a "structural" purpose of promoting accountability.

The Court has never recognized a First Amendment right to government information, but it has ruled repeatedly on cases involving the federal Freedom of Information of Act. The 1967 act requires access to federal agencies' records, but provides nine categorical exceptions. Most of the Supreme Court's decisions on the law have upheld agencies' refusal to release records under one or more of the exceptions.

ELECTRONIC MEDIA, ADVERTISING, AND THE COURT

Electronic media have also had a mixed record at the high court. Early in the history of broadcasting, the Court upheld the Federal Communications Commission's system of licensing radio and television stations as a necessary means to prevent interference by stations using the same frequency. "It is idle to posit an unbridgeable First Amendment right to broadcast," the Court wrote years later in *Red Lion Broadcasting Co. v. FCC* (1969). In that ruling, the Court rejected a First Amendment challenge to the so-called fairness doctrine, which required broadcasters to present both sides of public policy issues. (The FCC later repealed the doctrine.) The Court has upheld some government regulation of cable television by federal statute, FCC rule, or local government franchising. In addition, in a case pitting broadcasters against cable operators, the Court in 1997 upheld a law passed by Congress requiring cable companies to carry the signals of all local television stations. The 5-4 ruling in *Turner Broadcasting v. FCC* said the law was justified because the growing power of the cable industry threatened "the economic viability of free local broadcast television."

Advertisers, on the other hand, have won significant protection against government regulation in a series of decisions since the 1970s recognizing a First Amendment right to commercial speech.

In the seminal ruling, the Court in *Virginia State Board of Pharmacy v. Virginia Citizens Consumer Council* (1976) struck down a Virginia law that prohibited price advertising by pharmacists. In a free-market system, Justice Harry A. Blackmun wrote, "the free flow of commercial information is indispensable." Four years later, the Court in *Central Hudson Gas & Electric Corp. v. Public Service Commission of New York* (1980) established a multipart test permitting government regulation of advertising of a lawful product or service only if the regulation serves a substantial government interest, actually furthers that interest, and is no more restrictive than necessary to serve that goal. In cases applying the *Central Hudson* test, the Court has more often than not struck down challenged regulations.

OBSCENITY AND INDECENCY

The Court has also established somewhat strict tests for laws prohibiting obscenity or indecency. Obscenity was listed in a 1942 decision as one of several categories of constitutionally unprotected expression. Fifteen years later, the Court in *Roth v. United States* (1957) provided a definition. Material could be deemed obscene only if it met this test: "whether to the average person, applying contemporary standards, the dominant theme of the material taken as a whole appeals to the prurient interest." Over the next decade, the justices produced diverse opinions in obscenity cases, adding two requirements to the *Roth* test: "patently offensive to current community standards" and "utterly without redeeming social importance."

Miller v. California

> **Decided:** June 21, 1973
>
> **Vote:** 5 (Burger, B. White, Blackmun, Powell, Rehnquist)
>
>   4 (Douglas, Brennan, Stewart, T. Marshall)
>
> **Opinion of the Court:** Burger
>
> **Dissenting opinions (2):** Douglas; Brennan (Stewart, T. Marshall)

In 1973 a five-justice majority formed behind a new, slightly eased definition. In *Miller v. California,* Chief Justice Burger said that states could enact laws regulating obscenity if the definition was limited to materials "which, taken as a whole, appeal to the prurient interest in sex; which portray sexual conduct in a patently offensive way; and which, taken as a whole, do not have serious literary, artistic, political, or scientific value." Dissenting in a companion case, Justice Brennan—who had written the *Roth* decision—argued that no clear definition of obscenity could be written. He called for limiting anti-obscenity laws to prohibiting distribution to juveniles or "obtrusive exposure to unconsenting adults."

Twice in the 1970s, the Court also upheld the government's power to regulate material that is indecent but not obscene, in fragmented decisions by 5-4 votes. The Court in *Young v. American Mini Theatres, Inc.* (1976) ruled that local governments could use zoning ordinances to limit adult bookstores or movie theaters to a single area. Two years later, the Court in *FCC v. Pacifica Foundation* (1978) upheld the FCC's authority to punish radio or television stations for broadcasting indecent material, at least when children were likely to be listening or watching. The ruling upheld a sanction against a New York City radio station for the afternoon broadcast of a recording by comedian George Carlin, "Seven Dirty Words," that satirized social attitudes toward seven words that were repeatedly spoken during the monologue.

POLICING THE INTERNET

The indecency issue provided the background for the Court's initial brushes with the new world of the Internet. Concerned with the easy availability of sexually explicit material on the World Wide Web, Congress in 1996 passed the Communications Decency Act making it a crime to transmit any "obscene or indecent" material that could be received by children under the age of eighteen. Opponents called the requirement difficult to enforce, the definition of indecency vague, and the law a threat to the Internet's unique value: its unregulated, interactive availability to anyone with access to a computer.

The American Civil Liberties Union, representing a coalition of online users, and the American Library Association mounted parallel challenges to the law. In a mostly unanimous decision, the Court in *Reno v. American Civil Liberties Union* (1997) agreed that the law violated the First Amendment. Justice John Paul Stevens—who had written the plurality opinions in the two indecency cases in the 1970s—began by rejecting as inapt any of the justifications for regulating broadcasting or cable television. "Our cases provide no basis for qualifying the level of First Amendment scrutiny that should be applied to this medium," he wrote. He said the law's "many ambiguities" would necessarily silence speakers entitled to constitutional protection while the law's use of "community standards" could apply to discussions about such topics as safe-sex practices. He concluded by warning that any government regulation of the Internet "is more likely to interfere with the free exchange of ideas than to encourage it."

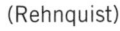

Reno v. American Civil Liberties Union

Decided: June 26, 1997

Vote: 7 (Stevens, Scalia, Kennedy, Souter, Thomas, Ginsburg, Breyer)

2 (Rehnquist, O'Connor)

Opinion of the Court: Stevens

Opinion concurring in part and dissenting in part: O'Connor (Rehnquist)

JUNE 27, 1997
COURT, 9-0, UPHOLDS STATE LAWS PROHIBITING ASSISTED SUICIDE; PROTECTS SPEECH ON INTERNET

DECENCY ACT FAILS

Effort to Shield Minors Is Said to Infringe the First Amendment

By LINDA GREENHOUSE

WASHINGTON, June 26—In a sweeping endorsement of free speech on the Internet, the Supreme Court today declared unconstitutional a Federal law making it a crime to send or display indecent material online in a way available to minors.

The decision, unanimous in most respects, marked the Court's first effort to extend the principles of the First Amendment into cyberspace and to confront the nature of a new, and—to most of the Justices—an unfamiliar medium.

The result left the coalition of Internet users, computer industry groups and civil liberties organizations that had challenged the Communications Decency Act exultant. The forceful opinion for the Court by Justice John Paul Stevens held that speech on the Internet is entitled to the highest level of First Amendment protection, similar to the protection the Court gives to books and newspapers. That stands in contrast to the more limited First Amendment rights accorded to speech on broadcast and cable television, where the court has tolerated a wide array of Government regulation.

"Content on the Internet is as diverse as human thought," Justice Stevens said in a quotation from a special three-judge Federal District Court in Philadelphia, which struck down the Communications Decency Act a year ago in a decision the Supreme Court affirmed today.

The Internet is a rapidly expanding global computer network, which allows as many as 60 million people to communicate online and connect with information and entertainment sources around the world. A large majority of its users live in the United States.

The decision makes it unlikely that any Government-imposed restriction on Internet content would be upheld as long as the material has some intrinsic constitutional value. Obscenity, which is outside the protection of the First Amendment, is also covered by the Communications Decency Act, and the Court left that provision intact today without even analyzing it.

The indecent material at issue today was not precisely defined by the 1996 law—one of its serious vulnerabilities, as the Court saw it—but was referred to in one section of the statute as "patently offensive" descriptions or images of "sexual or excretory activities."

Justice Stevens said that the Court regarded the law's goal of protecting children from indecent material as legitimate and important, but concluded that the "wholly unprecedented" breadth of the law threatened to suppress far too much speech among adults and even between parents and children. "The interest in encouraging freedom of expression in a democratic society outweighs any theoretical but unproven benefit of censorship," Justice Stevens wrote.

He noted that people could not "confidently assume" that discussions of birth control, homosexuality, or prison rape, or even the transmission of "the card catalogue of the Carnegie Library," would not violate the law and place computer network users at risk of severe criminal penalties. Violations of the Communications Decency Act, which never went into effect because of a stay issued by the lower court, carried penalties of two years in prison and a $250,000 fine. "The severity of criminal sanctions may well cause speakers to remain silent rather than communicate even arguably unlawful words, ideas, and images," Justice Stevens said.

The law made it a crime to use a computer to transmit indecent material to someone under 18 years old or to display such material "in a manner available" to a person under 18. Justice Stevens said that given the nature of the Internet, there was no way someone transmitting indecent material could be sure that a minor would not see it. He noted that most uses of the Internet, like chat rooms, newsgroups, and the World Wide Web, "are open to all comers."

ulation, similar to the "adult zones" for bookstores and X-rated movie theaters the Court has upheld in a series of decisions. But the analogy was inexact, she said, because there is no way in cyberspace to make sure that minors can be screened out while still allowing adults to have access to the regulated speech.

Justice O'Connor said the law was clearly unconstitutional because it was "akin to a law that makes it a crime for a bookstore owner to sell pornographic magazines to anyone once a minor enters his store."

The Communications Decency Act was a last-minute Senate amendment to another bill, the Telecommunications Act of 1996. It was adopted without hearings and amid substantial doubts about its constitutionality. For that reason, its sponsors agreed to add a provision guaranteeing quick Supreme Court review after a hearing by a single three-judge court, a shortcut through the normal appellate process.

President Clinton signed the bill and Administration lawyers defended the law vigorously. At the same time,

> " The interest in encouraging freedom of expression in a democratic society outweighs any theoretical but unproven benefit of censorship. "
> —Justice John Paul Stevens, *Reno v. American Civil Liberties Union*

Nor, Justice Stevens said, could people rely on a defense provided by the law for those who take "good faith, reasonable, effective and appropriate actions" to restrict access by minors. No current technology satisfied those demands, he said.

The opinion, Reno v. American Civil Liberties Union, No. 96-511, was signed by Justices Antonin Scalia, Anthony M. Kennedy, David H. Souter, Clarence Thomas, Ruth Bader Ginsburg, and Stephen G. Breyer.

In a separate opinion by Justice Sandra Day O'Connor, she and Chief Justice William H. Rehnquist, who signed her opinion, subscribed to much of the Court's approach. They said the law could be constitutionally applied, but only in the very limited circumstance of deliberate transmission of indecent material "where the party initiating the communication knows that all of the recipients are minors." If an adult might be among the recipients, the speech cannot constitutionally be suppressed, Justice O'Connor said.

Justice O'Connor said that on the surface, the Communications Decency Act was analogous to a zoning reg-

White House officials worked on a substitute Internet policy in the event the law was overturned, as some in the Administration hoped it would be.

The law was challenged by two main coalitions of plaintiffs, representing a wide spectrum of the Internet community. The United States Chamber of Commerce entered the case at the Supreme Court stage to argue that the law presented a threat to the country's ability to compete globally in an age of new communications, an argument that very likely got the attention of the free-market conservatives, including Justices Thomas and Scalia, who joined Justice Stevens's opinion.

The trial before the court in Philadelphia produced opinions by the three judges, Dolores K. Sloviter, Ronald L. Buckwalter and Stewart Dalzell, totaling 147 pages with 123 separate factual findings. The Court today relied heavily on these findings, including Justice Stevens's observation that the Internet was not as "pervasive" a medium as television or radio—where the Court has permitted greater Government regulation—because computer users have to actively search for indecent material and "seldom encounter such content accidentally."

Christopher A. Hansen, a lawyer for the American Civil Liberties Union, which organized one of the plaintiff groups, said today that in establishing the highest level of First Amendment protection, the Court's decision "was more about speech than about technology." That made the decision important for all future Internet cases even as the technology may change, Mr. Hansen said.

In his opinion, Justice Stevens was critical of several aspects of the Government's defense of the law, but singled out one in particular. That was the argument that unless the law was upheld, development of the Internet would be stifled by parents' fears about having online access if they could not shield their children from indecent material.

"We find this argument singularly unpersuasive," Justice Stevens said, adding that "the dramatic expansion of this new marketplace of ideas contradicts the factual basis of this contention" given the "phenomenal" growth of the Internet. "As a matter of constitutional tradition," he said, "in the absence of evidence to the contrary, we presume that governmental regulation of the content of speech is more likely to interfere with the free exchange of ideas than to encourage it."

* * * * * * * * * * * *

Congress responded in 1998 by passing a somewhat narrower law, the Children's Internet Protection Act, which the ACLU challenged before it could take effect. The Court in *Ashcroft v. American Civil Liberties Union* (2004) upheld a federal appeals court injunction against the law, but gave the government a chance to show that filtering software could be used to limit children's access to indecent materials without restricting access by adults. After a four-week trial, a federal district court judge in March 2007 again ruled the law unconstitutional; the federal appeals court in Philadelphia upheld the decision in July 2008. The government was expected to appeal to the Supreme Court.

FREEDOM OF RELIGION

The framers of the Constitution believed strongly in freedom of religion and included in the original charter a straightforward prohibition on the imposition of any "religious Test" as a qualification for "any Office or public Trust under the United States" (Art. VI, cl. 3). The First Amendment added two provisions that forbid Congress from making any "law respecting an establishment of religion, or prohibiting the free exercise thereof." The two religion clauses pose difficult questions of interpretation in practice, but the Supreme Court had few occasions to interpret them in its first 150 years. Since the 1940s, however, the Court has encountered an array of church-state issues with shifting results on the rules for permitting government support of religion or government regulation of religious practices.

Congress rarely legislated on religious subjects before the twentieth century, so the Supreme Court had almost no cases on the religion clauses as long as the Bill of Rights applied only to Congress and not to the states. In the one significant nineteenth century ruling, the Court upheld against a free exercise claim the bigamy conviction of a Mormon in the Utah territory, who argued that polygamy was a required practice under his faith. After citing the universal prohibition on multiple marriages in the states, the Court in *Reynolds v. United States* (1879) concluded, "it is impossible to believe that the constitutional guaranty of religious freedom was intended to prohibit legislation in respect to this most important feature of social life."

FREE EXERCISE CLAUSE

The Court's first brush with government aid to religious institutions came in a 1930 case from Louisiana challenging the use of tax funds to provide free textbooks to students in parochial as well as public schools. The plaintiffs, however, argued the expenditures amounted to an unlawful taking of property without directly raising an Establishment Clause claim. Five years earlier, the Court had ruled for the first time that the Free Press Clause applied to the states, but it did not consider specifically incorporating the religion clauses against the states until the 1940s.

The Court extended the religion clauses to the states in cases brought by Jehovah's Witnesses challenging various state or local laws aimed at restricting their proselytizing activities. In *Cantwell v. Connecticut* (1940), the Court struck down a state law requiring a permit for religious solicitation because it gave a state official discretion in determining whether the activity was in fact religious. Three years later, the Court in May 1943 ruled on both free speech and free exercise grounds that Jehovah's Witnesses could not be required to pay a daily tax on the privilege of door-to-door solicitation. The Court's ruling a month later sustaining the right of Jehovah's Witnesses to refuse to salute the flag in public schools also referenced both freedom of speech and religious liberty. (See page 186.)

The Court's early rulings stressed that individuals claiming a right to engage in religious practices were still subject to laws of general application. It restated that principle in a 1961 decision, *Braunfeld v. Brown,* upholding a state Sunday closing law. A law with a secular purpose is valid despite an "indirect burden on religious observance," the Court explained, unless the government can accomplish its purpose without imposing the burden.

In two later decisions, however, the Court significantly modified the *Braunfeld* holding. In *Sherbert v. Verner* (1963), the Court held that the government could infringe on religious practices only to further a "compelling interest." The decision backed a Seventh Day Adventist who sought unemployment compensation after she was fired for refusing to work on Saturday. Forcing the woman to choose between her religious principles and unemployment benefits, Justice Brennan wrote, "puts the same kind of burden upon the free exercise of religion as would a fine imposed against appellant for her Saturday worship." Nine years later, the Court in *Wisconsin v. Yoder* (1972) similarly backed a free exercise claim by parents of Amish children who ran afoul of the state's compulsory school attendance law by refusing to send their children to public schools past the eighth grade.

The Court in 1990 discarded the compelling interest standard and adopted a less protective test for religious practices. The 6-3 ruling in *Employment Division, Department of Human Resources of Oregon v. Smith* involved two men fired from their jobs with a private drug rehabilitation program because they took peyote as part of a Native American church ceremony. The Oregon Supreme Court had cited the Free Exercise Clause in reversing the state employment agency's decision to deny the two men unemployment benefits.

In his opinion reversing the Oregon high court's decision, Justice Antonin Scalia acknowledged that many states included exemptions from drug laws for use in religious ceremonies. Exemptions might be desirable, he said, but were not constitutionally required. "We have never held that an individual's religious beliefs excuse him from compliance with an otherwise valid law prohibiting conduct that the State is free to regulate," he wrote. Courts need not balance the state's interest against a free exercise claim, Scalia said, as long as the state was enforcing a neutral law of general application that was not targeted at a specific religious practice.

Four justices rejected Scalia's conclusion—three in dissent and the fourth, Sandra Day O'Connor, in an opinion agreeing with the result but not with the new test. The state had a legitimate interest in "uniform application" of its drug laws, O'Connor said, because of the "physical harm" caused to peyote users and the risk of illegal trafficking in the substance. But the state's interest had to be balanced against the free exercise claim, she said, to protect religious minorities. "The First Amendment was enacted precisely to protect the rights of those whose religious practices are not shared by the majority and may be viewed with hostility," she wrote. The three dissenters joined that portion of O'Connor's opinion.

APRIL 18, 1990
USE OF DRUGS IN RELIGIOUS RITUALS CAN BE PROSECUTED, JUSTICES RULE

By LINDA GREENHOUSE

Special to The New York Times

The Supreme Court ruled today that governments may prosecute those who use illegal drugs as part of religious rituals. It said such prosecutions were not a violation of the constitutional guarantee of religious freedom.

By a vote of 6 to 3, the Court refused to grant two men who are members of an American Indian church a religious exemption from an Oregon law that makes it a crime to possess or use peyote.

The decision, written by Justice Antonin Scalia, has broader implications for the Court's approach to resolving the conflicts that occur with some frequency between individual religious practice and generally applicable government policies.

The ruling overturned a decision by the Oregon Supreme Court that the First Amendment's protection for the "free exercise" of religion required an exemption in state law for the sacramental use of peyote.

A 'DESIRABLE' EXEMPTION

Oregon had not sought to prosecute the two men, who used peyote in the rituals of the Native American Church. Rather, the state's employment division refused to pay the men unemployment benefits after they were dismissed from their jobs for using peyote. The state agency said the criminal status of peyote use rendered the men ineligible for the benefits.

Peyote, a cactus that contains the hallucinogenic substance mescaline, has been used for centuries in Indian religious ceremonies. Federal law and the laws of 23 states, including many with substantial Indian populations, exempt the sacramental use of peyote from criminal penalties.

Justice Scalia said such an exemption was permissible, even "desirable," as a choice for legislators to make. But, he added, "the First Amendment's protection of religious liberty does not require this."

He noted that the Court ruled more than a century ago that Mormons could be prosecuted for polygamy even though their religion incorporated it. "We have never held that an individual's religious beliefs excuse him from compliance with an otherwise valid law prohibiting conduct that the State is free to regulate," he said.

"It may fairly be said that leaving accommodation to the political process will place at a relative disadvantage those religious practices that are not widely engaged in," Justice Scalia said, "but that unavoidable consequence of democratic government must be preferred to a system in which each conscience is a law unto itself."

A generally applicable law or regulation that places an incidental burden on religious practice is constitutional, Justice Scalia said, unless it is "specifically directed" at a religious act. As an example, he said, a law prohibiting "bowing down before a golden calf" would "doubtless be unconstitutional."

The majority's analysis drew strong dissents, not only from the three Justices who said the Constitution required an exemption for sacramental peyote use, but also from Justice Sandra Day O'Connor, who agreed with the outcome of the case but differed sharply with Justice Scalia's approach.

The three Justices who disagreed with the outcome as well as the approach were Thurgood Marshall, Harry A. Blackmun and William J. Brennan Jr. In her opinion concurring only in the result of the case, Justice O'Connor called the majority opinion "incompatible with our nation's fundamental commitment to individual religious liberty."

'VITALITY' OF FIRST AMENDMENT

She added: "If the First Amendment is to have any vitality, it ought not be construed to cover only the extreme and hypothetical situation in which a state directly targets a religious practice," she said.

"The essence of a free exercise claim," she said, "is relief from a burden imposed by government on religious practices or beliefs, whether the burden is imposed directly through laws that prohibit or compel specific religious practices, or indirectly through laws that, in effect, make abandonment of one's own religious or conformity to the religious beliefs of others the price of an equal place in the civil community.

"The history of our free-exercise doctrine amply demonstrates the harsh impact majoritarian rule has had on unpopular or emerging religious groups such as the Jehovah's Witnesses and the Amish."

In addition to filing their own dissenting opinion, Justices Blackmun, Marshall and Brennan signed much of Justice O'Connor's opinion. All four agreed that the Government must be required to justify a burden on religious practice by demonstrating that it served a "compelling state interest."

Justice O'Connor concluded that Oregon could have met that test in this case because of the state's compelling interest in curbing drug use. The three others concluded that the state's interest was not sufficiently compelling.

Justice Scalia's majority opinion rejected the "compelling state interest" test, saying it would "open the prospect of constitutionally required religious exemptions from civic obligations of almost every conceivable kind."

He said: "We cannot afford the luxury of deeming presumptively invalid, as applied to a religious objector, every regulation of conduct that does not protect an interest of the highest order."

The majority opinion, Employment Division v. Smith, No. 88-1213, was joined by Chief Justice William H. Rehnquist and Justices Byron R. White, John Paul Stevens and Anthony M. Kennedy.

* * * * * * * * * * * *

Establishment Clause

Establishment Clause claims—more numerous than free exercise cases—have arisen in a variety of contexts: government aid to religious institutions, especially parochial schools; government sponsorship of religious ceremonies, especially in public schools; and religious displays on government property, especially crèche scenes and the Ten Commandments. The Court has been strict in barring officially sponsored prayer in public schools, but since the 1990s has loosened restrictions in the other two areas.

"A WALL OF SEPARATION": THE COURT AND PAROCHIAL SCHOOLS

Ironically, the Court first embraced the controversial metaphor of "a wall of separation between church and state" in a decision that permitted the state of New Jersey to provide transportation to students in parochial as well as public schools. "The First Amendment has erected a wall between church and state," Justice Black wrote for the 5-4 majority in *Everson v. Board of Education* (1947). "We could not approve the slightest breach. New Jersey has not breached it here." Arthur Krock, *The Times'* Washington bureau chief, presciently said the decision appeared to be "the beginning of a grave judicial controversy."

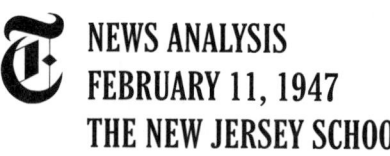

NEWS ANALYSIS
FEBRUARY 11, 1947
THE NEW JERSEY SCHOOL TRANSPORTATION CASE
By ARTHUR KROCK

WASHINGTON, Feb. 10—The vigor with which four justices of the Supreme Court today dissented from the legal reasoning, historical interpretation and final conclusion of the other five in the New Jersey case concerning publicly paid transportation of children to Catholic parochial schools suggests that, like the portal-to-portal issue, this is only the beginning of a grave judicial controversy.

This implication arises from the fact that, while the majority conceded that the New Jersey statute specifically providing transportation at public expense to children in non-public schools "approaches the verge" of a State's constitutional power, the minority contended that, under the majority's validation of the law, States may go much further. "If the State may aid these religious schools," commented Justice Jackson in his separate dissent, "it may therefore regulate them." And, speaking for the whole minority, Justice Rutledge said:

> We are told that the New Jersey statute is valid in its present application because the appropriation is for a public, not a private, purpose, namely the promotion of education, and the majority accept this idea in the conclusion that all we have here is "public welfare legislation." If that is true and the (First) Amendment's force can be thus destroyed, what has been said becomes all the more pertinent. For then there could be no possible objection to more extensive support of religious education by New Jersey.

> If the fact alone be determinative that religious schools are engaged in education, thus promoting the general and individual welfare, together with the Legislature's decision that the payment of public moneys for their aid makes their work a public function, then I can see no possible basis, except one of dubious legislative policy, for the State's refusal to make full appropriation for support of private, religious schools, just as is done for public instruction. There could not be, on that (the majority's) basis, valid constitutional objection.

ISSUE FOR ANOTHER DAY

This is more than an inference that a State could make such an attempt and rely on today's majority decision to uphold it in so doing. In that event, whatever encroachment on Jefferson's and Madison's First Amendment, forbidding an "establishment" of religion, was made by today's decision, there would be nothing left of the amendment at all. The Supreme Court, however, has often shown sufficient ingenuity in the use of lawyers' language and the shuffling of its own precedents to retreat from logical consequences when they become too destructive or unpopular, as its next move in the portal-to-portal issue once more may demonstrate.

The New Jersey case, decided today, came up from the Board of Education of Ewing Township and was based on a statute first outlawed and then sustained in the State courts. This statute provided that district school boards may, in effect, reimburse for transport costs the parents of children "living remote from any schoolhouse" who attend public and other schools except those operated for profit. The Ewing Township resolution, under this authority, paid the bus fares of such children attending public and Catholic parochial schools only.

A taxpayer charged violation of both the State and Federal Constitutions. Justice Black, noting for the majority that the statute was not challenged because of its exclusion of students at private schools, said that issue could be set aside in considering this case. Instead, he took up the charges that the statute and the township resolution violated the due process clause of the Fourteenth Amendment and those disestablishment provisions of the First Amendment which were made applicable to all the States by the Fourteenth.

"A MATTER OF PUBLIC WELFARE"

By this due process argument, he said, "a State's power to legislate for the public welfare might be seriously curtailed," and this disputed statute, he found, was passed as a matter of public welfare. The First Amendment, he added, did not—even inadvertently—"prohibit New Jersey from extending its general State law benefits to all its citizens without regard to their religious beliefs." If there are other religious schools in the district, for example, students living remote from them could not be excluded from getting the same paid transportation. But there was no accusation of this in the record.

As a matter of public welfare, commented Justice Black, the State gives fire, police and other protection to all property, including parochial schools, out of the tax revenues, and the bus fare is a part of the same pattern.

Justice Jackson, noting that his first inclination was to join the majority, said he had reluctantly decided otherwise. He made these points: "To render aid to its (Catholic) church schools is indistinguishable to me from rendering the same aid to the Church itself," and that violates the First Amendment. The test by which "the beneficiaries of this expenditure are selected" is "essentially religious," another plain violation. The effect of the amendment—"immeasurably compromised by today's decision"—"was to take every form of propagation of religion out of the realm of things * * * supported in whole or in part, at the taxpayers' expense."

The Chief Justice and Justice Reed joined the generally inseparable trio of Justices Black, Murphy and Douglas. . . .

• • • • • • • • • • • •

After the Court in 1968 approved a New York program of lending textbooks to parochial school students, parochial school supporters pushed on to win passage of laws in some states providing more direct assistance, including teacher salary subsidies and tuition reimbursements or tax credits. In 1971 the Court responded by striking down a Rhode Island teacher salary subsidy and a Pennsylvania law providing parochial schools with money for teacher salaries, text-books, and instructional materials. The decision in *Lemon v. Kurtzman* held that aid to parochial schools was permissible only if it had a secular purpose and did not entangle the government in religion.

The so-called *Lemon* test was applied strictly in a pair of decisions in 1985 that barred school districts from providing special educational services to parochial school students either during regular school hours or after the school day. Over the next decade, however, conservative justices called for loosening the rules. In 1997 the Court reopened one of the 1985 cases, overturned the decision, and allowed New York City to provide federally funded remedial services to parochial school students in school buildings. Three years later, the Court in *Mitchell v. Helms* (2000) overturned two other decisions from the 1970s in voting, 6-3, to permit federally financed loans of computers and other instructional equipment to religious as well as other private schools.

The trend culminated in a decision rejecting an Establishment Clause challenge to a school voucher program in Cleveland, which—like other voucher programs—principally benefited parochial schools. Writing for the 5-4 majority in *Zelman v. Simmons-Harris* (2002), Chief Justice Rehnquist said the program was constitutional because it was part of a general program to provide benefits to students without regard to religion and allowed families "to exercise genuine choice" between secular and religious schools.

Zelman v. Simmons-Harris

Decided: June 27, 2002

Vote: 5 (Rehnquist, O'Connor, Scalia, Kennedy, Thomas)

4 (Stevens, Souter, Ginsburg, Breyer)

Opinion of the Court: Rehnquist

Concurring opinions (2): O'Connor; Thomas

Dissenting opinions (3): Stevens; Souter (Stevens, Ginsburg, Breyer); Breyer (Stevens, Souter)

JUNE 28, 2002
SUPREME COURT, 5-4, UPHOLDS VOUCHER SYSTEM THAT PAYS RELIGIOUS SCHOOLS' TUITION

By LINDA GREENHOUSE

The Supreme Court, concluding that Cleveland's voucher plan was "a program of true private choice," today upheld the use of public money for religious school tuition in a decisive 5-to-4 ruling that the majority called a logical outgrowth of recent decisions and the dissenters described as a fundamental break with the past.

The most important ruling on religion and the schools in the 40 years since the court declared organized prayer in the public schools to be unconstitutional, the decision, issued on the final day of the court's 2001–2002 term, will not end the passionate debate over "school choice."

Rather, it will move that debate to state courts, in battles over state constitutional objections to voucher programs,

and to state legislatures and the ballot box. While a handful of voucher programs are now in operation, they have been defeated consistently in referendums.

Voucher supporters have attributed those defeats to the legal cloud over the concept that the court removed today.

"This allows the school choice movement to shift from defense to offense," said Clint Bolick, vice president of the Institute for Justice, a nonprofit group here that is a leading voucher supporter.

But voucher opponents said that their courtroom set-back did not mean they would lose the public opinion war. "The public mindset won't change," said Robert Chanin, general counsel of the National Education Association, the teachers union, who represented voucher opponents in the Supreme Court.

The decision also raises the prospect of new legal battles over what strings might be attached, in the form of nondiscrimination obligations or adherence to other public policies, to the public money that flows to religious school coffers.

Under Cleveland's six-year-old program, some 3,700 of the district's 75,000 children use vouchers of up to $2,250 to attend private schools, with nearly all—96 percent in the 1999–2000 school year that the court examined—attending religious schools.

Based in large part on that outcome, the federal appeals court in Cincinnati declared in December 2000 that the program had the "impermissible effect of promoting sectarian schools" and thus violated the First Amendment's prohibition against the "establishment" of religion.

a criterion with a practical capacity to screen something out," Justice David H. Souter said for himself and the three others, Justices John Paul Stevens, Ruth Bader Ginsburg and Stephen G. Breyer.

Chief Justice Rehnquist's majority opinion was joined by Justices Antonin Scalia, Anthony M. Kennedy, Clarence Thomas and Sandra Day O'Connor. It was significant that Justice O'Connor, while filing her own concurring opinion, fully subscribed to the majority opinion as well. In past church-state cases, as in a decision two years ago that upheld federal loans of computer equipment to parochial schools, Justice O'Connor has sometimes concurred only in the "judgment," leaving the dimensions of the ruling somewhat unclear.

In her opinion today, Justice O'Connor did suggest that the availability of other types of public school programs among the options presented to the Cleveland students helped persuade her that those eligible for vouchers "have a genuine choice between religious and nonreligious

> " If society cannot end racial discrimination, at least it can arm minorities with the education to defend themselves from some of discrimination's effects. "
>
> —Justice Clarence Thomas, *Zelman v. Simmons-Harris*

But the 96 percent figure lacked "constitutional significance," Chief Justice William H. Rehnquist wrote for the majority today, because the program was "neutral in all respects toward religion" and parents exercised "genuine choice" in where to use their vouchers.

Further, the chief justice said, the figure was misleading in not taking into account the thousands of children who exercised their choice under the Cleveland plan to leave their neighborhood public schools and attend publicly financed magnet or charter schools. When those were added to the denominator, he said, the proportion of voucher students attending religious schools dropped to 16.5 percent.

The four dissenters objected that it was the majority that made misleading use of statistics by counting students who attended nontraditional but tuition-free public schools as part of the voucher population.

"If the majority wishes to claim that choice is a criterion, it must define choice in a way that can function as

schools." She added, "In looking at the voucher program, all the choices available to potential beneficiaries of the government program should be considered."

But the dissenters did not find much comfort or a limiting principle in Justice O'Connor's approach; to the contrary, they expressed alarm at the ease with which the majority had relabeled the relevant categories in the case.

"The wide range of choices that have been made available to students within the public school system has no bearing on the question whether the state may pay the tuition for students who wish to reject public education entirely and attend private schools that will provide them with a sectarian education," Justice Stevens said in his dissenting opinion.

While also joining the majority, Justice Thomas filed a separate opinion emphasizing the role of school choice on the opportunities available to poor urban children.

"The promise of public school education has failed poor inner-city blacks," he said, adding, "If society cannot end racial discrimination, at least it can arm minorities with the education to defend themselves from some of discrimination's effects."

His opinion echoed Ohio's defense of the Cleveland program, which the State Legislature enacted after a federal court placed the failing school district, where fewer than one-third of the students graduate from high school, under state control. Many voucher supporters have argued that the program gives poor children the range of choices that middle-class families have enjoyed.

The school choice movement has drawn on many sources of support, including libertarian and free-market groups that see marketplace competition as the best way to force public schools to improve.

The dissenters today said that the $2,250 cap on tuition gave an illusion of choice that in fact steered children toward the religious schools, where tuition is below that limit, and away from secular private schools, where tuition is above it.

In his majority opinion, Zelman v. Simmons-Harris, No. 00-1751, Chief Justice Rehnquist described the court's holding as the logical if not inevitable outcome of a series of rulings dating to an opinion he wrote as an associate justice in 1983.

In that case, Mueller v. Allen, the court upheld a Minnesota law providing tax deductions for certain educational expenses that as a practical matter were incurred only by parents with children in private school. Given that nearly all private schools in Minnesota were religious, 96 percent of the beneficiaries were parents with children in religious schools.

The Minnesota program was not a constitutional violation, the court held then, because it was a neutral law that distributed money according to private parental choice. "We believe that the program challenged here is a program of true private choice," consistent with the Mueller decision and two similar rulings, the chief justice said today.

The dissenters objected that the ruling today was a sharp break from the past. Justice Breyer said voucher programs differed "in both kind and degree from aid programs upheld in the past" because they provided public money "to a core function of the church: the teaching of religious truths to young children."

Justice Breyer predicted that the decision would prove highly divisive in a country with "more than 55 different religious groups." He predicted many struggles, asking, "How will the public react to government funding for schools that take controversial religious positions on topics that are of current popular interest—say, the conflict in the Middle East or the war on terrorism?"

In reply, Chief Justice Rehnquist said "the program has ignited no 'divisiveness' or 'strife' other than this litigation."

* * * * * * * * * * * *

PRAYER IN PUBLIC SCHOOLS AND "EQUAL ACCESS"

Engel v. Vitale

> **Decided:** June 25, 1962
>
> **Vote:** 6 (Warren, Black, Douglas, Clark, Harlan II, Brennan)
>
> 1 (Stewart)
>
> **Opinion of the Court:** Black
>
> **Concurring opinion:** Douglas
>
> **Dissenting opinion:** Stewart
>
> **Did not participate:** Frankfurter, B. White

Even as church-state separationists were losing ground on the parochial school aid issue, they were holding on to the far more controversial victories that they had won in the 1960s against officially sponsored prayer in public schools. Classroom prayer and Bible reading had long been a regular practice in schools throughout the country, but in the early 1960s the Supreme Court ruled the practices an impermissible government establishment of religion. In the first of the rulings, the Court in *Engel v. Vitale* (1962) barred the daily classroom recital of a twenty-two word, nondenominational prayer written by the New York Board of Regents. Justice Black said the prayer violated the Establishment Clause because it was "composed by governmental officials as a part of a governmental program to further religious beliefs." A year later, the Court extended the decision in a challenge brought to daily Bible readings in public schools (*Abington School District v. Schempp*). Justice Stewart was the lone dissenter in both rulings.

JUNE 26, 1962
SUPREME COURT OUTLAWS OFFICIAL SCHOOL PRAYERS IN REGENTS CASE DECISION

RULING IS 6 TO 1

Suit Was Brought by 5 L.I. Parents Against Education Board

By ANTHONY LEWIS

Special to The New York Times

WASHINGTON, June 25—The Supreme Court held today that the reading of an official prayer in New York public schools violated the Constitution.

The prayer was drafted by the New York Board of Regents and recommended in 1951 for recital aloud by teachers and children in each classroom at the start of every school day. It is non-denominational and just twenty-two words long. It reads:

"Almighty God, we acknowledge our dependence upon Thee, and we beg Thy blessing upon us, our parents, our teachers and our country."

country. And beyond that, it might indicate a stricter attitude in the Supreme Court toward breaches of what it has called the "wall of separation" between church and state.

The prayer case was one of seventeen decided by the Supreme Court in a crowded final session today before it adjourned for the summer. In addition to those opinions the court issued hundreds of brief orders to clean up the docket. It returns next Oct. 1.

In an unusual ceremony at the start of today's session, Justice Hugo L. Black was honored for serving through twenty-five terms of the court. The Solicitor General,

> If there is any one thing clear in the First Amendment it is that the right of the people to pray in their own way is not to be controlled by the election returns.
>
> —Justice Hugo L. Black, *Engel v. Vitale*

By a vote of 6 to 1 the court held that the reading of the prayer was "an establishment of religion" forbidden by the First Amendment to the Constitution.

IMPACT FAR-REACHING

But the impact of the decision goes far beyond the New York prayer. The clear implication of the ruling was that any religious ceremony promoted by the state in public schools would be suspect. That would include, for example, reading of verses from the Bible—a practice now under challenge in Pennsylvania.

Many of the public school systems in the United States have such religious ceremonies. The practice is most common in the South, where chapel exercises and Bible readings are commonly used.

Thus, today's decision would have a major and controversial impact on public school practices across the

Archibald Cox, and Chief Justice Earl Warren joined in a brief but dramatic tribute to the justice.

Justice Black wrote the opinion of the court in the prayer case. He was joined by the Chief Justice and Justice Tom C. Clark, John Marshall Harlan and William J. Brennan Jr. Justice William O. Douglas concurred in a separate opinion.

Justice Potter Stewart was the sole dissenter. Not participating were Justices Felix Frankfurter, who is in the hospital, and Byron R. White, who joined the court after the case was argued.

The case was brought by five parents of children in the public schools of New Hyde Park, L.I., N.Y. Two of the parents were Jewish, one a member of the Ethical Culture Society, one a Unitarian and one a non-believer. They said the form of the prayer conflicted with their religious beliefs.

The highest New York State court, the Court of Appeals, rejected their protest against the prayer by a vote of 5 to 2.

ESTABLISH[MENT] CLAUSE VIOLATED

The complaint of these families, as Justice Black phrased it today, was that the prayer violated the establishment clause of the First Amendment because it was "composed by governmental officials as a part of a governmental program to further religious beliefs."

"We agree with that contention," Justice Black said.

"In this country, it is no part of the business of government to compose official prayers for any group of the American people to recite.

School officials had argued that the prayer was inoffensive because parents who did not want their children to say it could get them excused. The children could then either leave the room or remain seated and silent while their classmates stood and prayed.

In New Hyde Park, only one child had sought to be excused since the prayer was adopted in 1958.

Justice Black rejected this argument. He said, first, that placing "the power, prestige and financial support of government" behind a particular form of religious observance does tend to coerce religious minorities to conform.

PURPOSE OF BAN

But the purposes of banning "an establishment of religion go much further," Justice Black said. He declared that the clause "does not depend upon any showing of direct governmental compulsion and is violated by the enactment of laws which establish an official religion whether those laws operate directly to coerce nonobserving individuals or not."

In stating the opinion from the bench today, Justice Black added these extemporaneous comments:

"The prayer of each man from his soul must be his and his alone. That is the genius of the First Amendment.

"If there is any one thing clear in the First Amendment it is that the right of the people to pray in their own way is not to be controlled by the election returns."

Justice Stewart, in his dissent, criticized Justice Black's "uncritical invocation of metaphors like the 'wall of separation.' "

"I cannot see how an 'official religion' is established by letting those who want to say a prayer say it," Justice Stewart wrote.

"On the contrary, I think that to deny the wish of these school children to join in reciting this prayer is to deny them the opportunity of sharing in the spiritual heritage of our nation."

REVIEWS GOVERNMENT REFERENCES

Justice Stewart reviewed historical examples of references to God in American governmental proceedings. He noted that Congress begins its sessions with a prayer and that the crier of the Supreme Court itself says at every session: "God save the United States and this honorable court."

He said none of these amounted to establishing an "official religion," and neither did the New York prayer. All, he argued, simply recognized "the deeply entrenched and highly cherished spiritual traditions of our nation."

Justice Black, for his part, dismissed in a footnote the comparison of the New York prayer with references to God in such places as the Court and Congress. He said these were "patriotic or ceremonial occasions" bearing "no true resemblance to the unquestioned religious exercise" at issue today.

Justice Douglas, on the other hand, suggested in his concurring opinion that all these practices were unconstitutional. He said the audience for a prayer in a school, court or legislature was a "captive audience."

Some indication of the impact of the decision is given by the fact that twenty states came into the case as friends of the court to urge upholding of the prayer. The American Civil Liberties Union, which supported the case for the plaintiffs, and some Jewish and other groups were on the opposite side.

COMMENT BY SOUTHERNER

Immediate reaction in Congress was dominated by unfavorable comment from Southern members. Representative George Andrews, Democrat of Alabama, said:

"They put the Negroes in the schools and now they've driven God out."

The Supreme Court had a chance ten years ago to rule on a similar case. But it dismissed the case on procedural grounds.

That case, from New Jersey, challenged the reading of verses from the Bible in public schools. But the children involved had all graduated by the time the case reached the Supreme Court, and the court held that the complaining parents lacked standing to sue simply as taxpayers.

The first important church-state decision from the modern court came in 1947. By a vote of 5 to 4, the court upheld the use of state funds to provide bus service for parochial school pupils.

Interestingly, Justice Douglas—who was one of the majority of five in the Buas [sic] case—said in his opinion today that it should be overruled. In retrospect, he said, it seems "out of line with the First Amendment."

In 1948 the court held 8 to 1 that the use of public school classrooms for religious instruction in a "release time" program was unconstitutional. But in 1952 it approved, by vote of 6 to 3, a New York program releasing children from public school classes for religious instruction elsewhere. . . .

• • • • • • • • • • • •

The *Engel* and *Schempp* rulings provoked strong criticism, widespread noncompliance, and continuing efforts for the next two decades to overturn the decisions by constitutional amendment. Nevertheless, the Court has adhered to and even extended the decisions. In 1985 the Court struck down an Alabama law requiring a "moment of silence" in public schools, noting that the law's stated purpose was to promote "meditation or voluntary prayer." In 1992 the Court ruled, 5-4, against prayers at public high school graduation ceremonies; social conservatives were especially angry that the decision in *Lee v. Weisman* was written by Justice Kennedy, a Reagan appointee. And in 2000 the Court went one step further and barred school officials from sponsoring prayer at high school football games.

The Court has ruled, however, that religious groups are entitled to use public school buildings on the same basis as other organizations. The ruling in *Board of Education of Westside Community Schools v. Mergens* (1990) upheld a congressional statute, the Equal Access Act of 1984, requiring schools to provide "equal access" for religious groups as granted other extracurricular organizations. In a pair of cases in 2001, the Court ruled that denying religious groups equal access to school buildings also violated the Free Speech Clause.

RELIGIOUS DISPLAYS

In a third Establishment Clause area, the Court has struggled to find a coherent line for judging the constitutionality of religious displays in or around government buildings. In 1984 the Court upheld the display of a crèche, along with other traditional Christmas symbols, in a Pawtucket, Rhode Island, city park. Five years later, shifting majorities in companion cases from Pittsburgh barred the display of a crèche in the Allegheny County, Pennsylvania, courthouse but permitted the display on courthouse grounds of a menorah, symbolizing the Jewish holiday Hanukkah.

Writing for the different majorities in *County of Allegheny v. American Civil Liberties Union* (1989), Justice Blackmun said the display of the crèche with no other holiday symbols and in a prominent location sent "an unmistakable message that [the county] supports and promotes . . . the crèche's message." By contrast, Blackmun said, the menorah did not have an exclusively religious message because it was displayed with other symbols of the winter holidays, including a Christmas tree.

The decisions riled religious conservatives, who mocked the Court for establishing a "plastic reindeer" test for permitting Christmastime displays in government buildings. They became even more upset in the late 1990s as church-state separationists, including the ACLU, began challenging the placement of the Ten Commandments in government buildings. The Court in 1980 had summarily overturned a Kentucky law requiring the posting of the Ten Commandments in every public school classroom. The new challenges responded to active efforts by religious conservatives to display the Decalogue in local and state courthouses.

Two cases reached the Supreme Court in 2005—one challenging the recent posting of the Ten Commandments as part of a historical display in a Kentucky courthouse and the other challenging a

McCreary County v. American Civil Liberties Union

Decided: June 27, 2005

Vote: 5 (Stevens, O'Connor, Souter, Ginsburg, Breyer)

4 (Rehnquist, Scalia, Kennedy, Thomas)

Opinion of the Court: Souter

Concurring opinion: O'Connor

Dissenting opinion: Scalia (Rehnquist, Kennedy, Thomas)

monolith bearing the text of the commandments placed on the grounds of the Texas State Capitol in 1961. With Justice Stephen G. Breyer casting the pivotal vote in two 5-4 decisions, the Court ruled the courthouse display unconstitutional but refused to order the removal of the monolith. In *McCreary County v. American Civil Liberties Union* (2005), Justice David H. Souter stressed evidence that county officials had acted with a religious purpose in mounting the display. But Breyer changed sides in *Van Orden v. Perry* (2005), emphasizing the history of the monolith—a civic group had placed the granite marker as part of a nationwide program to combat juvenile delinquency—to conclude that it had a "predominantly secular message."

JUNE 28, 2005
JUSTICES ALLOW A COMMANDMENTS DISPLAY, BAR OTHERS

By LINDA GREENHOUSE

WASHINGTON, June 27—A fractured Supreme Court on Monday, struggling to define a constitutional framework for the government display of religious symbols, upheld a six-foot-high Ten Commandments monument on the grounds of the Texas Capitol while ruling that framed copies of the Commandments on the walls of two Kentucky courthouses were unconstitutional.

significance of the particular context in which the Commandments were displayed. The question was whether either display violated the First Amendment's prohibition against an official "establishment" of religion.

To the extent that the decisions provided guidelines for the further cases that are all but certain to follow, it appeared to be that religious symbols that have been on

> It is true that many Americans find the Commandments in accord with their personal beliefs. But we do not count heads before enforcing the First Amendment.
>
> —Justice Sandra Day O'Connor,
> *McCreary County v. American Civil Liberties Union*

The decisions in the two separate cases came on the final day of the court's 2004–2005 term, a term shadowed by Chief Justice William H. Rehnquist's illness and speculation about his retirement plans.

But if the 80-year-old chief justice, who has been battling thyroid cancer, has such plans, he gave no indication of them as he presided over the hourlong proceedings. He even joked at one point, observing after he described the complicated voting pattern in the Texas Ten Commandments case that "I didn't know we had that many people on our court."

The vote in each Ten Commandments case was 5 to 4, with both majorities emphasizing, to varying degrees, the

display for many years, with little controversy, are likely to be upheld, while newer displays intended to advance a modern religious agenda will be met with suspicion and disfavor from the court.

Only Justice Stephen G. Breyer agreed with both decisions, a development that appears to give him the balance of power in a contentious area of the court's docket that has been controlled most often in the past by Justice Sandra Day O'Connor.

For her part, Justice O'Connor voted in each case with the group that found the displays unconstitutional, a surprising development given her past voting record. She explained herself in a concurring opinion in the Kentucky case, McCreary County v. American Civil Liberties Union, No. 03-1693, which was decided with a majority opinion by Justice David H. Souter.

"It is true that many Americans find the Commandments in accord with their personal beliefs," Justice O'Connor said in her concurring opinion. "But we do not count heads before enforcing the First Amendment."

Justice O'Connor said the country had worked well, when compared with nations gripped by religious violence, by keeping religion "a matter for the individual conscience, not for the prosecutor or bureaucrat." She added: "Those who would renegotiate the boundaries between church and state must therefore answer a difficult question: why would we trade a system that has served us so well for one that has served others so poorly?"

The result in the Kentucky case provoked a particularly bitter dissenting opinion from Justice Antonin Scalia, who read from it at length on Monday morning. He accused the majority of expressing hostility to religion and deviating from the intent of the Constitution's framers. "Nothing stands behind the court's assertion that governmental affirmation of the society's belief in God is unconstitutional except the court's own say-so," Justice Scalia said.

Noting the court's inconsistency in the church-state area, in which decisions have upheld property-tax exemptions for churches and the employment of chaplains by state legislatures, Justice Scalia said the court had often deviated from the principle the majority now invoked of official neutrality between religion and nonreligion. What could be the reason for the inconsistency, he asked, and then gave this answer:

"I suggest it is the instinct for self-preservation, and the recognition that the court, which 'has no influence over either the sword or the purse,' cannot go too far down the road of an enforced neutrality that contradicts both historical fact and current practice without losing all that sustains it: the willingness of the people to accept its interpretation of the Constitution as definitive, in preference to the contrary interpretation of the democratically elected branches."

The two cases produced a total of 10 opinions, totaling 136 pages. Outside the court, the split decisions enabled each side in the larger debate over the role of religion in the public square to claim a measure of victory. It may take further litigation, not in these particular cases but in others that raise related questions, before the import of the decisions becomes clear.

For example, on Tuesday the justices are expected to announce the disposition in several cases they have held in abeyance while these were pending. One is an appeal by a South Carolina town, Great Falls, of a ruling that it could not constitutionally open sessions of its town council with a prayer invoking the name of Jesus Christ.

At the least, the ruling on Monday in the Texas case, Van Orden v. Perry, No. 03-1500, will immunize from constitutional challenge hundreds of granite Ten Commandments monuments that were erected in public places around the country by the Fraternal Order of Eagles, a national civic organization, in the 1950's and 1960's. According to the Eagles at the time, exposing the nation's youth to the Ten Commandments would lead to a decrease in juvenile delinquency.

The monument on the grounds of the Texas Capitol is one of 17 monuments and 21 historical markers that decorate the 22-acre park. The Ten Commandments monument was challenged by Thomas Van Orden, a law school graduate, now homeless, who passes it as he uses the library at the state Supreme Court, near the Capitol. Both the federal district court in Austin and the United States Court of Appeals for the Fifth Circuit, in New Orleans, found that the monument had a valid secular purpose and did not violate the Constitution.

The Supreme Court affirmed that ruling Monday with the combined opinions of Chief Justice Rehnquist and Justice Breyer. The Rehnquist opinion attracted three other votes, those of Justices Scalia, Anthony M. Kennedy and Clarence Thomas.

"Of course, the Ten Commandments are religious," Chief Justice Rehnquist said; some supporters of displaying the Commandments had tried to argue to the court that the monuments should essentially be regarded as codes of secular law. The chief justice said that in addition to their religious significance, "the Ten Commandments have an undeniable historical meaning." He added, "Simply having religious content or promoting a message consistent with a religious doctrine does not run afoul of the Establishment Clause."

Chief Justice Rehnquist drew a distinction between the Texas monument and a case from 1980 in which the court struck down a Kentucky law requiring copies of the Commandments to be posted in public school classrooms. The display on the Capitol grounds "is a far more passive use of those texts," he said.

Justice Breyer's concurring opinion said the case was a "borderline case" that depended not on any single formula but on context and judgment. The monument's physical setting, he said, "suggests little or nothing of the sacred." The fact that 40 years had passed without dispute, until Mr. Van Orden filed his lawsuit, suggested that the public had understood the monument not as a religious object but as part of a "broader moral and historical message reflective of a cultural heritage."

Further, Justice Breyer said, a contrary decision would lead to the removal of many longstanding depictions of the Ten Commandments in public places, and "it could thereby create the very kind of religiously based divisiveness that the Establishment Clause seeks to avoid."

The dissenters in the Texas case were the four justices who, along with Justice Breyer, found the Kentucky courthouse displays unconstitutional. They were Justices John Paul Stevens and Ruth Bader Ginsburg in addition to Justices Souter and O'Connor. Justice Stevens, in a dissenting opinion in the Texas case, said that the Ten Commandments were inherently religious and that by displaying them, Texas gave the message that "this state endorses the divine code of the Judeo-Christian God."

In his majority opinion in the Kentucky case, Justice Souter emphasized the history of the courthouse displays, which began as solitary displays of the Ten Commandments and became part of a broader display of historical documents only in the face of litigation. The claim by Pulaski and McCreary Counties that the displays had a secular purpose "was an apparent sham," he said, adding, "Reasonable observers have reasonable memories."

The decision upheld a ruling by the United States Court of Appeals for the Sixth Circuit, in Cincinnati.

THE RIGHTS OF POLITICAL PARTICIPATION

CHAPTER 6

As chairman of the Shelby County Quarterly Court in the 1950s, Charles Baker was the full-time chief executive of the governing body for the county that included Memphis, Tennessee's largest city. Like other big cities in the United States, Memphis had been growing rapidly since the end of World War II as the United States continued its transformation from a predominantly rural to a predominantly urban, and later suburban, country.

Tennessee's constitution, like those of almost all the states, required reapportionment of districts for the state House of Representatives and the state Senate every ten years "according to the number of qualified voters in each." But the requirement—comparable to the provision in the U.S. Constitution requiring decennial reapportionment among the states for the U.S. House of Representatives (Art. I, sec. 2, cl. 3)—

Protesters argue in front of the Supreme Court in December 2000 as the Court hears arguments in *Bush v. Gore.* The case was prompted by extremely close election results in the 2000 presidential race in Florida. The Court found an equal protection violation and ruled that the Florida ballot recount must cease. Democrat Al Gore conceded the race to Republican George W. Bush following the ruling.

had not been acted on since 1901. As a result, rural areas that once held most of the state's population still controlled a majority of seats in the Tennessee General Assembly despite the growth of the state's cities and suburbs.

As county executive, Baker saw the results of the legislature's failure to redistrict in proportionately lower funding for Shelby and other urban counties and less attention to urban problems generally. Along with others in Memphis and the state's capital city of Nashville, Baker decided to file a federal court lawsuit in 1959 aimed at forcing the legislature to comply with the reapportionment requirement. Joe Carr, who oversaw state elections as secretary of state, was the first-named defendant.

"I think everyone will agree that the Constitution of Tennessee has been ignored and violated continuously and systematically over a period of years," U.S. District Court judge William E. Miller said during arguments in the case. Along with the other two judges on the panel, however, Miller felt bound to dismiss the suit; a Supreme Court decision, *Colegrove v. Green* (1946), kept federal courts out of reapportionment cases because they presented a "political question."

The plaintiffs appealed to the Supreme Court, which heard two rounds of arguments in the case in April and October 1961. The decision came in March 1962. By a 6-2 vote, the Court held in *Baker v. Carr* that federal courts had jurisdiction to hear the case under the Fourteenth Amendment's Equal Protection Clause and that the plaintiffs had presented "a justiciable constitutional cause of action" upon which they "would be entitled to relief."

The ruling went no further, but the import was recognized immediately. "Rural Areas Facing Loss of Political Dominance," a *New York Times* headline declared. In a dissent, Justice Felix Frankfurter, who had written the Court's ruling in *Colegrove,* said that the high court's injecting itself into an "essentially political conflict" could "impair the Court's position as the ultimate organ of 'the supreme Law of the Land.'"

Within a matter of years, *Baker v. Carr* and a succession of three other rulings in 1963 and 1964 wrought a political revolution across the country. The Court's rulings—summarized in the now familiar phrase "one person, one vote"—required the redrawing of state legislative districts as well as congressional districts. Rural areas lost power to the nation's cities and suburbs: politics was changed, fundamentally and lastingly.

NEWS ANALYSIS
MARCH 27, 1962
RURAL AREAS FACING LOSS OF POLITICAL DOMINANCE

Court Ruling Expected to Bring Gradual Shift of Power to Suburbs and Cities and to Strengthen the Democrats

By JAMES RESTON

Special to The New York Times

WASHINGTON, March 26—The Supreme Court's decision in the Tennessee reapportionment case is expected to shift the balance of political power gradually against the rural conservatives.

The first reaction here was that the 6-to-2 decision authorizing voters to challenge the make-up of State Legislatures in Federal courts would probably do these things:

- Decrease the voting strength of rural conservatives in the many State Legislatures and increase the strength of city and suburban voters, who tend to be more sympathetic toward social change and government intervention.

- Increase, over all, the power of the Democratic party, which is better organized politically in the cities and is now engaged in a major drive to extend and strengthen its party organization in the suburbs.

- Expand the influence of the Federal courts as instruments of social change.

This expansion of the influence of the courts is in keeping with the trend of Federal judicial power in the last generation.

The Supreme Court, often the target of Presidential opposition for opposing social change, has increasingly led the fight for such change in recent years: First in the reorganization of the economic system under the antitrust laws; then in the reorganization of the public school system in the desegregation decision of 1954; and now in today's decision to take jurisdiction in the reorganization of the voting system in State Legislatures.

There was no unanimity here tonight on the political implications of the decision. Most observers seemed to be of the opinion that, by approving Federal judicial jurisdiction in state-legislature reapportionment cases, the Supreme Court had put pressure on the legislatures to bring about a more equal balance on the basis of population and geography.

Some experts in the field more impressed by the ingenuity and determination of the rural interests in the state legislatures, took another view, however. They said they expected a movement in some states to rewrite the state Constitution to give adequate population representation in the lower house of the state legislature and equal geographic representation—one representative for each county—in the upper chamber of the state legislature.

NEW JERSEY AN EXAMPLE

The system, which prevails in the New Jersey State Senate, would tend, it was pointed out, to meet the demand for population representation but retain an even more rigid veto by freezing the rural county representatives in the upper chamber.

This, however, was a minority view. The consensus seemed to be that the court decision would dramatize what is seldom denied here, namely, that the state legislatures are over-represented in the rural side, and that this, in turn, will lead in due course to larger and probably less conservative replacements in the state legislatures.

They said that malapportionment was "particularly pronounced" in the suburbs of the ten largest metropolitan areas—New York, Los Angeles, Philadelphia, Detroit, San Francisco-Oakland, Boston, St. Louis, Cleveland, Baltimore and Newark.

Until today's decision by the Supreme Court, however, the imbalance in the state legislatures had been primarily a local and state issue, with regional politicians and political scientists arguing it out without producing any major change.

This points up one of the odd paradoxes in the majority and dissenting opinions. Justice Felix Frankfurter, dissenting, argued that the court's intervention was wrong and would be ineffective.

"In this situation," he wrote, "as in others of like nature, appeal for relief does not belong here.

"Appeal must be to an informed, civically militant electorate. In a democratic society like ours, relief must come through an aroused popular conscience that sears the conscience of the people's representatives."

> " The consensus seemed to be that the court decision would dramatize what is seldom denied here, namely, that the state legislatures are over-represented in the rural side, and that this, in turn, will lead in due course to larger and probably less conservative replacements in the state legislatures. "

The most scientific study of malapportionment in the state legislatures was made recently by Professors Paul T. David and Ralph Eisenberg of the University of Virginia. It showed that between 1910 and 1960 the relative value of the right to vote (100 equals the average vote value) rose from 113 to 171 in the nation's least populated counties. During this same period, the relative vote value in counties with more than 500,000 persons dropped from 81 to 76.

Professors David and Eisenberg said in their report that malapportionment had been magnified in all suburban areas by "enormous" population gains.

FIND SUBURBS LAGGING

"The suburbs," their report said, "seemed never to catch up" in representation, even when they are given some more legislative seats."

Yet, when some experienced politicians looked over the court's decision tonight, their opinion seemed to be that the court's decision might very well produce that "informed, civically militant electorate" that local political and pedagogical analysis had failed to arouse in the past.

Justice Frankfurter was particularly critical of injecting the court into what he called the clash of political forces in political settlements.

"The court's authority—possessed neither of the purse nor the sword—ultimately rests," he argued, "on sustained public confidence in its moral sanction. Such feeling must be nourished by the court's complete detachment, in fact and appearance, from political entanglements."

There was little support here for the view that the courts, "possessed neither of the purse nor the sword," would decide these cases themselves. Many observers made the point that it would be much more difficult for the courts to come up with a formula for just representation in a state legislature than to produce a formula for public school integration.

Nevertheless, the political consensus seemed to be about as follows:

First, the court has dramatized a critical situation.

Second, the rise in the nation's population—up by 3,000,000 every year—and the movement of the people off the land into the cities and suburbs, have created urgent problems of city renewal, education, and transportation.

Third, the state legislatures, increasingly weighted to the farm areas, are not dealing with these problems effectively. Therefore, once the court has brought the issue to the center of national attention, public opinion will produce the pressure for greater representation from the urban and suburban areas.

That this will be a slow process nobody doubts—probably as slow as the school desegregation process. But the feeling here is that the process has now started, that it will proceed mainly in the headlines for a time, but that in due course it will move—probably leftward from where it is now.

• • • • • • • • • • • •

The reapportionment revolution played out in the 1960s simultaneously with the voting rights revolution for African Americans. Congress, not the Court, played the lead role in this second transformation by passing the Voting Rights Act of 1965. In fact, the Court in the late nineteenth century had thwarted Congress's efforts to enforce the post–Civil War Fifteenth Amendment's mandate that the right to vote not be abridged because of "race, color, or previous condition of servitude."

During the same period, the Court had also turned aside the plea of a women's suffragist to gain the right to vote as a "privilege or immunity" of U.S. citizenship protected by the Fourteenth Amendment. Women gained the right to vote nationwide only with the ratification of the Nineteenth Amendment in 1920.

By the end of the twentieth century, federal courts' role in reapportionment and redistricting was well established, if still controversial at times. The Court declined to police the partisan practice of "gerrymandering"—drawing legislative districts to benefit one party or disadvantage another. In the 1990s, however, the Court stepped in to limit the use of race in drawing district lines.

At the same time, the Court was drawn into a range of other voting and election disputes, including the dramatic case of *Bush v. Gore* (2000) that effectively settled one of the closest presidential election contests in the nation's history. The Court's decision to block the Florida recount that Democrat Al Gore was seeking to try to reverse Republican George W. Bush's apparent Electoral College majority was—and remains—controversial.

In its unsigned opinion, however, the Court insisted that it had no recourse to entering what Justice Frankfurter years earlier had called "the political thicket." In the concluding paragraph, the Court explained: "When contending parties invoke the process of the court . . . it becomes our unsought responsibility to resolve the federal and constitutional issues the judicial system has been forced to confront."

EARLY DEVELOPMENTS

The original Constitution left voting and elections almost completely up to the states. State legislatures were given the initial power to prescribe "the Times, Places and Manner of holding Elections for Senators and Representatives" (Art. I, sec. 4, cl. 1). Congress could "make or alter such Regulations," except that it could not change the place for choosing senators—who were elected by state legislatures until the ratification of the Seventeenth Amendment in 1913. States were free to set their own rules for state and local elections, but anyone eligible to vote for the most numerous branch of the state legislature could also vote for members of the U.S. House of Representatives.

When the Constitution was adopted, the right to vote was limited to adult, white, propertied men—a small fraction of the total population. Vermont, admitted to the Union in 1791, became the first state to expand the franchise to all adult white men regardless of property ownership. By 1840 almost all of the states had eliminated property requirements for voting. In Rhode Island, however, a dispute over efforts to broaden voting rights led to a unique legal fight pitting two groups that each claimed to be the state's legitimate government. The issue reached the Supreme Court in 1849, but the Court—in a seminal opinion by Chief Justice Roger B. Taney in *Luther v. Borden*—said the dispute turned on "political questions" that were not for the Court to decide.

POST–CIVIL WAR EXPANSION OF THE FRANCHISE

African Americans and white women, however, were still denied the right to vote—by law or custom. The feminist leader Elizabeth Cady Stanton helped give birth to the women's suffrage movement by organizing a historic conference in Seneca Falls, New York, in 1848; the movement succeeded seven decades later with the ratification of the Nineteenth Amendment (1920), which prohibits the United States or any state from abridging the right to vote "on account of sex."

The post–Civil War Fourteenth and Fifteenth Amendments laid the groundwork for extending the franchise to former slaves and possibly to others, but the Supreme Court's initial rulings blunted their impact. The Fourteenth Amendment, ratified in 1868, made "all persons born or naturalized in the United States" citizens of the United States and of their state of residence; it went on to prohibit any state from making or enforcing any law abridging "the privileges or immunities of citizens of the United States." The Fifteenth Amendment, ratified in 1870, specifically provided that no state could deny or abridge the right to vote "on account of race, color, or previous condition of servitude."

Both amendments included provisions authorizing Congress to pass enforcing legislation. Using that authority, Congress passed the Enforcement Acts of 1870 and 1871, which prescribed criminal penalties for anyone interfering with the right to vote under the 1870 amendment.

The Court, however, cut off any use of the Fourteenth Amendment to expand the franchise with a decision in 1875 rebuffing an effort by Virginia Minor, president of the Missouri Women's Suffrage Association, to register and vote. In a unanimous ruling, the Court held that the right to vote was not a "privilege or immunity" of U.S. citizenship. "The Constitution of the United States does not confer the right of suffrage upon anyone," Chief Justice Morrison R. Waite wrote in *Minor v. Happersett*.

A year later, the Court took a similarly narrow view of the Fifteenth Amendment in two decisions overturning criminal convictions under the Enforcement Act of 1870. In *United States v. Reese* (1876), the Court held that the act's operative section was invalid because it covered actions denying the right to vote for reasons other than race. On the same day, the Court threw out one of ninety-six indictments resulting from a massacre of sixty blacks in Colfax, Louisiana, in 1873 after a racially charged election dispute. The deaths occurred when a white mob supporting two white Democratic candidates for local offices attacked a band of African Americans who had massed around the Colfax courthouse to prevent the ouster of the Republican officeholders, including the black sheriff. In an 8-1 decision, Waite declared the indictment defective because it failed to allege that defendant William Cruikshank had acted with racial motive. "We may suspect that race was the cause of the hostility," Waite wrote in *United States v. Cruikshank* (1876), "but it is not so averred."

Reflecting the dominant political view in the country, *The New York Times* editorially praised the earlier ruling as well as both of the 1876 decisions. "The United States have neither the power nor the obligation to do police duty in the States," *The Times* wrote after the *Cruikshank* decision.

United States v. Cruikshank

Decided: March 27, 1876

Vote: 9 (Waite, Clifford, Swayne, Miller, Davis, Field, Strong, Bradley, Hunt)

0

Opinion of the Court: Waite

Concurring opinion: Clifford

EDITORIAL
MARCH 28, 1876

Two decisions of the Supreme Court of the United States bearing upon the scope and purpose of the Enforcement act, and on the proper methods of defining offenses arising under it, will be found in our columns to-day. The

The source of a good many of the blunders made in interpreting the legislation arising out of the Fourteenth and Fifteenth amendments is shown to be the tendency to confound the rights which one citizen must respect in another

> " The United States have neither the power nor the obligation to do police duty in the States—a fact which both Judges and legislators have committed serious mistakes in ignoring. "

decision in the Louisiana case points out with admirable clearness and emphasis the distinction between rights conferred by the Constitution and rights which the Constitution simply guards against infringement either by Congress on one hand or by State Governments on the other.

with the rights whose enjoyment the State must guarantee to all its citizens. The United States have neither the power nor the obligation to do police duty in the States—a fact which both Judges and legislators have committed serious mistakes in ignoring.

* * * * * * * * * * * *

THE CONTESTED 1876 ELECTION AND POST-RECONSTRUCTION VOTING BARRIERS

A year after *Cruikshank,* five of the justices played a critical role in halting the federal push for civil rights for African Americans by helping to settle the disputed 1876 presidential election between Republican Rutherford B. Hayes and Democrat Samuel J. Tilden. Hayes lost the popular vote, but the Electoral College vote turned on disputed counts in three southern states: Florida, Louisiana, and South Carolina. Congress created a fifteen-member electoral commission in January 1877 to settle the disputes. The commission was to include five members appointed by the Republican-controlled House, five selected by the Democratic-controlled Senate, and five justices—two Democratic appointees, two Republican appointees, and a fifth justice to be chosen by the full Court.

Initially, the Court chose independent David Davis for the final seat, but he withdrew after his election to the Senate from Illinois. In his place, the Court chose Joseph P. Bradley, a Republican, who eventually sided with the other Republicans in 8-7 votes that gave all three states to Hayes. Meanwhile, Hayes had promised his southern supporters that, if elected, he would withdraw federal troops from the South. By fulfilling his promise, he ended Reconstruction, giving southern states an open path to denying African Americans political and other legal rights.

OBITUARY
JANUARY 23, 1892
JUSTICE BRADLEY DEAD

The End of a Notable Career on the Bench

... When the Electoral Commission of 1877 was appointed, Justice Bradley was chosen fifth Judge by the two Democratic and two Republican Judges on the commission. In the matter of the Louisiana and Florida elections he cast the turning vote which made Rutherford B. Hayes President by his decision that "evidence aliunde [Latin: "evidence from another source"] the Governor's certificate could not be taken by the Electoral Commission," because in that commission were vested only such powers as reside in the two houses of Congress, and that it was law that the act of a sovereign State expressed through the regularly constituted authorities thereof having jurisdiction in the matter could not be inquired into by Congress. He wrote and rewrote several opinions on the subject, but his last word was to throw out the "evidence aliunde the Governor's certificate." From this legal phrase he was nicknamed "Aliunde Joe" by newspapers which disagreed with his judgment, and because the name sounded wise and its meaning was not clear to the vulgar it clung to him for some time. . . .

BALLOT BARRIERS

The Court in 1884 breathed some life into the Fifteenth Amendment by upholding the Enforcement Act conviction of a Ku Klux Klansman, Jasper Yarbrough, for attacking a black man, Berry Saunders, for attempting to vote in a congressional election in Georgia. The government "must have the power to protect the elections on which its existence depends, from violence and corruption," Justice Samuel F. Miller wrote in *Ex parte Yarbrough* (1884). Two decades later, however, the Court reversed itself by ruling in a Kentucky case that the Enforcement Act was unconstitutional because it went beyond the Fifteenth Amendment to punish private interference with voting rights (*James v. Bowman,* 1903).

In the meantime, the Court had given states permission to use one of the principal methods devised to deny African Americans the right to vote: literacy tests. The ruling in *Williams v. Mississippi* (1898) upheld the murder conviction of a black man who claimed that African Americans were excluded from voting by the use of literacy tests and, on that basis, excluded from the grand jury that indicted him. In a unanimous opinion, Justice Joseph McKenna explained that the literacy test laws "do not on their face discriminate between the races, and it has not been shown that their actual administration was evil."

In 1915, however, the Court ruled that Oklahoma's use of a so-called grandfather clause to exempt white voters from the state's literacy test did violate the Fifteenth Amendment. Oklahoma's literacy test required prospective voters to be able to read and write sections of the Constitution, but it exempted anyone who was a registered voter on January 1, 1866, and any "lineal descendant of such person." In an 8-0 decision, the Court in *Guinn v. United States* (1915) said that the law operated "in direct and positive disregard of the 15th Amendment" by preserving the right of suffrage as it had existed before ratification of the amendment.

THE RIGHT TO VOTE

Although the Court began to show a heightened concern about voting rights for African Americans, as evident in a protracted legal fight over all-white Democratic primaries in the one-party South, the effective enfranchisement of black voters occurred only after Congress took action—most notably, by passing the historic Voting Rights Act of 1965. The act—upheld a year later by the Supreme Court—put the power of the federal government behind voting registration of blacks in the Deep South. It also subjected states and localities with a history of voting discrimination to ongoing federal supervision of any election law changes that could disadvantage African Americans or other minorities. In the late twentieth century, the Court also ruled on the voting rights of eighteen-year-olds, felons, and residents of the District of Columbia.

African American Voting Rights

In the one-party politics that prevailed in the South for the first half of the twentieth century, victory in the Democratic primary was tantamount to winning the general election. Many of the region's states systematically excluded African Americans from voting. Texas passed a law in 1923 specifically forbidding blacks from voting in the Democratic primary. Lawrence A. Nixon, a black physician in El Paso and a member of the local chapter of the National Association for the Advancement of Colored People (NAACP), challenged the law after being barred from voting in the party's May 1924 primary.

In a unanimous decision, the Court agreed with Nixon's claim that the law violated the Fourteenth and Fifteenth Amendments. "A more direct and obvious infringement" of the equal protection guarantee would be hard to imagine, Justice Oliver Wendell Holmes Jr. wrote in *Nixon v. Herndon* (1927). The Texas legislature responded by authorizing state party committees to set their own qualifications for primary voting. Nixon successfully challenged that law as well. By a 5-4 vote, the Court held in *Nixon v. Condon* (1932) that the party's rules, adopted under authority of the state, constituted state action.

Smith v. Allwright

Decided: April 3, 1944

Vote: 8 (Stone, Black, Reed, Frankfurter, Douglas, Murphy, R. Jackson, W. Rutledge)

1 (O. Roberts)

Opinion of the Court: Reed

Concurring without opinion:

Frankfurter

Dissenting opinion: O. Roberts

The Texas Democratic Party responded to that ruling by adopting, on its own, a whites-only voting rule. This time, the Court in *Grovey v. Townsend* (1935) unanimously upheld the rule, viewing the party as a private association. A decade later, however, the Court overruled that decision and ended the two-decade-long fight. The right to vote, Justice Stanley F. Reed wrote in *Smith v. Allwright* (1944), "is not to be nullified by a State in a form which permits a private organization to practice racial discrimination in the election."

APRIL 9, 1944
THE DEEP SOUTH

Court Decision in Texas Case Stirs Up States' Rights
By JAMES E. CROWN

NEW ORLEANS, April 8—From Georgia to Texas, in virtually every Southern State, demands are growing for wider application of the States' rights doctrine. This is because of the decision of the United States Supreme Court which holds that Negroes cannot be barred from Texas primary elections.

The Registrar of Voters is the judge of whether or not a citizen has properly interpreted any section of the Constitution which he suggests. In this way, only about 3,000 Negroes out of a population of several hundred thousand have qualified to vote in Louisiana.

In Mississippi only a handful of Negroes vote, because of education tests. These two States and others in the South insist that they have the right to pass on the qualifications of voters. In all parts of the South an increasing number of educationally qualified Negroes is voting each year.

The effect of the Supreme Court ruling in the Texas case on the next national election is a matter of considerable speculation. It is argued by many that seven of the Supreme Court justices named by Mr. Roosevelt voted to upset the primary election laws of Texas. Some declare that this will have the effect of causing opposition to the President if he seeks a fourth term. . . .

APRIL 9, 1944
THE UPPER SOUTH

Seaboard Area Takes Calmly Question of Negro Voter
By VIRGINIUS DABNEY

RICHMOND, Va., April 8—The upper South is much less disturbed than the deep South by the United States Supreme Court's ruling that Negroes must be admitted to Democratic primaries. Virginia, North Carolina, Kentucky and Tennessee have admitted them for years, and have had no interracial disturbances or other complications.

North Carolina, which has neither the white primary nor the poll tax but has a population 27 per cent colored, is an example of how relatively liberal handling of the Negro voter operates in practice. The registration law there requires any registrant "to read or write" any section of the Constitution, and while it undoubtedly is used to exclude some qualified Negroes, the system is much fairer than that in some Southern States.

A Georgia editor has been quoted as saying that the Supreme Court's decision will be largely meaningless, "so long as the registration boards can ask a prospective voter to recite the Declaration of Independence, and then can throw him out for omitting the commas."

It is certain that many Negroes will be deprived of the franchise in some States despite the court's decision, by means of educational or property qualifications, or the poll tax, none of which has been pronounced unconstitutional. South Carolina politicians hope that they by-passed the whole problem by means of an act of the 1943 Legislature which instructed the solidly Democratic lawmaking body to eliminate all party rules from the State code." . . .

POLL TAXES

The Court in 1937 rejected an equal protection challenge to another practice that helped keep African Americans and others from voting: the poll tax. A white voter, Nolen Breedlove, challenged Georgia's $1 poll tax as a violation of the Fourteenth Amendment's Equal Protection and Privileges and Immunities Clauses. The Court's unanimous decision in *Breedlove v. Suttles* (1937) called poll taxes "a familiar form of taxation" and found no infringement of any federally protected right.

Harper v. Virginia State Board of Elections

Decided: March 24, 1966

Vote: 6 (Warren, Douglas, Clark, Brennan, B. White, Fortas)

3 (Black, Harlan II, Stewart)

Opinion of the Court: Douglas

Dissenting opinions (2): Black; Harlan II (Stewart)

Civil rights groups turned to Congress, where they finally succeeded in 1962 in winning approval of a proposed constitutional amendment to abolish poll taxes in federal, but not state, elections. By then, only five states imposed the levy: Alabama, Arkansas, Mississippi, Texas, and Virginia. The states completed ratification of the Twenty-fourth Amendment in 1964. Two years later, the Court outlawed poll taxes altogether. "Wealth or fee paying has, in our view, no relation to voting qualifications," Justice William O. Douglas wrote in the 6-3 decision *Harper v. Virginia State Board of Elections* (1966).

THE CIVIL RIGHTS ACT OF 1964

The Civil Rights Act of 1964 included provisions aimed at boosting African American participation in elections—for example, by requiring states to adopt standard procedures for voter registration. With progress still slow, Rev. Martin Luther King Jr. led a march from Montgomery, Alabama, to Selma on March 8, 1965, to dramatize the need for more blacks to register. The violent reaction of white police and white bystanders triggered a nationwide reaction that President Lyndon B. Johnson used to win congressional approval within five months of the most sweeping voting rights law in U.S. history.

THE VOTING RIGHTS ACT OF 1965

The Voting Rights Act of 1965 suspended literacy tests, established criminal penalties for interfering with voting rights of others, and placed federal voting registration machinery in seven Deep South states. State or local jurisdictions with a history of discrimination were subject to "preclearance" requirements—approval by the Justice Department or a three-judge federal court in the District of Columbia—for any election law changes that could affect minority voting.

South Carolina v. Katzenbach

Decided: March 7, 1966

Vote: 8 (Warren, Douglas, Clark, Harlan II, Brennan, Stewart, B. White, Goldberg)

1 (Black)

Opinion of the Court: Warren

Opinion concurring in part and dissenting in part: Black

The affected states challenged this assertion of federal authority. In a nearly unanimous decision, however, the Court emphatically upheld the law. "Congress has full remedial power to effectuate the constitutional prohibition against racial discrimination in voting," Chief Justice Earl Warren wrote in *South Carolina v. Katzenbach* (1966). In a partial dissent, Justice Hugo L. Black objected only to the preclearance requirement, saying it "distorts our constitutional structure."

The Court's decision cleared the way for full implementation of the law and produced optimistic predictions among civil rights supporters and many observers that politics in the South and elsewhere would be lastingly changed for the better. *The Times'* political reporter John Herbers, for example, went so far as to predict—perhaps overoptimistically—the end of racist politics in the region. The law did quickly boost voting registration among African Americans. Within four years, almost 1 million black voters had been registered under the act's provisions, helping set the stage over time for the election of an increasing number of African Americans to local and state offices in the South.

NEWS ANALYSIS
MARCH 13, 1966
VOTE: NOW FOR A NEW ERA IN SOUTH

By JOHN HERBERS

Special to The New York Times

WASHINGTON, March 12—One year ago when the Rev. Dr. Martin Luther King Jr. was leading demonstrations in Alabama for Federal voting legislation he noted that in many ways Southern Negroes had a better life than those who had migrated to the ghettos of the North. Many owned small farms, he said, and most participated in a stable community life that gave them a measure of emotional security. What was lacking, Dr. King said, was political power that would give Negroes a voice in the state capitals, the county court houses and the city halls.

This week, the Supreme Court removed the last obstacle to free participation by Negroes at the polls by upholding the main sections of the Voting Rights Act of 1965. The way is now clear for a long-awaited transformation of politics in the Deep South.

Under the automatic triggering device in the act, tests have been suspended in Louisiana, Mississippi, Alabama, Georgia, South Carolina, Virginia and 26 counties of North Carolina. Since the act was signed last Aug. 6, Attorney General Nicholas DeB. Katzenbach has assigned examiners to 37 counties and promised to send others wherever local officials in the seven-state area use literacy tests or other devices to prevent free and easy access to the registration books.

In the last seven months, Federal examiners have enrolled more than 100,00[0] Negro citizens. Local officials acting in voluntary compliance with the act have registered at least another 200,000 in the five Deep South states principally affected. This brings to about 950,000 the number of Negro names on the registration books, still only about 40 per cent of those eligible.

> **The South is not likely ever again to produce the kind of racist politics that marred the region much of this century. With rare exceptions the registration of Negroes in large numbers has eliminated race as an important issue in political campaigns.**

"After enduring nearly a century of widespread resistance to the 15th Amendment" to the Constitution, Chief Justice Earl Warren wrote in the controlling opinion, "Congress has marshaled an array of potent weapons against the evil. . . . We may finally look forward to the day when truly 'the right of citizens of the United States to vote shall not be denied or abridged by the United States or by any state on account of race, color or previous condition of servitude.' "

REASON FOR DISSENT

The lone dissent was on a minor section of the act. Justice Hugo L. Black said he did not think Congress had authority to tell states they must have the approval of the Attorney General or the Federal courts before enacting new laws governing voting qualifications.

But with legal resistance virtually at an end, with the coming of warm weather and political campaigns and with the renewal of registration drives the number registered may increase sharply in the next few months. Mr. Katzenbach told civil rights leaders in Atlanta the other day he hopes and expects that more than half of the voting-age Negro population in the five states will participate in this year's elections in each of the states.

REGISTRATION TRIPLED

Already the act has worked magic in some areas. Negro registrations have more than tripled in Mississippi. Birmingham, a center of resistance to Negro advances, may soon have more registered Negroes than Atlanta, where Negroes have long participated in political life.

No one, however, expects a transformation overnight. Civil rights groups face a tremendous task in politically activating an enormous reservoir of Negro citizens who have never voted and have never tried. Negro leaders have said demonstrations of the kind seen in Birmingham recently may be necessary in some areas to get the people out and to convince the Justice Department that more examiners are needed.

But the South is not likely ever again to produce the kind of racist politics that marred the region much of this century. With rare exceptions the registration of Negroes in large numbers has eliminated race as an important issue in political campaigns.

There is one possibility, however, that worries officials in Washington and in the South. It is that politics could become so polarized in some areas that a white party and a black party developed with each discouraging membership or support from the other race. It is too early to tell if this will happen.

A NEW MOOD

It has not happened in states like Tennessee and in pockets of the Deep South where Negroes have voted freely for some time. There they have sought to defeat the racists and elect both moderate whites and Negroes to office.

There is, however, a new mood of Negro militancy in the South and in many areas whites are still trying to keep both parties free of Negro participation. In the Alabama Black Belt, where Negroes generally outnumber whites, a number of Negro candidates have entered the spring primaries for local office.

The immediate responsibility for integration of politics, officials say, rests with both national parties, which can go a long way toward stamping out racism in their Southern branches and with Negro and white leaders in the areas involved.

• • • • • • • • • • • •

Through the 1970s, the Court backed expansive readings of the law. In 1980, however, the Court rejected a Voting Rights Act challenge to the use of at-large elections in Mobile, Alabama, to choose the three members of the city's governing body. The system effectively prevented African Americans—about one-third of the city's population—from winning a seat on the commission. In *City of Mobile v. Bolden* (1980), the Court held, 6-3, that the law forbade only deliberate and intentional discrimination and did not guarantee minorities the right to representation.

Congress responded by amending the law in 1982 to overturn the decision and to prohibit voting practices—intentionally discriminatory or not—that denied blacks or other minorities a chance "to elect representatives of their choice." Four years later, the Court applied the law in striking down the use of multimember legislative districts in North Carolina. The complex ruling in *Thornburg v. Gingles* (1986) established that in jurisdictions with racially polarized voting, large blocs of minority voters could not be divided among mostly white districts because the practice "diluted" minority voting strength.

As the 1990 census approached, the Justice Department adopted the position that states drawing new legislative or congressional districts could avoid vote dilution by concentrating African Americans or Hispanics in "majority-minority" districts. When white voters challenged the race-conscious redistricting, however, the Supreme Court narrowly ruled, in a series of decisions beginning in 1993, that the practice raised equal protection issues. (See page 239.) The rulings limited racial redistricting somewhat, but vote dilution remained illegal.

In 2006 the Court ruled that Texas had violated the Voting Rights Act by adding white voters from San Antonio to a predominantly Latino district that extended to the Mexico border. The ruling in *League of United Latin American Citizens v. Perry* upheld the rest of the district map, but Justice Anthony M. Kennedy said the change in the South Texas district "took away the Latinos' opportunity" to elect a candidate of their choice.

ENFRANCHISEMENT AND THE STATES

The Court played an incidental role in extending the right to vote to eighteen-year-olds in all elections, federal or state. A strong movement to lower the voting age arose in the 1960s when eighteen-year-olds were among those being sent to fight in Vietnam. Congress responded by including in the Voting Rights Act Amendments of 1970 a provision lowering the voting age to eighteen in all elections. The act also barred literacy tests in all elections for a five-year period and established a uniform, thirty-day residency requirement to vote in presidential elections.

Eighteen states joined in challenging the law as an unconstitutional intrusion on state control over elections. By different 5-4 majorities, the Court voted in *Oregon v. Mitchell* (1970) to uphold the lower voting age for federal elections but to strike down Congress's attempt to lower the voting age for state elections as well.

The decision—which upheld the literacy test ban and thirty-day residency requirement—created administrative difficulties for the forty-seven states that did not allow eighteen-year-olds to vote. Congress responded by proposing a constitutional amendment to lower the voting age for all elections; the states ratified the Twenty-sixth Amendment on July 1, 1971, only three months and seven days after it was submitted.

The Court has invalidated some other state restrictions on voting. In *Dunn v. Blumstein* (1972), the justices voted 8-1 to strike down Tennessee's one-year residency requirement. Justice Thurgood Marshall said the law burdened two fundamental rights—the right to vote and the right to travel—and the state had failed to show the compelling interest needed to uphold it. A thirty-day requirement "appears to be ample" to prevent voter fraud, Marshall said. Three years later, however, the Court upheld an Arizona law cutting off registration fifty days before party primaries.

The Court has also struck down on equal protection grounds property ownership qualifications imposed in some states or municipalities to vote on bond measures. In one ruling, the Court in *Phoenix v. Kolodziejski* (1970) found "no adequate reason to restrict the franchise on the issuance of general obligation bonds to property owners." A year earlier, the Court had also struck down a New York law limiting the right to vote in school district elections to persons who had children or who owned or leased property in the district (*Kramer v. Union Free School District*). Both decisions were by 6-3 votes.

States have been upheld, however, in denying the franchise to convicted felons. The 6-3 ruling in *Richardson v. Ramirez* (1974) noted that the Fourteenth Amendment includes a provision permitting disenfranchisement for "participation in rebellion, or other crime." Arguments that the restrictions are "outmoded" should be addressed to "the legislative forum," Justice William H. Rehnquist wrote. The Court in 2005 declined to hear a case seeking to reconsider the decision.

In October 2000, the Court rejected a legal effort by residents of Washington, D.C., to win voting representation for the District of Columbia in Congress. The Twenty-third Amendment gives Washingtonians the right to vote in presidential elections, but the District is allowed only a non-voting delegate in the House of Representatives. The Court summarily affirmed a lower court decision that no constitutional provision guarantees District residents the right to vote for members of the national legislature.

THE RIGHT TO AN EQUAL VOTE

The Constitution leaves the structure and composition of state legislatures up to each individual state. All the states followed the federal model in creating "bicameral" legislatures—with one chamber usually called the House of Representatives and a second called the Senate. (Nebraska changed to a one-chamber or "unicameral" legislature in 1937 as a cost-saving measure.) The Constitution also does not prescribe how states are to elect members of the U.S. House of Representatives. Congress did pass a law in 1842, however, requiring election from single-member districts instead of at-large. Later laws required that districts be approximately equal in population (1872) and compact and contiguous (1901, 1911).

DRAWING THE DISTRICTS: REAPPORTIONMENT

Drawing district lines emerged as a source of controversy early in U.S. history. In 1812 Massachusetts governor Elbridge Gerry proposed a map of legislative districts designed to help his Anti-Federalist allies. When a critic said that one irregularly shaped legislative district resembled a salamander, another called it instead a "gerrymander." The epithet stuck, and the practice has likewise endured.

Congress has reapportioned members in the House of Representatives on the basis of the federal census at the start of every decade but one; lawmakers stalemated in 1920 over a dispute about which of several mathematical formulas to use. The comparable requirements in state constitutions, however, proved to be less automatic. As of 1958, twenty-three of the then forty-eight states had not reapportioned for periods ranging from ten years to half a century or longer.

Initially, the Supreme Court was reluctant to get involved in reapportionment and redistricting disputes. The Court in 1932 unanimously rejected a challenge to Mississippi's congressional districting. Five justices said the requirements for equal, compact, and contiguous districts had lapsed when Congress omitted them from the 1929 apportionment law; four justices went further and said federal courts had no jurisdiction over such a challenge.

The Court in 1946 threw out a suit brought in the name of a Northwestern University political scientist, Kenneth Colegrove, aimed at forcing Illinois' rural-dominated legislature to redraw congressional districts. Colegrove and the other Chicago-area plaintiffs contended that numerical disparities between districts violated voters' rights under the Equal Protection Clause.

By a 4-3 vote, however, the Court declined to rule on the claim. "Courts ought not enter this political thicket," Justice Frankfurter wrote for three justices in *Colegrove v. Green* (1946). "The remedy for unfairness in districting is to secure State legislatures that will apportion properly, or to invoke the ample powers of Congress." Without joining Frankfurter's opinion, Justice Wiley B. Rutledge Jr. agreed that the suit should be dismissed because of the "delicate" character of the dispute.

THE REAPPORTIONMENT REVOLUTION

Baker v. Carr

Decided: March 26, 1962

Vote: 6 (Warren, Black, Douglas, Clark, Brennan, Stewart)
2 (Frankfurter, Harlan II)

Opinion of the Court: Brennan

Concurring opinions (3): Douglas; Clark; Stewart

Dissenting opinions (2): Frankfurter (Harlan II); Harlan II (Frankfurter)

Did not participate: Whittaker

In *Baker v. Carr,* the Court in 1962 effectively overruled that decision. "An unbroken line of our precedents sustains the federal courts' jurisdiction of the subject matter of federal constitutional claims of this nature," Justice William J. Brennan Jr. wrote. The plaintiffs had legal standing, he explained, in order to protect their "right to a vote free of arbitrary impairment by state action." As for the political nature of the case, Brennan deemed it irrelevant. "The mere fact that the suit seeks protection of a political right does not mean it presents a political question," he wrote.

The 6-2 ruling—with Frankfurter and John Marshall Harlan dissenting—sent the case back to Tennessee with no further guidance. A year later, the Court began to fill in the blanks with an 8-1 decision striking down Georgia's "county unit" voting system for electing governors, senators, and other statewide officers. The system heavily favored rural areas by giving each county a number of "units," which were then awarded to the candidate who carried the county.

Writing for the majority in *Gray v. Sanders* (1963), Justice Douglas said the Constitution did not permit the differential weighting of votes from one county to another. "The conception of political equality from the Declaration of Independence, to Lincoln's Gettysburg Address, to the Fifteenth, Seventeenth, and Nineteenth Amendments can mean only one thing—one person, one vote," Douglas wrote. When Frankfurter retired in August 1962, Harlan was left as the lone dissenter.

The Court finished laying the groundwork for the reapportionment revolution with two decisions in 1964 requiring equal-population districting for the House of Representatives and for both chambers of bicameral state legislatures. Under the Constitution, Justice Black wrote in *Wesberry v. Sanders* (1964), "one man's vote in a congressional election is to be worth as much as another's." The same principle, Chief Justice Warren explained in *Reynolds v. Sims* (1964), applied to state legislative districting. "Legislators represent people, not trees or acres," Warren said in rejecting any analogy to the constitutional provision giving each state two seats in the U.S. Senate. Three justices—Tom C. Clark, Harlan, and Potter Stewart—dissented on congressional districting; Harlan dissented alone in the state districting case.

Reynolds v. Sims

> **Decided:** June 15, 1964
> **Vote:**   8 (Warren, Black, Douglas,
>   Clark, Brennan, Stewart,
>   B. White, Goldberg)
>   1 (Harlan II)
> **Opinion of the Court:** Warren
> **Concurring opinions (2):** Clark; Stewart
> **Dissenting opinion:** Harlan II

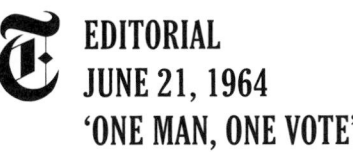

EDITORIAL
JUNE 21, 1964
'ONE MAN, ONE VOTE'

In the past decade, roughly corresponding to the period Earl Warren has been Chief Justice, the Supreme Court has handed down decisions affecting ever-broader areas of American life. One result has been a constriction of the power of the states over matters once considered wholly within their jurisdiction.

Last week, in an historic decision, the Supreme Court struck at one of the most fundamental areas of state power—apportionment of their legislatures. In a 6-to-3 ruling, the Court held that apportionment must be on a "one person, one vote" basis, with each legislative unit "substantially equal" in population.

in a number of states from one party to the other and making them more responsive to majority will of the electorate.

(3) The political complexion of a number of Congressional districts, which must be redrawn in accordance with an earlier Supreme Court decision, may also be affected since it is the revised state legislatures in many cases that will be doing the redrawing.

(4) New fuel will be added to the controversy over the role of the Supreme Court in relation to other branches of government.

 The weight of a citizen's vote cannot be made to depend on where he lives.

—Chief Justice Earl Warren, *Reynolds v. Sims*

Among some of the possible effects of the decision are:

(1) More than 40 of the 50 states may be required to reapportion their legislative districts.

(2) Urban and suburban areas, for the most part, will gain strength at the expense of rural districts, thus possibly shifting control of the legislatures

The legislatures affected by last week's decision are made up of two chambers in all but one of the 50 states (Nebraska's is unicameral). Their powers—taxation, public works, education, penal and civil codes, licensing of a broad range of activities, etc.—affect virtually every aspect of the citizen's life, far more, in fact, than does the Federal Government.

The representation in these legislatures is based on a variety of formulas, some—such as New York's—extremely complicated. And in most of the states, in one or both houses, population is not the controlling factor.

A typical formula, for example, calls for at least one representative from each county, regardless of how sparsely populated, while placing a maximum on the number of representatives from any one county, regardless of how densely populated. In some cases allocations are based on geographic units, such as islands or peninsulas or coastal areas; in others, economic or occupational factors, such as a concentration of dairy farmers, or fishermen or ranch or plantation owners, is controlling.

RURAL DOMINATION

In general the formulas tend to favor rural districts as against urban and suburban areas. Some weird disparities exist. In Nevada the population spread between the smallest and largest election district for the upper house, each with equal representation, is 568 to 127,016, and theoretically 8 per cent of the voters could elect a majority in the chamber. In Connecticut, the range in the lower house is 191 to 81,089, with 12 per cent able to elect a majority. In New York in the lower house it is 15,044 to 314,721, with 34 per cent needed for a majority. There is not a single state where a majority of the votes is required for the election of a majority in either house.

Such apportionment, and similar disparities in Congressional districts, has long been a controversial issue. But political or legislative remedy has been difficult since the systems, by their very nature, tend to be self-perpetuating.

Two years ago the Supreme Court for the first time ruled that legislative districts were subject to judicial scrutiny. A flock of suits resulted. Last February the Court, ruling on one such suit, held that Congressional districts must be based strictly on population. It cited Article I of the Constitution which states that "the House of Representatives shall be . . . chosen . . . by the people of the several states."

In last week's decision, the Court majority applied the same principle to apportionment for the state legislatures, although this time the basis was the 14th Amendment's provision that no state shall "deny to any person within its jurisdiction the equal protection of the laws."

WARREN'S OPINION

The Court, passing on apportionment in Alabama, New York, Colorado, Maryland, Virginia and Delaware (cases involving several other states are pending) found that all six violated the "equal protection" clause. Writing for the majority, Chief Justice Warren (joined by Justices Black, Douglas, Brennan, White and Goldberg) declared:

> "Legislators represent people, not trees or acres. Legislators are elected by voters, not farms or cities or economic interests. . . . To the extent that a citizen's right to vote is debased, he is that much less a citizen. The weight of a citizen's vote cannot be made to depend on where he lives."

Justice Warren rejected as "inapposite and irrelevant" the analogy with the Federal system in which each state has two Senate seats regardless of population. He said that system had been a necessary compromise as the price of union of a group of sovereignties under a Federal Government, but that counties or other political subdivisions within the states were not such sovereignties.

Justices Harlan, Stewart and Clark filed vigorous—and in some of the cases, separate—dissents. Justice Harlan wrote that "the equal protection clause was never intended to inhibit the states in choosing any democratic method they pleased for the apportionment of their legislatures" as long as the apportionment was "rational" rather than an arbitrary "crazy-quilt."

'NEEDS AND INTERESTS'

Justice Stewart, echoing Justice Warren's words, but reaching the opposite conclusion, wrote:

> "Legislators do not represent faceless numbers. They represent people . . . with identifiable needs and interests . . . which can often be related to the geographical districting."

There was some dispute about the over-all political effect of the decision, since it will vary from state to state. But the consensus seemed to be that the Democrats stood to benefit most because of the greater weight for urban areas. Some Republicans, however, were taking solace in the thought that suburban areas, which also will get greater representation, are Republican strongholds and may partially offset Democratic gains in the cities.

As for the controversy over the Court's role, in a series of decisions running from the 1954 school segregation ruling to the issue adjudicated last week, the current court probably has broken more new ground than any of its predecessors. Critics claim that the result has been a profound alteration in the powers of the various branches of Government, with the Court in ever growing ascendancy and taking upon itself the task of "amending" the Constitution. The Court's defenders argue that it has properly been correcting ills for which no other remedy exists.

• • • • • • • • • • • •

Despite criticism and opposition, states quickly began complying with the rulings. In later cases, the Court applied the one person, one vote principle to require very close mathematical equality among congressional districts but to permit somewhat greater variations in state legislative districting. In 1983 the Court even upheld, on a 5-4 vote, a Wyoming legislative districting plan that guaranteed each county at least one seat in the state's lower house.

PARTISAN GERRYMANDERING

The Court next confronted the issue of partisan gerrymandering, but its tentative rulings left the practice essentially unchanged. In a suit filed by Indiana Democrats against a Republican-written state legislative reapportionment, the Court held, 6-3, that challenges to partisan gerrymandering were "justiciable" in federal courts. But a different 7-2 majority went on in *Davis v. Bandemer* (1986) to uphold the challenged plan.

Over the next two decades, federal courts proved unreceptive to similar challenges. The Supreme Court eventually took up the issue again in a case brought by Pennsylvania Democrats challenging a Republican-written congressional districting scheme. Four justices in *Vieth v. Jubelirer* (2004) wanted to bar partisan gerrymandering cases altogether. Justice Kennedy, who cast the pivotal vote to uphold the plan, said he saw no "workable standards" for judging such claims but declined to completely rule out gerrymandering cases in the future.

Two years later, Kennedy again wrote the controlling opinion in a Texas case, *League of United Latin American Citizens v. Perry* (2006), rejecting a broad challenge to a congressional redistricting scheme that helped Republicans pick up six House seats. Kennedy acknowledged the GOP lawmakers' strictly partisan motivation, but found "no legally impermissible use of political classifications."

RACIAL REDISTRICTING

The Court in the 1990s showed less reluctance in dealing with another controversial issue: racial redistricting. After the 1990 census, several states created a number of "majority-minority" districts aimed at helping elect African Americans or Hispanics to Congress or state legislatures. White voters challenged some of the resulting districts as a violation of their rights under the Equal Protection Clause.

The first case to reach the Court involved an irregularly shaped North Carolina district that snaked almost across the state to include predominantly black neighborhoods in three major cities. By a 5-4 vote, the Court held in *Shaw v. Reno* (1993) that white voters could challenge a district that is "highly irregular" in shape and drawn to "segregate voters by race." For the majority, Justice Sandra Day O'Connor said the practice "bears an uncomfortable resemblance to political apartheid."

Shaw v. Reno

Decided: June 28, 1993

Vote: 5 (Rehnquist, O'Connor, Scalia, Kennedy, Thomas)
4 (B. White, Blackmun, Stevens, Souter)

Opinion of the Court: O'Connor

Dissenting opinions (4): B. White (Blackmun, Stevens); Blackmun; Stevens; Souter

JUNE 29, 1993
COURT QUESTIONS DISTRICTS DRAWN TO AID MINORITIES

JUSTICES SPLIT 5-4

Odd Shapes Are Likened to Past Schemes That Excluded Blacks

By LINDA GREENHOUSE

Special to The New York Times

WASHINGTON, June 28—A sharply divided Supreme Court ruled today that designing legislative districts to increase black representation can violate the constitutional rights of white voters.

The decision casts doubt on the redistricting that brought North Carolina its first black members of Congress since Reconstruction, and possibly on districts in other regions that have been given bizarre shapes to insure the election of minority representatives.

The 5-to-4 ruling gave a group of white North Carolina voters the chance to prove that the state's new 12th District is an unconstitutional racial gerrymander that violates the white voters' right to equal protection of the laws. The district connects small black population centers in a 160-mile ribbon no wider in some places than the interstate highway that it follows.

WHITE'S FINAL DAY

The majority opinion was joined by Chief Justice William H. Rehnquist and by Justices Antonin Scalia, Anthony M. Kennedy and Clarence Thomas. Justices Byron R. White, Harry A. Blackmun, John Paul Stevens and David H. Souter all wrote dissenting opinions.

On his final day after more than 31 years on the Court, Justice White, who began his public career handling civil rights issues as a Justice Department official in the Kennedy Administration, said it was "both a fiction and a departure from settled equal protection principles" to regard the white voters as having a case.

Justice White noted that even with the creation of two black-majority districts in North Carolina, whites were still a majority in 10 of 12 districts, or 83 percent of the

> " It is unsettling how closely the North Carolina plan resembles the most egregious racial gerrymanders of the past.
> —Justice Sandra Day O'Connor, *Shaw v. Reno*

O'CONNOR FOR THE MAJORITY

The decision overturned a ruling last year by a special three-judge Federal District Court in North Carolina, which dismissed the challenge on the ground that Supreme Court precedents made it clear that white voters generally have no cause for complaint about districts drawn for the purpose of electing blacks.

In her majority opinion, Justice Sandra Day O'Connor drew a different lesson from the Court's precedents. Noting that the Court had struck down districting plans that excluded blacks, she said, "It is unsettling how closely the North Carolina plan resembles the most egregious racial gerrymanders of the past." . . .

A reapportionment plan linking people who live far apart and who "may have little in common with one another but the color of their skin," Justice O'Connor said, "bears an uncomfortable resemblance to political apartheid."

districts, while constituting 76 percent of the state's people. "Surely they cannot complain of discriminatory treatment," he said.

In ordering the District Court to give the white plaintiffs their day in court, the Justices left unanswered many questions about the breadth of their ruling today.

Justice O'Connor said there may be "wholly legitimate purposes" for concentrating members of a racial group in one or more districts while excluding them from others. She said "traditional districting principles" like keeping districts compact, contiguous and within existing political subdivisions could provide such a "race-neutral" rationale.

'COMPELLING INTEREST' NEEDED

But the opinion cast doubt on the extent to which explicitly racial considerations of the sort frequently invoked in reapportionment cases, like the desire to remedy discrimination or avoid dilution of black voting strength, can justify districts that do not fit the traditional descriptions.

Justice O'Connor said the North Carolina district would have to be judged by the legal standard of "strict scrutiny" that the Court applies to discrimination on the basis of race. Under this standard, which can almost never be satisfied in practice, the state must show that a "compelling interest" made it necessary to treat people differently on the basis of race.

In one of the most potentially significant parts of the opinion, Justice O'Connor said that the fact that the North Carolina Legislature drew the disputed district to comply with the Federal Voting Rights Act was not, by itself, a "compelling state interest."

A FAMILIAR DIVIDE

The state came up with the 12th District after the Justice Department had rejected an initial plan that provided for only one majority-black district, saying the state's black population was big enough to support two districts. The Justice Department's refusal to approve the plan under Section 5 of the Voting Rights Act left the state with the option of going to court or complying; the Legislature's response was to draw the 12th District.

Justice O'Connor said today that while "the states certainly have a very strong interest in complying with Federal antidiscrimination laws that are constitutionally valid as interpreted and as applied," compliance with the Voting Rights Act does not provide immunity from constitutional challenge or give states "carte blanche to engage in racial gerrymandering."

The white plaintiffs in this case had argued that if the North Carolina plan was in fact required under the Voting Rights Act, then the law itself was unconstitutional. Justice O'Connor said that the District Court would be free to consider this argument when it reconsiders the case.

She also said that a district looking like North Carolina's 12th District could not be defended automatically as a remedy for past discrimination against black voters,

a defense that the state put forward in this case. "Racial gerrymandering, even for remedial purposes, may balkanize us into competing racial factions," she said.

The philosophical and constitutional divide on the Court in today's decision, Shaw v. Reno, No. 92-357, was familiar from the Court's bitter debates over affirmative action and similar race-conscious policies: whether distinctions made on the basis of race can ever be benign.

The dissenters stressed that white voters as a whole in North Carolina had suffered no injury from a relatively modest, though historic, step in equalizing power in the state. "The duty to govern impartially is abused when a group with power over the electoral process defines electoral boundaries solely to enhance its own political strength at the expense of any weaker group," Justice Stevens said, adding:

"That duty, however, is not violated when the majority acts to facilitate the election of a member of a group that lacks such power because it remains underrepresented in the state legislature—whether that group is defined by political affiliation, by common economic interests, or by religious, ethnic, or racial characteristics."

RISKS ARE SEEN

In the majority's view, however, "racial classifications of any sort pose the risk of lasting harm to our society," as Justice O'Connor said today. She said, "The very reason that the equal-protection clause demands strict scrutiny of all racial classifications is because without it, a court cannot determine whether or not the discrimination truly is benign."

Justice O'Connor said that one injury that districts of this type inflict is to perpetuate racial stereotypes and exacerbate patterns of racial-bloc voting. In addition, she said, representatives elected from such districts receive the "pernicious" message that their job is to represent only their racial group.

"This is altogether antithetical to our system of representative democracy," she said.

Ruling in a Georgia case two years later, the Court said redistricting plans were subject to challenge if race was "the predominant factor" in placing "a significant number of voters within or without a particular district." The 5-4 decision in *Miller v. Johnson* (1995) threw out a Georgia congressional map. In that case and two similar decisions in 1996, the Court rejected arguments that maximizing the number of majority-minority districts was necessary to comply with the federal Voting Rights Act. The Court softened its rulings somewhat in 2001, however, by requiring challengers seeking to throw out racially drawn lines to offer an alternative that would be consistent with "traditional districting principles" and bring about "significantly greater racial balance."

BUSH V. GORE (2000)

Unexpectedly, the Court also found an equal protection violation in its most dramatic intervention ever in an election case: the December 12, 2000, ruling in *Bush v. Gore* that cemented George W. Bush's election as president. The ruling ended a political and legal battle that began after returns on election night, November 7, gave Bush an apparent Electoral College majority only on the strength of a 1,784-vote victory in Florida. After a mandatory machine recount reduced the margin to 327 votes, Al Gore initiated a month-long battle for additional recounts in hopes of erasing Bush's lead.

The Supreme Court initially intervened on December 4 to set aside the Florida Supreme Court's ruling granting Gore's request to extend the deadline set by state law for certifying election returns. The unanimous, unsigned opinion in *Bush v. Palm Beach County Canvassing Board* (2000) said there was "considerable uncertainty" about the grounds for the state court's decision.

Four days later, the Florida Supreme Court gave Gore another victory by ordering an immediate, statewide manual recount to begin on Saturday, December 9. In Washington, however, the Supreme Court granted Bush's request for a stay to block the recount and scheduled arguments for Monday, December 11.

Bush's lawyer, Theodore B. Olson, argued before the justices that the Florida court's ruling amounted to a "wholesale revision" of the state's election law in violation of the provision in the U.S. Constitution that gave state legislatures authority to determine the method of selecting presidential electors (Art. II, sec. 1, cl. 2). He also argued that the state court had not specified standards to use in the manual recount.

Bush v. Gore

Decided: December 12, 2000

Vote: 5 (Rehnquist, O'Connor, Scalia, Kennedy, Thomas)

4 (Stevens, Souter, Ginsburg, Breyer)

Opinion: *Per curiam*

Concurring opinion: Rehnquist (Scalia, Thomas)

Dissenting opinions (4): Stevens (Ginsburg, Breyer); Souter (Stevens, Ginsburg, Breyer); Ginsburg (Stevens, Souter, Breyer); Breyer (Stevens, Souter, Ginsburg)

The Court issued its ruling to a crowd of waiting reporters late on the night of Tuesday, December 12. By a 5-4 vote, the Court held that the lack of clear standards for conducting the recount amounted to an equal protection violation. "The recount mechanisms . . . do not satisfy the minimum requirement for non-arbitrary treatment of voters necessary to secure the fundamental right," the unsigned opinion stated.

Later, O'Connor and Kennedy were reliably identified as the authors of the majority opinion. In a concurring opinion, the Court's other three conservatives—Chief Justice Rehnquist and Justices Antonin Scalia and Clarence Thomas—said they also agreed with Bush's argument that the Florida court had infringed the state legislature's power over selecting presidential electors.

Liberal justices bitterly complained about the decision. "Although we may never know with complete certainty the identity of the winner of this year's Presidential election," Justice John Paul Stevens wrote, "the identity of the loser is perfectly clear. It is the Nation's confidence in the judge as an impartial guardian of the rule of law."

In the aftermath, some critics depicted the ruling as unprincipled activism, citing in particular the Court's explicit description of the decision as "limited to the present circumstances." Supporters insisted, however, that the Court had acted properly to end a potentially paralyzing dispute over the election.

Gore conceded the election in a televised address the next evening after the ruling. "While I strongly disagree with the Court's decision," he said, "I accept it." Bush, who spoke to the nation immediately afterward, made no reference to the court fight.

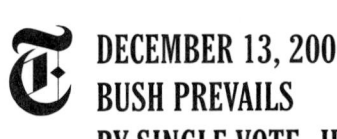

DECEMBER 13, 2000
BUSH PREVAILS
BY SINGLE VOTE, JUSTICES END RECOUNT, BLOCKING GORE AFTER 5-WEEK STRUGGLE

An Awareness of Hazards

By LINDA GREENHOUSE

WASHINGTON, Dec. 12—The Supreme Court effectively handed the presidential election to George W. Bush tonight, overturning the Florida Supreme Court and ruling by a vote of 5 to 4 that there could be no further counting of Florida's disputed presidential votes.

The ruling came after a long and tense day of waiting at 10 p.m., just two hours before the Dec. 12 "safe harbor" for immunizing a state's electors from challenge in Congress was to come to an end. The unsigned majority opinion said it was the immediacy of this deadline that made it impossible to come up with a way of counting the votes that could both meet "minimal constitutional standards" and be accomplished within the deadline.

the state the opportunity to try to count all the disputed ballots now." . . .

The six separate opinions, totaling 65 pages, were filled with evidence that the justices were acutely aware of the controversy the court had entered by accepting Governor Bush's appeal of last Friday's Florida Supreme Court ruling and by granting him a stay of the recount on Saturday afternoon, just hours after the vote counting had begun.

"None are more conscious of the vital limits on judicial authority than are the members of this court," the majority opinion said, referring to "our unsought responsibility to resolve the federal and constitutional issues the judicial system has been forced to confront."

> When a court orders a statewide remedy, there must be at least some assurance that the rudimentary requirements of equal treatment and fundamental fairness are satisfied.
>
> —*Per curiam* opinion in *Bush v. Gore*

The five members of the majority were Chief Justice William H. Rehnquist and Justices Sandra Day O'Connor, Antonin Scalia, Anthony M. Kennedy and Clarence Thomas.

Among the four dissenters, two justices, Stephen G. Breyer and David H. Souter, agreed with the majority that the varying standards in different Florida counties for counting the punch-card ballots presented problems of both due process and equal protection. But unlike the majority, these justices said the answer should be not to shut the recount down, but to extend it until the Dec. 18 date for the meeting of the Electoral College.

Justice Souter said that such a recount would be a "tall order" but that "there is no justification for denying

The dissenters said nearly all the objections raised by Mr. Bush were insubstantial. The court should not have reviewed either this case or the one it decided last week, they said.

Justice John Paul Stevens said the court's action "can only lend credence to the most cynical appraisal of the work of judges throughout the land."

His dissenting opinion, also signed by Justices Breyer and Ruth Bader Ginsburg, added: "It is confidence in the men and women who administer the judicial system that is the true backbone of the rule of law. Time will one day heal the wound to that confidence that will be inflicted by today's decision. One thing, however, is certain. Although we may never know with complete certainty the identity of the winner of this year's Presidential election, the identity of the loser is perfectly clear. It is the nation's confidence in the judge as an impartial guardian of the rule of law."

What the court's day and a half of deliberations yielded tonight was a messy product that bore the earmarks of a failed attempt at a compromise solution that would have permitted the vote counting to continue.

It appeared that Justices Souter and Breyer, by taking seriously the equal protection concerns that Justices Kennedy and O'Connor had raised at the argument, had tried to persuade them that those concerns could be addressed in a remedy that would permit the disputed votes to be counted.

Justices O'Connor and Kennedy were the only justices whose names did not appear separately on any opinion, indicating that one or both of them wrote the court's unsigned majority opinion, labeled only "per curiam," or "by the court." Its focus was narrow, limited to the ballot counting process itself. The opinion objected not only to the varying standards used by different counties for determining voter intent, but to aspects of the Florida Supreme Court's order determining which ballots should be counted.

"We are presented with a situation where a state court with the power to assure uniformity has ordered a statewide recount with minimal procedural safeguards," the opinion said. "When a court orders a statewide remedy, there must be at least some assurance that the rudimentary requirements of equal treatment and fundamental fairness are satisfied."

Three members of the majority—the Chief Justice, and Justices Scalia and Thomas—raised further, more basic objections to the recount and said the Florida Supreme Court had violated state law in ordering it.

The fact that Justices O'Connor and Kennedy evidently did not share these deeper concerns had offered a potential basis for a coalition between them and the dissenters. That effort apparently foundered on the two justices' conviction that the midnight deadline of Dec. 12 had to be met.

The majority said that "substantial additional work" was needed to undertake a constitutional recount, including not only uniform statewide standards for determining a legal vote, but also "practical procedures to implement them" and "orderly judicial review of any disputed matters that might arise." There was no way all this could be done, the majority said.

The dissenters said the concern with Dec. 12 was misplaced. Justices Souter and Breyer offered to send the case back to the Florida courts "with instructions to establish uniform standards for evaluating the several types of ballots that have prompted differing treatments," as Justice Souter described his proposed remand order. He added: "unlike the majority, I see no warrant for this court to assume that Florida could not possibly comply with this requirement before the date set for the meeting of electors, Dec. 18."

Justices Stevens and Ginsburg said they did not share the view that the lack of a uniform vote-counting standard presented an equal protection problem.

In addition to joining Justice Souter's dissenting opinion, Justice Breyer wrote one of his own, signed by the three other dissenters, in which he recounted the history of the deadlocked presidential election of 1876 and of the partisan role that one Supreme Court justice, Joseph P. Bradley, played in awarding the presidency to Rutherford B. Hayes.

"This history may help to explain why I think it not only legally wrong, but also most unfortunate, for the Court simply to have terminated the Florida recount," Justice Breyer said. He said the time problem that Florida faced was "in significant part, a problem of the Court's own making." The recount was moving ahead in an "orderly fashion," Justice Breyer said, when "this court improvidently entered a stay." He said: "As a result, we will never know whether the recount could have been completed."

There was no need for the court to have involved itself in the election dispute this time, he said, adding: "Above all, in this highly politicized matter, the appearance of a split decision runs the risk of undermining the public's confidence in the court itself. That confidence is a public treasure. It has been built slowly over many years, some of which were marked by a Civil War and the tragedy of segregation. It is a vitally necessary ingredient of any successful effort to protect basic liberty and, indeed, the rule of law itself."

"We do risk a self-inflicted wound," Justice Breyer said, "a wound that may harm not just the court, but the nation."

Justice Ginsburg also wrote a dissenting opinion, joined by the other dissenters. Her focus was on the implications for federalism of the majority's action. "I might join the chief justice were it my commission to interpret Florida law," she said, adding: "The extraordinary setting of this case has obscured the ordinary principle that dictates its proper resolution: federal courts defer to state high courts' interpretations of their state's own law. This principle reflects the core of federalism, on which all agree."

"Were the other members of this court as mindful as they generally are of our system of dual sovereignty," Justice Ginsburg concluded, "they would affirm the judgment of the Florida Supreme Court."

Unlike the other dissenters, who said they dissented "respectfully," Justice Ginsburg said only: "I dissent."

Nothing about this case, Bush v. Gore, No. 00-949, was ordinary: not its context, not its acceptance over the weekend, not the enormously accelerated schedule with argument on Monday, and not the way the decision was released to the public tonight.

When the court issues an opinion, the justices ordinarily take the bench and the justice who has written for the majority gives a brief oral description of the case and the holding.

Today, after darkness fell and their work was done, the justices left the Supreme Court building individually from the underground garage, with no word to dozens of journalists from around the world who were waiting in the crowded pressroom for word as to when, or whether, a decision might come. By the time the pressroom staff passed out copies of the decision, the justices were gone.

• • • • • • • • • • •

THE RIGHT TO SPEND

Money—aptly called the "mother's milk of politics"—has been important in political campaigns in the United States since the 1830s, when Jacksonian democracy ushered in the era of mass politics. Congress began regulating contributions and spending in congressional and presidential campaigns early in the twentieth century, but the laws proved ineffective in limiting spending after the advent of television advertising in the 1950s. When Congress sought to tighten campaign finance regulation after the Watergate scandals in the 1970s, however, the Supreme Court opened a big gap by invalidating on First Amendment grounds any mandatory spending limits for candidates or for individuals or groups operating independently of a candidate's campaign.

Federal Regulation of Campaign Finance

Congress began regulating campaign finance in the Progressive era by passing the Tillman Act of 1907 to prohibit corporate contributions to federal campaigns; the Taft-Hartley Act of 1947, officially the Labor-Management Relations Act, imposed a similar ban on labor union donations. The Publicity Act of 1910 required spending disclosures in congressional races, but only after the election. Spending limits—$5,000 for House races and $10,000 for Senate contests—were enacted in 1911. The Supreme Court weakened the laws by ruling in *Newberry v. United States* (1921) that primary elections were beyond Congress's authority—a decision that stood until the Court overruled it in *United States v. Classic* (1941). In the meantime, Congress in 1925 replaced the Publicity Act with a stronger Federal Corrupt Practices Act, which required quarterly spending reports and disclosure of contributions. It also raised spending limits for Senate races and brought presidential campaigns under regulation by requiring spending and contribution reports from any committee seeking to influence the selection of presidential electors in two or more states.

The rising cost of campaigns prompted Congress to enact the Federal Election Campaign Act of 1971, which required more disclosure from contributors and set more realistic spending limits on advertising. Three years later, Congress overhauled the law in the wake of the Watergate scandals. The Federal Election Campaign Act Amendments of 1974 established overall spending limits on congressional candidates and limited individual, political action committee, and party donations to candidates. It also provided for public financing of presidential campaigns. In addition, it established the Federal Election Commission (FEC) as an independent agency to enforce the law.

The Supreme Court in 1934 had upheld campaign finance regulation in presidential races—and, by implication, in congressional campaigns. "To say that Congress is without the power to pass appropriate legislation to safeguard such an election from the improper use of money is to deny to the nation in a vital particular the power of self-protection," Justice George Sutherland wrote in *Burroughs v. United States*. But the post-Watergate law brought a broader challenge that raised for the first time a First Amendment argument against campaign spending and contribution limits.

BUCKLEY v. VALEO (1976)

The plaintiffs in *Buckley v. Valeo* (1976) included Sen. James L. Buckley of New York, who had run on the Conservative and Republican party tickets; former senator Eugene J. McCarthy of Minnesota, a Democrat; the New York Civil Liberties Union; and *Human Events,* a conservative publication. Francis R. Valeo, secretary of the Senate, was the first named defendant. The challengers argued that campaign contributions or expenditures amounted to constitutionally protected "speech" and that Congress had inadequate grounds for the limits the law imposed on each.

Buckley v. Valeo

Decided: January 30, 1976

Vote: Multiple

Opinion: *Per curiam*

Dissenting opinions (5): Burger;
  B. White; T. Marshall;
  Rehnquist; Blackmun

Did not participate: Stevens

The Court handed down its ruling on January 30, 1976, in an unsigned, 137-page opinion that required a scorecard to sort out the votes on each of the major holdings. The opinion opened by acknowledging the challengers' point that the act imposed "direct quantity restrictions on political communication and association" by candidates, parties, groups, and individuals. It went on, however, to uphold contribution limits by a 6-2 vote. Contribution limits imposed only a "marginal" restriction on political communications, the Court said, and Congress had sufficient justification in seeking "to limit the actuality and appearance of corruption resulting from large individual financial contributions."

Spending limits were ruled unconstitutional, though, by votes of 6-2 as applied to candidates and 7-1 as applied to others. Those provisions, the Court said, "place substantial and direct restrictions on the ability of candidates, citizens, and associations to engage in protected political expression, restrictions that the First Amendment cannot tolerate." Dissenting, Justice Byron R. White said it made "little sense" to limit contributions without also limiting spending.

The ruling did uphold public financing of presidential campaigns, but it struck down the FEC's composition because Congress was given a role in appointing the members of the executive branch agency. Congress acted quickly to remedy the defect by giving the president the power to appoint FEC members. But new issues arose as candidates, parties, and others tested the parts of the law that remained intact.

JANUARY 31, 1976
HIGH COURT UPHOLDS PUBLIC FUNDS FOR PRESIDENTIAL ELECTION RACES, REMOVES MOST LIMITS ON SPENDING

LANDMARK RULING

30-Day Deadline Is Set for Restructuring of Federal Commission

By LESLEY OELSNER

Special to The New York Times

WASHINGTON, Jan. 30—In a landmark ruling on how political campaigns are to be waged, the Supreme Court today upheld public financing for Presidential contests, limits on how much individuals may contribute directly to a candidate in any Federal election race, and strict requirements for reporting both contributions and expenditures.

At the same time, the Court struck down as unconstitutional all limits on how much can be spent in a campaign for Congress by a candidate or in his behalf, and struck down nearly all limits on spending in a campaign for President.

The Court permitted one exception regarding unlimited spending for Presidential contenders: In upholding the public financing system, it also upheld the requirement that candidates who accept Federal financing must in return abide by limits on expenditures.

A WATERGATE REACTION

The spending limits had been a major part of the broad campaign financing reform legislation that was enacted last winter to prevent abuses and illegalities in campaigns of the kind disclosed by the Watergate scandal.

especially the First Amendment, have now been interpreted to contain.

While the Court did strike down portions of the new law, it sustained more than it knocked down. The new law drastically changed the rules for political contenders.

The law was enacted largely to prevent corruption and the appearance of corruption in the political process. It was challenged, in the lawsuit that led to today's ruling, by 12 persons and groups, including former Senator Eugene J. McCarthy, on the ground that it violated a series of con-

> " The First Amendment denies Government the power to determine that spending to promote one's political views is wasteful, excessive, or unwise.
>
> —*Per curiam* opinion in *Buckley v. Valeo* "

The Court also ruled that the new Federal Election Commission, created to implement the reform legislation, must either be restructured or, 30 days from now, cease exercising all but a few of its powers.

The Court ruled that many of the powers and duties that the new law gave to the commission—such as the power to initiate civil lawsuits to enforce the law—were powers and duties that could be constitutionally exercised only by Federal officers appointed by the President.

LACK OF AUTHORITY

The majority of commission members are named by officials of Congress. As a result, the Court said, the commission lacks authority to exercise those powers.

The Court stayed the effect of its ruling for 30 days to give Congress a chance to enact remedial legislation.

The current contenders in the Presidential primaries have already been operating under the new contribution, disclosure and public financing provisions. Since each has accepted public financing, each is bound by spending limits as a condition of that financing. The restructuring of the Federal Election Commission is all that must be done, at this point, as a result of the ruling.

The long-range effect of the ruling, though, is vast—both in terms of the practical rules for campaigns, and in terms of the extent of the guarantees that the Constitution,

stitutional provisions and particularly the First Amendment's guarantee of free speech.

What the Court did in today's ruling was balance the governmental interests underlying the law against constitutional guarantees—the need to prevent abuses such as Watergate, for example, against possible infringements by the law on free speech.

POSSIBLE PROBLEMS SEEN

The Court found that various portions of the law, particularly the limits on spending and contributions, but also the requirements regarding reporting and disclosure, posed possible First Amendment problems. But, except in the case of spending limits, it found that the interests underlying the legislation outweighed the need to prevent the First Amendment violation.

Speaking of the limits on contributions and spending, for instance, the Court majority—in an unsigned opinion, joined in some parts by five Justices and in other parts by six, seven or eight—said:

"The present act's contribution and expenditure limitations impose direct quantity restrictions on political communication and association by persons, groups, candidates and political parties."

However, the Court went on to distinguish between contributions and elections.

Limiting expenditures, the Court said, is a "substantial restraint on speech," adding that the limit of $1,000 on what an individual may spend relative to a clearly identified candidate—for example, such as placing a newspaper advertisement advocating that person's election—"would appear to exclude all citizens and groups except candidates, political parties, and the institutional press from any significant use of the most effective modes of communication."

Limiting the amount an individual may contribute to a candidate or party, however, the Court said, is only a "marginal" restriction, for the "quantity of communication by the contributor does not increase perceptibly with the size of his contribution."

After making that distinction, the court then weighed each of the limits against the governmental needs underlying the law.

In the case of contributions, it held that "it is unnecessary to look beyond the act's primary purpose—to limit the actuality and appearance of corruption resulting from large individual financial contributions"—to find sufficient justification.

"To the extent that large contributions are given to secure political quid pro quos from current and potential office holders, the integrity of our system of representative government is undermined," the Court said. "Although the scope of such pernicious practices can never be reliably ascertained, the deeply disturbing examples surfacing after the 1972 election demonstrate that the problem is not an illusory one."

Speaking of limitations on expenditures, however, the Court said:

"The First Amendment denies Government the power to determine that spending to promote one's political views is wasteful, excessive, or unwise. In the free society ordained by our Constitution it is not the Government but the people—individually as citizens and candidates and collectively as associations and political committees—who must retain control over the quantity and range of debate on public issues in a political campaign."

CRITICISM IN DISSENTS

The distinctions drawn by the majority drew some criticism from dissenting Justices—criticism that sometimes seemed ironic in that at least some of it expressed what might be considered a "civil libertarian view," urging more stringent First Amendment protection than did the majority, and it came from Justices who have been categorized as conservative.

Chief Justice Warren E. Burger, for example, said, "For me contributions and expenditures are two sides of the same First Amendment coin." Neither, he added, should be limited.

The majority opinion was "per curiam," or by-the-Court ruling that was not signed by any one Justice as the author.

A summary attached to the ruling indicated which Justice joined which parts; separate statements by five Justices also indicated points of agreement and disagreement. Eight Justices participated—Chief Justice Burger, and Justices William J. Brennan Jr., Potter Stewart, Thurgood Marshall, Lewis Powell Jr., Harry A. Blackmun, William H. Rehnquist and Byron R. White. John Paul Stevens, who was sworn in after the arguments in the case, did not participate.

The voting breakdown was as follows:

- Sustaining limits on contributions: The vote was 6-2, with Justices Burger and Blackmun dissenting.
- Striking down limitations on expenditures: The vote was 6-2 on limiting expenditures by a candidate or his family, with Justices White and Marshall dissenting; for other spending limits, the vote was 7-1, with only Justice White dissenting.
- Sustaining disclosure and reporting requirements: All the Justices agreed, with the exception that the Chief Justice opposed the requirements for reporting names and addresses of contributors of more than $10 and reporting names, addresses, and business occupations of those who contribute more than $100.
- Sustaining public financing: All but Chief Justice Burger agreed on the general principle; Justice Rehnquist dissented on the specifics of the financing plan under which, he said, minor party and independent candidates are discriminated against.
- The structure of the commission: All agreed, except that Chief Justice Burger dissented from the Court's sustaining the validity of actions the F.E.C. has taken to date.

In addition, there was disagreement among several Justices on the rationale of various parts of the holding. The only Justices who were in complete agreement on the entire majority opinion were Justices Brennan, Stewart and Powell.

The Court's ruling regarding the Federal Election Commission was generally based on the constitutional principle of separation of powers, and specifically on the so-called "appointments clause" of the Constitution, which provides for Presidential appointment of Federal officers.

The Court held that only some of the commission's powers could be considered legislative—such as information-gathering and investigating. Other powers, the Court said, such as rule-making, initiating civil lawsuits designed to enforce the statute, and deciding which matters to refer to the Justice Department for criminal prosecution, were powers reserved for other branches of Government.

To perform these latter non-legislative kinds of duties, the Court reasoned, the commission membership must be selected in accord with the appointments clause. So, the Court said, because the majority of the commission members are not now selected in this manner but are instead selected by legislative officials, the commission must cease performing all but the legislative type of work.

In discussing the requirements for disclosure and reporting, for example, the Court cited these purposes: To provide the electorate with information as to the source and use of political funds; to "deter actual corruption and avoid the appearance of corruption by exposing large contributions and expenditures to the light of publicity"; and to gather the data necessary for detecting violations of the law.

The Court conceded, as the various challengers had contended, that disclosure requirements might deter some people from giving money.

"It is undoubtedly true," it said, "that public disclosure of contributions to candidates and political parties will deter some individuals who otherwise might contribute. In some instances, disclosure may even expose contributors to harassment or retaliation."

The Court said, however, that serious infringements of First Amendment rights was [sic] still "speculative."

It also suggested that if a "reasonable probability" of harassment as a result of the disclosure requirements could be made out, the courts would undoubtedly be sympathetic to such contentions. Presumably the Court was thus opening the way for further litigation of the issue at a later date.

The matter is significant, for according to the challengers who brought the case to the high court, minor parties are particularly vulnerable to this provision.

The majority also agreed that the thresholds of $10 and $100 for the amounts of contributions that must be reported were "low." It said, however, that this was a determination for Congress to make.

Justice Burger, on the subject, said, "Congress has used a shotgun to kill wrens as well as Hawks."

• • • • • • • • • • •

"Soft Money" and Political Ad Regulation

Two major questions arose over the two decades following the *Buckley* decision. The first arose from an FEC regulation issued in 1978 allowing political parties to raise and spend funds for voter registration and turnout drives outside the provisions of the law. Parties turned to raising increasing sums of so-called soft money from, among others, corporations and unions, which were barred from directly contributing to federal candidates. The second issue arose after unions and corporations began to air election-time advertising that skirted the ban on paying for the ads out of their own treasuries instead of separately funded political action committees (PACs). The ads escaped regulation by avoiding what came to be called "express advocacy"—a direct call to vote for or against a particular candidate.

McCAIN-FEINGOLD ACT

Campaign finance reform advocates worked through the 1990s to close the two regulatory gaps. They succeeded in 2002 in winning enactment of the Bipartisan Campaign Reform Act—also called the McCain-Feingold Act after its two principal Senate sponsors, Republican John McCain of Arizona and Democrat Russell Feingold of Wisconsin. Title I of the law prohibited federal officeholders, candidates, and national political parties from soliciting, raising, or spending soft money. Title II allowed corporations or unions to pay for "electioneering communications"—defined as television advertising broadcast within sixty days of a federal election that referred to "a clearly identified candidate for Federal office"—only through PACs and not out of their own treasuries.

In signing the bill on March 26, 2002, President George W. Bush said some provisions raised "serious constitutional concerns." Separate constitutional challenges were filed almost immediately. Senate Republican leader Michael McConnell of Kentucky was the lead plaintiff in a broad complaint attacking both of the law's main titles; others participating in the suit included the Libertarian National Committee and interest groups ranging from the American Civil Liberties Union to the National Right to Life Committee. The Republican National Committee attacked the soft-money ban for political parties. The U.S. Chamber of Commerce and AFL-CIO also joined in an unlikely common cause to urge the justices to strike down the restriction on election-time issue advertising.

After a special three-judge court upheld most of the law in January 2003, the Supreme Court decided to hold an extraordinary four hours of argument in the case on September 8—four weeks before the scheduled start of the new term. The lineup of lawyers was extraordinary as well: Solicitor General Theodore Olson defended the law against one of his predecessors, Kenneth Starr—like Olson, a conservative Republican. Seth Waxman, a former Democratic solicitor general, represented McCain and Feingold, who had intervened to defend the law. The interest groups attacking the law retained Floyd Abrams, one of the nation's leading First Amendment experts whose private clients included *The New York Times*.

The oral arguments showed the justices clearly split between a liberal bloc of four inclined to uphold the law and a conservative bloc of four inclined to strike down many of its provisions. Justice O'Connor appeared to hold the decisive vote. The ruling, issued three months later, confirmed the speculation as O'Connor—a former state legislator who had generally voted to uphold campaign finance regulation—joined with the Court's senior liberal, Stevens, in writing a 5-4 opinion upholding the law's major provisions.

The soft-money restrictions, Stevens and O'Connor wrote in *McConnell v. Federal Election Commission* (2003), were an appropriate way to prevent "the potential for . . . undue influence" on federal officeholders by campaign donors. The new definition of "electioneering communications," they said, was also an appropriate way for Congress "to correct the flaws it found in the existing system." Conservative justices, including Chief Justice Rehnquist, said both provisions restricted political speech without adequate justification. "Today's decision breaks faith with our tradition of robust and unfettered debate," Justice Kennedy wrote in the longest dissent.

The law returned to the Court after the antiabortion group Wisconsin Right to Life sought a ruling to determine the legality of ads that it planned to run in advance of the 2004 election criticizing the state's Democratic senator, Feingold, for supporting filibusters to block votes on President Bush's judicial nominees. By the time the case was argued in April 2007, John G. Roberts Jr. was chief justice and O'Connor had been succeeded by Bush's second appointee, Samuel A. Alito Jr. They joined the three remaining dissenters from *McConnell* in a 5-4 decision, *Federal Election Commission v. Wisconsin Right to Life, Inc.* (2007), that significantly narrowed the law's limits on issue ads.

In a controlling opinion that only Alito joined, Roberts said that unions and corporations can pay for issue advertising out of their own treasuries provided the ads do not unmistakably advocate the election or defeat of a particular candidate. The restriction, Roberts said, is constitutional only if an ad "is susceptible of no reasonable interpretation other than as an appeal to vote for or against a specific candidate." The three other conservatives on the Court would have gone further and overruled *McConnell* outright; the four dissenters complained that the decision had "effectively" done just that.

Federal Election Commission v. Wisconsin Right to Life, Inc.

Decided: June 25, 2007

Vote: 5 (J. Roberts, Scalia, Kennedy, Thomas, Alito)

4 (Stevens, Souter, Ginsburg, Breyer)

Opinion of the Count: J. Roberts

Concurring opinion: Alito

Opinion concurring in part and in judgment: Scalia (Kennedy, Thomas)

Dissenting opinion: Souter (Ginsburg, Breyer)

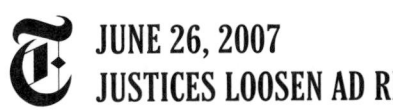

JUNE 26, 2007
JUSTICES LOOSEN AD RESTRICTIONS IN CAMPAIGN LAW

By LINDA GREENHOUSE AND DAVID D. KIRKPATRICK

The Supreme Court on Monday took a sharp turn away from campaign finance regulation, opening a wide exception to the advertising restrictions that it upheld when the McCain-Feingold law first came before it four years ago.

In a splintered 5-to-4 decision, Chief Justice John G. Roberts Jr. said that as interpreted broadly by federal regulators and the law's supporters, the restrictions on television advertisements paid for from corporate or union treasuries in the weeks before an election amounted to censorship of core political speech unless those advertisements explicitly urge a vote for or against a particular candidate.

court limited student speech and ruled that taxpayers do not have standing to challenge the administration's program of support for social service programs offered by religious institutions.

Coming as the 2008 presidential race takes off, the campaign finance decision has the effect of jettisoning a major part of the McCain-Feingold law, which Congress passed in 2002 to curb the flow of unregulated "soft money" into federal election campaigns.

While the decision did not deal directly with the soft-money ban, which is in a separate section of the law, elec-

> ❝ Where the First Amendment is implicated, the tie goes to the speaker, not the censor. ❞
> —Chief Justice John G. Roberts Jr., *FEC v. Wisconsin Right to Life, Inc.*

"Where the First Amendment is implicated," the chief justice said, "the tie goes to the speaker, not the censor."

Consequently, Chief Justice Roberts said, the only advertisements that can be kept off the air in the pre-election period covered by the law—the 30 days before a primary election and the 60 days before a general election—are those that are "susceptible of no reasonable interpretation other than as an appeal to vote for or against a specific candidate."

Describing and then dismissing the rationale for the advertising restrictions, Chief Justice Roberts used a phrase that seemed to sum up the new majority's view toward campaign finance regulation. "Enough is enough," the chief justice said.

The decision was a reminder of the ways in which the justices appointed by President Bush are moving the court. While Chief Justice Roberts's predecessor, Chief Justice William H. Rehnquist, was a dissenter when the court upheld the law four years ago, Justice Sandra Day O'Connor was in the 5-to-4 majority. Her successor, Justice Samuel A. Alito Jr., voted with Chief Justice Roberts on Monday, and in fact was the only justice to join his opinion fully.

Two other closely divided rulings announced on Monday also showed the influence of the new justices. The

tion experts said the effect would be to undercut the soft-money section as well by permitting a largely unlimited flow of money from corporate treasuries to pay for the all-important broadcast advertisements in the weeks before primary and general elections. Groups seeking to influence the outcome of the election could easily sidestep the prohibition on explicit appeals for or against candidates, supporters of the law said.

It is not clear which candidate or party is more likely to benefit from the ruling in 2008. But Senator John McCain, the Arizona Republican seeking his party's presidential nomination, may suffer the most in the short term. His sponsorship of the law, formally called the Bipartisan Campaign Reform Act, is unpopular with conservatives and Republican primary voters, and the Supreme Court's decision is a reminder of his role.

Although the court's five most conservative justices voted in the majority and the four more liberal justices were the dissenters, the outcome was not easy to categorize simply along ideological lines. Both sides of the campaign finance debate have always attracted unusual coalitions. Chief Justice Roberts pointed out in his opinion that among the groups supporting the challenge to the law, which was brought by the Wisconsin Right to Life, were the American Civil Liberties Union and the A.F.L.-C.I.O., as well as the United States Chamber of Commerce and the National Rifle Association.

The dissenters, Justices David H. Souter, John Paul Stevens, Ruth Bader Ginsburg and Stephen G. Breyer, said the decision stood the court's earlier interpretation of the statute "on its head" and would invite the "easy circumvention" of the sponsors' purpose.

The dissenters' argument that the court had effectively overruled its 2003 decision in McConnell v. Federal Election Commission, presented in an opinion by Justice Souter, found agreement among election law experts.

"Corporations received the victory that they did not achieve in 2003," said Edward B. Foley, a professor at the Moritz College of Law at Ohio State University.

It may be only a matter of time before the court reconsiders its 2003 decision upholding the constitutionality of the entire law, or at least expands its Monday decision to strike down any restriction on advertising. Three of the five justices in the majority, Antonin Scalia, Anthony M. Kennedy and Clarence Thomas, declined to sign the chief justice's opinion because it did not take that step.

In fact, Justice Scalia, in a footnote to his separate opinion, agreed with the dissenters that the court has in effect already reversed the 2003 decision when it came to the advertising restriction. The decision changed the law so substantially that it "effectively overrules" the 2003 decision "without saying so," Justice Scalia said. And demonstrating that he does not consider the new chief justice immune from the insults for which his opinions are famous, he added: "This faux judicial restraint is judicial obfuscation."

Justice Alito indicated in a separate opinion that he, too, would be open to reconsidering the earlier decision, as "we will presumably be asked in a future case" to do.

Legal experts and political advocates said the ruling, Federal Election Commission v. Wisconsin Right to Life Inc., No. 06-969, represented a swing back from a tighter approach toward regulating political contributions that peaked with passage of the 2002 law.

Congress enacted the law in part in reaction to a flood of special interest money into both parties. Throughout the 1990s, both parties had aggressively courted contributions to their allied party committees from corporations, unions and wealthy individuals for the express purpose of winning elections.

These donations, known as soft money, thus circumvented the limits on campaign contributions under older campaign laws. The McCain-Feingold law sought to end the use of soft money in part by barring corporations and unions from contributing to parties or political action committees.

The new decision brings back soft money, said Kenneth A. Gross, a Washington lawyer who represents corporations in election law matters. "The significance of it is, you can use soft money to do these ads," he said. "This is a clear shot over the bow by this court that there is going to be less regulation of money in politics. The fulcrum has now shifted."

It remains to be seen how the Federal Election Commission applies the new ruling. The decision held that Wisconsin Right to Life had a constitutional right to run three television commercials in 2004 that criticized Senator Russ Feingold, Democrat of Wisconsin, for helping to block Mr. Bush's judicial nominees. Contact the senator, the commercials said.

Wisconsin Right to Life conceded that the advertisements were prohibited by the statute because they named Mr. Feingold, who was seeking re-election; were intended to reach Wisconsin voters; and were to run during the law's 30-day blackout period before the primary. So the question was whether they were nonetheless permitted by the First Amendment, as a special three-judge Federal District Court here held that they were. The decision on Monday upheld that ruling.

In its decision in 2003, the Supreme Court ruled that the advertising restriction was not unconstitutional "on its face." Although many assumed that the ruling ended the matter, James Bopp Jr., Wisconsin Right to Life's counsel, pressed for the right to challenge the restriction "as applied" to his group and others like it, which he said were engaged in constitutionally protected issue advocacy, albeit with corporate contributions.

In its last term, the Supreme Court gave the go-ahead for "as applied" challenges, a signal that the court might soon be taking a different view of the law.

The law's supporters, including Fred Wertheimer, a longtime advocate of tighter campaign laws, asserted on Monday that a remaining part of the law, prohibiting federal officials from soliciting soft money, was still extremely important.

Mr. McCain agreed. While calling the decision "regrettable," he pointed out that the solicitation ban was unaffected. "Fortunately, that central reform still stands as the law," he said.

EQUAL PROTECTION OF THE LAW

CHAPTER 7

J. D. Shelley moved to St. Louis from Mississippi in 1930, not long after a young black girl his family knew was beaten by a group of white men. He lived with his wife and six children in racially segregated neighborhoods until he had saved enough money from his job at a government munitions factory to buy a house in the city's Fairground neighborhood.

Some African American families had lived in the neighborhood for years, including in the Labadie Avenue block where the Shelleys bought a house in fall 1945. In 1911, however, thirty of the block's thirty-nine families had signed a restrictive covenant, enforceable in court for fifty years, prohibiting the sale of any of the lots or parcels to a member of the "Negro or Mongolian race."

Carlotta Walls and Elizabeth Eckford, right, leave Central High School in Little Rock, Arkansas, in November 1957. National Guard troops were called in several months before to enforce desegregation of the school. Although the Court's 1954 ruling in *Brown v. Board of Education* prohibits racial segregation in public schools, desegregation battles continue to the present day.

Restrictive covenants had spread through the country in the early twentieth century as African Americans migrated from the rural South to cities in the North and in border states such as Missouri. Many whites who lived in those cities feared that the influx of African Americans—Negroes or colored people, as they were then called—would lower property values and bring social instability.

As early as the 1920s, African American groups were mobilizing against the practice. During and immediately after World War II, the National Association for the Advancement of Colored People (NAACP) worked with local groups to bring to court test cases in such cities as Chicago, Detroit, Los Angeles, and Washington, D.C.

The Supreme Court had dealt with racial segregation in housing twice in the early decades of the twentieth century. In 1918 the Court struck down a Louisville, Kentucky, ordinance that forbade members of one race to buy or reside on property on a street where most residents were of another race. The white plaintiff in *Buchanan v. Warley* sued to invalidate the ordinance after a black buyer backed out of a sales contract when he learned the law would prevent him from living in the house. Unanimously, the Court ruled the ordinance violated the post–Civil War Fourteenth Amendment by interfering with the property rights of both the white seller and the black buyer.

Eight years later, however, the Court rejected a legal challenge to the validity of private restrictive covenants in a case from Washington, D.C. A white homeowner sued to enforce a racial covenant after a white neighbor agreed to sell her house to an African American. Unanimously, the Court ruled in *Corrigan v. Buckley* (1926) that private racial discrimination presented no constitutional or statutory issue.

As late as the 1920s, the Supreme Court had done little to protect rights for African Americans. Before the Civil War, the Court had supported slavery—notably in 1857 in the Dred Scott decision, which held that blacks had no legal rights. After the Civil War, the Court narrowly interpreted the Fourteenth Amendment's Equal Protection Clause, which forbade the states from denying "equal protection of the laws" to "any person within its jurisdiction." Around the same time, the Court also ruled that women were not denied equal protection when they were not allowed to vote or to practice law.

By the 1940s, the Court was beginning to change its approach on racial issues. In 1938 it ruled that Missouri's all-white admissions policy at the state's only public law school violated the Equal Protection Clause. Even so, the Court in the early 1940s declined to hear any of the test cases challenging restrictive covenants.

J. D. Shelley did not know of the Labadie Avenue covenant when he agreed to buy the lower story of a two-family flat from a white family, the Fitzgeralds. On October 9, 1945, however, a white neighbor, Louis Kraemer, sued to block the sale. The judge refused because the racial covenant had not been signed by all the families on the block. On appeal, the Missouri Supreme Court disagreed. It said the covenant was valid and the Shelleys were not being denied rights under the Fourteenth Amendment or the Civil Rights Act of 1866, which guaranteed contract and property rights to all citizens without regard to race.

George Vaughn, a black lawyer practicing in St. Louis, took the case to the Supreme Court, which—to the NAACP's surprise—agreed in June 1947 to hear the appeal. In the arguments in January 1948, Vaughn called racially restrictive covenants "the Achilles heel" of democracy. The Justice Department supported the Shelleys' case—its first such intervention in a private civil rights suit.

Shelley v. Kraemer

Decided: May 3, 1948

Vote: 6 (Vinson, Black, Frankfurter, Douglas, Murphy, Burton)

0

Opinion of the Court: Vinson

Did not participate: Reed, R. Jackson, W. Rutledge

Four months later, the Supreme Court ruled in *Shelley v. Kraemer* (1948) that judicial enforcement of racially restrictive covenants constituted "state action" in violation of the Equal Protection Clause. "Because of the race or color of these petitioners they have been denied rights of ownership or occupancy enjoyed as a matter of course by other citizens of different race or color," Chief Justice Frederick (Fred) M. Vinson wrote. The vote was 6-0. Without explanation, three justices recused themselves; it has been supposed that they themselves owned properties subject to restrictive covenants.

NEWS ANALYSIS
MAY 4, 1948
THE CHIEF JUSTICE CLOSES A LOOPHOLE

By ARTHUR KROCK

WASHINGTON, May 3—The clearest insight which the Chief Justice of the United States has publicly given of his legal equipment and his political philosophy is to be found in two opinions he wrote for a unanimous Supreme Court today. They concern the widespread effort of householders to bar, on racial or similar grounds, specified groups of citizens from acquiring homes in reserved neighborhoods.

Chief Justice Vinson held that, while property owners may make private covenants of this type without violating any statute or constitutional provision, neither state nor federal courts may enforce them even when a signatory to the covenant breaks his pledge to his neighbors. Such enforcement, he said, is employing the public power for a purpose repugnant both to the spirit and the letter of the Fourteenth Amendment, which decrees that:

> No state shall make or enforce any law which shall abridge the privileges or immunities of citizens of the United States; nor shall any state deprive any person of life, liberty or property without due process of law; nor deny to any person within its jurisdiction the equal protection of the laws.

Answering the contention that this language applies only to the states, and therefore does not bind federal courts, which are the enforcement agencies of the central government, the Chief Justice wrote:

> It is not consistent with the public policy of the United States to permit federal courts in the nation's capital to exercise general equitable powers to compel action denied the state courts where such state action has been held to be violative of the guaranty of the equal protection of the laws. We cannot presume that the public policy of the United States manifests a lesser concern for the protection of such basic rights against the discriminatory action of federal courts than against such action taken by the courts of the states.

HIS LAW AND DOCTRINE

In these two rulings Chief Justice Vinson revealed his legal and political trend of mind. As a lawyer and judge he concluded that no arm of the public power, of which the courts are one, can legally be used to enforce a private compact which nullifies in any instance the broad requirement of any part of the Constitution. He pointed out that the Supreme Court has frequently held that no federal or state ordinance can legalize a contract of this kind because it violates the Fourteenth Amendment, asserting it must follow that what is unconstitutional for a Legislature

to pass is equally unconstitutional for a court to enforce. As a political philosopher, however, he said that if private citizens desire to make among themselves discriminatory agreements for the protection of their own properties, they violate no law in so doing. But in countenancing self-enforcement as an instrument at their disposal which breaks no law, he did not say at any point that suit for damages might not be brought against a covenanter who breached such a written agreement.

The cases were brought to the Supreme Court by persons, adjudged in the lower court to be Negroes, who had bought restricted property from willing sellers within the covenant area but not in every instance signers of the compact. (Many of these go into effect if 80 per cent of the property owners concerned are signers.) But it was clear from what the Chief Justice wrote that, even if all the property owners in an area sign the compact, neither state nor federal court procedure can be invoked to prevent any one of these from breaking the agreement or to require the purchaser to divest himself of his purchase.

A NEW QUESTION DECIDED

The Supreme Court was obliged to reverse a federal district panel in Washington and state courts in Missouri and Michigan in coming to its conclusions. The circumstances were slightly different in the case arising in St. Louis because there a trial court refused to divest Negro purchasers of their homes on the ground that the restrictive agreement was ineffective because it had not been signed by all the property holders in the district. But the legal issue and the issue in public policy that the Chief Justice stated and decided today were not resolved in the lower courts as he resolved them.

It was, he said, a new question for the Supreme Court— "whether the equal protection clause of the Fourteenth Amendment inhibits judicial enforcement by state [and federal] courts of restrictive covenants based on race or color." And he observed significantly that no litigant had contended such agreements as these could be "squared" with the amendment "if imposed by state or local ordinance." That being so, he found the judicial arm equally restrained.

To the argument that the courts could also bar white citizens from buying home property in certain areas restricted by Negroes to themselves, that therefore enforcement of such compacts is equitable, the Chief Justice coldly responded: "Equal protection of the laws is not achieved through indiscriminate imposition of inequalities."

The three justices who did not sign the opinions abstained for no reason that implies disagreement with the six for whom the Chief Justice delivered a judgment remarkable in that it forbids the government either to enforce private contracts repugnant to the general law or to interfere with them.

• • • • • • • • • • • •

Other race cases were moving toward the Court, including several local suits challenging legally segregated public schools. Six years later, the Court's landmark decision in *Brown v. Board of Education* (1954) outlawed "separate but equal" public schools. Ever since, the Supreme Court has played a critical role in efforts to promote equal rights for African Americans—strongly supportive into the 1970s, less so since. The Court in the 1970s also began to shape equal protection law to advance women's rights.

Despite *Brown,* the vast majority of African American as well as Latino pupils are now attending predominantly nonwhite schools. The percentage increased through the 1990s just as the Supreme Court, under Chief Justice William H. Rehnquist, was telling federal judges to wrap up ongoing school desegregation cases.

Some public school systems responded to the trend by developing assignment plans aimed at maintaining "racial balance" in individual schools. White families challenged some of those plans as depriving them of equal protection of the laws. In its first major civil rights ruling under Chief Justice John G. Roberts Jr., the Court in June 2007 agreed. The 5-4 ruling struck down two racial balance plans from Seattle, Washington, and Jefferson County (Louisville), Kentucky.

Dissenting justices said the ruling jeopardized efforts to promote racial diversity in the schools. In a pivotal concurrence, however, Justice Anthony M. Kennedy left school districts some room to develop "general policies" aimed at what he called school systems' "compelling interest" in racial diversity.

EARLY DEVELOPMENTS

The Declaration of Independence, written in 1776, proclaims that "all men [*sic*] are created equal." But the Constitution, written in 1787, includes no specific guarantee of individual equality under the law. In fact, without ever using the word *slavery,* the original Constitution sanctioned the institution by forbidding Congress for twenty years to limit the "Migration or Importation of such Persons as any of the States now existing shall think proper to admit" (Art. I, sec. 9). Article I also provided that for purposes of apportioning seats in the House of Representatives among the states, the number of these "other Persons" was to be multiplied by three-fifths (Art. I, sec. 2, cl. 3). Northern states insisted on the "Three-fifths Clause" to limit the South's ability to use the nonvoting slaves to gain additional clout in the new Congress.

THE COURT ON SLAVERY

The slave population stood at 680,000, a little over one-sixth of the young nation's population, at the time of the first census in 1790. Congress passed the Fugitive Slave Act in 1793, requiring the return of slaves who escaped across state lines. In 1808 Congress banned the importation of slaves, but their number continued to grow; the slave population reached 4 million—about one-eighth of the nation's total—as of 1860, on the eve of the Civil War.

The Supreme Court during this era generally tried to avoid entanglement in an issue that was visibly tearing the country apart. In its first ruling on the subject, the Court held in *The Antelope* (1825) that slavery was not illegal under international law. "This Court must not yield to feelings which might seduce it from the path of duty," Chief Justice John Marshall wrote, "but must obey the mandates of the law." The ruling returned to Spanish claimants thirty-seven Africans who had landed in Florida aboard a Spanish slave ship that privateers had seized off the coast of Africa.

In the 1840s and 1850s, the Court on several occasions buttressed enforcement of the fugitive slave law. In 1842 it invalidated a Pennsylvania law that required a judicial hearing before a runaway slave was to be returned to his or her state under the law. In reaffirming the law six years later, the Court expressly disclaimed any power to decide what it called "a political question." And in 1859 the Court in *Abelman v. Booth* reinstated the conviction of the Wisconsin abolitionist editor Sherman Booth for aiding a runaway slave after a state court judge had ruled the federal act unconstitutional and ordered him released.

THE DRED SCOTT DECISION

Two years earlier, the Court had departed from its passive stance by boldly attempting to settle the slavery question once and for all. The ruling in *Scott v. Sandford* (1857)—the Dred Scott case—was disastrous, legally and politically.

Dred Scott was a Missouri slave who traveled during the 1830s with his owner, army surgeon John Emerson, on postings to the free state of Illinois and the Wisconsin territory, where slavery was prohibited by federal law. He then returned with Emerson to St. Louis in 1838. After Emerson's death, his widow left Scott in the care of his original owner, Henry Blow, who opposed the extension of slavery and helped Scott test whether his stays in Illinois and Wisconsin made him a free man. The Missouri Supreme Court, however, ruled in 1852 that Scott was still a slave.

Emerson's widow then helped set up a federal court test case by selling Scott to her brother, John Sanford (whose name was misspelled in court records). The federal circuit court ruled that Scott was not a citizen and thus could not bring a suit in federal court. The Supreme Court heard the case first over four days in early February 1856 and then scheduled a second round of arguments to follow the November 1856 election. After hearing the first arguments, Justice Benjamin R. Curtis wrote to an uncle that the Court would decide the case narrowly without ruling on the constitutionality of the Missouri Compromise. That law, passed in 1820 but repealed in 1854, had prohibited the extension of slavery into virtually all of the vast territory acquired in the Louisiana Purchase.

The Court's 7-2 ruling—announced on March 6 and 7, 1857, just after the inauguration of the new president, James Buchanan—was by no means narrow. In the most important of the seven separate opinions from the majority, Chief Justice Roger B. Taney said that Scott's suit had to be dismissed because slaves and their descendants "are not included" as "citizens" in the Constitution and had "no rights that the white man was bound to respect." He went on to rule the Missouri Compromise unconstitutional. Congress has no power to prohibit slavery in the states or territories, Taney explained. The only two constitutional provisions directed at slavery "treat [slaves] as property and make it the duty of the Government to protect it."

Scott v. Sandford

Decided: March 6, 1857

Vote: 7 (Taney, Wayne, Catron, Daniel, Nelson, Grier, Campbell)

2 (McLean, Curtis)

Opinion of the Court: Taney

Concurring opinions (6): Wayne; Nelson (Grier); Grier; Daniel; Campbell; Catron

Dissenting opinions (2): McLean; Curtis

MARCH 7, 1857
LATEST INTELLIGENCE.

By Telegraph to the New-York Daily Times.

Magnetic Telegraph Co.'s Offices—5 Hanover-st., and 181 Broadway.

IMPORTANT FROM WASHINGTON.

Decision of the Supreme Court in the Dred Scott Case.

The Ordinance of 1787 and the Missouri Compromise Declared Unconstitutional.

WASHINGTON, Friday, March 6.

The opinion of the Supreme Court in the Dred Scott case was delivered by Chief Justice Taney. It was a full and elaborate statement of the views of the Court. They have decided the following important points:

First—Negroes, whether slaves or free, that is, men of the African race, are not citizens of the United States by the Constitution.

Second—The Ordinance of 1787 had no independent constitutional force or legal effect subsequently to the adoption of the Constitution, and could not operate of itself to confer freedom or citizenship within the Northwest Territory on negroes not citizens by the Constitution.

Third—The provisions of the Act of 1820, commonly called the Missouri Compromise, in so far as it undertook to exclude negro slavery from, and communicate freedom and citizenship to, negroes in the northern part of the Louisiana cession, was a Legislative act exceeding the powers of Congress, and void, and of no legal effect to that end.

Federal Government there depend on the general provisions of the Constitution, which defines in this, as in all other respects, the powers of Congress.

Third—As Congress does not possess power itself to make enactments relative to the persons or property of citizens of the United States, in a Federal Territory, other than such as the Constitution confers, so it cannot constitutionally delegate any such powers to a Territorial Government, organized by it under the Constitution.

Fourth—The legal condition of a slave in the State of Missouri is not affected by the temporary sojourn of such slave in any other State, but on his return his condition still depends on the laws of Missouri.

As the plaintiff was not a citizen of Missouri, he, therefore, could not sue in the Courts of the United States. The suit must be dismissed for want of jurisdiction.

The delivery of this opinion occupied about three hours, and was listened to with profound attention by a crowded Court-room. Among the auditors were gentlemen of eminent legal ability, and a due proportion of ladies.

> The delivery of this opinion occupied about three hours, and was listened to with profound attention by a crowded Court-room. Among the auditors were gentlemen of eminent legal ability, and a due proportion of ladies.

In deciding these main points, the Supreme Court determined the following incidental points:

First—The expression "territory and other property" of the Union, in the Constitution, applies "in terms" only to such territory as the Union possessed at the time of the adoption of the Constitution.

Second—The rights of citizens of the United States emigrating into any Federal territory, and the power of the

Judge Nelson stated the merits of the case. The question was whether or not the removal of Scott from Missouri with his master to Illinois, with a view to temporary residence there, worked his emancipation. He maintained that the question depended wholly on the law of Missouri, and for that reason the judgment of the Court below should be affirmed.

Judge Catron believed the Supreme Court has jurisdiction to decide the merits of the case. He argued that Congress could not do directly what it could not do indirectly. If it could exclude one species of property, it could exclude another. With regard to the Territories ceded, Congress could govern them only with the restrictions of the States which ceded them; and the Missouri act of 1820 violated the leading features of the Constitution, and was therefore void. He concurred with his brother Judges, that Scott is a slave, and was so when this suit was brought.

Several other Judges are to deliver their views to-morrow. . . .

APRIL 11, 1857
THE OPINIONS IN THE DRED SCOTT CASE.

Much inquiry is made in reference to the time when the opinion of the Supreme Court in the Dred Scott case will appear officially before the public. Hitherto only an abstract of the opinion has appeared, as reported for the Associated Press. I learn that the venerable Chief Justice Taney has not filed his opinion in the clerk's office, but was expected to do so to-day, or on Monday. The reporter of the decisions of the Court, Mr. Howard, has in readiness the volume in which the opinion of the several Justices in the Dred Scott case will appear. The volume will be published in this City.

The dissenting opinions of Justices McLean and Curtis have been spread before the public through the newspapers of Boston and New-York, and before they were filed. They were not obtained from the Clerk's office. As the reporter of the Court is entitled to a copyright, it will be a violation of that right to present the opinions in full in the newspapers. It is not certain, therefore, that the opinion of the Court, as presented by Chief Justice Taney and Justice Nelson, will reach the public through the popular press, and the impression made by the premature publication of the dissenting opinion will not be fully counteracted. It is unfortunate that the resolution offered in the Senate for printing, for the use of that body, twenty thousand copies of the series of opinions, was not taken up and adopted.

—*Washington Correspondence of the Baltimore Sun.*

• • • • • • • • • • • •

Taney hoped that the Court's decision on Dred Scott would eliminate slavery as a political issue. Instead, the ruling inflamed the issue. It was strongly attacked by opponents of slavery in the North as soon as newspaper summaries appeared. Criticism intensified after the dissenting justices—Curtis and John McLean—got their opinions printed in April, ahead of the official publication of all the opinions in May. Southerners defended the ruling, as did northern Democrats, who hoped with Taney that ending slavery as a political issue would keep their party together and stunt the growth of the fledgling antislavery Republican Party. But criticism by Republicans—including future president Abraham Lincoln—kept both slavery and the Supreme Court's role itself very much political issues.

EDITORIAL
OCTOBER 14, 1864
THE DEATH OF ROGER B. TANEY.

The demise of Chief-Justice Taney comes almost like some strange visitation. For one full generation he has occupied the highest judicial position in the United States, and it almost seems identified with his name. The disturbance of old associations is all the greater, because it happens at the very height of the civil conflict which is linked indissolubly with the most important act of his judicial life.

Judge Taney was a man of pure moral character, and of great legal learning and acumen. Had it not been for his unfortunate Dred Scott decision, all would admit that he had, through all those years, nobly sustained his high office. That decision itself, wrong as it was, did not spring from a corrupt or malignant heart. It came, we have the charity to believe, from a sincere desire to compose, rather than exacerbate, sectional discord. But yet it was none the less an act of supreme folly, and its shadow will ever rest on his memory. . . .

> " Judge Taney was a man of pure moral character, and of great legal learning and acumen. Had it not been for his unfortunate Dred Scott decision, all would admit that he had, through all those years, nobly sustained his high office. "

• • • • • • • • • • •

RECONSTRUCTION AMENDMENTS AND THE CIVIL RIGHTS ACTS

It took the Civil War to end slavery as a political issue. Using his powers as commander in chief, President Lincoln issued an executive order on September 22, 1862, ordering all slaves in Confederate states not then controlled by Union forces freed as of January 1, 1863. The Emancipation Proclamation did not free any slaves in Border or Northern states, but it did effectively commit the government to the elimination of slavery. On December 6, 1865—eight months after the war's end—the states completed ratification of the Thirteenth Amendment, which prohibited "slavery [or] involuntary servitude . . . within the United States, or any place subject to their jurisdiction."

The Fourteenth and Fifteenth Amendments—ratified in July 1868 and February 1870, respectively—were aimed at giving further protections to African Americans, including those who had been free as well as the emancipated former slaves. The Fourteenth overturned the Dred Scott decision by making "all persons born or naturalized in the United States" citizens of the United States and the state where they lived. It forbade any state from abridging the "privileges or immunities" of U.S. citizenship; depriving "any person of life, liberty, or property, without due process of law"; or denying "any person . . . the equal protection of the laws."

The Fifteenth provided: "The right of citizens of the United States to vote shall not be denied or abridged by the United States or by any State on account of race, color, or previous condition of servitude."

Each of the three amendments included a final section authorizing Congress to pass "appropriate legislation" to enforce its terms. Congress passed several major laws toward that end, but the Supreme Court rendered them largely useless by ruling provisions unconstitutional or limiting their scope on constitutional grounds.

The Civil Rights Act of 1866—enacted on April 9, 1866, over the veto of President Andrew Johnson—provided that all citizens "of every race and color" shall enjoy the same rights, among others, "to make and enforce contracts" or "to inherit, purchase, lease, sell, hold, and convey real and personal property" as white persons. Violations were misdemeanors punishable by a fine of up to $1,000 and up to one year's imprisonment.

The Enforcement Acts—three major laws passed in 1870 and 1871—were aimed at enforcing the right of African American suffrage under the Thirteenth Amendment in the face of evident obstruction in southern states by the newly formed Ku Klux Klan or similar groups. The Enforcement Act of 1870, or Force Act, specifically guaranteed citizens a right to vote in state or local elections without regard to race, color, or previous condition of servitude. The act provided penalties for hindering that right by "force, bribery, threats, or intimidation" and gave the newly established Justice Department power to enforce its provisions through the use of election supervisors in states and large cities.

The Enforcement Act of 1871 prohibited "fraudulent" activities used to deprive citizens of voting rights—thus reaching practices being used in northern states to keep blacks from the polls. The third of the acts—commonly called the Ku Klux Klan Act—made it a "high crime" for two or more persons to conspire to deprive citizens of the political and legal rights guaranteed in the previous laws, including the 1866 act.

Four years later, Congress passed the Civil Rights Act of 1875, which provided that "all persons" were entitled to "the full and equal enjoyment" of public accommodations, including "inns, public conveyances on land or water, theaters, and other places of public amusement," without regard to race, color, or previous condition of servitude. Violations were misdemeanors punishable by fines of $500 to $1,000 and imprisonment for thirty days to one year.

RULINGS ON CIVIL RIGHTS LAWS

The Court began weakening the laws with its 5-4 ruling in the *Slaughterhouse Cases* (1873) that the Privileges and Immunities Clause protected only the limited rights attributable to U.S. citizenship, not "the entire domain of civil rights heretofore belonging exclusively to the states." That decision rejected a challenge by New Orleans butchers to an ordinance granting a monopoly to certain slaughterhouses. Two years later, the Court specifically ruled that the right to vote was not a privilege of U.S. citizenship. The ruling in *Minor v. Happersett* was likewise not about race: it rejected an appeal by a Missouri suffragist, Virginia Minor. (See page 227.)

The next year, the Court gutted the 1870 voting rights law by ruling in *United States v. Reese* (1876) that the Fifteenth Amendment left it up to states to determine the right of suffrage. In a separate case decided the same day, *United States v. Cruikshank,* the Court threw out indictments that resulted from an election-related massacre of sixty blacks in Colfax, Louisiana, after they had seized control of the local courthouse. By turning a blind eye to evident racial discrimination, the Court allowed states and localities over the next century to adopt seemingly neutral laws such as literacy tests and poll taxes that effectively prevented most African Americans from voting. (See page 227.)

The Court ruled in 1883 on the constitutionality of the Civil Rights Act of 1875 in five consolidated cases challenging whites-only policies in theaters in New York and California, a hotel in Missouri, a restaurant in Kansas, and a train in Tennessee. The Court's 8-1 decision in the *Civil Rights Cases* (1883) held the act unconstitutional as exceeding Congress's authority under the Thirteenth or Fourteenth Amendment.

"Individual invasion of individual rights is not the subject-matter of the [Fourteenth] Amendment," Justice Joseph P. Bradley wrote. "It would be running the slavery argument into the ground," he continued, "to make it apply to every act of discrimination which a person may see fit to make as to guests he will entertain, or as to the people he will take into his coach or cab or car; or admit to his concert or theatre, or deal with in other matters of intercourse or business."

Civil Rights Cases

> **Decided:** October 15, 1883
>
> **Vote:**   8 (Waite, Miller, Field, Bradley, Woods, Matthews, Gray, Blatchford)
>
> 1 (Harlan I)
>
> **Opinion of the Court:** Bradley
>
> **Dissenting opinion:** Harlan I

OCTOBER 16, 1883
THE CIVIL RIGHTS DECISION.
NO CHANGE IN THE CONDITION OF COLORED PEOPLE INVOLVED.

WASHINGTON, Oct. 15.—The announcement to-day that the Supreme Court had decided the Civil Rights act to be unconstitutional provoked some comment among public men here. The general opinion, as gathered from the expressions of those who had only heard what the decision was but had not had [the] opportunity to learn the grounds upon which the opinion was based, was that the view of the Supreme Court would not entail any hardship upon the colored people or deprive them of any privileges which they have enjoyed since the war. Gov. Cameron, of Virginia, said that the decision would not alter their condition in his State. The colored people in that State, with the exception of a few persons who were disposed to be defensive by raising questions about social privileges which no law could regulate, were enjoying many privileges which had become theirs through the breaking of old party lines. These privileges they would continue to enjoy, unless political affairs should unhappily array blacks against whites, by a strict party division. Senator Riddleberger, who is also in the city, said that he did not see how the decision of the Supreme Court could make any practical change in the condition of the blacks in the South. No law could abolish the differences between races or compel white men of all kinds to associate intimately or conduct their business in any other way than that which seemed best for them. He believed that the colored people in Virginia would be treated as well with the civil rights act declared of no effect in that State as they would have been if all its provisions had been reaffirmed.

ATLANTA, Ga., Oct. 15.—The announcement of the decision of the Federal Supreme Court that the Civil Rights bill is unconstitutional was received with the wildest enthusiasm here. One year ago Haverly's Minstrels played an engagement in Atlanta. A well-dressed negro named Johnson seated himself in the dress circle from which he was escorted by police officers. Thus matters rested until a month ago, when a suit under the criminal clause of the Civil Rights bill was instituted against Mgr. Dequie [sic] and Haverly's Minstrels. Next day Prof. Chase, of the colored school here, was on his way to Atlanta from Augusta with several colored students. On being told the news of the suit against Degure, Prof. Chase ostentatiously brought the students into the ladies' car, when a great commotion was made and the Professor narrowly escaped violence. These events created a deep feeling here. By a strange coincidence the same troupe was playing here to-night when the end man announced to the audience the decision of the court. The entire house rose and gave three cheers for the result.

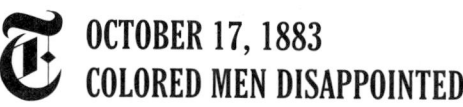

OCTOBER 17, 1883
COLORED MEN DISAPPOINTED.

THE CIVIL RIGHTS DECISION REGARDED AS A STEP BACKWARD.

WASHINGTON, Oct. 16.—The decision of the Supreme Court declaring the Civil Rights act unconstitutional has been the subject of much comment here to-day. Several of the most prominent colored men of the District have given their opinions as to the moral effect of the decision. Naturally the majority of them express regret that the Supreme Court has rendered such a decision, and are inclined to regard it as an obstacle to the progress of the colored race. Mr. Bruce, Register of the Treasury, declares it a most unfortunate decision, and one that "will carry the country backward fifteen years at least:" [sic] also, that it does not reflect the sentiment of the people, and is a revival of the theory of States' rights. Fred Douglass says the decision puts the colored people again outside of the law and

places them, when on a steam-boat or railroad train, or in a theatre, restaurant, or other public place, at the mercy of any white ruffian who may choose to insult them. Prof. Greener says that, in view of this decision, every colored man with any self-respect, must continue to demand the fullest protection of the law, both as a man and as an American citizen, and that he does not think the civilization of the age can be turned back even by the Supreme Court of the United States.

At a conference of colored people of the District to-day it was decided to hold a meeting on Monday night to express the sentiment of the colored race with respect to the decision, and to consider what course to pursue in view of that decision.

• • • • • • • • • • • •

"SEPARATE BUT EQUAL"

The ruling in the *Civil Rights Cases* did not settle the question of whether states could pass laws mandating racial segregation in public accommodations. That issue reached the Court in *Plessy v. Ferguson* (1896), which attracted limited attention at the time but came to be as infamous as the Dred Scott case in denying equal rights to African Americans.

Homer Plessy, who was one-eighth black and appeared white, was arrested in 1892 for violating a Louisiana law mandating racial segregation on trains by trying to take a seat in the coach reserved for whites on a trip from New Orleans to Covington. He unsuccessfully challenged the law in state courts as a violation of the Equal Protection Clause and then appealed to the Supreme Court. With one justice dissenting, the Court upheld the law.

The Fourteenth Amendment, Justice Henry B. Brown wrote, "could not have been intended . . . to enforce social, as distinguished from political equality." He then rejected as "a fallacy" Plessy's argument that legal segregation "stamps the colored race with a badge of inferiority." "If this be so," he wrote, "it is not by reason of anything found in the act, but solely because the colored race chooses to put this construction on it."

In a prophetic dissent, Justice John Marshall Harlan predicted the decision would prove "quite as pernicious" as the Dred Scott ruling. "Our Constitution is colorblind and neither knows or tolerates classes among citizens," he wrote. "The thin disguise of 'equal' accommodations for passengers will not mislead anyone, nor atone for the wrong this day done."

Plessy v. Ferguson

> **Decided:** May 18, 1896
>
> **Vote:** 7 (Fuller, Field, Gray, Brown, Shiras, E. White, Peckham)
> 1 (Harlan I)
>
> **Opinion of the Court:** Brown
>
> **Dissenting opinion:** Harlan I
>
> **Did not participate:** Brewer

MAY 19, 1896
LOUISIANA'S SEPARATE CAR LAW.

WASHINGTON, May 18.—The Supreme Court to-day, in an opinion read by Justice Brown, sustained the constitutionality of the law of Louisiana requiring the railroads of the State to provide separate cars for white and colored passengers. There was no inter-State commerce feature in the case, for the railroad upon which the incident occurred giving rise to the case—Plassy [*sic*] vs. Ferguson—the East Louisiana Railroad—was and is operated wholly within the State. The opinion states that by analogy to the laws of Congress and of many of the States, requiring the establishment of separate schools for children of the two races, and other similar laws, the statute in question was within the competency of the Louisiana Legislature, exercising the police power of the State. The judgment of the Supreme Court of the State, upholding the law, was therefore affirmed.

Mr. Justice Harlan announced a very vigorous dissent, saying that he saw nothing but mischief in all such laws. In his view of the case, no power in the land had the right to regulate the enjoyment of civil rights upon the basis of race. It would be just as reasonable and proper, he said, for States to pass laws requiring separate cars to be furnished for Catholics and Protestants, or for descendants of those of the Teutonic race and those of the Latin race.

RACIAL EQUALITY

Over the course of the twentieth century, the Supreme Court moved from a largely passive stance toward racial discrimination to a more activist posture by mid-century and then into a period of consolidation and retrenchment by century's end. The Court's rulings outlawing legally mandated racial segregation and permitting racial preferences in employment, government contracting, and higher education cheered civil rights advocates but produced a backlash that began in the South and later spread across the country. Polls taken in 2004 at the fiftieth anniversary of *Brown* showed widespread public support for school integration. Three years later, however, the Roberts Court cut back on school districts' discretion to fashion plans to reverse the growing racial isolation in urban and suburban systems.

The Supreme Court's few decisions on racial issues during the first half of the twentieth century formed no consistent pattern. The Court blocked officially established racial segregation in housing in 1918, but then permitted private racially restrictive covenants in 1926. The Court's voting rights decisions limited some measures to block voting by African Americans but permitted others—notably, literacy tests and poll taxes. (See page 229.) The Court used the racially charged rape convictions in the *Scottsboro Cases* (1932) to establish a constitutional rule against racial discrimination in jury selection, but took no further steps specifically aimed at combating racism in the criminal justice system. (See page 356.) And the Court's ruling in the Japanese American internment case, *Korematsu v. United States* (1944), declared racial classifications "inherently suspect," but still upheld the wartime relocation and detention of hundreds of thousands of U.S. citizens solely because of their national origin. (See page 85.)

CHALLENGES TO SCHOOL SEGREGATION

Through the first half of the twentieth century, the NAACP, formed in 1909, was mounting educational, political, and legal campaigns against racial discrimination in many settings. In the 1930s, it began developing a concentrated attack on segregation in education under the leadership of future Supreme Court justice Thurgood Marshall, a native of Baltimore who had graduated from the historically black Howard University Law School in Washington, D.C. In his home state, Marshall won a decision in 1935 striking down the all-white admissions policy at the University of Maryland Law School.

As chief counsel of the NAACP, Marshall then helped direct the campaign that won successive victories at the Supreme Court in higher education cases that put teeth into the second part of "separate but *equal.*" The Court in *Missouri ex rel. Gaines v. Canada* (1938) overturned the state's policy of barring blacks from the state's law school and instead paying for their costs at an out-of-state school. A decade later, the Court ruled that Oklahoma had to provide a law school for a black applicant, but it took no further action after the state established a "school" for the plaintiff in a roped off area of the state Capitol.

In two cases in 1950, however, the Court refused to accept such ruses. *Sweatt v. Painter* ordered Texas to admit Herman Sweatt to the previously all-white University of Texas Law School. *McLaurin v. Oklahoma State Regents for Higher Education* ordered the University of Oklahoma to lift restrictions on a black graduate student, George McLaurin, who had been admitted to the previously all-white school but was required to sit, eat, and study at specially designated desks and tables.

Marshall had focused first on higher education in part to minimize the anticipated resistance to interracial education for younger children. Through the 1940s, however, the NAACP was working with local families and groups challenging "separate but equal" school systems in the South and some border states. Generally, the suits sought to upgrade the evidently unequal facilities for black pupils. But the Court's *Sweatt* and *McLaurin* decisions convinced Marshall and others that the time had come for a direct challenge to the first half of "*separate* but equal."

BROWN AND "MASSIVE RESISTANCE"

To give the Court the full picture of racial segregation, the NAACP lawyers chose not one but five cases to press their argument: two from the South (Clarendon County, South Carolina, and Prince Edward County, Virginia); two from border states (New Castle County, Delaware, and Topeka, Kansas); and one from the District of Columbia. The first named plaintiff in the Topeka case was Oliver Brown, a railroad laborer, who complained that his eight-year-old daughter Linda had to attend an all-black elementary school a mile from their home instead of the nearby all-white school.

The Court heard arguments in December 1952; the justices were closely divided. As a temporizing measure, the Court adopted Justice Felix Frankfurter's suggestion to ask for new briefs on whether the Fourteenth Amendment was intended to abolish segregation. The cases were due to be reargued in December 1953. Three months before then, Chief Justice Vinson died—his legacy tarnished by his inability to unite a divided Court. On September 30, 1953, President Dwight D. Eisenhower chose Earl Warren, the popular governor of California, as chief justice—repaying Warren for supporting Eisenhower's nomination at the 1952 Republican convention. The recess appointment took effect immediately, without Senate confirmation.

Future Supreme Court justice Thurgood Marshall and his legal team from the National Association for the Advancement of Colored People arrive at the Supreme Court in December 1953 to successfully argue the school desegregation cases. The Court's decision in *Brown v. Board of Education* (1954) overturned *Plessy v. Ferguson*'s "separate but equal" doctrine of 1896 and prohibited racially segregated schools.

Source: George Tames/The New York Times

After the rearguments, Warren personally took on the task of writing an opinion and adopted the goal of getting all justices to sign it. He kept the opinion short—only thirteen pages—and free of accusatory rhetoric. He personally lobbied the two justices who balked—Stanley F. Reed and Robert H. Jackson—to join the opinion. He even persuaded Jackson to leave his hospital bed to be in the Court for the announcement of the decision in *Brown v. Board of Education* on May 17, 1954.

Warren dismissed as inconclusive the issue of the intention of the framers of the Fourteenth Amendment and proceeded instead to the present effects of "separate but equal" in public schools. "Does segregation of children in public schools solely on the basis of race, even though the physical facilities and other 'tangible' factors may be equal, deprive the children of the minority group of equal educational opportunities?" Warren asked. "We believe that it does."

Brown v. Board of Education

> **Decided:** May 17, 1954
> **Vote:** 9 (Warren, Black, Reed,
> Frankfurter, Douglas,
> R. Jackson, Burton, Clark,
> Minton)
> 0
> **Opinion of the Court:** Warren

Separating children solely because of their race "generates a feeling of inferiority," Warren explained, pointing in a controversial footnote to sociological studies on the detrimental effects of enforced segregation. Warren then stated: "We conclude that in the field of public education the doctrine of 'separate but equal' has no place. Separate educational facilities are inherently unequal." On that basis, he determined that plaintiffs in the four state cases had been denied rights under the Equal Protection Clause; in the District of Columbia case, *Bolling v. Sharpe* (1954), he said that racial segregation violated an equal protection requirement that was implicit in the Fifth Amendment's Due Process Clause, applicable to the federal government. (See "Supreme Court's Major School Desegregation Rulings, 1954–2007," opposite.)

Instead of issuing decrees, the Court asked for a new round of briefs and arguments on fashioning remedies. A year later, the Court's unanimous opinion in *Brown II* sent all five cases back to lower courts with the direction that school officials "make a prompt and reasonable start toward full compliance" and proceed to desegregate "with all deliberate speed."

Instead of conciliating segregationists, the delay gave them time to organize what came to be called "massive resistance" to *Brown*. The Court first addressed the resistance in *Cooper v. Aaron* (1958), a unanimous decision refusing a plea by Little Rock, Arkansas, officials to postpone further desegregation in the face of the hostility accompanying the integration of the city's Central High School. To emphasize their unanimity, each of the justices personally signed the opinion. Even so, Gov. Orval Faubus closed schools for a year rather than comply.

In other states, school officials devised "freedom of choice" plans for pupils to avoid desegregation. In 1963 the Court rejected one of those plans—in Knoxville, Tennessee—that allowed students assigned to schools where they would be in the minority to transfer to a school where they would be in the majority.

Over the next five years, the Court showed increasing impatience with the resistance. Then, in May 1968, the Court declared in *Green v. County School Board of New Kent County, Va.* that delays had to end. The ruling rejected a freedom of choice plan that had resulted in only 15 percent of black pupils attending integrated schools. School systems, the Court said, had to eliminate racial discrimination "root and branch" and develop a plan to create a unitary system "that promises realistically to work, and promises realistically to work now."

By then, Congress had passed and President Lyndon B. Johnson had signed three major civil rights laws: the Civil Rights Act of 1964, the Voting Rights Act of 1965, and the Fair Housing Act of 1968. The Court unanimously upheld the first of the acts in December 1964, less than six months after Johnson had signed it. It upheld the Voting Rights Act by an 8-1 vote on March 7, 1966. (See page 232.)

Then, two months after Johnson signed the housing law, the Court overturned its eighty-five-year-old ruling in the *Civil Rights Cases* (1883) that had barred Congress from prohibiting private racial discrimination. In passing the Civil Rights Act of 1866, Congress had properly exercised its authority under the Thirteenth Amendment to eliminate the "badges of slavery," Justice Potter Stewart wrote in *Jones v. Alfred H. Mayer Co.* (1968). "When racial discrimination herds men into ghettos and makes their ability to buy property turn on the color of their skin, then it too is a relic of slavery," he said.

Supreme Court's Major School Desegregation Rulings, 1954–2007

Decision (Date)	Vote	Main Opinion
Brown v. Board of Education (1954) Declares "separate but equal" schools for white and black students inherently unequal, unconstitutional	9-0	Warren
Brown v. Board of Education (1955) (Brown II) Requires racially segregated school systems to desegregate "with all deliberate speed"	9-0	Warren
Cooper v. Aaron (1958) Refuses to postpone desegregation of Little Rock schools; reaffirms Brown in opinion personally signed by all nine justices	9-0	*Per curiam*
Goss v. Board of Education of Knoxville (1963) Strikes down plan allowing white students to transfer out of previously all-black schools	9-0	Clark
Griffin v. County School Board of Prince Edward County (1964) Prohibits local governments from using public funds to finance segregated "private" schools	9-0	Black
Green v. County School Board of New Kent County (1968) Bars "freedom of choice" plans allowing all pupils to attend school of their choice	9-0	Brennan
Alexander v. Holmes County Board of Education (1969) Rejects Nixon administration's request to delay desegregation of thirty-three Mississippi school systems; declares "all deliberate speed" standard "no longer constitutionally permissible"	9-0	*Per curiam*
Swann v. Charlotte-Mecklenburg County Board of Education (1971) Permits federal courts to order use of busing, racial quotas, and gerrymandered school zones as interim steps to eliminate vestiges of racial segregation	9-0	Burger
North Carolina State Board of Education v. Swann (1971) Invalidates state antibusing law prohibiting use of busing for racial balance	9-0	Burger
Keyes v. School District No. 1, Denver (1973) Allows federal courts to bar "de facto" segregation if school district policies were "deliberately segregative"; recognizes Hispanics as "identifiable class" in school segregation cases	7-1	Brennan
Milliken v. Bradley (1974) Bars court-ordered plan requiring cross-district busing between Detroit and suburban school systems	5-4	Burger
Pasadena City Board of Education v. Spangler (1976) Rejects requirement to maintain racial balance in individual schools once a racially neutral plan is adopted and put into effect	6-2	Rehnquist
Runyon v. McCrary (1976) Bars racial segregation in private schools	7-2	Stewart
Bob Jones University v. United States (1983) Upholds Internal Revenue Service policy of denying tax exemption to racially segregated universities	8-1	Burger
Missouri v. Jenkins (1990) Allows federal courts to order local governments to levy taxes in excess of state statutory limits in order to correct school segregation	5-4	B. White

(continued)

Supreme Court's Major School Desegregation Rulings, 1954–2007 (continued)

Decision (Date)	Vote	Main Opinion
Board of Education of Oklahoma City Public Schools v. Dowell (1991) Allows formerly desegregated school districts to be freed of court orders if they prove that elements of past discrimination have been eliminated to all "practicable" extent	5-3	Rehnquist
Freeman v. Pitts (1992) Allows federal courts to give up control of school districts in incremental stages even if parts of desegregation decrees have not been achieved	8-0	Kennedy
Missouri v. Jenkins (1995) Rejects court-ordered plan requiring teacher salary increases, creation of "magnet schools" to attract suburban students to Kansas City schools; calls plan impermissible "interdistrict remedy"	5-4	Rehnquist
Parents Involved in Community Schools v. Seattle School Dist. No. 1 (2007) Bars use of race as determinative factor in assigning individual pupils to schools; concurring opinion by Kennedy allows use of general policies to promote racial diversity	5-4	Roberts

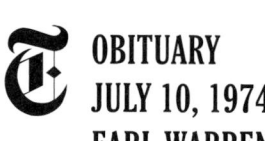

OBITUARY
JULY 10, 1974
EARL WARREN IS DEAD IN CAPITAL AT 83; CHIEF JUSTICE IN VAST SOCIAL CHANGE

His 16 Years on Court Had Profound Impact on Law and Life

By ANTHONY LEWIS

Special to The New York Times

. . . It was often said that no Chief Justice since John Marshall had had so profound an impact on American law and life. During the Warren years the Supreme Court, usually a conservative influence, became a force for libertarian reform.

The school segregation case, Brown v. Board of Education, was the best-known symbol of those years. Decided on May 17, 1954, just eight months after Mr. Warren took his seat, the case held segregated schools unconstitutional, overruling the 60-year-old separate-but-equal doctrine. Later cases applied the new rule to all racial barriers imposed by law.

The Chief Justice's role in the Brown case was hidden by the Supreme Court tradition of secrecy in deliberation. But many students of the period believe that he had a crucial role in achieving unanimity on the Court.

The public knew the racial segregation cases better than any others in the Warren years. But changes just as sweeping came in two other areas: criminal law and legislative apportionment.

The Warren Court interpreted the Constitution to provide many new rights for those suspected or accused of crime. For example, all poor defendants were for the first time guaranteed the right to free counsel. Evidence secured by illegal police methods was excluded from use at trials.

Then, in 1966, came the landmark case of Miranda v. Arizona. The Court held that all arrested persons had a right to see a lawyer before being questioned by the police— a free lawyer if they could not pay for one—and had to be advised of that right.

Chief Justice Warren once said himself that he regarded the apportionment cases as more important than those dealing with either race or criminal defendants' rights.

Precedents had barred Federal courts from even considering challenges to legislative districts that were gerrymandered or grossly unequal in population. Then, in 1962, the Court turned away from that history and said that Federal judges could consider apportionment cases.

Two years later, in a massive opinion by the Chief Justice, the Court held that every house of every state legislature had to be districted substantially on the basis of equal population. The result was the redistricting, in a short time, of almost all American state legislatures.

These cases made Earl Warren a highly controversial figure, very likely the most controversial judge of the century. Southern segregationists ran campaigns to "impeach Earl Warren." Liberals honored him more than they did most Presidents. . . .

THE BURGER COURT AND DESEGREGATION

Through Chief Justice Warren's retirement in 1969, the Court had been unanimous in every school desegregation case. In its first ruling under Chief Justice Warren E. Burger, the Court was again unanimous in upholding federal judges' power to order school districts to use busing plans to desegregate schools. "Bus transportation has been an integral part of the public education system for years," Burger wrote in *Swann v. Charlotte-Mecklenburg County Board of Education* (1971).

APRIL 21, 1971
SUPREME COURT, 9-0, BACKS BUSING TO COMBAT SOUTH'S DUAL SCHOOLS, REJECTING ADMINISTRATION STAND
OPINION BY BURGER

Segregation in North Based on Housing Is Not Affected

By FRED P. GRAHAM

Special to The New York Times

WASHINGTON, April 20—The Supreme Court unanimously upheld today the constitutionality of busing as a means to "dismantle the dual school systems" of the South.

But the Court made it clear that today's decision did not apply to Northern-style segregation, based on neighborhood patterns.

In a series of decisions written by Chief Justice Warren E. Burger and supported by the eight other Justices, the Court overrode the arguments of the Nixon Administration and the Justice Department, which had intervened on the side of Southern school systems in the four cases decided today.

DISMAY OVER U.S. VIEW

To the dismay of civil rights organizations and the delight of many white Southerners, the Justice Department lawyers had argued that Southern school systems should be allowed to assign students to schools in their own neighborhoods even if this resulted in slowing the pace of desegregation in the South.

Southern lawyers had contended that the Northern areas were permitted to have neighborhood schools and that it would be discriminatory if the South were not allowed the same "privilege."

"Desegregation plans cannot be limited to the walk-in school," the Court declared. It held that busing was proper unless "the time or distance is so great as to risk either the health of the children or significantly impinge on the educational process." Young children may be improper subjects for busing when the distances are long, the Court concluded.

LIMITS ON DECISION

The Court stopped short of ordering the elimination of all-black schools or of requiring racial balance in the schools. But it said that the existence of all-black schools created a presumption of discrimination and held that Federal district judges may use racial quotas as a guide in fashioning desegregation decrees.

This is expected to touch off a new wave of desegregation orders this summer in the cities of the South, where school segregation has persisted despite the 1954 Supreme Court decision that declared legally required segregation to be unconstitutional.

Chief Justice Burger excluded "de facto" segregation of the North from today's ruling by declaring, "We do not reach in this case the question whether a showing that school segregation is a consequence of other types of state action, without any discriminatory action by the school authorities, is a constitutional violation requiring remedial action by a school desegregation decree."

The major portion of what Mr. Burger described as "guidelines, however imperfect, for the assistance of school authorities and courts" came in a 28-page opinion upholding a busing decree governing the joint school system in Charlotte-Mecklenburg County, N.C.

The court upheld the judgment of Federal District Judge James B. McMillan, who required massive crosstown busing of children in an effort to approximate in each elementary school the ratio of 71 per cent whites and 29 per cent blacks that exists in the entire school system.

Judge McMillan's ruling was overturned by the United States Court of Appeals for the Fourth Circuit on the grounds that it was unreasonable and burdensome. In upholding Judge McMillan, the Supreme Court stressed that the school board had failed to propose an acceptable plan and that this had forced him to produce his own plan.

In such cases a district court has "broad powers to fashion a remedy," the Supreme Court said. It said that Judge McMillan's solution was acceptable under those particular circumstances, although it did not mean that other judges were required to order similar measures.

The Court's guidelines contained the following points:

- Desegregation does not require that every school in every community must always reflect the racial composition of the school system as a whole. However, if a judge wishes to use mathematical ratios, as Judge McMillan did, as "a starting point in the process of shaping a remedy," this may be within his equitable discretion.

- The existence of "some small numbers" of schools of one race, or virtually one race, is not alone proof of racial discrimination. "But in a system with a history of segregation" the courts may indulge in "a presumption against schools that are substantially disproportionate in their racial composition." If such school districts have any all-black schools, the burden will be on them "to satisfy the court that their racial composition is not the result of present or past discriminatory action on their part."

- It is not enough for school officials to draw school attendance lines that appear to be racially neutral. Officials must foster integration by such affirmative measures as gerrymandering school boundaries to include both races, pairing "white" and "Negro" schools, and drawing school zones that combine noncontiguous areas in racially diverse neighborhoods.

- The authority of Federal courts to require the assignment of students on the basis of race to achieve integration is not affected by antibusing language in the Civil Rights Act of 1964. The courts' obligation is to enforce the 14th Amendment's declaration that no state shall "deny any person within its jurisdiction the equal protection of the laws."

  Congress declared in the Civil Rights Act that it did not intend to enlarge the remedies of courts in enforcing the equal protection guarantee but that it also did not purport to diminish these remedies.

A companion case today concerned a ruling by the Supreme Court of Georgia, which upheld the contention by white parents in Athens, Ga., that school officials had violated the 14th Amendment by making racial assignments to achieve desegregation.

Chief Justice Burger said that, on the contrary, racial assignments were necessary to enforce the 14th Amendment rights by upsetting the segregated status quo.

Using similar reasoning in a third case, the Court declared unconstitutional an antibusing statute enacted by the North Carolina Legislature. A similar law passed by the New York Legislature has been declared unconstitutional by a three-judge Federal District Court and is pending before the Supreme Court.

In the fourth case the Court overturned the desegregation plan of Mobile, Ala., and ordered further desegregation. Mobile officials had avoided busing by adopting a neighborhood approach that left many Negroes in the eastern section of the city in predominantly black schools. The Court found this inadequate.

While the ruling today is its most sweeping school desegregation action since the 1954 case, it leaves some unanswered questions that may confound Federal District judges in the coming months.

The ruling said that "at some point" Southern school districts should have satisfied the 1954 ruling and become "unitary." However, it did not say how Southern communities would know when they had reached that point. Once there, the Court said the communities would not be "required to make year-by-year adjustments of the racial composition of student bodies."

The Court also did not say if communities can close their inner city schools and bus Negroes out, or, if they must bus children of both races equally.

But the most vexing aspect of the ruling is likely to be the broad discretion given to Federal District judges. Having been told that they must do more to break down racial imbalance, but that they are not required to eliminate all "black" schools or achieve racial balance, any ruling is likely to be attacked as either too strong or too weak. . . .

* * * * * * * * * * * *

The Court split after *Swann,* as a majority of justices—including Burger and the three others appointed by President Richard M. Nixon—began cutting back on desegregation remedies. In the most important case, the Court voted 5-4 in *Milliken v. Bradley* (1974) essentially to prohibit federal judges from ordering desegregation plans between central cities and outlying suburbs. The decision blocked an ambitious plan to desegregate schools in Detroit and adjacent suburbs. Two years later, the Court ruled in a case from Pasadena, California, that school districts had no need to juggle pupil assignments once a racially neutral plan was in place.

THE COURT ON AFFIRMATIVE ACTION

In line with *Brown,* the Court also began in the 1950s to require states to dismantle racial segregation in public colleges and universities. A separate issue arose later when some universities—public and private—adopted affirmative action plans designed to increase the admission of African Americans into predominantly white schools. Some white students challenged the plans as a violation of their equal protection rights. The Court ducked a case on the issue in 1974 but agreed three years later to hear an appeal by Allan Bakke, a white student who said he had been rejected from the University of California–Davis Medical School because sixteen places had been reserved for black applicants.

The justices split 4-1-4 in *Regents of the University of California v. Bakke* (1978), with Justice Lewis F. Powell Jr. in the middle. Four justices found the plan violated Title VI of the Civil Rights Act of 1964, which prohibited racial discrimination by state and local governments. Four others found no violation, either statutory or constitutional. In the controlling opinion, Powell found that the fixed set-aside for minority applicants violated both Title VI and the Equal Protection Clause. But he also said schools could make limited use of racial preferences to attain "a diverse student body."

Over the next decade, the Court produced a similarly nuanced rule on use of affirmative action in employment. In *United Steelworkers of America v. Weber* (1979), the Court ruled that Kaiser Aluminum did not violate the Civil Rights Act's job discrimination provisions in Title VII by reserving half of its trainee slots for minorities.

Regents of the University of California v. Bakke

Decided: June 28, 1978

Vote: Multiple

Judgment of the Court: Powell

Opinions concurring in part and dissenting in part (5):

Brennan, B. White, T. Marshall, Blackmun; Stevens (Burger, Stewart, Rehnquist); B. White; T. Marshall; Blackmun

In rulings in the early 1980s, however, the Court ruled that affirmative action plans violated the act if they required laying off more senior white workers to make room for minorities. Civil rights groups feared a retreat on the issue, but in 1987 the Court reaffirmed the legality of voluntary affirmative action plans. The 6-3 decision in *Johnson v. Transportation Agency, Santa Clara County* also cheered women's groups because it upheld a plan to move more women into higher-ranking positions in the government agency.

Under Chief Justice Rehnquist, the Court grew more skeptical of integration and affirmative action in the 1990s, especially after Justice Thurgood Marshall retired in 1991 and was succeeded by Clarence Thomas, an outspoken African American conservative. Three successive rulings limited court-ordered remedies in school cases in the face of what civil rights groups called "resegregation." In *Missouri v. Jenkins* (1995), Rehnquist wrote a 5-4 decision throwing out a plan ordering use of magnet schools to draw suburban pupils into the predominantly minority Kansas City school system.

The Court also clamped down on use of racial preferences in government contracting. In 1989 the Court ruled in *Richmond v. J. A. Croson Co.* that state and local governments had to meet the highest constitutional standard—strict scrutiny—to justify minority set-asides. *Adarand Constructors, Inc., v. Peña* (1995) extended that rule to federal government programs as well.

THE UNIVERSITY OF MICHIGAN CASES

Those affirmative action rulings encouraged opponents of racial preferences to urge the Court to reconsider the *Bakke* decision allowing public colleges and universities to consider the race of individual applicants in admissions decisions. The Court took up the issue in two cases brought by white students challenging race-conscious admissions policies at the University of Michigan's undergraduate college and its law school. The cases attracted an outpouring of briefs from supporters of affirmative action—including business groups and a group of retired military officers—and a smaller number from conservative groups opposed to racial preferences. The Bush administration sided with the students challenging the policies.

The decisions, announced on June 23, 2003, appeared at first to be a compromise—upholding the law school's admissions policies in *Grutter v. Bollinger* (5-4) but striking down the college's policies in *Gratz v. Bollinger* (6-3). On closer examination, however, supporters of affirmative action said that Justice Sandra Day O'Connor's opinion in *Grutter* established a clear holding that universities can use individualized race-conscious admissions procedures to promote what she called a "compelling government interest in attaining a diverse student body."

In support of that conclusion, O'Connor cited the briefs filed by business groups and military leaders. Applying strict scrutiny, she found the law school used race as only one factor in an individualized admissions process, not as a quota. By contrast, Rehnquist spoke for a majority in ruling the undergraduate admissions process unconstitutional in *Gratz* because it gave so much weight to race as to guarantee admission to "virtually every minimally qualified underrepresented minority applicant."

O'Connor closed *Grutter,* however, with a warning that racial preferences should not continue in perpetuity. Citing the twenty-five-year period since *Bakke,* O'Connor concluded, "We expect that 25 years from now, the use of racial preferences will no longer be necessary to further the interest approved today."

Grutter v. Bollinger

Decided: June 23, 2003

Vote: 5 (Stevens, O'Connor, Souter, Ginsburg, Breyer)

4 (Rehnquist, Scalia, Kennedy, Thomas)

Opinion of the Court: O'Connor

Concurring opinion: Ginsburg (Breyer)

Opinions concurring in part and dissenting in part (2): Scalia (Thomas); Thomas (Scalia)

Dissenting opinions (2): Rehnquist (Scalia, Kennedy, Thomas); Kennedy

Gratz v. Bollinger

Decided: June 23, 2003

Vote: 6 (Rehnquist, O'Connor, Scalia, Kennedy, Thomas, Breyer)

3 (Stevens, Souter, Ginsburg)

Opinion of the Court: Rehnquist

Concurring opinions (3): O'Connor (Breyer); Thomas; Breyer

Dissenting opinions (3): Stevens (Souter); Souter (Ginsburg); Ginsburg (Souter)

JUNE 24, 2003
JUSTICES BACK AFFIRMATIVE ACTION BY 5 TO 4, BUT WIDER VOTE BANS A RACIAL POINT SYSTEM

COLLEGES RELIEVED

U. of Michigan Ruling Endorses the Value of Campus Diversity

By LINDA GREENHOUSE

WASHINGTON, June 23—The Supreme Court preserved affirmative action in university admissions today by a one-vote margin but with a forceful endorsement of the role of racial diversity on campus in achieving a more equal society.

"In order to cultivate a set of leaders with legitimacy in the eyes of the citizenry, it is necessary that the path to leadership be visibly open to talented and qualified individuals of every race and ethnicity," Justice Sandra Day O'Connor wrote in her 5-to-4 majority opinion upholding the University of Michigan's consideration of race for admission to its law school. . . .

racial diversity, a position that had appeared undermined by the court's subsequent equal protection rulings in other contexts and that some lower federal courts had boldly repudiated, has now been endorsed by five justices and placed on a stronger footing than ever before.

President Bush had asked the court to declare the universities' policies unconstitutional.

Although the four dissenters in the law school case did not directly confront the continued validity of the Bakke precedent, it was clear that both Justices Clarence Thomas and Antonin Scalia would have overturned it if they could. "Every time the government places citizens on

> " Effective participation by members of all racial and ethnic groups in the civil life of our nation is essential if the dream of one nation, indivisible, is to be realized. "
>
> —Justice Sandra Day O'Connor, *Grutter v. Bollinger*

At the same time, by a vote of 6 to 3, and with Justice O'Connor in the majority as well, the court invalidated the same university's affirmative action program for admission to its undergraduate college. The difference was in the details: the undergraduate school uses a point system based in part on race.

As a result, the pair of decisions—the court's first in a generation to address race in university admissions—provided a blueprint for taking race into account without running afoul of the Constitution's guarantee of equal protection.

The law school engages in a "highly individualized, holistic review of each applicant's file" in which race counts as a factor but is not used in a "mechanical way," Justice O'Connor said. For that reason, she said, it was consistent with Justice Lewis F. Powell Jr.'s controlling opinion in the Bakke case in 1978, which permitted the use of race as one "plus factor."

The result of today's rulings was that Justice Powell's solitary view that there was a "compelling state interest" in

racial registers and makes race relevant to the provision of burdens or benefits, it demeans us all," Justice Thomas said in a dissenting opinion that Justice Scalia also signed.

Chief Justice William H. Rehnquist wrote the principal dissenting opinion that spoke for all four, including Justice Anthony M. Kennedy. He took a more oblique approach that attacked the law school program not so much for its premise as for how it works in practice, dismissing it as "a carefully managed program designed to ensure proportionate representation of applicants from selected minority groups."

Justice Kennedy, writing separately, said that Justice Powell's opinion in the Bakke case "states the correct rule for resolving this case," but that the court had not applied the "meaningful strict scrutiny" under which the program should have been found unconstitutional.

Joining Justice O'Connor's majority opinion in Grutter v. Bollinger, No. 02-241, were Justice Ruth Bader Ginsburg, who wrote a brief concurring opinion, and Justices John Paul Stevens, David H. Souter and Stephen G. Breyer.

By contrast with the law school, the admissions program for Michigan's College of Literature, Science, and the Arts awards 20 points on a scale of 150 for membership in an underrepresented minority group—blacks, Hispanics, and American Indians—with 100 points guaranteeing admission to the university's main undergraduate school. Fixed numbers of points are also awarded for other factors, including alumni connections, geography and athletics.

The inclusion of race on the scale, with the result that nearly all qualified minority applicants are admitted to the competitive program while many qualified white students are turned away, demonstrates the absence of the "individualized consideration" that the Bakke decision required, Chief Justice Rehnquist wrote. Justice O'Connor echoed that conclusion, describing the undergraduate program as a "nonindividualized, mechanical one."

Justice Breyer, concurring separately, did not sign the Rehnquist opinion. The dissenters were Justices Ginsburg and Souter, who said the majority opinion was incorrect on the merits, and Justice Stevens. He said the case should have been dismissed because the plaintiffs, two white students who had failed to win admission under an earlier version of the undergraduate admissions policy, lacked standing to challenge the current policy that the university adopted in 1998.

The rulings today came as an enormous relief to the civil rights community, as well as to public and private colleges and universities around the country, dozens of which had joined briefs supporting Michigan. Although the constitutional issue applied directly only to public institutions, federal law has given private colleges an equal stake in the outcome by forbidding racial discrimination by educational institutions that receive federal money.

President Bush issued a statement praising the court "for recognizing the value of diversity on our nation's campuses." He added, "Like the court, I look forward to the day when America will truly be a color-blind society."

The statement made no reference to the fact that the administration had asked the court to invalidate both Michigan programs as thinly disguised quota systems that violated the holding of the Bakke decision. Mr. Bush had personally announced in a televised address in January that his administration was siding against the university.

"A reader would never know that the administration's brief derided the law school's goal of having a critical mass of underrepresented students in each class," the liberal advocacy group People for the American Way said in a statement.

The administration's brief faulted the university for having failed to consider "race-neutral alternatives" before adopting its affirmative action plans. The only example the brief offered as an acceptable alternative was the plan now used in Texas, California and Florida, where admission is offered automatically to high school graduates above a particular class rank.

In her majority opinion today, Justice O'Connor was close to dismissive of the administration's analysis. She said the brief did not explain "how such plans could work for graduate and professional schools." She added: "Moreover, even assuming such plans are race-neutral, they may preclude the university from conducting the individualized assessments necessary to assemble a student body that is not just racially diverse, but diverse along all the qualities valued by the university."

The court's precedents, including the Bakke decision, made clear that any official consideration of race must survive a standard of judicial review known as strict scrutiny, meaning that the policy must serve a compelling state interest and be narrowly tailored to achieve that interest. Consequently, Michigan faced two analytical hurdles in defending its programs in lawsuits brought by three disappointed white applicants, Barbara Grutter in the law school case and Jennifer Gratz and Patrick Hamacher in the undergraduate case, Gratz v. Bollinger, No. 02-516. The university had to persuade the court that racial diversity was a compelling interest that was appropriately served by the challenged programs.

Justice O'Connor's opinion in the law school case embraced the diversity rationale. "Effective participation by members of all racial and ethnic groups in the civil life of our nation is essential if the dream of one nation, indivisible, is to be realized," she said. She added that law schools, in particular, served as gateways to economic and political leadership.

"Access to legal education (and thus the legal profession) must be inclusive of talented and qualified individuals of every race and ethnicity," she said, "so that all members of our heterogeneous society may participate in the educational institutions that provide the training and education necessary to succeed in America."

Her opinion cited a number of briefs from businesses, colleges and, with particular emphasis, two dozen retired senior military officers and former commandants of the service academies, who told the court that affirmative action was essential to maintaining an integrated officer corps.

The real debate came down to whether either program was narrowly tailored enough. With its 20-point formula, the undergraduate program had always appeared more vulnerable. The Federal District Court in Detroit had invalidated both programs. On appeal, the United States Court of Appeals for the Sixth Circuit, in Cincinnati, upheld the law school program but never issued an opinion after hearing arguments on the undergraduate program.

In concluding her opinion, Justice O'Connor noted that 25 years had passed since Bakke and said affirmative action should "no longer be necessary" 25 years from now. That led Curt A. Levey, director of legal and public affairs at the Center for Individual Rights, the law firm representing the plaintiffs, to observe that universities would start facing new lawsuits 20 years from now if they did not heed the court's advice.

"The court says affirmative action is not timeless, and it had better not be," Mr. Levey said in an interview.

• • • • • • • • • • •

Race-Based School Assignments

Meanwhile, white families had been filing similar challenges around the country against race-conscious assignment policies used by local school systems to produce racial balance in individual schools. Supported by conservative groups, they argued the policies violated *Brown*'s central premise by assigning students to schools based on the color of their skin. School systems that adopted such plans and the civil rights advocates supporting them argued the policies were essential to achieve *Brown*'s promise of educational equality for all students—black, white, or brown.

Near the end of Chief Justice Roberts's first term, the Court agreed to take up the issue in cases from Seattle, Washington, and Jefferson County (Louisville), Kentucky. As with affirmative action cases, these attracted a huge number of briefs—more than sixty in all—with supporters outnumbering opponents. The Bush administration again backed the challengers.

Roberts announced the Court's decisions on June 28, 2007, in a dramatic climax to a term that had already seen conservative victories on such issues as abortion and campaign finance. By a 5-4 vote, the Court ruled in *Parents Involved in Community Schools v. Seattle School District No. 1* (2007) that both school districts' plans violated the equal protection rights of the white families who had challenged them. "Classifying and assigning schoolchildren according to a binary conception of race is an extreme approach in light of our precedents and our Nation's history of using race in public schools, and requires more than . . . an amorphous end to justify it," Roberts wrote.

Roberts went further in a passage joined by three other conservatives, but not Justice Kennedy. "Racial balance, pure and simple" is an "illegitimate" objective, Roberts said. "The way to stop discrimination on the basis of race," he concluded, "is to stop discriminating on the basis of race."

In an unusual procedure, Kennedy summarized his concurring opinion from the bench. He criticized the Louisville and Seattle plans, but agreed with the four liberal dissenters in finding diversity—"depending on its meaning and definition"—to be "a compelling educational goal a school district may pursue." He pointed to permissible steps, including redrawn attendance zones, "strategic site selection," allocation of resources for special programs, and targeted recruitment of faculty.

Justice Stephen G. Breyer capped the dramatic reading with a twenty-minute summary of his dissenting opinion—at seventy-seven pages, the longest he had ever written. "The Court's decision today slows down and sets back the work of local school boards to bring about racially diverse schools," Breyer said. He concluded bluntly: "This is a decision that the Court and this Nation will come to regret."

Parents Involved in Community Schools v. Seattle School District No. 1

Decided: June 28, 2007

Vote: 5 (J. Roberts, Scalia, Kennedy, Thomas, Alito)

4 (Stevens, Souter, Ginsburg, Breyer)

Opinion of the Court: J. Roberts

Concurring opinions (2): Kennedy; Thomas

Dissenting opinions (2): Stevens; Breyer (Stevens, Souter, Ginsburg)

JUNE 29, 2007
JUSTICES LIMIT THE USE OF RACE IN SCHOOL PLANS FOR INTEGRATION

By LINDA GREENHOUSE

WASHINGTON, June 28—With competing blocs of justices claiming the mantle of Brown v. Board of Education, a bitterly divided Supreme Court declared Thursday that public school systems cannot seek to achieve or maintain integration through measures that take explicit account of a student's race.

Voting 5 to 4, the court, in an opinion by Chief Justice John G. Roberts Jr., invalidated programs in Seattle and metropolitan Louisville, Ky., that sought to maintain school-by-school diversity by limiting transfers on the basis of race or using race as a "tiebreaker" for admission to particular schools.

ity, Justice Anthony M. Kennedy, did not. Justice Kennedy agreed that the two programs were unconstitutional. But he was highly critical of what he described as the chief justice's "all-too-unyielding insistence that race cannot be a factor in instances when, in my view, it may be taken into account."

In a separate opinion that could shape the practical implications of the decision and provide school districts with guidelines for how to create systems that can pass muster with the court, Justice Kennedy said achieving racial diversity, "avoiding racial isolation" and addressing "the problem of de facto resegregation in schooling" were

> " The way to stop discrimination on the basis of race is to stop discriminating on the basis of race.
>
> —Chief Justice John G. Roberts Jr.,
>
> *Parents Involved in Community Schools v. Seattle School District No. 1* "

Both programs had been upheld by lower federal courts and were similar to plans in place in hundreds of school districts around the country. Chief Justice Roberts said such programs were "directed only to racial balance, pure and simple," a goal he said was forbidden by the Constitution's guarantee of equal protection.

"The way to stop discrimination on the basis of race is to stop discriminating on the basis of race," he said. His side of the debate, the chief justice said, was "more faithful to the heritage of Brown," the landmark 1954 decision that declared school segregation unconstitutional. "When it comes to using race to assign children to schools, history will be heard," he said.

The decision came on the final day of the court's 2006–7 term, which showed an energized conservative majority in control across many areas of the court's jurisprudence.

Chief Justice Roberts's control was not quite complete, however. While Justices Antonin Scalia, Clarence Thomas and Samuel A. Alito Jr. joined his opinion on the schools case in full, the fifth member of the major-

"compelling interests" that a school district could constitutionally pursue as long as it did so through programs that were sufficiently "narrowly tailored."

The four justices were "too dismissive" of the validity of these goals, Justice Kennedy said, adding that it was "profoundly mistaken" to read the Constitution as requiring "that state and local school authorities must accept the status quo of racial isolation in schools."

As a matter of constitutional doctrine and practical impact, Justice Kennedy's opinion thus placed a significant limitation on the full reach of the other four justices' embrace of a "colorblind Constitution" under which all racially conscious government action, no matter how benign or invidious its goal, is equally suspect.

How important a limitation Justice Kennedy's opinion proves to be may become clear only with time, as school districts devise and defend plans that appear to meet his test.

Among the measures that Justice Kennedy said would be acceptable were the drawing of school attendance zones, "strategic site selection of new schools," and directing resources to special programs. These would be permissible even if adopted with a consciousness of racial demographics, Justice Kennedy said, because in avoiding the labeling and sorting of individual children by race they would satisfy the "narrow tailoring" required to meet the equal protection demands of the 14th Amendment.

Justice Stephen G. Breyer, who wrote the principal dissenting opinion, was dismissive of Justice Kennedy's proposed alternatives and asserted that the court was taking a sharp and seriously mistaken turn.

Speaking from the bench for more than 20 minutes, Justice Breyer made his points to a courtroom audience that had never seen the coolly analytical justice express himself with such emotion. His most pointed words, in fact, appeared nowhere in his 77-page opinion.

"It is not often in the law that so few have so quickly changed so much," Justice Breyer said.

In his written opinion, Justice Breyer said the decision was a "radical" step away from settled law and would strip local communities of the tools they need, and have used for many years, to prevent resegregation of their public schools. Predicting that the ruling would "substitute for present calm a disruptive round of race-related litigation," he said, "This is a decision that the court and the nation will come to regret."

Justices John Paul Stevens, David H. Souter and Ruth Bader Ginsburg signed Justice Breyer's opinion. Justice Stevens wrote a dissenting opinion of his own, as pointed as it was brief.

He said the chief justice's invocation of Brown v. Board of Education was "a cruel irony" when the opinion in fact "rewrites the history of one of this court's most important decisions" by ignoring the context in which it was issued and the Supreme Court's subsequent understanding of it to permit voluntary programs of the sort that were now invalidated.

"It is my firm conviction that no member of the court that I joined in 1975 would have agreed with today's decision," Justice Stevens said. He did not mention, nor did he need to, that one of the justices then was William H. Rehnquist, later the chief justice, for whom Chief Justice Roberts once worked as a law clerk.

Justice Clarence Thomas was equally pointed and equally personal in an opinion concurring with the majority.

"If our history has taught us anything," Justice Thomas said, "it has taught us to beware of elites bearing racial theories." He added in a footnote, "Justice Breyer's good intentions, which I do not doubt, have the shelf life of Justice Breyer's tenure."

The justices had been wrestling for over a year with the two cases. It was in January 2006 that parents who objected to the Louisville and Seattle programs filed their Supreme Court appeals from the lower court decisions that had upheld the programs.

The Louisville case was Meredith v. Jefferson County Board of Education, No. 05-915, filed by the mother of a student who was denied a transfer to his chosen kindergarten class because the school he wanted to leave needed to keep its white students to stay within the program's racial guidelines.

The Seattle case, Parents Involved in Community Schools v. Seattle School District No. 1, No. 05-908, was filed by a group of parents who had formed a nonprofit corporation to fight the city's high school assignment plan.

Because a single Supreme Court opinion resolved both cases, the decision carries only the name of the Seattle case, which had the lower docket number.

The appeals provoked a long internal struggle over how the court should respond. Months earlier, when Justice Sandra Day O'Connor was still on the court, the justices had denied review in an appeal challenging a similar program in Massachusetts. With no disagreement among the federal appellate circuits on the validity of such programs, the new appeals did not meet the criterion the court ordinarily uses to decide which cases to hear. It was June of last year before the court, reconfigured by the additions of Chief Justice Roberts and Justice Alito, announced, over the unrecorded but vigorous objection of the liberal justices, that it would hear both appeals.

By the time the court ruled on Thursday, there was little suspense over what the outcome would be. Not only the act of accepting the appeals, but also the tenor of the argument on Dec. 4, gave clear indications that the justices were on course to strike down both plans.

The cases were by far the oldest on the docket by the time they were decided; the other decisions the court announced on Thursday were in cases that were argued in March and April. What consumed the court during the seven months the cases were under consideration, it appears likely, was an effort by each side to edge Justice Kennedy closer to its point of view.

While it is hardly uncommon to find Justice Kennedy in the middle of the court, his position there this time carried a special resonance. He holds the seat once occupied by Justice Lewis F. Powell Jr. who, 29 years ago to the day, announced his separate opinion in the Bakke case. That solitary opinion, rejecting quotas but accepting diversity as a rationale for affirmative action in university admissions, defined the law for the next 25 years, until the decision was refined and to some degree strengthened in the University of Michigan Law School decision.

Justice Kennedy was a dissenter from that 2003 decision. But, surprisingly, he cited it on Thursday, invoking it to rebut the argument that the Constitution must always be, regardless of context or circumstance, colorblind.

• • • • • • • • • • • • •

SEX DISCRIMINATION

Bradwell v. Illinois

> **Decided:** April 15, 1873
>
> **Vote:** 8 (Clifford, Swayne, Miller, Davis, Field, Strong, Bradley, Hunt)
>
> 1 (S. P. Chase)
>
> **Opinion of the Court:** Miller
>
> **Concurring opinion:** Bradley (Swayne, Field)
>
> **Dissenting without opinion:** S. P. Chase

As late as the 1960s, the Supreme Court viewed the rights of women—just as most Americans did—through the lens of their traditional roles as wife, mother, and homemaker. The Court took no note of the women's suffrage movement in 1875 when it rejected the suit by the Missouri suffragist Virginia Minor to gain the right to vote. Two years earlier, the Court had rejected a suit brought by Myra Bradwell, who had passed the Illinois bar exam, to invalidate an Illinois law barring women from being licensed as attorneys. "The natural and proper timidity and delicacy which belongs to the female sex evidently unfits it for many of the occupations of civil life," Justice Bradley wrote in *Bradwell v. Illinois* (1873).

Man's role, Bradley explained, "is, or should be, woman's protector and defender." This attitude of romantic paternalism led Congress and the states to pass laws limiting women's role in the workplace and civic life. The Court found no fault with such measures. Three years after striking down a New York law limiting the hours of bakery workers, the Court upheld an Oregon statute that limited the hours of laundry workers—virtually all of them women. The difference between the sexes, the Court wrote in *Muller v. Oregon* (1908), "upholds that which is designed to compensate for some of the burdens which rest upon [women]."

MARCH 16, 1873
WOMEN PRACTICE IN THE COURTS—A TEST CASE.

From the Chicago Journal, March 13.

Mrs. Myra Bradwell, of this city, the editor of the *Legal News,* whose application to be admitted to practice law was refused by the Illinois Supreme Court, and who some time since appealed the matter to the Supreme Court of the United States, expects a decision at an early day. The question is an important one. Mrs. Bradwell bases her case upon that provision of the Fourteenth Amendment of the Constitution which recognizes as citizens "all persons born or naturalized in the United States and subject to the jurisdiction thereof." She claims that this includes women as well as men, and we do not see why not.

> " Mrs. Bradwell bases her case upon that provision of the Fourteenth Amendment . . . which recognizes as citizens 'all persons born or naturalized in the United States and subject to the jurisdiction thereof.' She claims that this includes women as well as men, and we do not see why not. "

• • • • • • • • • • • • •

Women won the right to vote with ratification of the Nineteenth Amendment in 1920, but the Court's devotion to romantic paternalism continued. In 1948 it upheld a Denver ordinance that forbade a woman from working in a bar unless she was the wife or daughter of the owner. In 1961 the Court unanimously upheld a state law automatically exempting women from jury duty. "Woman is still regarded as the center of home and family life," Justice John Marshall Harlan, whose name-sake grandfather had argued for a "colorblind Constitution" sixty-five years earlier, wrote in *Hoyt v. Florida*. The ruling was overturned in 1975. (See page 379.)

CHANGING TIDE: THE WOMEN'S RIGHTS MOVEMENT

The reenergized women's rights movement that began to emerge in the 1960s made its presence felt first in Congress and then, in the next decade, at the Supreme Court. The Court's rulings included, most prominently, the landmark decision in *Roe v. Wade* (1973) legalizing abortion during most of a woman's pregnancy. (See page 319.) The Court also established constitutional limitations on laws treating men and women differently. The "intermediate scrutiny" standard that evolved barred some forms of sex discrimination, but stopped short of prohibiting any differential treatment of men and women under the law.

Congress began to recognize the reality of women's roles outside the home in 1963 by passing the Equal Pay Act, which required employers to pay men and women equally for equal work. Title VII of the Civil Rights Act of 1964 went further by barring any differential treatment in hiring, pay, or benefits based on sex, unless sex was a "bona fide occupational qualification." Paradoxically, opponents of the bill backed the sex discrimination provision, hoping to derail the bill by making it unpalatable to many moderates.

Even as the Court began developing constitutional limits on sex discrimination in the 1970s, the two civil rights laws remained the only legal instruments available to safeguard equal treatment for women in private employment. The Court's early rulings favored women who challenged pater-nalistic employment practices that limited their employment opportunities compared with men's. In *Phillips v. Martin Marietta Corp.* (1971) the Court summarily ordered a lower court to reconsider a challenge to the aircraft manufacturer's policy of refusing to hire women with preschool children even though it hired men regardless of the age of their children.

In an influential opinion six years later, the Court struck down an Alabama law that established height and weight requirements for prison guards because they disqualified a large proportion of women but hardly any men. The ruling in *Dothard v. Rawlinson* (1977) extended the so-called dis-parate impact theory first recognized in a race discrimination case in 1971 to sex discrimination cases as well.

Four years later, the Court in *County of Washington v. Gunther* (1981) read Title VII more broadly than the Equal Pay Act to prohibit any sex-based wage discrimination even if no member of the opposite sex held an equal but higher paying job. Justice William J. Brennan Jr. was careful to specify, however, that the Court was not endorsing the "comparable worth" theory pushed by women's rights advocates, which called for broadly reevaluating pay scales in jobs traditionally held primarily by women.

In a ruling on constitutional grounds, the Court in 1974 barred government employers from adopting blanket policies requiring pregnant women to take leaves from work for specified periods before or after childbirth. The "arbitrary" and "irrational" policies violated the Due Process Clause by penalizing women for exercising their right to bear children, Justice Stewart explained in *Cleve-land Board of Education v. LaFleur*. Six months later, however, Stewart wrote for a 6-3 majority in *Geduldig v. Aiello* in holding that states could refuse to pay disability benefits to women unable to work because of pregnancy-related conditions.

Congress responded to that ruling in 1978 by passing the Pregnancy Discrimination Act, which generally prohibits job discrimination based on pregnancy or childbirth. The Court gave the law a somewhat broad reading in a decision, *Automobile Workers v. Johnson Controls, Inc.* (1991), that prohibited employers from adopting so-called fetal protection policies. Policies excluding fertile women from jobs that entailed exposure to chemicals with a risk of creating birth defects may have been "benign" in purpose, Justice Harry A. Blackmun explained, but they violated the law. He noted that men also faced risks to their reproductive systems but were not subject to the job limitations.

Evolving Gender-Based Classifications

The Court's constitutional rulings on gender-based classifications evolved in a succession of cases over a decade's time in areas ranging from probate law to university admissions. The first of the decisions, *Reed v. Reed* (1971), struck down an Idaho law that preferred men over women in appointing an administrator for the estate of a minor child who died without a will. Sally Reed, who was separated from her husband Cecil, challenged the law as a violation of the Equal Protection Clause. By a 7-0 vote, the Court agreed. Gender-based classifications "must be reasonable" and "must rest upon some ground having a fair and substantial relation to the object of the legislation," Chief Justice Burger wrote.

Two years later, the Court applied the rational basis test to strike down a Utah measure requiring divorced fathers to support their sons to age twenty-one but their daughters only to age eighteen. Using the same test, however, the Court upheld gender-based classifications in four other cases between 1974 and 1976. In *Kahn v. Shevin* (1974), for example, the Court said that a Florida property tax exemption for widows but not widowers was "reasonably designed" to cushion the financial impact of spousal loss for women "for whom that loss imposes a disproportionately heavy burden."

GINSBURG AND A STRICTER APPROACH

Meanwhile, the American Civil Liberties Union had given its backing to a law professor with an ingenious litigation strategy for leading the Court to take a stricter approach to sex classifications in the law. Future Supreme Court justice Ruth Bader Ginsburg, who had begun handling sex discrimination cases for the ACLU while teaching at Rutgers Law School, moved to New York City to become the first female tenured professor at Columbia Law School and the head of the ACLU's newly established women's rights project. Ginsburg had the insight that laws extending special benefits or exemptions to women hurt women by preserving outmoded conceptions of their roles in society and also had the immediate effect of disadvantaging men.

In the first of her cases representing the ACLU before the Court, Ginsburg challenged a federal statute that allowed all married men in the armed forces to claim dependent benefits for their wives, but denied the dependent benefits to married women unless they proved their husbands relied on them for more than half the family income. By an 8-1 vote, the Court in *Frontiero v. Richardson* (1973) ruled the statute unconstitutional on equal protection grounds. In the main opinion, Justice Brennan adopted Ginsburg's argument that sex classifications—like racial classifications—were inherently suspect; the opinion commanded only four votes, however.

Frontiero v. Richardson

Decided: May 14, 1973

Vote: 8 (Burger, Douglas, Brennan, Stewart, B. White, T. Marshall, Blackmun, Powell)

1 (Rehnquist)

Judgment of the Court: Brennan

Opinions concurring in judgment (2): Stewart; Powell (Burger, Blackmun)

Dissenting opinion: Rehnquist

MAY 22, 1973
A 'FLAMING FEMINIST' LAUDS COURT

Special to The New York Times

GLOUCESTER, Mass.—When Mrs. Sharron Frontiero, who describes herself as "a flaming feminist," heard about the recent Supreme Court judgment that female military personnel were entitled to the same dependency benefits for their husbands as servicemen for their wives, she burst out with a joyous, "Hot damn!"

The High Court's judgment came as somewhat of a surprise to the 26-year-old physical therapist, who was a first lieutenant at Maxwell Air Force Base, Ala., when she filed the class action suit in December, 1970.

A three-judge Federal District Court had rejected her argument that refusing a dependency allowance for her husband, Joseph, who was a fulltime student at Huntingdon College, Montgomery, amounted to an unconstitutional discrimination that deprived her of property without due process.

The couple had spent about $800 in legal fees, and a costly appeal to the Supreme Court seemed a financial impossibility.

"It was a lot of money for us," she said. "We told our lawyer [Joseph Levin of Montgomery, Ala.] that we couldn't afford more than $1,000, so he got us the backing of the American Civil Liberties Union and the Southern Poverty Law Center."

Mrs. Frontiero said she had originally applied for dependency benefits because she believed that her paycheck was the principal support for her husband while he attended college. After the Air Force refused the request, the former Air Force nurse brought suit.

The Federal District Court then upheld the Defense Department regulation on a point of fact, since it was

> When Mrs. Sharron Frontiero, who describes herself as 'a flaming feminist,' heard about the recent Supreme Court judgment that female military personnel were entitled to the same dependency benefits for their husbands as servicemen for their wives, she burst out with a joyous, 'Hot damn!'

"I was really put down when the decision first went against us, really crushed," Mrs. Frontiero said. "I wasn't looking forward to the Supreme Court decision."

But now that it's over, Mrs. Frontiero says "it was worth the fight." Her husband feels the same way. When she called him at work and told him of the Supreme Court's decision, he, too, burst out with a loud whoop.

"Hot damn, honey," he shouted, "we did it!"

In a moment of reflection, Mr. Frontiero added that while it took time and money, "the one real good thing about it was that it gave a real lift to the feminist movement. We like to think we've helped do something concrete rather than just talk."

"Some of the guys at work find it hard to believe that I do half the housework and iron my own shirts," Mr. Frontiero said. "But it doesn't bother me. I mean, Sharron works too, and is just as tired when she gets home."

proven that Mr. Frontiero's veteran benefits—he had been a Navy electronics specialist—covered at least half his monthly expenses.

The Supreme Court, however, ruled that female members of the armed services were entitled to the same dependency benefits as servicemen were.

Mrs. Frontiero called her suit "really a matter of principle." It asked only for remuneration of the expenses not provided during her service tour, amounting to about $2,200.

Mrs. Frontiero left the Air Force in October, 1972, when her husband graduated and took a job as an industrial hygienist at the Portsmouth Naval Shipyard in New Hampshire. Mrs. Frontiero is a visiting nurse in their new home town of Gloucester, where her husband was born (she comes from Greenfield, Mass., a small town in the western part of the state).

President Ronald Reagan and Justice Sandra Day O'Connor walk outside the Supreme Court after she was sworn in on September 25, 1981. O'Connor, the first female justice, was the only woman on the bench until Ruth Bader Ginsburg joined the Court in 1993.

Source: AP Images

Two years after the *Frontiero* ruling, Brennan led a unanimous Court in *Weinberger v. Wiesenfeld* (1975) in striking down a Social Security Act provision giving survivors' benefits to widows with small children but not widowers. The distinction between surviving mothers and surviving fathers was "entirely irrational," Brennan said. He added that it resulted in the "denigration" of the efforts of working women to contribute to their families' support.

"INTERMEDIATE SCRUTINY"

In 1976 Brennan found majority support for a compromise standard between rational basis and strict scrutiny. The decision in *Craig v. Boren* struck down an Oklahoma law allowing women but not men to drink 3.2 percent, "nonintoxicating" beer at age eighteen. Writing for six justices, Brennan said that "classifications by gender must serve important governmental objectives and must be substantially related to achievement of those objectives." Oklahoma's law failed that test, he said, because it was not substantially related to the stated goal of achieving traffic safety.

The Court followed this "intermediate scrutiny" test in two decisions in 1981 that nevertheless upheld sex-based classifications. The ruling in *Michael M. v. Superior Court of Sonoma County* upheld California's statutory rape law allowing prosecution of a male for having sex with a female younger than eighteen; the law furthered the state's aim of preventing teenage pregnancies, the 5-4 majority said. In *Rostker v. Goldberg,* the Court gave no more than lip service to the test in voting 6-3 to uphold exempting women from the military draft. Justice Rehnquist emphasized the great deference given to Congress on national security matters.

O'Connor and Ginsburg Take the Bench

In August 1981 President Ronald Reagan fulfilled a campaign pledge by naming a woman to serve on the Supreme Court: Sandra Day O'Connor, an appellate judge and former legislator in Arizona. In her first major opinion at the end of the 1981–1982 term, O'Connor led a closely divided Court in striking down a Mississippi law that barred men from enrolling at the state university's school of nursing. Adding a gloss to the *Craig v. Boren* standard, O'Connor said that a party seeking to uphold a gender-based classification must show "an exceedingly persuasive justification" for the classification. Mississippi's admission policy—justified as a means to promote educational opportunities for women—failed the test, O'Connor said, because it "tends to perpetuate the stereotyped view of nursing as an exclusively women's job." Rehnquist was among the four dissenters.

Fifteen years later, Ginsburg—who had become the second woman to serve on the Court in 1993—reaffirmed the standard from O'Connor's opinion in a decision striking down the all-male admissions policy at Virginia Military Institute, the state's prestigious military academy. Virginia vigorously defended the need for an all-male environment to impart military discipline and sought to derail the litigation by creating a military training institute for women at the nearby Mary Baldwin College.

In *United States v. Virginia* (1996), Ginsburg forcefully rejected both of the state's defenses. The all-male admissions policy improperly relied on "overbroad generalizations about the different talents, capacities, or preferences of males and females," she said. Further, the alternative provided at the women's college was inadequate. "Women seeking and fit for a VMI-quality education cannot be offered anything less, under the State's obligation to afford them genuinely equal protection," she concluded.

United States v. Virginia

> **Decided:** June 26, 1996
> **Vote:** 7 (Rehnquist, Stevens, O'Connor, Kennedy, Souter, Ginsburg, Breyer)
> 1 (Scalia)
> **Opinion of the Court:** Ginsburg
> **Opinion concurring in judgment:** Rehnquist
> **Dissenting opinion:** Scalia
> **Did not participate:** Thomas

JUNE 27, 1996
MILITARY COLLEGE CAN'T BAR WOMEN, HIGH COURT RULES

By LINDA GREENHOUSE

The Supreme Court ruled today that under the "skeptical scrutiny" that applies to government action that treats men and women differently, the State of Virginia cannot justify keeping women out of its state-supported military college, the Virginia Military Institute.

"Women seeking and fit for a V.M.I.-quality education cannot be offered anything less under the state's obligation to afford them genuinely equal protection," Justice Ruth Bader Ginsburg said in a majority opinion for six Justices.

A seventh member of the Court, Chief Justice William H. Rehnquist, agreed in a separate opinion that the all-male admissions policy at the 157-year-old military college violated the Constitution and that the remedy accepted by the lower courts, a women's "leadership" program supported with state money at a nearby women's college, was inadequate.

The vote was therefore 7 to 1 on the basic constitutional holding in one of the Court's most important sex discrimination cases in years.

The lone dissenter was Justice Antonin Scalia, who objected that "change is forced upon Virginia, and reversion to single-sex education is prohibited nationwide, not by democratic processes but by order of this Court." Justice Clarence Thomas, whose son attends V.M.I., did not take part in the case.

The opinion leaves the state with the theoretical option of turning the college into a private institution, which would be free to exclude women. But officials at the school in Lexington, Va., indicated today that this option was probably not realistic.

"Whether or not it is feasible is very problematical," Maj. Gen. Josiah Bunting 3d, the superintendent of V.M.I., said at a news conference there this afternoon. "I must discourage speculation about that."

The board of trustees will meet July 12 and 13 and decide how to proceed, General Bunting said. A 1963 graduate of V.M.I., he described the ruling as a "savage disappointment."

Also at stake is the future of the Virginia Women's Institute for Leadership at Mary Baldwin College in Staunton, Va., where 42 students have just completed their first year of a program accepted by the lower courts as a valid alternative to admission to V.M.I.

Justice Ginsburg said that the women's program was only a "pale shadow" of what V.M.I. offered to male students and that it provided none of the considerable benefits of a degree from V.M.I., long one of the most prestigious educational institutions in the South. Chief Justice Rehnquist called the women's program "distinctly inferior."

General Bunting said a foundation supported by V.M.I. alumni would continue to provide financing for the Mary Baldwin program for four more years.

The country's only other state supported all-male college, The Citadel in South Carolina, will also be governed by the ruling today. South Carolina has also proposed a separate women's program at a private college, which is awaiting review in Federal District Court in Charleston.

The case presented the Court with two questions. The first was whether the exclusion of women violated the equal protection guarantee of the 14th Amendment, as the Justice Department charged when it sued the State of Virginia in Federal District Court in Roanoke in 1990. Once the Court found the all-male admissions policy to be unconstitutional, the second question was whether the alternative women's program was sufficient to remedy the violation.

The case had a complicated history in the lower courts, with the most recent ruling, a 1995 decision by the United States Court of Appeals for the Fourth Circuit, in Richmond, answering yes to both questions. The appeals court said that while the admissions policy deprived women of equal protection, the Mary Baldwin program was "sufficiently comparable" to a V.M.I. education to solve the problem.

For women actually to enroll at V.M.I. and take part in the rigorous military-style training there would destroy "any sense of decency that still permeates the relationship

Justice Ginsburg said. The state's alternative program "affords no cure at all for the opportunities and advantages withheld from women who want a V.M.I. education and can make the grade," she said.

Justice Ginsburg said Virginia's concern, as endorsed by the appeals court, that it would be destructive to place men and women together at V.M.I. reflected the same "ancient and familiar fear" that kept women out of law and other professions until well into modern times. She said the fact that women had graduated at the top of their classes from each of the Federal military academies and were serving successfully in the military indicated that "Virginia's fears for the future of V.M.I. may not be solidly grounded."

For Justice Ginsburg, a pioneer in the field of women's rights who as a private lawyer argued and won many of the Supreme Court precedents she cited in her opinion today, this was surely a moment of deep personal satisfaction.

There was a dramatic moment in her five-minute announcement when she began discussing a 1982 precedent, Mississippi University for Women v. Hogan—not one of her own cases—that held unconstitutional the

> " Generalizations about 'the way women are,' estimates of what is appropriate for most women, no longer justify denying opportunity to women whose talent and capacity place them outside the average description. "
>
> —Justice Ruth Bader Ginsburg, *United States v. Virginia*

between the sexes," the appeals court said in an opinion that emphasized the spartan nature of barracks life and the brutalities of the "rat line" in which older students scream at and harass first-year cadets.

In her opinion today, Justice Ginsburg dismantled the appeals court's analysis in a manner both methodical and sweeping. While it might be true that most women would neither choose nor benefit from the educational methods at V.M.I., that was beside the point, she said, noting that the state never declared that a V.M.I. education was suitable for most men either.

"Generalizations about 'the way women are,' estimates of what is appropriate for most women, no longer justify denying opportunity to women whose talent and capacity place them outside the average description,"

exclusion of men from a state-supported nursing school. A state could not base admissions decisions on "archaic and stereotypic notions" of "proper" roles for men and women, the Hogan decision held.

The author of that decision was Justice Sandra Day O'Connor, then the junior Justice and still a curiosity as the first woman to serve on the Court. When Justice Ginsburg first referred to the Hogan case this morning, she lifted her eyes from the memo she was reading and gazed for a moment at Justice O'Connor. With just the barest hint of a smile, Justice O'Connor stared straight ahead.

The Clinton Administration had asked the Court to use this case, United States v. Virginia, No. 94-1941, to establish that official distinctions on the basis of sex should be just according to the same "strict scrutiny" that applies to distinctions based on race. The Court narrowly rejected taking that step in a case Justice Ginsburg argued in the 1970's.

Justice Ginsburg referred only obliquely to the issue today, instead applying what she called a "skeptical scrutiny" under which the state must demonstrate an "exceedingly persuasive justification" for any official action that treats men and women differently.

"The justification must be genuine, not hypothesized or invented post hoc in response to litigation," she said. "And it must not rely on overbroad generalizations about the different talents, capacities, or preferences of males and females."

She said that in its willingness to accept Virginia's alternative women's program as "sufficiently comparable," the appeals court ignored the Supreme Court's insistence on searching scrutiny in sex discrimination cases and "substituted a standard of its own invention."

The opinion today did not so much make new law on this issue as apply the existing standard in a forceful way. The Court's standard of review in sex discrimination cases "seemed to mean different things to different appeals courts" before today's decision, said Judith Lichtman, the president of the Women's Legal Defense Fund.

In his concurring opinion, Chief Justice Rehnquist objected that the Court had unnecessarily chosen a new verbal formulation, introducing an "element of uncertainty" into sex discrimination analysis.

The Chief Justice addressed Virginia's argument that an all-male V.M.I. served a policy of diversity in education. "The difficulty with its position is that the diversity benefited only one sex," the Chief Justice said, adding that while the Hogan decision "placed Virginia on notice" 14 years ago that the V.M.I. admissions policy was possibly unconstitutional, "the state did nothing." A high-quality, fully financed women's alternative program might have sufficed, he said.

In his dissenting opinion, which at 40 pages was a page shorter than the majority opinion, Justice Scalia described the decision as "not the interpretation of a Constitution, but the creation of one." He said that the rationale of the majority opinion threatened the continued existence of private single-sex colleges that receive various forms of Federal aid including tax-exempt status. But he said there was "substantial hope, I am happy and ashamed to say," that the Court would never take its analysis that far.

Cadets on the V.M.I. parade ground expressed deep disappointment today, saying the ruling would disturb the cohesion of the cadets.

"We don't have doors on the stalls in the bathrooms," said David F. Nash, a 20-year-old international studies major from Virginia Beach, who this fall will be a second-classman, or junior. "We have a group shower, and we have windows on our doors. There's virtually no place where you're really alone. It helps break you down. Everyone's equal: No one is behind a closed door, and no one is better."

- - - - - - - - - - - -

THE COURT ON SEXUAL HARASSMENT

Beginning in the mid-1980s, the Court also expanded the reach of Title VII by interpreting it to ban sexual harassment in the workplace. In *Meritor Savings Bank v. Vinson* (1986), Justice Rehnquist wrote for a unanimous Court in holding that "severe or pervasive sexual harassment" could be found to create "an abusive working environment" and thereby amount to discrimination on the basis of sex. The ruling reinstated a complaint by a former employee of a Washington, D.C., bank, who said one of her supervisors repeatedly pressed her for sexual favors over a four-year period. The supervisor denied the allegations; a lower court had dismissed the suit on the ground that any sexual relations had been voluntary.

The Supreme Court ruling spawned a substantial increase in sexual harassment claims before the Equal Employment Opportunity Commission and in federal courts. The Court took up several cases in the 1990s to settle secondary issues that had arisen. In *Harris v. Forklift Systems, Inc.* (1993), the Court ruled that an employee need not prove serious psychological injury to hold an employer liable for a hostile work environment. In *Oncale v. Sundowner Offshore Services, Inc.* (1998), the Court ruled that men could also sue for sexual harassment. The ruling reinstated a claim by a Louisiana oil rig worker who said he had to quit his job after being subjected to sexual abuse, humiliation, and threats by two male supervisors.

In a pair of companion cases the same year, the Court also clarified when an employer could be found responsible for sexual harassment of an employee by a supervisor. *Faragher v. City of Boca Raton* (1998) and *Burlington Industries, Inc. v. Ellerth* (1998) each held that an employer could avoid liability if it showed that it "exercised reasonable care to prevent and correct promptly any sexually harassing behavior" and that the plaintiff "unreasonably failed to take advantage of any preventive or corrective opportunities provided." Employment law experts forecast the ruling would lead most big employers to institute sexual harassment reporting and compliance procedures.

"SUSPECT" CLASSES; "FUNDAMENTAL" INTEREST

The Supreme Court's equal protection decisions give heightened scrutiny to some other classifications besides those based on race, nationality, or sex. Alienage is the only other category specifically designated as inherently suspect, but even in modern times the Court has upheld some state and federal laws burdening aliens' rights. Conversely, the Court has overturned a number of laws that disadvantage the poor in regard to "fundamental" rights or interests without ruling poverty a suspect classification. In a few other instances, the Court has overturned laws challenged on equal protection grounds because they singled out a class of persons for unfavorable treatment for no legitimate reason.

THE RIGHTS OF ALIENS

Through the years, federal and state governments have enacted various laws limiting employment of, land ownership by, and government benefits to aliens. Challenges have produced various results. The Court in 1915 struck down an Arizona law requiring private employers to hire aliens as no more than 20 percent of their workers. In 1927, however, the Court upheld a Cincinnati ordinance that barred aliens from working in pool halls. The city claimed that aliens operating pool halls posed a special menace to society.

The Court in 1914 upheld a Pennsylvania law barring aliens from game hunting. In 1923 it upheld state laws barring Japanese and other Asian aliens from owning land. The Court changed directions on both issues after the end of World War II, however. In *Oyama v. California* (1948), the Court limited the scope of the state's Alien Land Law, and stripped it of its effectiveness, by ruling in favor of a U.S. citizen of Japanese ancestry who received land as a gift from his noncitizen father. Six months later, the Court invalidated another California law that prohibited Japanese aliens from fishing in the state's coastal waters. State laws discriminating against lawful aliens conflict with the federal government's power to regulate immigration, the Court said in *Takahashi v. Fish and Game Commission* (1948).

ALIENAGE AS A "SUSPECT" CLASSIFICATION

The modern era began with a 1971 decision, *Graham v. Richardson*—the Supreme Court's first declaration that alienage is an "inherently suspect" classification. The unanimous ruling struck down an Arizona law restricting certain welfare benefits to citizens or aliens who had resided in the United States for at least fifteen years. "Aliens as a class are a prime example of a 'discrete and insular' minority . . . for whom heightened judicial solicitude is appropriate," Justice Blackmun wrote. In 1976, however, the Court ruled that the federal government could bar Medicare benefits to aliens unless they had been permanent residents for at least five years.

Through the 1970s, the Court followed the stricter approach in striking down state laws barring aliens from becoming lawyers (Connecticut), engineers (Puerto Rico), state civil servants (New

York), or notaries public (Texas). In 1976, the Court ruled in *Hampton v. Mow Sun Wong* that the U.S. Civil Service Commission could not bar aliens from the federal civil service. In 1979, however, the Court voted 5-4 to sustain a New York law prohibiting aliens who refuse to become U.S. citizens from working as public school teachers. "Some state functions are so bound up with the operation of the State as a governmental entity as to permit the exclusion from those functions of all persons who have not become part of the process of self-government," Justice Powell wrote for the majority in *Ambach v. Norwick*.

In perhaps the most controversial of the decisions, the Court in 1982 ruled, 5-4, that children of illegal aliens cannot be denied public education. The ruling in *Plyler v. Doe* struck down a Texas law under the lax rational-basis test. For the majority, Justice Brennan said that any savings in educational costs were "wholly insubstantial in light of the costs involved to these children, the State, and the Nation." Chief Justice Burger led four dissenters.

Plyler v. Doe

Decided: June 15, 1982

Vote: 5 (Brennan, T. Marshall, Blackmun, Powell, Stevens)

4 (Burger, B. White, Rehnquist, O'Connor)

Opinion of the Court: Brennan

Concurring opinions (3): T. Marshall; Blackmun; Powell

Dissenting opinion: Burger (B. White, Rehnquist, O'Connor)

JUNE 16, 1982
JUSTICES RULE STATES MUST PAY TO EDUCATE ILLEGAL ALIEN PUPILS

By LINDA GREENHOUSE

Special to The New York Times

WASHINGTON, June 15—The Supreme Court ruled today, 5 to 4, that children who are illegal aliens have a constitutional right to a free public education.

The Court said that a Texas law, which was declared unconstitutional earlier in two separate rulings by the . . . United States Court of Appeals for the Fifth Circuit, violated the children's constitutional right to equal protection of the laws.

In an opinion by Associate Justice William J. Brennan Jr., the Court struck down the statute, which cut off state funds from local school districts for educating children who had not been "legally admitted" to the United States. Under that law, the local districts could either charge the children tuition or bar them from school.

The decision marked the first time that the Supreme Court had held explicitly that the 14th Amendment's equal protection guarantee "extends to anyone, citizen or stranger," who is within a state's boundaries, regardless of immigration status.

The Court was unanimous in rejecting the argument of Texas that the equal protection clause did not apply to illegal aliens. But while it was essential to the outcome, that issue was only a preliminary one in the case. The Justices split sharply on the ultimate issue before the Court: whether the alien children's right to "equal protection" encompassed the right to the same education offered to all other children in Texas.

In concluding that it does, Justice Brennan wrote of the fundamental role of education "in maintaining the fabric of our society," of the "inestimable toll" exacted by a lack of basic literacy and of the unfairness of penalizing children for their parents' illegal status. "Legislation directing the onus of a parent's misconduct against his children does not comport with fundamental conceptions of justice," Justice Brennan said.

In a dissenting opinion, Chief Justice Warren E. Burger charged that the majority "employs, and in my view abuses, the 14th Amendment in an effort to become an omnipotent and omniscient problem solver."

Justice Brennan and Chief Justice Burger have for years opposed each other on many issues. But rarely have the differences in their basic view of the Constitution and the courts been as sharply etched.

DISSENT BY CHIEF JUSTICE

The equal protection clause, the Chief Justice said, "is not an all-encompassing 'equalizer' designed to eradicate every distinction for which persons are not 'responsible.'" He said, "The Constitution does not provide a cure for every social ill, nor does it vest judges with a mandate to try to remedy every social problem."

Justice Brennan's opinion was joined by Associate Justices Thurgood Marshall, Harry A. Blackmun, Lewis F. Powell and John Paul Stevens. The Chief Justice's dissenting opinion was also signed by Associate Justices Byron R. White, William H. Rehnquist and Sandra Day O'Connor.

The decision, Plyler v. Doe (No. 80-1538), concerned only children and only public education. The close vote, as well as the majority's emphasis on the special role of education and the special needs of children, indicated that a majority of the Court would be unlikely to extend the analysis to a ruling that adult illegal aliens are constitutionally entitled to Government benefits, such as welfare.

The Texas law, the only one cutting off school funds for illegal aliens in the nation, had been challenged in separate lawsuits by the Mexican-American Legal Defense and Educational Fund and by a group of legal aid lawyers.

Illegal immigration is a heated political issue in Texas. The state defended the law in the lower courts in part on the ground that its school system would be overwhelmed by the cost of educating an estimated 110,000 children who are illegal aliens. However, in 1980, when Justice Powell ordered the state not to enforce the law while the case was on appeal, only 11,000 illegal aliens enrolled in the state's schools out of a total enrollment of 2.2 million.

protection cases, and the level applied almost always determines the result. At the lowest level, for which Chief Justice Burger argued in his dissent, a challenged law will be upheld if it is merely "rational," a test that can almost always be met.

The highest level, "strict scrutiny," appeared foreclosed by the Court's precedents, including a 1973 decision by Justice Powell in which the Court ruled that education was not a "fundamental right." To prevail, Justice Brennan had to persuade a majority of the Court, including Justice Powell, to apply the middle level of scrutiny, under which a challenged law is struck down unless it furthers a "substantial," rather than a merely rational, interest of the state.

He succeeded by arguing that although education is not a fundamental right in the abstract, the Texas law should be subjected to heightened scrutiny because it "imposes a lifetime hardship on a discrete class of children not accountable for their disabling status."

"By denying these children a basic education," he said, "we deny them the ability to live within the structure of our civic institutions, and foreclose any realistic possi-

> By denying these children a basic education, we deny them the ability to live within the structure of our civic institutions, and foreclose any realistic possibility that they will contribute in even the smallest way to the progress of our Nation.
>
> —Justice William J. Brennan Jr., *Plyler v. Doe*

JUSTICE DEPT. BACKED PLAINTIFFS

The case moved through the lower courts in the Carter Administration, and the Justice Department supported the plaintiffs' equal protection challenge. Before the Supreme Court heard the argument last fall, however, the department abandoned that position. It told the Court that while it believed the equal protection clause applied to illegal aliens, the Federal Government had no legal "interest" in the constitutionality of the Texas law and would therefore take no position.

For the Court, the key analytical issue in the case was the standard by which to judge the Texas law. The Court applies three distinct levels of scrutiny to equal

bility that they will contribute in even the smallest way to the progress of our nation." In reviewing the law, he said, "we may appropriately take into account its costs to the nation and to the innocent children who are its victims."

Once the majority subjected the law to "heightened scrutiny," it quickly decided that Texas had failed to defend the law as serving a "substantial" interest. Justice Brennan said the state had failed to show that illegal immigration was a "significant burden" on the state's economy or school system, or that the prospect of free education was a spur to would-be migrants.

"It is difficult to understand," he said, "precisely what the state hopes to achieve by promoting the perpetuation of a subclass of illiterates within our boundaries, surely adding to the problems and costs of unemployment, welfare and crime."

Any fiscal savings, the justice said, "are wholly insubstantial in light of the costs involved to these children, the state and the nation."

. . . .

WEALTH-BASED CLASSIFICATIONS

Without ruling poverty a suspect classification, the Court in several cases has found wealth-based classifications to violate equal protection when they deprive poor people of fundamental rights without sufficient justification. In the first such decision, the Court ruled, 5-4, that Illinois was violating indigent defendants' rights in felony cases by refusing to provide a free trial transcript—as needed to appeal a conviction. "In criminal trials a State can no more discriminate on account of poverty than on account of religion, race, or color," Justice Hugo L. Black wrote in a plurality opinion for four justices in *Griffin v. Illinois* (1956).

The Court expanded the ruling to misdemeanor cases in 1971; that decision was unanimous. Two decades later, the Court held that a state could not prevent an indigent from challenging a parental termination order if she could not afford to pay for a transcript. "We place decrees forever terminating parental rights in the category of cases in which the State may not 'bolt the door to equal justice,' " Justice Ginsburg wrote in *M.L.B. v. S.L.J.* (1996), quoting from the *Griffin* decision. The vote was 6-3.

In an earlier criminal case, the Court had ruled that California was violating indigent defendants' rights by providing a free lawyer on appeal only if a court determined that legal counsel would be advantageous. The ruling in *Douglas v. California* (1963) was a companion to the landmark decision, *Gideon v. Wainwright* (1963), guaranteeing indigent defendants free legal counsel in felony trials based on due process grounds. (See page 376.)

The Court expanded safeguards for indigent litigants in three other cases in the early 1970s. *Williams v. Illinois* (1970) held that a state cannot keep poor people in jail past the expiration of a sentence merely to work off a fine they were unable to pay. In 1971 the Court said that a "30 days or $30" sentence also violated indigent defendants' rights.

In the same year, the Court ruled in *Boddie v. Connecticut* (1971) that states could not prevent indigent persons from seeking a divorce if they were unable to pay a filing fee—$60 in the specific case. The state's interest in discouraging frivolous suits, Justice Harlan wrote in the 8-1 decision, was insufficient to overcome the indigents' interest "in having access to the only avenue open for dissolving their . . . marriages." But two years later the Court upheld, 5-4, a federal law requiring indigents to pay a fee—then $50—to declare bankruptcy. "There is no constitutional right to obtain a discharge of debts in bankruptcy," Justice Blackmun wrote in *United States v. Kras* (1973).

Equal rights advocates suffered a narrow defeat that same year in a case that they had hoped could produce a major victory for educational equity. By a 5-4 vote, the Court upheld the nearly universal practice of using property taxes to finance public elementary and secondary education. The system resulted in more money for schools in wealthy districts and less in poorer districts—including urban districts with disproportionate numbers of minority students.

Writing for the majority in *San Antonio Independent School District v. Rodriguez* (1973), Justice Powell said that the Constitution does not guarantee a right to education and that Texas's school financing system did not deny an education to any identifiable group of poor persons. "At least where wealth is involved," Powell wrote, "the Equal Protection Clause does not require absolute equality or precisely equal advantages." Justice Marshall, architect of the successful school desegregation litigation decades earlier, led the four dissenters.

San Antonio Independent School District v. Rodriguez

Decided: March 21, 1973

Vote: 5 (Burger, Stewart, Blackmun, Powell, Rehnquist)

4 (Douglas, Brennan, B. White, T. Marshall)

Opinion of the Court: Powell

Concurring opinion: Stewart

Dissenting opinions (3): Brennan; B. White (Douglas, Brennan); T. Marshall (Douglas)

MARCH 22, 1973
COURT, 5-4, BACKS SCHOOLS IN TEXAS ON PROPERTY TAX

Holds State Laws Are Not Void Just Because Their Benefits 'Fall Unevenly'

MARSHALL IN A DISSENT

He Terms Ruling a Retreat From the Commitment to Equality of Opportunity

By WARREN WEAVER Jr.

Special to The New York Times

WASHINGTON, March 21—The Supreme Court held today that the states could finance their public school systems in part with property taxes that provided more money and better educational facilities for pupils who lived in wealthier districts.

The decision, by a 5-to-4 vote, upheld the constitutionality of the Texas school finance system, which effectively prevents districts with relatively low property values from spending as much money on education as do those with higher property values.

The minority consisted of four Democrats, with Associate Justices Byron R. White and Thurgood Marshall writing minority opinions, joined by William O. Douglas and William J. Brennan Jr.

SCHOOL QUALITY VARIES

Justice Marshall called the decision "a retreat from our historic commitment to equality of educational opportunity and . . . unsupportable acquiescence in a system which

> " The Justices of this Court lack both the expertise and the familiarity with local problems so necessary to the making of wise decisions with respect to the raising and disposition of public revenues. "
>
> Justice Lewis F. Powell Jr.,
> *San Antonio Independent School District v. Rodriguez*

If a single Justice had shifted his vote, reversing the Court's ruling, the school system of every state except that of Hawaii would have been materially affected, with residents of richer districts paying more taxes to help support comparable standards in poorer districts.

'BURDENS FALL UNEVENLY'

But a bare majority of the Court concluded that state laws for financing public services should not be declared unconstitutional "merely because the burdens or benefits thereof fall unevenly, depending upon the relative wealth of the political subdivisions in which citizens live."

All five Republicans, four of them appointees of President Nixon, voted to sustain the Texas school plan. Associate Justice Lewis F. Powell Jr. wrote the majority opinion in which Chief Justice Warren E. Burger and Associate Justices Potter Stewart, Harry A. Blackmun and William H. Rehnquist concurred.

deprives children in their earliest years of the chance to reach their full potential as citizens."

The majority, he said, decided "that a state may constitutionally vary the quality of education which it offers its children in accordance with the amount of taxable wealth located within the school districts within which they reside."

Challenging the constitutionality of the Texas law were 15 Mexican-American families living in the Edgewood district of San Antonio, where the total public school expenditure in 1967–68, from Federal, state and local sources, was $356 per pupil.

In San Antonio's most affluent district, Alamo Heights, the comparable figure was $594 per pupil. The difference was largely attributable to the amount that the wealthier district was able to raise by property taxes.

Justice Powell wrote in the majority opinion that the equal protection clause of the Constitution did not require "absolute equality or precisely equal advantages," and that the relative poverty of the Edgewood parents "has not occasioned an absolute deprivation of the desired [educational] benefit."

"The Justices of this Court lack both the expertise and the familiarity with local problems so necessary to the making of wise decisions with respect to the raising and disposition of public revenues," the majority continued.

When educational experts disagree on how and where to raise and spend money, Justice Powell wrote, "the judiciary is well advised to refrain from interposing on the states inflexible constitutional restraints that could circumscribe or handicap . . . continued research and experimentation."

Although the majority felt it necessary to declare that its action "is not to be viewed as placing its judicial imprimatur on the status quo" in educational finance, the same justices said that recommendations in the dissent would have produced "an unprecedented upheaval in public education."

The court's decision was criticized by the acting executive secretary of the National Educational Association, Allan M. West, who said, "The yield of crops and concentration of wealth in individual communities will continue to determine the kind of education each child receives."

He emphasized that the Court's ruling did not prevent individual states from adopting school financing plans designed to produce greater equality than property tax systems generally do.

In his dissent, Justice Marshall did not hold out much hope that parents—like the plaintiffs in this case—could persuade a legislature to rewrite the education spending formulas in their favor.

"I, for one, am unsatisfied," he wrote, "with the hope of an ultimate 'political' solution sometime in the indefinite future while, in the meantime, countless children unjustifiably receive inferior educations that 'may affect their hearts and minds in a way unlikely ever to be undone.' "

The last phrase was a quotation from the Supreme Court's landmark decision of 1954 prohibiting segregation in the public schools.

In deciding the case, the Court produced five separate opinions totaling 136 pages.

MARCH 22, 1973
PLAINTIFF IS BITTER
Special to The New York Times

SAN ANTONIO, Tex., March 21—Demetrio P. Rodriguez, the original signer of the petition that lead to the Supreme Court's ruling, said today:

"I cannot avoid at this moment feeling deep and bitter resentment against the supreme jurists and the persons who nominated them to that high position. The poor people have lost again, not only in Texas but in the United States, because we definitely need changes in the educational system." . . .

• • • • • • • • • • • •

The Court has been more skeptical of laws imposing wealth-based restrictions on political rights. After initially upholding state poll taxes in 1937, the Court reversed itself and outlawed the practice in 1966. (See page 232.) Twice, the Court has ruled that states may not use filing fee requirements to keep poor people off the ballot. *Bullock v. Carter* (1972) struck down a Texas statute that based the filing fee in party primaries on the costs of conducting those elections. The fees ran as high as $8,900 for some races. The Court expanded the ruling in *Lubin v. Parish* (1974) by holding that California could not deny an indigent a spot on the ballot simply because he could not pay the fee, no matter how reasonable the amount.

RESIDENCY REQUIREMENTS

The Court has struck down some state residency requirements for receiving government benefits as an impermissible burden on the fundamental right to travel. In *Shapiro v. Thompson* (1969), the Court struck down one-year residency requirements in Connecticut, Pennsylvania, and the District of Columbia. A classification that penalizes the right to travel is unconstitutional unless necessary to promote a compelling governmental interest, the 6-3 majority said. In 1974 the Court similarly struck down an Arizona law requiring one year's residency to be eligible for free nonemergency medical care.

Twenty-five years later, the Court ruled on slightly different grounds that California could not limit new residents' level of welfare benefits to that received in their former state. *Saenz v. Roe* (1999) held the differential violated the new residents' right to travel under the Fourteenth Amendment's Privileges and Immunities Clause because they were treated less favorably than longtime residents of the state.

OTHER CLASSES

Romer v. Evans

Decided: May 20, 1996

Vote: 6 (Stevens, O'Connor, Kennedy, Souter, Ginsburg, Breyer)

3 (Rehnquist, Scalia, Thomas)

Opinion of the Court: Kennedy

Dissenting opinion: Scalia (Rehnquist, Thomas)

The Court has never treated homosexuals as a suspect class. But in *Romer v. Evans* (1996), the Court struck down a Colorado initiative that barred the state or any municipality from passing a law to prohibit discrimination on the basis of sexual orientation. The measure "classifies homosexuals not to further a proper legislative end but to make them unequal to everyone else," Justice Kennedy wrote for the 6-3 majority. "This Colorado cannot do." Later, Kennedy wrote the opinion for the Court in 2003 that ruled laws criminalizing gay sex as unconstitutional on privacy grounds. (See page 331.)

MAY 21, 1996
RULING SIGNALS MORE FIGHTS TO COME
By DAVID W. DUNLAP

Ordinarily, Suzanne B. Goldberg, a lawyer with the Lambda Legal Defense and Education Fund, measures her words painstakingly and pronounces them softly. Yesterday, she allowed herself some jubilation.

"This is the most important victory ever for lesbian and gay rights," said Ms. Goldberg, a member of the legal team that prevailed as the Supreme Court struck down Amendment 2 of the Colorado state constitution, which would have forbidden local laws protecting homosexuals from discrimination.

Another member of the legal team, Matt Coles of the American Civil Liberties Union, said the ruling "ought to put an end" to similar initiatives in other states and would weaken the Government's position in barring homosexuals from serving openly in the military.

"For the first time," Mr. Coles said, "the Supreme Court has said that the Government cannot justify discrimination simply out of hostility and fear." He and Ms. Goldberg said the outcome might also affect challenges to sodomy laws, custody battles involving gay parents and laws foreclosing recognition of same-sex marriages.

Conservatives, who believe that anti-bias laws effectively create special rights for homosexuals, said the decision would not necessarily have such a broad legal impact. But they acknowledged its social magnitude.

"What the majority opinion has done is undercut the right of citizens to preserve their view of sexual morality," said Jay A. Sekulow of the American Center for Law and Justice in Virginia Beach, Va., a conservative organization founded and headed by Pat Robertson. "This does send a signal to America that there has been a shift of momentum towards the homosexual community, there's no doubt about it."

Mayor Wellington Webb of Denver, where an anti-bias law had been overturned by Amendment 2, declared "a day of celebration for our city, state and the nation."

Before they could begin their parties, advocates of civil-rights measures for lesbians and gay men simply marveled at the outcome, given that the Supreme Court had ruled only 10 years ago that the Constitution did not protect homosexual relations between consenting adults.

"I'm in shock more than anything else," said Richard G. Evans, a gay man who works for Mayor Webb and who was the plaintiff whose name was given to the Amendment 2 case, captioned Romer vs. Evans.

The Romer in the case, Gov. Roy Romer of Colorado, said: "It is helpful to have a final answer. Now let's find out how we can live together under the law."

"The fact that the Court did not agree with the 'special-rights' argument is important," she said. "And it's really important for gay people that the Court is talking about us in line with equal protection under the law."

Despite the decision, Carolyn H. T. Cosby of Concerned Maine Families, the chief proponent of last year's ballot measure, said she would press on with her new campaign to prohibit recognition of same-sex marriage in the state.

And Will Perkins, the executive board chairman of Colorado for Family Values, which sponsored Amendment 2, raised the possibility of an impeachment drive against the six Supreme Court justices in the majority.

"When the American people see what has happened today and begin to understand how this goes into every aspect of our culture," he said, "then I think it's very possible that kind of call will be made.

"Today is a truly chilling day for people of conscience across America," Mr. Perkins said. "Those forces bent on

> " The Romer in the case, Gov. Roy Romer of Colorado, said: 'It is helpful to have a final answer. Now let's find out how we can live together under the law.' "

"The amendment is not operable and not enforceable," the Governor said.

Because of legal challenges, Amendment 2 never took effect. But in the four years since it was enacted, similar initiatives have passed in Cincinnati; Alachua County, Fla., and in nearly 30 counties and towns in Oregon.

But other statewide initiatives have failed. Last November, voters in Maine defeated a ballot measure that would have nullified and prohibited local laws protecting homosexuals from discrimination.

Patricia A. Peard, a lawyer in Portland, Me., who was a leading opponent of the ballot measure, said yesterday's decision would be "helpful to all of us trying to fight these clearly discriminatory referenda."

forcing a deviant life style down the throats of the American people have moved a long step forward in making Government their pet bully."

Mr. Sekulow did not go nearly so far. "This is not Roe v. Wade for gays and lesbians," he said. "This is the first case of many to come."

In one respect, Frank Whitworth, the executive director of a gay support group known as Ground Zero in Colorado Springs, agreed with that assessment.

"This is not the end to this fight by gays and lesbians for equality under the law," he said. But he added that the battle could be interrupted long enough for a celebration. "Our community—which wasn't a community until this all happened—will come out in force, I'm sure," he said.

· · · · · · · · · · · ·

In another equal protection case, the Court refused to make developmentally disabled people a suspect class, but appeared to use somewhat heightened scrutiny in striking down a city's decision to deny a special use permit for a group home for mentally retarded adults in a residential neighborhood. Requiring a permit for this group home but not for others was based on "an irrational prejudice against the mentally retarded," the Court said in *City of Cleburne v. Cleburne Living Center, Inc.* (1985).

LIBERTY, PROPERTY, AND DUE PROCESS

CHAPTER 8

Estelle Griswold had a curious hope on the morning of November 2, 1961, when she opened a family planning clinic for married women in a former nineteenth-century mansion at 79 Trumbull Street in New Haven, Connecticut. She wanted to get arrested.

As executive director of the Planned Parenthood League of Connecticut, Griswold had been fighting for years to get rid of an 1879 state law that made it a crime to use contraceptive devices or drugs or, by inference, to give advice on their use. Twice, the organization had taken the issue to the Supreme Court of the United States, only to have the justices turn the cases away on the ground that the plaintiffs lacked legal standing to challenge the law.

Abortion has become one of the most socially charged issues that the Supreme Court faces today. The core constitutional right to an abortion, decided in *Roe v. Wade* (1973) remains, but the Court has narrowed the impact of the ruling in several cases. Any decision will draw impassioned protesters to the sidewalk in front of the Supreme Court plaza. Here, a group kneels, holding copies of the Court's decision in *Gonzales v. Carhart* (2007), which upheld a federal ban on "partial-birth abortion."

In a June 19, 1961, ruling, however, the Court was closely divided. The five justices who voted in *Poe v. Ullman* (1961) to dismiss the case explained that Connecticut had never enforced the law except in response to litigation. Among the four justices who wanted to decide the case, one—the moderate conservative John Marshall Harlan—called the law "an intolerable and unjustifiable invasion of privacy in the conduct of the most intimate concerns of an individual's personal life."

The plaintiffs in *Poe*—a married couple and a housewife, suing under pseudonyms, and a Yale Medical School obstetrician, Dr. C. Lee Buxton—had been unable to convince a majority of the justices that they were at risk of prosecution under the unenforced law. Griswold responded to the nonruling by deciding to open a clinic, advertise for patients, and challenge law enforcement to come and get her.

Happily for Griswold, the news conference announcing the opening of the clinic was enough to prompt a citizen complaint that resulted ten days later in charges filed against her and Buxton, who was the clinic's medical director. To avoid further liability, Griswold closed the clinic. She and Buxton were later convicted and fined $100 each. As expected, the Connecticut Supreme Court upheld the convictions—setting the stage for the hoped-for, real-stakes showdown at the U.S. Supreme Court.

Justices across the ideological spectrum made clear their discomfort with the law during the March 30, 1965, arguments. When the state's attorney, Joseph Clark, said the law's goal was to "act as a deterrent to sexual intercourse outside marriage," Justice Potter Stewart noted that the clinic claimed to be advising only married women. But to persuade the justices to strike the law down, Yale law professor Thomas Emerson had to attack it not merely as illogical but also as unconstitutional.

Emerson told the justices that the law amounted to an invasion of privacy—a right that he said could be traced to several of the provisions of the Bill of Rights. In addition, he argued that the law violated the broadly phrased constitutional prohibition against depriving anyone of "life, liberty, or property without due process of law."

Early in the twentieth century, the Due Process Clause—found in both the Fifth and Fourteenth Amendments—had been used by the Court to protect property rights against laws passed by Congress or state legislatures regulating economic affairs. Since the late 1930s, however, the doctrine of "substantive due process" had fallen into disfavor as an invitation for judges to second-guess policy decisions of the political branches of government.

Three months after arguments, the Court's 7-2 ruling in *Griswold v. Connecticut* (1965) gave birth control advocates their long-sought victory as the Court wiped the contraceptives law off the books. The justices, however, failed to reach complete agreement on the reasons for striking down the statute. Justice William O. Douglas agreed with Emerson's primary argument and recognized a right of privacy that he said could be seen in "the penumbras" of several provisions in the Bill of Rights. But three of the four justices who joined Douglas's opinion wrote separately to emphasize specifically the Ninth Amendment's protection for "unenumerated" rights not listed elsewhere in the Bill of Rights. Two others rested their conclusions on what Harlan called the law's intrusion on "values implicit in the concept of ordered liberty" as protected by the Due Process Clause.

JUNE 8, 1965
HIGH COURT BARS CURBS ON BIRTH CONTROL; FINDS CONNECTICUT LAW INVADES PRIVACY

7-to-2 Ruling Establishes Marriage Privileges—Stirs Debate

By FRED P. GRAHAM

Special to The New York Times

WASHINGTON, June 7—The Supreme Court struck down the Connecticut birth-control law today in a sweeping decision that established a new constitutional "right of privacy."

In a 7-to-2 ruling the Court invalidated the 1879 law, which forbids the use of contraceptives by anyone, including married couples.

The seven justices in the majority were divided on the proper constitutional provision to use in striking down the law, but they agreed that married couples had private rights that could not be abridged in such a manner.

The majority ruling was written by Justice William O. Douglas. It touched off a controversy as the two dissenters, Justice Potter Stewart and Justice Hugo L. Black, charged that the decision revived the Court's earlier policy of strik-

ing down legislation that it considered unreasonable, even when the law did not violate a specific provision of the Constitution.

The dissenters said that in lieu of a specific constitutional prohibition against laws invading a citizen's privacy, the Court should not rely on vague concepts of "fundamental rights" or "liberty" to strike down a repugnant law.

The Court had avoided striking down the Connecticut law in two previous cases by holding that the law was not properly before it.

In 1942 it refused to rule on a doctor's claim that the law violated his rights to counsel his patients about contraceptives. The Court held he could not challenge the law on behalf of his patients, but only for himself.

In 1961 a group of women contended they could not get birth control advice needed for reasons of health. The Court said their claim presented no real controversy because the law had never been enforced against users of contraceptives, but only against birth control clinics.

In the case decided today two leaders of the Connecticut Planned Parenthood League had been fined $100 each for operating a birth control clinic in New Haven.

THE CLINIC IS CLOSED

Mrs. Estelle T. Griswold, executive director of the league, and Dr. C. Lee Buxton, a professor at the Yale Medical School and medical director of the clinic, were arrested on Nov. 10, 1961 and charged with aiding and abetting their patients to violate the law. After the arrests the clinic was closed.

Five justices joined in three concurring opinions holding there was a constitutional right of privacy, but disagreed upon which provision of the Constitution created it.

Justice Arthur J. Goldberg said in a concurring opinion signed by Chief Justice Earl Warren and Justice William J. Brennan that the Ninth Amendment protected "fundamental rights" not specifically mentioned in the Constitution and the Bill of Rights.

The Ninth Amendment says: "The enumeration in the Constitution, of certain rights, shall not be construed to deny or disparage others retained by the people."

Justice Goldberg said: "The Ninth Amendment shows a belief of the Constitution's authors that fundamental rights exist that are not expressly enumerated in the first eight amendments and an intent that the list of rights included there not be exhaustive."

> " We deal with a right of privacy older than the Bill of Rights—older than our political parties, older than our school system.
> —Justice William O. Douglas, *Griswold v. Connecticut* "

In the majority opinion, Justice Douglas said the arrests of the Planned Parenthood leaders created a controversy that the Court could properly decide, one involving "the constitutional rights of married people with whom they had a professional relationship."

He said "the specific guarantees in the Bill of Rights have penumbras" that reached areas not specifically mentioned in the amendments. He cited six different amendments—the First, Third, Fourth, Fifth, Ninth, and Fourteenth—that create a "zone of privacy" violated by the law's restrictions on married couples.

A VIEW OF MARRIAGE

Justice Douglas declared:

"We deal with a right of privacy older than the Bill of Rights—older than our political parties, older than our school system. Marriage is a coming together for better or for worse, hopefully enduring, and intimate to a degree of being sacred. The association promotes a way of life, not causes; a harmony in living, not political faiths; a bilateral loyalty, not commercial or social projects. Yet it is an association for as noble a purpose as any involved in our prior decisions."

BLACK'S DOCTRINE REJECTED

Justice Goldberg rejected the doctrine long advocated by Justice Black that the Fourteenth Amendment incorporated all of the Bill of Rights into the amendment's due-process clause and made them applicable to the states. This would limit the list of constitutionally protected rights of those specifically listed in the Bill of Rights, he said.

Instead, the due-process clause absorbs only "those specifics of the first eight amendments which express fundamental personal rights," Justice Goldberg said. All other "fundamental rights" are protected by the Ninth Amendment, he said.

In a separate concurring opinion Justice John M. Harlan agreed that the Constitution's guarantees against state restrictions on personal liberty should not be limited to those parts of the Bill of Rights that have been "incorporated" into the Fourteenth Amendment by Supreme Court decisions.

He said the Fourteenth Amendment's due-process clause alone protects persons against state laws that violate "basic values 'implicit in the concept of ordered liberty.' "

Justice Byron R. White's concurring opinion agreed that the due-process clause, which prohibits states from depriving any person of "liberty" without due process of law, was clearly violated by the restrictions of the Connecticut law.

The willingness of the five concurring justices—Warren, Goldberg, Brennan, Harlan and White—to strike down a state law for violating such concepts as "ordered liberty," "liberty," and "fundamental rights," drew bristling dissents from Justices Black and Stewart.

They saw the case as a turning point toward increased judicial activism similar to the early years of this century, when the court struck down many state laws as "unreasonable" deprivations of property without due process of law.

Justice Black—who has been known as a "judicial activist" himself in recent years—recalled a list of cases in which the Court held invalid state and Federal laws regulating business and labor matters as "unreasonable."

These decisions eventually brought the court into conflict with the New Deal and precipitated President Roosevelt's "court-packing" plan. The Court abandoned the due-process approach in 1937 in the famous turnabout under which the Court took a "hands off" attitude toward economic legislation.

Privacy is a "broad, abstract and ambiguous concept" that can be expanded or shrunken by later court decisions, Justice Black declared.

He said the Ninth Amendment was not intended to give the Court a veto over state and Federal legislation.

In a separate dissent Justice Stewart said there was nothing in general in the Constitution that protected citizens against invasion of their privacy by state laws. Although he thought the law was "silly," he felt it could be eliminated only by the Connecticut Legislature.

Since the decision was based on the violation of private rights by prohibiting use of contraceptives, constitutional lawyers were uncertain as to its effect on other birth control laws.

On May 13, the Hempstead, L.I., police arrested a former medical student, William R. Baird of 1269 G Street, Valley Stream, for dispensing birth control devices and advice. He told reporters that he would appeal his conviction under the New York law in an attempt to have it declared unconstitutional. . . .

* * * * * * * * * * * *

Griswold had an immediate impact on only one state: Connecticut's law was unique in the country. Some commentators immediately grasped the potential for broader implications, though. In *The New York Times,* one commentator suggested the ruling laid the foundation to prohibit wiretapping by the government.

The Court in fact made only a glancing reference to *Griswold* two years later when it ruled that the Fourth Amendment generally prohibits wiretapping without a search warrant. (See page 362.) But *Griswold* was central to the Court's more controversial decision in 1973 legalizing abortion throughout the country. In recognizing a woman's right to an abortion during most of her pregnancy, the landmark decision in *Roe v. Wade* cited both lines of thought from *Griswold*— a right of marital and sexual privacy and a substantive liberty protected under the Due Process Clause.

More than thirty-five years later, *Roe v. Wade* remains controversial not merely for its result but also for its legal doctrine. Yet the Court has reaffirmed the use of the Due Process Clause to protect individual liberties not specifically mentioned elsewhere in the Constitution—most recently, in its decision in 2003 striking down state laws prohibiting gay sex. The Court has also applied the doctrine to recognize a right of medical autonomy to refuse lifesaving treatment, but has not gone further to allow terminally ill patients a right to physician-assisted suicide.

The Roberts Court has had no occasion yet to reexamine this legal doctrine. In its first substantive abortion-related ruling, however, the Court in 2007 upheld a federal law banning a specific late-term procedure that opponents call "partial-birth abortion." Antiabortion groups hope—and abortion-rights advocates fear—that the ruling could foretell a full reconsideration of *Roe* if a case squarely raising the issue should reach the Court.

Far from retreating from the rights-protecting business, the Roberts Court in 2008 opened up a new field of constitutional litigation by recognizing under the Second Amendment a right to own and possess guns within one's home for self-defense. The 5-4 ruling—pitting the conservative majority against four liberal dissenters—struck down a ban on handguns in the District of Columbia. It also immediately generated similar lawsuits aimed at gun control laws in other cities, including Chicago and San Francisco.

EARLY DEVELOPMENTS

The original Constitution contained no general protection for property rights, only the Contracts Clause's prohibition against any state law "impairing the Obligation of Contracts" (Art. I, sec. 10, cl. 1) and several provisions protecting the institution of slavery, though not by name. (See page 256.) The Fifth Amendment, part of the Bill of Rights, adds two protections. It provides that "no person" may be "deprived of life, liberty, or property, without due process of law," nor can "private property be taken for public use, without just compensation."

The Due Process Clause can be traced back to the provision in the English Magna Carta in 1215 that no free man be imprisoned "except by the lawful judgment of his peers or by the law of the land." Legal historians disagree whether the phrasing "due process of law"—introduced in 1354—had the same, substantive meaning or referred only to procedural regularity. In America, James Madison was the first to introduce the phrase into a constitutional provision; he did not define it in the congressional debate on what became the Fifth Amendment.

Madison's intention in drafting the Ninth Amendment, on the other hand, is known. He initially opposed a Bill of Rights for fear that any rights not included might be deemed unprotected. To guard against that possibility, the Ninth Amendment provides: "The enumeration in the Constitution, of certain rights, shall not be construed to deny or disparage others retained by the people."

DUE PROCESS IN THE NINETEENTH CENTURY

In the years before the Civil War, the Court invoked the Contracts Clause in several decisions to limit state actions impinging on property rights. But in its first ruling on the Takings Clause, *Barron v. Baltimore* (1835), the Court unanimously held that the just compensation requirement applied only to the national government, not to states and localities. (See page 148.)

When the Supreme Court first construed the Due Process Clause in *Murray's Lessee v. Hoboken Land & Improvement Co.* (1856), the justices defined it only in procedural terms. A year later, however, Chief Justice Roger B. Taney gave the clause substantive meaning in ruling that the slave Dred Scott remained the "property" of his owner when they traveled to a free state or territory. "An act of Congress which deprives a citizen of the United States of his liberty or property merely because he came himself or brought his property into a particular Territory of the United States . . . could hardly be dignified with the name of due process of law," Taney wrote in *Scott v. Sandford* (1857).

The Fourteenth Amendment made the Due Process Clause applicable to the states, but Congress again provided scant evidence as to its meaning. In the Court's first important ruling on the amendment, the justices narrowed the scope of the Privileges and Immunities Clause by ruling that it protected only the few rights of U.S. citizenship and left other rights up to the states' discretion. The ruling in the *Slaughterhouse Cases* (1873) upheld a Louisiana law that granted a private company an exclusive franchise to operate slaughterhouses in New Orleans and adjoining parishes.

In a significant dissent, however, Justice Joseph P. Bradley said the law violated due process. The fundamental rights of life, liberty, and property, he said, "can only be taken away by due process of law" and "can only be interfered with . . . by lawful regulations necessary or proper for the mutual good of all."

In two later cases, the Court again rejected due process arguments to limit states' economic regulations. The decision in the *Granger Cases* (1877) upheld state regulation of railroad rates and grain elevator fees on the ground that those businesses were "affected with a public interest." In *Mugler v. Kansas* (1887), the Court upheld a Kansas law prohibiting the manufacture or importation of liquor, but Justice John Marshall Harlan—grandfather of the namesake justice of the mid-twentieth century—specified in a separate opinion that a law that had no "substantial relation" to its objects could be struck down as a violation of "rights secured by the fundamental law."

The Court became more protective of economic rights beginning in the 1890s. In *Chicago, Milwaukee and St. Paul R.R. Co. v. Minnesota* (1890), the Court held that the state's rate-setting agency had violated the railroad's due process rights by a lack of procedure: the railroads were given no notice, no hearing, and no opportunity to challenge the reasonableness of the rates. In *Smyth v. Ames* (1898), the Court went further, overturning a Nebraska statute on the ground that the maximum rates specified did not allow the railroads a "fair return." That ruling used due process to extend the Takings Clause to the states in the first example of the incorporation doctrine that proved so important later in free speech and criminal law cases. (See "Cases Incorporating Provisions of the Bill of Rights," page 355.)

Due Process and Personal Liberty in the "Lochner Era"

Seven years after *Smyth* came the decision that gave its name to the Court's use of substantive due process to strike down laws regulating economic affairs: *Lochner v. New York* (1905). "The general right to make a contract in relation to his business is part of the liberty of the individual protected by the 14th Amendment of the Federal Constitution," Justice Rufus W. Peckham Jr. wrote. New York's law limiting bakery workers to ten hours a day violated the rights of both employers and employees, he explained, because it was not necessary to protect the health of workers or the public. Among the four dissenters, Justice Oliver Wendell Holmes Jr. acidly observed, "The constitution is not intended to embody a particular economic theory."

The Court retreated by upholding two later maximum-hour statutes, including an Oregon measure limiting all workers to ten hours (*Bunting v. Oregon,* 1917). But it relied on *Lochner* in its decisions striking down minimum-wage laws in *Adkins v. Children's Hospital* (1923) and *Morehead v. New York* (1936).

Meanwhile, the Court had issued rulings at tension with each other on the power of the states and municipalities to impose land-use requirements affecting property rights. The Court in 1915 upheld a Los Angeles ordinance prohibiting brickyards within the city limits even though the law put a brickmaker out of business. A decade later, the Court upheld a general zoning statute that prohibited businesses, hotels, and apartment houses in residential areas. Cities could limit property rights to protect the community's peace, health, and safety, Justice George Sutherland explained in *Euclid v. Ambler Realty Co.* (1926).

Four years earlier, however, the Court had ruled that some land-use restrictions could go "too far" and amount to an unconstitutional taking of property. The law at issue in *Pennsylvania Coal Co. v. Mahon* (1922) barred the underground mining of coal in areas of severe subsidence in order to protect the owners of nearby homes. "The general rule is that

Pennsylvania Coal Co. v. Mahon

Decided: December 11, 1922

Vote: 7 (Taft, McKenna, Holmes, Van Devanter, Pitney, McReynolds, Sutherland)

1 (Brandeis)

Opinion of the Court: Holmes

Dissenting opinion: Brandeis

while property may be regulated to a certain extent," Justice Holmes wrote, "if regulation goes too far it will be recognized as a taking." The decision established the concept of a "regulatory taking" and allowed the coal company to resume underground operations, but gave little guidance in deciding how far was "too far."

BEYOND PROPERTY RIGHTS

The Court in the 1920s also extended substantive due process to protect more than property rights. In *Meyer v. Nebraska* (1923), the Court struck down an anti-alien law prohibiting the teaching of modern languages other than English to children who had not passed the eighth grade. Robert Meyer had been convicted after using a German-language Bible to teach at a private, Lutheran school in a rural county in southeastern Nebraska.

By a 7-2 vote, the Court found that the law violated not only Meyer's liberty to teach but also parents' liberty to shape their children's education. The liberty protected by the Due Process Clause, Justice James C. McReynolds wrote,

> denotes not merely freedom from bodily restraint but also the right of the individual to contract, to engage in any of the common occupations of life, to acquire useful knowledge, to marry, to establish a home and bring up children, to worship God according to the dictates of his own conscience, and generally to enjoy those privileges long recognized at common law as essential to the orderly pursuit of happiness by free men.

McReynolds said the goals of promoting assimilation and civic development were legitimate during wartime but inadequate during "a time of peace and domestic tranquility." Dissenting in a companion case, Justice Holmes argued that promoting a common language was a legitimate goal.

Meyer v. Nebraska

Decided: June 4, 1923

Vote: 7 (Taft, McKenna, Van Devanter, McReynolds, Brandeis, Butler, Sanford)

2 (Holmes, Sutherland)

Opinion of the Court: McReynolds

Dissenting without opinion: Holmes, Sutherland. (The dissent is found in the companion case, *Bartels v. State of Iowa*)

JUNE 5, 1923
ENDS 21 STATES' BAN ON FOREIGN TONGUES

Supreme Court Decides Pupils Have Constitutional Right to Be Taught Them.

ISSUE RAISED ON GERMAN

Justice McReynolds in Opinion Upholds Freedom to Acquire Knowledge.

Special to The New York Times.

WASHINGTON, June 4.—State statutes preventing the teaching of foreign languages to pupils below the eighth grade in the public, private and parochial schools of Iowa, Nebraska, Ohio and eighteen other States were declared unconstitutional by the United States Supreme Court today.

Justice McReynolds in a majority opinion held that the Nebraska Supreme Court erred in sustaining the conviction of Robert T. Meyer, a parochial school teacher, who instructed a ten-year-old child in German. The Meyer conviction was originally obtained under an act passed by the Nebraska State Legislature forbidding the teaching of any language except English in the schools.

On the ground of the Meyer decision today, the Supreme Court reversed the Supreme Courts of Iowa, Ohio and Nebraska in four cases, based on the same complaint. These cases were those of August Bartels against Iowa, H. H. Bohning against Ohio, Emil Pohl against Ohio and the Nebraska District of Evangelical Lutheran Synod of Missouri, Ohio and other States and others against Governor McKelvie of Nebraska and other officers.

In his opinion on the Meyer case, Justice McReynolds denied the right of the State to restrict the liberty of the individual and went on to say that mere knowledge of the German language cannot be regarded as injurious.

Although the Legislature was actuated by a desire to make better Americans of school children, he said, yet it had attempted materially to interfere with the work of modern language teachers, with the chances of pupils to acquire an education and with the power of parents to control their children's school courses.

No sudden emergency had arisen to make the knowledge of a language other than English harmful, the Justice said.

Justice Holmes and Justice Sutherland dissented from the majority of the court, Mr. Holmes holding in a written opinion that Nebraska had power to enact the statute which the Supreme Court today declared objectionable. They further held that the laws should be tested for their effect on extending the use of English.

reasonable relation to some purpose within the competency of the State to effect. Determination by the Legislature of what constitutes proper exercise of police power is not final or conclusive, but is subject to supervision by the courts.

"The American people have always regarded education and acquisition of knowledge as matters of supreme importance which should be diligently promoted. The ordinance of 1787 declares 'religion, morality and knowledge being necessary to good government and the happiness of mankind, schools and the means of education shall forever be encouraged.' Corresponding to the right of control, it is the natural duty of the parent to give his children education suitable to their station in life and nearly all the States, including Nebraska, enforce this obligation by compulsory laws.

> "No sudden emergency has arisen which renders knowledge by a child of some language other than English so clearly harmful as to justify its inhibition, with the consequent infringement of rights long freely enjoyed.
>
> —Justice James C. McReynolds, *Meyer v. Nebraska*

FREEDOM TO ACQUIRE KNOWLEDGE.

Justice McReynolds said in part:

"The problem for our determination is whether the statute as construed and applied unreasonably infringes the liberty guaranteed the plaintiff in error by the Fourteenth Amendment: 'No State * * * shall deprive any person of life, liberty or property without due process of law.'

"While this court has not attempted to define with exactness the liberty thus guaranteed, the term has received much consideration and some of the included things have been definitely stated. Without doubt, it denotes not merely freedom from bodily restraint but also the right of the individual to contract, to engage in any one of the common occupations of life, to acquire useful knowledge, to marry, establish a home and bring up children, to worship God according to the dictates of his own conscience, and generally to enjoy those privileges long recognized by common law as essential to the orderly pursuit of happiness by free men.

"The established doctrine is that this liberty may not be interfered with, under the guise of protecting the public interest by legislative action which is arbitrary or without

UPHOLDS RIGHTS OF TEACHERS.

"Practically, education of the young is only possible in schools conducted by especially qualified persons who devote themselves thereto. The calling always has been regarded as useful and honorable, essential, indeed, to the public welfare. Mere knowledge of the German language cannot reasonably be regarded as harmful. Heretofore it has been commonly looked upon as helpful and desirable.

"The plaintiff in error taught this language in school as part of his occupation. His right thus to teach and the right of parents to engage him so to instruct their children, we think, are within the liberty of the amendment.

"Evidently the Legislature has attempted materially to interfere with the calling of modern language teachers, with the opportunities of pupils to acquire knowledge and with the power of parents to control the education of their own.

"It is said the purpose of the legislation was to promote civic development by inhibiting training and education of the immature in foreign tongues and ideals before they could learn English and acquire American ideals, and that 'the English language should be and become the mother tongue of all children reared in this State.'

"It is also affirmed that the foreign-born population is very large, that certain communities commonly use foreign words, follow foreign leaders, move in a foreign atmosphere, and that the children are thereby hindered from becoming citizens of the most useful type and the public safety is imperiled.

CAN'T COERCE LEARNING OF ENGLISH.

"That the State may do much—go very far, indeed—in order to improve the quality of its citizens physically, mentally and morally is clear, but the individual has certain fundamental rights which must be respected. The protection of the Constitution extends to all, to those who speak other languages as well as those born with English on the tongue.

"Perhaps it would be highly advantageous if all had ready understanding of our ordinary speech, but this cannot be coerced by methods which conflict with the Constitution—a desirable end cannot be promoted by prohibitive means.

"The desire of the Legislature to foster a homogeneous people with American ideals prepared readily to understand current discussions of civic matters is easy to appreciate. Unfortunate experiences during the late war and aversions toward every characteristic of truculent adversaries were certainly enough to quicken that aspiration.

"But the means adopted, we think, exceed the limitations upon the power of the State and conflict with rights assured to the plaintiff in error. The interference was plain enough, and no adequate reason therefor in time of peace and domestic tranquillity has been shown.

"The power of the State to compel attendance at some school and to make reasonable regulations for all schools, including a requirement that they shall give instructions in English, is not questioned. Nor has challenge been made of the State's power to prescribe a curriculum for institutions which it supports.

"Those matters are not within the present controversy. Our concern is with the prohibition approved by the Supreme Court. Adams vs. Tanner . . . pointed out that mere abuse incident to an occupation ordinarily useful is not enough to justify its abolition, although regulation may be entirely proper.

"No sudden emergency has arisen which renders knowledge by a child of some language other than English so clearly harmful as to justify its inhibition, with the consequent infringement of rights long freely enjoyed. We are constrained to conclude that the statute as applied is arbitrary and without reasonable relation to any end within the competency of the State.

"As the statute undertakes to interfere only with teaching which involves modern languages, leaving complete freedom as to other matters, there seems no adequate foundation for the suggestion that the purpose was to protect the child's health by limiting his mental activities. It is well known that proficiency in a foreign language seldom comes to one not instructed at an early age, and experience shows that this is not injurious to the health, morals or understanding of the ordinary child.

"The judgment of the court below must be reversed and the cause remanded for further proceedings not inconsistent with this opinion."

FOREIGN TONGUES TAUGHT AT HOME.

Justice Holmes dissenting in the foreign language case, said:

"We all agree, I take it, that it is desirable that all the citizens of the United States should speak a common tongue and therefore that the end aimed at by the statute is a lawful and proper one.

"The only question is whether the means adopted deprived teachers of the liberty secured to them by the Fourteenth Amendment. It is with hesitation and unwillingness that I differ from my brethren with regard to a law like this, but I cannot bring my mind to believe that in some circumstances, and circumstances existing, it is said, in Nebraska, the statute might not be regarded as a reasonable or even necessary method of reaching the desired result.

"The part of the act with which we are concerned deals with the teaching of young children. Youth is the time when familiarity with a language is established, and if there are sections of the State where a child would hear only Polish or French or German spoken at home, I am not prepared to say that it is unreasonable to provide in his early years that he shall hear and speak only English at school. But if it is reasonable, it is not an undue restriction of the liberty, either of teachers or scholar."

Justice Holmes concluded with a statement that he was unable to say whether the Constitution prevented the experiment being tried.

Two years later, McReynolds wrote for a unanimous Court in striking down an anti-Catholic initiative in Oregon requiring children between the ages of eight and sixteen to be educated only in public schools. "The fundamental theory of liberty . . . excludes any general power of the state to standardize its children by forcing them to accept instruction from public teachers only," McReynolds wrote in *Pierce v. Society of Sisters* (1925).

JUNE 2, 1925
OREGON SCHOOL LAW DECLARED INVALID BY SUPREME COURT

Bench Unanimously Upholds Right of Parent to Dictate Child's Education.

STATE CONTROL REJECTED

Justice McReynolds, in Opinion, Calls Law "Standardizing Children" Unconstitutional.

PRIVATE SCHOOLS JUSTIFIED

State Law Is Characterized as Destructive of "Useful and Meritorious" Institutions.

Special to The New York Times.

WASHINGTON, June 1.—The inherent right of a parent to send his boy or girl to any school he deems best was upheld and the right of a State to insist that the children must attend certain institutions was sharply denied when the Supreme Court declared unconstitutional this afternoon the Oregon law prescribing that children between 8 and 16 years of age must be educated in the public schools.

the Society of the Sisters of the Holy Name of Jesus and Mary in opposing the State authorities, who were officially listed as Walter M. Pierce, the Governor; Isaac H. Van Winkle, the Attorney General, and Stanley Myers, the District Attorney for Multnomah County.

The dual fight of the parochial and the secular schools had already been won in the Federal Court for the District

 We think it entirely plain that the Act of 1922 unreasonably interferes with the liberty of parents and guardians to direct the upbringing and education of children under their control.

—Justice James C. McReynolds, *Pierce v. Society of Sisters*

The Court, at the same time, declared that to sustain the Oregon law would mean the destruction of thousands of dollars worth of property belonging to the parochial and secular schools, and that this would amount to depriving them of their possessions without due process of law.

Few decisions in years have attracted as much attention as the present one which was rendered unanimously and was handed down by Associate Justice McReynolds.

Charges that the law was backed by the Ku Klux Klan and was aimed at the Roman Catholic Church have been heard on every side since the statute was enacted. The law, however, makes no distinction against parochial schools, and in the case which was decided this afternoon, the Hill Military Academy, a non-sectarian institution, joined with

of Oregon, but the State officials appealed from that decision to the Supreme Court, which today upheld the lower court's dictum.

HOLDS CHILD "NOT CREATURE OF STATE."

"The child is not the mere creature of the State," declared Justice McReynolds in that part of his opinion which dealt with the right of the parent to dictate the school to which his child should go.

"Those who nurture him and direct his destiny have the right, coupled with the high duty, to recognize and prepare him for additional obligations," he continued, speaking for the court.

"We think it entirely plain that the (Oregon) act of 1922 unreasonably interferes with the liberty of parents and guardians to direct the upbringing and education of children under their control. As often heretofore pointed out, rights guaranteed by the Constitution may not be abridged by legislation which has no reasonable relation to some purpose within the competency of the State.

"The fundamental theory of liberty upon which all Governments in this Union repose excludes any general power of the State to standardize its children by forcing them to accept instruction from public teachers only."

It could not be expected that the Supreme Court would touch on the Ku Klux Klan issue because it had not been spread officially on the records of the case, but at one point Justice McReynolds stated:

"The appellees are engaged in a kind of undertaking not inherently harmful, but long regarded as useful and meritorious. Certainly there is nothing in the present records to indicate that they have failed to discharge their obligations to patrons, students of the State. And there are no peculiar circumstances or present emergencies which demand extraordinary measures relative to primary education." . . .

. . . .

The Lochner-era Court was less protective of what has come to be called medical autonomy. In *Jacobson v. Massachusetts* (1905), the Court voted 7-2 to uphold a compulsory vaccination law. Easily rejecting a personal liberty argument, Justice Harlan said the police power included the "authority of a state to enact quarantine laws and 'health laws of every description.' "

Two decades later—after *Meyer* and *Pierce*—the Court was similarly dismissive in upholding a Virginia law permitting involuntary sterilization of "feeble-minded" persons. The plaintiff, Carrie Buck, was—as Holmes recites in his opinion—"a feeble-minded white woman" committed to the Virginia State Colony for Epileptics and Feeble-Minded in Lynchburg. At age eighteen, Buck had already given birth to an illegitimate child and was pregnant again when the institution's review board approved the superintendent's request to sterilize her.

"The principle that sustains compulsory vaccination is broad enough to cover cutting the Fallopian tubes," Justice Holmes wrote in *Buck v. Bell* (1927). Holmes, an advocate of the then popular race-improving theory of eugenics, added an allusion to the fact that Buck's mother herself had been institutionalized. "Three generations of imbeciles are enough," Holmes said.

MAY 3, 1927
UPHOLDS OPERATING ON FEEBLE-MINDED

Supreme Court Majority Finds Virginia's Sterilization Law Valid.
RIGHT TO PROTECT SOCIETY
Justice Holmes Draws Analogy to Compulsory Vaccination in Woman's Case.
Special to The New York Times.

WASHINGTON, May 2—The authority of the State of Virginia to order the sterilization of mental defectives was upheld by the United States Supreme Court in an opinion handed down today by Associate Justice Holmes for the majority of the court.

The case was that of Carrie Buck, a feeble-minded white woman, committed to the Virginia State Colony for Epileptics and Feeble-Minded. Her mother, also feeble-minded, is in the same institution. Carrie Buck, now about 21 years old, is the mother of an illegitimate feeble-minded child.

R. G. Shelton, guardian for the young woman, brought the action against J. H. Bell, Superintendent of the colony, to prevent the operation of salpingotomy.

The Circuit Court of Amherst County had ordered it performed in accordance with the Virginia State law, and the Supreme Court of that State affirmed the lower court. The case came to the United States Supreme Court's finding, the contention being made that the Virginia law was void under the Fourteenth Amendment because it denied the woman due process of law and the equal protection of the laws.

SEES PROTECTION FOR SOCIETY.

"It is better for all the world," Justice Holmes said in the decision, "if instead of waiting to execute degenerate offspring for crime, or to let them starve for their imbecility, society can prevent those who are manifestly unfit from continuing their kind."

The principle sustaining compulsory vaccination was broad enough to cover the proposition of sterilization, Justice Holmes declared.

Associate Justice Butler noted a dissent from the majority decision, but did not hand down a written opinion.

The Virginia act, Justice Holmes declared, recited that the patient's health and society's welfare might be pro-

that in that respect the plaintiff in error has had due process of law."

Dealing with the contention that under no circumstances could an order for sterilization be justified, Justice Holmes stated:

LAW "DOES ALL THAT IT CAN."

"In view of the general declarations of the Legislature and the specific findings of the Court, obviously we cannot say as matter of law that the grounds do not exist, and if they exist they justify the result. We have seen more than once that the public welfare may call upon the best citizens for their lives. It would be strange if it could not call upon those

> " It is better for all the world, if instead of waiting to execute degenerate offspring for crime, or to let them starve for their imbecility, society can prevent those who are manifestly unfit from continuing their kind. "
> —Justice Oliver Wendell Holmes Jr., *Buck v. Bell*

moted in certain instances by sterilization of mental defectives under careful safeguard. The sterilization, the opinion stated, could be carried out without serious pain or substantial danger to life. The State of Virginia, it was asserted, supported many defectives in various instances who if discharged now would become a menace, but who if sterilized might be set at liberty.

"The very careful provisions" by which the act protected the patients from abuse were referred to by Mr. Holmes. "These provisions," he wrote, "include requirements for public hearings, reduction of all evidence to writing, appeal to the Circuit Court of the county, and finally appeal to the highest court of the State."

"There can be no doubt," the Justice added, "that so far as procedure is concerned the rights of the patients are most carefully considered, and as every step in this case was taken in scrupulous compliance with the statute and after months of observation there is no doubt

who already sap the strength of the State for these lesser sacrifices, often not felt to be such by those concerned, in order to prevent our being swamped with incompetence."

Taking up the contention that the argument for sterilization failed when confined to the small number who are in institutions, and not applied to the "multitude outside," Justice Holmes said:

"It is the usual last resort of constitutional arguments to point out shortcomings of this sort. But the answer is that the law does all that is needed when it does all that it can; indicates a policy; applies it to all within the lines, and seeks to bring within the lines all similarly situated so far and so fast as its means allow."

The Virginia Supreme Court held that Carrie Buck "is the potential parent of socially inadequate offspring, likewise afflicted; that she may be sterilized without detriment to her general health and that her welfare and that of society will be promoted by her sterilization."

. . . .

Buck's attorney argued not personal liberty, but equal protection, saying that the law discriminated against people in state institutions. Holmes dismissed the equal protection claim as "the usual last resort of constitutional arguments." In 1942, however, the Court in *Skinner v. Oklahoma* did find an equal protection violation in a law authorizing involuntary sterilization of habitual criminals. "Marriage and procreation are fundamental to the very existence and survival of the race," Justice Douglas wrote in the unanimous opinion. The law violated equal protection, he explained, because it did not treat all persons convicted of similar crimes the same way.

JUNE 2, 1942
HIGH COURT VOIDS STERILIZATION LAW

Hits Oklahoma Discrimination, Applying Statute to Chicken Thief, Not Embezzler
PERSONAL LIBERTY CITED
Negroes Win Cases, One for Forced Confession, Other on All-White Jury Issue
Special to The New York Times.

WASHINGTON, June 1—In a series of opinions dealing with personal liberties the Supreme Court unanimously invalidated today the Oklahoma law for sterilization of habitual criminals on the ground that it was discriminatory, applying to such offenders as chicken thieves but not embezzlers.

The nine justices reversed the conviction of a Negro for murder and of another for rape, finding that one was moral turpitude," and exempted violation of the liquor laws, embezzlement and political offenses.

"A person who enters a chicken coop and steals chickens commits a felony and he may be sterilized if he is thrice convicted," Justice Douglas stated.

"If, however, he is a bailee of the property and fraudulently appropriates it, he is an embezzler. Hence, no matter how habitual his proclivities, he may not be sterilized.

 When the law lays an unequal hand on those who have committed intrinsically the same quality of offense and sterilizes one and not the other, it has made as invidious a discrimination as if it had selected a particular race or nationality for oppressive treatment.
—Justice William O. Douglas, *Skinner v. Oklahoma*

coerced into a confession and that the other was indicted by an all-white grand jury; held that a Marylander convicted of robbery was not necessarily entitled to a lawyer when he could not afford one, and refused to a Florida slayer a fourth stay of execution.

Justice Douglas wrote the Oklahoma opinion, applying to an order for sterilization of Jack T. Skinner, convicted in 1928 of chicken stealing and in 1929 and 1934 of robbery with firearms, and released in 1939 after serving his third sentence.

EXEMPTIONS IN THE LAW

Passed in 1935, the law ordered sterilization for those convicted thrice for "crime amounting to felonies involving

"When the law lays an unequal hand on those who have committed intrinsically the same quality of offense and sterilizes one and not the other, it has made as invidious a discrimination as if it had selected a particular race or nationality for oppressive treatment."

Concurring, Chief Justice Stone said, however, that the real question was "wholesale condemnation of a class to such an invasion of personal liberty" without a chance to show whether heredity entered into the matter. . . .

PROPERTY RIGHTS

The Lochner era, with its solicitude for property rights, ended abruptly in 1937. Over the next fifty years, economic rights remained largely in eclipse as the Supreme Court imposed only minimal "rational basis" standards for economic regulations and gave wide berth to states and cities in land-use policies. A property rights movement emerged in the 1980s, however, and won some significant victories at the Court through the 1990s. But in 2005, property rights advocates suffered a bitter disappointment with the Court's decision in a closely watched case that broadly upheld the government's exercise of eminent domain to take private property for public uses, including private economic development.

THE "RATIONAL BASIS" STANDARD

Only months after striking down a New York minimum wage statute in 1936, the Court took up the issue again in a case from the state of Washington. In upholding a minimum wage law, the Washington Supreme Court had directly questioned the continuing validity of the Court's 1923 decision in *Adkins*. On that basis, the Court decided to reconsider *Adkins* and then to overrule it so as to uphold the Washington law.

　　Writing for the 5-4 majority in *West Coast Hotel Co. v. Parrish* (1937), Chief Justice Charles Evans Hughes rejected the broad freedom of contract theory used in striking down the earlier minimum wage laws. "The Constitution does not speak of freedom of contract," Hughes wrote. Further,

Susette Kelo's New London, Connecticut, home took center stage when the Supreme Court in 2005 upheld the city's seizure of the property by eminent domain for private economic development. The Court ruled such seizures legal as long as they provide "appreciable benefits to the community."

Source: Suzanne DeChillo/The New York Times

the liberty protected under the Due Process Clause, he explained, is not absolute. "Regulation which is reasonable in relation to its subject and is adopted in the interests of the community is due process," he concluded.

A year later, the Court fortified the new doctrine by establishing "rational basis" as the presumptive standard for reviewing economic measures. The decision in *United States v. Carolene Products Co.* (1938) upheld a federal law prohibiting the shipment in interstate commerce of "filled milk"—skim milk reconstituted with nondairy fillers such as palm oil. Henceforth, Justice Harlan Fiske Stone declared, an economic regulation challenged on substantive due process grounds would be upheld unless demonstrated facts "preclude the assumption that it rests upon some rational basis within the knowledge and experience of legislators."

Stone added—in the now famous "Footnote 4"—that closer scrutiny might be required for laws that appear to violate a specific constitutional prohibition; that interfere with political rights, such as the right to vote; or that are directed against religious, racial, or other "discrete and insular" minorities. Combined with the main holding, the footnote in effect signaled the start of an individual rights revolution. But the import of the ruling was so subtly stated that *The New York Times,* among other papers, had no story on the decision the next day.

Applying the rational basis test, the Court proceeded to reject due process and equal protection challenges to any number of laws favoring some economic interests and disfavoring others, even if the justices saw reasons to doubt their wisdom. The decision in *Ferguson v. Skrupa* (1963), for example, sustained a Kansas law that prohibited nonlawyers from engaging in the business of "debt adjusting"—credit counseling, debt consolidation, and the like. Allowing nonlawyers to provide debt adjustment services may have social utility, Justice Hugo L. Black wrote, "but such arguments are properly addressed to the legislature, not to us."

PROPERTY OWNERSHIP AND EMINENT DOMAIN

Meanwhile, the Court had also signaled all but unlimited deference to the government's use of eminent domain to take private property for public use. In *Berman v. Parker* (1954), the Court unanimously rejected a plea by a store owner to block the taking of his property as part of an "urban renewal" project in a slum-ridden section of Washington, D.C. Justice Douglas explained that legislatures—Congress, in this instance—could exercise power of eminent domain for any number of public purposes, including "public safety, public health, morality, peace and quiet, law and order." The judiciary has only "an extremely narrow" role in determining whether the purpose is proper, he said. In addition, a legislature has discretion to transfer private property to another "private enterprise" for redevelopment purposes. "We cannot say that public ownership is the sole method of promoting the public purposes of community redevelopment projects," he concluded.

NOVEMBER 23, 1954
CONGRESS UPHELD ON SLUM CLEARING
Supreme Court Says Federal and State Legislatures Have Wide Redevelopment Power
Special to The New York Times.

WASHINGTON, Nov. 22—The Supreme Court unanimously ruled today that Federal and State Legislatures had broad powers to authorize redevelopment of slum areas.

It upheld the constitutionality of the District of Columbia Redevelopment Act of 1945. This law authorized the acquisition of large areas in Washington for slum clearance and their sale or lease for redevelopment to private interests.

The law was challenged by the owners of seventy-six acres of commercial and residential property in southwest Washington. They asserted that the law authorized seizure of private property for other than public use in violation of the due process clause of the Fifth Amendment to the Constitution.

This amendment says that no person shall be "deprived of life, liberty or property without due process of law."

Justice William O. Douglas, who wrote the high court's opinion, held that Congress, in passing the law, had made "legislative determination" that it was "the policy of the United States to protect and promote the welfare of the inhabitants of the seat of Government" by eliminating injurious conditions by "all means necessary and appropriate for the purpose."

"Once the object is within the authority of Congress," Justice Douglas asserted, "the means by which it will be attained is also for Congress to determine. Here one of the means chosen is the use of private enterprise for redevelopment of the area.

"Subject to specific constitutional limitations, when the Legislature has spoken, the public interest has been declared in terms well-nigh conclusive. In such cases, the Legislature, not the judiciary, is the main guardian of the public needs to be served by social legislation, whether it be Congress legislating concerning the District of Columbia or the states legislating concerning local affairs."

Justice Douglas said that the "concept of public welfare is broad and inclusive," and that it was not the function of the judiciary "to determine whether a particular housing project is or is not desirable."

The decision in the Washington case was regarded as clearing the way for similar programs in other states and municipalities. Such programs have been adopted in thirty-four states and sustained in court proceedings in twenty of them. . . .

• • • • • • • • • • • •

The ruling in the Washington, D.C., case gave a green light to municipalities across the country to take private property for economic redevelopment. In one of the most controversial instances, the city of Detroit displaced more than 4,000 families from its "Poletown" neighborhood in 1981 in order to transfer the land to General Motors for a new auto assembly plant. The Michigan Supreme Court rejected an effort to block the use of eminent domain for the project. The U.S. Supreme Court was equally permissive. In *Hawaii Housing Authority v. Midkiff* (1984), for example, the Court unanimously upheld a Hawaii land-redistribution law that transferred property from a few large landowners to many smaller owners.

Earlier, the Court had given cities broad discretion to impose restrictions on private owners' uses of their property. In *Penn Central Transportation Co. v. New York City* (1978), the Court rejected, 6-3, a regulatory takings claim for compensation brought by the owners of Grand Central Terminal because the city's Landmark Preservation Law prevented demolition of the terminal to make way for construction of a multistory office building on the midtown Manhattan site. For the majority, Justice William J. Brennan Jr. said the government can impose land-use restrictions that adversely affect economic values without its action amounting to a taking. The case established a three-part, government-friendly test that called for examining the extent to which a regulation inflicts "economic losses" on the owner, the extent to which it interferes with "reasonable investment-backed expectations," and the character of the government action. Justice William H. Rehnquist led the three dissenters.

Penn Central Transportation Co. v. New York City

Decided: June 26, 1978

Vote: 6 (Brennan, Stewart, B. White, T. Marshall, Blackmun, Powell)

3 (Burger, Rehnquist, Stevens)

Opinion of the Court: Brennan

Dissenting opinion: Rehnquist (Burger, Stevens)

THE REHNQUIST COURT AND EMINENT DOMAIN

After being elevated to chief justice, Rehnquist led the Court in a different direction. In his first term as chief, the Court held in *First English Evangelical Lutheran Church v. County of Los Angeles* (1987) that an owner may be entitled to compensation for a "temporary taking," even if the government later changes a regulation to permit use of the property. In a second California case, *Nollan v. California*

Coastal Commission (1987), the Court blocked the state's coastal commission from requiring a landowner to grant public access to his beachfront in return for a construction permit.

Property rights advocates won some additional victories in the 1990s. In *Lucas v. South Carolina Coastal Council* (1992), the Court backed a beachfront property owner's claim to compensation because a coastal protection scheme destroyed all economically viable use of the site. In *Dolan v. City of Tigard* (1994), the Court ruled that a landowner or developer can be required to set aside part of a property to offset the impact of new construction only if the government shows a "rough proportionality" between the conditions it imposes and the projected harm from the project. In 1999 the Court ruled that property owners with "regulatory takings" claims have the right to a jury trial in federal court under the federal civil rights law (*City of Monterey v. Del Monte Dunes*).

NEWS ANALYSIS
JULY 21, 1996
COMMUNITY INTERESTS VS. PROPERTY RIGHTS
By DAVID W. DUNLAP

. . . What the United States Supreme Court has done is to expand the concept of regulatory "takings." The underlying premise is that land-use controls can effectively deprive owners of the use [of] their property every bit as much as outright seizure, leaving owners to pick up the tab for common benefits—like waterfront access or undeveloped open space—that should be borne by the public at large.

As a general proposition, a regulation must substantially advance a legitimate government interest and not deprive a property of all of its economic value. It was long ago established by the Supreme Court that if a regulation went "too far," it would be recognized as a taking. But for most of this century, the Court was largely silent on the subject.

"It used to be that when you talked about the Fifth Amendment, people thought you were talking about self-incrimination," said Roger J. Marzulla, who heads the environmental law section at the influential Washington firm of Akin, Gump, Strauss, Hauer & Feld. . . . "As few as five years ago, when you talked about the just-compensation clause, people had no idea what you were talking about."

He said the new cases "indicated that the Supreme Court is serious about property rights, that compensation is indeed due and that government at all levels must take into account the extent of private property rights."

But Jerold S. Kayden, associate professor of urban planning at the Harvard Graduate School of Design, said that recent legislative action "reflects a recognition by property-rights advocates that they have not yet achieved the victory they wanted in the judicial branch."

"We're still left scratching our heads about what happens when a regulation has a severe impact but the property value isn't diminished to zero," Mr. Kayden said. "The fact that millions of dollars may be foregone [*sic*] by the impact of regulation doesn't automatically trigger a constitutional finding of a taking. But between the cup and the lip is a large area for further exploration." . . .

• • • • • • • • • • • •

In 2002, however, the Court ruled, 6–3, that the government ordinarily does not have to compensate an owner for a temporary moratorium restricting use of property. "A rule that required compensation for every delay in the use of property would render routine government processes prohibitively expensive or encourage hasty decision-making," Justice John Paul Stevens wrote for the majority in *Tahoe-Sierra Preservation Council, Inc. v. Tahoe Regional Planning Agency*.

Three years later, the Court dealt property-rights advocates a bigger blow by upholding a plan by the economically distressed city of New London, Connecticut, to take most of the city's working-class Fort Trumbull neighborhood for use in an ambitious commercial and residential

Kelo v. City of New London

    Decided: June 23, 2005

    Vote: 5 (Stevens, Kennedy, Souter,

               Ginsburg, Breyer)

           4 (Rehnquist, O'Connor, Scalia,

               Thomas)

    Opinion of the Court: Stevens

    Concurring opinion: Kennedy

    Dissenting opinions (2): O'Connor

              (Rehnquist, Scalia, Thomas);

              Thomas

development project. A handful of homeowners challenged the city's use of eminent domain to take their properties, including Susette Kelo, who had distinctively restored a nineteenth-century riverfront cottage near the New London Harbor.

Property rights advocates viewed the case as an ideal vehicle for challenging what they called "eminent domain abuse"—the taking of private property under government authority only to turn it over to private developers. The Court disagreed. Its 5-4 decision in *Kelo v. City of New London* (2005) emphatically reaffirmed the government's discretion in determining the public uses for eminent domain. "Promoting economic development is a traditional and long accepted function of government," Stevens wrote for the majority.

JUNE 24, 2005
JUSTICES UPHOLD TAKING PROPERTY FOR DEVELOPMENT

By LINDA GREENHOUSE

WASHINGTON, June 23—The Supreme Court ruled on Thursday, in one of its most closely watched property rights cases in years, that fostering economic development is an appropriate use of the government's power of eminent domain.

The 5-to-4 decision cleared the way for the City of New London, Conn., to proceed with a large-scale plan to replace a faded residential neighborhood with office space for research and development, a conference hotel, new residences and a pedestrian "riverwalk" along the Thames River.

taking would be unconstitutional. The Connecticut Supreme Court upheld the use of eminent domain in a ruling last year.

In affirming that decision, the majority opinion by Justice John Paul Stevens resolved a question that had surprisingly gone unanswered for all the myriad times that governments have used their power under the Fifth Amendment to take private property for public use. The question was the definition of "public use."

The homeowners, represented by a public-interest law firm, the Institute for Justice, which has conducted

> **Promoting economic development is a traditional and long accepted function of government.**
>
> —Justice John Paul Stevens, *Kelo v. City of New London*

The project, to be leased and built by private developers, is intended to derive maximum benefit for the city from a $350 million research center built nearby by the Pfizer pharmaceutical company.

New London, deemed a "distressed municipality" by the state 15 years ago, has a high unemployment rate and fewer residents today than it had in 1920.

The owners of 15 homes in the Fort Trumbull neighborhood, including one woman who was born in her house 87 years ago and has lived there since, had resisted the plan and refused the city's offer of compensation.

After the city condemned the properties in November 2000, the homeowners went to state court to argue that the

a national litigation campaign against what it calls eminent domain abuse, argued that taking property to enable private economic development, even development that would provide a public benefit by enhancing the tax base, could never be a "public use."

In its view, the only transfers of property that qualified were those that gave actual ownership or use to the public, like for a highway or a public utility.

But the majority concluded on Thursday that public use was properly defined more broadly as "public purpose." Justice Stevens noted that earlier Supreme Court decisions interpreting the public use clause of the Fifth Amendment had allowed the use of eminent domain to redevelop a blighted neighborhood in Washington, to redistribute land ownership in Hawaii and to assist a gold-mining company, in a decision by Justice Oliver Wendell Holmes in 1906.

"Promoting economic development is a traditional and long accepted function of government," Justice Stevens said, adding, "Clearly, there is no basis for exempting economic development from our traditionally broad understanding of public purpose."

In a dissenting opinion, Justice Sandra Day O'Connor objected that "the words 'for public use' do not realistically exclude any takings, and thus do not exert any constraint on the eminent domain power."

Justice O'Connor said, "Under the banner of economic development, all private property is now vulnerable to being taken and transferred to another private owner, so long as it might be upgraded."

Justice Stevens, examining the New London plan in light of the majority's general analysis, said the plan "unquestionably serves a public purpose," even though it was intended to increase jobs and tax revenue rather than remove blight.

He described the plan as "carefully formulated" and comprehensive. Sounding a federalism note, Justice Stevens said that state legislatures and courts were best at "discerning local public needs" and that the judgment of the New London officials was "entitled to our deference."

Justices Stephen G. Breyer, Ruth Bader Ginsburg, Anthony M. Kennedy and David H. Souter joined the majority opinion in Kelo v. City of New London, No. 04-108. Justice Kennedy also wrote a separate concurring opinion to emphasize that while there was no suggestion in this instance that the plan was intended to favor any individual developer, "a court confronted with a plausible accusation of impermissible favoritism to private parties should treat the objection as a serious one and review the record to see it if has merit."

Justice O'Connor's dissenting opinion was joined by Chief Justice William H. Rehnquist and by Justices Antonin Scalia and Clarence Thomas. She wrote that rather than adhering to its precedents, the court had strayed from them by endorsing economic development as an appropriate public use.

"Who among us can say she already makes the most productive or attractive use of her property?" Justice O'Connor asked.

She added: "The specter of condemnation hangs over all property. Nothing is to prevent the state from replacing any Motel 6 with a Ritz-Carlton, any home with a shopping mall or any farm with a factory."

Both Justice O'Connor and Justice Thomas, who also filed his own dissent, said the decision's burden would fall on the less powerful and wealthy.

"The government now has license to transfer property from those with fewer resources to those with more," Justice O'Connor said. "The founders cannot have intended this perverse result."

Justice Thomas, who called the decision "far reaching and dangerous," cited several studies showing that those displaced by urban renewal and "slum clearance" over the years tended to be lower-income minority residents.

"The court has erased the Public Use Clause from our Constitution," he said.

In the majority opinion, Justice Stevens said, "The necessity and wisdom of using eminent domain power to promote economic development are certainly matters of legitimate public debate."

The court did not "minimize the hardship that condemnations may entail," he said, despite the fact that the homeowners will receive "just compensation."

Justice Stevens said that states remained free to place restrictions on their own use of eminent domain power through their own constitutions and laws, as many have; California, for example, has a law restricting to blighted areas the use of eminent domain for economic development.

Scott G. Bullock, the lawyer who argued the case for the New London homeowners, said in an interview that his organization, the Institute for Justice, would accept the court's invitation and "continue the fight in the state supreme courts." As a result of the decision, he said, "we are going to see more eminent domain abuse and a growing grass-roots rebellion against this type of government action."

Allan B. Taylor, a partner in the Hartford law firm Day, Berry & Howard who filed a brief on New London's behalf for the Connecticut Conference of Municipalities and organizations of cities in 31 other states, said an opposite outcome in this case would have ushered in an "extraordinary revolution."

If the court had not upheld the Connecticut Supreme Court, he said in an interview, "it would greatly limit what cities and towns all over the country could do." Mr. Taylor said he read the opinion not as a green light for the wholesale use of eminent domain, but as "a green light for continuing to do careful and responsible planning."

The decision was a clear defeat for the long-term effort by Chief Justice Rehnquist and Justice Scalia to limit government control over private property. Although a series of decisions from the mid-1980's through the early 90's had appeared to indicate a major shift in the court's traditional deference to government land-use policies, that effort has stalled in recent cases.

By the same token, the decision was the latest success for Justice Stevens, the 85-year-old senior associate justice, who appears to be having one of the most productive terms in his 30 years on the Supreme Court.

The New London case was among the final decisions the court was expected to make in this term. The court indicated that Monday would be the final day of the term.

. . . .

Stevens rejected the homeowners' arguments that courts should, as he phrased it, "second guess" governmental decisions about the likely success of a project or the specific properties to be acquired. But, he added, states were free to impose stricter requirements than the "federal baseline" either through court decisions or legislation.

In a significant concurrence, Justice Anthony M. Kennedy said that the Public Use Clause prohibits transfers "intended to confer benefits on particular, private entities" or "with only incidental or pretextual public benefits." He said courts should apply "meaningful rational basis review" if confronted with "plausible accusation of impermissible favoritism to private parties."

Writing for four dissenters, Justice Sandra Day O'Connor argued the decision amounted to abandoning a "long-held, basic limitation on government power" and effectively deleting the words "public use" from the Takings Clause. "Under the banner of economic development," she wrote, "all private property is now vulnerable to being taken and transferred to another private owner, so long as it might be upgraded—i.e., given to an owner who will use it in a way that the legislature deems more beneficial to the public—in the process."

The ruling provoked a firestorm of criticism from members of Congress and other public officials, commentators, and the public at large. Within a year, some twenty-five states had acted on Stevens's suggestion and passed laws placing some new limits on use of eminent domain for private development. In New London itself, the city pressed forward with its plans, but in a compromise suggested by Kelo agreed to move her house to a nearby location still close to the harbor.

PRIVACY RIGHTS

Connecticut's ban on using contraceptives represented an extreme version of laws enacted in many states in the nineteenth century regulating sexual conduct. Although some of the laws restricting contraceptives were eased by the mid-twentieth century, laws making it a crime to engage in "sodomy"—understood to mean oral or anal sex and sometimes limited to conduct between persons of the same sex—remained on the books in most states as of 1960. Most states also had retained laws first enacted in the nineteenth century that banned abortion with only limited exceptions.

These laws were challenged in legislative bodies and in the courts by proponents of a succession of political and cultural movements: the sexual revolution, the women's rights movement, and the gay rights movement. With its ruling in *Griswold* in 1965, the Supreme Court stepped into the middle of these culture wars. Less than a decade later, the Court broadly construed the right of privacy to encompass, with some limitations, a woman's right to abortion. Later, the Court also extended privacy rights to safeguard individual autonomy in medical decisions. And, in a major victory for gay rights, the Court in 2005 ruled unconstitutional the few remaining state antisodomy laws—statutes used infrequently and only against homosexuals.

ACCESS TO CONTRACEPTIVES

The Griswold case reached the Supreme Court only a few years after birth control pills had become widely available as an alternative to the centuries-old barrier techniques of preventing conception: diaphragms for women, condoms for men. When Griswold was arrested, she had gladly explained the details of birth control to the two New Haven detectives. At the Supreme Court, however, neither the justices nor the lawyers uttered the words "diaphragm" or "condom" once during the arguments.

In the majority opinion, Justice Douglas controversially found a protection for "zones of privacy" implicit in several of the amendments in the Bill of Rights: the First (freedom of speech), Third (no peacetime quartering of soldiers), Fourth (no unreasonable search or seizure), Fifth (privilege against self-incrimination), and Ninth (unenumerated rights). "Specific guarantees in the Bill of Rights have penumbras, formed by emanations from those guarantees that help give them life and substance," Douglas wrote.

Four justices joined Douglas's opinion, but Justice Arthur J. Goldberg wrote for three of them in a longer opinion specifically relying on the Ninth Amendment. Two other justices—Harlan and Byron R. White—wrote separate opinions relying solely on the Due Process Clause. The two dissenters—Black and Stewart—rejected the claimed privacy right. "The Court talks about a constitutional 'right of privacy' as though there is some constitutional provision or provisions forbidding any law ever to be passed which might abridge the 'privacy' of individuals," Justice Black wrote. "But there is not."

Griswold v. Connecticut

Decided: June 7, 1965

Vote: 7 (Warren, Douglas, Clark, Harlan II, Brennan, B. White, Goldberg)

2 (Black, Stewart)

Opinion of the Court: Douglas

Concurring opinion: Goldberg (Warren, Brennan)

Opinions concurring in judgment (2): Harlan II; B. White

Dissenting opinions (2): Black (Stewart); Stewart (Black)

NEWS ANALYSIS
JUNE 13, 1965
A JUDICIAL GAME OF MUSICAL CHAIRS

By ARTHUR KROCK

WASHINGTON, June 12—The Supreme Court's 7 to 2 ruling, that planned parenthood in wedlock by the use of contraceptive devices cannot constitutionally be forbidden (as in the Connecticut law the court struck down), was a sharp and sudden check on the mounting judicial and legislative regimentation of the private choices of individuals. And, though the application of the ruling was restricted, the majority opinions defined "privacy" as an implicit constitutional right in terms broader than the court has employed in the social area for many years.

To a people beset by restriction on acts reflecting individual preferences that for generations were held to be within their constitutional rights, the decision marks a reversion to the less-inhibited past. But, while the sweeping language of the majority opinions can and will be quoted hereafter in legal actions against limitations of private

choice that have been imposed by the Court and by Congress in the name of equal rights, the odds remain against the success of such litigation.

PLAUSIBLE EITHER WAY

The line-up of the nine justices on the planned parenthood issue supplies sufficient evidence that, case by case, they can assert constitutional propositions with as much plausibility as when previously they denied them. For example, it could reasonably be argued from the opinions extolling freedom of choice and of association, that the court will outlaw the effort to attain a racial balance in the schools in many localities by transporting children far from their places of residence. The expansive and approving phraseology with which the majority championed "privacy" in general as within the "penumbra" of the specific constitutional guarantees of individual rights may encourage hopeful speculation that the court ultimately will narrow its validation of the 1964 Act of Congress which forbids nearly all private owners of public facilities to practice racial segregation in any form.

But that would be the acme of wishful thinking. The shifts of position by several of the Supreme Court brethren in the planned parenthood case is a sufficient warning. Justice Black, who has consistently maintained an "absolutist" concept of the constitutional guarantees of individual rights against claims that this was injurious to the general interest in the particular circumstances, upheld the Connecticut legislation forbidding planned parenthood based on that self-same claim. In what resembled a game of musical chairs, several justices who had opposed Black's "absolutist" position on the ground that its usual effect was to make

choice—whether public or private or parochial—is also not mentioned . . . Yet the First Amendment has been construed to include certain of those rights.

To the latter Justice Douglas added "a right of privacy older than the Bill of Rights—older than our political parties, older than our school system. . . . Marriage [is] . . . intimate to the degree of being sacred. [It] is an association for as noble a purpose as any involved in our prior decisions." For parents who, for any number of reasons, object to the transport of their children to distant schools in very different types of neighborhoods, their attitude is equally an assertion of the right of choice and association.

One Federal Circuit Court of Appeals has agreed; another will pass on a contrary ruling by a district judge.

> " To a people beset by restriction on acts reflecting individual preferences that for generations were held to be within their constitutional rights, the decision marks a reversion to the less-inhibited past. "

the Court a "super-legislature," left themselves open to his charge that this was the role in which they cast the Court by joining in outlawing the Connecticut statute.

TO GUESS IS FUTILE

In view of the school desegregation ruling of 1954 and others in which Justice Douglas has approved restrictions imposed by the Court and by Congress on individual preferences, the following from his opinion on behalf of the majority in the Connecticut case demonstrates the futility of trying to guess on instant evidence what the Court will hold hereafter in the same category:

> We do not sit as a super-legislature to determine the wisdom, need and propriety of laws that touch economic problems, business affairs or *social* conditions. (italics supplied). This law, however, operates directly on an intimate relation of husband and wife, and their physician's role in one aspect of that relation.
>
> The association of people is not mentioned in the Constitution nor in the Bill of Rights. The right to educate a child in a school of the parents'

The issue, therefore, is moving toward the Supreme Court. But experience discounts a confident conclusion that Justice Douglas, who considered sociological grounds sufficient for the outlawing of compulsory state racial segregation in the public schools that the court had long sustained as constitutional, necessarily will hold that these parents are asserting rights which, like marital "privacy," also exist in the "penumbra" of the Constitution.

PREDICTING DANGEROUS

The shifting of position by members of the court in the Connecticut case also warns against another confident assumption drawn from the majority's dicta on the rights of privacy, particularly as respecting married persons. This is that, since the anti-miscegenation laws in a number of states collide headlong with these comments, the laws are sure to be held unconstitutional. But this assumption is the more tempting because of the sweep of verbiage in which the court proclaimed the implicit constitutional right of all choices pertaining to the marriage state.

No right, wrote Justice Goldberg in his separate concurrence, is "so basic and fundamental and so deep-rooted in our society as the right of privacy in marriage . . . to 'marry, establish a home and bring up children,' . . . (and, as the court recognized in *Meyer v. Nebraska* is) . . . an essential part of the liberty guaranteed by the 14th Amendment." But in the following quote by Justice Goldberg from an earlier dissent by Justice Harlan there is at least one suggestion that the court will not be unanimous in striking down the anti-

miscegenation laws, whose objective is to prevent Negro-Caucasian intermarriage:

"It is one thing when the state exerts its power . . . to say who may marry . . . but quite another . . . when it undertakes to regulate . . . the intimacies of a marriage it has acknowledged."

Seven years later, the Court relied on the Equal Protection Clause to extend the right to use contraceptives to unmarried persons. The decision in *Eisenstadt v. Baird* (1972) overturned the conviction of birth control advocate William Baird under a Massachusetts law prohibiting the distribution of contraceptives to unmarried persons for the purpose of preventing pregnancy. For the majority, Justice Brennan said the law did not further the state's claimed interest in preventing premarital sex because it did not prohibit distributing contraceptives aimed at preventing disease.

Eisenstadt v. Baird

> **Decided:** March 22, 1972
> **Vote:** 6 (Douglas, Brennan, Stewart, B. White, T. Marshall, Blackmun)
> 1 (Burger)
> **Opinion of the Court:** Brennan
> **Concurring opinion:** Douglas
> **Concurring in judgment:** B. White (Blackmun)
> **Dissenting opinion:** Burger
> **Did not participate:** Powell, Rehnquist

MARCH 23, 1972
COURT VOIDS AN ANTI-CONTRACEPTIVE LAW

Special to The New York Times

WASHINGTON, March 22—The Supreme Court ruled today that a state could not outlaw the distribution of contraceptives to single persons when birth control devices are legally available to married couples.

In a 4-to-3 decision, the Court declared unconstitutional Massachusetts's 93-year-old law that authorized prison terms of up to five years for persons who sold or gave birth control devices to unmarried persons.

The ruling is expected to have minimal direct impact upon state laws, because only Wisconsin has a similar law applying to unmarried persons only.

The Supreme Court ruled in 1965 that states could not make it illegal to make contraceptives available to married persons, and many states that had anti-contraceptive laws subsequently repealed them.

16 STATES HAVE LAWS

A spokesman for Planned Parenthood-World Population in New York said today that as of last September, 34 states had no anti-contraceptive law. Of the remaining 16 states, Massachusetts's and Wisconsin's laws are unconstitutional under today's ruling and the archaic statutes of three other states—Louisiana, Nebraska and Pennsylvania—are widely considered to be unconstitu-

tionally vague. They outlaw "secret drugs or nostrums," which is considered an inexact description of modern contraceptives.

Today's decision did not remove the authority of states to limit the distribution of contraceptives to physicians or druggists. Thus it apparently will not affect New York's law, which says that only doctors and druggists can dispense contraceptives and that druggists cannot sell them to persons under 16 years of age. According to Planned Parenthood, similar laws exist in Arkansas, Idaho, Minnesota, Montana, New Jersey, Oregon and Texas.

The three other states that regulate contraceptive sales—Maryland, North Dakota and South Dakota—only prohibit vending machine sales.

BAIRD CONVICTION INVALIDATED

The decision today overturned the conviction of William R. Baird, a 39-year-old birth control crusader from Valley Stream, L.I., who received a three-month jail sentence for giving an unmarried woman a packet of vaginal foam after he lectured at Boston University in 1967. The state courts upheld his conviction, but the United States Court of Appeals for the First Circuit struck down the law.

Justice William J. Brennan Jr., the only Roman Catholic on the Supreme Court, wrote the opinion today affirming the Court of Appeals.

He rejected the state's argument that the law was a proper exercise of the state's power to discourage fornication and to protect people from harmful products. Justice Brennan noted that this could not have been the state's real purpose, because the law leaves married persons exposed to both.

shows the population crisis has finally been recognized by our Government."

Justices William O. Douglas, Thurgood Marshall and Potter Stewart joined Justice Brennan in the opinion.

Justices Byron R. White and Harry A. Blackmun joined in overturning Mr. Baird's conviction, but they did not join the majority opinion. They said that if Mr. Baird had given away birth control pills they would have upheld the con-

> " If the right of privacy means anything, it is the right of the individual, married or single, to be free from unwarranted governmental intrusion into matters so fundamentally affecting a person as the decision whether to bear or beget a child.
> —Justice William J. Brennan Jr., *Eisenstadt v. Baird* "

He concluded that when the state respected married people's right of privacy, it denied single people equal protection of the laws by treating them differently.

"If the right of privacy means anything," he said, "it is the right of the individual, married or single, to be free from unwarranted governmental intrusion into matters so fundamentally affecting a person as the decision whether to bear or beget a child."

Mr. Baird called the decision "a great victory for the people of Massachusetts and the nation, a victory which

viction under the state's power to control harmful products. But they said there was no proof that vaginal foam was harmful.

The lone dissenter against overturning the conviction was Chief Justice Warren E. Burger. He said the state had acted properly in punishing Mr. Baird "for dispensing medicinal material without a license."

Justices Lewis F. Powell Jr. and William H. Rehnquist did not participate because they were not on the Court when the case was argued. . . .

. . . .

In 1977 Justice Brennan again wrote the main opinion in *Carey v. Population Services International,* striking down a New York law prohibiting distribution of contraceptives to minors under the age of sixteen. The law burdened minors' rights to use contraceptives and served no compelling state interest, Brennan said. Chief Justice Warren E. Burger and Justice Rehnquist dissented.

ABORTION RIGHTS

States began enacting laws to ban abortion in the mid-nineteenth century, primarily to protect women from unsafe medical procedures. By the 1960s, an abortion reform movement was arguing that the laws had the opposite effect. Women with means could circumvent the bans one way or another, it was contended, but poor women seeking an abortion had to resort to physicians or unlicensed practitioners of uncertain training and skills who worked—figuratively if not literally—in "back alleys."

The abortion reform movement drew from the work of family planning groups such as Planned Parenthood, antipoverty organizations, and the nascent women's liberation movement. But these groups' efforts collided against the strong opposition of the Roman Catholic Church and the significant public ambivalence about the morality of what were then called "elective" abortions.

By 1970, however, twelve states had enacted liberalized abortion laws. In the first six months of 1970, three states, including New York, adopted "repeal laws" that virtually eliminated any barriers to a woman's choice to terminate a pregnancy.

Reformers also challenged abortion laws on constitutional grounds, often successfully. Yet in its first ruling on the issue, the Supreme Court in 1971 upheld a law for the District of Columbia that banned all abortions except those necessary to save the life or health of the mother. The 5-4 decision in *United States v. Vuitch* found the law not to be unconstitutionally vague, but only after construing the health exception to encompass protection for the woman's mental well-being.

ROE v. WADE (1973)

With abortion law challenges pending in many states and federal circuits, the Court agreed only two weeks after *Vuitch,* on May 3, to hear appeals from Texas and Georgia, which were seeking to overturn decisions striking down their laws as unconstitutional. Texas had banned all abortions except those to save the life of the mother; Georgia's liberalized law allowed abortions if there was danger to the life or health of the mother, if the child would be physically or mentally defective, or if the woman had been raped. Georgia also required that abortions be performed in an accredited hospital and approved by two licensed physicians other than the woman's own and by a hospital review committee.

The plaintiff in the Texas case, "Jane Roe"—years later identified as Norma McCorvey—was an unmarried pregnant woman in Dallas who wanted to terminate her pregnancy. She brought suit in 1970 against the Dallas County prosecutor, Henry Wade, to block enforcement of the law. By the time the case was argued before the Supreme Court in December 1971, she had delivered the baby and given it up for adoption.

The close vote in *Vuitch* encouraged abortion rights advocates. Then in September, two of the justices in the majority—Black and Harlan—retired, both of them gravely ill. As their successors, President Richard M. Nixon nominated Lewis F. Powell Jr., a Virginia lawyer and former president of the American Bar Association, and Rehnquist, then head of the Justice Department's Office of Legal Counsel. The Senate confirmed both in early December, though not in time for them to be on the bench for the scheduled December 13 arguments in the abortion cases. Lawyers for Texas asked that arguments be postponed to allow a full bench to hear the cases, but the Court decided to stick with the schedule.

Representing Roe, Sarah Weddington, a twenty-six-year-old lawyer who herself had earlier had an illegal abortion in Mexico, told the justices that both the Ninth and Fourteenth Amendments protected a woman's right to end a pregnancy. Jay Floyd, an assistant state attorney general, began his argument by depicting the case as moot since Roe had already delivered the baby. Under questioning, he gave hesitant answers concerning the state's interest in banning abortions and the choices available to a woman seeking to terminate a pregnancy.

The vote in the justices' private conference appeared to favor striking down the Texas law and upholding the Georgia statute, with Chief Justice Burger voting to leave both laws on the books. Even though Burger was in the minority in the Texas case, he assigned the opinion to the junior justice in the majority, Harry A. Blackmun, a childhood friend from Minnesota whom Nixon had appointed in 1970. The breach of protocol angered Douglas, who thought he should have assigned the opinion as the senior justice in the majority. In any event, Blackmun was dissatisfied with his draft by the end of the term and proposed a second round of arguments in the cases with a full bench—in part to have more time to work on his opinions.

Blackmun spent the summer doing research at the Mayo Center in Minnesota and put the fruits of his work into the final opinion in *Roe v. Wade,* which was issued—following a second round of arguments in October 1972—on January 22, 1973. After acknowledging "the sensitive and emotional nature of the issue," Blackmun recited the Court's precedents on marriage and contraception to conclude that the constitutional right to privacy—based on the Fourteenth Amendment's Due Process Clause—was "broad enough to encompass a woman's decision whether or not to terminate her pregnancy."

Abortion had been legal through much of history, Blackmun recounted, and was made illegal in the United States mainly to protect women's health. With that consideration reduced, he continued, the major justification for making abortion illegal was "the state's interest . . . in protecting prenatal life." But that interest, he said, had to be calibrated with the woman's interest during the course of the pregnancy. This reasoning led Blackmun to the controversial trimester approach: permitting no regulations during the first trimester and only regulations "reasonably related to maternal health" until fetal viability, roughly at the end of the second trimester. The state's "interest in the potentiality of human life" could justify a ban on postviability abortions, he concluded, but only if exceptions were permitted "for the preservation of the life or health of the mother."

Six justices from across the ideological spectrum joined Blackmun's opinion, with only two dissenters: White and Rehnquist. In a concurring opinion, however, Burger said the ruling did not legalize "abortion by demand." By the same vote in the second case, *Doe v. Bolton* (1973), the Court ruled the Georgia law unconstitutional. The various procedural requirements were unrelated to the state's interest in protecting health, Blackmun said, and unduly restricted the woman's right to an abortion as well as physicians' rights to practice.

Roe v. Wade

Decided: January 22, 1973

Vote: 7 (Burger, Douglas, Brennan, Stewart, T. Marshall, Blackmun, Powell)

2 (B. White, Rehnquist)

Opinion of the Court: Blackmun

Concurring opinions (3): Burger; Douglas; Stewart

Dissenting opinions (2): B. White (Rehnquist); Rehnquist

JANUARY 23, 1973
HIGH COURT RULES ABORTIONS LEGAL THE FIRST 3 MONTHS
State Bans Ruled Out Until Last 10 Weeks

NATIONAL GUIDELINES SET BY 7-TO-2 VOTE

By WARREN WEAVER Jr.

Special to The New York Times

WASHINGTON, Jan. 22—The Supreme Court overruled today all state laws that prohibit or restrict a woman's right to obtain an abortion during her first three months of pregnancy. The vote was 7 to 2.

In a historic resolution of a fiercely controversial issue, the Court drafted a new set of national guidelines that will result in broadly liberalized anti-abortion laws in 46 states but will not abolish restrictions altogether.

Establishing an unusually detailed timetable for the relative legal rights of pregnant women and the states that would control their acts, the majority specified the following:

- For the first three months of pregnancy the decision to have an abortion lies with the woman and her doctor, and the state's interest in her welfare is not "compelling" enough to warrant any interference.

- For the next six months of pregnancy a state may "regulate the abortion procedure in ways that are reasonably related to maternal health," such as

licensing and regulating the persons and facilities involved.

- For the last 10 weeks of pregnancy, the period during which the fetus is judged to be capable of surviving if born, any state may prohibit abortions, if it wishes, except where they may be necessary to preserve the life or health of the mother.

Today's action will not affect existing laws in New York, Alaska, Hawaii and Washington, where abortions are now legally available in the early months of pregnancy. But it will require rewriting of statutes in every other state.

The basic Texas case decided by the Court today will invalidate strict anti-abortion laws in 31 states; a second decision involving Georgia will require considerable rewriting of more liberal statutes in 15 others.

Justice Harry A. Blackmun wrote the majority opinion in which Chief Justice Warren E. Burger and Justices

William O. Douglas, William J. Brennan Jr., Potter Stewart, Thurgood Marshall and Lewis F. Powell Jr. joined.

Dissenting were Justices Byron R. White and William H. Rehnquist.

Justice White, calling the decision "an exercise of raw judicial power," wrote that "the Court apparently values the convenience of the pregnant mother more than the continued existence and development of the life or potential life which she carries."

The Court's decision was at odds with the expressed views of President Nixon. Last May, in a letter to Cardinal Cooke, he opposed "liberalized abortion policies" and spoke out for "the right to life of literally hundreds of thousands of unborn children."

But three of the four Justices Mr. Nixon has appointed to the Supreme Court voted with the majority, with only Mr. Rehnquist dissenting.

ments that a woman seeking to terminate her pregnancy in that state would have to meet.

DECISION FOR DOCTORS

Among them were a flat prohibition on abortions for out-of-state residents and requirements that hospitals be accredited by a private agency, that applicants be screened by a hospital committee and that two independent doctors certify the potential danger to the applicant's health.

The Georgia law permitted abortions when a doctor found in "his best clinical judgment" that continued pregnancy would threaten the woman's life or health, that the fetus would be likely to be born defective or that the pregnancy was the result of rape.

The same Supreme Court majority, with Justice Blackmun writing the opinion again, emphasized that this medical

> The Court's decision was at odds with the expressed views of President Nixon. . . . But three of the four Justices Mr. Nixon has appointed to the Supreme Court voted with the majority, with only Mr. Rehnquist dissenting.

The majority rejected the idea that a fetus becomes a "person" upon conception and is thus entitled to the due process and equal protection guarantees of the Constitution. This view was pressed by opponents of liberalized abortion, including the Roman Catholic Church.

Justice Blackmun concluded that "the word 'person,' as used in the 14th Amendment, does not include the unborn," although states may acquire, "at some point in time" of pregnancy, an interest in the "potential human life" that the fetus represents, to permit regulation.

It is that interest, the Court said, that permits states to prohibit abortion during the last 10 weeks of pregnancy, after the fetus has developed the capacity to survive.

In both cases decided today, the plaintiffs had based their protest on an assertion that state laws limiting the availability of abortion had circumscribed rights and freedoms guaranteed them by the Constitution: due process of law, equal protection of the laws, freedom of action and a particular privacy involving a personal and family matter.

In its decision on the challenge to the Georgia abortion law, the high court majority struck down several require-

judgment should cover all relevant factors—"physical, emotional, psychological, familial and the woman's age."

In some of the 15 states with laws similar to Georgia's, doctors have tended to take a relatively narrow view of what constituted a woman's health in deciding whether an abortion was legally justified.

The Texas law that the Court invalidated entirely was typical of the criminal statutes passed in the last half of the 19th century prohibiting all abortions except those to save a mother's life. The Georgia law, approved in 1972 and altered by the Court today, was patterned after the model penal code of the American Law Institute.

In the Texas case, Justice Blackmun wrote that the constitutional right of privacy, developed by the Court in a long series of decisions, was "broad enough to encompass a woman's decision whether or not to terminate her pregnancy."

He rejected, however, the argument of women's rights groups that this right was absolute "and she is entitled to terminate her pregnancy at whatever time, in whatever way and for whatever reason she alone chooses."

"With this we do not agree," the Justice declared.

"A state may properly assert important interests in safeguarding health in maintaining medical standards and in protecting potential life," Mr. Blackmun observed. "At some point in pregnancy, these respective interests become sufficiently compelling to sustain regulation of the factors that govern the abortion decision."

The majority concluded that this "compelling" state interest arose at the end of the first three months of pregnancy because of the "now established medical fact" that until then, fewer women die from abortions than from normal childbirth.

During this three-month period, the Court said, a doctor can recommend an abortion to his patient "without regulation by the state" and the resulting operations can be conducted "free of interference by the state."

The "compelling state interest" in the fetus does not arise, however, until the time of "viability," Justice Black-mun wrote, when it has "the capability of meaningful life outside the mother's womb." This occurs about 10 weeks before delivery.

In reading an abbreviated version of his two opinions to the Court this morning, Justice Blackmun noted that most state legislatures were in session now and would thus be able to rewrite their states' abortion laws to conform to the Court's decision.

Both of today's cases wound up with anonymous parties winning victories over state officials. In the Texas case, "Jane Roe," an unmarried pregnant woman who was allowed to bring the case without further identity, was the only plaintiff after the Supreme Court disqualified a doctor and a childless couple who said that the wife's health would be endangered by pregnancy.

In the Georgia case, the surviving plaintiff was "Mary Doe," who, when she brought the action, was a 22-year-old married woman 11 weeks pregnant with her fourth child.

* * * * * * * * * * * *

The ruling touched off a political and legal debate that continues more than thirty years later. Abortion rights advocates cheered the ruling, but some came later to accept the criticism that a more tempered decision might have avoided the backlash that resulted. Abortion opponents criticized the legal basis for the ruling and quickly mobilized to try to overturn the decision and in the meantime to lobby for whatever legislative restrictions the ruling might permit.

EDITORIAL
JANUARY 24, 1973
RESPECT FOR PRIVACY

The Supreme Court has made a major contribution to the preservation of individual liberties and of free decision-making by its invalidation of state laws inhibiting a woman's right to obtain an abortion in the first three months of pregnancy.

The Court's seven-to-two ruling could bring to an end the emotional and divisive public argument over what always should have been an intensely private and personal matter. It will end that argument if those who are now inveighing against the decision as a threat to civilization's survival will pause long enough to recognize the limits of what the Court has done.

It has not ordered any mother to have an abortion. It has left the decision where it belongs—to the woman and her physician—with the power of the state to interfere, at later stages of pregnancy, governed essentially by considerations of maternal health. The Court has performed a useful historical function by recalling that the spur for the initial adoption of state laws banning abortion nearly a century ago was the great risk of maternal death involved in the surgical procedures then used. Now the risk arises out of perpetuating such archaic statutory prohibitions. The effect of these laws has been to force women, especially the young and the poor, to resort to abortion mills instead of expert hospital care when they are determined not to have an unwanted child.

The majority opinion by Justice Blackmun stops short of the absolutist view that a woman is entitled to terminate her pregnancy whenever, however and why ever she alone chooses. Instead, it affirms the legitimate interest of the state in putting such limits on that right of privacy as are needed in advanced phases of gestation to safeguard health, maintain medical standards or protect potential life. In the process, the Court wisely avoids the quicksand of attempting a judicial pronouncement on precisely when life begins, an endeavor that has long baffled scientists, theologians and philosophers.

Nothing in the Court's approach ought give affront to persons who oppose all abortion for reasons of religion or individual conviction. They can stand as firmly as ever for those principles, provided they do not seek to impede the freedom of those with an opposite view.

President Nixon, who intervened so gratuitously last year in an effort to upset New York State's liberal abortion law, can exercise a healing role now by acting to uphold the Court's ruling. In so doing he would be following the admirable precedent set by President Eisenhower nearly two decades ago in backing the Supreme Court's school desegregation decision, despite his own private reservations.

The Court's verdict on abortions provides a sound foundation for final and reasonable resolution of a debate that has divided America too long. As with the division over Vietnam, the country will be healthier with that division ended.

• • • • • • • • • • •

THE COURT AFTER *ROE V. WADE*

Over the next two decades, the Court upheld some legislative restrictions and struck many others down. (See "Supreme Court's Major Abortion-Related Rulings, 1973–2007," page 324.) In two of the rulings with the broadest impact, the Court upheld state and federal restrictions on using Medicaid funds to pay for abortions for poor women. As Powell wrote in *Maher v. Roe* (1977), *Roe v. Wade* did not prevent the government from "favoring childbirth over abortion." The ruling upheld a Connecticut regulation that barred funding unless the abortion was "medically necessary" for the woman's physical or mental health. Three years later, the Court's ruling in *Harris v. McRae* (1980) upheld a more severe federal restriction that barred funding for abortions except if the woman's life would be endangered or in cases of rape or incest.

The Court decided early on that spousal consent provisions violated a woman's right to abortion, but it took several cases before settling on an approach to parental consent and notification provisions for minors. Companion decisions in 1990 in *Hodgson v. Minnesota* and *Ohio v. Akron Center for Reproductive Health* struck down a two-parent notice requirement but upheld a one-parent notice provision as long as a "mature" minor could use a "judicial bypass" to circumvent the requirement and show that an abortion was in her best interest.

By the late 1980s, the Court's composition had changed with Rehnquist's elevation to chief justice and three other appointments by President Ronald Reagan, who opposed the *Roe* decision: Sandra Day O'Connor, Antonin Scalia, and Anthony M. Kennedy. Antiabortion groups hoped that a Missouri case would give the transformed Court a chance to uphold a broad set of abortion restrictions and perhaps even to overturn *Roe*. The decision in *Webster v. Reproductive Health Services* (1989) upheld all of the provisions in the challenged Missouri law, but in a pivotal concurring opinion, O'Connor refused to provide a fifth vote for Rehnquist's call to replace *Roe*'s "rigid framework" with a more flexible test for judging abortion restrictions. In a dissent, however, Blackmun warned that *Roe* and the right to an abortion "survive but are not secure."

Abortion opponents were again disappointed three years later, when the Court upheld all except one of the challenged abortion restrictions in a Pennsylvania law but fell one vote short of overturning *Roe*. The Pennsylvania law included several provisions— a twenty-four-hour waiting period, an informed consent provision, and a spousal notification requirement—that seemed at odds with the Court's precedents. But the Court had two new justices since the earlier ruling: David H. Souter and Clarence Thomas, both appointed by President George H. W. Bush and both confirmed over the opposition of abortion-rights groups.

Webster v. Reproductive Health Services

Decided: July 3, 1989

Vote: 5 (Rehnquist, B. White, O'Connor, Scalia, Kennedy)

4 (Brennan, T. Marshall, Blackmun, Stevens)

Judgment of the Court: Rehnquist

Concurring in judgment (2): O'Connor; Scalia

Dissenting opinions (2): Blackmun (Brennan, T. Marshall); Stevens

Supreme Court's Major Abortion-Related Rulings, 1973–2007

Decision (Date)	Vote	Main Opinion
Roe v. Wade (1973), _Doe v. Bolton_ (1973) Finds women have qualified constitutional right to terminate a pregnancy; no regulation permitted in first trimester, only health-related regulations permitted in second; bans permitted after viability if exceptions allowed to protect life or health of woman	7-2	Blackmun
Planned Parenthood v. Danforth (1976) Strikes down spousal consent provision (6-3), parental consent provision (5-4)	Mixed	Blackmun
Maher v. Roe (1977) Upholds state regulation denying funding for non-medically necessary abortions for indigent women	6-3	Powell
Bellotti v. Baird (1979) Strikes down two-parent parental consent provision, subject to judicial override	8-1	Powell
Harris v. McRae (1980) Upholds federal law (Hyde Amendment) denying funding for abortions for indigent women except in cases of rape or incest or if the woman's life is endangered	5-4	Stewart
Planned Parenthood v. Ashcroft (1983) Upholds parental consent provision with right of minor to use judicial bypass procedure	5-4	Powell
Akron v. Akron Center for Reproductive Health (1983) Strikes down twenty-four-hour waiting period, informed consent provision	6-3	Powell
Thornburgh v. American College of Obstetricians and Gynecologists (1986) Strikes down informed consent provision, postviability degree of care requirement	5-4	Blackmun
Webster v. Reproductive Health Services (1989) Upholds "life begins at conception" preamble, bans on state employees performing abortions or on abortions performed at public facilities, requirement for viability testing after twentieth week of pregnancy; four votes for substantially modifying or overruling _Roe_	5-4	Rehnquist
Hodgson v. Minnesota (1990) Strikes down two-parent notification provision (5-4), but as modified upholds parental consent provision with judicial bypass (5-4)	Mixed	Stevens; O'Connor
Ohio v. Akron Center for Reproductive Health (1990) Upholds provision requiring physician to notify one of minor's parents before performing abortion; law included judicial bypass procedure	6-3	Kennedy
Rust v. Sullivan (1991) Upholds prohibition on federally funded family planning clinics from engaging in abortion counseling or referrals	5-4	Rehnquist
Planned Parenthood of Southeastern Pennsylvania v. Casey (1992) Reaffirms "essential holding" of _Roe_ (5-4); upholds one-parent parental consent with judicial bypass, informed consent, twenty-four-hour waiting period, reporting requirements (7-2); strikes down spousal notification (5-4)	Mixed	O'Connor, Kennedy, Souter
Stenberg v. Carhart (2000) Strikes down Nebraska law banning partial-birth abortions	5-4	Breyer
Gonzales v. Carhart (2007) Upholds federal law banning partial-birth abortions	5-4	Kennedy

Despite the hopeful signs for antiabortion groups, the decision in *Planned Parenthood of Southeastern Pennsylvania v. Casey* (1992) left *Roe* on the books, at least in modified form. Justices O'Connor, Kennedy, and Souter coauthored an unusual joint opinion that rejected the calls to overrule *Roe*. "The ability of women to participate equally in the economic and social life of the Nation has been facilitated by their ability to control their reproductive lives," the justices wrote. Besides hurting this reliance interest, the justices explained, overruling *Roe* in the face of the sustained criticism of the decision would "seriously weaken the Court's capacity to exercise the judicial power and to function as the Supreme Court of a Nation dedicated to the rule of law."

Nonetheless, the three justices agreed that *Roe*'s trimester framework "undervalues the State's interest in potential life." They replaced it with a more flexible test—long advocated by O'Connor—for upholding abortion regulations unless they imposed "an undue burden" on a woman's right to choose. Applying that standard, the three justices provided the pivotal votes to find the spousal notification provision unconstitutional by a 5-4 margin. The other provisions were left standing by a 7-2 vote.

Planned Parenthood of Southeastern Pennsylvania v. Casey

Decided: June 29, 1992

Vote: 5 (Blackmun, Stevens, O'Connor, Kennedy, Souter)
4 (Rehnquist, B. White, Scalia, Thomas)

Judgment of the Court: O'Connor, Kennedy, Souter

Concurring opinion: Stevens

Opinion concurring in judgment: Blackmun

Dissenting opinions (2): Rehnquist (B. White, Scalia, Thomas); Scalia (Rehnquist, B. White, Thomas)

JUNE 30, 1992
HIGH COURT, 5-4, AFFIRMS RIGHT TO ABORTION BUT ALLOWS MOST OF PENNSYLVANIA'S LIMITS

SURPRISING DECISION

Majority Issues Warning on White House Effort to Overturn Roe

By LINDA GREENHOUSE

Special to The New York Times

WASHINGTON, June 29—By the narrowest of margins, and in words reflecting anger and anguish alike at its continuing role in the center of the storm over abortion, the Supreme Court today reaffirmed what it called the "essence" of the constitutional right to abortion while at the same time permitting some new state restrictions.

The 5-to-4 ruling redefined and limited the abortion right to some degree. But it left it stronger than many abortion-rights supporters had expected and opponents had hoped for from a Court that had appeared for the last three years to be on a course leading inevitably to the evisceration, if not complete overruling, of Roe v. Wade, the 1973 decision that established abortion as a fundamental right. . . .

UNCONSTITUTIONAL PROHIBITIONS

While the ruling upheld part of a Pennsylvania law regulating access to abortions, the majority left no doubt that laws prohibiting all or most abortions are unconstitutional. Louisiana, Utah and Guam have passed such laws and other states have been considering them.

In the opinion for the Court, unusual for being written jointly by Justices Sandra Day O'Connor, Anthony M. Kennedy and David H. Souter, and joined in part by Justices Harry A. Blackmun and John Paul Stevens, the majority said that Roe v. Wade established a "rule of law and a component of liberty we cannot renounce."

The majority said the 1973 decision had acquired a "rare precedential force" and could be overturned "under fire" only "at the cost of both profound and unnecessary damage to the Court's legitimacy, and to the nation's commitment to the rule of law."

There was little doubt that the "under fire" comment was aimed, at least in part, at the White House, both under President Bush and his predecessor, Ronald Reagan. In the first paragraph of its 60-page opinion, the majority noted pointedly that "the United States, as it has done in five other cases in the last decade, again asks us to overrule Roe."

A NEW ANALYSIS

The decision upheld parts of Pennsylvania's Abortion Control Act and struck down another part, applying for the first time a new analysis that asks whether a state abortion regulation has the purpose or effect of imposing an "undue burden." This was defined as a "substantial obstacle in the path of a woman seeking an abortion before the fetus attains viability."

Under this analysis, the Court said that four sections of Pennsylvania's law did not impose an undue burden on the right to abortion and were constitutional. These sections require a woman to delay an abortion for 24 hours after listening to a presentation at the medical office intended to persuade [her] to change her mind; require teenagers to have the consent of one parent or a judge; specify the medical emergencies in which the other requirements

Justices Blackmun and Stevens, in separate opinions of their own, said that four provisions should be held unconstitutional. And they joined the O'Connor-Kennedy-Souter group to strike down the husband-notification provision.

This provision contained several exceptions, including one for women who believed their husbands would physically injure them on learning of a planned abortion.

But the Court said that this did not sufficiently protect women who face psychological as well as physical abuse and who may have "very good reasons for not wishing to inform their husbands of their decision to obtain an abortion."

> " The majority said [Roe v. Wade] had acquired a 'rare precedential force' and could be overturned 'under fire' only 'at the cost of both profound and unnecessary damage to the Court's legitimacy, and to the nation's commitment to the rule of law.' "

will be waived, and require the doctor or clinic to make statistical reports to the state. At the same time, by a 5-4 vote, the Court struck down a fifth provision requiring a married woman to tell her husband of her intent to have an abortion.

Gov. Robert P. Casey of Pennsylvania, a Democrat whose opposition to abortion has made him something of a pariah in his party, said the Court's analysis vindicated his state's approach to regulating abortion. "Today's decision upholding the Pennsylvania law is a victory for the unborn child, the most powerful member of the human family," he said.

Abortion-rights supporters said the ruling would encourage more state restrictions and that the waiting period, in particular, would make abortions more difficult and expensive for women who would have to make two trips to abortion clinics that might be hundreds of miles from their homes.

Seven Justices supported these requirements. In addition to Justices O'Connor, Kennedy and Souter, they were Chief Justice William H. Rehnquist and Justices Antonin Scalia, Byron R. White and Clarence Thomas. These four Justices said that the Court should not only have upheld these regulations, but should also have overturned Roe v. Wade itself.

The Court added, "A state may not give to a man the kind of dominion over his wife that parents exercise over their children."

SCATHING DISSENTS

In dissenting opinions, Chief Justice Rehnquist and Justice Scalia offered scathing critiques of the Court's opinion. Each signed the other's opinion, and both opinions were also signed by Justices White and Thomas. The overlap was somewhat puzzling, because the two opinions expressed very different, even contradictory, views about what the majority had accomplished.

Chief Justice Rehnquist said the Court had not actually reaffirmed Roe v. Wade, but had rendered it a "facade," replacing its framework with a standard "created largely out of whole cloth" and "not built to last."

"Roe v. Wade stands as a sort of judicial Potemkin village," the Chief Justice said, "which may be pointed out to passersby as a monument to the importance of adhering to precedent."

Justice Scalia, on the other hand, declared that "the imperial judiciary lives," and appeared to concede to the majority its assertion that abortion remained on a solid constitutional foundation, although one he strongly disagreed with.

"By foreclosing all democratic outlet for the deep passions this issue arouse," Justice Scalia said, "by banishing the issue from the political forum that gives all participants, even the losers, the satisfaction of a fair hearing and an honest fight, by continuing the imposition of a rigid national rule instead of allowing for regional differences, the Court merely prolongs and intensifies the anguish."

The case, Planned Parenthood v. Casey, No. 91-744, gave the two newest Justices their first opportunity to rule in an abortion case. Both Bush nominees—Justice Souter, who joined the Court in 1990, and Justice Thomas, who told the Senate Judiciary Committee last September that he had never discussed Roe v. Wade—had been careful to avoid giving their views on abortion during their confirmation hearings.

SURPRISE FROM 2 JUSTICES

The real surprise in the decision, however, lay not in their votes but in the votes of two Justices chosen by Ronald Reagan, Justices O'Connor and Kennedy, who in previous opinions were sharp critics of Roe v. Wade.

Just three years ago, when the Court upheld portions of a restrictive Missouri abortion law in Webster v. Reproductive Health Services, Justice Kennedy joined a plurality opinion by Chief Justice Rehnquist that would have essentially overturned Roe v. Wade and replaced it with the lowest level of constitutional protection.

Justice O'Connor was a consistent dissenter during her early years on the Court. In her first abortion opinion in 1983, she was sharply critical of the precedent, declaring that it had established a doctrine "at war with itself" because the date of fetal viability was, she said, moving ever earlier toward the first months of pregnancy.

In her early opinions, Justice O'Connor proposed replacing Roe v. Wade with an "undue burden" test that would have allowed more restrictions than the test she, Justice Kennedy and Justice Souter adopted today. Because she had initially referred to the state's interest in the life of the fetus as "compelling," it had not been clear whether her original "undue burden" test would find it unconstitutional for a state to ban abortion.

Today's opinion made no reference to a "compelling" state interest in fetal life and acknowledged that some of her previous statements had been "inconsistent." "We answer the question, left open in previous opinions discussing the undue burden formulation, whether a law designed to further the state's interest in fetal life which imposes an undue burden on the woman's decision before fetal viability could be constitutional," the three Justices wrote. "The answer is no."

The important difference between today's decision and Roe v. Wade lay in the standard of review by which courts are to evaluate abortion restrictions. As the Court had interpreted Roe v. Wade until the Webster decision three years ago, abortion was a "fundamental" right that could not be restricted except to serve a "compelling" state interest, a standard of review known as "strict scrutiny" under which nearly all restrictions on abortion during the first two trimesters of pregnancy were found invalid.

But the new "undue burden" standard will permit considerably more regulation during that period. The Court today overruled two decisions, one from 1983 and the other from 1986, that had struck down, applying strict scrutiny analysis, 24-hour waiting periods and informed consent provisions much like the ones the Court upheld today.

The decision today upheld a ruling last fall by the United States Court of Appeals for the Third Circuit, in Philadelphia.

MORE WRANGLING AHEAD

The decision today was certainly not the Court's final word on the abortion issue, and it may not even be the final word on the Pennsylvania law. The majority indicated that because the law had not yet taken effect, and because the abortion clinics that challenged the law had not had occasion to document the effects of the waiting period and other provisions, the Court's door would be open to the argument that provisions that did not appear to impose an "undue burden" in theory might do so in fact.

Justice Blackmun, in his separate opinion, said he was "pleased" that the Court was open to reconsidering its conclusion and "confident" that the evidence would prove the clinics' case.

The opinion of Justice Blackmun, the author of Roe v. Wade, took an extraordinarily personal tone, reflecting relief that the Court had not flatly overturned Roe v. Wade as he had publicly predicted, and disappointment that his legacy still remained under attack.

In a bitter dissenting opinion in the Webster case three years ago, he warned that darkness was approaching and "a chill wind blows." Today, he said, "But now, just when so many expected the darkness to fall, the flame has grown bright." He commended Justices O'Connor, Souter and Kennedy for "an act of personal courage and constitutional principle."

But he warned that Roe v. Wade was only one vote away from being completely overruled. "I am 83 years old," he said. "I cannot remain on this Court forever." He predicted a fierce confirmation battle over the nomination of a successor. Justice Blackmun, the oldest member of the Court, has said within the past few days that he is not planning to retire at this point.

Given the Justices' personal feelings, the scene in the courtroom this morning, on the last day of the Court's term, was one of drama. Justice O'Connor read a section of the joint opinion, stressing that abortion was a difficult personal issue for the members of the Court. But she said, "Our obligation is to define the liberty of all, not to mandate our own moral code."

. . . .

President Bill Clinton's appointment of two abortion rights supporters—Ruth Bader Ginsburg and Stephen G. Breyer—dashed antiabortion groups' hopes for a different result for the rest of the decade. But abortion opponents found a new issue by seeking to ban a rarely used late-term procedure that doctors called "intact dilation and extraction," or intact D&E, but that antiabortion groups provocatively labeled "partial-birth abortion." The procedure entailed the partial delivery of a fetus through the vaginal canal followed by the piercing of the fetal skull to complete the removal. Abortion opponents, who often displayed graphic pictures of the procedure, won enactment of laws banning the procedure in some thirty states by the end of the decade.

The *Carhart* Decisions

Stenberg v. Carhart

Decided: June 28, 2000

Vote: 5 (Stevens, O'Connor, Souter, Ginsburg, Breyer)

4 (Rehnquist, Scalia, Kennedy, Thomas)

Opinion of the Court: Breyer

Concurring opinions (3): Stevens (Ginsburg); O'Connor; Ginsburg (Stevens)

Dissenting opinions (4): Rehnquist; Scalia; Kennedy (Rehnquist); Thomas (Rehnquist, Scalia)

In 2000, however, the Court ruled, 5-4, that Nebraska's partial-birth abortion law—typical of such state statutes—was unconstitutional. Writing for the majority in *Stenberg v. Carhart* (2000), Justice Breyer said the law's failure to include an exception allowing the procedure to protect a woman's health would "place some women at unnecessary risk of tragic health consequences." In addition, he said, the law imposed an "undue burden" on women's rights because the vague definition of the procedure could be used to prosecute doctors for performing more common abortion procedures. Justice O'Connor provided a critical fifth vote for the decision, but wrote separately to say that a narrower law might be sustained.

Congress and President George W. Bush responded by passing and signing into law the federal Partial-Birth Abortion Ban Act of 2003. The act included a more detailed definition of the banned procedure along with a lengthy refutation of the need for a health exception. Federal appeals courts in St. Louis, New York City, and San Francisco all ruled the measure unconstitutional. The government's appeals reached the Supreme Court after two appointments had been made by President Bush: Roberts as chief justice and Samuel A. Alito Jr. as O'Connor's successor. Abortion rights advocates opposed the nominees, who both stopped short in their testimony of endorsing *Roe v. Wade*.

Gonzales v. Carhart

Decided: April 18, 2007

Vote: 5 (J. Roberts, Scalia, Kennedy, Thomas, Alito)

4 (Stevens, Souter, Ginsburg, Breyer)

Opinion of the Court: Kennedy

Concurring opinion: Thomas (Scalia)

Dissenting opinion: Ginsburg (Stevens, Souter, Breyer)

By a 5-4 vote, the Court in *Gonzales v. Carhart* (2007) upheld the federal ban, with both Roberts and Alito in the majority. Justice Kennedy, who had written a strong dissent in the earlier case, voted to uphold the federal act. In the majority opinion, he wrote that the definition in the law was neither vague nor overbroad and did not cover the standard D&E procedure. He went on to reject the need for a health exception in the law, citing the "documented medical disagreement" on the issue. And in a passage that stirred resentment among abortion rights advocates, Kennedy said the ban was justified in part by the "grief more anguished and sorrow more profound" that a woman would feel upon learning the details of the procedure.

In an impassioned dissent read from the bench, Justice Ginsburg called the ruling "alarming." She particularly criticized Kennedy for adopting what she called the "anti-abortion shibboleth" that women suffer from depression and a loss of self-esteem after undergoing an abortion.

APRIL 19, 2007
IN REVERSAL OF COURSE, JUSTICES, 5-4, BACK BAN ON ABORTION METHOD

By LINDA GREENHOUSE

The Supreme Court reversed course on abortion on Wednesday, upholding the federal Partial-Birth Abortion Ban Act in a 5-to-4 decision that promises to reframe the abortion debate and define the young Roberts court.

The most important vote was that of the newest justice, Samuel A. Alito Jr. In another 5-to-4 decision seven years ago, his predecessor, Justice Sandra Day O'Connor, voted to strike down a similar state law. Justice Alito's vote to uphold the federal law made the difference in the outcome announced Wednesday.

The decision, the first in which the court has upheld a ban on a specific method of abortion, means that doctors who perform the prohibited procedure may face criminal prosecution, fines and up to two years in prison. The federal law, enacted in 2003, had been blocked from taking effect by the lower court rulings that the Supreme Court overturned.

The banned procedure, known medically as "intact dilation and extraction," involves removing the fetus in an intact condition rather than dismembering it in the uterus. Both methods are used to terminate pregnancies beginning at about 12 weeks, after the fetus has grown too big to be removed by the suction method commonly used in the first trimester, when 85 percent to 90 percent of all abortions take place.

While the ruling will thus have a direct impact on only a relatively small subset of abortion practice, the decision has broader implications for abortion regulations generally, indicating a change in the court's balancing of the various interests involved in the abortion debate.

Most notable was the emphasis in the majority opinion, by Justice Anthony M. Kennedy, on the implication of abortion's "ethical and moral concerns."

"The act expresses respect for the dignity of human life," Justice Kennedy said.

The decision was a major victory for the Bush administration and its vigorous defense of the law, which President Bill Clinton had vetoed twice before President Bush signed it.

Mr. Bush welcomed the ruling, saying: "The Supreme Court's decision is an affirmation of the progress we have made over the past six years in protecting human dignity and upholding the sanctity of life. We will continue to work for the day when every child is welcomed in life and protected in law."

It was also a vindication for the strategic choice the anti-abortion movement made 15 years ago, when the prospect of persuading the Supreme Court to reconsider the right to abortion seemed a distant dream. . . .

By identifying the intact procedure and giving it the provocative label "partial-birth abortion," the movement turned the public focus of the abortion debate from the rights of women to the fate of fetuses. In short order, 30 states banned the procedure.

> Mr. Bush welcomed the ruling, saying: 'The Supreme Court's decision is an affirmation of the progress we have made over the past six years in protecting human dignity and upholding the sanctity of life. We will continue to work for the day when every child is welcomed in life and protected in law.'

The decision on Wednesday came seven years after the court struck down one of those state laws, from Nebraska. Justice Kennedy was a strong dissenter from that decision. With Justice Alito's vote, he was in a position this time to write not for the dissenters but for the new majority.

Chief Justice John G. Roberts Jr. and Justices Antonin Scalia and Clarence Thomas also voted in the majority. Justices Thomas and Scalia also filed a brief concurring opinion reiterating their opposition to the court's abortion precedents and expressing their continued desire to overturn them.

Neither Chief Justice Roberts nor Justice Alito signed this statement. There was no way of knowing whether their silence meant they disagreed with it or whether, not having previously expressed their views as Justices Thomas and Scalia had, they had no need at this point to stake their ground.

The court did not explicitly overturn any of its precedents, although Justice Ruth Bader Ginsburg, writing for the four dissenters, said the decision was "so at odds with our jurisprudence" that it "should not have staying power." Justice Ginsburg called the decision "alarming" and said the majority's "hostility" to the right to abortion was "not concealed."

Justices John Paul Stevens, David H. Souter and Stephen G. Breyer signed Justice Ginsburg's opinion, portions of which she read from the bench at a slow pace that caused every syllable to resonate.

Justice Kennedy took pains to describe the decision as faithful to the court's earlier rulings, including the one in the Nebraska case. He said that by defining the prohibited procedure more precisely, the federal law avoided the vagueness the court had found in the Nebraska statute and thus did not place doctors at risk of violating it inadvertently.

Congress passed the law in response to the court's ruling in the Nebraska case, responding specifically to the majority's insistence in that case that the law must include an exception for circumstances when the banned procedure was necessary for the sake of a pregnant woman's health. Congress provided an exception only to save a pregnant woman's life, as Nebraska had, declaring that the procedure was never necessary for a woman's health.

Justice Kennedy, in addressing the need for the health exception, said on Wednesday that it was acceptable for Congress not to include one because there was "medical uncertainty" over whether the banned procedure was ever necessary for the sake of a woman's health. He said that pregnant women or their doctors could assert an individual need for a health exception by going to court to challenge the law as it applied to them.

Justice Ginsburg said that this approach was unrealistic and "gravely mistaken." She said that requiring "piecemeal" litigation "jeopardizes women's health and places doctors in an untenable position."

Clarke D. Forsythe, president of Americans United for Life, a leading anti-abortion group, said approvingly that while the court did not technically overturn the Nebraska decision, the new ruling "effectively gutted it."

Dr. LeRoy H. Carhart, the Nebraska doctor who challenged both the state law in 2000 and the federal law in this case, Gonzales v. Carhart, No. 05-380, said that "those who support this law are trying to outlaw all abortions, one step at a time."

In his discussion of the court's precedents, Justice Kennedy went so far as to suggest that the new ruling was in fact compelled by the court's decision in Planned Parenthood v. Casey, the 1992 case that reaffirmed the basic holding of Roe v. Wade that women have a constitutional right to abortion. Justice Kennedy supported that result and helped write the decision's unusual joint opinion.

On Wednesday, he said that "whatever one's views concerning the Casey joint opinion, it is evident a premise central to its conclusion—that the government has a legitimate and substantial interest in preserving and promoting fetal life—would be repudiated were the court now to affirm the judgments of the courts of appeals" that struck down the federal law.

In describing the federal law's justifications, Justice Kennedy said that banning the procedure was in fact good for women, protecting them against terminating their pregnancies by a method they might not fully understand in advance and would come to regret later.

"Respect for human life finds an ultimate expression in the bond of love the mother has for her child," he said, adding: "It is self-evident that a mother who comes to regret her choice to abort must struggle with grief more anguished and sorrow more profound when she learns, only after the event, what she once did not know: that she allowed a doctor to pierce the skull and vacuum the fast-developing brain of her unborn child, a child assuming the human form."

Justice Ginsburg objected vehemently that "this way of thinking reflects ancient notions of women's place in the family and under the Constitution—ideas that have long since been discredited."

She cited century-old Supreme Court cases that upheld a paternalistic view of women's place in society and contrasted those with more recent cases, including one she successfully argued to the court in 1977 and one in which she wrote the majority opinion in 1996, that rejected "archaic and overbroad generalizations" and assumptions about women's inherent dependency.

One law professor, Martin S. Lederman of Georgetown University, commented after reading Justice Ginsburg's response on this point that Justice Kennedy's opinion "was an attack on her entire life's work."

In her opinion, Justice Ginsburg said the majority had provided only "flimsy and transparent justifications" for upholding the law, which she noted "saves not a single fetus from destruction" by banning a single method of abortion. "One wonders how long a line that saves no fetus from destruction will hold in face of the court's 'moral concerns,' " she said.

• • • • • • • • • • • •

GAY RIGHTS

The Supreme Court was indifferent or hostile toward gay rights for several decades after cases involving homosexuals first appeared on its docket in the 1950s. A series of actions in the 1960s generally upheld the government's right to fire employees or deport immigrants on grounds of homosexuality. In the 1970s the Court twice set aside lower court rulings that had struck down antisodomy laws as too broad or too vague. In 1976 the Court issued a summary decision upholding Virginia's antisodomy statute. Unlike the previous actions, the ruling in *Doe v. Richmond* (1976) amounted to a legal precedent even though no opinion was issued.

A decade later, the Court gave full consideration to the issue in a case challenging Georgia's antisodomy statute, but the result was the same. Michael Hardwick was arrested in his Atlanta apartment after police officers serving a warrant for drinking in public found him in bed engaged in oral sex with another man. The district attorney declined to prosecute, but Hardwick filed a federal court suit challenging the constitutionality of the law.

By a 5-4 vote in *Bowers v. Hardwick* (1986), the Court upheld the statute. For the majority, Justice White rejected as "facetious" any notion that the Constitution conferred on homosexuals the right to engage in sodomy. He acknowledged the Court's various privacy-related precedents, but concluded they were irrelevant because there was "no connection between family, marriage, or procreation on the one hand and homosexual activity on the other."

 ## JULY 1, 1986
HIGH COURT, 5-4, SAYS STATES HAVE THE RIGHT TO OUTLAW PRIVATE HOMOSEXUAL ACTS
DIVISION IS BITTER
By STUART TAYLOR JR.
Special to The New York Times

A bitterly divided Supreme Court ruled 5 to 4 today that the Constitution does not protect homosexual relations between consenting adults, even in the privacy of their own homes.

The Court held that a Georgia law that forbids all people to engage in oral or anal sex could be used to prosecute such conduct between homosexuals.

The majority said it would not rule on whether the Constitution protected married couples and other hetero-

sexuals from prosecution under the same law. Associate Justice John Paul Stevens, however, said in a dissent that such laws were "concededly unconstitutional with respect to heterosexuals" under the reasoning of previous Supreme Court rulings.

WEAKENS LEGAL POSITION

The decision is unlikely to curb the growing visibility of homosexuality as a fact of daily life in America, but it weakens the legal arguments of homosexual activists against various forms of discrimination.

This does not necessarily mean it would allow discrimination against homosexuals in other contexts. However, both homosexual groups and their opponents agreed the ruling would slow the advancement of homosexual rights. . . . The announcement of the decision was unusually dramatic, with Associate Justices Byron R. White, author of the majority opinion, and Harry A. Blackmun, author of an impassioned dissent, both reading detailed passages from the bench.

LIMITS EFFECT OF PAST RULINGS

The ruling limited past Supreme Court decisions by rejecting what Justice White called the view "that any kind of private sexual conduct between consenting adults is constitutionally insulated from state proscription."

WAS NOT PROSECUTED IN CASE

Mr. Hardwick was not prosecuted, but he challenged the law on the ground that it violated his constitutional right to privacy.

Justice White's opinion declined to extend to homosexuals a line of decisions involving heterosexuals—in particular a 1965 decision striking down a Connecticut law against contraception—in which the Court has recognized constitutional rights to sexual privacy. While the court did not specifically refer to homosexual acts between women, its reasoning would apparently apply to such acts.

Justice White stressed the "ancient roots" in English common law of statutes criminalizing homosexual relations, noting that all 50 states outlawed homosexual sodomy until 1961 and that 24 states and the District of Columbia still do.

> " The Court is most vulnerable and comes nearest to illegitimacy when it deals with judge-made constitutional law having little or no cognizable roots in the language or design of the Constitution. "
> —Justice Byron R. White, *Bowers v. Hardwick*

While the Court has previously upheld a vague right of sexual privacy for heterosexuals, it has never specified, and did not say today, whether that right protects oral or anal sex between men and women.

Criminal prosecutions for private sexual conduct between consenting adults are rare in the case of homosexuals, the Court noted today, and almost unheard of in the case of heterosexuals.

The case ruled on today was a civil suit challenging the Georgia sodomy law brought by Michael Hardwick, a homosexual who had been arrested in his Atlanta bedroom while having sexual relations with another man.

The law defines sodomy as "any sex act involving the sex organs of one person and the mouth or anus of another."

A police officer had gone to his home to serve a warrant because Mr. Hardwick had not paid a fine for public drunkenness. The officer was given permission by someone who answered the door to enter the house and find Mr. Hardwick.

"The Court is most vulnerable and comes nearest to illegitimacy when it deals with judge-made constitutional law having little or no cognizable roots in the language or design of the Constitution," Justice White said in explaining why it should not create a right to homosexual sodomy.

Justice Blackmun, in his dissent, said, "The right of an individual to conduct intimate relationships in the intimacy of his or her own home seems to me to be the heart of the Constitution's protection of privacy."

Justice Stevens, in a separate dissent, said the Court's rationale, like the Georgia statute and the English common law from which it was derived, "applies equally to the prohibited conduct regardless of whether the parties who engage in it are married or unmarried, or of the same or different sexes."

He said that the court's prior decisions indicated the Constitution barred governmental intrusion into private heterosexual relationships, and that the same protections should apply to homosexuals.

SEVERITY OF PUNISHMENT CITED

One member of the majority, Associate Justice Lewis F. Powell Jr., said in a separate concurrence that while states may criminalize homosexual sodomy, those who commit such acts may enjoy some protection from the Eighth Amendment's ban on "cruel and unusual punishments."

Noting that the Georgia law authorizes prison sentences of one to 20 years for a single homosexual act, he said, "In my view, a prison sentence for such conduct—certainly a sentence of long duration—would create a serious Eighth Amendment issue."

Others joining the majority opinion were Chief Justice Warren E. Burger and Associate Justices William H. Rehnquist and Sandra Day O'Connor.

Associate Justices William J. Brennan Jr., Thurgood Marshall and Stevens joined Justice Blackmun's dissent. The first two also joined Justice Stevens's dissent.

Twenty-six states have decriminalized sodomy, and five of the 24 that still make homosexual sodomy a crime have decriminalized heterosexual sodomy, at least in some contexts.

The New York Court of Appeals, in a 1980 decision apparently in conflict with today's Supreme Court decision, held the state's law barring sodomy unconstitutional. But a state official said the ruling would have no direct bearing on New York law.

"The New York State statute was struck down by our own state court of appeals, and that statute remains unconstitutional," said Timothy Gilles, a spokesman for State Attorney General Robert Abrams. Mr. Gilles said the Supreme Court had declined to rule on the New York case in 1981, letting stand the state court ruling.

New Jersey and Connecticut have decriminalized sodomy by legislation.

NONCOMMITAL ON DESIRABILITY

Justice White stressed today that the case, Bowers v. Hardwick, No. 85-140, "does not require a judgment on whether laws against sodomy between consenting adults in general, or between homosexuals in particular, are wise or desirable," or about whether states should repeal such laws.

"The issue presented is whether the Federal Constitution confers a fundamental right upon homosexuals to engage in sodomy and hence invalidates the laws of the many states that still make such conduct illegal and have done so for a very long time," he said.

Justice White said that homosexual activity was not protected by previous decisions that have interpreted the 14th Amendment right not to be deprived of "liberty" without "due process of law" as including various "fundamental rights" not specified in the Constitution. He said these rights were limited to those "deeply rooted in this nation's history or tradition" or "implicit in the concept of ordered liberty."

In light of the law's longstanding condemnation of homosexual conduct, Justice White said, it would be "at best, facetious" to suggest that homosexual conduct qualified as a "fundamental right."

PRIVACY ARGUMENT REJECTED

Justice White also rejected the argument that homosexual conduct should be protected at least where it occurs in the privacy of the home. "Otherwise illegal conduct is not always immunized whenever it occurs in the home," he said, citing laws against possession of narcotics and stolen goods as well as "adultery, incest and other sexual crimes."

In response to arguments that the Constitution bars majorities from imposing their view of morality on minorities, he said the law "is constantly based on notions of morality, and if all laws representing essentially moral choices are to be invalidated under the Due Process Clause, the courts will be very busy indeed."

A Federal appellate court in Atlanta had held that the Georgia law "infringes upon the fundamental constitutional rights of Michael Hardwick" to have private sexual relations, indicating it was likely to strike the law down after further proceedings. The state appealed to the Supreme Court.

Justice White noted that a husband and wife who had challenged the law along with Mr. Hardwick had been held by the lower courts not to have standing to sue because they had never been arrested.

He said: "The only claim properly before the Court, therefore, is Hardwick's challenge to the Georgia statute as applied to consensual homosexual sodomy. We express no opinion on the constitutionality of the Georgia statute as applied to other acts of sodomy."

. . . .

The Court adopted a different tone toward homosexuals in the 1990s. In 1995 the Court upheld the right of the organizers of Boston's St. Patrick's Day parade to refuse to let a gay and lesbian Irish group march, but the opinion took a respectful tone toward the message that the group wanted to convey. More substantively, the next year the Court struck down a Colorado initiative that sought to prevent the enactment of state or local laws prohibiting discrimination on the basis of sexual orientation. (See page 292.)

Lawrence v. Texas

Decided: June 26, 2003

Vote: 6 (Stevens, O'Connor, Kennedy,
Souter, Ginsburg, Breyer)

3 (Rehnquist, Scalia, Thomas)

Opinion of the Court: Kennedy

Concurring opinion: O'Connor

Dissenting opinions (2): Scalia
(Rehnquist, Thomas); Thomas

The sodomy issue returned to the Court in a case brought by two Texas men, John Lawrence and Tyron Garner, challenging their convictions and $200 fines under a state law that banned oral or anal sex between persons of the same sex. In *Lawrence v. Texas* (2003), the Court overturned the convictions by a 6-3 vote in a decision that explicitly overruled *Bowers v. Hardwick*. For the majority, Justice Kennedy said that under the Due Process Clause homosexuals had "the full right to engage in private conduct without government intervention." "The State cannot demean their existence or control their destiny by making their private sexual conduct a crime," he wrote.

JUNE 27, 2003
JUSTICES, 6-3, LEGALIZE GAY SEXUAL CONDUCT IN SWEEPING REVERSAL OF COURT'S '86 RULING

By LINDA GREENHOUSE

The Supreme Court issued a sweeping declaration of constitutional liberty for gay men and lesbians today, overruling a Texas sodomy law in the broadest possible terms and effectively apologizing for a contrary 1986 decision that the majority said "demeans the lives of homosexual persons." The vote was 6 to 3.

two Houston men who were prosecuted for having sex in their home, few people on either side of the case expected a decision of such scope from a court that only 17 years ago, in Bowers v. Hardwick, had dismissed the same constitutional argument as "facetious." The court overturned that precedent today.

 Gays are 'entitled to respect for their private lives,' Justice Anthony M. Kennedy said for the court. 'The state cannot demean their existence or control their destiny by making their private sexual conduct a crime.'

Gays are "entitled to respect for their private lives," Justice Anthony M. Kennedy said for the court. "The state cannot demean their existence or control their destiny by making their private sexual conduct a crime."

Justice Kennedy said further that "adults may choose to enter upon this relationship in the confines of their homes and their own private lives and still retain their dignity as free persons." . . .

While the result had been widely anticipated since the court agreed in December to hear an appeal brought by

In a scathing dissent, Justice Antonin Scalia accused the court of having "taken sides in the culture war" and having "largely signed on to the so-called homosexual agenda." He said that the decision "effectively decrees the end of all morals legislation" and made same-sex marriage, which the majority opinion did not discuss, a logical if not inevitable next step. Chief Justice William H. Rehnquist and Justice Clarence Thomas signed Justice Scalia's dissent.

While some gay rights lawyers said that there were still abundant legal obstacles to establishing a right either to gay marriage or to military service by gay soldiers, there was no doubt that the decision had profound legal and political implications. A conservative Supreme Court has now identified the gay rights cause as a basic civil rights issue.

Ruth Harlow, legal director of the Lambda Legal Defense and Education Fund and the lead counsel for the two men, John G. Lawrence and Tyron Garner, called the decision "historic and transformative." Suzanne Goldberg, a professor at Rutgers Law School who had represented the men in the Texas courts, said that the decision would affect "every kind of case" involving gay people, including employment, child custody and visitation, and adoption.

"It removes the reflexive assumption of gay people's inferiority," Professor Goldberg said. "Bowers took away the humanity of gay people, and this decision gives it back."

The vote to overturn Bowers v. Hardwick was 5 to 4, with Justice Kennedy joined by Justices John Paul Stevens, David H. Souter, Ruth Bader Ginsburg and Stephen G. Breyer.

"Bowers was not correct when it was decided, and it is not correct today," Justice Kennedy said. "Its continuance as precedent demeans the lives of homosexual persons."

Justice Sandra Day O'Connor, who was part of the 5-to-4 majority in Bowers v. Hardwick, did not join Justice Kennedy in overruling it. But she provided the sixth vote for overturning the Texas sodomy law in a forcefully written separate opinion that attacked the law on equal protection grounds because it made "deviate sexual intercourse"—oral or anal sex—a crime only between same-sex couples and not for heterosexuals.

"A law branding one class of persons as criminal solely based on the state's moral disapproval of that class and the conduct association with that class runs contrary to the values of the Constitution and the Equal Protection Clause," Justice O'Connor said.

Texas was one of only four states—Kansas, Oklahoma and Missouri are the others—to apply a criminal sodomy law exclusively to same-sex partners. An additional nine states—Alabama, Florida, Idaho, Louisiana, Mississippi, North Carolina, South Carolina, Utah and Virginia—have criminal sodomy laws on their books that in theory, if not in practice, apply to opposite-sex couples as well. As a result of the majority's broad declaration today that the government cannot make this kind of private sexual choice a crime, all those laws are now invalid.

Twenty-five states had such laws at the time the court decided Bowers v. Hardwick. The Georgia sodomy law the court upheld in that case was overturned by a state court ruling in 1998. Some of the other state laws have been repealed and others invalidated by state courts.

In the Texas case, Mr. Lawrence and Mr. Garner were discovered by the Houston police while having sex in Mr. Lawrence's apartment. The police entered through an unlocked door after receiving a report from a neighbor of a "weapons disturbance" in the apartment. The neighbor was later convicted of filing a false report.

The men were held in jail overnight. They later pleaded no contest, preserving their right to appeal, and were each fined $200. The Texas state courts rejected their constitutional challenge to the law.

Asked today for the Bush administration's reaction to the ruling, Ari Fleischer, the White House press secretary, noted that the administration had not filed a brief in the case. "And now this is a state matter," he said. In fact, the decision today, Lawrence v. Texas, No. 02-102, took what had been a state-by-state matter and pronounced a binding national constitutional principle.

The delicacy of the moment for the White House was apparent. Groups representing the socially conservative side of the Republican Party reacted to the decision with alarm and fury. On the other hand, important libertarian groups had supported the challenge to the Texas law. Justice Thomas, who is often in sympathy with libertarian arguments, wrote a brief separate dissenting opinion today with a nod in that direction.

He said he would vote to repeal the law if he were a member of the Texas Legislature. "Punishing someone for expressing his sexual preference through noncommercial consensual conduct with another adult does not appear to be a worthy way to expend valuable law enforcement resources," Justice Thomas said, but added that he could not overturn the law as a judge because he did not see a constitutional basis for doing so.

Charles Francis, co-chairman of the Republican Unity Coalition, a group of gay and heterosexual Republicans seeking to defuse the issue within the party, said today, "I hope the giant middle of our party can look at this decision not as a threat but as a breakthrough for human understanding." The group includes prominent Republicans like former President Gerald R. Ford, David Rockefeller and Alan K. Simpson, the former senator from Wyoming, who is its honorary chairman. No member of the Bush administration has joined the group, Mr. Francis said.

As the court concluded its term today, the absence of any sign of a retirement meant that the issue was not likely to surface in judicial politics anytime soon. There was a tense and ultimately humorous moment in the courtroom this morning when, after the announcements of decisions, Chief Justice Rehnquist brought the term to a close with his customary words of thanks to the court staff.

"The court today notes the retirement," he then said drily as those in the audience caught their breath, "of librarian Shelley Dowling." A collective sigh and audible chuckles followed as the marshal, Pamela Talkin, banged her gavel and the nine justices left the bench, all of them evidently planning to return when the court meets on Sept. 8 for arguments in the campaign finance case.

Earlier, as Justice Kennedy was reading excerpts from his decision, the mood in the courtroom went from enormous tension and then—on the part of the numerous gay and lesbian lawyers seated in the bar section—to visible relief. By the time he referred to the dignity and respect to which he said gays were entitled, several were weeping, silently but openly.

The majority opinion was notable in many respects: its critical dissection of a recent precedent; its use of a decision by the European Court of Human Rights, supporting gay rights, to show that the court under Bowers v. Hardwick was out of step with other Western countries; and its many citations to the court's privacy precedents, including the abortion rights cases.

The citations to Roe v. Wade and Planned Parenthood v. Casey appeared particularly to inflame Justice Scalia. If Bowers v. Hardwick merited overruling, he said, so too did Roe v. Wade. He also said that laws against bigamy, adultery, prostitution, bestiality and obscenity were now susceptible to challenges.

The majority opinion did not precisely respond to that prediction, noting instead that the right claimed by Mr. Lawrence and Mr. Garner did not involve prostitution, public behavior, coercion or minors.

The fundamental debate on the court was over the meaning of the Constitution's due process guarantee, which Justice Kennedy said was sufficiently expansive so that "persons in every generation can invoke its principles in their own search for greater freedom."

• • • • • • • • • • •

Kennedy stressed that the decision covered only private, consensual conduct between adults and that the case did not raise the question of recognition for gay marriages. In a bitter dissent, Justice Scalia said the ruling undermined all laws regulating sexual conduct and left laws limiting marriage to heterosexuals "on pretty shaky grounds."

NEWS ANALYSIS
NOVEMBER 19, 2003
SUPREME COURT PAVED WAY FOR MARRIAGE RULING WITH SODOMY LAW DECISION

By LINDA GREENHOUSE

In its gay rights decision five months ago striking down a Texas criminal sodomy law, the Supreme Court said gay people were entitled to freedom, dignity and "respect for their private lives." It pointedly did not say they were entitled to marry.

In fact, both Justice Anthony M. Kennedy, in his majority opinion for five justices, and Justice Sandra Day O'Connor, in her separate concurring opinion, took pains to demonstrate that overturning a law that sent consenting adults to jail for their private sexual behavior did not imply recognition of same-sex marriage, despite Justice Antonin Scalia's apocalyptic statements to the contrary in an angry dissent proclaiming that all was lost in the culture wars.

The Texas case "does not involve whether the government must give formal recognition to any relationship that homosexual persons seek to enter," Justice Kennedy wrote. And Justice O'Connor wrote: "Unlike the moral disapproval of same-sex relations—the asserted state interest in this case—other reasons exist to promote the institution of marriage beyond mere moral disapproval of an excluded group."

And yet, despite the majority's disclaimers, it is indisputable that the Supreme Court's decision in Lawrence v. Texas also struck much deeper chords. It was a strikingly inclusive decision that both apologized for the past and, looking to the future, anchored the gay-rights claim at issue in the case firmly in the tradition of human rights at the broadest level.

And it was this background music that suffused the decision Tuesday by the Massachusetts Supreme Judicial Court that same-sex couples have a state constitutional right to the "protections, benefits, and obligations of civil marriage." The second paragraph of Chief Justice Margaret Marshall's majority opinion included this quotation from the Lawrence decision: "Our obligation is to define the liberty of all, not to mandate our own moral code."

doctrine. The Goodridge decision "is absolutely consistent with and responsive to Lawrence," Suzanne Goldberg, a professor at Rutgers University Law School who represented the two men who challenged the Texas sodomy law in the initial stages of the Lawrence case, said in an interview. Ms. Goldberg added: "It's impossible to overestimate how profoundly Lawrence changed the landscape for gay men and lesbians."

Professor Goldberg said that sodomy laws, even if not often enforced, had the effect of labeling gays as "criminals who deserved unequal treatment." With that argument removed, discriminatory laws have little left to stand on, she said, adding that the Supreme Court "gave state courts not only cover but strength to respond to unequal treatment of lesbians and gay men."

> The marriage ban works a deep and scarring hardship on a very real segment of the community for no rational reason.
> —Massachusetts Chief Justice Margaret Marshall,
> *Goodridge v. Department of Public Health*

"You'd have to be tone deaf not to get the message from Lawrence that anything that invites people to give same-sex couples less than full respect is constitutionally suspect," Professor Laurence H. Tribe of Harvard Law School said in an interview. Professor Tribe said that had the Texas case been decided differently—or not at all—"the odds that this cautious, basically conservative state court would have decided the case this way would have been considerably less."

The Massachusetts decision was based on the state's Constitution, which Chief Justice Marshall described as "if anything, more protective of individual liberty and equality than the federal Constitution." She said the Massachusetts Constitution "may demand broader protection for fundamental rights; and it is less tolerant of government intrusion into the protected spheres of private life."

Clearly, the state ruling, Goodridge v. Department of Public Health, was not compelled by the Supreme Court's decision in Lawrence v. Texas and, given its basis in state law, cannot be appealed to the Supreme Court. Whether it will influence other state high courts remains to be seen. A similar case in the New Jersey state courts was dismissed this month at the trial level and is now on appeal.

Yet just as clearly, the Massachusetts decision and the Lawrence ruling were linked in spirit even if not as formal

The Massachusetts court considered and rejected the various rationales the state put forward to defend opposition to same-sex marriage. These included providing a "favorable setting for procreation" and child-rearing and defending the institution of marriage.

"It is the exclusive and permanent commitment of the marriage partners to one another, not the begetting of children, that is the sine qua non of civil marriage," Chief Justice Marshall said. Noting that the plaintiffs in this case "seek only to be married, not to undermine the institution of civil marriage," she said, "The marriage ban works a deep and scarring hardship on a very real segment of the community for no rational reason."

The decision will usher in a new round of litigation. The federal Defense of Marriage Act anticipated this development by providing that no state shall be required to give effect to another state's recognition of same-sex marriage.

On the books since 1996, the law has gone untested in the absence of any state's endorsement of same-sex marriage. With 37 states having adopted laws or constitutional provisions defining marriage as between a man and a woman, same-sex couples with Massachusetts marriage licenses may soon find themselves with the next Supreme Court case in the making.

MEDICAL AUTONOMY

The Supreme Court in the 1990s also became embroiled in the political and legal debate over a claimed "right to die"—understood either as a right to refuse life-sustaining medical treatment or as a right to physician-assisted suicide. In the name of individual autonomy, the Court gave qualified approval to the former. Regarding the latter, the Court cited the state's interest in preserving life in rejecting a constitutional right for someone with a terminal illness to a doctor's assistance in ending his or her life.

A RIGHT TO DIE

The "right-to-die" issue first gained national prominence in 1976 with the case of a young New Jersey woman, Karen Ann Quinlan, who fell into a long-lasting, possibly drug-induced coma after a party. Ruling on a petition filed by her parents, the New Jersey Supreme Court said that Quinlan had the right to terminate life support "as a matter of self-determination" and that her father could represent her wishes because she was unable to speak for herself.

The U.S. Supreme Court never ruled on Quinlan's case, but the same issue reached the justices in 1990 in the case of a Missouri woman, Nancy Beth Cruzan, who had been left in a persistent vegetative state after an automobile accident in 1983. When her parents sought to remove water and feeding tubes, the Missouri Supreme Court ruled that they could be removed only on the basis of "clear and convincing evidence" of the patient's wishes.

By a 5-4 vote, the U.S. Supreme Court ruled in *Cruzan v. Director, Missouri Department of Health* (1990) that states could establish a strict standard of proof in such cases, but all the justices acknowledged what Rehnquist called "the right of a competent individual to refuse medical treatment." The ruling sent the case back to Missouri courts, where testimony from two of Cruzan's friends convinced a judge that she would not have wanted to remain on life support if left in a coma. The state did not contest the ruling. With life support removed, Cruzan died on December 26—six months and a day after the Supreme Court decision.

Cruzan v. Director, Missouri Department of Health

> **Decided:** June 25, 1990
>
> **Vote:** 5 (Rehnquist, B. White, O'Connor, Scalia, Kennedy)
>
> 4 (Brennan, T. Marshall, Blackmun, Stevens)
>
> **Opinion of the Court:** Rehnquist
>
> **Concurring opinions (2):** O'Connor; Scalia
>
> **Dissenting opinions (2):** Brennan (Marshall, Blackmun); Stevens

JUNE 26, 1990
JUSTICES FIND A RIGHT TO DIE, BUT THE MAJORITY SEES NEED FOR CLEAR PROOF OF INTENT

By LINDA GREENHOUSE
Special to The New York Times

Eight members of the Supreme Court, venturing for the first time into the sensitive "right to die" issue, said in a ruling today that a person whose wishes are clearly known has a constitutional right to the discontinuance of life-sustaining treatment.

But the Justices differed over how specific people must be in making their wishes known. In the case before them today, the Justices ruled, by a vote of 5 to 4, that the state of Missouri can sustain the life of a woman, comatose for more than seven years, because her family had not shown by "clear and convincing evidence" that she would have wanted the treatment stopped.

Nevertheless, all the Justices but one, Antonin Scalia, clearly endorsed the view that there is a constitutional right, as part of the "liberty" guaranteed by the 14th Amendment, to avoid unwanted medical treatment. The Amendment's due process clause prohibits the Government from depriving any person of "life, liberty, or property without due process of law."

DEFEAT FOR MISSOURI FAMILY

The decision today stated clearly for the first time what the court said could be inferred from prior decisions: "that a competent person has a constitutionally protected liberty interest in refusing unwanted medical treatment." The court specifically applied that princi-

mits a person to call off life-sustaining care. The ruling gave strong encouragement for the use of living wills and other increasingly popular techniques by which people try to insure that their medical wishes will be carried out if they become incompetent.

Chief Justice William H. Rehnquist wrote the majority opinion, which was joined by Justices Byron R. White, Anthony M. Kennedy, Sandra Day O'Connor and, with evident reluctance, Justice Scalia. Dissenting opinions were filed by Justices John Paul Stevens and William J. Brennan Jr., who was joined by Justices Thurgood Marshall and Harry A.

An innocent person's constitutional right to be free from unwanted medical treatment is thereby categorically limited to those patients who had the foresight to make an unambiguous statement of their wishes while competent.

—Justice John Paul Stevens, dissenting,
Cruzan v. Director, Missouri Dept. of Health

ple to all patients who have made their wishes clearly known, those who are comatose as well as those who are still conscious.

The decision was a defeat for the family of Nancy Cruzan, a 32-year-old woman who has been in a type of coma known as a persistent vegetative state since an automobile accident seven years ago. Her family had sought legal permission to disconnect the feeding tube that is providing the nutrients keeping her alive.

The Court held that when a permanently unconscious person has left no clear instructions, a state is free to carry out its interest in "the protection and preservation of human life" by denying a request by family members to terminate treatment. . . .

LIVING WILLS ENCOURAGED

Doctors have said that Ms. Cruzan could live 30 more years in her unconscious condition. There are 10,000 people in the United States who are in the same type of coma as she is.

But in deciding the Cruzan case, the Court—in both majority and minority opinions—made clear that it overwhelmingly supports the view that the Constitution per-

Blackmun. The dissenters said the Court should have permitted the termination of Nancy Cruzan's treatment.

Before the automobile accident that destroyed part of her brain, Ms. Cruzan had indicated in a general way to friends and family members that she would never want to live as a "vegetable." The Missouri Supreme Court rejected her family's request to cut off artificial feeding, ruling that there was not "clear and convincing evidence" of Ms. Cruzan's own wishes.

RIGOROUS STANDARD FOR STATE

In his opinion upholding that ruling, Chief Justice Rehnquist said that while a state need not apply such a rigorous evidentiary standard, "we cannot say that the Supreme Court of Missouri committed constitutional error in reaching the conclusion that it did."

The standard of "clear and convincing evidence" is the highest standard of proof that courts use in civil cases. Only the courts in New York and Maine, in addition to Missouri, have required this standard in cases involving medical treatment for unconscious people.

Although the Supreme Court rejected the Cruzan family's argument that the Constitution prohibited the use

of such a rigorous standard, the decision was nonetheless seen as a breakthrough.

"There are some wonderful things here," M. Rose Gasner, director of legal services for the Society for the Right to Die, said today. "The Constitution is being applied in a brand new and revolutionary way."

On the other hand, Ms. Gasner said, "it's more clear than ever before that people had better write down their wishes."

Significantly, the Court drew no distinction between providing food and water and other forms of treatment like surgical intervention or mechanical assistance with breathing. Ms. Cruzan can breathe on her own but cannot swallow, so she has been fed through a tube that is surgically implanted in her abdomen.

ISSUE OF 'HEROIC' MEASURES

One argument in the case had been that providing food and water is not medical treatment, and could not be cut off no matter what other "heroic" measures doctors might forgo. But a number of medical organizations filed briefs arguing that providing and regulating the formula needed by a person in Ms. Cruzan's condition was actually a delicate medical procedure, and the Court appeared to accept that assertion without addressing it directly.

Missouri has a living will statute, which, like those in several other states, does not provide for the withdrawal of food and water. Alan Meisel, a medical ethics specialist at the University of Pittsburgh Law School, said today's decision would provide legal grounds for challenging the distinction made in these laws between nutrition and other kinds of treatment.

Missouri's law was not in effect at the time of Ms. Cruzan's accident, so it was not directly at issue today.

The Court had never before addressed any aspect of the right-to-die issue that has commanded considerable attention from state courts and legislatures for the past 15 years. This case, Cruzan v. Missouri, No. 88-1503, has commanded more public attention that any other matter on the Court's docket since the Justices agreed to hear the family's appeal last July.

'PERPLEXING QUESTION'

The majority opinion had a solemn, even tentative tone. Chief Justice Rehnquist said the case presented "a perplexing question with unusually strong moral and ethi-

cal overtones." He disavowed any effort "to cover every possible phase of the subject."

"The principle that a competent person has a constitutionally protected liberty interest in refusing unwanted medical treatment may be inferred from our prior decisions," the Chief Justice said. He referred to a series of decisions examining the rights of prisoners and inmates of state institutions to refuse various kinds of forced treatment.

When the Court agreed to hear the Cruzan case, it had been widely expected that the Justices would examine whether the asserted right to die was part of the constitutional right of privacy, a right that the Court has applied to abortion and contraception. Many state courts have invoked the right to privacy in finding constitutional protection for the right to terminate medical treatment.

However, Chief Justice Rehnquist said, without further explanation, that the Court would not analyze the issue as a privacy question in this case. "We believe this issue is more properly analyzed in terms of a 14th Amendment liberty interest," he said.

The majority traced the "liberty interest" in being free of unwanted medical attention to English common law when, the Chief Justice noted, "even the touching of one person by another without consent and without legal justification was a battery."

PATIENT'S 'INFORMED CONSENT'

The Court said that this concept was the basis for the modern doctrine that medical treatment cannot proceed without a patient's "informed consent." The "logical corollary" of that doctrine "is that the patient generally possesses the right not to consent," the Chief Justice said. He said the conflict arose when an incompetent patient could not express his wishes.

Chief Justice Rehnquist noted that a number of states had imposed a lower burden of proof in these cases than had the Missouri court. He said that this was a decision that the Constitution left states free to make.

"We believe that Missouri may permissibly place an increased risk of an erroneous decision on those seeking to terminate an incompetent individual's life-sustaining treatment," the Chief Justice said.

He added that "an erroneous decision not to terminate results in a maintenance of the status quo" while an erroneous decision to end treatment "is not susceptible of correction."

STRONG DISSENT BY BRENNAN

This analysis drew a strong dissent from Justice William J. Brennan Jr. He said that while a mistaken decision to cut off treatment "to be sure, will lead to failure of that last remnant of physiological life, the brain stem," the impact of erroneously continuing treatment was also severe.

Such a decision, Justice Brennan said, "robs a patient of the very qualities protected by the right to avoid unwanted medical treatment."

He added: "His own degraded existence is perpetuated; his family's suffering is protracted; the memory he leaves behind becomes more and more distorted. Even a later decision to grant him his wish cannot undo the intervening harm."

In a separate dissenting opinion, Justice Stevens said that by focusing solely on a patient's previous statements, the Court "fails to respect the best interests of the patient." He said: "An innocent person's constitutional right to be free from unwanted medical treatment is thereby categorically limited to those patients who had the foresight to make an unambiguous statement of their wishes while competent."

Justice O'Connor made much the same point in her concurring opinion. She noted that because "few individuals provide explicit oral or written instructions regarding their intent to refuse medical treatment should they become incompetent," states that require such expressions "may frequently fail to honor a patient's intent."

But she said that the decision today raised the prospect that the Constitution might be read to require states to honor instructions left through living wills or persons designated as surrogate decision-makers.

O'CONNOR LOOKS AHEAD

"In my view," she said, "such a duty may well be constitutionally required to protect the patient's liberty interest in refusing medical treatment."

Since the four dissenters would clearly view such advance instructions as constitutionally enforceable, Justice O'Connor's opinion provided a fifth vote for that approach.

Of the five separate opinions, the most bitter in tone was Justice Scalia's concurring opinion. He said the Court should have ruled that there was no constitutional component to the right to die issue. "I would have preferred that we announce, clearly and promptly, that the Federal courts have no business in this field," he said.

He added: "This Court need not, and has no authority to, inject itself into every field of human activity where irrationality and oppression may theoretically occur, and if it tries to do so it will destroy itself."

In its ruling, the Court did not address the rights of a patient who seeks assistance in committing suicide, an issue that has received wide publicity since a Michigan doctor helped an Alzheimer's patient kill herself earlier this month with a suicide device. Chief Justice Rehnquist noted in passing that as part of their policies for protecting human life, "the majority of states in this country have laws imposing criminal penalties on one who assists another to commit suicide." . . .

PHYSICIAN-ASSISTED SUICIDE

The issue of physician-assisted suicide reached the Court in a pair of cases from the states of Washington and New York, where physicians and others challenged laws that banned the practice. The Court in 1997 upheld the laws in companion decisions—*Washington v. Glucksberg* and *Vacco v. Quill*—that were unanimous in result but divided in reasoning. In *Glucksberg*, Chief Justice Rehnquist explained that the Court should "exercise the utmost care" in expanding the Due Process Clause into "this uncharted area." Four justices joined his opinion; the other four indicated misgivings about an absolute ban on physician-assisted dying. In one concurring opinion, Justice O'Connor said she saw "no legal barriers" to a patient's obtaining medication to alleviate pain "even to the point of causing unconsciousness and hastening death."

Washington v. Glucksberg

Decided: June 26, 1997

Vote: 9 (Rehnquist, Stevens, O'Connor, Scalia, Kennedy, Souter, Thomas, Ginsburg, Breyer)

0

Opinion of the Court: Rehnquist

Concurring opinion: O'Connor (Ginsburg, Breyer)

Opinions concurring in judgment (4): Stevens; Souter; Ginsburg; Breyer

JUNE 27, 1997
COURT, 9-0, UPHOLDS STATE LAWS PROHIBITING ASSISTED SUICIDE; PROTECTS SPEECH ON INTERNET

NO HELP FOR DYING

But Justices Leave Door Open to Future Claim of a Right to Aid

By LINDA GREENHOUSE

WASHINGTON, June 26—Stepping for the first time into the wrenching political and moral debate over doctor-assisted suicide, the Supreme Court ruled today that states may continue to ban the practice but at the same time suggested that the door remained open to constitutional claims for assistance by dying patients in the future.

In a pair of 9-to-0 decisions, the Court rejected constitutional challenges to laws in New York and Washington that made doctor-assisted suicide a crime. But the Court's tone was that of a tentative first step rather than a definitive final ruling on the issue.

In concurring opinions that accounted for a majority of the Court, various Justices suggested that at least some terminally ill people in intractable pain might be able to claim in the future that they had a constitutional right to a doctor's assistance in hastening their deaths. . . .

"Our opinion does not absolutely foreclose such a claim," Chief Justice William H. Rehnquist said in the Court's principal opinion, which was signed by four other Justices.

New York's and Washington's criminal prohibitions against assisted suicide to be unconstitutional.

Throughout the opinions today, the Court's tone was measured and sober, in contrast to the sharp language that sometimes pervades the Court's constitutional debates. The Court seemed to be inviting further developments. Chief Justice Rehnquist noted that "throughout the nation, Americans are engaged in earnest and profound debate about the morality, legality and practicality of physician-assisted suicide." He said the Court's approach "permits this debate to continue, as it should in a democratic society."

Although the Court did not address the question directly, there was at least a strong suggestion in Chief Justice Rehnquist's opinion, as well as an explicit discussion in a concurring opinion by Justice David H. Souter, that states were free to experiment and permit doctor-assisted suicide if they chose to do so. The Court should "stay its hand to allow reasonable legislative consideration," Justice Souter said.

> " The inconclusive nature of the ruling on doctor-assisted suicide was perhaps the most surprising aspect of a decision that was widely seen, in its bottom line, as a foregone conclusion. "

One of those four, Justice Sandra Day O'Connor, said that while she agreed there was "no generalized right to 'commit suicide,'" she viewed as still open the question of whether "a mentally competent person who is experiencing great suffering" that cannot otherwise be controlled has a constitutionally based "interest in controlling the circumstances of his or her imminent death." . . .

The inconclusive nature of the ruling on doctor-assisted suicide was perhaps the most surprising aspect of a decision that was widely seen, in its bottom line, as a foregone conclusion. The Court was never likely to embrace the expansive views of due process or equal protection taken by the two Federal appeals courts whose decisions were reversed today. The lower courts had declared

Only one state, Oregon, has voted to permit doctor-assisted suicide, in a referendum that has yet to go into effect because of prolonged court challenges. The Justices have been asked by opponents of the measure to hear a challenge to its constitutionality, but that case will not come up for consideration until the Court's next term. Meanwhile, the Oregon Legislature decided to put the question to voters again, in November.

One reason for the somewhat inconclusive outcome today was the way in which Chief Justice Rehnquist structured his opinion in the Washington State case, which dealt with the question of whether a right to doctor-assisted suicide should be recognized as an aspect of the "liberty" protected by the 14th Amendment's guarantee of due process.

The Chief Justice essentially reframed the question that five doctors had raised when they brought their lawsuit on behalf of three dying patients. The question, as the lower court interpreted it, was whether mentally competent, terminally ill adults had a right to a doctor's assistance in determining the time and manner of their death.

The United States Court of Appeals for the Ninth Circuit, in San Francisco, answered yes in a 1996 opinion that drew on the Court's constitutional precedents on the right to abortion and the right to reject unwanted life-sustaining treatment.

Chief Justice Rehnquist, however, put the question in the case on a higher level of generality: "Whether the protections of the due process clause include a right to commit suicide with another's assistance." The answer to that question was no, he said, given several factors that he said were relevant: a 700-year history of disapproval of suicide and assisted suicide in the Anglo-American legal tradition; "the considered policy choice of almost every state," and strong state interests in protecting vulnerable people and avoiding the "path to voluntary and perhaps even involuntary euthanasia."

In their concurring separate opinions other Justices objected to the Chief Justice's formulation of the question. Justice Stephen G. Breyer said the Court should have considered a different way of describing the question, one "for which our legal tradition may provide greater support." He said: "That formulation would use words roughly like a 'right to die with dignity.' But irrespective of the exact words used, at its core would lie personal control over the manner of death, professional medical assistance, and the avoidance of unnecessary and severe physical suffering—combined."

Justice Breyer said there was no need to decide in this case whether a right described in that way was protected by the Constitution because in both New York and Washington, doctors are permitted to prescribe pain-killing drugs, even in potentially lethal doses, so that "the laws before us do not force a dying person to undergo that kind of pain."

In a separate opinion, Justice John Paul Stevens said he viewed the decision today as being in much the same posture as the Court's decisions that upheld the death penalty 20 years ago. "Just as our conclusion that capital punishment is not always unconstitutional did not preclude later decisions holding that it is sometimes impermissibly cruel," Justice Stevens said, "so is it equally clear that a decision upholding a general statutory prohibition of assisted suicide does not mean that every possible application of the statute would be valid." He said there were "situations in which an interest in hastening death is legitimate" and "entitled to constitutional protection."

Justice Stevens said he did not agree with the appeals court that there was a categorical right involved, but said he recognized "the possibility that an individual plaintiff seeking to hasten her death, or a doctor whose assistance was sought, could prevail in a more particularized challenge."

It was this assertion that Chief Justice Rehnquist acknowledged in his opinion, at the same time adding that "such a claim would have to be quite different" from ones involved in this case. He did not elaborate.

In both the Washington case, Washington v. Glucksberg, No. 96-110, and the New York case, Vacco v. Quill, No. 95-1858, the Chief Justice's opinions for the Court were joined by Justices O'Connor, Antonin Scalia, Anthony M. Kennedy, and Clarence Thomas. In addition to the separate opinions by Justices O'Connor, Stevens, Souter and Breyer, Justice Ruth Bader Ginsburg indicated in a brief statement that she agreed with Justice O'Connor's approach.

In the New York case, which also began as a lawsuit by doctors and terminally ill patients, the United States Court of Appeals for the Second Circuit, in Manhattan, took a different approach to striking down the New York law. The appeals court said that because New York permitted terminally ill patients to hasten their death by ordering withdrawal of life-sustaining medical treatment, the prohibition against doctor-assisted suicide violated the rights of other dying patients who were not dependent on particular equipment or treatment.

In his opinion overturning this decision, Chief Justice Rehnquist said that "unlike the Court of Appeals, we think the distinction between assisting suicide and withdrawing life-sustaining treatment, a distinction widely recognized and endorsed in the medical profession and in our legal traditions, is both important and logical." He added: "It is certainly rational."

The Chief Justice was the author of the Court's decision in 1990, in Cruzan v. Missouri Department of Health, that for the first time recognized a right to forgo unwanted treatment. As with the decisions today, the Cruzan decision left important issues unsettled and divisions within the Court unresolved.

The dispute over the Cruzan decision flared up again in a very telling way today in an oblique debate between the

Chief Justice, who said the decision was based on little more than the common-law rule that "forced medication was a battery," and Justice Stevens, who interpreted the decision as a much more affirmative recognition of a "more basic concept of freedom that is even older than the common law."

Justice Stevens said the right recognized in the 1990 decision, which concerned a young woman being kept alive in a persistent vegetative state, was "not merely a person's right to refuse a particular kind of unwanted treatment, but also her interest in dignity, and in determining the character of the memories that will survive long after her death."

Reaction to the rulings today was voluminous, reflecting the intense interest the cases had generated. More than 60 briefs were filed, a near record for the Court. Among those expressing satisfaction with the decision was President Clinton, who opposes assisted suicide and who recently signed into law a prohibition against using any Federal money, including Medicaid money, to pay for doctor-assisted suicide.

JUNE 27, 1997
2 WITH INTIMATE KNOWLEDGE OF HOW TO LOOK AT DEATH
By NEIL A. LEWIS

The question of how to approach death is as universal as any faced by Americans today, and two of the Justices who decided the doctor-assisted suicide case have had intense exposure to the issue.

The author of today's main opinion, Chief Justice William H. Rehnquist, saw his wife die in 1991 after a long fight with ovarian cancer. Justice Stephen G. Breyer's wife, Joanna Hare Breyer, is a psychologist at Boston's Dana Farber Cancer Institute, where she counsels terminally ill children and their families.

Members of the Court are famously protective of their personal lives and rarely talk about how their experiences may have affected their rulings. But one leading authority on dying said it was inevitable that the Justices would be influenced by their own observations about how people die.

"There can be no objectivity in any decision involving the end of life," said Dr. Sherwin B. Nuland of the Yale-New Haven Hospital and an authority on facing death. "It is so emotional it is almost instinctual so; whether one is a Supreme Court Justice or not, that person cannot help but be influenced by personal experiences involving death." . . .

* * * * * * * * * * * *

The Court considered the issue again after the Bush administration tried to use the federal Controlled Substances Act to prevent doctors in Oregon from prescribing lethal drugs for terminally ill patients under the state's "Death with Dignity" initiative approved by voters in 1994. By a 5-4 vote, the Court ruled in *Gonzales v. Oregon* (2006) that the move was an unauthorized attempt to intrude on the states' traditional powers to define the rules of medical practice.

THE RIGHT TO KEEP AND BEAR ARMS

The Second Amendment states: "A well regulated Militia, being necessary to the security of a free State, the right of the people to keep and bear Arms, shall not be infringed." The amendment's prefatory clause makes clear that the provision was included in the Bill of Rights to protect the states' rights to maintain militias. The meaning of the operative clause is not so clear, and the ambiguity helped fuel a raging debate in the late twentieth century over gun rights versus gun control.

Gun control advocates argued that the amendment did nothing more than safeguard states' militias and imposed no limits on regulation of firearms. Gun owners and gun rights organizations contended that the amendment also established an individual right to own and possess firearms and limited the scope of government regulation.

The Supreme Court seemed to adopt the narrower so-called collective view of the amendment in what stood for nearly seventy years as its only detailed discussion of the provision. The unanimous decision in *United States v. Miller* (1939) rejected a suspected moonshiner's effort to use the Second Amendment to overturn his conviction for possessing a sawed-off shotgun in violation of the National Firearms Act of 1934. To be a protected "arm" under the amendment, Justice McReynolds explained, a defendant had to show that the weapon had "some reasonable relationship to the preservation or efficiency of a well-regulated militia."

Gun regulation became a major issue after the assassinations and racial unrest of the 1960s. Gun control advocates won passage of important new regulations—notably, the federal Gun Control Act of 1968, which banned interstate sale of firearms. Beginning in the 1970s, gun rights advocates countered with strong and often effective lobbying to block new regulations and launched a parallel effort to revitalize the Second Amendment through political advocacy and academic scholarship. The issue reached the Supreme Court again after the federal appeals court in Washington, D.C., struck down the District of Columbia's near total ban on possession of handguns in 2007.

The Supreme Court's 5-4 decision in *District of Columbia v. Heller* (2008), upholding the appeals court's decision, gave gun rights advocates a seminal victory. For the majority, Justice Antonin Scalia said that the amendment's text and history both pointed to the right to keep and bear arms as an individual right. Without specifying a standard of review, he said the District's handgun ban infringed that right because it prevented residents from having "the quintessential self-defense weapon" in their homes.

Scalia specified, however, that the ruling did not jeopardize many gun regulations, including laws against carrying concealed weapons or prohibiting gun possession by felons or minors. Dissenting justices warned that the decision would hamper local governments' efforts to deal with what Justice Breyer called the "serious, indeed life-threatening problem" of gun violence. Gun rights advocates in fact filed a Second Amendment suit challenging a similar Chicago ordinance the same day and another in San Francisco the next day.

District of Columbia v. Heller

> **Decided:** June 26, 2008
> **Vote:**   5 (Roberts, Scalia, Kennedy, Thomas, Alito)
>   4 (Stevens, Souter, Ginsburg, Breyer)
> **Opinion of the Court:** Scalia
> **Dissenting opinions (2):** Stevens; Breyer

JUNE 27, 2008
JUSTICES, RULING 5-4, ENDORSE PERSONAL RIGHT TO OWN GUN

By LINDA GREENHOUSE

WASHINGTON—The Supreme Court on Thursday embraced the long-disputed view that the Second Amendment protects an individual right to own a gun for personal use, ruling 5 to 4 that there is a constitutional right to keep a loaded handgun at home for self-defense.

The landmark ruling overturned the District of Columbia ban on handguns, the strictest gun-control law in the country, and appeared certain to usher in a new round of litigation over gun rights throughout the country.

The court rejected the view that the Second Amendment's "right of the people to keep and bear arms" applied to gun ownership only in connection with service in the "well regulated militia" to which the amendment refers.

Justice Antonin Scalia's majority opinion, his most important in his 22 years on the court, said that the justices were "aware of the problem of handgun violence in this country" and "take seriously" the arguments in favor of prohibiting handgun ownership.

"But the enshrinement of constitutional rights necessarily takes certain policy choices off the table," he said, adding, "It is not the role of this court to pronounce the Second Amendment extinct."

Justice Scalia's opinion was signed by Chief Justice John G. Roberts Jr. and Justices Anthony M. Kennedy, Clarence Thomas and Samuel A. Alito Jr.

In a dissenting opinion, Justice John Paul Stevens took vigorous issue with Justice Scalia's assertion that it was the Second Amendment that had enshrined the individual right to own a gun. Rather, it was "today's law-changing decision" that bestowed the right and created "a dramatic upheaval in the law," Justice Stevens said in a dissent joined by Justices David H. Souter, Ruth Bader Ginsburg and Stephen G. Breyer. Justice Breyer, also speaking for the others, filed a separate dissent.

Justice Scalia and Justice Stevens went head to head in debating how the 27 words in the Second Amendment should be interpreted. The majority opinion and two dissents ran 154 pages.

It has been nearly 70 years since the court last examined the meaning of the Second Amendment. In addition to their linguistic debate, Justices Scalia and Stevens also sparred over what the court intended in that decision, United States v. Miller.

In the opaque, unanimous five-page opinion in 1939, the court upheld a federal prosecution for transporting a sawed-off shotgun. A Federal District Court had ruled that the provision of the National Firearms Act the defendants were accused of violating was barred by the Second Amendment, but the Supreme Court disagreed and reinstated the indictment.

For decades, an overwhelming majority of courts and commentators regarded the Miller decision as having rejected the individual-right interpretation of the Second Amendment. That understanding of the "virtually unreasoned case" was mistaken, Justice Scalia said Thursday.

> " It is not the role of this court to pronounce the Second Amendment extinct.
>
> —Justice Antonin Scalia, *District of Columbia v. Heller* "

Justice Stevens said the majority opinion was based on "a strained and unpersuasive reading" of the text and history of the Second Amendment, which provides: "A well regulated militia, being necessary to the security of a free state, the right of the people to keep and bear arms, shall not be infringed."

According to Justice Scalia, the "militia" reference in the first part of the amendment simply "announces the purpose for which the right was codified: to prevent elimination of the militia." The Constitution's framers were afraid that the new federal government would disarm the populace, as the British had tried to do, Justice Scalia said.

But he added that this "prefatory statement of purpose" should not be interpreted to limit the meaning of what is called the operative clause—"the right of the people to keep and bear arms, shall not be infringed." Instead, Justice Scalia said, the operative clause "codified a *pre-existing* right" of individual gun ownership for private use.

Contesting that analysis, Justice Stevens said the Second Amendment's structure was notable for its "omission of any statement of purpose related to the right to use firearms for hunting or personal self-defense," in contrast to the contemporaneous "Declarations of Rights" in Pennsylvania and Vermont that did explicitly protect those uses.

He said the Miller decision meant "only that the Second Amendment does not protect those weapons not typically possessed by law-abiding citizens for lawful purposes, such as short-barreled shotguns."

Justice Stevens said the majority's understanding of the Miller decision was not only "simply wrong," but also reflected a lack of "respect for the well-settled views of all of our predecessors on the court, and for the rule of law itself."

Despite the decision's enormous symbolic significance, it was far from clear that it actually posed much of a threat to the most common gun regulations. Justice Scalia's opinion applied explicitly just to "the right of law-abiding, responsible citizens to use arms in defense of hearth and home," and it had a number of significant qualifications.

"Nothing in our opinion," he said, "should be taken to cast doubt on longstanding prohibitions on the possession of firearms by felons and the mentally ill, or laws forbidding the carrying of firearms in sensitive places such as schools and government buildings, or laws imposing conditions and qualifications on the commercial sale of arms."

The opinion also said prohibitions on carrying concealed weapons would be upheld and suggested somewhat less explicitly that the right to personal possession did not apply to "dangerous and unusual weapons" that are not typically used for self-defense or recreation.

The Bush administration had been concerned about the implications of the case for the federal ban on possessing machine guns.

President Bush welcomed the decision. "As a long-standing advocate of the rights of gun owners in America," he said in a statement, "I applaud the Supreme Court's historic decision today confirming what has always been clear in the Constitution: the Second Amendment protects an individual right to keep and bear firearms."

The opinion did not specify the standard by which the court would evaluate gun restrictions in future cases, a question that was the subject of much debate when the case was argued in March.

Among existing gun-control laws, just Chicago comes close to the complete handgun prohibition in the District of Columbia's 32-year-old law. The district's appeal to the Supreme Court, filed last year after the federal appeals court here struck down the law, argued that the handgun ban was an important public safety measure in a congested, crime-ridden urban area.

On the campaign trail on Thursday, both major-party presidential candidates expressed support for the decision—more full-throated support from Senator John McCain, the presumptive Republican nominee, and a more guarded statement of support from Senator Barack Obama, his presumptive Democratic opponent.

Mr. McCain called the decision "a landmark victory for Second Amendment freedom in the United States" that "ended forever the specious argument that the Second Amendment did not confer an individual right to keep and bear arms."

Mr. Obama, who like Mr. McCain has been on record as supporting the individual-rights view, said the ruling would "provide much-needed guidance to local jurisdictions across the country."

He praised the decision for endorsing the individual-rights view and for describing the right as "not absolute and subject to reasonable regulations enacted by local communities to keep their streets safe."

Unlike the court's ruling this month on the rights of the Guantánamo detainees, this decision, District of Columbia v. Heller, No. 07-290, appeared likely to defuse, rather than inflame, the political debate. The Democratic Party platform in 2004 included a plank endorsing the individual-rights view of the Second Amendment.

The case reached the court as a result of an assumption by the Cato Institute, a libertarian organization here, that the time was right to test the prevailing interpretation of the Second Amendment. Robert A. Levy, a lawyer and senior fellow of the institute, looked for law-abiding district residents rather than criminal defendants appealing convictions, to challenge the law.

Mr. Levy, who financed the case, recruited six plaintiffs. Five were dismissed for lack of standing. But the United States Court of Appeals for the District of Columbia Circuit ruled in favor of one, Dick Anthony Heller. He is a security guard who carries a gun while on duty at a federal judicial building here and was denied a license to keep his gun at home. The court said Thursday that assuming Mr. Heller was not "disqualified from the exercise of Second Amendment rights," the district government must issue him a license.

CRIME AND PUNISHMENT

CHAPTER 9

Cleveland police came to Dollree Mapp's home early on the morning of May 23, 1957, looking for a suspect in a recent firebombing tied to the city's numbers rackets. They found the suspect—who was later cleared—along with a batch of betting slips and four dirty books. Mapp said the books belonged to a roomer who had moved away.

Dolly Mapp had hardly consented to the police search of the two-story house, where she lived on the top floor with her eleven-year-old daughter. When three officers first arrived, Mapp called her lawyer, who told her not to let the police

Ernesto Miranda, right, was convicted of kidnapping and rape after he confessed to the crimes while in police custody. In a landmark decision, *Miranda v. Arizona* (1966), the Supreme Court reversed the conviction, ruling that suspects must be informed of their constitutional rights when arrested.

in without a warrant. Police tried again several hours later, after reinforcements arrived. When Mapp did not come to the door immediately, the officers broke in.

Mapp asked the officers to show her a search warrant. One of the officers displayed a piece of paper, which Mapp grabbed and put down the front of her dress. As the Supreme Court later described the scene, "A struggle ensued in which the officers recovered the piece of paper and as a result of which they handcuffed appellant because she had been 'belligerent' in resisting their official rescue of the 'warrant' from her person."

The officers continued to struggle with Mapp as they took her upstairs. They ransacked the apartment, found nothing incriminating, and then went down to the basement. There, they came upon a trunk, opened it, and found betting slips and four books that were lurid by 1950s standards. Mapp was arrested on a misdemeanor gambling count and later indicted on a felony charge under the state's recently broadened obscenity statute.

No search warrant was ever produced at trial, but the problem did not matter in Ohio courts. In 1949 the U.S. Supreme Court had ruled that states had to follow the Fourth Amendment, part of the Bill of Rights, which prohibits "unreasonable" searches and requires "probable cause" for a judge to issue a search warrant. But the Court in that decision did not require states to follow the so-called exclusionary rule—the rule in federal courts since 1914 that barred the use of any evidence seized in violation of the Fourth Amendment.

Mapp was acquitted on the gambling charge but convicted and sentenced to up to seven years in the obscenity case. On appeal, a majority of the Ohio Supreme Court thought the state's obscenity statute unconstitutional, but the state constitution required a supermajority ruling to strike down a state law. In addition, Ohio had no rule excluding illegally obtained evidence. So the state high court upheld Mapp's conviction after observing that police had not used "brutal or offensive physical force" in obtaining the evidence.

Alexander Kearns, Mapp's lawyer, succeeded in persuading the U.S. Supreme Court to hear an appeal. In oral arguments on March 30, 1961, Kearns argued that the books were far from obscene. Both Kearns and a lawyer from the American Civil Liberties Union touched only briefly on questions about the search.

In their private conference, the justices agreed unanimously that the conviction had to be reversed because the statute improperly covered mere possession of obscene materials. With little discussion, three justices also observed that the case could be an opportunity to reconsider the 1949 decision, *Wolf v. Colorado*, and apply the exclusionary rule to the states. Chief Justice Earl Warren assigned the opinion to Justice Tom C. Clark, who surprised two of his colleagues immediately afterward by taking up the idea of overruling *Wolf*.

Over the next two months, Clark won approval from a bare majority of five justices for doing just that. And so it was that on June 19—with hardly any warning—the Supreme Court instructed state court judges around the country to prohibit the use of any evidence that police had obtained without following the Fourth Amendment's command. "Nothing can destroy a government more quickly than its failure to observe its own laws, or worse, its disregard of the charter of its own existence," Clark wrote in *Mapp v. Ohio* (1961).

JUNE 20, 1961
HIGH COURT BARS EVIDENCE STATES SEIZE ILLEGALLY
BENCH SPLIT 5 TO 4

Reversal of an Earlier Ruling Invalidates Local Practices

Special to The New York Times

WASHINGTON, June 19—The Supreme Court overruled today a landmark decision of 1949 and held that the Constitution forbids the use of illegally seized evidence in state criminal trials.

The vote was 5 to 4 for taking this historic step. Of the four justices in the minority, three disagreed on the constitutional issue. The fourth did not reach the issue.

This was the final day of the Supreme Court's term.

The search-and-seizure decision is expected to have sweeping effects on local law enforcement throughout the country. Some observers quickly described it as the most significant limitation ever imposed on state criminal procedure by the Supreme Court in a single decision.

The effect of the decision is to eliminate a long-standing difference in the rules for state and Federal courts.

24 STATES INVOLVED

A 1914 case, Weeks v. United States, decided that Federal courts must exclude illegally seized evidence. But in 1949, in the case of Wolf v. Colorado, the Supreme Court said that state courts were not bound by the same rule.

At the time of the Wolf case, twenty-nine of the forty-eight states admitted illegally seized evidence. Today, twenty-four of the fifty do so, including New York, Connecticut and New Jersey.

The decision today effectively wipes out the local practice in the latter group of states. From now on in New York, for example, a defendant in a narcotics case will be able to move for exclusion of evidence of heroin found in his home on the ground that the police had no warrant or other legal basis for the search that produced the evidence.

Justice Tom C. Clark wrote the opinion of the court today. He was joined by Chief Justice Earl Warren and Justices Hugo L. Black, William O. Douglas and William J. Brennan Jr.

A dissent by Justice John Marshall Harlan was joined in by Justices Felix Frankfurter and Charles E. Whittaker. Justice Potter Stewart did not reach the search-and-seizure question but joined the majority for other reasons.

The decision does not directly affect the wiretapping problem.

In recent years the Supreme Court has held that the Communications Act of 1934 bars all tapping. But it has construed the same statute to let the state courts admit illegal wiretap evidence.

The court held in 1928 that tapping was not a search or seizure covered by the Constitution. That 5-to-4 decision has been much attacked. If it were ever overruled, the fruits of illegal tapping would be barred.

The case decided today arose from the prosecution of a Cleveland boarding house owner, Dollree Mapp, under an Ohio law making it a crime to possess obscene literature.

In 1957 three policemen went to Miss Mapp's house to look for gambling materials. They entered without a search warrant. When she resisted, they handcuffed her. They found no gambling material, but they did find some obscene books that she said belonged to a tenant.

the oral argument, had said that he had never even heard of the Wolf case.

By deciding so important a question without real argument Justice Harlan said, "our voice becomes only a voice of power, not of reason."

Justice Clark said simply that the Wolf case had been criticized ever since it was decided in 1949. He remarked that "no term of court ever passes that someone doesn't holler Wolf."

One reason given for overruling the Wolf decision was that some of its own arguments had weakened. Two of these arguments were that a majority of states preferred to admit illegal evidence and that there were other ways to deal with illegal searches besides excluding their fruits.

In fact, Justice Clark said, some states have found since 1949 that any remedies but exclusion of evidence are "worthless and futile," and they have decided despite strong police protest to rule out the fruits of illegal searches.

> The ignoble short cut to conviction left open to the state tends to destroy the entire system of constitutional restraints on which the liberties of the people rest.
>
> —Justice Tom C. Clark, *Mapp v. Ohio*

The seized books were admitted at Miss Mapp's trial and she was convicted. She drew a sentence of from one to seven years.

It is always unusual for the Supreme Court to overrule one of its earlier decisions. But the result today was the more surprising because the search-and-seizure question had hardly been mentioned in the briefs and oral argument.

The major argument had been that the state law was unconstitutional. This law makes possession of obscene matter a crime even though it is not to be shown to anyone else. In fact a majority of the Ohio Supreme Court thought the law unconstitutional but did not overturn it because of a peculiar Ohio rule requiring a special majority to strike down a state statute.

HARLAN SCORES DECISION

One basis for Justice Harlan's dissent was a charge that the majority had "reached out" to decide a point not even argued before it. He observed that Miss Mapp's lawyer, in

Justice Clark said that it was common sense and morality to require the same rule for Federal and state trials. He said that re-examination of the Wolf case had led the majority "to close the only courtroom door remaining open to evidence secured by official lawlessness."

'IGNOBLE SHORT CUT'

"The ignoble short cut to conviction left open to the state," he said, "tends to destroy the entire system of constitutional restraints on which the liberties of the people rest."

Justice Harlan, for the three dissenters, said that, quite the contrary, the nature of the American political system counseled against imposing rigid Federal restraints on local police practices. He called the decision "bewildering, unfortunate, ill-considered, far-reaching."

Justice Stewart agreed to the reversal of Miss Mapp's conviction, but without considering the search-and-seizure question. He found the Ohio obscenity law unconstitutional. . . .

Mapp v. Ohio

Decided: June 19, 1961

Vote: 5 (Warren, Black, Douglas,
         Clark, Brennan)

     3 (Frankfurter, Harlan II,
         Whittaker)

     1 (Stewart)

Opinion of the Court: Clark

Concurring opinions (2): Black; Douglas

Memorandum opinion: Stewart

Dissenting opinion: Harlan II
         (Frankfurter, Whittaker)

The Court's decision in *Mapp* ushered in what came to be called the due process or criminal procedure revolution—a series of decisions through the 1960s that fundamentally transformed law enforcement and criminal trials throughout the United States. Chief Justice Warren, a former district attorney and state attorney general in California, led a five-vote majority in telling the states that they must accord suspects and criminal defendants virtually all of the protections set out in the Bill of Rights. In the most dramatic decision, the Court ruled in *Miranda v. Arizona* (1966) that police must tell suspects of their right to remain silent during interrogation, their right to a lawyer, and their right to have a lawyer appointed for them if they cannot afford one.

Police practices before the 1960s were often rough and tumble—as in Mapp's case and a succession of search and interrogation cases that the Court had considered over the previous three decades. The Warren Court's decisions disturbed law enforcement and alarmed much of the public, who believed the dissenting justices' warnings that the rulings would handcuff the police and turn criminals out on the streets.

More than forty years later, the Court's rulings have survived, and law enforcement has adapted. Under two conservative chief justices—Warren E. Burger and William H. Rehnquist—the Court narrowed some of the decisions without overruling them. Rehnquist, in fact, wrote an opinion in 2000 that reaffirmed *Miranda*.

On the other hand, another decision that the Warren Court liberals helped produce early in Burger's tenure did not survive: the 1972 ruling that overturned all existing death sentences in the country as violating the Eighth Amendment's prohibition against "cruel and unusual punishments." Four years later, the Court upheld rewritten capital punishment statutes that narrowed jurors' discretion in imposing the death penalty. Since then, the Court has been closely divided in reviewing capital cases. In three decisions since 2000, the justices divided either 6-3 or 5-4 in prohibiting the death penalty for mentally retarded or juvenile offenders or for child rape.

Under Chief Justice John G. Roberts Jr., the Court continues to have a pro–law enforcement majority in most criminal cases. In one significant decision, *Hudson v. Michigan* (2006), the Court eased enforcement of the exclusionary rule in cases where police fail to "knock and announce" before entering a home to execute a search. For the majority, Justice Antonin Scalia said the costs of imposing the exclusionary rule in such cases—including "the risk of releasing dangerous criminals"—outweighed any benefits in deterring police misconduct. Dissenting justices said the ruling diminished the "high value" that the Fourth Amendment places "in protecting the privacy of our homes."

EARLY DEVELOPMENTS

The original Constitution included only a few provisions relating to crime and punishment. It required jury trials for all federal crimes except in cases of impeachment and specified that trials be held in the state where the offense was committed (Art. III, sec. 2, cl. 3). It also defined the crime of treason and required for a conviction the testimony of "two Witnesses to the same overt Act" or the defendant's "Confession in open Court" (Art. III, sec. 3, cl. 1). It further required each state to extradite a fugitive from justice from another state "on Demand of the executive Authority" (Art. IV, sec. 2, cl. 2).

The Bill of Rights added the array of protections that have become familiar since the Warren Court's criminal procedure revolution:

- The Fourth Amendment prohibits "unreasonable searches and seizures." It goes on to specify that no warrant may be issued unless supported by "probable cause" and "particularly describing the place to be searched, and the persons or things to be seized."

- The Fifth Amendment requires "a presentment or indictment of a Grand Jury" for any "capital, or otherwise infamous crime." It prohibits double jeopardy—that is, being tried twice for the same crime—or being "compelled in any criminal case to be a witness against himself." It also includes a general prohibition against being "deprived of life, liberty, or property, without due process of law."
- The Sixth Amendment adds specific provisions regarding trials. It guarantees a defendant a "speedy and public trial" by "an impartial jury" in the state or district where the offense was committed. It specifies the right "to be informed of the nature and cause of the accusation" as well as the right "to be confronted with the witnesses against him" and the right to have "compulsory process for obtaining witnesses in his favor." It concludes by establishing the right to "the assistance of Counsel for his Defense."
- The Eighth Amendment prohibits "excessive bail," "excessive fines," and "cruel and unusual punishments."

The Supreme Court had only few occasions to enforce or interpret these provisions until the twentieth century. Law enforcement was—and remains—primarily the responsibility of the states. During the nineteenth century, the federal government played a very limited role in prosecuting crime, and the Supreme Court heard relatively few criminal appeals. Further, the Court had ruled since its decision in *Barron v. Baltimore* (1833) that the Bill of Rights applied only to the national government, not to the states.

Even after the Fourteenth Amendment imposed the Due Process and Equal Protection Clauses on the states, the Court continued to say that the states did not have to accord criminal defendants the protections set out in the Bill of Rights. In 1884, for example, the Court upheld the murder conviction and death sentence of Joseph Hurtado, who had been brought to trial in California without an indictment.

Writing for the majority in *Hurtado v. California* (1884), Justice Stanley Matthews reasoned that an indictment was not part of due process because the Fifth Amendment included separate clauses for those two requirements. The ruling merited only a single paragraph in *The New York Times,* but it prompted a long opinion from the lone dissenter, John Marshall Harlan, who said the same reasoning would free the states from other Bill of Rights provisions. "Will it be claimed that these rights were not secured by 'the law of the land' or by 'due process of law'?" Harlan asked.

MARCH 4, 1884
THE GREENBACK ACT VALID
THE SUPREME COURT DECIDES THE LEGAL TENDER CASE.
THE CONSTITUTIONALITY OF THE LAW OF 1878 AFFIRMED—JUSTICE FIELD DISSENTS—
KUKLUX AND OTHER CASES.

WASHINGTON, March 3.— . . . A decision was also rendered in the murder case of Joseph Hurtado, plaintiff in error, against the State of California. In error to the Supreme Court of California. The Federal question presented by this case is whether a man who has been prosecuted for murder by information, without indictment by a Grand Jury, has been tried by due process of law, as those words are to be understood in the fourteenth amendment to the Federal Constitution. The court holds, first, that the words "due process of law," in the fourth amendment, do not necessarily require indictment by a Grand Jury in a prosecution by a State for murder; second, that a conviction for murder upon an information as prescribed by the Constitution and penal code of California, and a sentence of death thereon, are not illegal or in violation of the fourteenth amendment. The judgment of the court below is affirmed. Opinion by Justice Matthews, Justice Harlan dissenting. . . .

Harlan anticipated what later came to be called the "incorporation doctrine"—the view that the Fourteenth Amendment's Due Process Clause "incorporated" some or all of the provisions of the Bill of Rights. But Harlan was seventy-five years ahead of his time. In case after case through the late 1940s, the Court declined to hold the states to the Bill of Rights provisions. Thus, *Twining v. New Jersey* (1908) found no violation of the Fifth Amendment's privilege against self-incrimination when a state judge commented on a defendant's failure to testify.

In *Palko v. Connecticut* (1937), the Court ruled, 8-1, that states could appeal a defendant's acquittal despite the Fifth Amendment's prohibition against double jeopardy. The ruling upheld a defendant's first-degree murder conviction and death sentence in a retrial after the state had successfully appealed his original conviction on a lesser charge of second-degree murder. Writing for the majority, Justice Benjamin N. Cardozo set out the theory of "selective incorporation"—the view that some procedural rights were "implicit in the concept of ordered liberty." He determined, however, that double jeopardy, indictments, and even jury trials were not among them. Justice Pierce Butler was the lone dissenter.

The Court continued to reject incorporation through the 1940s, though with more dissents. In *Betts v. Brady* (1942), three justices—Hugo L. Black, William O. Douglas, and William Francis (Frank) Murphy—disagreed with the Court's refusal to require states to provide lawyers for indigent defendants in all felony cases.

Five years later, the Court divided 5-4 in reaffirming that the Fifth Amendment did not apply to the states. The ruling in *Adamson v. California* (1947) upheld the murder conviction and death sentence of an illiterate black man after the prosecution had commented to the jury on his failure to take the stand in his own defense. "For a state to require testimony from an accused," Justice Stanley F. Reed wrote, "is not necessarily a breach of a state's obligation to give a fair trial."

In a concurring opinion, Justice Felix Frankfurter reiterated Cardozo's view that the Fourteenth Amendment's Due Process Clause required states to abide only by "those canons of decency and fairness which express the notions of justice of English-speaking peoples." In his dissenting opinion, Black argued that the Fourteenth Amendment incorporated all of the provisions of the Bill of Rights against the states. In the 1960s, the Court began incorporating the Bill of Rights provisions one by one—as Frankfurter suggested—but eventually applied almost all of them, as Black had advocated. (See "Cases Incorporating Provisions of the Bill of Rights into the Due Process Clause of the Fourteenth Amendment," opposite.)

Earlier, the Court's rulings in federal cases had provided some protections for criminal defendants. In *Boyd v. United States* (1886), the Court ruled that the Fourth Amendment protected individuals against subpoenas as well as searches for private business papers. The Court established the exclusionary rule for federal cases in *Weeks v. United States* (1914)—a decision that *The Times* said could "revolutionize" criminal prosecutions. Seven years later, the Court provided even greater Fourth Amendment protections by holding that even with a warrant, police could not search for "mere evidence." The ruling in *Gouled v. United States* (1921) essentially limited police searches to contraband or the instrumentalities of crime. The limitation stood until the Warren Court discarded it in *Warden v. Hayden* (1967).

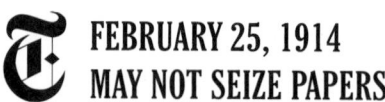

FEBRUARY 25, 1914
MAY NOT SEIZE PAPERS.

Supreme Court Makes Ruling That May Affect Dynamiters' Case.

WASHINGTON, Feb. 24.—Criminal prosecutions in the United States may be revolutionized by a decision to-day of the Supreme Court restricting the conditions under which prosecuting officials may seize papers belonging to persons accused of crime. The immediate result of the decision was that Fremont Weeks, an express messenger at Kansas City, Mo., will receive a new trial on a charge of using the mails to further an alleged lottery scheme. The United States Marshal entered his house and seized 600 letters, which were used against him at the trial.

Cases Incorporating Provisions of the Bill of Rights into the Due Process Clause of the Fourteenth Amendment

Constitutional Provision	Case	Year
First Amendment		
Freedom of speech and press	*Gitlow v. New York*	1925
Freedom of assembly	*De Jonge v. Oregon*	1937
Freedom of petition	*Hague v. Committee for Industrial Organization*	1939
Free exercise of religion	*Cantwell v. Connecticut*	1940
Establishment of religion	*Everson v. Board of Education*	1947
Fourth Amendment		
Unreasonable search and seizure	*Wolf v. Colorado*	1949
Exclusionary rule	*Mapp v. Ohio*	1961
Fifth Amendment		
Payment of compensation for the taking of private property	*Chicago, Burlington and Quincy R. Co. v. Chicago*	1897
Self-incrimination	*Malloy v. Hogan*	1964
Double jeopardy	*Benton v. Maryland*	1969
When jeopardy attaches	*Crist v. Bretz*	1978
Sixth Amendment		
Public trial	*In re Oliver*	1948
Due notice	*Cole v. Arkansas*	1948
Right to counsel (felonies)	*Gideon v. Wainwright*	1963
Confrontation and cross-examination of adverse witnesses	*Pointer v. Texas*	1965
Speedy trial	*Klopfer v. North Carolina*	1967
Compulsory process to obtain witnesses	*Washington v. Texas*	1967
Jury trial	*Duncan v. Louisiana*	1968
Right to counsel (misdemeanor when jail is possible)	*Argersinger v. Hamlin*	1972
Eighth Amendment		
Cruel and unusual punishment	*Louisiana ex rel. Francis v. Resweber*	1947
Ninth Amendment		
Privacy[a]	*Griswold v. Connecticut*	1965

Source: Lee Epstein and Thomas G. Walker, *Constitutional Law for a Changing America,* 5th ed. (Washington, D.C.: CQ Press, 2004).

Note: Provisions the Court has not incorporated: Second Amendment right to keep and bear arms; Third Amendment right against quartering soldiers; Fifth Amendment right to a grand jury hearing; Seventh Amendment right to a jury in civil cases; and Eighth Amendment right against excessive bail and fines.

[a]The word *privacy* does not appear in the Ninth Amendment (nor anywhere in the text of the Constitution). In *Griswold* several members of the Court viewed the Ninth Amendment as guaranteeing (and incorporating) that right.

The point that the Government improperly seized papers in the "dynamiters" cases against Frank M. Ryan and other Bridge Union officials in a raid in Indianapolis has been raised, and the decision to-day may enter into that prosecution if a new trial is granted, as sought in an application for review filed to-day with the Supreme Court.

Justice Day, in announcing the court's unanimous decision, held that Weeks's constitutional guarantee against unreasonable search had been violated.

"If letters and private documents can thus be seized and held and used in evidence against a citizen accused of an offense," said Justice Day, "the protection of the Fourth Amendment declaring his right to be secure against such searches and seizures is of no value, and, so far as those thus placed are concerned, might as well be stricken from the Constitution."

Since 1904 the courts of the country have restricted prosecuting officials little in presenting in evidence papers secured by searching houses without search warrants. It was in that year that the Supreme Court, in the case of Al Adams, the "Policy King," of New York, laid down the principle that a trial court need not stop in the midst of a trial to question a witness as to how be had obtained possession of papers, but would admit the papers into evidence, no matter how possession was obtained.

* * * * * * * * * * *

Federal law had also established the right to counsel to all defendants in capital cases ever since 1790. In 1938 the Court extended that right to all federal defendants. "The Sixth Amendment . . . embodies a realistic recognition of the obvious truth that the average defendant does not have the professional legal skill to protect himself when brought before a tribunal with the power to take his life or liberty," Justice Black wrote for the 6-2 majority in *Johnson v. Zerbst*.

Meanwhile, the Court in the first several decades of the twentieth century had begun to review some state court convictions to determine whether judicial abuses amounted to due process violations. The Court in *Frank v. Mangum* (1915) found no due process violation in the controversial case of Leo Frank, a Jewish factory owner convicted in Georgia on the basis of disputed evidence of the murder of a teenage girl who worked at his plant. Yet eight years later, the Court in *Moore v. Dempsey* (1923) ordered the release of five African American tenant farmer activists who were convicted of murder in Arkansas after perfunctory trials—just forty-five minutes long in one case—that Justice Oliver Wendell Holmes Jr. described as "swept to the fatal end by an irresistible wave of public passion."

The Court intervened more dramatically in the 1930s in another racially charged case: the convictions of nine illiterate, young black men for raping two white women aboard a freight train passing through Tennessee and Alabama. Amidst intense community hostility, the "Scottsboro Boys" were convicted in a trial where their local counsel put up only a pro forma defense. They appealed to the Supreme Court, arguing a Sixth Amendment violation because they had had no chance to consult with their locally appointed lawyer or prepare a defense.

In a 7-2 decision in the first of the *Scottsboro Cases, Powell v. Alabama* (1932), the Court agreed. Justice George Sutherland concluded that the judge's refusal to give the defendants "reasonable time and opportunity to secure counsel" constituted a violation of the Fourteenth Amendment's Due Process Clause. Sutherland limited the ruling to capital cases, however.

On retrial, two of the defendants, Clarence Norris and Haywood Patterson, moved to quash the indictment and the pool of potential jurors on the ground that African Americans had been systematically excluded. The judge denied the motion, and both were convicted again. In unanimous decisions— *Norris v. Alabama* and *Patterson v. Alabama*—the Court in 1935 threw out the convictions. Chief Justice Charles Evans Hughes said the jury commissioners' acknowledged practice of refusing to call blacks for jury service was "evidence of the discrimination that the Constitution forbids."

NOVEMBER 8, 1932
NEW TRIAL ORDERED BY SUPREME COURT IN SCOTTSBORO CASE

Ruling Finds Seven Negroes Condemned in Alabama Were Denied Right of Counsel.

TWO OF 9 JUSTICES DISSENT

Police Wield Clubs Freely on Radicals Attempting to Picket Court Chamber.

MANY HURT, 14 ARRESTED

Alabama Judge Expects New Trial In March—Holds Move for Change of Venue Likely.

Special to The New York Times

WASHINGTON, Nov. 7.—New trials were ordered by the Supreme Court today for seven Negroes condemned to death at Scottsboro, Ala., on charges of attacking two white girls.

Seven members of the court joined in the opinion handed down by Justice Sutherland, asserting that the Negroes had been denied the right of counsel. Justices

Butler and McReynolds, the other two members of the bench, dissented, saying that the youths had not been deprived of any of their constitutional rights in the Alabama court.

An hour before the decision was announced, Capitol and metropolitan policemen and a corps of detectives vigorously wielding clubs, had driven 100 Communists and other radical demonstrators off the plaza at the East front of the Capitol. Tear gas and clubs were used to quell the Reds, many of whom were injured. Their banners were torn up, and fourteen of them were arrested.

In contrast to this stormy scene, the Supreme Court chamber was clothed in its customary dignity as the opinion was read. Not a whisper disturbed the solemnity. Present were many sympathizers with the Scottsboro defendants.

WORLD RADICALS AWAIT DECISION.

Interest in the outcome was intense. Like the Sacco-Vanzetti and Mooney cases, the Scottsboro trials have attracted world-wide attention among radicals, who contend that the Negro youths were "railroaded" through the Alabama courts. Foreign capitals, notably Moscow, where the Soviet celebrated its fifteenth anniversary, eagerly awaited the Supreme Court's decision.

ally in danger of mob violence; but it does appear that the attitude of the community was one of great hostility. The Sheriff thought it necessary to call for the militia in safeguarding the prisoners. Chief Justice Anderson pointed out in his opinion that every step taken from the arrest and arraignment to the sentence was accompanied by the military.

"It is perfectly apparent that the proceedings from beginning to end took place in an atmosphere of tense, hostile and excited public sentiment. During the entire time the defendants were closely confined or were under military guard.

"The record does not disclose their ages, except that one of them was 19 and another only 14 or 15 years of age; but the record clearly indicates that most, if not all of them, were youthful and they are constantly referred to as 'the boys.' They were ignorant and illiterate. All of them were residents of other States, where alone members of their families or friends resided."

However guilty the defendants may have been proved to be, they were presumed to be innocent until convicted, Justice Sutherland stated.

"It was the duty of the court having their cases in charge to see that they were denied no necessary incident of a fair trial," he continued.

> " It is perfectly apparent that the proceedings from beginning to end took place in an atmosphere of tense, hostile and excited public sentiment. During the entire time the defendants were closely confined or were under military guard.
>
> —Justice George Sutherland, *Powell v. Alabama* "

Critical language was used by Justice Sutherland in his opinion. At one point he recited the dialogue between the judge in an Alabama court and prospective counsel for the Negroes, and then remarked:

"In this casual fashion, the matter of counsel in a capital case was disposed of."

Describing the atmosphere in Scottsboro, where the Negroes were taken off a freight train after the alleged assault, he said:

"It does not sufficiently appear that the defendants were seriously threatened with or that they were actu-

"It is hardly necessary to say that the rights of counsel being conceded, a defendant should be afforded a fair opportunity to secure counsel of his own choice. Not only was that not done here, but such designation of counsel as was attempted was either so indefinite or so close upon the trial as to amount to a denial of effective and substantial aid in that regard. This will be amply demonstrated by a brief review of the record.

"It thus will be seen that until the very morning of the trial no lawyer had been named or definitely designated to represent the defendants."

COURT'S POWERS DEFINED.

After tracing precedents for right of counsel for prisoners, the opinion continued.

"In the light of the facts outlined in the forepart of this opinion—the ignorance and illiteracy of the defendants, their youth, the circumstances of public hostility, the imprisonment and the close surveillance of the defendants by the military forces, the fact that their friends and families were all in other States and communication with them necessarily difficult, and, above all, that they stood in deadly peril of their lives—we think the failure of the trial court to give them reasonable time and opportunity to secure counsel was a clear denial of due process.

"The duty of the trial court to appoint counsel under such circumstances is clear, as it is clear under circumstances such as are disclosed by the record here, and its power to do so, even in the absence of a statute, cannot be questioned.

"The judgments must be reversed and the causes remanded for further proceedings not inconsistent with this opinion."

BUTLER HOLDS TRIAL WAS FAIR.

On the other hand, Justices Butler and McReynolds, in the dissenting opinion written by the former, insisted that a fair trial had been given to the Negroes and that they were represented by "an able member of the local bar of long and successful experience in the trial of criminal as well as civil cases."

The two justices sharply criticized the majority of their colleagues, saying Justice Sutherland and those agreeing with him had taken a position "extending Federal authority into a field hitherto occupied exclusively" by the States.

"If correct, the ruling that the failure of the trial court to give petitioners time and opportunity to secure counsel was denial of due process is enough, and with this the opinion should end," Justices Butler and McReynolds said on this point, "but the court goes on to declare that 'the failure of the trial court to make an effective appointment of counsel was likewise a denial of due process within the meaning of the Fourteenth Amendment.'

"This is an extension of Federal authority into a field hitherto occupied exclusively by the several States. Nothing before the Court calls for a consideration of the point.

It was not suggested below and petitioners do not ask for a decision here. The court, without being called upon to consider it, adjudges without a hearing an important constitutional question concerning criminal procedure in State courts.

"It is a wise rule firmly established by a long course of decisions here that constitutional questions even when properly raised and argued—are to be decided only when necessary for a determination of the rights of the parties in controversy before it."

The seven defendants in the Scottsboro case are: Charley Weems, 19 years old; Willie Roberson, 17; Andy Wright, 18; Olen Montgomery, 17; Haywood Patterson, 18; Ozie Powell, 16; and Clarence Norris, 20. The crime with which they are charged dates back to March 25, 1931, when, as Justice Sutherland states, they with two others were on a freight train on its way through Alabama. According to the records in the case the youths climbed into an open freight gondola where there were seven white boys and two white girls, and ejected the white boys, except one.

From the record, Justice Sutherland pointed out that messages were sent ahead "asking that every Negro be taken off the train." When the train arrived at Paint Rock, the youths were arrested by a sheriff's posse. The girls swore that each of them was attacked by six Negroes, and identified the defendants.

The group was taken to Scottsboro, the county seat, where feeling ran high, and where the sheriff found it necessary to call for the militia. Once the prisoners were taken to Gadsden for safekeeping, but were later returned to Scottsboro for trial.

Indictments were returned March 31, and the defendants were arraigned on the same day in three groups.

The prisoners pleaded not guilty, but the trials were all concluded in a single day and death penalties were imposed upon eight, including one youth named Williams whose conviction was reversed on appeal. The ninth defendant, Roy Wright, was acquitted.

The trial court overruled motions for new trials and the Alabama Supreme Court eventually affirmed the seven convictions. Chief Justice Anderson, however, "thought the defendants had not been accorded a fair trial and strongly dissented," Justice Sutherland observed.

Radicals became deeply interested in the case and the International Labor Defense played a big part in bringing the issue to the Supreme Court. . . .

APRIL 2, 1935
NEW TRIAL ORDERED BY SUPREME COURT IN SCOTTSBORO CASE

Chief Justice Hughes Rules Negroes Were Barred From Juries in Norris Ruling.

SECOND CASE SENT BACK

If Alabama Does Not Grant New Trial to Patterson, High Court Will Order It.

Special to The New York Times

WASHINGTON. April 1.—Clarence Norris and Haywood Patterson, Negroes condemned to death on charges of having assaulted a white woman in the celebrated Scottsboro case, must have new trials, the Supreme Court held today in two opinions by Chief Justice Hughes.

The whole weight of the opinion in the Norris case was that Negroes had for years been barred from jury duty in Jackson and Morgan Counties, Alabama, where the Scottsboro cases were tried. The opinion on Patterson dealt almost entirely with Alabama's protest that the Supreme Court had no jurisdiction.

Asserting that Negroes had been arbitrarily and systematically barred from jury duty, Justice Hughes in the Norris case held that court proceedings were invalid where citizens were excluded because of race and color from jury duty. He reviewed the evidence that Negroes had not been called for jury duty and the addition of Negroes' names to the jury rolls after the first trial.

"While there was testimony which cast doubt upon the qualifications of some of the Negroes who had been named, and there was also general testimony as to the lack of 'sound judgment' of the 'good Negroes' in Jackson County," the Chief Justice said, "we think that the definite testimony as to the actual qualifications of individual Negroes, which was not met by any testimony equally direct, showed that there were Negroes in Jackson County qualified for jury service."

HOLDS DISCRIMINATION SHOWN.

"We think that the evidence that for a generation or longer no Negro had been called for service on any jury in Jackson County; that there were Negroes qualified for jury service; that according to the practice of the jury commission their names would normally appear on the preliminary list of male citizens of the requisite age, but that no names of Negroes were placed on the jury roll, and the testimony with respect to the lack of appropriate consideration of the qualifications of Negroes established the discrimination which the Constitution forbids," the opinion added.

Chief Justice Hughes condemned the "sweeping characterization of the qualification" of Negroes in Alabama as stated by the authorities of Morgan County.

"Upon the proof contained in the record now before us, a conclusion that their continuous and total exclusion from juries was because there were none possessing the requisite qualifications cannot be sustained," he declared.

In the case of Norris the court specifically ordered that he must be tried again, but in the Patterson case the issue was sent back to the Alabama courts for "further proceedings." Lawyers and court officials agreed that if a new trial should be refused to Patterson he could approach the Supreme Court for a direct order for a new trial.

In other Scottsboro reviews the court had set aside the convictions of seven of the nine Negroes accused of assaulting two white girls in a box car in 1931. The court then held that the defendants had not had full opportunity to consult counsel.

Norris and Patterson alone were tried the second time in Alabama. Two of the other Negroes were not brought to trial and the remaining five whose convictions were set aside still await trial.

Justice McReynolds did not hear argument and took no part in the consideration and decision of either of the cases ruled on today.

SEARCHES AND SEIZURES

Supreme Court decisions applying the Fourth Amendment to law enforcement searches are as varied as the circumstances in the myriad cases the justices consider. After imposing the exclusionary rule on states, the Warren Court tightened some of the specific requirements for police searches but loosened others. The Burger and Rehnquist Courts generally moved to loosen rules, with some significant exceptions.

While the Court has generally given police more leeway in making arrests, either with or without a warrant, it has invoked due process principles to limit arrests for undefined offenses, such as loitering or vagrancy. It has also applied the Fourth Amendment to prohibit some other police practices—including some automobile checkpoints—as unreasonable seizures under the Fourth Amendment.

ARRESTS

The Supreme Court has upheld the common law rule that permits warrantless arrests by law enforcement officers for crimes committed in their presence and for other crimes where there are reasonable grounds for an arrest. Imposing a warrant requirement for all arrests would be "an intolerable hardship" for law enforcement, the Court said in *Gerstein v. Pugh* (1975). A year later, the Court voted 6-2 in *United States v. Watson* (1976) specifically to permit the warrantless arrest of a felony suspect found in a public place.

A quarter century later, the Court divided 5-4 in allowing warrantless arrests for minor offenses, including nonjailable traffic violations. The decision in *Atwater v. City of Lago Vista* (2001) rejected a federal civil rights suit by a Texas woman, Gail Atwater, who contended that her arrest for not wearing a seat belt and failing to have her children seat-belted while driving to soccer practice was an unreasonable seizure under the Fourth Amendment.

APRIL 25, 2001
DIVIDED JUSTICES BACK FULL ARRESTS ON MINOR CHARGES
By LINDA GREENHOUSE

A sharply divided Supreme Court ruled today that a police officer who observes someone breaking a law, even a minor infraction for which the maximum penalty is a small fine, can make a full custodial arrest without violating the Fourth Amendment's prohibition against unreasonable seizure.

The 5-to-4 decision rejected a lawsuit against a Texas city that was brought by a woman who was stopped for driving without a seat belt. The woman, Gail Atwater, was placed under arrest, taken in handcuffs to the police station and held in a jail cell until she posted $310 bond. The maximum fine for the offense, a misdemeanor under Texas law, was $50.

Justice David H. Souter said that although Ms. Atwater had been subjected to "gratuitous humiliations" and "pointless indignity," what happened to her did not violate the Fourth Amendment. He said that to "mint a new rule of constitutional law" would be to turn many ordinary arrests into occasions for constitutional litigation.

The case fractured the court's usual alliances, provoking a dissenting opinion by Justice Sandra Day O'Connor, who warned that "such unbounded discretion" for the police "carries with it grave potential for abuse."

Justice O'Connor added that "as the recent debate over racial profiling demonstrates all too clearly, a relatively minor traffic infraction may serve as an excuse for stopping and harassing an individual."

Ms. Atwater is white, and race was not an element in the case, Atwater v. City of Lago Vista, No. 99-1408. That made the dissent's reference to racial profiling particularly striking; five years ago, before the police practice of focusing on black motorists for traffic stops became the subject of widespread discussion and official concern, the court ruled unanimously in a case called Whren v. United States that as long as a police officer had an objective reason for stopping a driver, the officer's subjective motive was irrelevant.

Referring to that decision today, Justice O'Connor said that "it is precisely because these motivations are beyond our purview that we must vigilantly ensure that officers' post-stop actions—which are properly within our reach—comport with the Fourth Amendment's guarantee of reasonableness."

The incident that led to the ruling today took place in 1997. Ms. Atwater was bringing her two young children home from soccer practice, driving her pickup truck at about 15 miles an hour on the local streets near her home. None of the three was wearing a seat belt. The officer who ordered her out of the car refused to let her take her crying children to a neighbor's house and said he would take them into custody as well, but a neighbor came along in time to take the children.

The officer searched the truck, finding two tricycles, a bicycle, an Igloo cooler, a bag of charcoal, toys, food and two pairs of children's shoes. After Ms. Atwater was released from jail, she found that the truck had been towed.

The lawsuit that she and her husband brought against Lago Vista, its police chief, and the officer who arrested her was dismissed by the federal district court in Austin. A three-judge panel of the United States Court of Appeals for the Fifth Circuit, in New Orleans, reinstated the suit, but the full appeals court vacated that decision and ruled against the Atwaters by a vote of 11 to 5.

In writing the majority opinion today, Justice Souter was joined by the four most conservative justices, with whom he is almost always at odds in divided cases: Chief Justice William H. Rehnquist and Justices Antonin Scalia, Clarence Thomas and Anthony M. Kennedy.

Justice O'Connor, who is most often allied with that group, was joined in her dissent this time by Justices John Paul Stevens, Ruth Bader Ginsburg and Stephen G. Breyer.

There was no obvious explanation for the voting pattern beyond the frank and quite personal responses that both Justice O'Connor and Justice Souter offered when the case was argued in early December.

"You've got the perfect case!" Justice O'Connor exclaimed then to Ms. Atwater's lawyer, and she indicated that she saw little difficulty in drafting a rule that would make custodial arrests for minor offenses the exception rather than the rule.

On the other hand, Justice Souter, a former attorney general of New Hampshire, pressed Ms. Atwater's lawyer, Robert C. DeCarli, for information about how widespread a problem such arrests were, and appeared unpersuaded that there was a problem for the Supreme Court to fix. In his opinion today, he said "there simply is no evidence of widespread abuse of minor-offense arrest authority."

He noted that some states had passed laws to limit police authority to make arrests for minor offenses, and said that this trend, as well as the "good sense" and "political accountability" of local officials, should take care of any problem.

A spokesman for the New York City Police Department said it was too early to comment about how the court's decision might affect the department, which since the election of Mayor Rudolph W. Giuliani has focused intensely on so-called quality of life offenses, like smoking on the subways and urinating in public. For such offenses, as well as for motor vehicle violations, the police will issue summonses rather than make arrests.

For more serious misdemeanors like shoplifting or property damage, New York police typically bring suspects back to the stationhouse, where they are fingerprinted and checked for outstanding warrants.

"We have to review it, then we'll go from there," said Lt. Elias Nikas, a police spokesman, said of the ruling. "The New York City police department will continue to adhere to department policies, and our legal bureau will review the Supreme Court decision."

Susan N. Herman, a law professor at Brooklyn Law School who filed a brief in the case for the American Civil Liberties Union and other groups, said today that the majority's assumption that a substantial problem did not exist was naïve.

"The reported cases are just the tip of the iceberg," she said, explaining that police officers who make an arrest and then conduct a search without finding anything incriminating often let the person go with a citation. The major purpose served by abusive arrests for minor offenses was to authorize the "search incident to arrest," essentially fishing expeditions, she said.

Emily Whitfield, a spokeswoman for the New York office of the A.C.L.U., raised concerns about the consequences of the decision on minorities. "There is a real fear that this new authority will be used by the police in a racially discrimina-tory fashion," she said. "Now we have a situation where the government, even if they can't put you in jail after you're convicted, can put you in jail before you're tried."

Ms. Atwater's lawyer had argued that under early English law, ordinary misdemeanors were not seen as jus-tifying arrest in the absence of some other element, like a breach of the peace. Justice Souter rejected this argu-ment as a basis for finding that the Constitution's fram-ers would have regarded such arrests as constitutionally unreasonable, saying that the historical evidence was ambiguous.

. . . .

On the other hand, the Court ruled in *Payton v. New York* (1980) that police ordinarily need a warrant to enter a house to make an arrest. The Court also limited police practices in 1985 by ruling that officers may not use deadly force to stop a fleeing felon unless they have reason to believe the suspect might kill or seriously injure persons nearby. "A police officer may not seize an unarmed, non-dangerous suspect by shooting him dead," Justice Byron R. White wrote in *Tennessee v. Garner* (1985).

Later, however, the Court ruled in *Scott v. Harris* (2001) that police can use force to terminate a high-speed vehicular chase that threatens innocent bystanders even if the action places the flee-ing suspect at risk of serious injury or death. The ruling rejected a federal civil rights suit by a Geor-gia man, Victor Harris, who was left permanently paralyzed in March 2001 after a deputy sheriff rammed his car off the road in order to bring a ten-minute high-speed chase to an end.

The Court has also applied the prohibition on unreasonable seizures to some law enforcement–related automobile stops. The decision in *Delaware v. Prouse* (1979) barred police from randomly stopping motorists to check for licenses and registration. Justice Rehnquist was the lone dissenter. As chief justice a decade later, however, Rehnquist wrote the majority opinion in *Michigan Depart-ment of State Police v. Sitz* (1990) upholding the use of sobriety checkpoints to apprehend drunken drivers. The strong interest in highway safety outweighed the "slight" intrusion on motorists' rights, Rehnquist said in the 6-3 decision.

After another decade, the Court ruled in *City of Indianapolis v. Edmond* (2000) that police could not set up similar checkpoints to look for illegal drugs. The primary purpose was not highway safety, but law enforcement, Justice Sandra Day O'Connor explained for the majority. Rehnquist led three dissenters.

In a pair of decisions separated by almost three decades, the Court struck down on due process grounds a broad anti-loitering ordinance in Jacksonville, Florida (*Papachristou v. City of Jackson-ville,* 1972) and a narrower Chicago law targeting suspected gang members. "The freedom to 'loiter' for innocent purposes is part of the liberty protected by the Due Process Clause of the 14th Amend-ment," Justice John Paul Stevens wrote in *Chicago v. Morales* (1999).

SEARCHES

Thirty-five years after creating the exclusionary rule for federal cases in *Weeks,* the Supreme Court specifically decided that due process did not require that the same rule be applied to the states. The 6-3 decision in *Wolf v. Colorado* (1949) upheld Julius Wolf's conviction for performing illegal abortions; police used evidence from patients whose names they found after seizing the doctor's appointment book without a warrant. All of the justices agreed the Fourth Amendment was binding on the states, but Justice Felix Frankfurter concluded for the majority that the exclusionary rule was not "an essential ingredient" of individual rights under the amendment.

In *Mapp v. Ohio* (1961), the Court concluded instead that the exclusionary rule was constitution-ally mandated. As Justice Clark wrote, "Having once recognized that the right to privacy embodied in the Fourth Amendment is enforceable against the states, and that the right to be secure against rude invasions of privacy by state officers is, therefore, constitutional in origin, we can no longer permit that right to remain an empty promise."

The Warren Court followed with two decisions in the 1960s aimed at tightening judicial practices in issuing search warrants requested by police. *Aguilar v. Texas* (1964) and *Spinelli v. United States* (1969) established a rule that police must provide specific information and an independent basis for judging the reliability of the informant who provided the information for a magistrate to determine whether there is probable cause to issue a search warrant.

The Court in 1968 also extended the Fourth Amendment's warrant requirement to wiretapping. Forty years earlier, the Court had ruled in *Olmstead v. United States* (1928) that wiretapping is neither a search nor a seizure because police neither enter a suspect's house nor take away any material items. In an often quoted dissent, Justice Louis D. Brandeis said the ruling undermined the Fourth Amendment's purpose of protecting "the sanctities of a man's home and the privacies of his life."

In *Katz v. United States* (1967), the Court adopted Brandeis's approach by blocking the use of information obtained from telephone calls that federal agents had monitored by means of a listening device placed on the outside of a public phone booth. "The Fourth Amendment protects people, not places," Justice Potter Stewart wrote in the 8-1 decision. The ruling led Congress the same year to include provisions for obtaining wiretap warrants in the Omnibus Crime Control and Safe Streets Act.

In other cases, however, the Warren Court stopped short of strictly interpreting Fourth Amendment requirements. A five-vote majority combined in *Warden v. Hayden* (1967) to abolish the eighty-year-old "mere evidence" rule that allowed police to search only for contraband and instrumentalities of crime. Justice William J. Brennan Jr. called the distinction "irrational" and unrelated to the amendment's goal of protecting privacy.

A year later, the Court ruled that the Fourth Amendment allows police to stop suspicious persons on the street, "frisk" them for weapons, and use any evidence found in the limited pat-down search. In writing the majority opinion in *Terry v. Ohio* (1968), Chief Justice Warren stressed that police must have reasonable grounds to suspect criminal activity and could do no more than search the suspect's outer clothing for weapons. As the lone dissenter, Justice Douglas said police needed probable cause for the initial stop.

Under Chief Justice Burger, the Court changed from viewing the exclusionary rule as constitutionally mandated and instead treated it as a judicially created remedy that need not be applied to every illegal search. On that basis, the Court ruled that prosecutors could use illegally obtained evidence to question grand jury witnesses (*United States v. Calandra,* 1974) and that federal courts need not apply the exclusionary rule in habeas corpus cases (*Stone v. Powell,* 1976). Meanwhile, the Court had also ruled in 1973 that—in contrast to the rights outlined seven years earlier in *Miranda*—police need not inform the target of a search of the right to refuse consent unless police have a warrant (*Schneckloth v. Bustamonte*).

The Court eased the application of the exclusionary rule further in the 1980s. The decision in *Illinois v. Gates* (1983) eased the *Aguilar-Spinelli* rule to permit magistrates to issue search warrants as long as the "totality of the circumstances" indicated the police information was reliable. In 1984 the Court created two exceptions to the exclusionary rule: The "good faith" exception from *United States v. Leon* allows use of evidence if police use a warrant later found to be defective. The "inevitable discovery" rule of *Nix v. Williams* allows use of illegally obtained evidence if police can show it ultimately would have been discovered by lawful means.

Katz v. United States

> **Decided:** December 18, 1967
> **Vote:** 7 (Warren, Douglas, Harlan II, Brennan, Stewart, B. White, Fortas)
> 1 (Black)
> **Opinion of the Court:** Stewart
> **Concurring opinions (3):** Douglas (Brennan); Harlan II; B. White
> **Dissenting opinion:** Black
> **Did not participate:** T. Marshall

Terry v. Ohio

> **Decided:** June 10, 1968
> **Vote:** 8 (Warren, Black, Harlan II, Brennan, Stewart, B. White, Fortas, T. Marshall)
> 1 (Douglas)
> **Opinion of the Court:** Warren
> **Concurring opinions (3):** Black; Harlan II; B. White
> **Dissenting opinion:** Douglas

Board of Education v. Earls

Decided: June 27, 2002

Vote: 5 (Rehnquist, Scalia, Kennedy,
            Thomas, Breyer)
            4 (Stevens, O'Connor, Souter,
            Ginsburg)

Opinion of the Court: Thomas

Concurring opinion: Breyer

Dissenting opinions (2): O'Connor;
            Ginsburg (Stevens, O'Connor,
            Souter)

Under Rehnquist, the Court alternated between strict and relaxed application of Fourth Amendment rules. In a series of decisions, the Court upheld drug testing of transportation workers (*Skinner v. Railway Labor Executives' Association,* 1989), federal law enforcement agents (*National Treasury Employees Union v. Von Raab,* 1989), and high school athletes (*Vernonia School District No. 47J v. Acton,* 1995). In *Board of Education v. Earls* (2002), the Court extended the schools decision to permit drug testing of any student participating in extracurricular activities. On the other hand, the Court ruled in *Kyllo v. United States* (2001) that police need a warrant to use a high-tech "thermal imager" to scan a house looking for evidence of indoor marijuana cultivation.

JUNE 28, 2002
JUSTICES ALLOW SCHOOLS WIDER USE OF RANDOM DRUG TESTS FOR PUPILS

By LINDA GREENHOUSE

WASHINGTON, June 27—The Supreme Court today upheld the widespread use of random drug testing of public school students in a significant expansion of an earlier ruling that endorsed drug testing for student athletes.

The 5-to-4 decision upheld a program in a rural Oklahoma district that required students engaged in "competitive" extracurricular activities, a category that includes the future homemakers' club, the cheerleading squad and the choir, to submit to random drug testing.

In emphasizing the "custodial responsibilities" of a public school system toward its students, rather than the details of how the program was organized, the majority opinion by Justice Clarence Thomas appeared to encompass random drug testing of an entire student population.

But one member of the majority, Justice Stephen G. Breyer, who wrote a concurring opinion while also signing Justice Thomas's, said it was significant that the program in the Tecumseh, Okla., school district "preserves an option for a conscientious objector" by limiting the scope to students in extracurricular activities. A student "can refuse testing while paying a price (nonparticipation) that is serious, but less severe than expulsion," Justice Breyer said.

Students who are found to be using drugs at Tecumseh High School are barred from their activities and referred for counseling, but are not otherwise disciplined or reported to the police. The policy was challenged by Lindsay Earls, an honor student active in several activities who is now attending Dartmouth College.

Ms. Earls lost her case in federal district court in Oklahoma City but won last year in the United States Court of Appeals for the 10th Circuit, in Denver. That court examined the Supreme Court's 1995 ruling in Vernonia School District v. Acton and said that the athletes-only precedent did not validate the broader Tecumseh policy. The Tecumseh program violated the Fourth Amendment's prohibition against unreasonable searches, the appeals court ruled.

In his opinion overturning that decision today, Justice Thomas said the Tecumseh program was "entirely reasonable" in light of the "nationwide epidemic of drug use" among school-age children. While the Tecumseh district did not now appear to have a serious problem, he said, "it would make little sense to require a school district to wait for a substantial portion of its students to begin using drugs before it was allowed to institute a drug testing program designed to deter drug use."

The decision, Board of Education v. Earls, No. 01-332, was joined by Chief Justice William H. Rehnquist and Justices Antonin Scalia and Anthony M. Kennedy as well as Justice Breyer. The dissenters were Justices Sandra Day O'Connor, John Paul Stevens, and David H. Souter, all of whom were in the minority in the court's athletes-only ruling in 1995, and Ruth Bader Ginsburg, who had concurred in the earlier decision. In a dissenting opinion today, which the other three dissenters joined, Justice Ginsburg said the two cases were significantly different.

In the first, she said, the court "concluded that a public school district facing a disruptive and explosive drug abuse problem sparked by members of its athletic teams had 'special needs' that justified suspicionless testing of district athletes as a condition of their athletic participation." But she said the 1995 opinion "cannot be read to endorse invasive and suspicionless drug testing of all students."

Had the court in the Vernonia case "agreed that public school attendance, in and of itself, permitted the state to test each student's blood or urine for drugs," she continued, "the opinion in Vernonia could have saved many words."

Justice Thomas said in the majority opinion that the differences in the two cases were "not essential." The earlier decision did not depend on the program's details but on "the school's custodial responsibility and authority," he said.

Justice Thomas added that it would not necessarily be less intrusive to require that drug testing be based on suspicions of particular students. That approach "might unfairly target members of unpopular groups" and place added burdens, including fear of lawsuits, on teachers and administrators, he said. . . .

• • • • • • • • • • •

The Rehnquist Court generally continued to ease application of the exclusionary rule to evidence found in cars after arrests or traffic stops. In *Whren v. United States* (1996), the Court unanimously ruled that police officers can use evidence found in plain view in a car even if they stopped it only as a pretext to look for drugs. Two years later, though, the Court ruled in *Knowles v. Iowa* (1998) that the police cannot conduct a full search of a car after a routine traffic stop.

In another unanimous decision, the Court in *Wilson v. Arkansas* (1995) said the Fourth Amendment required police executing a search warrant at a private home to announce their presence and give residents a brief time to respond before entering. A decade later, however, the Roberts Court significantly weakened the "knock-and-announce" rule by holding in *Hudson v. Michigan* (2006) that evidence found could be used even if police did not follow the procedure. "The social costs of applying the exclusionary rule to knock-and-announce violations are considerable; the incentive to such violations is minimal to begin with, and the extant deterrences against them are substantial," Scalia wrote in the 5-4 ruling. For the dissenters, Justice Stephen G. Breyer called Scalia's position "an argument against the Fourth Amendment's exclusionary principle itself. And it is an argument that this Court, until now, has consistently rejected."

JUNE 16, 2006
COURT LIMITS PROTECTION AGAINST IMPROPER ENTRY
By LINDA GREENHOUSE

WASHINGTON, June 15—Evidence found by police officers who enter a home to execute a search warrant without first following the requirement to "knock and announce" can be used at trial despite that constitutional violation, the Supreme Court ruled on Thursday.

The 5-to-4 decision left uncertain the value of the "knock-and-announce" rule, which dates to 13th-century England as protection against illegal entry by the police into private homes.

Justice Antonin Scalia, in the majority opinion, said that people subject to an improper police entry remained free to go to court and bring a civil rights suit against the police.

But Justice Stephen G. Breyer, writing for the dissenters, said the ruling "weakens, perhaps destroys, much of the practical value of the Constitution's knock-and-announce protection." He said the majority's reasoning boiled down to: "The requirement is fine, indeed, a serious matter, just don't enforce it."

The decision followed a reargument less than a month ago, with the newest justice, Samuel A. Alito Jr., evidently casting the decisive vote. Justice Breyer's dissenting opinion was clearly drafted to speak for a majority that was lost when Justice Sandra Day O'Connor left the court shortly after the first argument in January.

The justices' lineup in this case, which upheld a Detroit man's conviction for drug possession, may become a familiar one as the court proceeds through its criminal-law docket. In addition to Justice Alito, those who joined the majority opinion by Justice Scalia were Chief Justice John G. Roberts Jr. and Justices Clarence Thomas and Anthony M. Kennedy. Justice Breyer's dissenting opinion was joined by Justices John Paul Stevens, David H. Souter and Ruth Bader Ginsburg.

The decision answered a question that the court had left open in 1995, when it held in a unanimous opinion by Justice Thomas that the traditional expectation that the police should knock and announce their presence was part of what made a search "reasonable" within the meaning of the Fourth Amendment. The amendment bars unreasonable searches.

In that case, Wilson v. Arkansas, the court declined to say what the remedy should be for a violation of the knock-and-announce rule. Ordinarily, evidence that is seized illegally—in the absence of a warrant, for example—may not be used at trial, under what is known as the exclusionary rule.

By a strong majority, most state and federal courts that have considered the issue have applied the exclusionary rule to violations of the knock-and-announce requirement. In its decision on Thursday in Hudson v. Michigan, No. 04-1360, the Supreme Court upheld a ruling by the Michigan Court of Appeals, one of the few courts to have rejected the exclusionary rule in this context.

In the case, the Detroit police had a warrant to search for drugs in the home of Booker T. Hudson Jr. At his unlocked door, they announced their presence, but did not knock and waited only three to five seconds before entering, not the 15 to 20 seconds suggested by the Supreme Court's precedents.

Had the police observed a longer wait, they would have executed the search warrant and found the evidence anyway, Justice Scalia said. That made the connection between the improper entry and the discovery of the evidence "too attenuated" to justify the "massive remedy of suppressing evidence of guilt."

Justice Scalia said the knock-and-announce rule was designed to protect life, property and dignity by giving the homeowner time to respond to the knock and eliminating the need for the police to break down the door. But he said the rule has never protected "one's interest in preventing the government from seeing or taking evidence described in a warrant."

Throughout his opinion, Justice Scalia made clear his view that the right at issue was a minimal, even trivial, one—"the right not to be intruded upon in one's nightclothes," he said at one point—that could not hold its own when balanced against the "grave adverse consequences that exclusion of relevant incriminating evidence always entails."

The majority opinion was sufficiently dismissive of the exclusionary rule as to serve as an invitation to bring a direct challenge to the rule in a future case.

Justice Scalia surveyed changes in the legal landscape since 1961, when the court in the landmark case Mapp v. Ohio made the exclusionary rule binding on the states. Noting that the purpose of the exclusionary rule was to deter constitutional violations by making them costly for the prosecution, Justice Scalia said there was less need for deterrence today, when the police are better trained and when the ability to bring civil rights suits against the government has greatly expanded. Under current federal law, he noted, successful civil rights plaintiffs are reimbursed for their attorney fees.

The conditions that made deterrence necessary "in different contexts and long ago" no longer exist, Justice Scalia said, adding that a strict application of the exclusionary rule as envisioned by the court in 1961 "would be forcing the public today to pay for the sins and inadequacies of a legal regime that existed almost half a century ago."

It is rare to find Justice Scalia, a self-described "originalist," incorporating evolving conditions into his constitutional analysis. Almost always, when the court in a constitutional case takes account of changing conditions, the result is an expansion of constitutional rights, rather than, as Justice Scalia advocated in this case, a contraction.

One puzzling aspect of the decision was a concurring opinion by Justice Kennedy, who said that he wished to underscore the point that "the continued operation of the exclusionary rule, as settled and defined by our precedents, is not in doubt." Nonetheless, he signed the part of Justice Scalia's opinion that suggested that the exclusionary rule rested on an increasingly weak foundation.

Justice Breyer argued that "the court destroys the strongest legal incentive to comply with the Constitution's knock-and-announce requirement. And the court does so without significant support in precedent."

He called the majority's argument "an argument against the Fourth Amendment's exclusionary principle itself," adding, "And it is an argument that this court until now has consistently rejected."

INTERROGATION AND CONFESSIONS

The Supreme Court has called confessions "among the most effectual proofs in the law," but within the same sentence in an 1884 decision stressed that confessions must be "subjected to careful scrutiny" to determine whether they were both "deliberate" and "voluntary." Before holding the Fifth Amendment applicable to the states, the Court barred the use of coerced confessions in state courts as a due process violation and invoked its supervisory power over federal courts to throw out confessions obtained after a prolonged delay before a suspect's first appearance in court.

In rapid succession in the 1960s, the Court held the Fifth Amendment applicable to the states, gave suspects the right to counsel during police interrogation, and then laid down the now familiar *Miranda* guidelines requiring police to advise suspects of their rights before custodial interrogation. The latter ruling produced intense public criticism and a law passed by Congress in 1968 aimed at overturning it. Since the 1970s, the Court has limited *Miranda* but refused to overrule it. In fact, the Court in 2000 forcefully reaffirmed *Miranda* by striking down Congress's attempt to override the decision.

THE ROAD TO MIRANDA

The Court's first decisions barring the use of coerced confessions came in two cases involving African American death row inmates in southern states. In *Brown v. Mississippi* (1936), three black suspects were subjected to prolonged beatings before giving confessions that they later repudiated. "The rack and torture chamber cannot be substituted for the witness stand," Chief Justice Hughes wrote in a unanimous opinion. Four years later, in *Chambers v. Florida* (1940), the Court recognized the danger of psychological coercion by reversing the convictions of four black men who had confessed after being held incommunicado for several days.

In the next three decades, the Court decided thirty state confession cases, examining the "totality of the circumstances" of the police interrogation to determine whether a statement was voluntary and therefore admissible. No clear rule emerged.

Meanwhile, the Court had set out a rule for federal courts to bar the use of confessions obtained after "unnecessary delay" in a suspect's arraignment. In *McNabb v. United States* (1943), the Court overturned the convictions of several men who had confessed to killing a federal revenue agent after they were questioned by federal officers for three days. The Court reaffirmed the *McNabb* ruling in *Mallory v. United States* (1957), which barred a confession obtained in a rape case after an eighteen-hour delay between arrest and arraignment.

The Court based its rulings on a federal statute requiring a "prompt" arraignment as well as on its supervisory power over federal courts. Amidst strong criticism, Congress eventually revised the law in 1968 to permit some use of evidence obtained during such delays. Meanwhile, the Court in 1958 had ruled in a pair of state cases that confessions could be voluntary and admissible even if a suspect had been denied the opportunity to consult with a lawyer during interrogation.

The Court reversed direction in a pair of decisions in 1964 that recognized a right to counsel during interrogation. In *Massiah v. United States,* the Court barred the use of incriminating statements that a defendant in a drug smuggling case made after indictment to his codefendant, who was cooperating with federal agents in surreptitiously recording the conversation. By a 6-3 vote, the Court held that the Sixth Amendment right to counsel barred the use of statements that the federal agents "had deliberately elicited from him after he had been indicted and in the absence of his counsel."

Ostensibly, *Massiah* applied only to federal and not to state cases. A month later, however, the Court held in *Malloy v. Hogan* (1964) that the Fifth Amendment's privilege against self-incrimination applied to the states. The unanimous ruling set aside a contempt citation for a labor union official who had cited the Fifth Amendment in refusing to testify before a state investigation of gambling in Connecticut.

The Court proceeded only one week later to extend the *Massiah* right-to-counsel rule to police interrogation of suspects in state cases. Danny Escobedo repeatedly asked to see his lawyer while Chicago police were interrogating him about the ambush shooting of his brother-in-law. Escobedo's lawyer, at the station house, was also asking to see his client. In the interrogation, Escobedo implicated himself after police told him an accomplice had blamed the whole shooting on him; he answered by accusing the accomplice of being the triggerman—an admission that then allowed police to get a full statement from him.

By a 5-4 vote in *Escobedo v. Illinois* (1964), the Court held that the police refusal to allow Escobedo to consult with his lawyer violated his Sixth Amendment right. For the majority, Justice Arthur J. Goldberg said the right to counsel attached before any charge because interrogation was a "critical stage" of a criminal case. He dismissed concerns from the four dissenters that fewer confessions would be obtained. "The right to counsel would indeed be hollow if it began at a period when few confessions were obtained," Goldberg wrote.

JUNE 23, 1964
USE OF CONFESSION IN TRIAL IS CURBED

Court Bars it as Evidence if Suspect Can't See Lawyer or Is Not Told of Rights
Special to The New York Times

WASHINGTON, June 22—A 5-to-4 majority of the Supreme Court placed a sharp new restriction today on the use of confessions in criminal trials.

the country. The ruling was based on the integrity of the right to counsel—a right applied in full force just last year to state as well as to Federal trials.

> A system of criminal law enforcement which comes to depend on the 'confession' will, in the long run, be less reliable and more subject to abuses than a system which depends on extrinsic evidence independently secured through skillful investigation.
>
> —Justice Arthur J. Goldberg, *Escobedo v. Illinois*

If the police focus on a principal suspect, the Court said, and question him without letting him see his lawyers or without warning him that his answers may be used against him, any resulting confession must be barred from evidence.

Justice Arthur J. Goldberg wrote the decision, which is likely to have broad effects on law enforcement across

A strong dissent by Justice Byron R. White was joined by Justices Tom C. Clark and Potter Stewart. Justice John Marshall Harlan dissented separately, and Justice Stewart also wrote his own dissenting opinion.

"I do not suggest for a moment that law enforcement will be destroyed by the rule announced today," Justice

White said. "The need for peace and order is too insistent for that.

"But it will be crippled and its task made a great deal more difficult—all, in my opinion, for unsound, unstated reasons which can find no home in any of the provisions of the Constitution." . . .

The confession case today came from Illinois. Danny Escobedo had been arrested on suspicion of the murder of his brother-in-law but released after his lawyer obtained a writ of habeas corpus.

Ten days later Escobedo was arrested again, after an alleged accomplice had implicated him. He was questioned at police headquarters later at night until, finally, he confessed.

While he was being questioned, in handcuffs, his lawyer—told of the arrest by Escobedo's family—came to headquarters and tried to see him. The police would not allow a visit until after the questioning had been concluded.

It was also shown that no one had advised Escobedo, a 22-year-old man of Mexican extraction, of his constitutional right to remain silent.

Justice Goldberg found, on these facts, that Escobedo's right to counsel had been violated. His opinion also contained some general strictures against police dependence on confessions.

"We have learned the lesson of history, ancient and modern," he said, "that a system of criminal law enforcement which comes to depend on the "confession" will, in the long run, be less reliable and more subject to abuses than a system which depends on extrinsic evidence independently secured through skillful investigation."

"We hold only," he concluded, "that when the process shifts from investigatory to accusatory—when its focus is on the accused and its purpose is to elicit a confession—our adversary system begins to operate and, under the circumstances here, the accused must be permitted to consult with his lawyer."

Justice White said today's decision was "another major step in the direction of the goal which the Court seemingly has in mind—to bar from evidence all admissions obtained from an individual suspected of crime, whether involuntarily made or not." . . .

- - - - - - - - - - - -

Despite renewed criticism, the Court agreed to hear five more confession cases in its 1965–1966 term. Among them was the rape-kidnap conviction of Ernesto Miranda, a young and emotionally troubled truck driver who had confessed after two hours of interrogation without having asked for a lawyer or having endured any evident mistreatment by Phoenix police. The other cases included more questionable police tactics—such as prolonged interrogation or isolation of the suspect from friends or relatives. But, as the Court later acknowledged, none of the statements would have been ruled involuntary under existing law.

By the same 5-4 margin as in *Escobedo,* however, the Court in *Miranda v. Arizona* (1966) established what Chief Justice Warren called "concrete constitutional guidelines" for police interrogation of suspects. In contrast to his spare opinion in *Brown v. Board of Education* (1954) a decade earlier, Warren expounded at length on the compulsion inherent in "incommunicado interrogation of individuals in a police-dominated atmosphere," with tactics aimed at enabling the police to "persuade, trick, or cajole [the suspect] out of exercising his constitutional rights."

Basing the decision on the Fifth as well as the Sixth Amendment, Warren said that a suspect must be told "in clear and unequivocal terms" of the right to remain silent as well as the government's right to use any statement made in court. Since police can "quickly . . . overbear" a suspect's will, Warren continued, the presence of counsel was "indispensable." The lawyer could help prevent police "coercion," he explained, and assist in making any statement more "reliable." Also, because many suspects are poor, Warren said, they must be told not only of the right to consult with a lawyer but also of the right to have one appointed for them if they cannot afford to hire their own.

Warren showed evident emotion as he summarized his opinion in the June 13 session. Justice Harlan was equally animated as he summarized his dissent from the

Miranda v. Arizona

Decided: June 13, 1966

Vote: 5 (Warren, Black, Douglas, Brennan, Fortas)

4 (Clark, Harlan II, Stewart, B. White)

Opinion of the Court: Warren

Opinion concurring in part, dissenting in part: Clark

Dissenting opinions (2): Harlan II (Stewart, B. White); B. White (Harlan II, Stewart)

bench. The ruling, Harlan said, was "poor constitutional law" that would entail "harmful consequences." In his written dissent, Justice White argued the ruling was "a deliberate calculus to prevent interrogation, to reduce the incidence of confessions and pleas of guilty, and to increase the number of trials." "In some unknown number of cases," White warned, the result would be to "return a killer, a rapist or other criminal to the streets . . . to repeat his crime whenever it pleases him."

JUNE 14, 1966
HIGH COURT PUTS NEW CURB ON POWERS OF THE POLICE TO INTERROGATE SUSPECTS

DISSENTERS BITTER

Four View Limitation on Confessions as Aid to Criminals

By FRED P. GRAHAM

Special to The New York Times

WASHINGTON, June 13—The Supreme Court announced today sweeping limitations on the power of the police to question suspects in their custody.

The justices split 5 to 4. In stinging dissents the minority denounced the decision as helping criminals go free to repeat their crimes.

The majority opinion, by Chief Justice Earl Warren, broke new constitutional ground by declaring that the Fifth Amendment's privilege against self-incrimination comes into play as soon as a person is within police custody.

If the suspect confesses after receiving the required warnings but without having counsel, the burden is on the prosecution to prove a knowing waiver of rights. And any prolonged interrogation will be taken to show a lack of waiver.

Moreover, the majority opinion said, if the suspect makes a knowing waiver but later asks to see a lawyer, all questioning must stop until he sees one. If the suspect is alone and starts to talk, but then indicates "in any manner" that he wants to remain silent, the police must stop questioning him.

> Justice Harlan, his face flushed and his voice occasionally faltering with emotion, denounced the decision as 'dangerous experimentation' at a time of a 'high crime rate that is a matter of growing concern.'

Consequently, under the ruling, the prosecution cannot use in a trial any admissions or confessions made by the suspect while in custody unless it first proves that the police complied with a detailed list of safeguards to protect the right against self-incrimination.

The suspect, the Court said, must have been clearly warned that he may remain silent, that anything he says may be held against him and that he has a right to have a lawyer present during interrogation.

COURT-APPOINTED COUNSEL

If the suspect desires a lawyer but cannot afford one, he cannot be questioned unless a court-appointed lawyer is present.

RULLING CALLED 'DANGEROUS'.

Although Chief Justice Warren stressed that the ruling did not outlaw confessions, the majority's opinion drew bitter dissenting remarks from Justices Tom C. Clark, John M. Harlan, Potter Stewart and Byron R. White.

Justice Harlan, his face flushed and his voice occasionally faltering with emotion, denounced the decision as "dangerous experimentation" at a time of a "high crime rate that is a matter of growing concern."

He said it was a "new doctrine" without substantial precedent, reflecting a balance in favor of the accused.

Justice White said: "In some unknown number of cases the Court's rule will return a killer, a rapist or other criminal to the streets and to the environment which produced him, to repeat his crime whenever it pleases him.

"As a consequence, there will not be a gain, but a loss in human dignity."

Both the White and the Harlan dissents and one by Justice Clark insisted that the self-incrimination privilege did not apply at such an early stage in criminal proceedings. The self-incrimination clause of the Fifth Amendment says no person "shall be compelled in any criminal case to be a witness against himself."

Today's court action disposed of four appeals by prisoners who had confessed after having been interrogated by the police. They are Ernesto A. Miranda, convicted of rape in Phoenix, Ariz.; Michael Vignera, convicted of robbery in New York; Roy Allen Stewart, convicted of murder in Los Angeles; and Carl Calvin Westover, convicted of Federal charges of robbery in Sacramento, Calif.

All four convictions were reversed in today's action. The vote was 5 to 4 in each case except that of Stewart. Here it was 6 to 3: Justice Clark joined the majority because he thought the confession was involuntary, although he rejected in this case as in the others the Court's new limitations on interrogation.

Chief Justice Warren indicated that the Court would rule next Monday on a fifth confession case, which will determine whether the rules announced today will be applied retroactively to void old convictions.

In reading his 61-page opinion Chief Justice Warren recounted a number of instances of the use of police brutality to obtain confessions. He also condemned psychological pressures.

At times the emotion in his voice equaled that of the dissenters and bespoke the deep division in the Court over the new doctrine.

WARREN LAUDS POLICE

The Chief Justice departed from his written opinion to praise the police "when their services are honorably performed." But he said that when they abandon fair methods "they can become as great a menace to society as any criminal we have."

He emphasized that the decision did not rule out questioning of witnesses at the scene of a crime or detention of a suspect while his story was being checked out.

He made it clear that, despite some prediction by legal experts, the ruling did not require the presence of lawyers at police stations.

Spontaneous admissions of guilt also can be offered as evidence, he said, so long as they do not come after illegal interrogation without counsel.

By stating that police "custody" exists whenever a person is "deprived of his freedom of action in any significant way," the majority opinion makes clear that the police cannot avoid the new rules by conducting their interrogations during long rides in squad cars.

However, the opinion did seem to leave room for more litigation on the meaning of "custody" and on the circumstances under which a statement is truly spontaneous.

Also, it did not say specifically what proof would be necessary to show that a suspect had waived his rights—whether, ultimately, a suspect must have a lawyer to waive a lawyer.

The opinion also did not say whether other evidence than a confession, discovered as the fruits of an illegal interrogation, would be legally admissible.

Chief Justice Warren's reliance upon the Fifth Amendment surprised some legal authorities, because the famous parent case of today's decision, Escobedo v. Illinois, had ruled out a confession primarily because the defendant's Sixth Amendment right to see his lawyer had been violated.

The decision today tends to merge the two rights, to assure a person a right to counsel whenever he is in a situation that might cause him to incriminate himself. The doctrine applies to all felony and misdemeanor trials, in both Federal and state courts.

In support of his view that these rules would not cripple law enforcement, Chief Justice Warren pointed out that the Federal Bureau of Investigation has for years warned all suspects of their right to counsel and to remain silent. He said England, Scotland and India had not suffered from observing similar procedures.

Replying to the dissenters' complaint that the Court should have waited for the completion of pending confession studies by the American Bar Association, the American Law Institute and the President's Commission on Law Enforcement and Administration of Justice, Mr. Warren said:

"The issues presented are of constitutional dimensions and must be determined by the courts." . . .

• • • • • • • • • • • •

POST-*MIRANDA* RULINGS

The *Miranda* decision provoked strong, mostly negative reactions from politicians, police and law enforcement groups, and the general public. Two years later, Congress included a provision in the Crime Control and Safe Streets Act of 1968 that any "voluntary" confession was admissible in federal courts. That same year, Republican Richard M. Nixon made law and order a major theme of his successful campaign for the presidency.

As president, Nixon made four appointments to the Court—including Burger as chief justice in 1969—creating a 5-4 conservative majority in place of the one-vote liberal margin that had prevailed on criminal law issues. The Burger Court quickly began moving to rein in some of the broad implications of the *Miranda* decision. Even though *Miranda* said "no use" could be made of a statement given without full warnings, the Court voted 5-4 in *Harris v. New York* (1971) to allow the use of statements obtained in violation of *Miranda* to impeach a defendant who decided to testify. In *Michigan v. Tucker* (1974), the Court similarly said that a suspect's statement could be used as a lead to obtain further evidence, despite a *Miranda* violation.

In other rulings, the Court established guidelines for police in dealing with suspects who assert their rights. The Court ruled in *Michigan v. Mosley* (1975) that police can resume questioning of a suspect who asserts the right to remain silent if they wait for an interval and then advise the suspect again of his or her rights. In 1981, however, the Court ruled in *Edwards v. Arizona* that police must stop interrogation if a suspect asks for a lawyer and cannot resume until the suspect has actually conferred with counsel unless the suspect initiates further interrogation. Justice White, one of the *Miranda* dissenters, wrote the decision.

As an associate justice, Rehnquist wrote some of the decisions narrowing *Miranda*. After he became chief justice in 1986, the Court continued to interpret *Miranda* narrowly in some cases though without overruling or fundamentally altering it. Early in 1987, for example, the Court ruled that police need not advise a suspect of all the crimes to be covered in an interrogation (*Colorado v. Spring*). In 1994 the Court ruled that an ambiguous request—"Maybe I should talk to a lawyer"—was not enough to require police to stop questioning (*Davis v. United States*).

Dickerson v. United States

Decided: June 26, 2000

Vote: 7 (Rehnquist, Stevens, O'Connor, Kennedy, Souter, Ginsburg, Breyer)

2 (Scalia, Thomas)

Opinion of the Court: Rehnquist

Dissenting opinion: Scalia (Thomas)

A direct opportunity to overrule *Miranda* reached the Court in 2000 after the federal appeals court in Virginia cited the 1968 federal law to permit the use of a confession obtained without complying with *Miranda*. Despite the conservative majority, the Court in *Dickerson v. United States* (2000) instead reaffirmed *Miranda* in an emphatic 7-2 opinion written by Rehnquist himself. Congress has no authority to "legislatively supersede" a Court decision on constitutional law, Rehnquist said. He also declared the *Miranda* controversy effectively over. "*Miranda* has become embedded in routine police practice to the point where the warnings have become part of our national culture," he wrote.

JUNE 27, 2000
JUSTICES REAFFIRM MIRANDA RULE, 7-2; A PART OF 'CULTURE'
By LINDA GREENHOUSE

WASHINGTON, June 28—The Supreme Court reaffirmed the Miranda decision today by a 7-to-2 vote that erased a shadow over one of the most famous rulings of modern times and acknowledged that the Miranda warnings "have become part of our national culture."

The court said in an opinion by Chief Justice William H. Rehnquist that because the 1966 Miranda decision "announced a constitutional rule," a statute by which Congress had sought to overrule the decision was itself unconstitutional.

Miranda had appeared to be in jeopardy, both because of that long-ignored but recently rediscovered law, by which Congress had tried to overrule Miranda 32 years ago, and because of the court's perceived hostility to the original decision.

The chief justice said, though, that the 1968 law, which replaced the Miranda warnings with a case-by-case test of whether a confession was voluntary, could be upheld only if the Supreme Court decided to overturn Miranda. But with Miranda having "become embedded in routine police practice" without causing any measurable difficulty for prosecutors, there was no justification for doing so, he said.

Justices Antonin Scalia and Clarence Thomas cast the dissenting votes.

The decision overturned a ruling last year by the federal appeals court in Richmond, Va., which held that Congress was entitled to the last word because Miranda's presumption that a confession was not voluntary unless preceded by the warnings was not required by the Constitution.

right to remain silent," he intoned in a firm voice, moving on to the other familiar warnings without further introduction. Some in the courtroom audience wondered whether they might be hearing these phrases as the official words of the court for the last time.

By the time the chief justice finished delivering his opinion, there was no ringing endorsement of Miranda, but the message was clear: "Whether or not we would agree with Miranda's reasoning and its resulting rule, were we addressing the issue in the first instance," he said, "the principles of stare decisis weigh heavily against overruling it now." The Latin phrase "stare decisis," meaning "to stand by things decided," is the court's standard reference for the doctrine of adherence to precedent.

Both in his courtroom announcement and in his written opinion, Chief Justice Rehnquist made only passing reference to a series of opinions throughout the 1970's, 80's and 90's suggesting that Miranda was not itself embedded directly in the Constitution but was rather just a "prophy-

> " Whether or not we would agree with *Miranda*'s reasoning and its resulting rule, were we addressing the issue in the first instance, the principles of *stare decisis* weigh heavily against overruling it now. "
> —Chief Justice William H. Rehnquist, *Dickerson v. United States*

The decision today—only 14 pages long, in Chief Justice Rehnquist's typically spare style—brought an abrupt end to one of the odder episodes in the court's recent history, an intense and strangely delayed refighting of a previous generation's battle over the rights of criminal suspects. Miranda v. Arizona was a hallmark of the Warren Court, and Chief Justice Rehnquist, despite his record as an early and tenacious critic of the decision, evidently did not want its repudiation to be an imprint of his own tenure.

There was considerable drama in the courtroom today as the chief justice announced that he would deliver the decision in the case, Dickerson v. United States, No. 99-5525. The announcement meant that he was the majority opinion's author. Given his statements over more than 25 years about Miranda's lack of constitutional foundation, there was the distinct possibility that he was about to announce that Miranda had been overruled.

The way Chief Justice Rehnquist chose to begin his announcement did little to clarify matters. "You have the

lactic" effort to protect the underlying Fifth Amendment right against compelled self-incrimination.

One of his own early opinions, Michigan v. Tucker in 1974, said the "procedural safeguards" adopted in Miranda "were not themselves rights protected by the Constitution"— a quotation that Justice Scalia flung back at the chief justice today in his bitter dissenting opinion. These post-Miranda decisions permitted prosecutors to use statements obtained in violation of Miranda to impeach a defendant's credibility or for other purposes beyond the prosecution's direct case.

"These decisions illustrate the principle—not that Miranda is not a constitutional rule—but that no constitutional rule is immutable," the chief justice said, describing the "modifications represented by these cases" as "a normal part of constitutional law."

In his stinging dissent, which Justice Thomas joined, Justice Scalia accused the majority of playing intellectually dishonest "word games" to justify going beyond the court's authority to apply the Constitution's commands.

"Since there is in fact no other principle that can reconcile today's judgment with the post-Miranda cases that the court refuses to abandon," he wrote, "what today's decision will stand for, whether the justices can bring themselves to say it or not, is the power of the Supreme court to write a prophylactic, extraconstitutional Constitution, binding on Congress and the states."

The decision was a vindication for the Clinton administration, and particularly for Attorney General Janet Reno. In the face of opposition from parts of her law enforcement constituency within the Justice Department, she put the department on the side of an indicted bank robber in arguing that Miranda was a statement of constitutional law and that the 1968 statute, known as Section 3501, was not a valid exercise of Congressional authority.

"Today's decision recognizes Miranda has been good for law enforcement," the attorney general said today, adding: "Most importantly, it will continue to provide a public sense of fairness in our criminal justice system."

Justices John Paul Stevens, Sandra Day O'Connor, Anthony M. Kennedy, David H. Souter, Ruth Bader Ginsburg, and Stephen G. Breyer joined the chief justice's majority opinion today. There were no separate concurring opinions, a rare expression of unanimity among the majority in a major case.

As much as anything else, the decision reflected the court's deep suspicion, expressed in several recent decisions, of Congressional incursions into the realm of constitutional law-making, which the justices regard as reserved for the court alone.

In this, the decision was reminiscent of the 1992 decision that reaffirmed the constitutional right to abortion, joined by justices who might well not have voted for Roe v. Wade in 1973 as an original matter but who thought the court would weaken itself by repudiating the precedent.

The validity of Section 3501 had not come before the court until now because no administration, of either party, sought to apply it. The law was injected into the case against Charles T. Dickerson, accused of participating in a 1997 bank robbery in Alexandria, Va., by a career federal prosecutor who asked the Federal District Court there to use the law to admit incriminating statements that Mr. Dickerson had given in the absence of Miranda warnings.

The District Court refused, and the Justice Department would not permit Section 3501 to be pressed on appeal. A conservative legal organization here, the Washington Legal Foundation, won permission to make the argument as a friend of the court from the United States Court of Appeals for the Fourth Circuit, which admitted the confession and accused the department of abdicating its responsibility.

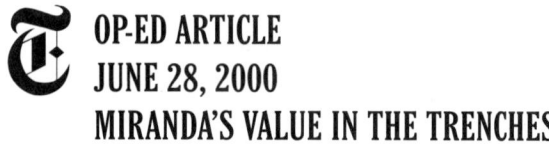

OP-ED ARTICLE
JUNE 28, 2000
MIRANDA'S VALUE IN THE TRENCHES
By SCOTT TUROW

I was delighted by the Supreme Court's decision on Monday to uphold Miranda, the 34-year old constitutional mandate that requires the police to advise anyone arrested of the right to remain silent. Miranda retains an almost sacramental value; it is a vivid emblem of central ideas about the law. But the truth is that by now, Miranda has little practical impact on the interaction between suspects and cops.

To whatever degree Miranda ever impeded law enforcement, its effect abated a long time ago. I have been practicing criminal law for nearly 22 years now, eight years as a federal prosecutor and 14 years in private practice. In that time, I have been involved in exactly one case where the result was changed after a confession was declared inadmissible under Miranda, and that matter involved a juvenile who, in addition to not being told his rights, did not enjoy the benefit of a number of other safeguards applied in Illinois to the questioning of minors.

Nor is my experience idiosyncratic. After a couple of hours of computer research, I could not find a single reported decision in Illinois in the last 12 months in which a confession was suppressed or a conviction reversed because of a Miranda violation.

To a great extent, as the court recognized on Monday in Dickerson v. United States, courts and cops have accommodated themselves to the rule. The more conservative justices who ascended to the Supreme Court after the Warren years have narrowed the decision's grand mandate, refining, for example, what amounts to interrogation for Miranda purposes, or sometimes allowing subsequent statements to be admitted even if a defendant initially claimed his Miranda rights.

As for the police, the court is right when it says that law enforcement practices have adjusted to Miranda's strictures. As a prosecutor, I never noted that federal agents much resented Miranda, even though some, like those in the Internal Revenue Service, were required to give warning when simply questioning someone.

In eight years, I never had a statement excluded from evidence because of the Miranda rule. The agents accepted the standard and often applied it skillfully. I remember a veteran F.B.I. agent dispensing the Miranda warnings to a suspect before we took him before a grand jury, a practice required by the Justice Department. As one of my colleagues commented, the warning sounded

ture, well understood by anyone who has ever watched TV. Confronted with an accusation, most people can't resist the impulse to explain, probably fearing that remaining silent would make them look guilty.

So if Miranda makes little difference in the daily world of law enforcement, why is it so heartening to see it still standing? Because Miranda is an expression of some fundamental concepts about the law we all should hold dear. One is equality before the law. Miranda, in essence, says that despite the vast disparities in education and income in our society, everyone in a confrontation with the state will possess the same critical knowledge about how the system works.

Second, the fact that some cops resent giving warnings has always been evidence in my mind of the warnings' value. Miranda's requirements are, in the most stereotypical police view, the intrusive work of nosy outsiders from

> " Catching bad guys is important, but it is not the only thing this society values; we also care about certain minimal standards of decency in the government's treatment of citizens and limits on the authority of the state. "

so avuncular, you just about expected the agent to put his arm around the prospective defendant's shoulders.

Granted, the federal agents with whom I worked were most often investigating white-collar crime, while most of the objections to Miranda have come from urban police, whose confrontations with suspects are often far more spontaneous. They are frequently faced with sorting out on the fly whether they intend to let a suspect go, which determines whether the Miranda warnings are required.

In the last decade, I've talked to enough people arrested in Chicago who said they were not read their rights during their initial interrogation that I wonder if some cops have reached a different accommodation with Miranda.

While I resent these kinds of tactics, I don't think many of these defendants, if given the Miranda warnings, would have shut up or asked for a lawyer. As the Supreme Court noted, Miranda by now is part of our national cul-

the world of the law, people sitting in the serene comfort of their cushy offices and judicial chambers, telling the police how to handle things on the dangerous streets.

But cops should recognize that no matter how noisy their protests, or how much they chafe, they are always going to be subject to civilian authority. Catching bad guys is important, but it is not the only thing this society values; we also care about certain minimal standards of decency in the government's treatment of citizens and limits on the authority of the state.

The requirement to recite Miranda is an important reminder to the police that the war on lawlessness is always subject to the guidance of the law. This week's decision, by a court that is not perceived as particularly hostile to law enforcement, is a needed reaffirmation of that message.

Scott Turow is the author of "Presumed Innocent" and "Personal Injuries."

TRIALS

The Sixth Amendment's rules aimed at ensuring fair trials for criminal defendants were all made applicable to the states in decisions dating from 1948 and resuming in the 1960s. Some of the earliest rulings seem self-evident and noncontroversial. *In re Oliver* (1948) imposed the public trial requirement; the decision overturned the contempt of court sentence a judge imposed on a witness after an in-chambers hearing. In the same year, *Cole v. Arkansas* incorporated the notice requirement; the ruling set aside verdicts against three defendants convicted in a labor dispute under a code section that was different from the one charged in the indictment.

Other provisions have been more complicated and more expensive for the states to follow. None are more important than the right to "assistance of counsel" and the right to "an impartial jury." States had no general obligation to provide lawyers to indigent defendants until the Supreme Court's landmark decision of *Gideon v. Wainwright* (1963). Today, that right is well established if the reality is still less than equal justice. Until the 1960s, jury selection procedures fell well short of ensuring a fair cross-section of the community even after Supreme Court decisions barred systematic exclusion of minority groups or others from jury service. Today, jury selection procedures are rigorously inclusive for the most part but controversies remain—especially in qualifying jurors in death penalty cases.

RIGHT TO COUNSEL

The Supreme Court's 1932 decision in the *Scottsboro Cases* found a due process violation in the judge's flagrant failure to permit the defendants time and opportunity to secure counsel, but it established no general rule governing the right to counsel in state cases. A decade later, the majority in *Betts v. Brady* (1942) specifically declined to impose on the states the same federal rule established four years earlier to require appointment of counsel for all indigent defendants (*Johnson v. Zerbst,* 1938).

In upholding Smith Betts's robbery conviction in Maryland, Justice Owen J. Roberts said the Due Process Clause did not impose "an inexorable command" to require counsel in all criminal cases. Roberts noted that in contrast to the young and illiterate defendants in the *Scottsboro Cases,* Betts was a middle-aged man "of ordinary intelligence and ability" who had defended himself by cross-examining witnesses and presenting his own.

Over the next two decades, the Court used a *Betts*-type totality of circumstances analysis to reverse a number of convictions involving young or unsophisticated defendants or overbearing judges. In 1962 justices dissatisfied with the case-by-case approach seized on a handwritten plea by an indigent Florida inmate, Clarence Earl Gideon, as an opportunity to consider overruling *Betts* in favor of an absolute rule.

Gideon had been convicted of the felony offense of breaking and entering into a poolroom to commit a misdemeanor and sentenced to five years in prison. He had asked for an appointed lawyer, but the judge had refused because the offense was not a capital crime. In prison, Gideon taught himself enough law to file a habeas corpus petition with the state's supreme court and then a petition for review with the U.S. justices. The Court appointed Abe Fortas, a prominent Washington lawyer and future justice, to represent him.

The unanimous decision in *Gideon v. Wainwright* (1963) overruled *Betts* and required states to provide lawyers to indigent defendants in all felony cases. "Any person haled into court, who is too poor to hire a lawyer, cannot be assured a fair trial unless counsel is provided for him," Justice Black wrote. "This seems to us to be an obvious truth." In a telling postscript, Gideon was acquitted when he was tried again—this time with a court-appointed attorney.

Gideon v. Wainwright

Decided: March 18, 1963

Vote: 9 (Warren, Black, Douglas, Clark, Harlan II, Brennan, Stewart, B. White, Goldberg)

0

Opinion of the Court: Black

Concurring opinions (3): Douglas; Clark; Harlan II

MARCH 19, 1963
SUPREME COURT EXTENDS RULING ON FREE COUNSEL

Holds States Must Provide Lawyers for All Poor in Serious Criminal Cases

REVERSES 1942 DECISION

Unanimous Opinion Could Permit Many Now Jailed to Ask for New Trials

By ANTHONY J. LEWIS

Special to The New York Times

WASHINGTON, March 18—The Supreme Court held today that the states must supply free lawyers to all poor persons facing serious criminal charges.

The court unanimously overruled its own 1942 decision in the landmark case of Betts v. Brady. There the ruling was that the Constitution required appointed counsel only in cases involving a death sentence or "special circumstances," such as an illiterate defendant.

Justice Hugo L. Black, who dissented in 1942, wrote the opinion for the majority today. He said Betts v. Brady was incorrectly decided.

"Reason and reflection," Justice Black said, "require us to recognize that in our adversary system of criminal justice any person haled into court who is too poor to hire a lawyer cannot be assured a fair trial unless counsel is provided for him. This seems to us to be an obvious truth."

At present only five states have no regular provision for appointment of counsel except in capital cases—those with possible death sentences. These states are Florida, Alabama, Mississippi and North and South Carolina.

In a number of other states, however, appointing practices vary according to localities, with no regular provision in less populous areas for non-capital cases. And quite a few states do not provide counsel in misdemeanors or petty offenses.

MANY COULD ASK RELEASE

Thus today's decision could have a great impact across the country. Among other things it could permit many thousands of persons now in prison to demand new trials.

Justice Black's opinion did not say whether the new constitutional doctrine was to be applied to those already

> Florida estimated, in this case, that perhaps 5,000 prisoners in her jails had had no lawyers at their trials and might ask for release. The state made this a strong ground for pleading with the court not to overturn Betts v. Brady.

FLORIDA CASE INVOLVED

The decision, one of the most important ever made by the Supreme Court in the criminal law field, was provoked by Clarence Earl Gideon, a 52-year-old inmate of the Florida State Prison.

Gideon was convicted of breaking and entering the Bay Harbor Poolroom in Panama City, Fla., with intent to commit petty larceny. He asked for a lawyer at his trial but was turned down.

The Florida Supreme Court rejected a habeas corpus petition from Gideon. He then sent a hand-written petition to the United States Supreme Court, which agreed to hear the case and to reconsider the correctness of Betts v. Brady.

jailed. But there was nothing to indicate that others in Gideon's position could not seek their release on habeas corpus as he did, because he had no lawyer at his trial.

Florida estimated, in this case, that perhaps 5,000 prisoners in her jails had had no lawyers at their trials and might ask for release. The state made this a strong ground for pleading with the court not to overturn Betts v. Brady.

One restriction on the effect of the decision may be the doctrine of waiver—the rule that a man may waive his right to a lawyer by not demanding one. Gideon specifically asked for a lawyer at this trial, but many prisoners may not have done so.

Justice Black's opinion did not settle, either, whether the new rule will apply to the most petty crimes, such as traffic offenses. That will presumably be worked out in later cases.

'RESPECTFUL BURIAL'

Justice John Marshall Harlan, in a concurring opinion, said he agreed that Betts v. Brady should be overruled but thought it deserved "a more respectful burial" than Justice Black's opinion saying it was wrong to start with.

Justice Harlan was persuaded by the fact that the Supreme Court in recent years had repeatedly found "special circumstances" requiring counsel. He said that "to continue a rule which is honored by this court only with lip service is not a healthy thing."

Justice Tom C. Clark also filed a separate concurrence, based on his conclusion that the Constitution made no distinction between capital and noncapital crimes.

In several other cases today the court took major steps to provide new protections for state criminal defendants.

It held, 6 to 3, that when a state provides a right to appeal criminal convictions, it must supply counsel on appeal for indigents. The dissenters were Justices Harlan, Clark and Potter Stewart.

The Justices divided 5 to 4 in deciding that Washington State had not given two prisoners an adequate record of their trial as a basis for appeal. Justice Byron White wrote the dissent, joined by Justices Harlan, Clark and Stewart.

A unanimous decision struck down an Indiana procedure under which the public defender might prevent a poor man from appealing by declaring the appeal frivolous.

By a vote of 6 to 3, with Justices Harlan, Clark and Stewart dissenting, the court held that Federal courts may release on habeas corpus a state prisoner who was turned down in the state courts because he failed to follow required procedure.

This case, which has great significance for the relations of state and Federal courts, involved Charles Noia of New York, serving a life sentence for murder.

Two co-defendants of Noia's were eventually released because confessions were found to have been coerced from all three. But Noia had never appealed—because, he said, he feared a death sentence in a new trial.

The New York courts said this failure to appeal barred any relief for him after his two co-defendants went free. The Supreme Court said today that, whatever restricted the New York judiciary, Federal courts could and should free Noia.

Finally, by a vote of 5 to 4, the court said an Indiana prisoner should have a full hearing before a Federal court on his assertion that he had confessed after he was given a "truth serum" drug.

The dissenters—Justices Stewart, Harlan, Clark and White—agreed that a confession obtained by drugs would be invalid. But they said the prisoner had had ample chance to prove his claim in the state criminal proceedings, failed and should not be given a new chance in the Federal courts.

This barrage of criminal law decisions, especially the Gideon case, should spur state efforts to set up new methods of providing counsel for indigents. . . .

. . . .

In contrast to the *Mapp* exclusionary rule decision or the later police interrogation rulings, *Gideon* produced general public approval and willing compliance by the states. Twenty-two states in fact had urged the Court to overrule *Betts;* only Alabama had sided with Florida.

A decade later, the Court extended the *Gideon* rule to any misdemeanor case that actually results in imprisonment (*Argersinger v. Hamlin,* 1972). More recently, the Court ruled in *Alabama v. Shelton* (2002) that an indigent defendant cannot be given a suspended jail sentence unless he or she is provided appointed counsel at trial or waives the right.

The Court has not provided the same clear-cut test for claims that an appointed lawyer provided so inadequate a defense as to deprive a defendant of "effective assistance" of counsel. In *Strickland v. Washington* (1984), the Court established a somewhat strict test that a defendant must show that a lawyer's conduct fell below an "objective standard of reasonableness" and that but for the lawyer's "professional errors," the result of the trial probably would have been different. Justice O'Connor specifically said the decision imposed no "mechanical rules."

The Court applied the *Strickland* test the same day in rejecting a lower court's finding of ineffective assistance when an inexperienced lawyer had little time to confer with his client. A year later, the Court ruled that a lawyer's failure to file a notice of appeal by the deadline constituted ineffective assistance. But in 2000, the Court in *Roe v. Flores-Ortega* said that failure to file an appeal had to be judged on a case-by-case basis.

Only once since *Strickland* has the Court found ineffective assistance of counsel in a trial setting. In *Wiggins v. Smith* (2003), the Court ruled, 7-2, that two public defenders provided deficient representation by failing to uncover the defendant's long history of sexual and physical abuse. The information should have been available as mitigating evidence in his death penalty hearing, Justice O'Connor said.

Right to an Impartial Jury

The Supreme Court relied on the Fourteenth Amendment's Equal Protection Clause in a nineteenth-century decision striking down laws in Virginia and West Virginia that barred blacks from jury service (*Strauder v. West Virginia,* 1880). Later, in the second *Scottsboro Cases* decision, the Court held that even without a statutory disqualification, jury selection practices that resulted in an "unvarying" exclusion of African Americans amounted to an equal protection violation (*Norris v. Alabama,* 1935).

The Court applied that principle in *Hernandez v. Texas* (1954) to hold that the Fourteenth Amendment forbids the systematic exclusion of any substantial racial group—in the instant case, Latinos, who comprised 14 percent of the population in the county. In other decisions, the Court struck down practices that identified potential jurors by race. In *Whitus v. Georgia* (1967), for example, jurors were chosen from racially separated tax records.

Until then, the Court had not held the Sixth Amendment's right to jury trial applicable to the states. In 1968, however, the Court finally ruled in *Duncan v. Louisiana* that defendants charged with serious crimes must be accorded a jury trial in state courts. "Trial by jury is fundamental to the American scheme of justice," Justice White wrote in the 7-2 decision. Gary Duncan had been sentenced to two years in prison for battery; Louisiana law provided jury trials only for crimes punishable by death or hard labor.

Over the next decade, the Court played numbers games with jury size and verdicts. *Williams v. Florida* (1970) held that six-person juries were constitutionally permissible in either state or federal courts. In companion 1972 decisions—*Johnson v. Louisiana* and *Apodaca v. Oregon*—the Court held by a 5-4 vote that nonunanimous juries were also constitutionally permissible in state though not in federal courts. Louisiana permitted verdicts by 9-3 votes, Oregon by 10-2 margins. In 1979, however, the Court ruled in *Burch v. Louisiana* that a six-person jury had to be unanimous in reaching a verdict.

With sex discrimination law still in the future, the Court held in *Hoyt v. Florida* (1961) that states could excuse women from jury service without violating a defendant's right to an impartial jury. The unanimous ruling upheld Gwendolyn Hoyt's second-degree murder conviction by an all-male jury for killing her abusive husband with a baseball bat. *Taylor v. Louisiana* (1975) reversed that ruling—ironically, by favoring a male defendant's right to have a jury chosen from "a representative segment" of the community. Since "women are sufficiently numerous and distinct from men," Justice White explained, the fair cross-section requirement cannot be met if women are systematically excluded. Rehnquist was the lone dissenter.

As long as the jury pool is representative, a defendant has no constitutional right to a particular makeup of the jury in his or her trial. In two recent decisions, however, the Court ruled that prosecutors may not use so-called peremptory challenges during the jury selection process to strike out prospective jurors because of their race or sex. The Equal Protection Clause "forbids the States to strike black veniremen [members of a jury panel] on the assumption that they will be biased in a particular case simply because the defendant is black," Justice Lewis F. Powell Jr. wrote in *Batson v. Kentucky* (1986). Eight years later, the Court in *J.E.B. v. Alabama ex rel. T.B.* (1994) applied the same principle to the use of peremptory challenges to exclude women from individual juries.

MAY 1, 1986
HIGH COURT LIMITS EXCLUDING BLACKS AS JURY MEMBERS

By STUART TAYLOR JR.
Special to The New York Times

In one of its most important criminal law rulings in years, the Supreme Court today acted to protect the rights of black defendants by making it more difficult for prosecutors to exclude blacks from juries.

The 7-to-2 decision, which overturned in part a major 1965 ruling by the Court, held that prosecutors may not exclude blacks from juries because of concern that they will favor a defendant of their own race.

The Court also established an evidentiary standard that made it easier for black defendants to prove unconstitutional discrimination by prosecutors who exclude blacks from juries.

The ruling will prompt defense lawyers to challenge prosecutors' use of peremptory challenges in many cases with black defendants. It may also be used by lawyers representing members of other racial minorities and even whites to challenge exclusion of prospective jurors of the defendants' race. The extent to which such challenges will be successful remains to be seen.

Left unresolved today was whether the Court will apply its decision retroactively. If so, it could give thousands of black prisoners a basis for challenging their convictions.

The Court's action in overruling the 1965 decision in the case Swain v. Alabama was considered especially

> **[The Equal Protection Clause] forbids the prosecutor to challenge potential jurors solely on account of their race or on the assumption that black jurors as a group will be unable impartially to consider the State's case against a black defendant.**
>
> —Justice Lewis F. Powell Jr., *Batson v. Kentucky*

The case involves the use of a legal device, the peremptory challenge, to prevent seating a juror. Under Federal and state laws, prosecutors and defense lawyers alike may use such challenges to exclude specified numbers of prospective jurors from a panel without giving a reason. Lawyers can also ask the trial judge to exclude other jurors on the ground that their answers to questions disclose potential bias; that is, "for cause."

EFFECT ON CRIMINAL CASES

The decision will have a broad effect because prosecutors use peremptory challenges to exclude at least some prospective black jurors in a large percentage of the many criminal cases in which blacks are defendants.

The decision today was a major victory for defense lawyers and civil libertarians. It was a defeat for prosecutors, including the Reagan Administration and the National District Attorneys Association, who had urged the Court not to fetter the historically unrestricted powers of prosecutors.

unusual. This is because the earlier decision was made in an era when the Court's liberal majority under Chief Justice Earl Warren is generally thought to have been far more sympathetic to the rights of criminal defendants than the Court's current majority.

Justice Lewis F. Powell Jr., who was appointed by President Nixon, wrote the majority opinion today, rejecting the "crippling burden of proof" he said was placed on black defendants in the Swain case. Among those joining his opinion were Justices Sandra Day O'Connor, the only member of the court appointed by President Reagan, and Byron R. White, an appointee of President Kennedy and the author of the Swain decision.

Chief Justice Warren E. Burger and Justice William H. Rehnquist, both Nixon appointees, dissented strenuously, saying the Court had "casually cast aside" centuries of law.

The dissenters said the Constitution did not bar prosecutors or defense lawyers from excluding blacks "from a particular jury based upon the assumption or belief that they would be more likely to favor a black defendant," or from excluding members of other racial groups for similar reasons.

WHAT THE SWAIN CASE SAID

In the Swain decision, the Court said that it might be a violation of the Fourteenth Amendment guarantee of equal protection of the laws for prosecutors systematically to exclude blacks from juries solely on account of their race "for reasons wholly unrelated to the outcome of the particular case on trial."

But the Swain decision at least suggested, as the two dissenters argued today, that it was not unconstitutional for a prosecutor to exclude blacks in a particular case on a hunch that they would be more sympathetic to a black defendant.

The Swain decision also held that the Constitution did not give a black defendant any basis for requiring a prosecutor to justify his use of peremptory challenges in any given case, even if he excludes all blacks from the jury panel, unless the defendant can prove systematic racially motivated exclusion of blacks in case after case.

Today, Justice Powell held that the equal protection clause "forbids the prosecutor to challenge potential jurors solely on account of their race or on the assumption that black jurors as a group will be unable impartially to consider the State's case against a black defendant."

He also said that "a defendant may establish a prima facie case of purposeful discrimination in selection of the petit jury solely on evidence concerning the prosecutor's exercise of peremptory challenges at the defendant's trial."

If a defendant who is "a member of a cognizable racial group" can convince the trial judge that circumstances "raise an inference" that the prosecutor's exclusion of potential jurors of the defendant's race was racially motivated, then "the burden shifts to the State to come forward with a neutral explanation" for excluding those jurors.

The case, Batson v. Kentucky, No. 84-6263, involves James K. Batson, a black man convicted by an all-white jury of burglary and receipt of stolen goods. The prosecutor in the case used four of his six peremptory challenges to exclude all of the potential black jurors.

The justices sent the case back to the Kentucky courts, saying they should decide under the standards announced today whether these exclusions were racially motivated. If so, the court said, the conviction should be reversed.

Justices White and O'Connor and the two dissenters said the decision should not be retroactive. The five other Justices in the majority expressed no view on the issue.

In suggesting a wide range of factors that might bear on the question of whether racial motivation had been proved, the Court left trial judges with wide latitude in individual cases. Justice White's concurring opinion said "much litigation will be required to spell out the contours" of the decision.

Justice Thurgood Marshall, the Court's only black member, applauded the decision as "a historic step," but said it did not go far enough. He called for "banning the use of peremptory challenges by prosecutors and allowing the states to eliminate the defendant's peremptory as well." . . .

. . . .

Batson established a three-step process for considering claims of racial (or gender) bias. First, the defendant must make a preliminary showing that the prosecutor systematically struck out prospective jurors because of race or sex, without cause. The prosecutor can then try to show legitimate race- or gender-neutral reasons for excluding the juror. The defendant can then try to refute the explanation. A prosecutor's explanation need not be rational as long as it is not racially based (*Purkett v. Elem,* 1995). In 2008, however, the Court specified that appellate courts can determine on their own that a prosecutor's race-neutral explanation for excluding jurors is "implausible" (*Snyder v. Louisiana*).

The representative cross-section requirement poses a special difficulty in capital cases because many Americans oppose the death penalty. In *Witherspoon v. Illinois* (1968), the Court ruled that judges cannot systematically exclude jurors because of their "general scruples" about capital punishment. *Wainwright v. Witt* (1985), however, allows judges to excuse a juror whose opposition to the death penalty might "prevent or substantially impair" his or her ability to follow the law.

The rulings combine to make jury selection in capital cases time-consuming and appeals contentious. In the most recent ruling on the matter, the Court in *Uttecht v. Brown* (2007) divided 5-4 in telling federal courts in habeas corpus cases to defer to state judges' decisions to disqualify jurors with general concerns about the death penalty. The ruling reinstated a death sentence for a Washington State defendant after a federal appeals court found that one prospective juror was improperly disqualified during the eleven days of jury selection. The four dissenters accused the majority of "choosing to defer blindly" to the trial judge's rulings.

SENTENCING

Historically, the Supreme Court has given broad discretion to judges in determining sentences for criminal defendants and to states in choosing between judge or jury sentencing. The Court's first decision finding a state to have violated the Eighth Amendment's prohibition against cruel and unusual punishment came in 1962: *Robinson v. California* struck down a state law permitting prison sentences for persons found to be drug addicts. Six years later, however, the Court refused by a 5-4 vote to forbid states to punish chronic alcoholics for public drunkenness (*Powell v. Texas*, 1968).

The Court forcefully interjected itself into the issue of capital punishment in 1972 by throwing out all existing death sentences because the penalty was—as one of the justices put it—"wantonly and freakishly" imposed. The Court permitted the resumption of capital punishment four years later. Since then, the justices have narrowed the use of the death penalty while rejecting broad challenges to the practice.

Meanwhile, the Court opened up a new issue in 2000, when it began to limit the role of judges in fact-finding used to increase defendants' sentences. An unusual coalition of liberal and conservative justices found the practice to infringe defendants' right to jury trials. The line of decisions upset the use of sentencing guideline systems in state courts and changed the system that had been used in federal courts since the 1980s from mandatory to merely advisory guidelines.

CAPITAL PUNISHMENT

The Constitution recognizes capital punishment in two places. The Fifth Amendment provides that a grand jury indictment or presentment is required for any "capital, or otherwise infamous crime." Both the Fifth and Fourteenth Amendments prohibit depriving any person of "*life*, liberty, or property, without due process of law" (emphasis added).

The Supreme Court sanctioned the firing squad as one method of execution in a nineteenth-century case from what was then the territory of Utah (*Wilkerson v. Utah*, 1878). Seventy years later, the Court assumed for the first time that the Eighth Amendment applied to the states. Its ruling in *Louisiana ex rel. Francis v. Resweber* (1948), however, allowed the state to execute death row inmate Willie Francis after a botched first attempt at electrocuting him.

The Court began to oversee state criminal justice systems in the first half of the twentieth century in part because of patent injustices in capital cases such as the *Scottsboro* trials. As the Warren Court began systematically reforming criminal law in the 1960s, the NAACP Legal Defense Fund initiated a full-fledged campaign to abolish capital punishment because of the disproportionate use of the death penalty against African Americans. Meanwhile, public support for capital punishment was falling to as low as 42 percent in a 1966 poll.

The developments combined to produce the Court's stunning decision in *Furman v. Georgia* (1972) to invalidate all existing death sentences throughout the country. The five Warren Court justices in the majority each wrote separately to explain his reasons for finding capital punishment as then administered to be "cruel and unusual" under the Eighth Amendment. Douglas found the current practices "pregnant with discrimination." Brennan called the death penalty "degrading to human dignity," and Thurgood Marshall declared it to be "morally unacceptable." Stewart said it was "cruel and unusual in the same way that being struck by lightning is cruel and unusual." Finally, White said that the death penalty was "so infrequently imposed" that it had ceased to have any deterrent value. Chief Justice Burger and President Nixon's three other appointees—Harry A. Blackmun, Powell, and Rehnquist—dissented.

Many states turned to rewriting their death penalty statutes to try to meet the Court's objections. Two—Louisiana and North Carolina—eliminated discretion by making the death penalty mandatory for specified crimes. Twenty-five others instead adopted "guided discretion" laws that provided for a separate death penalty hearing before a jury after a guilty verdict. At this hearing, the prosecution and defense were free to introduce evidence of "aggravating" or "mitigating" factors in the individual case.

Furman v. Georgia

Decided: June 29, 1972

Vote: 5 (Douglas, Brennan, Stewart, B. White, T. Marshall)

4 (Burger, Blackmun, Powell, Rehnquist)

Opinion: *Per curiam*

Opinions concurring in judgment (5): Douglas; Brennan; Stewart; B. White; T. Marshall

Dissenting opinions (4): Burger (Blackmun, Powell, Rehnquist); Blackmun; Powell (Burger, Blackmun, Rehnquist); Rehnquist (Burger, Blackmun, Powell)

JUNE 30, 1972
SUPREME COURT, 5-4, BARS DEATH PENALTY AS IT IS IMPOSED UNDER PRESENT STATUTES

COURT SPARES 600

4 Justices Named by Nixon All Dissent in Historic Decision

By FRED P. GRAHAM

Special to The New York Times

WASHINGTON, June 29—The Supreme Court ruled today that capital punishment, as now administered in the United States, is unconstitutional "cruel and unusual" punishment

The historic decision came on a vote of 5 to 4.

Although the five Justices in the majority issued separate opinions and did not agree on a single reason for their

EIGHTH AMENDMENT CITED

The decision pitted the five holdovers of the more liberal Warren Court against the four appointees of President Nixon, who dissented. The ruling came as the Supreme Court handed down its final decisions of the year and recessed until Oct. 2.

> As Justice Stewart put it, the death penalty is 'so wantonly and so freakishly imposed' that those who are sentenced to death receive excessively harsh treatment.

action, the effect of the decision appeared to be to rule out executions under any capital punishment laws now in effect in this country.

The decision will also save from execution 600 condemned men and women now on death rows in the United States, although it did not overturn their convictions. Most will be held in prison for the rest of their lives, but under some states' procedures some of the prisoners may eventually gain their freedom.

Three Justices in the majority, William O. Douglas, William J. Brennan Jr. and Thurgood Marshall, concluded that executions in modern-day America necessarily violate the Eighth Amendment's prohibition against "cruel and unusual punishments."

The other two in the majority, the two "swing men" of the Court, Justices Potter Stewart and Byron R. White, reasoned that the present legal system operates in a cruel and unusual way, because it gives judges and juries the discretion to decree life or death and they impose it erratically.

As Justice Stewart put it, the death penalty is "so wantonly and so freakishly imposed" that those who are sentenced to death receive excessively harsh treatment.

VIEW OF CHIEF JUSTICE

"These death sentences are cruel and unusual in the same way that being struck by lightning is cruel and unusual," he said.

As the dissenters pointed out, this alignment means that no death sentence can pass muster before the present Supreme Court unless it satisfies the objections voiced by Justices Stewart and White.

Chief Justice Warren E. Burger suggested that legislatures could attempt to do this in two ways. One is to state in statute books in detail the conditions under which a judge or jury can impose the death penalty—such as rape accompanied by a vicious assault, or a convict's murder of a prison guard.

The second would be to revert to the practice of more than a century ago, and impose mandatory death sentences for those convicted of certain crimes.

In any event, Chief Justice Burger said, Congress and the state legislatures will be required to "make a thorough re-evaluation of the entire subject of capital punishment," including a serious inquiry into whether it serves as a deterrent.

All four dissenters also filed separate opinions, in a judicial outpouring that required 243 pages to express the view of all nine Justices.

The gist of the dissenters' position was that the Eighth Amendment has been in effect for 191 years and has not, until today, been held to rule out executions. They charged that the majority had usurped the prerogative of the legislatures in the decision today.

Justice Lewis F. Powell Jr. said the action would have a "shattering effect" upon the rule that prior decisions should be followed, as well as on the principles of "Federalism, judicial restraint, and—most importantly—separation of powers."

DECISION IN CALIFORNIA

Justice Harry A. Blackmun implied strongly that the majority had been "propelled toward its result" to stroke

down capital punishment by the recent decision of the Supreme Court of California, which outlawed executions under the state constitution's prohibition against "cruel or unusual" punishments.

Justice Blackmun added an unusually personal insight by saying that while he had an "abhorrence" of capital punishment he felt only the legislatures could abolish it.

Justice William H. Rehnquist's dissent said the decision had underscored a fundamental question about the Supreme Court's role in reviewing the nation's laws. While overreaching legislatures may encroach upon individual rights, he said an overreaching Supreme Court can "sacrifice the equally important right of the people to govern themselves."

The decision today culminated a campaign initiated by the N.A.A.C.P. Legal Defense and Educational Fund, Inc., five years ago, when the liberal coloration of the Warren Court made success appear much more likely than it had been presumed to be before the present Court.

Although the Supreme Court had never directly ruled that the death penalty was not cruel and unusual punishment, this was because it had been assumed throughout most of the country's history that it was not. The Court had said so, in passing, without actually making a ruling to that effect.

In his 50-page concurring opinion today, Justice William J. Brennan Jr. traced the evolution of the "cruel and unusual" punishment concept, and pointed out that the Supreme Court has traditionally considered it a growing concept, which develops with the changing mores of the times.

Therefore, even though the framers of the Bill of Rights did not intend to outlaw executions when they adopted the Eighth Amendment, Justice Brennan asserted that present conditions bring the death penalty within the prohibition.

His reasoning was that the penalty was unusually severe and degrading, it appeared to be arbitrarily imposed. It was widely condemned by contemporary society, and it might be no better a deterrent than prison.

Justice Thurgood Marshall expressed similar arguments, adding that the penalty was "morally unacceptable," if for no other reason than that it most frequently fell upon blacks, "the poor, the ignorant, and the underprivileged members of society."

Justice Douglas asserted that it is "implicit" in the ban on cruel and unusual punishment that executions cannot be imposed indiscriminately. Because it is the poor and minority groups that most often are executed, he concluded, capital punishment violates the 14th Amendment's guarantee of equal protection of the laws, as well as the Eighth Amendment.

Prior to today's decision, 11 state legislatures had abolished capital punishment completely, or with such narrow exceptions as the murder of a prison guard by a life convict. Thirty-nine states, the District of Columbia and the Federal Government had laws that authorized executions for various crimes.

The defendants before the Court today were William Henry Furman, sentenced to death for a robbery-murder in Georgia and Lucius Jackson Jr. of Georgia, and Elmer Branch of Texas, both condemned to death for rape. . . .

• • • • • • • • • • •

Four years after *Furman*—with Stevens now on the Court in place of Douglas—the Court approved the guided discretion statutes while disapproving the mandatory approach. Writing the main opinion in the 7-2 decision in *Gregg v. Georgia* (1976), Justice Stewart cited "considerations of federalism," "the moral consensus concerning the death penalty," and "its social utility as a sanction" in concluding that capital punishment for murder was "not invariably disproportionate to the crime." Brennan and Marshall dissented.

Gregg v. Georgia

Decided: July 2, 1976

Vote: 7 (Burger, Stewart, B. White, Blackmun, Powell, Rehnquist, Stevens)

2 (Brennan, T. Marshall)

Judgment of the Court: Stewart

Concurring opinion: B. White (Burger, Rehnquist)

Concurring in judgment: Blackmun

Dissenting opinions (2): Brennan; T. Marshall

JULY 3, 1976
JUSTICES UPHOLD DEATH PENALTY; REQUIRE GUIDANCE FOR IMPOSING IT, LIMIT LAWS MAKING IT MANDATORY

DECISION IS 7 TO 2

Punishment Is Ruled Acceptable, at Least in Murder Cases

By LESLEY OELSNER

Special to The New York Times

WASHINGTON, July 2—In a somber and dramatic session, the Supreme Court ruled by a vote of 7 to 2 today that the death penalty is not inherently cruel or unusual.

The Court found that it is a constitutionally acceptable form of punishment, at least for murder.

In 1972, the Court ruled, 5 to 4, that capital punishment as then practiced in America violated the Constitution's Eighth Amendment ban on cruel and unusual punishment, citing the arbitrary and "freakish" way in which some defendants were sentenced to die and others were allowed to live.

Today, however, reviewing five of the state statutes that were passed in response to the 1972 ruling in attempts to meet the Court's objections, the Court said that judges and juries may impose the penalty so long as they have been given adequate information and guidance for determining whether the sentence is appropriate in a particular case.

SOME STATUTES PERMISSIBLE

Statutes that provide for this information and guidance—requiring judges and juries to take account of mitigating as well as aggravating circumstances, for instance—are permissible under the 1972 ruling, the Court found.

It also ruled, by a vote of 5 to 4, that states may not impose "mandatory" capital punishment laws requiring the death penalty for every defendant convicted of murder. But its 7-to-2 judgment on the issue of the penalty's inherent constitutionality, and the various opinions of the seven Justices who joined in that judgment, make clear that statutes that come close to being mandatory will be permissible.

The impact of the Court action on the New York death penalty law was not clear. A spokesman for the NAACP Legal Defense and Educational Fund Inc. described the law as "a unique statute." Joseph Gormley Jr., Connecticut's chief state's attorney, said the decision appeared to indicate that his state's capital punishment law was constitutional. New Jersey does not have a death penalty.

3 STATUTES UPHELD

The Court upheld three of the state statutes before it today—those of Georgia, Florida and Texas—and struck down two, Louisiana's and North Carolina's. The Louisiana and North Carolina laws imposed blanket mandatory rules.

The Texas statute, however, also has a form of mandatory death penalty: Death is required as the penalty in murder cases, if the jury in a separate trial on the issue

Opponents have contended that it is not a deterrent, and that it is barbaric, a relic of the past that has no place in civilized society.

NO DEATHS SINCE 1967

Because of this dispute and because of the legal battles over the penalty's constitutionality, led in large part by the NAACP Legal Defense and Educational Fund Inc., no one has been executed in America since June 2, 1967. On that day Louis Jose Monge was put to death in the gas chamber in Colorado after pleading guilty to murdering his pregnant wife and three of his seven children.

It will probably be some months before the next execution, because of efforts by lawyers to get stays, and because of litigation. And there will still be legal battles ahead as lawyers challenge particular laws as inconsistent

> " We cannot say that [capital] punishment is invariably disproportionate to the crime; it is an extreme sanction, suitable to the most extreme of crimes.
>
> —Justice Potter Stewart, *Gregg v. Georgia* "

of sentence answers affirmatively each of three specific questions about the defendant and the crime. The Court found that this procedure required the jury to consider the particular case, including mitigating circumstances, and that this satisfied the Court's standard.

After the 1972 ruling, 35 states and the Federal Government imposed various kinds of death penalty legislation. The high court of Illinois subsequently struck down its state's law. Approximately 600 persons are on Death Row as a result of those laws.

Today's ruling may invalidate slightly more than half of the statutes and, in so doing, save some 300 persons from execution. However, it opens the way for every state to have a statute that is acceptable to the Supreme Court, simply by modifying or revising its law to approximate one of the three specifically upheld today.

Capital punishment has been the source of a bitter and emotional dispute for years, on legal grounds as well as for philosophical and religious reasons.

Prosecutors have traditionally demanded it, saying it is necessary as a deterrent. Substantial portions of the public have assented, according to public opinion polls, and their agreement has often made the issue a political one.

with today's ruling. But the judgment today means that the main legal battle is over.

In the 1972 ruling there were nine separate opinions, one for each of the nine Justices. That meant that the Supreme Court's holding was the lowest common denominator of the rulings of the five majority Justices—that it was the wantonless and discretionless way in which juries applied the death penalty that made it unconstitutional.

Today, the Court again split and there was no one opinion joined by a majority. In the five separate cases, each involving one state law, there were a total of 24 opinions.

DIFFERENT GROUPINGS

The holding of the Court today is thus the view again represented in the lowest common denominator, the view taken jointly by Justices Potter Stewart, Lewis F. Powell Jr. and John Paul Stevens, On the issue of the penalty's inherent constitutionality, they were joined by Chief Justice Warren E. Burger and Justices Byron R. White, Harry A. Blackmun and William H. Rehnquist. On the issue of the validity of blanket mandatory rules, they were joined by Justices William J. Brennan Jr. and Thurgood Marshall.

In 1972, Justices Stewart and White were among those who voted to strike down capital punishment, as it then existed. The other members who made up the five-man majority in 1972 were Justices Brennan, Marshall and William O. Douglas, who retired last year and was replaced by Justice Stevens.

The basic positions of the various groups of Justices on today's ruling broke down thus:

Justices Stewart, Powell and Stevens contended that for the penalty to be valid, the statute had to specify the discretion of whoever metes out the penalty, whether judge or jury, so as to eliminate arbitrary results. The judge or jury has to make a particularized finding regarding the defendant's character or the circumstances of the crime.

Justices White, Burger and Rehnquist would allow the states more leeway, requiring them only to enact laws that would result in the penalty's being imposed with some reasonable consistency.

Justice Blackmun for his part apparently would also give the states broad leeway. He did not issue any opinions today, however, other than brief statements referring to his dissent in the 1972 case.

Justices Brennan and Marshall would ban the death penalty altogether.

The Stewart-Powell-Stevens views, the ones that are now the law of the land, were laid out most fully in the opinions involving the Georgia and North Carolina laws.

The Georgia case involved a statute that was signed in 1972 by Jimmy Carter, the prime contender for the Democratic presidential nomination. The Justices made a three-part finding on this law. First, they found that the death penalty was not inherently unconstitutional; next, they found that statutes could be drafted to comply with the 1972 decision, and third, that Georgia's was satisfactory.

NO BAN CONSTRUED

At the time the Eighth Amendment was passed, it was not construed to ban death. The Justices noted that this was not decisive, for under a long series of rulings, the Court has established the principle that the penalty is to be viewed in relation to evolving standards of decency.

The test established by the Court over the years, they said was instead whether a punishment was excessive either as unnecessary and wanton infliction of pain, or as grossly disproportionate to the severity of the crime.

The Justices found basically that the death penalty would not always be considered excessive. They relied heavily on the fact that many state legislatures had enacted laws reflecting contemporary standards of decency, and that legislatures had considered the penalty necessary as a deterrent, and as retribution.

Of retribution, they said: "In part, capital punishment is an expression of society's moral outrage at particularly offensive conduct. This function may be unappealing to many, but it is essential in an ordered society that asks its citizens to rely on legal procedures rather than self-help to vindicate their wrongs."

DETERRENT INCONCLUSIVE

The justices said that the value of capital punishment as a deterrent was unknown, studies of it having come to "inconclusive" results. They said they assumed that it might have no deterrent effect in crimes of passion, but that it might in cases of "carefully contemplated murders, such as murder for hire." The matter, they said, was best left to the legislatures.

The final question was thus whether death was a disproportionate penalty for murder, the one crime that the Court said it was considering.

"There is no question that death as a punishment is unique in its severity and irrevocability," the Justices said. But considered against murder, they said, "we cannot say that the punishment is invariably disproportionate to the crime; it is an extreme sanction, suitable to the most extreme of crimes."

In dissent, Justice Brennan, the one Justice who was not in Court this morning, quoted from Albert Camus: "Justice of this kind is obviously no less shocking than the crime itself, and the new 'official' murder, far from offering redress for the offense committed against society, adds instead a second defilement to the first."

RETRIBUTION QUESTIONED

Justice Marshall, in his dissent, conceded that the recent enactment of many death penalty laws had some relevance to gauging the current standards of what is "cruel and unusual." But he argued that society had other effective means of deterrence, and he disputed as well the plurality's views of retribution.

"The mere fact that the community demands the murderer's life in return for the evil he has done cannot sustain the death penalty," he said.

On the issue of the validity of broad mandatory death penalty laws, the Stewart-Powell-Stevens opinions again stressed the history of the death penalty in the United

States—but to different ends. They noted that at the start, punishment was mandatory for many offenses. Juries often acquitted defendants rather than send them to their death by a conviction. States then began to limit the number of crimes for which death was the punishment: they later began to allow juries discretion as well even regarding those crimes.

Hence, the three Justices said, the nation had repudiated the concept of mandatory laws.

The Justices also found that both of the laws before them, North Carolina's and Louisiana's, were invalid under the 1972 ruling because they did not provide standards for the jury.

The dissenters questioned the majority's view of history. They also pointed out that in 1971 the High Court said in another death penalty case, "To identify before the fact those characteristics of criminal homicides and their perpetrators which call for the death penalty, and to express these characteristics in language which can be fairly understood and applied by the sentencing authority, appear to be tasks which are beyond present human ability."

- - - - - - - - - - - -

Woodson v. North Carolina

Decided: July 2, 1976

Vote: 5 (Brennan, Stewart, T. Marshall, Powell, Stevens)

4 (Burger, B. White, Blackmun, Rehnquist)

Judgment of the Court: Stewart

Opinions concurring in judgment (2): Brennan; T. Marshall

Dissenting opinions (3): B. White (Burger, Rehnquist); Blackmun; Rehnquist

Stewart also wrote the main opinion in the 5-4 decision in *Woodson v. North Carolina* (1976) to strike down the mandatory death penalty laws. The approach was unconstitutional, he said, because it "accords no significance" to facts about the individual offender or the circumstances of the particular offense. White joined Burger, Blackmun, and Rehnquist in dissent.

Through the 1980s, the Court applied the Eighth Amendment to prohibit use of the death penalty for rape (1977) or for some accomplices in murder cases (1982). It prohibited the death penalty for defendants who were under the age of sixteen at the time of the crime (1988), but allowed it for older teenagers (1989). It barred the execution of insane persons (1985), but not mentally retarded offenders (1989). (See "Supreme Court's Major Death Penalty Decisions, 1972–2008," opposite.)

The Court also rejected two broad challenges to the operation of death penalty laws. In *Pulley v. Harris* (1984), the Court voted 7-2 that states need not ensure that an individual death sentence is proportional to punishment for similar crimes. In *McCleskey v. Kemp* (1987), the Court turned aside a statistical study that supported a claim of racial discrimination by showing that the death penalty was used in Georgia disproportionately in cases with white victims. For the majority, Justice Powell said the study did not demonstrate "a constitutionally significant risk of racial bias."

Justices Brennan and Marshall stuck to their view of the death penalty as invariably "cruel and unusual" under the Eighth Amendment until their retirements in 1990 and 1991, respectively. In February 1994 Justice Blackmun said he would no longer vote to uphold death sentences, but he retired at the end of the term. Following Blackmun's departure, the Rehnquist Court had no justice unalterably opposed to the death penalty and a reliable majority skeptical of many death penalty appeals.

Atkins v. Virginia

Decided: June 20, 2002

Vote: 6 (Stevens, O'Connor, Kennedy, Souter, Ginsburg, Breyer)

3 (Rehnquist, Scalia, Thomas)

Opinion of the Court: Stevens

Dissenting opinions (2): Rehnquist (Scalia, Thomas); Scalia (Rehnquist, Thomas)

Even so, the Court imposed two new limits on use of the death penalty by barring its use against mentally retarded offenders in 2002 and against juvenile offenders three years later. The decisions—*Atkins v. Virginia* (2002) and *Roper v. Simmons* (2005)—relied on the infrequent use of the death penalty in similar cases as evidence of a national consensus against executing these two types of offenders. Both rulings stirred controversy among conservatives by citing the prevailing international practice against executing offenders in those categories.

Supreme Court's Major Death Penalty Decisions, 1972–2008

Decision (Date)	Vote	Main Opinion
Furman v. Georgia (1972) Bars existing death sentences as "cruel and unusual punishments" under Eighth Amendment	5-4	Unsigned
Gregg v. Georgia (1976) Allows death penalty if imposed in two-stage trial with "guided" jury discretion	7-2	Stewart
Woodson v. North Carolina (1976) Bars mandatory death penalty statutes	5-4	Stewart
Coker v. Georgia (1977) Bars death penalty for rape of an adult woman	7-2	White
Lockett v. Ohio (1978) Requires juries be able to consider any "mitigating" factor in defendant's behalf	7-1	Burger
Enmund v. Florida (1982) Bars death penalty for accomplices (in this case, a getaway driver) in felony murders	5-4	White
Ford v. Wainwright (1986) Bars death penalty for insane defendants	5-4	Marshall
Tison v. Arizona (1987) Permits death penalty for "major" participants in felony murders	5-4	O'Connor
McCleskey v. Kemp (1987) Upholds death penalty despite disproportionate use in cases with white victims	5-4	Powell
Thompson v. Oklahoma (1988) Bars death penalty for offenders under sixteen years old at time of crime	5-3	Stevens
Stanford v. Kentucky (1989) Permits death penalty for offenders aged sixteen or seventeen at time of crime	5-4	Scalia
Penry v. Lynaugh (1989) Permits death penalty for mentally retarded offenders	5-4	O'Connor
Atkins v. Virginia (2002) Bars death penalty for mentally retarded offenders	6-3	Stevens
Roper v. Simmons (2005) Bars death penalty for offenders under eighteen at time of crime	5-4	Kennedy
Baze v. Rees (2008) Upholds three-drug lethal injection protocol	7-2	Roberts
Kennedy v. Louisiana (2008) Bars death penalty for child rape	5-4	Kennedy

JUNE 21, 2002
CITING 'NATIONAL CONSENSUS,' JUSTICES BAR DEATH PENALTY FOR RETARDED DEFENDANTS

COURT IS SPLIT 6-3

Dissenters Call Decision Arrogant and Dispute Support by Public

By LINDA GREENHOUSE

WASHINGTON, June 20—The Constitution bars the execution of mentally retarded offenders, the Supreme Court declared today in a landmark death penalty ruling based on the majority's view that a "national consensus" now rejected such executions as excessive and inappropriate.

Of the 38 states that have a death penalty, 18 now prohibit executing the retarded, up from 2 when the court last considered the question in 1989. This "dramatic shift in the state legislative landscape," especially when anticrime legislation is extremely popular, "provides powerful evidence that today our society views mentally retarded offenders

ion that he read from the bench, Justice Scalia said that 18 states out of 38 was only 47 percent, not even half.

In the absence of an authentic consensus, the majority had simply enshrined its own views as constitutional law, he said, adding, "The arrogance of this assumption of power takes one's breath away."

Further, he said, "there is something to be said for popular abolition of the death penalty; there is nothing to be said for its incremental abolition by this court."

Chief Justice Rehnquist said the majority had improperly gone beyond looking at state legislative action to consider poll-

> " Today our society views mentally retarded offenders as categorically less culpable than the average criminal. "
>
> —Justice John Paul Stevens, *Atkins v. Virginia*

as categorically less culpable than the average criminal," Justice John Paul Stevens wrote for the 6-to-3 majority.

The decision, in the case of a Virginia man with an I.Q. of 59 who was convicted of committing a murder and robbery at the age of 18, could ultimately move 200 or more people off death row. Mental health experts believe that as many as 10 percent of those convicted of capital murder are mentally retarded, although states often dispute the claim in individual cases.

In fact, Virginia is disputing the evidence that the defendant in this case, Daryl R. Atkins, is retarded. The Supreme Court said today that it would be up to the states to develop "appropriate ways" to apply the new constitutional prohibition. The generally accepted definition of mental retardation is an I.Q. of approximately 70 or less accompanied by limitations on abilities like communication or caring for oneself.

The dissenters today, Chief Justice William H. Rehnquist and Justices Antonin Scalia and Clarence Thomas, disputed that there was a real or lasting consensus against executing the retarded. In a dissenting opin-

ing data and international opinion as well. "If it is evidence of a national consensus for which we are looking, then the viewpoints of other countries simply are not relevant," he said.

The 15 countries of the European Union filed a brief on behalf of Mr. Atkins, as did a group of senior American diplomats who told the court that the practice of executing retarded offenders was out of step with much of the world and was a source of friction between the United States and other countries.

Amnesty International said that since 1995, only three countries were reported to have executed mentally retarded people: Kyrgyzstan, Japan and the United States, which the organization said had executed 35 mentally retarded defendants since the court allowed states to reinstate the death penalty in 1976. The court's decision today "will provide the U.S. criminal justice system with a critical tool to uphold human rights standards," the organization said.

The decision overturns a ruling of the Virginia Supreme Court.

While the justices disputed the outcome, there was no dispute on the basic analytic approach, unique to the

Eighth Amendment, that depends on a sense of community norms to decide whether a practice violates the prohibition against cruel and unusual punishment. All agreed with the statement of Chief Justice Earl Warren in a 1958 case, Trop v. Dulles, that "the amendment must draw its meaning from the evolving standards of decency that mark the progress of a maturing society." Rather, the debate was over whether the evidence supported the evolution that the majority discerned.

The court's previous examination of the retardation question came in 1989 in a Texas case, Penry v. Lynaugh, in which Justice Sandra Day O'Connor's controlling opinion said that there was no current consensus against executing the retarded but kept the court's door open to future developments.

The developments came quickly. From the original two states, Georgia and Maryland, the list of states exempting retarded people from capital punishment grew to include New Mexico, Kentucky, Tennessee, Arkansas, Colorado, Washington, Indiana, Kansas, Nebraska, South Dakota, Arizona, Connecticut, Florida, Missouri and New York, which excluded the retarded when it reinstated its death penalty in 1995. The federal death penalty, reinstated in 1988, exempted the retarded.

When the court agreed last year to revisit the issue, it did so in a case from North Carolina, but North Carolina abolished the death penalty for the retarded last summer, before that case, McCarver v. North Carolina, No. 00-8727, could be argued. The justices then substituted the case they decided today, Atkins v. Virginia, No. 00-8452. It appeared earlier this year that the Atkins case might become moot as well. In February, the Virginia State Senate voted unanimously to abolish capital punishment for the retarded, but the House decided to delay action until after the Supreme Court decision.

Surveying this rapidly changing landscape, Justice Stevens noted that the numbers alone did not tell the full story.

"It is not so much the number of these states that is significant, but the consistency of the direction of change," especially in a strong anticrime climate, he said.

Even most states that nominally allow executing the retarded were not actually carrying out such executions, Justice Stevens said, concluding, "The practice, therefore, has become truly unusual, and it is fair to say that a national consensus has developed against it."

The opinion, joined by Justices O'Connor, Anthony M. Kennedy, David H. Souter, Ruth Bader Ginsburg and Stephen G. Breyer, did not end there. Justice Stevens went on to consider whether there was any reason the court should disregard or disagree with the legislative judgments. He concluded that, to the contrary, the state judgments were supported by a review of various factors making the death penalty particularly inappropriate for retarded defendants.

"Some characteristics of mental retardation undermine the strength of the procedural protections that our capital jurisprudence steadfastly guards," Justice Stevens said, adding that as a result, "mentally retarded defendants in the aggregate face a special risk of wrongful execution."

Among the factors he cited were their "diminished capacities to understand and process information" and to reason logically and control impulses. These characteristics do not mean that retarded defendants who are competent to stand trial should not face criminal punishment, Justice Stevens said, "but they do diminish their personal culpability" and indicate that the usual justifications for capital punishment, retribution and deterrence, are less applicable than to defendants with normal intelligence.

This part of the opinion might have broader significance for the court's death penalty jurisprudence, said one death penalty expert, Professor Michael Mello of Vermont Law School.

"It shows that a majority of the court is willing to take a fresh look at the real capital punishment, how the system really works," said Professor Mello, a former defense lawyer who opposes the death penalty.

He predicted that the court might be open to revisiting precedents that make it all but impossible for appellate courts to consider assertions of actual innocence if the defendant has not followed exacting procedures.

None of the current members of the court hold a position in flat opposition to the death penalty.

Neither the majority nor the dissenters discussed the retroactive implications of the decision. Under the court's constitutional jurisprudence, the decision applies retroactively as a general matter, but states could raise objections to granting relief to defendants who had not argued the retardation issue in earlier appeals. If the lower federal courts disagree on how such cases should be handled, the question could conceivably come back to the Supreme Court, where a majority appears ready to grant full retroactivity.

MARCH 2, 2005
SUPREME COURT, 5-4, FORBIDS EXECUTION IN JUVENILE CRIME
RETREAT FROM '89

Ruling, Citing 'Evolving Standards,' Affects 72 on Death Row

By LINDA GREENHOUSE

WASHINGTON, March 1—Concluding that the United States and the world have turned against the death penalty for youthful offenders, the Supreme Court ruled on Tuesday that the Constitution categorically bars capital punishment for crimes committed before the age of 18.

The 5-to-4 decision, which upheld a ruling by the Missouri Supreme Court, will move 72 people off death row in 12 states. It represented an about-face for a court that only 16 years ago rejected the argument that the execution of those who kill at the age of 16 or 17 violated the Eighth Amendment's prohibition against "cruel and unusual punishments."

Writing for the court on Tuesday, Justice Anthony M. Kennedy, who voted with the majority 16 years ago, said the new decision was necessary to keep pace with the "evolving standards of decency" that for the last 50 years have shaped the Supreme Court's view of what constitutes cruel and unusual punishments.

executions that stood to be affected by the decision were put on hold.

Justice Antonin Scalia, author of the court's last ruling on the subject, Stanford v. Kentucky, filed a dissent on the new decision in Roper v. Simmons, No. 03-633. Joined by Chief Justice William H. Rehnquist and Justice Clarence Thomas, Justice Scalia disputed nearly all of the majority's points, from how to count the various states to whether reference to the views of foreign legal systems had relevance or legitimacy.

"I do not believe that the meaning of our Eighth Amendment, any more than the meaning of other provisions of our Constitution, should be determined by the subjective views of five members of this court and like-minded foreigners," Justice Scalia said.

Justice Sandra Day O'Connor wrote a separate dissenting opinion that took issue both with the majority's assessment of the existence of a national consensus and

> " When a juvenile offender commits a heinous crime, the state . . . cannot extinguish his life and his potential to attain a mature understanding of his own humanity. "
>
> —Justice Anthony M. Kennedy, *Roper v. Simmons*

Justice Kennedy said that not only did 30 states—five more than 16 years ago—now reject the death penalty for juveniles, but that "it is fair to say that the United States now stands alone in a world that has turned its face against the juvenile death penalty."

Since 1990, he noted, only seven countries outside the United States have executed people for crimes they committed as juveniles, and all seven—Iran, Pakistan, Saudi Arabia, Yemen, Nigeria, China and Congo—have disavowed the practice.

There have been 19 such executions in the United States since 1990, most recently in 2003. Once the Supreme Court agreed in January of last year to decide the issue, all

with its view that the execution of juveniles was always disproportionate to their moral culpability. She noted that while as a legislator she would be "inclined to support" a minimum age of 18 for capital punishment, she could not find a constitutional basis for doing so as a judge.

Justice O'Connor pointedly disagreed, however, with her fellow dissenters' opposition to taking into account foreign legal developments. "This nation's evolving understanding of human dignity certainly is neither wholly isolated from, nor inherently at odds with, the values prevailing in other countries," she said.

Justice Kennedy's majority opinion was joined by Justices John Paul Stevens, David H. Souter, Ruth Bader

Ginsburg and Stephen G. Breyer. Justices Stevens and Ginsburg filed a concurring opinion to say that "perhaps even more important than our specific holding today is our re-affirmation of the basic principle that informs the court's interpretation of the Eighth Amendment"; namely, that the amendment's meaning was not frozen at the time of its adoption but has evolved.

That evolution has been on lively display in recent years with respect to the death penalty. In 1988, in Thompson v. Oklahoma, the court barred the execution of those under 16 at the time of the crime. Three years ago, in Atkins v. Virginia, the court ruled that the Eighth Amendment categorically barred the execution of the mentally retarded. The contrary precedent that the Atkins decision overruled was handed down on the same day in 1989 as the ruling that the court repudiated on Tuesday, permitting the execution of those who killed at 16 or 17.

The court based the Atkins decision on its perception that a new consensus had formed in the country to reject the execution of the retarded; 16 states that had permitted such executions in 1989 had rejected them by the time the issue came back to the Supreme Court in 2000. After that decision, the attention of opponents of the death penalty immediately turned to the juvenile question, on which the development in the states since 1989 had been slower, but steady and uniformly in the direction of raising the age.

The defendant in the new case, Christopher Simmons, who was sentenced to death for a murder he committed in 1993 at 17, went back to the Missouri courts after the Atkins decision to argue that the reasoning of the retardation case should be applied to juvenile offenders.

The Missouri Supreme Court agreed, noting that five states since 1989, by legislation or judicial decision, had raised the age to 18. It ordered Mr. Simmons re-sentenced to life in prison without parole.

In their dissenting opinions on Tuesday, both Justice O'Connor and Justice Scalia were highly critical of the Missouri court, saying that it lacked authority to depart, on its own, from the Supreme Court's binding precedent. "Allowing lower courts to reinterpret the Eighth Amendment whenever they decide enough time has passed for a new snapshot leaves this court's decisions without any force," Justice Scalia said, adding, "The result will be to crown arbitrariness with chaos."

The majority did not engage in this particular debate. Instead, Justice Kennedy took the Missouri Supreme Court's opinion as a given and then proceeded through his own analysis of the factual and legal landscape.

That analysis had three parts. First was an assessment of whether American society had formed a consensus against juvenile executions. While the change was "less dramatic" than the change on the retardation question, Justice Kennedy said, it nonetheless provided the "objective indicia of consensus" that the court found to be enough in the retardation case. He noted that Congress had set a minimum age of 18 when it passed the Federal Death Penalty Act in 1994. Counting the 12 states with no death penalty, he said, a majority of the states have rejected capital punishment for juvenile crimes.

In his dissent, Justice Scalia said it made little sense to include the non-death-penalty states in this calculation, calling the majority's approach "rather like including old-order Amishmen in a consumer-preference poll on the electric car." He continued: "Of course they don't like it, but that sheds no light whatever on the point at issue." Without counting the non-death-penalty states, he said, only 18 states had legislatively rejected the execution of 16- and 17-year-olds.

The second step in the majority's analysis was to move beyond counting by states to decide, in Justice Kennedy's words, "in the exercise of our own independent judgment, whether the death penalty is a disproportionate punishment for juveniles."

He said that "three general differences between juveniles under 18 and adults demonstrate that juvenile offenders cannot with reliability be classified among the worst offenders." The differences were: "a lack of maturity and an underdeveloped sense of responsibility"; vulnerability to peer pressure; and a personality that is still in formation, making it "less supportable to conclude that even a heinous crime committed by a juvenile is evidence of irretrievably depraved character."

Justice Kennedy concluded: "When a juvenile offender commits a heinous crime, the state can exact forfeiture of some of the most basic liberties, but the state cannot extinguish his life and his potential to attain a mature understanding of his own humanity."

This analysis, too, provoked Justice Scalia's strong dissent. "By what conceivable warrant can nine lawyers presume to be the authoritative conscience of the nation?" he asked. After describing details of Mr. Simmons's crime, which involved breaking into a woman's home, binding her with tape and wire and throwing her off a bridge into a river, where she drowned, Justice Scalia said the majority had failed to justify "a constitutional imperative that prevents legislatures and juries from treating exceptional cases in an exceptional way by determining that some murders are not just the acts of happy-go-lucky teenagers, but heinous crimes deserving of death."

Justice Scalia reserved his strongest dissent for the final stage of the majority's analysis, its reference to international developments that have left the United States alone in supporting juvenile executions. In the majority opinion, Justice Kennedy said that while the court was not bound by foreign developments, "it is proper that we acknowledge the overwhelming weight of international opinion" for its "respected and significant confirmation for our own conclusions."

Justice Scalia objected that while the court had determined that "the views of our own citizens are essentially irrelevant," it had wrongly given "center stage" to the "so-called international community."

. . . .

In 2008 the Court in *Kennedy v. Louisiana* again limited capital punishment by prohibiting the death penalty for child rapists. The 5-4 decision overturned a death sentence imposed by Louisiana on Patrick Kennedy for raping his young stepdaughter. For the majority, Justice Kennedy noted that Louisiana was one of only six states to authorize the death penalty for child rape and that Patrick Kennedy was one of only two convicted child rapists to be given death sentences under the state's 1995 law. The ruling went further by prohibiting capital punishment for any nonhomicide offense against an individual victim; it allowed the death penalty for "offenses against the State," such as treason, espionage, terrorism, or drug kingpin activity.

Earlier in the same year, however, the Court in *Baze v. Rees* (2008) cleared the way for states to use what had become the standard procedure for lethal injection executions. The 7-2 decision rejected a claim by two Kentucky inmates that the three-drug protocol—an anesthetic followed by a paralytic agent and then a drug that causes cardiac arrest—created an unacceptable risk that the inmate would suffer substantial pain during the execution. States had imposed a de facto moratorium on executions while the case was before the Court.

Despite agreeing with the result, Justice Stevens used the case to announce that he had come to believe the death penalty should be prohibited as cruel and unusual punishment. Stevens said the death penalty provided only marginal benefits in terms of the traditional goals of incapacitation, retribution, or deterrence, while capital cases entailed a significant risk of error or discrimination.

JUDGE AND JURY

Congress and many state legislatures acted in the 1980s to overhaul criminal sentencing by adopting "guideline" systems aimed at reducing disparities among sentences for similar types of offenses. Liberals supported the reforms on grounds of equity; conservatives joined because the new laws also either abolished or reduced the importance of parole. In a series of decisions beginning in 2000, however, the Supreme Court unexpectedly undercut the guideline systems by limiting the fact-finding authority of judges in meting out sentences under the laws.

The Court laid the groundwork for the development in a 5-4 decision, *Apprendi v. New Jersey* (2000), that narrowed a state hate crime law by requiring a jury instead of a judge to make the factual finding of racial motivation needed to trigger an enhanced penalty. The justices' lineup in finding the law to violate the defendant's right to a jury trial was unusual: Conservatives Scalia and Clarence Thomas joined liberals Stevens, David H. Souter, and Ruth Bader Ginsburg in the majority. Breyer, an architect of the federal sentencing system in the 1980s, joined Rehnquist, O'Connor, and Kennedy in dissent.

Four years later, the Court dropped a second shoe in its decision in *Blakely v. Washington* (2004). Ralph Blakely had pleaded guilty to kidnapping his estranged wife. Under the state of Washington's guideline system, he would ordinarily have faced a sentence of up to fifty-three months, but the judge raised the sentence to ninety months after finding Blakely had acted with "deliberate cruelty." For the same five-justice majority as in *Apprendi*, Scalia said the Sixth Amendment required that any factual finding needed to raise a defendant's sentence above the maximum prescribed for the offense must be made by a jury and must be proved beyond a reasonable doubt instead of by the lesser "preponderance of the evidence" standard.

The ruling cast doubt not only on state guideline systems but also on the federal system approved by Congress in 1984 and put into effect in 1987. The Court promptly agreed to hear two cases raising Sixth Amendment challenges to the federal system. The result—in January 2005—was a mixed ruling that allowed the federal guidelines to stand as advisory rather than mandatory for federal judges. In the first part of the decision in *United States v. Booker,* the *Apprendi-Blakely* majority held that mandatory use of the guidelines violated defendants' jury trial rights. But in the second part, Ginsburg switched sides to join the first part's dissenters to produce a different five-vote majority allowing judges to continue using the guidelines on an advisory basis.

Blakely v. Washington

Decided: June 24, 2004

Vote: 5 (Stevens, Scalia, Souter, Thomas, Ginsburg)

4 (Rehnquist, O'Connor, Kennedy, Breyer)

Opinion of the Court: Scalia

Dissenting opinions (3): O'Connor (Rehnquist, Kennedy, Breyer); Kennedy (Breyer); Breyer (O'Connor)

United States v. Booker

Decided: January 12, 2005

Vote: Multiple

Opinion of the Court in part: Stevens (Scalia, Souter, Thomas, Ginsburg)

Opinion of the Court in part: Breyer (Rehnquist, O'Connor, Kennedy, Ginsburg)

Opinions dissenting in part (4): Stevens (O'Connor, Scalia); Scalia; Thomas; Breyer (Rehnquist, O'Connor, Kennedy)

JANUARY 13, 2005
SUPREME COURT TRANSFORMS USE OF SENTENCE GUIDELINES
By LINDA GREENHOUSE

WASHINGTON, Jan. 12—The Supreme Court on Wednesday transformed federal criminal sentencing by restoring to judges much of the discretion that Congress took away 21 years ago when it put sentencing guidelines in place and told judges to follow them.

The guidelines, intended to make sentences more uniform, should be treated as merely advisory to cure a constitutional deficiency in the system, the court held in an unusual two-part decision produced by two coalitions of justices.

In the first part, five justices declared that the current guidelines system violated defendants' rights to trial by jury by giving judges the power to make factual findings that increased sentences beyond the maximum that the jury's findings alone would support.

That portion of the opinion had been widely anticipated, growing directly out of a similar conclusion the same five justices—John Paul Stevens, Antonin Scalia,

David H. Souter, Clarence Thomas and Ruth Bader Ginsburg—reached last June in invalidating the sentencing guidelines system in the state of Washington.

The real question hanging over the case, which the court granted on an expedited basis over the summer and heard in October on the opening day of its new term, was how the justices would solve the problem.

So it was the second part of the decision—the remedy—that was the surprise and that will shape the continuing debate over sentencing policy. With Justice Ginsburg joining the four justices who dissented from the first part—Stephen G. Breyer, Sandra Day O'Connor, Anthony M. Kennedy and Chief Justice William H. Rehnquist—a separate coalition said the problem could be fixed if the guidelines were treated as discretionary rather than mandatory.

From now on, Justice Breyer said, writing for the majority in this portion of the decision, judges "must consult" the guidelines and "take them into account" in imposing sentences. But at the end of the day the guidelines will be advisory only, with sentences to be reviewed on appeal for "reasonableness." Lawmakers and legal experts predicted Wednesday that the court's decision would renew the struggle between Congress and the judiciary for control over sentencing. On Capitol Hill, some members of Congress made it clear that they were bracing for a fight over how much discretion federal judges should have.

The decision leaves many unanswered questions and much work for the federal courts of appeals. It is in the appeals courts that its real meaning will emerge, as those courts handle sentencing appeals and build a body of law evaluating the "reasonableness" of sentences.

Thousands of federal defendants who have been sentenced since the decision in the Washington State case have effectively been in limbo awaiting clarification of the situation. People whose sentences are still on appeal will be immediately affected by the ruling.

The guidelines provide judges with a grid with the offense for which the defendant has been convicted on one axis and the offender's history and other details on another. The grid gives the judges a range of possible sentences and the system instructs them to go above that range if they make certain factual findings. It was this mandatory aspect of the system that was at issue in the case.

The remedy devised by Justice Breyer's five-member majority had not been proposed by any party, although the Justice Department suggested a form of advisory guidelines as a fallback position to its defense of the system's constitutionality. Christopher A. Wray, an assistant attorney general, said Wednesday that the department was relieved to see the guidelines remain in place but concerned that sentencing disparities might increase now that they were no longer mandatory.

The decision, United States v. Booker, No. 04-104, had its roots in a series of intensely disputed sentencing rulings that began with Apprendi v. New Jersey in 2000. In a series of cases, the court has held that given the Sixth Amendment right to trial by jury, judges cannot impose sentences beyond the "prescribed statutory maximum" unless the facts supporting such an increase are found by a jury beyond a reasonable doubt.

Under that analysis, the constitutional cloud over federal criminal sentencing derived from the mandatory nature of the guidelines, which instruct judges to consider various facts, like a defendant's leadership role in a criminal enterprise, and to increase sentences beyond the guidelines accordingly. The court made it clear in the Washington State case last June that the top of an ordinary guideline range was the equivalent of a statutory maximum.

But if judges simply exercise their traditional sentencing discretion, advised by guidelines but not bound by them, the defendant's Sixth Amendment right is not implicated, a conclusion on which all nine justices agreed on Wednesday. In other words, as judges' flexibility grows, defendants' Sixth Amendment protections shrink.

The dispute on the court was not over that paradoxical proposition, but rather over how Congress would have chosen to proceed if it had known of the Sixth Amendment issue when it put the guidelines system in place in the Sentencing Reform Act of 1984. When the Supreme Court finds a statute unconstitutional, the court's next step is to see whether there is a solution consistent with the legislators' original intent.

Dissenting from the remedy portion of the decision, Justice Stevens, with Justices Souter, Scalia and Thomas, said in effect that the last thing Congress would have done would be to give judges back the power that the guidelines were intended to constrain.

Rather, the dissenters said, if the problem was a violation of the right to trial by jury, the solution also lay with the jury: to require prosecutors to make indictments more specific and to present to the jury any factor that would increase a sentence beyond the ordinary range. Justice Stevens said that in avoiding this solution and instead changing the nature of the guidelines themselves, it was "clear that the court's creative remedy is an exercise of legislative, rather than judicial, power," one that "violates the tradition of judicial restraint."

Justice Breyer insisted, however, that his was the solution that "would deviate less radically from Congress's intended system." He said that to make jury findings the basis for sentencing would shift too much power to prosecutors and "undermine the sentencing statute's basic aim of ensuring similar sentences for those who have committed similar crimes in similar ways."

Justice Breyer spoke with some authority; as chief counsel of the Senate Judiciary Committee in the 1970's, he played a leading role in the passage of the Sentencing Reform Act and later was a member of the United States Sentencing Commission. He had been on the losing side of the Apprendi decision and the subsequent rulings.

Though the outcome Wednesday was not one he would have wished—he argued in dissent from the first part of the decision that guidelines were different than statutes and that the analysis of the earlier rulings should not apply—the decision was in some ways a personal triumph. The Sentencing Commission remains intact and the guidelines are still on the books, with the presumption that most judges will follow them most of the time.

The mystery in the case was Justice Ginsburg, who joined the Stevens group, as she consistently has, in applying the Sixth Amendment to the guidelines. She then provided Justice Breyer with his fifth vote to preserve the system's architecture. She did not write a separate opinion to explain herself. The court took considerably longer on the case than had been expected. Many people thought a decision would be out by Thanksgiving, and it is possible that Justice Ginsburg's vote, and therefore the outcome, was in play until late in the process.

The portion of Justice Breyer's opinion that dealt with appeals had the effect of overturning a 2003 Congressional amendment to the sentencing law that instructed appeals courts to give no deference to the decisions of trial judges when reviewing sentences shorter than those called for by the guidelines. That provision, known as the Feeney Amendment for its sponsor, Representative Tom Feeney, Republican of Florida, was an expression of Congressional impatience with the judiciary and in turn angered many federal judges.

It was not clear Wednesday whether Freddie J. Booker and Ducan Fanfan, the two defendants in the case before the court, would benefit from the ruling. Mr. Booker, convicted in Federal District Court in Madison, Wis., of possessing 50 grams of cocaine base, received an extra 8 years on a 22-year sentence when the judge found that he had distributed 10 times that amount.

After Mr. Fanfan was found guilty by a jury in Portland, Me., of distributing 500 grams of cocaine, the judge refused the government's request to increase the sentence, predicting that the Supreme Court would soon find the guidelines unconstitutional. Both defendants will now go back to district court for possible resentencing, with an appeal available to both sides.

· · · · · · · · · · · ·

In a pair of decisions, the Roberts Court buttressed federal trial judges' discretion by ruling that appellate courts could treat sentences within the guidelines as presumptively reasonable (*Rita v. United States*, 2007) and could not impose a heightened standard of review to sentences below the guidelines range (*Gall v. United States*, 2007). Roberts joined the majority in both rulings, while President George W. Bush's other appointee—Samuel A. Alito Jr.—dissented.

APPEALS AND HABEAS CORPUS

The Supreme Court reviews criminal convictions either on direct appeal from state or federal courts or in post-conviction challenges to state convictions called "habeas corpus"—the centuries-old English judicial writ permitting a court to consider whether a prisoner is being legally incarcerated. The justices have virtually unlimited discretion in deciding which cases the Court will consider. In recent years, criminal cases have comprised roughly one-third of the Court's formal decisions each year.

APPEALS

The Supreme Court has never specifically required states to permit appeals in criminal cases, but it said in the Leo Frank case that states must afford some "corrective procedure" to allow convicted defendants to pursue remedies for federal constitutional violations (*Frank v. Mangum*, 1915). Today, all states permit appeals in criminal cases.

The Court in 1956 began a line of cases based on the Equal Protection Clause to safeguard the right of indigent defendants to an appeal. In *Griffin v. Illinois* the Court ruled, 5-4, that states must provide a free trial transcript to an indigent defendant in a felony case for use in preparing an appeal. (*The Times'* Washington bureau chief, Arthur Krock, agreed with the dissenters that the ruling was an unwarranted intrusion on the states' prerogatives.) Nine years later, the Court followed the same principle in a decision, *Douglas v. California* (1963), that struck down a state law providing court-appointed attorneys on appeal only if an appellate court determined legal counsel would be advantageous on appeal. In *Ross v. Moffitt* (1971), the Court extended the requirement for a free trial transcript to misdemeanor cases as well as felonies.

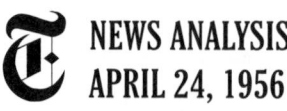

NEWS ANALYSIS
APRIL 24, 1956
ANOTHER DISCOVERY IN THE FOURTEENTH AMENDMENT
By ARTHUR KROCK

WASHINGTON, April 23—On another expedition among the clauses of the Fourteenth Amendment the Supreme Court today, by a vote of 5 to 4, discovered a wholly new effect of the mandates for "due process" and "equal protection." The latter is the same clause in which the court, in 1954, also, but unanimously, found a new meaning: that racial segregation in the state public schools was unconstitutional.

of the finding, agreed this was noble music but did not change the fact that the majority had subordinated the Federal system and ancient state authority to an ethical and sociological concept.

"As I view this case," wrote Justice Harlan, "it contains none of the elements hitherto regarded as essential to justify action by this Court under the Fourteenth Amendment. In truth what we have here is but the failure of Illinois to

> ## Why then fix bail at any reasonable sum if a poor man can't make it?
> —Justice Harold H. Burton, dissenting, *Griffin v. Illinois*

The ruling today was that, on a plea of indigence, defendants in non-capital criminal cases who for purposes of appeal demand from a state a stenographic transcript of the trial wherein they were convicted must be furnished with a free copy by the state. In Illinois, whence this case arose, such copies are furnished gratis to defendants under death sentence, but in non-capital cases (these defendants were convicted of armed robbery) the transcript must be paid for. The issue, said the majority, was simply that of the poor vs. the rich. And Magna Charta (1215 A. D.) was only one of the authorities cited.

'BEYOND OUR PROVINCE'

The opinion by Justice Black (in which he was joined by the Chief Justice, Justices Douglas and Clark, and by Justice Frankfurter separately) pulled out all the stops on the organ of equal rights and human compassion. The dissenters (Justices Burton, Reed and Minton, and Harlan separately), in their analysis of the constitutional basis

adopt as promptly as other states a desirable reform in its criminal procedure. Whatever might be said were this a procedure in the Federal courts, regard for our system of federalism requires such as this be left to the states. * * * I think it is beyond the province of this Court to tell Illinois that it must provide such procedures."

'IF WE KNEW THE FACTS'.

The majority noted that it was not instructing Illinois "to purchase a stenographer's transcript in every case where a defendant cannot buy it: the [State] Supreme Court may find other means of affording adequate and effective appellate review of indigent defendants." But, retorted the dissenters, "the constitutional question should not be decided without knowing the circumstances underlying the * * * allegation of need. Indigence, the only underlying 'fact' alleged, did not in itself necessarily preclude [the convicted robbers] from preparing a narrative bill of exceptions. * * * Who can say that if we knew the facts we might not have before us a much narrower constitutional question than the one decided today? * * * A decision having such wide impact should not be made on a record as obscure as this, especially when there are ready means at hand to have clarified the issue sought to be presented."

'WE MUST THEREFORE ASSUME'

The majority, however, in a familiar line-up where abstractions about the "underprivileged" are concerned, found it enough to know that the convicted robbers said they were too poor to buy the transcript, and that the state, under its statute, declined to make them a gift of it. Since counsel for Illinois conceded that a transcript was necessary for the defendants "to get adequate appellate review' of alleged trial errors, and since their request was made promptly and the Illinois courts did not deny review on the ground of insufficient allegations of trial errors—

We must, therefore, assume for the purposes of this decision [said the majority] that errors were committed in the trial which would merit rever-

sal, but that the petitioners could not get appellate review of those errors solely because they were too poor to buy a stenographic transcript.

'WHY THEN FIX BAIL?'

"To sanction such a ruthless consequence," wrote Justice Frankfurter, "inevitably resulting from a money hurdle erected by the state, would justify a latter-day Anatole France" to expand his ironic comment that the law "forbids the rich as well as the poor to sleep under bridges," etc. But, observed Justice Burton, while supply of free transcript to the poor by Illinois would be as desirable as it is in the states where this is done, "it is one thing for Congress and this Court to prescribe such procedure for the Federal courts, and quite another * * * to hold that the Constitution of the United States has prescribed it for all state courts. * * * Why then fix bail at any reasonable sum if a poor man can't make it?"

The present Supreme Court, in further Fourteenth Amendment discoveries, may hold that unconstitutional also.

• • • • • • • • • • • •

A defendant who wins a reversal of a conviction on appeal can be retried without violating the Double Jeopardy Clause. The Court ruled in *North Carolina v. Pearce* (1969), however, that a judge cannot impose a greater sentence in a retrial except on the basis of objective reasons related to the defendant's conduct after the first trial. Four years later, the Court decided that rule does not apply to juries in those states where they have sentencing authority. But the Court held in *Bullington v. Missouri* (1981) that the government cannot seek the death penalty in a retrial if the jury refused to impose the death sentence in the first trial.

HABEAS CORPUS

The Constitution states, "The Privilege of the Writ of Habeas Corpus shall not be suspended, unless when in Cases of Rebellion or Invasion the public Safety may require it" (Art. I, sec. 9, cl. 2). The Court has held that federal courts' use of habeas corpus depends on congressional action. Before the Civil War, Congress authorized habeas corpus only for federal prisoners and in other limited circumstances.

After the Civil War, Congress extended habeas corpus to state cases. Beginning in the 1880s, the Court ruled that habeas corpus relief could be granted to someone imprisoned under an unconstitutional law. Later, it held that prisoners were also entitled to relief if they had been unconstitutionally convicted or punished. In the *Frank* case in 1915, the Court went further and said that a state prisoner was entitled to "a judicial inquiry . . . into the very truth and substance of the causes of his detention."

Over the next five decades, the Court continued to expand the scope of habeas corpus review of state convictions. In *Townsend v. Sain* (1963), the Court said that federal courts should ordinarily conduct "a full and fair evidentiary hearing" on a prisoner's claims and need not defer to a state judge's legal findings. In another decision, *Fay v. Noia* (1963), the Court eased a previous rule that a state prisoner could not use federal habeas corpus without first having exhausted all remedies in state courts.

Beginning in the 1970s, the Court began cutting back on federal habeas corpus relief. *Stone v. Powell* (1976) barred the use of habeas corpus to relitigate Fourth Amendment claims about illegally obtained evidence. In *Wainwright v. Sykes* (1977), the Court ruled—in an opinion by Rehnquist—that inmates had to show special justification for raising a federal claim in a habeas corpus case if they could have raised it earlier but had failed to do so.

Teague v. Lane

Decided: February 22, 1989

Vote: 7 (Rehnquist, B. White, Blackmun, Stevens, O'Connor, Scalia, Kennedy,)
2 (Brennan, T. Marshall)

Opinion of the Court: O'Connor

Concurring in judgment (3): B. White; Blackmun; Stevens

Dissenting opinion: Brennan

After Rehnquist became chief justice, the Court continued to chip away at habeas corpus. In the most important ruling, *Teague v. Lane* (1989), the Court ruled—in a fractured decision—that state inmates could not use rulings issued after their convictions as the basis for habeas corpus relief unless the principle of the new case was "fundamental to the integrity of the criminal proceeding." Over the next few years, the Court also limited state inmates ordinarily to one federal habeas corpus petition and limited relief except in cases where errors had "substantial and injurious effect or influence in determining the jury's verdict."

Congress decided to codify many of these restrictions in a broad rewrite of habeas corpus law contained in the Antiterrorism and Effective Death Penalty Act of 1996. Along with a rule against "successive" habeas corpus petitions, the law set a one-year deadline for inmates to file a habeas corpus case except with permission of an appellate panel. The act also barred federal courts from granting habeas corpus relief unless a state court decision was "contrary to, or involved an unreasonable application of, clearly established Federal law, as determined by the Supreme Court of the United States."

President Bill Clinton, who had requested the counterterrorism parts of the bill but not the habeas corpus rewrite, signed the measure into law on April 24, 1996. The Court agreed only nine days later to hear a case challenging the act. A Georgia death row inmate claimed that a provision barring the Court itself from hearing appeals in some instances amounted to an unauthorized "suspension" of habeas corpus or an unconstitutional abridgment of the Court's appellate jurisdiction.

In a short and unanimous decision, *Felker v. Turpin* (1996), the Court rejected the challenge and upheld the law. Chief Justice Rehnquist explained that the Court still had original jurisdiction to hear an inmate's habeas corpus petition, though he stressed that the power would be used only in "exceptional circumstances."

JUNE 29, 1996
JUSTICES UPHOLD NEWLY SET LIMIT ON FEDERAL APPEALS BY INMATES

By LINDA GREENHOUSE

Ruling unanimously and with unusual speed, the Supreme Court today upheld a new law's strict limits on Federal court appeals by state prisoners, on the understanding that the Supreme Court itself retains jurisdiction to hear these cases.

Central to the decision was the Justices' view that Congress had left intact a route by which inmates can bring their appeals directly to the Supreme Court, bypassing obstacles to review in the Federal district and appellate courts that were imposed by the new Federal law.

That interpretation—which was urged on the Court both by the Georgia death row inmate who brought the case and by the Clinton Administration in defense of the new law—obviated a looming constitutional question that the law had appeared to raise: whether Congress had the ability to strip the Court of jurisdiction over a category of cases.

While affirming its own jurisdiction to hear habeas corpus petitions from state prisoners, the Court also made clear, in an opinion by Chief Justice William H. Rehnquist, that the Court would use that jurisdiction very sparingly, only in "exceptional circumstances."

Without defining those circumstances further, the Court then said that the Georgia inmates' appeal did not fit within that category, and denied the petition.

A petition for a writ of habeas corpus is a challenge to the constitutionality of a prisoner's conviction or sentence, and these petitions are the principal means by which state inmates can obtain Federal court review. Habeas corpus petitions have been responsible for overturning a substantial proportion of state-court death sentences and for years have been the target of critics, both within the Supreme Court and in Congress, on the ground that they result in unduly prolonging death row appeals.

law that any second or subsequent petition had to meet a particularly high standard and could not be filed at all unless it passed a special "gatekeeping" mechanism. Under this system, a Federal appeals court must grant a motion giving the inmate permission to file the petition in Federal District Court. Denial of the motion is not appealable to the Supreme Court.

That provision posed two constitutional questions: first, whether the new law amounted to a "suspension" of the writ of habeas corpus, which the Constitution forbids; and second, whether the denial of Supreme Court review was an abrogation by Congress of the Supreme Court's appellate jurisdiction, as defined in Article III of the Constitution.

To resolve these issues, the Court on May 3 granted the first case to reach it under the new law and ordered argument to be held in a month. Four Justices—John Paul Stevens, Ruth Bader Ginsburg, Stephen G. Breyer and David H. Souter—objected that the Court was acting in "unseemly haste," but they were overruled.

> ❝ The decision today, a spare 13 pages long, was an anticlimactic ending to what had at one point seemed to be a great constitutional battle in the making. ❞

The decision today, Felker v. Turpin, No. 95-8836, addressed one section of the Antiterrorism and Effective Death Penalty Act of 1996, which limits the ability of state prisoners who have already filed one habeas corpus petition in Federal court to file subsequent ones.

There are a number of other provisions relating to habeas corpus in the new law, which President Clinton signed on April 24. Challenges to other sections of the law, including limits on initial petitions by death-row inmates, are quickly making their way through the lower courts. The Supreme Court is almost certain to take these up in future cases.

So while the practical effect of today's ruling may be to shorten some death penalty appeals eventually, appeals are likely to be prolonged by additional litigation for some time.

The decision today, a spare 13 pages long, was an anticlimactic ending to what had at one point seemed to be a great constitutional battle in the making.

To achieve its goal of curbing repetitive habeas corpus petitions, Congress provided in Section 106 of the new

As the case was briefed and argued to the Court, it appeared that in its own haste to curb habeas corpus, Congress had overlooked the fact that for more than 200 years the Supreme Court had possessed jurisdiction to accept "original" habeas corpus petitions from inmates who have not gone through the lower Federal courts. While the Court has exercised that jurisdiction only very rarely, if it in fact remains, the new law would not have the court stripping elements that had raised the constitutional doubts.

"We conclude that although the Act does impose new conditions on our authority to grant relief, it does not deprive this Court of jurisdiction to entertain original habeas petitions," Chief Justice Rehnquist said in his opinion today.

Noting that "repeals by implication are not favored" and that Congress had not even addressed the issue, he said "there can be no plausible argument that the Act has deprived this Court of appellate jurisdiction in violation of Article III."

The Court dealt only obliquely with the further question of whether, in the exercise of its original habeas corpus jurisdiction, the Court itself was bound by the restrictive standards that the new law applies to eligibility to file a second habeas corpus petition. For example, under the law the inmate must be prepared to show by "clear and convincing evidence" that he would have been found not guilty if not for a constitutional error in his trial.

"Whether or not we are bound by these restrictions, they certainly inform our consideration of original habeas petitions," the Chief Justice said. He noted that the Court's current rules already limit these petitions to "exceptional circumstances." It was clear from the opinion that the Court wants to avoid having to give substantive review to every death-row habeas petition it receives.

In decisions over the last several years, the Court itself has set so many limits on multiple habeas-corpus petitions that the lower courts have granted very few of them, so as a practical matter this avenue of relief for state-court inmates was already essentially reserved for unusual cases with convincing evidence of innocence.

* * * * * * * * * * * *

Over the next decade, the Court alternated between tightening and loosening the law's restrictions. In 1998 the Court in two cases loosened the law's restrictions on successive petitions and on the Court's power to review appellate court actions in habeas cases. The fractured decision in *Williams v. Taylor* (2000) adopted a somewhat strict interpretation of the law's "unreasonable application" standard for setting aside state court decisions, but ruled that Virginia courts had been unreasonable in rejecting a death row inmate's claim of ineffective assistance of counsel. In many other cases, however, the Court set aside lower courts' decisions to grant habeas relief on the ground that the judges had failed to defer to state court rulings as required under the law.

THE ROBERTS COURT

CHAPTER 10

Unlike presidents or members of Congress, Supreme Court justices hold office indefinitely. "I was appointed for life, and I intend to serve out my term," Justice Thurgood Marshall was quoted as saying when asked about retirement.

Age and illness, however, eventually create vacancies on the Court. Marshall, in fact, retired in 1991 at age eighty-three. "I'm old," he explained at a news conference. "I'm falling apart." He died less than two years later. A year after that—in 1994—Justice Harry A. Blackmun retired at age eighty-five. His successor, Stephen G. Breyer, became the Court's fifth new member in seven years.

Stephen Crowley/The New York Times

Chief Justice John G. Roberts Jr., far right, congratulates Justice Samuel A. Alito Jr. after swearing him in on February 1, 2006, to succeed retired justice Sandra Day O'Connor. Since their appointments by President George W. Bush, Roberts and Alito have strengthened the Court's conservative bloc and helped produce significant shifts in such areas as abortion, campaign finance, and school integration.

The Court that Breyer joined was closely divided between blocs of conservative and liberal justices—just as the Court had been since the 1970s. It remained closely divided, with its membership unchanged, for the next eleven years—the longest period without a vacancy on the Court since the early 1800s.

Age and illness finally gave President George W. Bush the opportunity at the start of his second four-year term to reshape the Court in his own political image. On July 1, 2005, Justice Sandra Day O'Connor announced her intention to retire at age seventy-five in order to help care for her husband, who was suffering from Alzheimer's disease. O'Connor, the Court's first female justice, had cast pivotal votes on such ideologically charged issues as abortion, affirmative action, and church-state relations. Conservatives hoped—and liberals feared—that Bush would appoint a more reliably conservative jurist to succeed her.

Bush turned to a young federal appeals court judge, John G. Roberts Jr., who was known primarily as a consummate Supreme Court advocate from his four years in the solicitor general's office and more than a decade in private practice in Washington, D.C. Roberts also had conservative political credentials from his six years as a lawyer in the White House and Justice Department under President Ronald Reagan.

Roberts was awaiting his Senate confirmation hearing when Chief Justice William H. Rehnquist died on September 3, 2005, one month short of his eighty-first birthday, after a nearly year-long fight against thyroid cancer. Two days later, Bush decided to nominate Roberts, who had been a law clerk for Rehnquist, to succeed him as chief justice. Roberts won Senate confirmation on the strength of his résumé and a dazzling performance before the Senate Judiciary Committee.

O'Connor agreed to stay on until Bush could make another choice for her seat. Bush failed with his first choice: White House counsel Harriet Miers, who had neither the résumé nor the conservative credentials that Bush's supporters had expected. She withdrew. The president then turned to Samuel A. Alito Jr., who—like Roberts—had come of age as a lawyer in the Reagan administration. Alito had then been appointed to a federal appeals court seat in 1990 by Bush's father, President George H. W. Bush.

Alito won confirmation in January 2006 in a closer Senate vote than that on Roberts. Senate Democrats and liberal interest groups worked hard to defeat him, fearing that as O'Connor's successor he would shift the balance of power on the Court.

With Alito's confirmation, the Roberts Court began to take shape—still closely divided but leaning somewhat more to the right than the Court had been under Rehnquist or his predecessor, Warren E. Burger. Along with Roberts and Alito, the Court included two other staunch conservatives: Antonin Scalia and Clarence Thomas. Both had served in Republican administrations before being named to federal appeals courts and then to the Supreme Court: Scalia by President Reagan and Thomas by the first President Bush.

On the other side of the ideological spectrum were four justices who typically took liberal positions on civil rights and civil liberties issues. Two had been elevated from federal appeals court seats by Republican presidents: John Paul Stevens, chosen by President Gerald Ford, and David H. Souter, appointed by the first President Bush. The other two, Ruth Bader Ginsburg and Breyer, had been chosen by President Bill Clinton as the first Democratic appointees since the 1960s.

In the middle sat Anthony M. Kennedy, a moderate conservative who—like O'Connor—had gained a reputation as a sometimes swing vote after joining the Court in 1988. Reagan nominated Kennedy after the Senate rejected his first choice, Robert H. Bork, at the end of a dramatic and still controversial confirmation fight. Kennedy came to be seen as somewhat more conservative than O'Connor, but he also strongly supported First Amendment claims and voted occasionally to strengthen trial safeguards for criminal defendants.

Bush's opportunity to fill two Supreme Court vacancies did not guarantee success in shifting the Court's ideological orientation. For one thing, Roberts and Alito were to have only two votes out of nine. In addition, once on the bench, some justices have taken positions quite different from what the president or the Senate may have expected. Chief Justice Earl Warren is the most commonly cited historical example of the so-called surprise justice; on the current Court, Souter is viewed as taking positions that would not have been anticipated from his previous career. But the surprise justice is the exception, not the rule. Indeed, the profiles of the current Supreme Court justices published in *The New York Times* immediately after their nominations generally yield an accurate foretaste of the kind of justice each has become.

As Roberts ended his third term in 2008, observers generally agreed that the Court had moved to the right on a number of issues. Most dramatically, the Court in 2007 issued three 5-4 rulings that diverged from prior decisions to uphold a federal ban on so-called partial-birth abortions, limit school districts' ability to engineer racial diversity in pupil enrollment, and ease restrictions on special-interest spending in presidential and congressional elections. Alito provided a critical vote for each of the rulings; O'Connor had taken the opposite position in earlier cases on the same issues.

With O'Connor gone, Kennedy became the pivotal justice, and his influence has been evident throughout Roberts's tenure. He provided critical votes for the major conservative rulings, but also sided with the four liberal justices to produce, among others, the two rulings in 2006 and 2008 that rejected the Bush administration's legal strategy for dealing with suspected enemy combatants held at Guantánamo Bay Naval Base in Cuba.

The Roberts Court's flurry of conservative decisions in 2007 combined with a record percentage of one-vote rulings to produce much speculation that the justices' ideological divisions were hardening. A year later, the 2008 term ended with fewer 5-4 rulings overall and with each side claiming significant victories. Conservatives hailed the Court's first-ever ruling that the Second Amendment establishes an individual right to own and possess guns, at least in the home. Liberals counted as major victories the decision guaranteeing habeas corpus rights to Guantánamo detainees and the ruling barring the death penalty for child rape or most other nonhomicide offenses.

JUNE 29, 2008
ON COURT THAT DEFIED LABELING, KENNEDY MADE THE BOLDEST MARK

By LINDA GREENHOUSE

WASHINGTON—It was not last year's spectacularly divided Supreme Court. The term that ended Thursday lacked last term's gory display of 5-to-4 decisions, with only 11 cases out of 67 decided this time by one-vote margins.

Neither was it the Roberts court, at least not yet. Although Chief Justice John G. Roberts Jr. was in the majority in 90 percent of the decisions, more than any other member of the court, the more liberal justices won their share of the high-profile cases. The rulings granting the

vote in the Second Amendment case was cast by Justice Anthony M. Kennedy.

So if the Roberts court in its third term—one that left a complicated and, to some extent, blurred imprint—were to be summed up in a sound bite, it would be this: It was, once again, Justice Kennedy's court.

Justice Kennedy, who marked his 20th anniversary on the court in February, did not compile quite the pitch-perfect voting record in this term that he did in the last, when he dissented only twice in 68 decisions and voted

> If the Roberts court in its third term—one that left a complicated and, to some extent, blurred imprint—were to be summed up in a sound bite, it would be this: It was, once again, Justice Kennedy's court.

Guantánamo detainees access to federal court and rejecting capital punishment for those who rape children were issued over the dissent of the chief justice.

Nor was it a court in repose in the third year under Chief Justice Roberts. There was, in fact, less unanimity: just under 30 percent of the cases were decided without dissent, compared with just over 40 percent in the term before, and just over half in 2005–6. Over all, the court decided the fewest cases since the 1953–54 term.

In the case for which history may ultimately remember the term—the decision interpreting the Second Amendment to protect the right to own a gun for private use—the court's conservative bloc won a stunning, if narrow, victory. As in the Guantánamo decision, the crucial

with the majority in all 24 of the cases decided by votes of 5 to 4. This term, Justice Kennedy dissented 10 times (compared with the chief justice's seven), including in four of the 5-to-4 decisions.

And his vote was not always as essential. Two of the major decisions of the term, in which the court upheld Kentucky's method of execution by lethal injection and Indiana's law requiring voters to produce photo identification at the polls, were decided by more comfortable margins of 7 to 2 and 6 to 3.

In those decisions, the justices gave some evidence of trying to find a modicum of middle ground. In both the lethal injection case, Baze v. Rees, and the voter ID case, Crawford v. Marion County Election Board, the court found the evidence insufficient to declare the challenged practices unconstitutional, but left the door open, at least theoretically, for more fully substantiated lawsuits in the future. First principles, in other words, were not necessarily in play.

But there were no such signs of a search for middle ground in the term's signature cases, the rulings on Guantánamo and guns. The justices spoke at each other across a wide gulf of instinct and perception. In each case, the dissenters accused those in the majority of indulging in rank judicial activism, of injecting the court into a realm where it did not belong.

Justice Kennedy wrote the majority opinion in the Guantánamo case, Boumediene v. Bush, joined by Justices John Paul Stevens, David H. Souter, Ruth Bader Ginsburg and Stephen G. Breyer. He silently joined Justice Antonin Scalia's majority opinion in the gun case, District of Columbia v. Heller, along with Chief Justice Roberts and Justices Clarence Thomas and Samuel A. Alito Jr. Joined by the liberal justices, he wrote the 5-to-4 majority opinion in Kennedy v. Louisiana, the case that ruled out the death penalty for child rape, and in Dada v. Mukasey, a 5-to-4 decision that granted additional procedural rights to immigrants facing deportation.

There is no reason to suppose that Justice Kennedy's role will be any less important in the near future. In striking down the District of Columbia's ban on handguns, the court began writing a new chapter of constitutional law. The decision raised more questions than it answered, and it may take many more cases to flesh out how far the court intends to go to displace legislative choices for gun regulations.

Since Justice Kennedy did not write separately, there is no way of knowing whether he is in full agreement with Justice Scalia's historically based analysis, or whether he would accept as reasonable some restrictions that lack the historical pedigree that language in Justice Scalia's opinion appears to demand. For example, it is not clear whether Justice Scalia's analysis would permit licensing and background checks of gun owners or, if it would not, whether Justice Kennedy would regard such measures as acceptable.

The term, which began on Oct. 1 and ended on June 26, included some unanticipated developments, like a string of victories for employees in workplace discrimination cases. In the previous term, a 5-to-4 decision that imposed tight time limits on workers' ability to file pay discrimination cases drew a strong response, including an unsuccessful effort in Congress to overturn it by amending the statute the court had interpreted.

But the plan by liberal groups to use that decision, Ledbetter v. Goodyear Tire and Rubber Company, as a focus for generating concern about the future of the court was blunted by the rulings in five discrimination cases that favored employees in this term. In two cases, the court ruled by votes of 7 to 2 and 6 to 3 that federal statutes cover claims of retaliation against employees who complain to management about discrimination.

Further defying easy categorization, the term also included a number of favorable rulings for criminal defendants. Overturning a Louisiana death-row inmate's conviction by a vote of 7 to 2, with only Justices Scalia and Thomas dissenting, the court gave added teeth to its rule against racial discrimination in jury selection. By wide margins, the court also narrowed the application of two federal money-laundering statutes and gave federal judges added discretion to show leniency in sentencing defendants for crimes involving crack cocaine.

"It's not as if every case that's visible turns on ideology," Christopher L. Eisgruber, a Supreme Court scholar who is provost at Princeton University, said in an interview. He said many cases present questions about "other kinds of values, about process and precedent." But he added that the term demonstrated that "in cases that really raise ideological questions, the court remains ideologically divided."

Students of the court across the ideological spectrum made similar points. There was no "new 'era of good feelings' " on the court, said Ilya Shapiro, senior fellow in constitutional studies at the libertarian Cato Institute, which sponsored the successful lawsuit that led to the gun-control ruling.

But, Mr. Shapiro added, unanimity was not necessarily an end in itself. While "we would prefer the highest court in the land to speak with one voice in resolving the nation's deepest disputes," he said, "it is better for five justices to hold to their constitutional duty to say what the law is than to have nine produce a lukewarm opinion that either splits the baby or, worse, legislates from the bench."

There was nothing lukewarm about the justices' performances in the cases that mattered the most to them. The Guantánamo decision, the court's third consecutive rebuff to the Bush administration's efforts to keep the detainees outside the jurisdiction of the federal courts, prompted Justice Scalia's warning that the ruling "will almost certainly cause more Americans to be killed."

Justice Stevens and Justice Breyer, in dissenting opinions in the Second Amendment case on handguns, refrained from leveling such a charge against Justice Scalia's majority opinion, although Justice Breyer described at length the landscape of urban violence that he said gave "compelling" support for the District of Columbia's effort at gun control. Addressing process rather than outcome, Justice Stevens said that in bypassing "judicial restraint, the majority had thrown the Supreme Court into the 'political thicket' " that Justice Felix Frankfurter, a conservative judicial hero, had warned against in a different context long ago.

Justice Stevens announced his dissent from the bench on Thursday morning, a signal of the depth of feeling on a dissenter's part and a step none of the liberal justices had felt impelled to take earlier in the term. Justice Scalia's announcement of the decision and the eight-point rebuttal Justice Stevens read in response offered the courtroom audience 23 minutes of drama before Chief Justice Roberts announced, with a smile that might have signified relief, that the term was over.

In past years, the final morning on the bench has been the occasion for the announcement of a justice's retirement. No such announcement was expected in the midst of a presidential election year. It may be a different story next year. But as this term demonstrated, each Supreme Court term is in some respects a different story.

* * * * * * * * * * * *

With justices appointed for life, however, three terms are too short a period to definitively gauge the Court's direction or measure its impact. The Roberts Court "is still evolving," commented Steven Shapiro, national legal director of the American Civil Liberties Union. "It's a little early to be discussing trends and putting stamps on a Court that is relatively new and working out its internal dynamics."

JOHN G. ROBERTS JR.

John Glover Roberts Jr. (1955–) became the nation's seventeenth chief justice—and the youngest in more than two hundred years—after stellar accomplishments as a student at Harvard, a government lawyer in both the Reagan and George H. W. Bush administrations, and a private attorney with a reputation as one of the country's premier Supreme Court advocates.

President George W. Bush included Roberts in an initial batch of nominees for federal appeals courts in May 2001, but partisan warfare over judicial nominations stalled his confirmation until May 2003. Questioned about abortion during his confirmation hearing, Roberts said he had no personal views that would prevent him from following *Roe v. Wade* as precedent. Roberts's opinions in his two years on the D.C. Circuit Court of Appeals were viewed as well written and largely noncontroversial with a slight conservative tilt.

Although Roberts was near the top of Bush's short list of potential Supreme Court nominees, the president surprised Court watchers when he nominated Roberts instead of a woman to succeed Justice O'Connor in July 2005. The Senate Judiciary Committee was set to begin Roberts's confirmation hearings in September 2005, when Chief Justice William H. Rehnquist died of thyroid cancer. Bush quickly withdrew Roberts's original nomination and instead nominated him for chief justice.

During his confirmation hearings, Roberts displayed thorough knowledge of Supreme Court decisions and procedures. He described himself as nonideological and answered questions about controversial positions he took during the Reagan era by emphasizing his role as an advocate for the administration. The Senate approved the nomination, 78–22, with Democrats casting the only no votes.

JULY 20, 2005
AN ULTIMATE CAPITAL INSIDER

John Glover Roberts

By NEIL A. LEWIS

WASHINGTON, July 19—In nominating Judge John G. Roberts for the Supreme Court, President Bush, who likes to portray himself as an outsider to Washington and its culture, chose an ultimate insider in the capital.

Mr. Bush considered candidates from around the country, his aides had said. But his choice, Judge Roberts, 50, owns the kind of résumé and experience that is prized in Washington; a driven student, he graduated from Harvard College in only three years and went on to Harvard Law School. That was followed by a clerkship on the Supreme Court with William H. Rehnquist when he was an associate justice.

Mr. Bush's father wanted to put Judge Roberts on the United States Court of Appeals for the District of Columbia Circuit, regarded as second in importance only to the

Patricia A. Brannan, a partner at Hogan & Hartson who attended Harvard Law School with Mr. Roberts, said her former colleague possessed what she called a "Midwest calm."

"He would wear very well" in the cloistered world of the Supreme Court, Ms. Brannan added.

Judge Roberts and his wife, Jane Marie Sullivan, also a lawyer, live in Chevy Chase, Md., and have two children, Jack, 4, and Josephine, 5. Friends described the couple as devout Catholics.

If he is confirmed to the Supreme Court, he will find himself on familiar ground. He has stood in the well of the court 39 times arguing cases before the justices he may soon join on the other side of the bench.

> He looks relaxed and spontaneous. But it's all based on an extraordinary amount of work and preparation.
>
> —Richard Lazarus, Georgetown University

Supreme Court, when he was 36. When the Democrats who controlled the Senate at the time balked, he went out and developed a lucrative private practice at Hogan & Hartson, a top-tier Washington firm, attracting a flock of corporate clients.

Judge Roberts, widely described as cordial and wry, has been comfortable in the Washington world in which top lawyers, journalists and others mix easily.

"John is one of those guys who is almost always the smartest one in the room, but you'd never know it," said J. Warren Gorrell Jr., chairman of Hogan & Hartson. "He doesn't take himself too seriously and is always careful to acknowledge the accomplishments of other people. He has a great legal mind."

Mr. Gorrell and others who know Mr. Roberts, who grew up in Indiana, describe him as unassuming and modest.

"It sounds a little awkward to say that a person who was just nominated to the Supreme Court of the United States is a regular guy, but he is," Mr. Gorrell said.

The number of cases, some on behalf of the government when he was a deputy solicitor general, the rest representing private clients, puts him in an elite company of lawyers who regularly appear before the court.

In winning 25 of those cases, he has gained a reputation as one of the handful of lawyers in the nation who are at the top of their game when the game is making a clearheaded argument and remaining cool when nine justices can fire questions at you.

Even though Judge Roberts has practiced law in the headiest of environments, he has generally avoided revealing much about his personal views on issues or some of the hot-button cases that are often at the center of confirmation battles.

Even in the last two years as a judge on the United States Court of Appeals for the District of Columbia Circuit he has not produced any especially provocative writings.

The one arguable exception in his career is that as deputy solicitor general in 1991, he signed a legal brief to the Supreme Court arguing on behalf of the first President George Bush: "We continue to believe that Roe v. Wade was wrongly decided and should be overruled," a reference to the 1973 opinion that first found a Constitutional right to abortion.

That brief is sure to become a topic of debate in his confirmation hearings as abortion rights advocates have already suggested it will be their prime exhibit in opposing his nomination. His supporters will almost certainly respond by raising the issue as to whether it is fair to attribute to a lawyer the views of his client, in that case the president.

In his first year on the appeals court he seemed to throw in his lot in one case with advocates of the new federalism, that is, judges and scholars who believe Congress is limited in the laws it may enact, leaving some issues to states.

In the case in which a California resort sued the Interior Department over a regulation governing arroyo toads, he wrote that the full court should reconsider the resort's claim because the toads had no effect on interstate commerce, the rationale for federal intervention. The toad, he wrote, "for reasons of its own, lives its entire life in California."

Judge Roberts also upheld the arrest of a 12-year-old girl who was handcuffed by transit police on the Washington area subway system for eating a single French fry. "No one is very happy about the events that led to this litigation," he wrote, but that the police did not violate the girl's rights under the constitution's Fourth Amendment guarantee against unreasonable searches.

Last week, Judge Roberts was one of three judges who ruled unanimously that the Bush administration and the White House could conduct war crimes trials against suspected terrorists detained at the naval base in Guantánamo Bay, Cuba. The opinion reversed a ruling from a lower court judge that the military commissions used to try detainees on war crimes violated the Constitution and international law.

Because he has such a scant record on many of the social issues that come before the courts, some conservatives have suggested that his political profile is similar to that of Justice David H. Souter. When Justice Souter was nominated by President Bush's father in 1990, the White House and others said he would prove a reliable conservative; instead, he proved a profound disappointment. But unlike Justice Souter, who hailed from New Hampshire, Judge Roberts is well known in Washington legal circles;

has been active in the Federalist Society, the conservative lawyers group; and has many people to vouch for his conservative instincts.

On the other side of the political equation, he is likely to be confirmed, at least with far less trouble than many of the other candidates who had been listed as possible Bush choices. Even as Democrats were resisting many of Mr. Bush's other appeals court candidates with filibusters, Mr. Roberts was approved by a vote of 16 to 3 in the Judiciary Committee and confirmed unanimously by voice vote on May 9, 2003. As befits a Washington player, he brought endorsements from many Democrats, including Seth P. Waxman, President Bill Clinton's former solicitor general, who described the nominee as "an exceptionally well-qualified appellate advocate."

Since he served inside the Reagan White House, where he helped choose judges, Mr. Roberts has helped strengthen the conservative hold on the federal judiciary. But as an established member of the Washington legal scene, Mr. Roberts also learned how to navigate a bipartisan capital, working alongside many Democrats at Hogan & Hartson.

John Glover Roberts was born in Buffalo and grew up in Indiana, the son of an executive for the Bethlehem Steel Company and a homemaker. When Mr. Bush presented Judge Roberts in the Cross Hall on Tuesday night, he made special mention of the judge's having worked summers in steel mills, an apparent effort to give him some working-class cachet.

When Justice Stephen G. Breyer was nominated to the court by Mr. Clinton, he stressed that he once dug ditches for a summer.

Judge Roberts attended the La Lumiere School, a small, nominally Catholic boys' boarding school in La Porte, Ind., where he quickly outpaced his classmates and was given a special curriculum.

Rob MacLaverty, a Chicago businessman who went to the school with Judge Roberts, recalled that he was admired by the faculty as well as his fellow students.

"They figured out pretty quickly that he was ahead of the rest of us," Mr. MacLaverty said. "He pretty much finished high school by his junior year and they put together some individual tutorials to keep him occupied."

Mr. MacLaverty said that Judge Roberts, who was captain of the football team, was remarkable in that while he was clearly special he never behaved as [if] he was.

"He had a nice, friendly demeanor then," he said. "Just as he has now."

Although it was a boarding school, Judge Roberts' family lived nearby in Long Beach, a quiet lakeside town.

Richard Lazarus, a law professor at Georgetown University, described himself as a liberal but said that was no impediment to being a good friend to Judge Roberts. Judge Roberts' mode and mentor, he said, was not Chief Justice Rehnquist, but rather the appeals court judge for whom he clerked, Henry J. Friendly, who served on the appeals court based in New York until his death in 1986.

"They were very much alike," Professor Lazarus said. "He was hired by Judge Friendly without an interview because John's credentials were like his. They won the same history prize at Harvard and each had the same position on the law review there."

Professor Lazarus said that as an advocate before the court, Judge Roberts had a precise practice regimen. He would divide up his argument into about eight sections and first memorize them and then practice reciting them in random order to account for the justices' questions.

"He looks relaxed and spontaneous," he said. "But it's all based on an extraordinary amount of work and preparation."

John Files and Glen Justice contributed reporting for this article.

. . . .

Roberts was sworn in on September 29, 2005, just in time to preside over the opening of the 2005–2006 term on October 3. At age fifty, he was the youngest chief justice since John Marshall took office at age forty-five in 1801. Nevertheless, Roberts appeared poised and assured from the first day, presiding over arguments with a firm but light touch.

As his first term neared its end, Roberts gave a widely noticed law school commencement speech in which he pointed to benefits from unanimous or near unanimous decisions by the Court. His first term ended with unanimous decisions in nearly half of the Court's signed opinions— a slightly higher percentage than usual. A wide range of observers and experts credited Roberts with helping promote agreement among the justices and, more generally, with managing the Court's transition to a new chief justice fairly and efficiently. Liberal groups pointed to Roberts's conservative votes in the term's most divisive cases, however, as evidence that he was moving the Court somewhat to the right on civil liberties and civil rights issues.

Over the next two terms, the Roberts Court issued a number of rulings that conservatives cheered and liberals criticized. Roberts himself wrote the 2007 decisions that hampered school districts' ability to engineer racial diversity in pupil enrollment and allowed corporations, labor unions, and special interest groups to pay for thinly veiled campaign advertising during presidential and congressional election seasons.

Roberts has continued to strive to bring the justices together when possible, as Justice Scalia confirmed in a TV interview with PBS's Charlie Rose in June 2008. "The chief may say, 'Why don't you come along with a very narrow opinion. We can get seven votes for that. It will look a lot better,' " Scalia said.

JOHN PAUL STEVENS

Since his nomination to the Supreme Court in 1975, Justice John Paul Stevens (1920–) has resisted efforts to be pegged as either a liberal or a conservative. In his early years, he took centrist positions and developed a reputation for writing scholarly opinions and assuming individualist stances. As the Court shifted to the right, Stevens adopted more liberal views and emerged as the Court's most frequent dissenter, often dissenting alone.

Stevens was appointed to the Seventh Circuit Court of Appeals in 1970 by President Richard M. Nixon. In his five years on the appeals court, he earned a reputation as an independent-minded judicial craftsman. Although he was a registered Republican, he had never been active in partisan politics. His moderate, apolitical background was the key to his nomination to the Court in 1975 by President Gerald R. Ford, who wanted to select a nominee of impeccable reputation in the wake of the Watergate scandals and Nixon's forced resignation the previous year. The Senate confirmed Stevens without dissent, 98–0.

NOVEMBER 29, 1975
THE PRESIDENT'S CHOICE

John Paul Stevens

By ROBERT D. McFADDEN

Twenty-eight years ago, as a young Chicagoan with a sheaf of references, an unprepossessing manner and a new law degree, John Paul Stevens went to Washington to begin two years of service, as law clerk to Associate Justice Wiley B. Rutledge of the United States Supreme Court. Yesterday the former clerk was selected by President Ford to return to the Court, this time as an Associate Justice and the successor to William O. Douglas.

The man picked by the President is the 55-year-old judge of the United States Court of Appeals for the Seventh Circuit in Chicago, to which he was appointed in 1970 by President Nixon.

Judge Stevens's five years on the appellate court constitute his only experience in the judiciary, but they have generated more than 200 opinions and earned him a reputation as a man with a thoughtful intellect and a solid and scholarly, if unspectacular, approach to the law.

It was a style developed during more than two decades of private law practice in Chicago, primarily in the antitrust

"He's a first-rate lawyer, a first-rate judge and a first-rate person—more than that you can't ask for," Philip Kurland, an authority on constitutional law at the University of Chicago, said yesterday.

Another University of Chicago professor, Kenneth Dam, who is a specialist in antitrust law, said Judge Stevens was "considered one of the strongest judges on the Federal bench," and added: "He will easily be able to hold his own on the Court."

Judge Stevens is a quiet, mild-mannered man whose modesty is sometimes taken for shyness. He is 5 feet 10 inches tall, weighs about 170 pounds, has graying hair and blue eyes and likes to wear bow ties.

He underwent open heart surgery several years ago but is said to have recovered fully and plays golf occasionally, although he has given up the more energetic game of squash.

Judge Stevens also flies his own small airplane, is a good bridge player, takes an occasional mixed drink and, according to friends, has a quiet humor.

> " He's a first-rate lawyer, a first-rate judge and a first-rate person—more than that you can't ask for. "
>
> —Philip Kurland, University of Chicago

and corporate fields, a practice interrupted occasionally for service as counsel to various state and Federal agencies.

His cases, as a lawyer and as a judge, have not been widely publicized, but among his colleagues on the bench and in the law profession, Judge Stevens is regarded as a moderate with nominally Republican credentials but little background or interest in politics.

Several persons interviewed yesterday declined to characterize Judge Stevens in political terms, saying that the customary labels did not seem to suit him.

The judge is a member of a prominent Chicago family that prospered in the insurance business and once owned the Sevens Hotel, now the Chicago Hilton. He was born on April 20, 1920, the son of Ernest James and Elizabeth Street Stevens.

He had a brilliant academic record, graduating Phi Beta Kappa from the University of Chicago in 1941. After serving in the Navy from 1942 to 1945, and earning the Bronze Star Medal, he obtained his law degree from Northwestern University in 1947, graduating first in his class.

For the next two years, he was Justice Rutledge's law clerk at the Supreme Court. He then returned to Chicago to enter law practice, spending his first few years with a firm that is now headed by Albert E. Jenner, who was the chief minority counsel to the House Judiciary Committee last year, when it recommended the impeachment of Mr. Nixon.

In 1950, Judge Stevens was an associate counsel for a Congressional subcommittee studying monopoly and, from 1954 to 1955, was a member of the Attorney General's National Committee to Study the Antitrust Laws. In 1969, he was general counsel for a special Illinois Supreme Court commission that investigated allegations of misconduct against two State Supreme Court justices who subsequently resigned.

From 1952 until his appointment to the Federal bench in 1970, he was a partner in the Chicago law firm of Rothschild, Stevens, Barry & Myers.

The judge was a lecturer on antitrust and other law subjects at the University of Chicago and Northwestern University in the early 1950's. During his years of private practice, he has also written numerous articles for law and other journals on antitrust matters.

Judge Stevens and his wife, the former Elizabeth Jane Sheeren, were married in Washington in 1942 during his Navy service. They live in the Chicago suburb of Burr Ridge with the two youngest of their four children—John, 26, of Phoenix, Ariz.; Kathryn, 25, of Clarendon Hills, Ill.; and Elizabeth, 14, and Susan, 12.

After receiving word of her husband's nomination yesterday, Mrs. Stevens said she was "slightly hysterical" with happiness. The Judge calmly said that, if confirmed by the Senate, he would promptly get to work and do his best.

"He doesn't pontificate," said a jesting friend of the judge, "which means he might be qualified for the job."

• • • • • • • • • • • •

In his first year on the Court, Stevens wrote pivotal opinions in companion decisions that upheld capital punishment as long as states gave juries some guided discretion in imposing the death penalty. He also wrote an important opinion upholding the power of the Federal Communications Commission to limit indecency on radio and television. Later in the 1970s, he joined conservatives in voting to limit affirmative action and uphold limits on federal funding for abortions.

By the 1980s Stevens was taking more liberal positions. In one of his major opinions, Stevens led the Court in striking down an Alabama law allowing a moment of silence for prayer or meditation at the beginning of each school day. He also dissented from the 1986 decision upholding state antisodomy laws and the 1989 decision permitting the death penalty for juveniles who committed murders.

Through the next decade, Stevens continued to move toward the left, shifting his position on such issues as affirmative action and capital punishment. In 1997 he led the Court in striking down a newly enacted law aimed at preventing children from having access to sexually explicit material on the Internet. The same year he also wrote the Court's opinion holding that presidents have no immunity from civil suits while in office.

Following Justice Harry A. Blackmun's retirement in 1994, Stevens became the second most senior justice and gained the power to assign opinion-writing when the chief justice was in dissent. On the Roberts Court, Stevens used that power in a case where Roberts was recused to assign himself the main opinion in the 2006 decision that the military tribunals established to try suspected terrorists at Guantánamo Bay violated U.S. law and the Geneva Conventions. Two years later, Stevens wrote—and delivered from the bench—the main dissent in the ruling recognizing individual gun rights under the Second Amendment.

ANTONIN SCALIA

Upon joining the Supreme Court in 1986, Antonin Scalia (1936–) quickly became known as one of its most conservative members. He developed a reputation for a quick mind, outspoken views, and sharply written opinions. A strong opponent of abortion and affirmative action, he has voiced bitter disappointment at the Court's failure to overturn liberal precedents on these and other issues.

President Ronald Reagan appointed Scalia to the U.S. Court of Appeals for the District of Columbia Circuit in 1982 and nominated him to the Supreme Court in 1986 for the seat left vacant by Rehnquist's promotion to chief justice. With attention focused on Rehnquist's confirmation, Scalia's similarly conservative views provoked no substantial controversy. The Senate confirmed him for the post, 98–0. He became the first Italian American to serve on the Court.

JUNE 18, 1986
JUDGE WITH TENACITY AND CHARM

Antonin Scalia

By IRVIN MOLOTSKY

Special to The New York Times

WASHINGTON, June 17—To Judge Abner J. Mikva, a liberal member of the United States Court of Appeals for the District of Columbia Circuit, his colleague Antonin Scalia is a conservative but not antigovernment.

To Richard W. Pogue, the managing partner of the Cleveland law firm in which Judge Scalia once was a partner, he is a consensus builder despite his strongly held views.

"He was a strident opponent of the legislative veto," Mr. Simms said, referring to a law that permitted Congress to overturn some Presidential decisions. "He testified against it before legislative committees, notwithstanding President Reagan's support of them at first. He was prepared to express a view of the unconstitutionality of legislation at a time when he had nothing to gain. A lot of people would have kept their mouths shut."

> [Scalia] was a conservative when he was 17 years old. . . . He was brilliant, way above everybody else.
>
> —William Stern

To Larry L. Simms, who worked for Judge Scalia when he was an Assistant Attorney General in the Justice Department, he can hold to positions on important issues with great tenacity.

These and other views of Judge Scalia emerged today as President Reagan announced he intended to nominate him as an Associate Justice of the United States Supreme Court. The views came from his colleagues, friends and adversaries, all of whom predicted that his scholarship and charm would lead to his speedy approval by the Senate.

TENACIOUS ADVOCATE

Mr. Simms said that once Judge Scalia arrived at a position, he would hold to it, even at the risk of future advancement.

As it turned out, Judge Scalia's view prevailed, with the Supreme Court ruling such legislative vetoes unconstitutional.

William Stern, the former chairman of Urban Development Corporation in New York State, said of Judge Scalia, his former classmate at Xavier High School, a Catholic military academy in Manhattan:

"This kid was a conservative when he was 17 years old. An archconservative Catholic. He could have been a member of the Curia. He was the top student in the class. He was brilliant, way above everybody else."

Antonin Scalia (pronounced AN-tuh-neen Skuh-LEE-yuh) was born March 11, 1936, in Trenton, to Catherine and S. Eugene Scalia, both of whom died in the past year. His mother was born in the United States and his father in Italy, and the White House noted in his official biography today that his father was an immigrant. The Supreme Court said that, if confirmed, Judge Scalia would become the first Italian-American to serve on the Court.

Mr. Scalia, known to his friends as Nino, graduated summa cum laude from Georgetown University in 1957, where he was first in his class. In 1960 he graduated from Harvard Law School, where he had been an editor of the Law Review, and the next year he held a Sheldon Fellowship at Harvard.

He has taught law at the University of Chicago, Stanford University, Georgetown University and the University of

Virginia, and he served as an Assistant Attorney General from 1974 to 1977. In 1982, President Reagan named Judge Scalia to the appeals court, which is second in importance only to the Supreme Court.

Judge Scalia lives with his wife, the former Maureen McCarthy, and the younger of their nine children in the nearby suburb of McLean, Va.

Judge Mikva often found himself on the opposite sides of decisions from Judge Scalia, but he said he found him "a delightful colleague."

. . . .

Scalia's forthright conservative positions since taking the bench have endeared him to conservative Court watchers and advocacy groups. He has advocated a textual and historical approach on constitutional issues that emphasizes the "original meaning" of the charter's provisions and scorns the idea of a "living Constitution." He has opposed any use of international law in interpreting constitutional terms. President George W. Bush cited Scalia and Justice Clarence Thomas as models for his own Supreme Court appointments.

Scalia energetically questions counsel during oral argument. He often writes acerbic opinions, especially in dissent. He strongly criticized the Court's refusal in 1989 and again in 1992 to overturn the *Roe v. Wade* abortion rights decision. Dissenting from two gay rights decisions in 1995 and 2003, Scalia accused the majority of taking sides in the "culture wars." A graduate of an all-male military prep school, he also sharply criticized the 1996 decision requiring the Virginia Military Institute to admit women.

Under Rehnquist, Scalia helped form narrow majorities favoring states' rights on federalism issues and easing the separation of church and state. Among his major opinions was the 1997 ruling striking down a federal law requiring local law enforcement agencies to conduct background checks on gun purchasers.

In some instances, Scalia's strict reading of constitutional provisions leads him away from conservative positions. He voted with mostly liberal majorities in 1989 and 1990 to strike down laws banning desecration of the U.S. flag. He has opposed use of the Due Process Clause to limit state court damage awards. He also led the way in a series of rulings that invoked the Sixth Amendment to strengthen the role of juries instead of judges in criminal sentencing.

Despite his strong views, Scalia appears to be popular among his colleagues. He and his wife are especially close to Justice Ruth Bader Ginsburg, a former colleague on the D.C. Circuit, and her husband. Scalia and Ginsburg, both opera fans, once appeared together as extras in a performance by the Washington National Opera Company.

Under Roberts, Scalia has continued to hew to conservative positions for the most part. In 2008 he wrote the 5-4 decision that relied heavily on history and constitutional text to recognize an individual right to own firearms under the Second Amendment. Admirers saw the ruling as a decisive affirmation of Scalia's approach to constitutional interpretation.

ANTHONY M. KENNEDY

President Reagan chose Anthony McLeod Kennedy (1936–) for the Supreme Court in 1987 after the Senate's rejection of his first nominee for the vacancy, Robert H. Bork, and the withdrawal of his second choice. Kennedy's moderate conservatism and low-key demeanor helped him win unanimous confirmation by the Senate in January 1988. On the Court, he generally has hewed to conservative positions, but drew bitter reaction from conservatives in 1992 for voting to reaffirm the controversial *Roe v. Wade* abortion rights ruling.

President Gerald R. Ford appointed Kennedy to the Ninth Circuit Court of Appeals in 1975, where he served twelve years. He became Reagan's fourth and last appointee to the Court after two other, more prominent conservative federal judges failed to win confirmation. When Reagan nominated Kennedy, both the administration and the Senate were eager for an easy confirmation. He was approved 97–0.

NOVEMBER 12, 1987
RESTRAINED PRAGMATIST

Anthony M. Kennedy
By ROBERT REINHOLD
Special to The New York Times

SAN FRANCISCO, Nov. 11—In the modern world of family turmoil, the life of Judge Anthony McLeod Kennedy seems almost like a living Norman Rockwell portrait of provincial constancy and familial loyalty. He has been married to the same woman for 24 years, has sent all three of his children to his alma mater, Stanford University, and lives in the same white colonial-style house in Sacramento, behind a camellia bush and a neat row of gardenias, where he was born 51 years ago.

Judge Kennedy sits well to the right of center of the 36 regular and senior judges of the Ninth Circuit, which has been badly divided on such issues as immigration and criminal rights. But he is by no means on the extreme.

"It is very hard to read Tony's opinions and see his personal philosophy come through, but if you add up the results you can tell he is a conservative," said a fellow appeals judge, a liberal who often disagrees with Judge Kennedy and who requested anonymity. "But he is thoughtful and

> " While Tony Kennedy, as friends call him, is clearly a political and legal conservative, he strikes those who know him as a quiet pragmatic one, open to persuasion. "

Such restraint and respect for precedent find an echo in the legal opinions of the man President Reagan has picked as his third choice to fill the vacant seat on the Supreme Court. And if the President had originally hoped to fill the seat with a doctrinaire conservative, he will not find that in Judge Kennedy, an energetic, self-effacing and immensely polite man who likes to read history, complain about his deteriorated golf game and taste fine California wines.

While Tony Kennedy, as friends call him, is clearly a political and legal conservative, he strikes those who know him as a quiet pragmatic one, open to persuasion. His 500 or so written opinions in 12 years on the Court of Appeals for the Ninth Circuit in San Francisco are cautiously and narrowly crafted, sticking close to precedent and avoiding sweeping statements on social issues.

fair. You can talk to and reason with him. He may come back with the wrong position, but he'll go and think about it. You don't say it was a waste of time. His ideology does not hang all over him."

Another fellow judge, Alex Kozinski, a conservative who was once a clerk to Judge Kennedy, said, "He does not have some broad theory of the law that he tries to fit every case into." He added that the judge was, above all, "a lawyer."

Judge Kennedy is an active member of the Roman Catholic Church, which has led opposition to abortion and homosexual behavior, but his personal views on those issues could not be readily determined. And while some of his court opinions have offended women's and homosexual groups, colleagues say he has no rigid positions on these issues.

'DOES NOT GO OFF ON TANGENTS'

"He reaches opinions only to the extent you need to," said another former clerk, J. Clark Kelso. "He does not go off on tangents about social policy." Mr. Kelso cited the case in which Judge Kennedy upheld the right of the Navy to discharge a sailor for homosexual conduct but avoided the broader question of the legality of sexual relations between consenting adults.

Lawyers describe Judge Kennedy as extremely bright but not brilliant in the way that Judge Robert H. Bork is. While they have not all liked his decisions, liberal and conservative lawyers alike praise Judge Kennedy's temperament.

"If you picture a Federal judge, he does not fit it," said Ronald Zumbrun, director of the conservative Pacific Legal Foundation in Sacramento. "He has a low ego threshold, he has no airs about him. He is a normal person."

Although he seldom prevails with Judge Kennedy, Barry Portman, the Federal public defender in San Francisco, concurs, calling him "one of the most pleasant judges to argue before." He added: "I never found he had a private agenda or ideology. He was conservative but never tried to reach some holding not justified by the facts. If he has a consistent criminal judicial philosophy, I am not prepared to say what it is."

The 1987 edition of The Almanac of the Federal Judiciary gives this distillation of lawyers' views of him: "Courteous, stern on the bench, somewhat conservative, bright, well prepared, filled with nervous energy, asks many questions, good analytical mind, not afraid to break new ground, open minded, good business lawyer, hard to peg, an enigma, tends to agonize over opinions."

'HE'S MORE PROVINCIAL'

Colleagues say his style, marked by boyish enthusiasm, contrasts markedly with the apparently more worldly Judges Robert H. Bork and Douglas H. Ginsburg, who were chosen ahead of him for the job.

"Nobody will find anything in his opinions or personal life that will raise any problems," said the liberal Federal judge who asked anonymity. "You won't find anything very dramatic, very provocative or very controversial. He is not a big liver. He's more provincial. I wouldn't think Tony goes to the opera."

Judge Kennedy was born into Republican politics on July 23, 1936. His mother, Gladys, was a prominent civic booster, and his father, Anthony J. Kennedy, was a politically connected lawyer and lobbyist in Sacramento who was associated with Artie Samish, a powerful lobbyist and fixer who ultimately went to jail for tax evasion. At the age of 10 the youth took a year off from school to serve as a page in the State Senate.

He was graduated, Phi Beta Kappa in political science, from Stanford University in 1958. Prof. Robert A. Horn, now emeritus, who taught the young Mr. Kennedy constitutional law, remembers him as "extremely intelligent" and scholarly even as an undergraduate. "He was conservative but not a right-wing ideologue," Professor Horn said. "His personality is such that I cannot imagine his being a zealot or a fanatic." The professor said he was struck by how "courteous" the student was.

After Stanford, Mr. Kennedy went to the Harvard Law School, graduating in 1961. His roommate at Harvard, R. Dobie Langenkamp, now in the oil business in Tulsa, recalls that his friend "wanted to be a judge virtually all the time I knew him." Mr. Langenkamp said his roommate was deeply influenced by his parents' Republicanism. He recalls Mr. Kennedy as the hardest-working and most purposeful of his classmates, saying he was impressed with his breadth of reading, "and he wrote so exceedingly well."

TURNING POINT FOR LAWYER

After graduation, Mr. Kennedy joined a law firm in San Francisco, and in 1963 married Mary Jeanne Davis, who now teaches elementary school in Sacramento. That year was a turning point in the young lawyer's life. His father died of a heart attack, leaving his personal financial affairs in extraordinary disarray. The son returned to Sacramento, sacrificing a potentially lucrative practice in San Francisco, to take over his father's solo practice and help the family.

In his confirmation hearings for the Federal appeals court in 1975 Mr. Kennedy characterized his law practice as "widely diversified," including "people with individual legal problems, divorce, minor criminal, probate matters, my acquaintances from my many years in Sacramento" and "some very major companies." But the bulk of his practice, he told the committee, was representing businesses in the "middle of the spectrum."

His cases were mostly garden variety disputes, such as a condemnation case involving a development company whose owners included family friends and his mother.

He also worked as a lobbyist at the Capitol, representing Schenley Industries Inc., the liquor distillers; the California Association of Dispensing Opticians and Capitol Records Inc. A state audit in 1975 indicated that he devoted about 10 percent of his time to lobbying.

TIES TO REAGAN AND MEESE

Meanwhile, Mr. Kennedy also developed working ties to Ronald Reagan, when he was Governor of California and to his executive secretary, Edwin Meese 3d, now the Attorney General. As a private lawyer, he was asked to draw up a tax-cutting referendum that failed to win passage in 1973. He was appointed to the appeals court in 1975 by President Ford.

Judge Kennedy does not appear to have accumulated much wealth. His Federal financial disclosure statements show he has no more than $200,000 in assets, not including his residence.

An issue that may arise in confirmation hearings is his membership in the all-male Olympic Club, a private social group in San Francisco since 1962. According to press reports here, he resigned from the club last month when he was under consideration for the nomination before Judge Ginsburg was chosen. Such exclusionary clubs have come under increasingly wide criticism, particularly from women's groups.

His life in recent years has been marked by sorrow. His only brother died in a surfing accident in Hawaii, his only sister died of cancer and his mother died shortly thereafter. "The death of his brother, sister and mother coming so soon after each other was an awful lot to bear," said Robert M. Wheatley, a former law partner.

The Kennedys have two sons, Justin A., who was graduated from Stanford last year, and Gregory D., a senior at Stanford, and a daughter, Kristin M., a sophomore at the same school.

Off the bench, the judge is an avid reader of history and classic literature, such as Shakespeare, and occasionally plays golf at a local country club. His approach to life suggests a small-town innocence. When his local gas station closed down after 24 years, he lamented to The Sacramento Bee, "It is the kind of place where I can get my car serviced and talk about politics and law and life all at the same time."

For the last 22 years, Judge Kennedy has taught constitutional law once a week at the McGeorge School of Law at the University of the Pacific in Sacramento. He is a hard grader, but much admired by his students. "They are stunned to see this man walk in and give a three-hour dissertation and Socratic dialogue without ever looking at a note," said the dean, Gordon D. Schaber, who called the energetic judge "a human hydroelectric project."

It was a way of life Judge Kennedy appeared fated to continue when he was passed over in favor of Judge Ginsburg, commuting from Sacramento to the court's seat in San Francisco and traveling the circuit of nine states, Guam and Northern Mariana Island. But then, with the disclosure of Judge Ginsburg's marijuana use, the fates twisted again and Anthony Kennedy was called to Washington to be offered the post he was refused just two weeks ago.

∙ ∙ ∙ ∙ ∙ ∙ ∙ ∙ ∙ ∙ ∙ ∙

In Kennedy's first full term on the Court, he provided critical votes for a number of important conservative rulings. The decisions upheld state restrictions on abortion procedures, permitted executions of juveniles and mentally retarded persons, restricted minority contractor set-asides, and cut back on job discrimination remedies

Kennedy disappointed conservatives on several other issues. He provided critical votes in 1989 and 1990 for striking down state laws banning flag desecration—an early indication of his strong support for First Amendment claims in areas ranging from campaign finance regulation to sexual expression. Kennedy shocked conservatives in 1992 when he joined Justices O'Connor and Souter in a pivotal opinion that upheld a woman's right to an abortion but gave somewhat greater leeway for state regulation of the procedure. In the same year, he wrote the Court's decision barring government-sponsored prayer at high school graduations.

A decade later, Kennedy wrote the Court's landmark gay rights ruling in 2003 striking down state antisodomy laws. He also changed his positions from earlier cases by voting to bar execution of mentally retarded offenders in 2002 and writing the Court's opinion to prohibit the death penalty for juvenile offenders in 2005. Kennedy continued to take generally conservative positions, however, on issues such as affirmative action, government aid to parochial schools, criminal procedure, and states' rights.

Along with O'Connor, Kennedy was viewed as being a swing vote between the Court's conservative and liberal blocs. Throughout the 1990s, one or the other of them ended the Court's terms with the fewest dissenting votes of all the justices. With O'Connor's retirement in January 2006, Kennedy's position became more important. Although he sided most often with the conservative bloc, Kennedy cast a critical vote with the liberal justices in the 5-3 ruling in 2006 against the system of military tribunals that President Bush had established to try suspected enemy terrorists.

Kennedy's critical position became unmistakable in the 2007 term when he was in the majority in every 5-4 decision and dissented only twice overall. He wrote the 5-4 decision upholding a federal ban on "partial-birth" abortions and joined the conservative rulings on school integration and campaign finance. He also sided with liberals, however, in a 5-4 ruling requiring the Environmental Protection Agency to regulate greenhouse gases to try to control global warming. In 2008 Kennedy again generally voted with the conservative bloc, but joined with liberals to write two high-profile decisions granting habeas corpus rights to Guantánamo detainees and barring the death penalty for child rape.

DAVID H. SOUTER

Despite intense investigation by interest groups and probing questions from members of the Senate Judiciary Committee, the Senate knew relatively little about David H. Souter (1939–) when it considered his nomination to the Supreme Court in October 1990. He won confirmation even though lingering questions led some skeptics to call him "the stealth nominee." Once on the Court, Souter's liberal stands on many issues disappointed conservatives who had supported him, but pleased liberals who had harbored doubts about him.

In early 1990 President George H. W. Bush appointed Souter to the First Circuit Court of Appeals. When Bush nominated him to the Supreme Court just a few months later, Souter had not yet written an opinion as an appeals court judge. More than any other Supreme Court nominee in modern history, Souter was a person without a paper trail. As interest groups and Senate staff investigated Souter, they found little to indicate how he would vote as a Supreme Court justice.

Souter took great pains not to enlighten them during three days of testimony before the Senate Judiciary Committee. While impressing the senators with his intelligence, Souter told them little about his views concerning the issues likely to come before the Court. The senators were particularly eager to learn Souter's view about abortion, but he continually sidestepped questions on the subject. The Senate voted 90–9 to confirm Souter.

JULY 24, 1990
AN 'INTELLECTUAL MIND'
David Hackett Souter
By LINDA GREENHOUSE
Special to The New York Times

WASHINGTON, July 23—In the 22 years since he left private law practice to work as a government lawyer, David H. Souter, President Bush's Supreme Court nominee, has not given a speech, written a law review article or, as far as anyone knows, taken a position on the correctness of the Supreme Court's precedents on abortion or any other issue.

"We don't discuss politics because he doesn't know about politics," Senator Warren G. Rudman, the New Hampshire Republican who is Judge Souter's principal champion and sponsor, said today.

In all these ways, the 50-year-old Federal judge who stood next to President Bush at a White House news conference this afternoon could scarcely have been more different from Robert H. Bork, the outspoken nominee whom President Ronald Reagan introduced to the country under similar circumstances three years ago.

Judge Souter's published opinions from his seven years on the New Hampshire Supreme Court mainly concern interpretations of state law, topics like negligence, family law and criminal procedure. Confirmed by the Senate only two months ago to the United States Court of Appeals for the First Circuit, in Boston, Judge Souter had barely moved into his chambers and had not participated in any of the court's cases.

Judge Souter said: "The obligation of any judge is to decide the case before the court, and the nature of the issue presented will largely determine the appropriate scope of the principle on which its decision should rest."

"Where that principle is not provided and controlled by black letter authority or existing precedent," he said, referring to laws or established precedents, "the decision must honor the distinction between personal and judicially cognizable values."

His answers to other questions on the committee's form were more conversational in tone, particularly when

 He is about 135 pounds—and about 120 pounds of brain.
—John T. Broderick, New Hampshire Bar Association

BACKING IN BOTH PARTIES

The Senate and members of interest groups at both ends of the political spectrum will spend the next few weeks trying to fill in some of the blanks. But it is clear that the nominee has won the respect of Republicans and Democrats alike.

"He is about 135 pounds—and about 120 pounds of brain," said John T. Broderick, counsel for the New Hampshire State Democratic Party and president of the New Hampshire Bar Association. "I think he is an enormous intellectual. And the fact that I support him should tell you something."

Senator Rudman said his friend and protege, a former Rhodes scholar, "is the single most brilliant intellectual mind I have ever met."

Senator Rudman was Attorney General of New Hampshire from 1970 to 1976. Judge Souter, a Republican who joined the Attorney General's office in 1968, was his assistant and later his deputy.

Introduced by President Bush today as a judge who "will interpret the Constitution and not legislate from the Federal bench," Judge Souter declined to answer questions. But he did answer questions earlier this year, when the Senate was considering his nomination to the Federal appeals court.

A Senate Judiciary Committee questionnaire he filled out in February asked his for his views on "judicial activism." His answer, which was noncommittal, apparently did not raise alarms on either side; the vote to confirm him was unanimous.

he was asked to describe the most important cases he had handled before becoming a state court judge.

With evident enthusiasm, he discussed what he called a "simple automobile collision case" that was "tried on the afternoon of Dec. 19, 1967" in State Superior Court. He noted that the case was "not significant for any novelty except to me," because it was the "first chance for me to stand up in a courtroom all by myself."

"I had reason, despite my over-preparation, to be grateful for the court's patience," he said.

LIVES ON A FARM

David Hackett Souter was born Sept. 17, 1939, in Melrose, Mass. He now lives in Weare, N.H., in a farmhouse he valued on a recent financial disclosure form at $150,000. He placed his net worth at $621,000 as of last Dec. 31.

If confirmed by the Senate, Judge Souter would become the 105th Justice in the nation's history and the sixth unmarried one, The Associated Press reported. He would be the first bachelor member of the Court since Justice Frank Murphy, who served from 1940 to 1949.

Judge Souter graduated from Harvard College in 1961 and spent two years at Magdalen College, Oxford, as a Rhodes Scholar. He entered Harvard Law School when he returned to the United States and received his law degree in 1966.

He spent only two years in private law practice, at the Concord firm of Orr and Reno. He served three years as an assistant and five years as deputy attorney general.

He became Attorney General, an appointive office in New Hampshire, in 1976.

He became a judge on the state trial court in 1978. Five years later, Gov. John H. Sununu, now President Bush's chief of staff, accepted Senator Rudman's recommendation and named him to the State Supreme Court.

HAS WIDE INTERESTS

Thomas Rath, a Republican and former state Attorney General who was Judge Souter's deputy, said his old boss likes to work seven days a week, taking time out for classical music and hikes in the outdoors.

The nominee is an Episcopalian. He has never served in the military. If confirmed, he would be the first New Englander on the High Court since Justice Felix Frankfurter retired in 1962. He would be the Court's second Rhodes scholar, joining Justice Byron R. White.

Judge Souter served for 14 years as a trustee and for six years as president of Concord Hospital in Concord, N.H. He also served from 1981 to 1987 as an overseer of the Dartmouth Medical School. He has been a trustee and vice president of the New Hampshire Historical Society.

FOCUS ON TWO OPINIONS

Two of Judge Souter's opinions as an associate justice on the New Hampshire Supreme Court attracted some attention today.

One was a medical malpractice case the court decided in 1986, permitting a lawsuit against an obstetrician by a woman who contracted measles during her pregnancy and gave birth to a baby with severe defects. The woman argued that her doctor was negligent in failing to warn her of the possibility of birth defects so that she could have undergone prenatal testing in time to terminate the pregnancy.

Justice Souter concurred in the majority opinion by Justice William Batchelder, who noted that while abortion "involves controversial and divisive social issues," the United States Supreme Court had upheld the constitutional right to abortion.

Justice Souter also wrote a separate concurring opinion, noting that the majority opinion had failed to raise "a significant issue."

He said: "The trial court did not ask whether, or how, a physician with conscientious scruples against abortion, and the testing and counseling that may inform an abortion decision, can discharge his professional obligation without engaging in procedures that his religious or moral principles condemn.

"To say nothing about this issue could lead to misunderstanding," Justice Souter said. He noted that doctors in such a position might be able to discharge their duty to their patients by referring them for testing and counseling to another doctor.

The court's majority responded that it had not addressed the question Justice Souter raised "because it has not been raised, briefed, or argued in the record before us."

RAPE CASE IN SPOTLIGHT

The second case that drew comment today concerned a rape prosecution. Two years ago, Justice Souter wrote an opinion for a unanimous court overturning a rape conviction on the ground that the trial judge had erroneously excluded evidence about the victim's "sexually provocative" behavior. The defendant had testified that the victim had left a bar with him voluntarily and had consented to sexual intercourse.

Justice Souter's opinion said that the state's rape-shield law, intended to prevent victims from themselves being put on trial, had to be interpreted in light of a defendant's right to a fair trial.

- - - - - - - - - - - -

In his first years on the Court, Souter appeared to be taking mostly conservative positions. Then, in a pivotal decision in 1992, he joined with Justices O'Connor and Kennedy in an opinion reaffirming the *Roe v. Wade* abortion rights ruling that antiabortion groups had hoped he would help overturn. The three justices' stance in that ruling, along with votes in another case to bar government-sponsored prayers at high school graduations, sparked speculation that they might form a centrist coalition on the Court.

Over the next several terms, however, Souter split from his Republican-appointed colleagues by adopting more liberal positions on issues such as affirmative action, racial redistricting, federalism, church-state issues, and individual rights. He wrote lengthy, history-based dissents from several important rulings that eased the restrictions on government aid to religion and overturned congressional statutes in favor of states' rights. He also wrote an important separate opinion in the 1997 assisted suicide decision, calling for a more expansive view of substantive due process than the Court recognized.

Souter continues to be a mainstay of the liberal bloc as the Roberts Court takes shape. In 2008, however, he split from his liberal colleagues by writing the 5-3 opinion to reduce the punitive damage award in the *Exxon Valdez* oil spill case.

CLARENCE THOMAS

Charges of sexual harassment made the 1991 confirmation hearing for Supreme Court nominee Clarence Thomas (1948–), a prominent black conservative, one of the most tumultuous in the nation's history. When the Senate finally confirmed Thomas, the vote was the closest in more than a century. Thomas then staked out a position at the conservative end of the Court's ideological spectrum, calling at times for scrapping well-established, liberal precedents in areas such as civil rights, federalism, and individual rights.

President George H. W. Bush appointed Thomas to the D.C. Circuit Court of Appeals in 1989. Two years later, Bush nominated Thomas to succeed Justice Marshall, the Court's first African American justice and the architect of the school desegregation litigation in the 1940s and 1950s.

During his confirmation hearing, Thomas sidestepped senators' questions about his personal views, particularly concerning abortion. Civil rights and women's groups strongly opposed the nomination. The Senate Judiciary Committee deadlocked, 7–7, on whether to confirm Thomas, instead voting to send his name to the full Senate without a recommendation.

Two days before the scheduled Senate vote, *Newsday* and National Public Radio reported that Anita Hill, a law professor at the University of Oklahoma, had told Judiciary Committee staff that Thomas had sexually harassed her when they worked together at the Department of Education and the Equal Employment Opportunity Commission. The committee reopened the hearing and summoned Hill as a witness. She graphically described what she depicted as Thomas's advances and suggestive comments. Thomas followed with an adamant denial; he called the new hearing "a high-tech lynching for an uppity black."

The committee closed the hearing without resolving the conflict. After a contentious debate, the Senate voted to confirm Thomas, 52–48. The vote was largely along party lines: forty-one Republicans and eleven Democrats, primarily southerners, voted for Thomas; forty-six Democrats and two Republicans voted against him.

JULY 2, 1991
FROM POVERTY TO U.S. BENCH

Clarence Thomas
By NEIL A. LEWIS
Special to The New York Times

WASHINGTON, July 1—Judge Clarence Thomas, President Bush's choice to succeed Thurgood Marshall on the Supreme Court, has always been quick to tell his friends and colleagues about the grinding poverty into which he was born in coastal Georgia.

His father abandoned the family to go north when Judge Thomas was 7 years old, and his harried mother sent him to live with his grandparents in Savannah, the first time he lived in a house with a toilet. His success, he has told friends, was due to his grandfather's insistence that he go to school and work hard.

It was this sense that he had earned everything, and that nothing was given him because of his race, that has made him an impassioned opponent of affirmative action.

"I was raised to survive under the totalitarianism of segregation, not only without the active assistance of government but with its active opposition," he once said in a speech entitled, "Why Black Americans Should Look to Conservative Policies."

He has attacked with relish quotas, timetables and nearly all varieties of racial preference as having the insidious effect of enforcing a notion that blacks cannot compete with whites on an equal footing. Although his personal outlook on that issue probably extends into his judicial philosophy he has not yet had the chance to express it as a judge.

His grandfather made him stand up at meetings of the local chapter of the National Association for the Advancement of Colored People and read his grades aloud.

He enrolled at the all-white St. John Vianney Minor Seminary in Savannah. He once told an interviewer that the bigotry among some of the seminary students dismayed him but he was shocked that everyone tolerated it. Still, he thought about becoming a priest and enrolled for a time at another seminary, Immaculate Conception, in Conception, Mo., but decided against a religious career after encountering more discrimination.

> It was this sense that he had earned everything, and that nothing was given him because of his race, that has made him an impassioned opponent of affirmative action.

'DIFFERENT VIEW OF THE MEANS'

"He made it strictly on the merits, and he resents the notion that he's ever gotten anywhere because he's black," said Lovida H. Coleman Jr., a Washington lawyer and friend of Judge Thomas's from the days when they both attended Yale Law School. She said his views of the goals of civil rights are the same as most black Americans. "It's just that he has a different view of the means to those ends," she said.

It was his opposition to preference programs for members of minority groups, friends say, that first brought him into the orbit of a small group of black conservatives who delighted in questioning the views of the traditional civil rights groups. Eventually he came to the attention of the Reagan Administration.

Principally because of his solid legal background and his views as a black opponent of affirmative action he has long been regarded as a hot prospect for the Republican Party, which he joined shortly after Ronald Reagan was elected President.

Clarence Thomas, 43 years old, was born in Savannah on June 23, 1948, then moved to the small segregated town of Pinpoint, Ga., where, he has recalled, everyone lived in rickety shacks.

DISCRIMINATION AT SEMINARIES

His grandfather, Myers Anderson, could not read but saw to it that Clarence went to a Catholic school that a group of white nuns had established for poor black children.

Judge Thomas expressed frustration at such discrimination later in life when he told Juan Williams in an interview for The Atlantic magazine: "There is nothing you can do to get past black skin. I don't care how educated you are, how good you are at what you do. You'll never have the same contacts or opportunities."

He graduated from Holy Cross College, then Yale Law School. About that time his first marriage, from which he has one son, Jamal, began to come apart. He has since married Virginia Lamp, who works on legislation for the United States Labor Department. They live in Alexandria, Va.

PROTEGE OF DANFORTH

One of Mr. Thomas's first jobs was as an assistant attorney general to John Danforth, then the Missouri Attorney General and now the state's senior Senator. Like many successful people, Clarence Thomas flourished as a protege.

He has often said he was deeply grateful to Mr. Danforth because he felt he paid no attention to his race.

In his assignments as an assistant attorney general, he assiduously avoided working on anything to do with race. He worked on tax and environment cases. He left government briefly, and with a recommendation from Mr. Danforth, he went to work for the Monsanto Chemical Corporation as an in-house counsel. Friends say it was typical of him that he wanted to take a peek at the corporate world.

When Mr. Danforth went to Washington, Mr. Thomas followed as a legislative assistant.

CRITICAL OF CIVIL RIGHTS LEADERS

The Reagan Administration then tapped him to be the assistant secretary for civil rights at the recently formed Department of Education. In May 1982 he became the chairman of the Equal Employment Opportunity Commission, the agency charged with enforcing Federal laws against discrimination based on race, gender, color, national origin and, eventually, age.

At the commission, he became an ever more forceful spokesman against the traditional civil rights approach. Friends said that he often feuded privately with senior officials in the Justice Department over race issues. Yet in a 1984 interview with The Washington Post, he complained that all the nation's traditional civil rights leaders do is "bitch, bitch, bitch, moan and whine."

In an article for the Howard Law Journal and in speeches and interviews he also criticized some aspects of the Supreme Court's landmark 1954 ruling ordering school desegregation, Brown v. Board of Education. The ruling, he said, was based too much on sentiment and suggested that black schools were automatically inferior to white schools. The ruling, revered by many blacks, came in a case brought by Thurgood Marshall, the man whose seat Judge Thomas would replace.

When Mr. Thomas was named to the Court of Appeals for the District of Columbia, which is widely viewed as the nation's second-most influential court, opponents and supporters saw him as a likely Supreme Court appointment if Justice Marshall retired. His nomination caused muted anxiety among traditional civil rights groups and leaders who, in the end, lent quiet but unenthusiastic support.

FEW CONTROVERSIAL CASES

In his 15 months on the appellate court, he has not had a chance to rule on any affirmative action cases or on most of the other issues that are at the center of the nation's social agenda like abortion, obscenity and the proper dividing line between church and state.

Most of the circuit's caseload involves direct appeals from Federal regulator[y] agencies, and Judge Thomas's opinions on the bench include many administrative law rulings that generally upheld the agency. In criminal rulings, he has joined with both conservatives and liberals.

A regular cigar smoker, Judge Thomas reads briefs in a small smoking room off his main office. He has recently adopted an exercise regimen in the court's basement gym.

When the Senate Judiciary Committee held hearings on his nomination to the appeals court in 1990, it was his tenure at the employment commission that produced the most criticism.

Senator Howard M. Metzenbaum, an Ohio Democrat, voted against confirmation, saying that Mr. Thomas refused to enforce a recent law against age discrimination. He said that Mr. Thomas allowed 1,700 complaints filed with state anti-discrimination agencies to lapse without investigation, a charge Mr. Thomas denied.

CHANGING FOCUS OF COMMISSION

But it was Mr. Thomas's general stewardship of the agency that was behind much of the complaints by his opponents. Instead of the large-scale class-action suits the agency had brought in the past, he scaled down its mission, focusing on individual complaints.

During the confirmation hearings, under friendly questioning from Republican committee members, Mr. Thomas spoke of how he felt about being outside the mainstream of blacks in public life.

"I have taken positions which are at odds with what I have perceived in the past as expected orthodoxy and you can say orthodoxy or stereotype for black Americans," he said at one point. "I have problems with that."

He said that his grandfather, in his last conversation with him before his death in 1988, told him to choose between principle and popularity. That's what he felt he was doing, Mr. Thomas said.

- - - - - - - - - - -

On the Court, Thomas closely aligned himself with fellow conservative Antonin Scalia; they have voted together more than 90 percent of the time. Even when in the majority, they sometimes urge a more conservative stance than the Court adopted. In affirmative action cases, for example, Thomas and Scalia both have called for a complete ban on the use of racial preferences. When the Court upheld racial preferences in university admissions in 2003, Thomas wrote a strong and highly personal dissent complaining that affirmative action created a "stigma" for all African Americans.

Thomas also has called for overturning precedents expanding Congress's power in interstate commerce and allowing inmates to sue over prison conditions. He has advocated changing the Court's doctrines to give greater protection to commercial speech and to make it harder to regulate campaign contributions. He has uniformly rejected pleas to set aside death penalty convictions or sentences.

Since Roberts became chief justice, Thomas has continued to stake out positions at the conservative end of the ideological spectrum. In 2006 he was the only justice to support President George W. Bush's power to detain suspected enemy combatants without any hearings. When the Court in 2007 limited school districts' integration plans, Thomas wrote a concurring opinion questioning the benefits of "coerced racial mixing." In 2008 he went further than a Roberts-led plurality in limiting challenges to the methods used in lethal injection executions.

RUTH BADER GINSBURG

As a student, law professor, advocate, and judge, Ruth Bader Ginsburg (1933–) struggled against the legal profession's prevailing institutional discrimination against women. She surmounted those hurdles for herself and helped chart the litigation strategy that resulted in the Supreme Court's first constitutional rulings limiting sex discrimination in the law. Since her appointment to the Court in 1993, she has continued to be a strong champion for women's rights. She has adopted liberal positions in several other areas, but emerged as a voice for judicial restraint in some cases.

President Jimmy Carter named Ginsburg to the D.C. Circuit Court of Appeals in 1980. There she earned a reputation as a judicial moderate on a sharply divided court. She was among several candidates President Bill Clinton considered for his first appointment to the Court. Aides said later that Clinton was especially impressed with Ginsburg's life story. She was confirmed by the Senate, 96–3, and sworn in August 10, 1993, as the Court's second female justice and the first Jewish justice since 1969.

JUNE 15, 1993
REJECTED AS A CLERK, CHOSEN AS A JUSTICE
Ruth Joan Bader Ginsburg
By NEIL A. LEWIS
Special to The New York Times

WASHINGTON, June 14—In 1960, a dean at the Harvard Law School, Albert Sacks, proposed one of his star students to Justice Felix Frankfurter of the Supreme Court as a law clerk. Justice Frankfurter told Professor Sacks that while the candidate was impressive, he just wasn't ready to hire a woman and so couldn't offer a job to Ruth Bader Ginsburg.

Judge Ginsburg, who now sits on the Federal appeals court and was chosen today by President Clinton for the Supreme Court, recently told that story to her own law clerks to explain how she became interested in the role of women in the eyes of the law.

FORCE BEFORE THE COURT

In the years between that rebuff by Justice Frankfurter and her appointment to the United States Court of Appeals for the District of Columbia Circuit in 1980, Ruth Ginsburg was a major force on the other side of the Supreme Court's high bench.

From 1973 to 1976 she argued six women's rights cases before the Court and won five of them, profoundly changing the law as it affects women.

"She is the Thurgood Marshall of gender equality law," said Janet Benshoof, the president of the Center for Reproductive Law and Policy, an abortion-rights advocacy group, repeating a common description of Judge Ginsburg. Like Justice Marshall, who shaped the legal strategy of the civil rights movement for the NAACP Legal and Educational Defense Fund before he joined the Court, Ruth Ginsburg organized the cases, found the plaintiffs and delivered the oral arguments.

form had to show that her husband received more than half his support from her to qualify for the extra housing allowance.

A NEW JURISPRUDENCE

In her brief and argument, Ms. Ginsburg presented the Court with an array of evidence that women were branded inferior through such treatment. The Justices voted 8 to 1 in her favor, embarking on the road to a new jurisprudence that made it harder for the law to treat women differently.

> She is the Thurgood Marshall of gender equality law.
> —Janet Benshoof, Center for Reproductive Law and Policy

As the director of the Women's Rights Project of the American Civil Liberties Union, Ms. Ginsburg adopted a strategy intended to convince the Justices that laws that discriminated between men and women—even those laws that were meant to help women—were based on unfair and harmful stereotypes and were in most cases unconstitutional. To do that, she often used men as plaintiffs, showing that both men and women suffered from such stereotypes.

"Her strategy was an especially ingenious one, relying on male, often married, plaintiffs," said David Cole, a professor at Georgetown University Law School who recently wrote a law review article discussing Ms. Ginsburg's approach to the Supreme Court.

He said many of the regulations or laws she opposed ostensibly helped women, giving them some extra benefit in recognition of the prevailing notion that women were generally dependent on men.

"But she set out to prove that those kinds of laws in fact harmed women by contributing to a stereotyped view of their role," he said.

The first case she argued and won before the Court, in 1973, involved a female Air Force lieutenant, Sharron Frontiero, and her husband, Joseph, who challenged a statute that treated male and female service members differently. Under the law, a serviceman could claim his wife as a dependent and qualify for increased housing even if she did not depend on his income, while a woman in uni-

In 1976, in another case in which Ms. Ginsburg had filed a brief, the Justices set a standard that is still used today in sex discrimination cases. In that case, Craig v. Boren, the Court struck down an Oklahoma statute that said women as young as 18 could buy 3.2 percent beer while men had to be at least 21.

In its ruling, the Court declined to impose what is known as "strict scrutiny" of such discriminatory laws, which places a high burden on a state to justify making distinctions. But the Court did create a category known as "intermediate scrutiny," meaning that states could not enact laws that discriminated on the basis of sex without showing a substantial government interest.

Behind all the categorizing, the ruling's effect was to make it far harder to enact laws based on sexual stereotypes.

"Ruth Ginsburg was as responsible as any one person for legal advances that women made under the Equal Protection Clause of the Constitution," said Marcia Greenberger, the co-president of the National Women's Law Center. "As a result, doors of opportunity have been opened that have benefited not only the women themselves but their families."

REMEMBERING HER MOTHER

Ruth Joan Bader was born March, 15, 1933, in the Flatbush section of Brooklyn, and graduated from James

Madison High School. Her father, Nathan Bader, owned small clothing stores. Her mother, Celia Bader, died of stomach cancer when Ruth was 17; at the White House today, Judge Ginsburg paid tribute to her mother.

At Cornell University, she met Martin D. Ginsburg, a fellow pre-law student, and they were married in June 1954, the same month she graduated from college. "They had a marvelous romance in her senior year," recalled a cousin, Jane Gevirtz of Manhattan.

Ms. Gevirtz said she recently came upon a letter that Ms. Ginsburg had written to her in 1953 in which she said she wanted to be a lawyer but had deep doubts on whether she had sufficient aptitude for the law. Ms. Gevirtz said her cousin nonetheless wrote that she was determined to see if she could get into law school, despite being told from all sides that it was more appropriate for a woman to be a teacher.

Her first child, Jane, was born the year after she married. Her aptitude for the law was sufficient for Harvard Law School, and she found herself caring for an infant and attending Harvard for the next two years.

When her husband found a job in New York, she transferred to Columbia Law School. Ms. Ginsburg was elected to the law reviews of both Harvard and Columbia.

Years later she became the first tenured female professor at Columbia University Law School, where her daughter, Jane, an authority on copyright law, is now on the faculty. She also has a son, James.

Mr. Ginsburg, an expert on tax law who has been Ross Perot's tax lawyer for years, was an economic adviser in Mr. Perot's Presidential campaign.

While Judge Ginsburg is modest in demeanor, even shy, her husband is an ebullient sort, friends said.

VIEWS ON ROE

Despite her long record as a champion of women's rights, Judge Ginsburg has occasionally disappointed some of her former allies in the liberal advocacy groups. In her 13 years on the appeals court, she has often gone out of her way to mediate between the court's warring liberal and conservative factions.

But what has most dismayed some of her natural allies are her comments criticizing some aspects of Roe v. Wade, the 1973 Supreme Court ruling that declared there was a constitutional right to abortion.

In a speech in March at New York University, Judge Ginsburg outlined her objections to the 1973 ruling, which she said was too sweeping and thus contributed to the bitter debate over the last 20 years.

In essence, Judge Ginsburg argued that it was unwise of the Court majority to impose a detailed scheme prescribing how states may regulate abortion in each trimester of a pregnancy. Instead, she suggested, the Court should simply have overturned the law at issue, a Texas statute that outlawed nearly all abortions.

"Suppose the Court had stopped there, declaring unconstitutional the most extreme brand of law in the nation and had not gone on, as the Court did in Roe, to fashion a regime blanketing the subject," Ms. Ginsburg said, adding that a narrower ruling would have "served to reduce rather than to fuel controversy."

In that case, she went on, states would have more latitude to resolve the public dispute about abortion by creating their own abortion statutes, testing the Court's limits on how far they could go to restrict abortion.

Judge Ginsburg also said she believed the decision should have been grounded in a broad concept of equality for women. The Roe v. Wade decision was based instead on the idea that there is a constitutional right of privacy, which she did not discuss in the speech. Some abortion-rights advocates said today that the speech gave them concerns about her position in disputes over whether states can inhibit abortions with restrictions like waiting periods.

Kate Michelman, the president of the National Abortion Rights Action League, hinted at her group's displeasure with Judge Ginsburg's reservations about Roe. "Judge Ginsburg has been a strong advocate for women's equality," she said, "but her criticism of Roe v. Wade is cause for concern. We look forward to a thorough Senate Judiciary Committee hearing to determine whether Judge Ginsburg will protect a woman's fundamental right to privacy."

Supporters like Ms. Benshoof insist that Judge Ginsburg is a reliable supporter of abortion rights. In a 1989 opinion, in fact, Judge Ginsburg dissented from a ruling that allowed the Bush Administration to continue its policy of denying financing to international family planning groups that counsel abortion.

As a new justice, Ginsburg initially startled observers with her unusually active questioning during oral arguments. Later, she chafed when lawyers confused her with the Court's other female justice, O'Connor, during oral arguments. In her most important early opinion, she wrote the landmark ruling in 1996 ordering that women be admitted to the previously all-male Virginia Military Institute.

Despite generally liberal stands on civil rights, federalism, and church-state issues, Ginsburg often favors law enforcement in criminal cases. Many observers have commented on Ginsburg's frequent preference for deciding cases on procedural grounds rather than broad principles of social justice.

Ginsburg publicly voiced regret after O'Connor's retirement in January 2006 left her as the only female justice. "The word I would use to describe my position on the bench is lonely," she remarked a year later in an interview with *USA Today*.

Over the next several months, Ginsburg made headlines by delivering passionate dissents from the bench in two closely divided rulings affecting women's rights. She decried the April 2007 ruling to uphold a federal ban on "partial-birth" abortions as reflecting "hostility" to abortion rights. Then, in June, she denounced a decision tightening the time limits in wage discrimination suits as "totally at odds" with Congress's intent in prohibiting sex discrimination in the workplace.

STEPHEN G. BREYER

When President Clinton introduced Stephen G. Breyer (1938–) as his second Supreme Court nominee in May 1994, he described the federal appeals court judge as a "consensus builder." The reaction to the nomination proved his point: Breyer won immediate praise from Republican and Democratic senators alike and a range of legal experts. After joining the Court, Breyer generally aligned himself with the moderate-to-liberal bloc of justices and earned a reputation for carefully balanced questions from the bench and judiciously written opinions.

In his confirmation hearings, Breyer faced criticism for decisions made during his tenure on the First Circuit Court of Appeals, to which he was nominated by President Jimmy Carter. Among senators' concerns were his casting pro-business votes in regulatory cases and failing to disqualify himself from cases that might have affected his investment in the British insurance syndicate, Lloyd's of London. After promising to dispose of the Lloyd's investment, Breyer won Senate confirmation easily, 87–9. He joined Ginsburg as the Court's second Jewish member. Not since the 1930s, when Louis D. Brandeis and Benjamin N. Cardozo served together for six years, had there been two Jewish justices on the Court.

MAY 14, 1994
SCHOLARLY CONSENSUS BUILDER
Stephen Gerald Breyer
By DAVID MARGOLICK

By nature and personality, Judge Stephen G. Breyer, whom President Clinton named yesterday to the United States Supreme Court, is professorial. But rather than become enmeshed solely in ideas, Judge Breyer has chosen to harness his considerable intelligence to solve problems, to clean up messes.

Rather than stake out fixed positions, he has built coalitions and achieved consensus. As generously endowed with political savvy, pragmatism, personal charm and energy as intelligence—and unencumbered by any overarching ideology—he has won a reputation for doing as well as thinking.

While serving on the United States Court of Appeals for the First Circuit, where Judge Breyer has been chief judge since 1990, he used the same combination of skills to put together something as complicated as the Federal sentencing guidelines, as three-dimensional as a plan for an environmentally correct Federal courthouse on Boston Harbor and as crucial as coalitions of his fellow judges. He hates dissenting opinions, whether his own or others, and his court produces few of them.

Admirers see for him a moderate, consensus-building role like that of the man for whom he once clerked, Justice Arthur J. Goldberg, reaching out to Justices Sandra Day O'Connor, David H. Souter and Anthony M. Kennedy, the High Court's current middle, as Justice Goldberg once reached out to Justices Tom C. Clark and Potter Stewart.

strand in the best version of the American judiciary, and that's what all these Jewish Justices stood for, Breyer doesn't stand for that," he said. "The words 'social justice' would somewhat embarrass him."

As intellectually acute and agile as he is energetic, a man who writes his own opinions and selects as his law clerks not those he can most easily lean on but those who are most interesting to talk to, Judge Breyer possesses one trait that Democrats and liberals starved of High Court appointments for a generation still seek: the raw brain power to match Justice Antonin Scalia, commonly

> " There are different kinds of intelligence, and his is the kind that tries to take complicated issues, cut to the core and explain them to people who are not nearly so intelligent.
>
> —Akhil Amar, Yale Law School "

"There are different kinds of intelligence, and his is the kind that tries to take complicated issues, cut to the core and explain them to people who are not nearly so intelligent," said Prof. Akhil Amar of Yale Law School, one of Judge Breyer's former law clerks. "He's always been smarter than most of those around him, so he's had to learn how to get along with other people."

But for liberals seeking a kindred spirit on the Court after a generation of conservatives and moderate appointees—and a fitting replacement for Justice Harry A. Blackmun, the current Court's most liberal member—Judge Breyer could disappoint.

"Breyer's basic social instincts are conservative," said Morton Horwitz, a legal historian and former faculty colleague at Harvard Law School. "His legal culture is more liberal, and his very flexible pragmatism will enable him to give things a gentle spin in a liberal direction. But he's a person without deep roots of any kind. He won't develop a vision."

RAW BRAIN POWER

Judge Breyer is Jewish, but Mr. Horwitz said he had little in common with Louis Brandeis, Benjamin Cardozo, Felix Frankfurter and other Jews who have served on the High Court. "If we still believe there is this social justice

acknowledged to be the Rehnquist Court's intellectual leader.

"He's smarter than Scalia, but not nearly as bombastic," said Alan Dershowitz, who has taught with Judge Breyer at Harvard Law School and argued before him. "He will dominate the Court by his quiet intellect, not by brashy, noisy intrusions. He doesn't need to prove he's the smartest person in the courthouse."

But while an intellectual counterweight to Judge Scalia, Judge Breyer is not necessarily a philosophical one. The labels most often used to describe him are "centrist" and "technocrat." His critics consider him brilliant but bloodless, more gamesman than statesman, more clever than humane. They say he lacks passion and compassion, is too centered on economic efficiency and a cost-benefit view of life, and prefers tidying up things, be it the airline industry or sentencing or the way judges choose their clerks, over articulating a sweeping constitutional vision. . . .

President Clinton first met Judge Breyer last year, when he was a front-runner for the court seat vacated by Justice Byron White. Judge Breyer hobbled to Washington for a job interview, nursing broken ribs and a punctured lung suffered when struck by a car as he bicycled across Harvard Square. When Mr. Clinton tapped Judge Ruth Bader Ginsburg instead, there was speculation the two men had not hit it off.

There are those who find him snippy and snooty, caustic or condescending to those he considers not quite as smart as he, but they are a distinct minority. A good listener and able negotiator, he has won over almost everyone else. He may have won over even President Clinton with his conspicuous chipperness and grace after Judge Ginsburg beat him out. "A great pick," he called her.

THE INTELLECT MIXING THEORY AND PRACTICE

From an early age, Judge Breyer blended the theoretical and the practical. At Stanford University—his mother discouraged him from attending Harvard, for fear that he would bury himself there in books—he played Secretary General at a model United Nations. At Harvard, where he went on to study law and has taught for nearly 30 years, he planted himself where legal principles and politics merged, specializing in the law of administrative agencies and economic regulation.

By design, he periodically left his Cambridge cocoon for Washington, where he worked as a Watergate prosecutor, played a pivotal role in airline deregulation and became chief counsel to the Senate Judiciary Committee. In the process, he cemented his ties to Senator Edward M. Kennedy, who in 1980, in the waning days of the Carter Administration, shepherded him into his seat on the appellate court. . . .

THE DECISIONS ERUDITE AND METHODICAL

Judge Breyer is a man of great range. He served on a Federal judicial study committee contemplating the relationship between law and science, read all of Proust's "Remembrance of Things Past" in French a year ago and studied the Italian architect Borromini to pick up ideas for the new Federal courthouse, on which construction is to start this summer. Judge Breyer's decisions, narrowly tailored and generally deferential to lower courts, are less notable for their content than for their style: methodical, lucid, with no footnotes and little lofty rhetoric—what Professor Amar called "Hemingwayesque." . . .

More than any ruling, however, it is Judge Breyer's role in helping to devise the intricate Federal sentencing guidelines, then defending them against accusations that they are rigid, mechanical and unduly harsh, that his critics find alarming. Both as architect and apologist, they contend,

Judge Breyer provided liberal legitimacy to a cornerstone of Reagan-era law-and-order forces.

Stephen Gerald Breyer was born in San Francisco on Aug. 15, 1938. His father, Irving, was a lawyer and administrator with the school board. He starred debating [sic] at Lowell High School—one of his rivals was Edmund G. Brown Jr., later Governor of California—and was voted most likely to succeed in the Class of 1955.

"He was always sort of a peacemaker," said Stuart Pollock, a high school and college classmate, and now a Municipal Court judge in San Francisco. "He was not anyone you'd expect to see on the steps of Sproul Hall."

Judge Breyer graduated from Stanford in 1958, then spent two years studying philosophy, politics and economics as a Marshall Scholar at Oxford. He then enrolled at Harvard Law School, where he graduated magna cum laude and was articles editor of the Harvard Law Review. He then clerked for Justice Goldberg.

In 1967 he returned to Harvard Law School, where he taught and wrote on antitrust, administrative law, and economic regulation. Interested in policy matters, he developed ties to the John F. Kennedy School of Government. He started teaching a course on law and economics, which led to his interest in regulatory reform.

He saw Harvard as congenial but a bit remote. "Life there is important but doesn't affect 99.9999 percent of the people who get up, go to work, have to educate their children, and get their health insurance," he said in an interview.

His third and longest foray to Washington came in 1979, as counsel to the Senate Judiciary Committee, then headed by Senator Kennedy. There, he worked on a Federal criminal code, the F.B.I. charter, fair housing law and legislation to deregulate the trucking industry. He also helped select judges and get them confirmed. In addition, he had the politically sensitive task of drafting a policy barring Federal judges from belonging to private clubs that discriminated.

In 1979, after the Carter Administration balked at naming Archibald Cox, the former Watergate prosecutor, to a newly created seat on the First Circuit, Judge Breyer got the nod. His nomination was pending on Election Day, 1980, and appeared doomed once Ronald Reagan won. With help from, among others, various Republican members of the Committee, his nomination was salvaged, the only Democratic choice to do so. On Dec. 18, 1980, he was sworn in.

Along with Ginsburg, Breyer has taken liberal views on a range of issues before the Court, including civil rights, women's rights, federalism, and church-state issues. He wrote the Court's 5–4 decision in 2000 striking down a Nebraska law banning so-called partial-birth abortions and penned a strong dissent from the 2002 decision upholding vouchers for parochial school students. His record on civil liberties and criminal issues has been generally liberal with some exceptions. He has given police somewhat greater leeway than the other liberal justices in Fourth Amendment search cases. And he has adopted a flexible approach on First Amendment issues to permit government regulation in a range of areas, including campaign finance, commercial speech, and sexual expression.

As a former Senate staff member, Breyer has shown a special sensitivity to congressional prerogatives. In 1995 he wrote a strongly worded dissent from the Court's decision to strike down a law passed by Congress to prohibit possession of firearms near schools. He dissented again when the Court in 2000 struck down a law allowing victims of gender-motivated crimes to sue their attackers in federal court and when the Court in 2001 protected state governments from private damage suits for violations of the federal disability rights law.

In his most dramatic dissent, Breyer sharply criticized the 2007 decision to limit school districts' ability to consider race in pupil assignments as contrary to precedent and likely to lead to further resegregation. From the bench, he added a pungent critique not included in the printed opinion. "It's not often in the law," he said of the conservative majority, "that so few have changed so much so quickly."

SAMUEL A. ALITO JR.

As a young Justice Department lawyer in the Reagan administration in the 1980s, Samuel Anthony Alito Jr. (1950–) described himself as a lifelong conservative. Two decades later, conservatives looked to Alito to change the Court's balance of power after he succeeded Justice O'Connor, who had held a pivotal position between the Court's conservative and liberal blocs.

President George H. W. Bush nominated Alito for a vacancy on the Third Circuit Court of Appeals in 1990; the Senate confirmed him without controversy. On the bench, Alito gained a reputation as a careful and conscientious judge with a strong conservative orientation.

Alito was frequently mentioned as a potential Supreme Court nominee after President George W. Bush took office in 2001, but Bush chose Roberts for O'Connor's seat in July 2005. Then, after nominating Roberts instead to succeed the late Chief Justice William H. Rehnquist, Bush turned to his White House counsel, Harriet E. Miers, to fill O'Connor's position. Miers withdrew three weeks later, following stinging criticism of her qualifications from both liberals and conservatives. Despite calls to name a woman, Bush nominated Alito for the seat. In selecting Alito, Bush noted that he had more judicial experience than any Supreme Court nominee in the previous seventy years.

Conservative and liberal interest groups mounted strong lobbying campaigns for and against Alito. At the start of his Senate Judiciary Committee hearing, Alito said he had no "agenda" as a judge other than "the rule of law." Republicans praised his qualifications, while Democrats critically questioned him about his judicial record and his views on abortion rights and presidential power.

In a strictly party-line vote, the committee voted 10–8 to approve Alito's nomination. Some Democrats waged a last-minute filibuster against the nomination, but the Senate voted 72–25 to cut off debate on January 30, 2006. Alito won confirmation the next day, 58–42, with four Democrats voting for him and one Republican breaking party ranks to vote no.

NOVEMBER 1, 2005
THE METHODICAL JURIST

Samuel Anthony Alito Jr.

By NEIL A. LEWIS and SCOTT SHANE

WASHINGTON, Oct. 31—One weekend in 1986, two young lawyers working for Samuel A. Alito Jr., then a deputy assistant attorney general in the Justice Department, faced a looming deadline for a legal analysis and realized they would have to work all night to get it done.

"In the legal world, most bosses would say, 'This is what I want on my desk in the morning,' " said John F. Manning, one of the lawyers. "Sam stayed with us. He went out and got pizza and he pulled the all-nighter with us. I've never seen anything like that before or since."

firmation as chief justice, or Harriet E. Miers, the White House counsel, who withdrew after withering attacks on her credentials and conservative bona fides.

Judge Alito's jurisprudence has been methodical, cautious, respectful of precedent and solidly conservative, legal scholars said. In cases involving the great issues of the day—abortion, the death penalty and the separation of church and state—Judge Alito has typically taken the conservative side.

Yet he has not flaunted his political views inside or outside the courthouse. Friends say Judge Alito seems to

> " Sam is conservative because he's a straightforward believer in judicial restraint—that is, a judge's personal views should not dictate the outcome of the case.
>
> —Mark Dwyer "

Throughout his life—ever since he resolved his high school indecision between his dream of a career in baseball or a life in law—the self-effacing Judge Alito, President Bush's new choice for the Supreme Court, has made his mark with quiet dedication rather than showy display. He has cloaked his formidable intellect in modesty, an attribute both surprising and endearing to colleagues in high-octane legal circles.

While Judge Alito, 55, has built a reputation for decency, he has also compiled a conservative record that is coming under intense scrutiny from activists on the left and the right who understand his potential for shifting the balance on the bench.

Larry Lustberg, a former federal prosecutor who has known Judge Alito for 22 years, called him "totally capable, brilliant and nice."

But Mr. Lustberg added, "Make no mistake: he will move the court to the right, and this confirmation process is really going to be a question about whether Congress and the country wants to move this court to the right."

As a federal appeals court judge for 15 years, Judge Alito has amassed a more extensive paper record than either John G. Roberts Jr., who sailed through his con-

have inherited a distaste for shows of ideology from his father, an Italian immigrant who became research director for the New Jersey Legislature and had to rigorously avoid partisanship.

Judge Alito won prestigious academic prizes while at Princeton and Yale Law School, where he stood out for his conservative views, which were in the minority, as well as for his civility in engaging ideological opponents.

"The notion that he's an extreme conservative is wrong," said Mark Dwyer, Judge Alito's fellow student at Princeton and roommate at Yale. "Sam is conservative because he's a straightforward believer in judicial restraint—that is, a judge's personal views should not dictate the outcome of the case."

Even in the Reagan Justice Department, where a palpable sense of conservative triumph was in the air, "I never got the sense that he thought about legal issues in an ideological way," said Mr. Manning, now a professor at Harvard Law School.

But Walter F. Murphy, an emeritus professor at Princeton who supervised Judge Alito's undergraduate thesis on the Italian Constitutional Court and has kept up with him in the years since, said his former student believed in ruling according to an "original understanding" of the Constitution.

The phrase is generally used to describe legal theorists, like Justice Antonin Scalia, who believe judges should try to figure out what the Constitution's drafters would have ruled in contemporary cases.

Friends say references to Judge Alito as "Scalito," a name meant to suggest that he is a clone of Justice Scalia, the court's most robust conservative, are off the mark and demeaning.

Like Justice Scalia, Judge Alito is an Italian-American from Trenton, whose jurisprudence is indisputably conservative. But while Justice Scalia is known for his caustic writing and argumentative manner, Judge Alito is described by clerks, lawyers and former schoolmates as a man who takes extraordinary care to be gentle with others and is quick to help a struggling lawyer arguing before his court.

"He's got a powerful intellectual humility, is the way I'd put it," said Clark Lombardi, who clerked for Judge Alito in 1999 and 2000 on the United States Court of Appeals for the Third Circuit, the judge's current seat.

Judge Alito grew up in the Mercerville section of Hamilton Township, a postwar suburb that came to life as residents abandoned Trenton in the 1950's. The unassuming homes have small front lawns, and like so many of its New Jersey neighbors, the town's outskirts are lined with strip malls.

During the judge's childhood, Mercerville was populated by blue- and white-collar families: state employees, steel and porcelain workers, a mix of ethnic Europeans dominated by Italians, Poles and Hungarians.

The Alito family house on Fenwood Avenue, where Judge Alito's mother still lives, is a brick Cape Cod with a screened porch. An American flag is planted on the front lawn.

The judge's late father, Samuel A. Alito, came to America as a boy from Italy and worked as the research director of a nonpartisan agency that analyzed legislation for state lawmakers. The judge's mother, Rose, who will be 91 in December, worked as principal of the local elementary school.

The small family was close, and Sam Jr. and his sister, Rosemary, who worked as a television reporter and is now a lawyer, got along well, friends say. Ted Fort, 66, the former band director at Steinert High School, remembered Judge Alito as quiet and intensely focused on school and family. . . .

Judge Alito attended Princeton just as it was opening its doors to women, but classmates said he was not among those voicing opposition. Professor Murphy said he had predicted that the young Sam Alito would become a judge.

"He thought in judicial opinions even then," Professor Murphy said, adding that it was "not as clear then as now" that Judge Alito was a staunch conservative. . . .

With campuses nationwide embroiled in Vietnam War protests, Princeton decided in 1970 to phase out the R.O.T.C., allowing those already enrolled to finish up. When Judge Alito graduated in 1972, he was just one of 12 R.O.T.C. members in the class.

He was commissioned as an Army second lieutenant at graduation, but went to law school and served on active duty for just three months in 1975, though he remained in the Army Reserve until 1980.

At Yale Law School, where he was in the class behind Justice Clarence Thomas, Judge Alito was widely regarded as one of the smartest students, said Peter Goldberger, a classmate. Mr. Goldberger, who describes himself as a staunch liberal, said it was always enjoyable to get into a discussion with the young Mr. Alito.

"We fundamentally disagreed over just about everything," he said, "but it led to cheerful jousting." . . .

After Yale, Mr. Alito clerked for a Trenton law firm and then for an appellate judge, Leonard I. Garth of the Third Circuit. He then worked for four years in New Jersey as an assistant United States attorney before departing in 1981 for a seven-year stint in the Justice Department. First, as assistant to the solicitor general, he argued several cases before the Supreme Court involving criminal, communications and labor law.

While some talented young lawyers reveled in the conservative camaraderie of the Justice Department under Attorney General Edwin Meese III, Mr. Alito was not among them.

"Nobody tagged Sam as a fire-breathing conservative," said Mark Levy, a self-described Clinton Democrat who worked with him there. "He had friends across every divide."

Charles J. Cooper, the assistant attorney general in charge of the Office of Legal Counsel, recruited him to become a deputy assistant attorney general.

Mr. Cooper, who has remained friendly with Mr. Alito, said: "The power of his intellect is the most striking thing about him. I'd imagine there are about six lawyers in the country who are John Roberts's equal, and Sam is one of them." . . .

In 1987, Mr. Alito returned to New Jersey as United States attorney, where in three years he handled cases involving organized crime, child pornography and even terrorism, in a case against a member of the Japanese Red Army who was sentenced to 30 years in prison for plotting to bomb a Navy recruiting center.

While in that job, Mr. Alito met and married the librarian in the United States attorney's office, Martha-Ann Bomgardner. They have a son, Philip, now in college, and a daughter, Laura, in high school.

Since the first President Bush appointed him to the Third Circuit in 1990, Judge Alito's unaffected, low-key style has remained unchanged. Katherine Huang, a Los Angeles lawyer who was a law clerk to Judge Alito in 2000, said: "He's just a regular, approachable guy. He's a truly gentle sort." . . .

Reporting for this article was contributed by James Barron and Daniel J. Wakin from New York; Alison Leigh Cowan from Stamford, Conn.; Andrew Jacobs, Richard Lezin Jones and Laura Mansnerus from Trenton; Patrick McGeehan from West Caldwell, N.J.; and Ronald Smothers from Newark.

• • • • • • • • • • •

After being sworn in, Alito quickly aligned himself with the Court's conservative bloc. He cast decisive votes in 2006 in three cases reargued after O'Connor's departure—presumably because the eight other justices were evenly divided. Conservatives prevailed in each of the three, including a ruling to allow police to use evidence obtained in an unannounced, no-knock search of a suspect's home.

Over the next two terms, Alito continued to provide a critical fifth vote for the conservative-backed decisions on abortion rights, race-based school assignments, campaign finance, and gun rights. He also wrote the main opinion in a significant 5-4 ruling in 2007 that limited taxpayer suits challenging use of federal funds to promote religion. In that case and some others, however, Alito—like Roberts—separated himself from calls by Justices Scalia and Thomas to explicitly overturn prior decisions.

Besides strengthening the conservative majority, Alito's appointment also established a historic milestone. With five Catholic justices, the Court has a conservative majority for the first time: Roberts, Scalia, Kennedy, Thomas, and Alito.

INDEX

Italic page numbers indicate illustrations. Alphabetization is letter-by-letter (e.g., "Grandfather clauses" precedes "Grand jury").

*Abington School District
   v. Schempp* (1962),
   216, 219
Ableman v. Booth (1859),
   135–136, 257
Abolitionists, 124, 135, 257
Abortion rights. *See also
   Roe v. Wade*
   Alito and, 433
   Burger Court and, 126
   Court after *Roe v.
      Wade*, 323–331
   due process and, 314,
      318–331
   electioneering
      communications
      and, 250–252
   equal protection and,
      153
   Kennedy and, 417
   major abortion-related
      rulings (1973–2007),
      324
   partial-birth abortion,
      295, 298, 328–331,
      418, 430
   protests at clinics, 194
   public opinion and,
      127
   reaffirmation of, 66
   Stevens and, 412
   women's rights
      movement, 279
Abrams, Floyd, 250

Abrams v. United States
   (1919), 179
Academic freedom, 191
Access to public facilities
   by disabled
   persons, 168
ACLU. *See* American Civil
   Liberties Union
Actual malice standard for
   libel, 201
Adams, John
   Marbury v. Madison
      and, 107
   Sedition Act and, 177
   Supreme Court
      appointments of, 61
   war powers and, 56
Adamson v. California
   (1947), 354
*Adarand Constructors, Inc.
   v. Peña* (1995), 272
*Adkins v. Children's
   Hospital* (1923), 17,
   21, 300, 308
Adkins v. Virginia (2002),
   388
Adler v. Board of Education
   (1952), 188
Adult bookstores and
   movie theaters,
   regulation of, 206
Adulterated food, 14, 309
Advertising
   false, 168

freedom of press and,
   205–206
political ad regulation,
   249–252
Affirmative action,
   271–275, 412,
   423–424
Afghanistan, war in, 92
AFL-CIO, 250
African Americans. *See
   also* Affirmative
   action; Civil
   Rights Acts;
   Equal Protection
   Clause
   capital punishment
      and, 382, 388
   criminal proceedings
      against, 356–359
   impartial jury, right to,
      264, 379, 381
   poll taxes, 232, 261,
      264, 291
   racial redistricting, 234,
      239–242
   Reconstruction-era
      civil rights statutes,
      13
   restrictive covenants,
      253–256, 264
   "Scottsboro Boys,"
      356–359
   voting rights, 226–234,
      261, 264, 280

Age Discrimination in
   Employment Act of
   1967 (ADEA), 168
Agricultural Adjustment
   Act of 1933, 7, 20, 32
Agricultural Adjustment
   Act of 1938, 32
Aguilar v. Texas (1964),
   363
Air bags, failure to install,
   147
Alcohol, minimum legal
   age to drink, 33–34,
   157
Alden v. Maine (1999),
   130–133, 168
*Alexander v. Holmes
   County Board of
   Education* (1969),
   267
Aliens
   Alien Registration Act
      of 1940, 188
   detainees, rights of, 1–4
   immigrant labor, 139
   rights of, 153, 286–289
Alito, Samuel A., Jr., *403*
   exclusionary rule
      decision, 365
   federal court
      appointment of, 430
   habeas corpus writs
      for detainees
      decision, 3, 4

issue ads decision, 250, 251
military commissions decision, 96, 97
partial-birth abortion decision, 328, 329, 330
race-based school assignment decision, 276
Roberts Court and, 430–433
sentencing guidelines decision, 394
Supreme Court appointment of, 67, 119, 328, 403, 404, 430
voting record of, 67
Allegheny, County of v. American Civil Liberties Union (1989), 219
Allgeyer v. Louisiana (1897), 152
Alliance, Treaty of (1778), 56
Allied Structural Steel Co. v. Spannaus (1937), 139
al Qaeda, 1, 2
Ambach v. Norwick (1976), 287
American Civil Liberties Union (ACLU), 207–209, 219, 280
American Library Association, 207
American Railway Union, 59–60
American Sugar Refinery Co., breakup of, 14, 140
Americans with Disabilities Act of 1990 (ADA), 168
Amish children and compulsory school attendance, 210
The Antelope (1825), 257
Anti-loitering ordinances, 362
Anti-Semitism, 62, 182
Antisodomy laws, 314, 331–333, 334–337
Antiterrorism and Effective Death Penalty Act of 1996, 400
Antitrust law, 125
Apodaca v. Oregon (1972), 379
Appeals, criminal, 397–399, 402

Appellate jurisdiction of Court, 106
Appointments Clause, 73
Apprendi v. New Jersey (2000), 394, 395
Argentina and Falkland Islands, 99
Argersinger v. Hamlin (1972), 355, 378
Armband war protests in schools, 191–193
Arms, right to keep and bear, 298, 299, 344–347, 405, 410. *See also* Gun control; Second Amendment
Arms embargo, conviction for violation of, 99–100
Arraignments, delay in, 367
Arrests, 360–362
Arver v. United States (1918), 40–42
Ashcroft v. American Civil Liberties Union (2004), 209
Ashwander v. Tennessee Valley Authority (1936), 105
Assembly, freedom of, 181, 184, 193, 355
Atkins v. Virginia (2002), 389
Attorneys
  aliens as, 286–287
  for indigent defendants, 127
  women's licensure as, 278
Atwater v. City of Lago Vista (2001), 360–362
Authorization to Use Military Force, 92, 95
Automakers' failure to install air bags, suits against, 147
Automobile stops by police, 362, 365
Automobile Workers v. Johnson Controls, Inc. (1991), 280

Background checks for gun purchases, 24, 26, 130, 161
Bad tendency test for speech restrictions, 180, 181
Bail, excessive, 353
Bailey v. Drexel Furniture Co. (1922), 15, 16, 30
Baird, William, 317

Baker, Charles, 223
Baker v. Carr (1962), 126, 223–226, 236
Bakke decision. *See Regents of the University of California v. Bakke*
Baldwin v. G.A.F. Seelig, Inc. (1935), 142
Bank of the United States, state taxation of. *See McCulloch v. Maryland*
Bankruptcy
  filing fees, 289
  state entities, recovering funds from, 133
Barbary Wars (1801–1805, 1815), 56
Barron, John, 148
Barron v. Baltimore (1833), 148, 299, 353
Barry v. United States ex rel. Cunningham (1929), 47
Batson v. Kentucky (1986), 379–381
Baze v. Rees (2008), 389, 394
Beachfront property, public access to, 310–311
Beatings and torture, confessions from, 367
Belmont; United States v., 100
Benton v. Maryland (1969), 355
Berman v. Parker (1954), 309–310
Betts, Smith, 376
Betts v. Brady (1942), 354, 376, 378
Bible reading in public schools, 216
Bicameral legislatures, 235
Bigamy conviction of Mormons, 209
Bill of Attainder Clause, 147–148
Bill of Rights. *See also specific amendments*
  application of, 353
  criminal procedure and, 352–353
  early development of, 174
  incorporation doctrine, 180, 354, 355
  states and, 147, 148–151
bin Laden, Osama, 2

Bipartisan Campaign Reform Act of 2002, 249
Bishop, Joseph W., Jr., 126
Bituminous Coal Conservation Act of 1935, 19–20, 76
Black, Hugo L.
  black armband war protests in school decision, 192
  contraceptive access decision, 296, 298, 315, 316
  exclusionary rule decision, 350
  flag salute decision, 184, 186
  gambling taxation decision, 31
  incorporation doctrine and, 354
  Pentagon Papers decision, 175–176, 202, 203, 204
  prayer in public schools decision, 217, 218
  public officials libel decision, 197, 200
  reapportionment decision, 238
  retirement of, 319
  right to counsel decision, 354, 376, 377
  right to counsel in capital cases decision, 356
  steel mills seizure decision, 89, 90
  on Tenth Amendment, 157
  transcripts for criminal defendants decision, 398
  transportation of parochial school children decision, 213
  U.S. military courts in Great Britain executive agreement decision, 44
  Voting Rights Act decision, 232
  wealth-based classifications decision, 289
Black Monday, 7, 20, 70, 76
Blackmun, Harry A.
  abortion rights decision, 319–320, 321–322, 323, 325–327

aliens as suspect
classification
decision, 286
antisodomy law
decision, 332
bankruptcy filing fee
decision, 289
campaign finance
decision, 248
capital punishment
decision, 383, 384,
386, 388
children of illegal aliens
public education
decision, 287
cigarette smokers'
damage suits
decision, 145
executive privilege
decision, 53
fetal protection policies
decision, 280
flag desecration
decision, 194–195
FSLA application to
states decision, 157,
158–159
independent counsel
decision, 74
legislative veto
decision, 78
nuclear-waste disposal
decision, 161
Pentagon Papers
decision, 174–175,
176, 203, 204
peyote use in religious
ceremonies
decision, 211, 212
pharmacist advertising
decision, 206
property tax funding
of schools decision,
290
racial redistricting
decision, 240
religious display
decision, 219
retirement of, 403
Supreme Court
appointment of, 64,
115–116
Blakely v. Washington
(2004), 395
Blow, Henry, 257
Board of Education v. Earls
(2002), 364
*Board of Education of
Oklahoma City
Public Schools v.
Dowell* (1991), 268
*Board of Education of
Westside Community
Schools v. Mergens*
(1990), 219

*Board of Trustees of
the University of
Alabama v. Garrett*
(2001), 168
Bodie v. Connecticut
(1971), 289
Bolivia and arms embargo,
99–100
Bolling v. Sharpe (1954),
266
Bolton; Doe v. (1973), 320
Bong Hits for Jesus, 177
Booth, Sherman, 135, 257
Bork, Robert H., 66, 115,
118–119, 126, 404,
414
Bosnia, sleeper cells in, 1
Boumediene v. Bush
(2008), 2–4, 7, 98,
115
Bowers v. Hardwick (1968),
331–333
Boyd v. United States
(1886), 354
Bradley, Joseph P.
Civil Rights Act
decision, 151, 261
Electoral Commission
of 1876 and, 228–229
railroad regulation
decision, 140
slaughterhouse
decision, 300
Supreme Court
appointment of, 10
Bradwell, Myra, 278
Bradwell v. Illinois (1873),
278
Brady Handgun Violence
Prevention Act of
1993, 130, 161
Brandeis, Louis D.
freedom of speech
decision, 179, 180,
181
National Labor
Relations Act
decision, 22
New Deal legislation
and, 20
press gag law decision,
182, 183
removal power
decision, 68, 69
Supreme Court
appointment of, 62,
119
Supreme Court's rules
of restraint and, 105
wiretapping decision,
363
Brandenburg, Clarence,
191
Brandenburg v. Ohio
(1969), 191

Branzburg v. Hayes (1972),
205
Braunfeld v. Brown (1961),
210
Breedlove, Nolen, 232
Breedlove v. Suttles (1937),
232
Brennan, William J., Jr.
abortion rights
decision, 321
academic freedom
decision, 191
campaign finance
decision, 248
capital punishment
decision, 383, 384,
385, 386, 387, 388
children of illegal aliens
public education
decision, 287,
288–289
contraceptive access
decision, 297,
317–318
exclusionary rule
decision, 350
executive privilege
decision, 54
flag desecration
decision, 194, 195
Fourth Amendment
search requirements
decision, 363
free exercise decision,
210
FSLA application to
states decision, 158
gender-based
classifications
decision, 282
independent counsel
decision, 74
land restrictions
by governments
decision, 310
legislative veto
decision, 78
minimum legal age for
drinking decision,
33
obscenity decision, 206
Pentagon Papers
decision, 175, 176,
202, 203
peyote use in religious
ceremonies
decision, 211, 212
prayer in public
schools decision,
217
press at criminal trials
decision, 205
public officials libel
decision, 197, 199,
200

reapportionment
decision, 236, 238
right to die decision,
341
sex discrimination
decision, 279
Supreme Court
appointment of, 62,
188
Taiwan mutual defense
treaty decision,
43–44
Brewer, David J.
income tax decision, 11
Pullman strike, federal
troop use decision,
59
Breyer, Stephen G.
affirmative action
decision, 273–274
death of wife of, 344
election of 2000
decision, 243, 244
enemy combatant
decision, 93, 94
exclusionary rule
decision, 365–366,
367
Gun-Free School Zone
Act decision, 162,
163
habeas corpus for
detainees decision,
3, 4, 401
handgun ban decision,
345
Indian Gaming
Regulatory Act
decision, 166
issue ads decision, 252
juvenile offender
capital punishment
decision, 393
line-item veto decision,
35
medical marijuana
decision, 28
mentally retarded
capital punishment
decision, 391
military commissions
decision, 97
Miranda decision, 373
online indecency
decision, 208
partial-birth abortion
decision, 328
physician-assisted
suicide decision,
343
presidential immunity
decision, 82, 84
private developers and
eminent domain
decision, 313

race-based school
assignment
decision, 275, 277
random drug tests in
schools decision,
364
Roberts Court and, 404,
427–430
school voucher
program decision,
215, 216
seat belt arrest
decision, 361
sentencing guidelines
decision, 395–396,
397
state immunity from
citizen suit decision,
130
Supreme Court
appointment of, 68,
327, 403, 427
Ten Commandments
display decision,
220, 222
Violence Against
Women Act
decision, 165
Brooker; United States v.
(2005), 395–397
Brown, Henry B.
income tax decision,
11, 12
public accommodation
segregation
decision, 263
*Brown v. Board of
Education* (1954),
126, 127, *253*, 256,
265, 265–269
Brown v. Mississippi
(1936), 367
Buchanan, James, 257
Buchanan v. Warley (1918),
253–254
Buckley, James L., 246
Buckley v. Valeo (1976),
245–249
Building for Supreme
Court, 109–111, *110*
Bullock v. Carter (1972), 291
Bunting v. Oregon (1917),
300
Burch v. Louisiana (1979),
379
Burger, Warren E.
abortion rights
decision, 319, 320
antisodomy law
decision, 333
campaign finance
decision, 248
capital punishment
decision, 383, 384,
386, 387, 388

children of illegal aliens
public education
decision, 287–288
criminal procedure
under, 127, 352
death of, 65–66
exclusionary rule and,
360, 363
exclusion of member of
Congress decision,
48
executive privilege
decision, 52, 53, 54,
80, 114
FSLA application to
states decision, 158
gender-based
classifications
decision, 280
impartial jury decision,
380
legislative veto
decision, 76, 77, 78
Miranda decision, 372
obscenity decision, 206
Pentagon Papers
decision, 174–175,
176, 202, 203, 204
press at criminal trials
decision, 205
property tax funding
of schools decision,
290
public opinion and the
Court leadership
of, 126
school desegregation
and, 269–271
Supreme Court
appointment of, 64,
115, 126
Taiwan mutual defense
treaty decision, 43
*Burlington Industries, Inc. v.
Ellerth* (1998), 286
Burma, sanctions on, 99
Burnside, Ambrose E.,
177–178
Burroughs v. United States
(1934), 245–246
Burton, Harold H.
steel mills seizure
decision, 90
transcripts for
criminal defendants
decision, 398, 399
Bush, George H.W.
federal court appoint-
ments of, 430
Supreme Court
appointments of,
66, 67, 129, 323, 404,
418, 421
Bush, George W. *See also
Bush v. Gore*

campaign finance
reform, 250
Court's judicial power
and, 115
enemy combatants and,
1, 2, 55, 84, 108, 404
on habeas corpus
writs for detainees
decision, 4
on Scalia and Thomas,
414
Supreme Court
appointments of,
3, 67, 119, 328,
403–404, 407, 430
war on terror, 1–4, 84,
91–98, 108
Bush v. Gore (2000), 223,
226, 242–245
Busing for school
desegregation, 127
Butler, Elizur, 109, 135
Butler, Pierce
as conservative, 17
double jeopardy
decision, 353
New Deal legislation
and, 20
public school
education
requirement
decision, 305
removal power
decision, 69
"Scottsboro Boys"
decision, 357, 358
Butler; United States v.
(1936), 32
Buxton, C. Lee, 295

Cable television,
regulation of, 205
*C. A. Carbone, Inc. v.
Town of Clarkstown*
(1994), 144
Cahn, Edmond, 107–108
Calandra; United States v.
(1974), 363
Calder v. Bull (1792), 147
Campaign finance
Buckley v. Valeo,
246–249
federal regulation of,
194, 245–249
McCain-Feingold Act,
249–252
"soft money" and
political ad
regulation, 249–252
Canada, migratory bird
treaty with, 44
Cantwell v. Connecticut
(1940), 210, 355
Capital punishment,
382–394

ban on, overturning,
352
jury selection in,
381–382
juvenile offenders, 388,
389, 392–394, 412,
417–418
major death penalty
decisions
(1972–2008), 389
mentally retarded
offenders, 388, 389,
390–391, 417
Cardozo, Benjamin N.
Commerce Clause
decision, 142
double jeopardy
decision, 353
National Labor
Relations Act
decision, 22
New Deal legislation
and, 20
NIRA unconstitu-
tionality decision,
17, 76
selective incorporation
and, 354
Social Security taxation
decision, 32
Supreme Court
appointment of, 62
Carlin, George, 206
Carolene; United States v.
(1938), 309
Carswell, G. Harrold,
64–65, 115
Carter, Jimmy
Iran hostage crisis and,
101–102
judicial appointments
by, 60, 424
Taiwan mutual defense
treaty and, 43–44
Carter v. Carter Coal Co.
(1936), 19–20, 21, 76
Cartoons. *See* Political
cartoons
Catron, John
Dred Scott decision,
258–259
Prize Cases, 37, 39
*Central Hudson Gas &
Electric Corp. v.
Public Service
Commission of New
York* (1980), 206
Chada, Jagdish Rai, 76–78
Chambers v. Florida
(1940), 367
Champion v. Ames (1903),
14
*Charles River Bridge v.
Warren Bridge*
(1837), 137

Chase, Salmon P.
  habeas corpus appeal
      decision, 103, 105
  impeachment of, 108,
      123–124
  on jurisdiction of
      Court, 122
  Legal Tender Act
      decision, 10
  military tribunals of
      civilians decision,
      59
  Supreme Court
      appointment of, 61
Cherokee Nation v. Georgia
    (1831), 135
Chicago v. Morales (1999),
    362
Chicago, Burlington &
    Quincy R.R. v.
    Chicago (1897), 153,
    355
Chicago, Milwaukee and
    St. Paul R.R. Co. v.
    Minnesota (1890),
    300
Child Labor Act of 1916, 15
Child Labor Tax Law of
    1919, 30
Child rapists, capital
    punishment
    prohibition for, 389,
    394
Children. See also Schools
    labor, 15–16, 17, 21, 23,
      30, 109
  online protection of,
      196, 206–209
  radio and television
      programming and,
      206
Children's Internet
    Protection Act of
    1998, 209
Chinese laundrymen,
    discriminatory
    enforcement
    or licensing
    requirements, 152
Chisholm v. Georgia
    (1793), 106, 124,
    133–134
Cigarette Labeling and
    Advertising Act of
    1965, 144–147
Cipollone v. Ligget Group,
    Inc. (1992), 144–147
Circuit riding, Supreme
    Court justices
    requirement for, 56
Citizens as detainees, 2,
    92–95
Citizen suits against
    states, 122, 130, 154,
    165, 168

City of. See name of
    specific city
Civil rights
  alienage, 286–289
  constitutionality of
      statutes, 13
  Dred Scott and,
      257–260
  early developments,
      256–263
  gay rights, 292–293
  public demonstrations,
      193
  racial equality,
      264–278
  "separate but equal,"
      256, 263–265
  sex discrimination,
      278–286
  slavery, 256–257
Civil Rights Act of 1865,
    120
Civil Rights Act of 1866,
    260, 266
Civil Rights Act of 1875,
    151–152, 261–262
Civil Rights Act of 1964,
    24, 120–122, 232,
    266, 271, 279
Civil Rights Cases (1883),
    151–152, 261–262,
    263, 266
Civil War
  Bill of Attainder Clause
      and, 147
  Congress and, 37–39,
      40
  presidency during,
      56–59
  slavery and, 260
  speech, freedom of,
      177–178
Clark, Tom C.
  contraceptive access
      decision, 296
  exclusionary rule
      decision, 350, 351,
      362
  Miranda decision, 371
  prayer in public
      schools decision,
      217
  public officials libel
      decision, 197
  reapportionment
      decision, 237, 238
  right to counsel
      decision, 368, 378
  steel mills seizure
      decision, 90
  transcripts for
      criminal defendants
      decision, 398
Classic; United States v.
    (1941), 245

Clear and present danger
    test for speech
    restrictions, 179,
    181, 188, 191
Cleburne, City of v.
    Cleburne Living
    Center, Inc. (1985),
    293
Cleveland, Grover, use
    of troops in labor
    conflicts by, 59–60
Cleveland Board of
    Education v. LaFleur
    (1974), 279
Clifford, Nathan
  Legal Tender Act
      decision, 10–11
  Prize Cases, 37, 39
Clinton, Bill
  Court's judicial power
      and, 114
  impeachment of, 84
  line-item veto and,
      34–36, 79
  presidential immunity
      and, 55, 82–84, 114
  Supreme Court
      appointments of, 68,
      327, 404, 424, 427
Clinton v. City of New York
    (1998), 34–36, 79
Clinton v. Jones (1997),
    82–84, 114
Clymer, Adam, 120–121
Coal industry, regulation
    of, 14, 19, 300–301
Coerced confessions, 367
Cohen, P. J. & M. J., 134–135
Cohens v. Virginia (1908),
    108, 134–135
Coker v. Georgia (1977),
    389
Cold War, 100, 126, 188
Cole v. Arkansas (1948),
    355, 376
Colegrove, Kenneth, 236
Colegrove v. Green (1946),
    224, 236
Colfax, Louisiana
    massacre, 227, 261
College admission
    policies. See
    University
    admissions, racial
    preferences in
Combatant Status Review
    Tribunals, 2
Commerce power
  check of expansive
      power of, 24–29
  Congress and, 14–29
  enumerated powers
      and, 8
  "Lochner Era," 14–17,
      141

New Deal and, 17–25
  revolution of 1937,
      17–20
  states and, 137,
      139–147
Commercial speech,
    regulation of,
    205–206
Commissions, military.
    See Military
    commissions
Common Article 3 of
    Geneva Convention,
    2, 95
Communications Decency
    Act of 1996, 206–209
Communist Party, 47, 126,
    181, 188
Community standards test
    for obscenity, 206,
    207
Compassionate Use Act of
    1996 (Calif.), 27–29
Compelling state interest
    standard, 210
Confidential sources, 196,
    205
Confirmation process
    for Supreme Court
    justices, 115–119
Congress, 7–50
  bicameral legislatures,
      235
  commerce power,
      14–29
  confirmation process,
      115–119
  congressional affairs,
      45–50
  congressional powers,
      14–50
  contempt of Congress,
      45, 47, 189
  Court's judicial power
      and, 115–124
  District of Columbia
      and, 235
  early developments,
      8–14
  election of members of,
      226–227
  fiscal powers, 8, 28–36
  foreign affairs, 8, 36,
      42–44
  internal affairs, 47–50
  investigative powers,
      45–47, 189
  Marshall Court, 8–9
  national defense, 8,
      36–42, 56
  relationship between
      branches of govern-
      ment and, 6–7
  reversals of rulings of,
      120–122

"self-inflicted wounds," 9–14
senators, election of, 226
voting for members of, 235–236
Conscription. *See* Draft law
Consent to search, 363. *See also* Searches and seizures
Constitutional amendments, reversal of rulings by, 120–122
Contempt of Congress, 45, 47, 189
Contraceptives, access to, 153, 295–298, 314–318
Contract Clause, 137–139, 299
Contribution limits in political campaigns, 245–249. *See also* Campaign finance
Cooley v. Board of Wardens of the Port of Philadelphia (1852), 139
Cooper v. Aaron (1958), 266, 267
Cooperative federalism, 157–159
"Copperhead" newspaper, 177
Corporate income tax, 30
Corrigan v. Buckley (1926), 254
Counsel, right to
appeals and, 398
early developments and, 353, 354, 356
effective assistance of counsel, 378–379
during interrogations, 367–369
public opinion and, 127
requirements of, 376–379
wealth-based classification and, 289
County of. See specific name of county
Courthouse, disabled access to, 168
Court-packing plan, *103*
Court's size and, 122
Evans and, 112, 113, 114
motivation for, 21, 62
public opinion and, 125–126

timeline of, 112–113
withdrawal of, 7
Cox Broadcasting Corp. v. Cohn (1975), 201
Craig v. Boren (1976), 282
Crèche scenes. *See* Religious displays
Crime and punishment, 349–402
appeals, 397–399, 402
criminal procedure revolution, 133, 352
early developments, 352–359
habeas corpus, 399–402
interrogation and confessions, 127, 352, 367–375
retroactive changes in criminal laws, 147
searches and seizures, 352, 360–367
sentencing, 382–397
trials, 127, 205, 354, 376–382
Crime Control and Safe Street Acts of 1968, 372
Criminal syndicalism, 181, 191
Crist v. Bretz (1978), 355
Crock, Arthur, 212–213, 254–256, 315–317, 398–399
Crosby v. National Trade Council (2000), 99
Crown, James E., 231
Cruel and unusual punishment. *See* Eighth Amendment
Cruikshank, William, 227
Cruikshank; United States v. (1870), 227–228, 261
Cruzan, Nancy Beth, 338
Cruzan v. Director, Missouri Department of Health (1990), 338–341
Cuba, extradition to, 99
Cummings, John, 147–148
Curfews for Japanese Americans during World War II, 85, 87
Currency, printing of, 9–10
Curtis, Benjamin R.
Dred Scott decision, 259
Missouri Compromise, 257
Curtiss-Wright Export Corp.; United States v., 99–100
Cushing, William, 134

Cyberspace, regulation of. *See* Internet

Dabney, Virginius, 231
Dames & Moore v. Regan (1981), 101–102
Darby Lumber Co.; United States v. (1941), 23, 157
Dartmouth v. Woodward (1819), 137
Daugherty, Harry M. & Mally S., 45–47
Davis, David
Electoral Commission of 1876 and, 228
military tribunals of civilians decision, 58
Davis v. Bandemer (1986), 239
Davis v. Federal Election Commission (2008), 8
Day, William R., 15
Deadly force, use by police officer, 362
Death penalty. *See* Capital punishment
Debs, Eugene V., 59, 178, 179
Debs, In re (1895), 59–60
Debs v. United States (1919), 179
The Decision of 1789, 55
Declaration of Independence, 256
De Jonge, Dirk, 181
De Jonge v. Oregon (1937), 181, 355
Delaware v. Prouse (1979), 362
Delay between arrest and arraignment, confession during, 367
Democratic Party, 230
Democratic-Republicans, 107
Dennis, Eugene, 188
Dennis v. United States (1951), 188
Dependent benefits, gender-classifications and, 280–282
Deportation proceedings, 76–78
Desegregation, 24. *See also* School desegregation
Detainees. *See* Enemy combatants and detainees
Detainee Treatment Act of 2005, 2, 3–4, 95

Dickerson v. United States (2000), 372–377
Die, right to, 338–341
Direct tax, 106
"Dirty bomb" plot, 92
Disabilities
access to courthouse, 168
discrimination and states, 168
equal protection and, 292
Disclosures, campaign spending, 245
Disparate impact theory of discrimination, 279
Displays, religious, 212, 219–222
District of Columbia, voting rights for, 235
Diversity jurisdiction, 106
Divorce filing fee, 289
Doe v. See name of opposing party
Dolan v. City of Tigard (1994), 311
Door-to-door solicitation, 210
Dormant Commerce Clause, 142
Dothard v. Rawlinson (1977), 279
Double jeopardy, 353, 354, 355, 399
Douglas, William O.
abortion rights decision, 319, 321
capital punishment decision, 382–383, 384
contraceptive access decision, 296, 297, 315, 316
counsel for indigent defendants decision, 354
eminent domain decision, 309, 310
exclusionary rule decision, 350
executive privilege decision, 54
flag salute decision, 184, 186, 188
gambling taxation decision, 31
impeachment proceedings and, 123–124
on jurisdiction of Court, 122
Pentagon Papers decision, 175, 176, 202, 203, 204

poll tax decision, 232
prayer in public schools decision, 218, 219
public officials libel decision, 197
reapportionment decision, 237, 238
steel mills seizure decision, 90
sterilization of habitual criminals decision, 307
stop and frisk decision, 363
transcripts for criminal defendants decision, 398
transportation of parochial school children decision, 213
Vietnam policy decision, 40
Douglas v. California (1963), 289
Draft cards, burning of, 191
Draft law, 40–42, 282
Dred Scott decision
    Due Process Clause and, 299
    Reconstruction Amendments and Civil Rights Acts, 122, 254, 257–260
    as "self-inflicted wound," 9
    Taney Court and, 61, 124, 257, 258, 259
Drugs
    automobile checkpoints for, 362
    testing, 364–365
Dual federalism, 154–157
Due Process Clause
    arms, right to keep and bear, 344–347
    contraceptives, right to, 153, 295–298, 314–318
    dual federalism and, 154
    early developments, 299–307
    economic rights, 152, 300
    eminent domain, *308*, 309–314
    equal protection and, 147, 151–153
    First Amendment and, 180
    gay rights, 289, 331–337
    incorporation doctrine, 355

indictments, 353
medical autonomy, 298, 338–344
in nineteenth century, 299–300
privacy rights, 314–344
property rights, 296, 300, 308–314
rational basis standard, 308–309
school desegregation, 266
substantive due process, 296–307
Duncan, Gary, 379
Duncan v. Louisiana (1968), 355, 379
Dunlap, David W., 292–293, 311
Dunn v. Blumstein (1972), 235
Dunne, Finely Peter, 126

Eckford, Elizabeth, *253*
E. C. Knight Co.; United States v. (1895), 14, 19, 140
Economically distressed cities, eminent domain for, 311–312
Economic rights and Due Process Clause, 152, 300
Economic sanctions, 99
Educational equity reforms, 153
Edwards v. Arizona (1981), 372
EEOC (Equal Employment Opportunity Commission), 285
Effective assistance of counsel, 378–379
Eichman; United States v. (1990), 196
Eighteen, right to vote at, 230, 234
Eighth Amendment, 153, 352, 353, 355, 382. *See also* Capital punishment, Sentencing
Eisenhower, Dwight D.
    executive privilege and, 79
    Supreme Court appointments of, 62, 188
Eisentadt v. Baird (1972), 317–318
Election disputes, congressional investigation of, 47
Electioneering communications, 249–252

Election of 1876, 228
Election of 2000. *See Bush v. Gore*
Electoral College, 226, 228, 242
Electoral Commission of 1876, 228–229
Electronic media, 205
Eleventh Amendment
    effect of, 122
    immunity from suit and, 168
    public opinion and adoption of, 106, 124
    ratification of, 134
    state sovereignty and, 154–156
    tribal gaming and, 165
Ellsberg, Daniel, 173, 201
Emancipation Proclamation, 260
Embargoes, 99
Emergency Price Control Act of 1942, 42, 85
Emerson, John, 257
Emerson, Thomas, 296
Eminent domain, *308*, 309–314
Employee Retirement Income Security Act of 1974 (ERISA), 144
Employers' Liability Cases, 14
Employers' liability for sexual harassment by supervisor, 286
Employment, aliens and, 286–287
Employment Division, Department of Human Resources of Oregon v. Smith (1990), 210
Endo, Ex parte (1942), 88
Enemy combatants and detainees. *See also* Habeas corpus; Military tribunals
    neutral decision maker requirement for, 2
    presidential power and, 1, 2, 55, 84, 108, 404
    Roberts Court and, 412, 424
    treatment of, 1–4, 55, 95, 115
Enforcement Act of 1870, 227, 229, 260–261
Enforcement Act of 1871, 261
Engel v. Vitale (1962), 216–219
Enmund v. Florida (1982), 389

Enumerated powers, 8, 31–32, 40
Environmental Protection Agency (EPA), 79
Equal Access Act of 1984, 219
Equal access to public facilities by religious groups, 216–219
Equal Employment Opportunity Commission (EEOC), 285
Equal Pay Act of 1963, 279
Equal Protection Clause, 147, 151–153
    alienage, 286–289
    appeals, criminal, 397–398
    contraceptives, access to, 317
    disability, 293
    Dred Scott decision and, 257–260
    early developments, 254, 256–263
    gay rights, 292–293
    impartial jury, right to, 379
    poll taxes, 232
    racial equality, 264–278
    reapportionment and, 224
    residency requirements, 292
    restrictive covenants, 254
    "separate but equal," 263–265
    sex discrimination, 278–286
    slavery, 256–257
    suspect classes, 286–293
    voting rights, 235, 239
    wealth-based classifications, 153, 289–291
Equal vote, right to, 235–245
ERISA (Employee Retirement Income Security Act of 1974), 144
Escobedo, Danny, 368
Escobedo v. Illinois (1964), 368–369
Espionage Act of 1917, 178
Establishment Clause, 212–222
    incorporation doctrine, 355
    parochial schools and, 212–216

prayer in public schools and, 216–219
religious displays and, 219–222
Ethics in Government Act of 1978, 73–75
Euclid v. Ambler Realty Co. (1926), 300
Everson v. Board of Education (1947), 212–213, 355
Excise tax, 30
Exclusionary rule. *See* Searches and seizures
Exclusion of member of Congress, 47–50
Executive agreements, 44, 100–102
Executive orders, 1, 85, 87, 89, 102, 260
Executive privilege, 51–55, 79–81, 114
Ex parte. See name of party
Ex Post Facto Clause, 147
Express advocacy, 249
Extradition, 352

Fairfax, Lord, 134
Fairfax's Devisee v. Hunter's Lessee (1813), 134
Fair Housing Act of 1968, 266
Fair Labor Standards Act of 1938 (FLSA), 23, 24, 129, 131, 157–159
Fairness doctrine, 205
Falkland Islands, 99
False advertising, 168
Family and Medical Leave Act of 1993 (FMLA), 168
Faragher v. City of Boca Raton (1998), 286
Farm relief program, 32–33
Faubus, Orval, 266
FCC v. Pacifica Foundation (1978), 206
FEC. *See* Federal Election Commission
Federal aid to states, conditions on, 33, 157
Federal Communications Commission (FCC), 205–206
Federal Corrupt Practices Act of 1925, 245
Federal Election Campaign Act Amendments of 1974, 7, 245
Federal Election Campaign Act of 1971, 245

Federal Election Commission (FEC), 245–249
Federal Election Commission v. Wisconsin Right to Life (2007), 250–252
Federalism, 154–159. *See also* States and the Court
Federalist Papers, 106
Federalists, 107, 177
Federal judge, impeachment of, 50
Federal law enforcement officers, drug testing of, 364
Federal Trade Commission (FTC), 7, 70–72, 412
Feingold, Russell, 249, 250
Felker v. Turpin (1996), 400–402
Felons, voting rights of, 235
Fetal protection policies and sex discrimination, 280
Field, Stephen J.
income tax decision, 11
trial of niece of, 181
Field v. Clark (1892), 75
Fifteenth Amendment
African Americans and, 149
enforcement of, 226, 227, 229
ratification of, 260
voting rights and, 230, 261
Fifth Amendment. *See also* Due Process Clause; Interrogation and confession
capital punishment and, 382
double jeopardy, 353, 354
early development under, 354
grand jury and, 353
incorporation doctrine, 153, 355
indictment under, 353
just compensation requirement, 148, 152–153, 154, 299
out-of-state businesses and, 152
property rights and, 299
provisions of, 353
Railroad Retirement Act of 1934 and, 20
school desegregation and, 266

self-incrimination, privilege against, 47
Waite and Fuller Courts and, 13
Filing fees for elections, 291
Filtering software for Internet, requirement of, 209
Fines, 289, 353
Firearms. *See* Gun control
Firing squads, 382
First Amendment, 153, 173, 430. *See also* Freedom of ideas
First English Evangelical Lutheran Church v. County of Los Angeles (1987), 310
Fiscal powers, 28–36
spending power, 29, 31–36
taxing power, 9, 11–13, 20, 28–31
Fitzgerald, A. Ernest, 81–82
Flag desecration, 177, 194–196, 412
Flag Protection Act of 1989, 196
Flag salute, 184–188, 210
Fletcher v. Peck (1810), 137
The Florida Star v. B.J.F. (1989), 201
Floyd, Jay, 319
FLSA. *See* Fair Labor Standards Act of 1938
FMLA (Family and Medical Leave Act of 1993), 168
Food
adulterated, 14, 309
prices, control of, 42
Food and Drug Administration, lawsuits for medical devices approved by, 147
Football games, prayer at public high schools, 219
Footnote 4 of *Carolene Products*, 309
Force Act of 1870, 260–261
Ford, Gerald R.
Douglas and, 123
federal court appointments of, 415
Supreme Court appointments of, 404, 411
Ford v. Wainwright (1986), 389

Foreign affairs
Congress and, 8, 36, 42–44
president and, 56, 98–102
Foreign governments, sovereignty of, 99
Foreign language, teaching in schools, 153, 301–303
Fortas, Abe
black armband war protests in school decision, 191, 193
confirmation process, 115, 116
criminal syndicalism decision, 191
Supreme Court appointment of, 62
Fourteenth Amendment. *See also* Due Process Clause; Equal Protection Clause
age discrimination and, 168
capital punishment and, 382
disability discrimination and, 168
early developments, 9, 261
felons' voting rights and, 235
First Amendment and, 180
impartial jury right and, 379
incorporation doctrine, 180, 354, 355
individual rights and, 147
post–Civil War Amendments and, 148–151
public accommodations and, 151–152, 263
racial segregation and, 254
ratification of, 260
reversal of legislative rulings and, 120
voting rights and, 227, 230, 232, 235
women's suffrage and, 226
Fourth Amendment. *See also* Searches and seizures
Breyer and, 430
incorporation doctrine and, 153, 354, 355

Waite and Fuller Courts and, 13
France, naval war with U.S. (1798–1800), 56
Francis, Willie, 382
Frank, Leo, 356, 397
Frank v. Mangum (1915), 356, 397, 399
Frankfurter, Felix
  exclusionary rule decision, 350, 362
  flag salute decision, 184–188
  gambling taxation decision, 31
  immunity for witness before Congress decision, 47
  incorporation doctrine and, 354
  NIRA unconstitutionality decision, 18
  prayer in public schools decision, 217
  reapportionment decision, 224, 236
  retirement of, 237
  school desegregation decision, 265
  steel mills seizure decision, 90
  transcripts for criminal defendants decision, 398, 399
Frazier-Lemke farm mortgage relief act, 20
Freedom of ideas, 173–222
  early developments, 177–183
  free press and states, 181–183
  incorporation doctrine, 355
  Internet and, 206–209
  obscenity and indecency, 196, 206
  press, freedom of, 196–209, 355
  religion, freedom of, 209–222, 355
  speech, freedom of, 183–196, 355
  speech and states, 179–181
  war and speech, 177–179
Freedom of information, 205
Freedom of Information Act of 1967, 205
Freedom of speech. *See* Freedom of ideas; Speech, freedom of

Free Exercise Clause, 209–212, 355
Freeman v. Pitts (1992), 268
Friedman, Barry, 127
Frontiero v. Richardson (1973), 280–282
Fugitive Slave Act of 1793, 256
Fugitive Slave Act of 1850, 135–136
Fuller, Melville W.
  Congress's authority over interstate commerce and, 14, 140
  constitutional amendment violations and, 13
  death of, 13
  income tax decision, 11, 12
Furman v. Georgia (1972), 382–385, 389

Gag law, 181–183
Gall v. United States (2007), 397
Gambling, taxation, 30–31
Gang members, laws targeting, 362
Garbage, interstate shipment of, 144
Garcia v. San Antonio Metropolitan Transit Authority (1985), 24, 157–1159
Gay rights
  Due Process Clause and, 298, 314, 331–337
  Kennedy and, 417
  sexual orientation discrimination, 292–293
Gender-based classifications, 280–283
Gender discrimination. *See* Sex discrimination
General Welfare Clause. *See* Spending power
Geneva Conventions, 1, 2, 95, 115, 412
German-language newspapers, wartime articles of, 179
German saboteurs during World War II, 86–87
Gerrymandering, 226, 236, 239
Gerstein v. Pugh (1975), 360

Gibbons v. Ogden (1824), 9, 139
Gideon, Earl, 376
Gideon v. Wainwright (1963), 127, 289, 376–378
Gillem, Alvin, 103
Ginsburg, Ruth Bader
  as ACLU attorney, 280
  affirmative action decision, 273
  antisodomy law decision, 335
  detainee decision, 3, 4, 94, 95, 401
  election of 2000 decision, 243, 244
  Gun-Free School Zone Act decision, 163
  habeas corpus for detainees decision, 3, 4, 401
  Indian Gaming Regulatory Act decision, 166
  issue ads decision, 252
  juvenile offender capital punishment decision, 392–393
  line-item veto decision, 35
  medical marijuana decision, 28
  mentally retarded capital punishment decision, 391
  military commissions decision, 97
  Miranda decision, 373
  online indecency decision, 208
  partial-birth abortion decision, 329, 330–331
  physician-assisted suicide decision, 343
  private developers and eminent domain decision, 313
  race-based school assignment decision, 277
  random drug tests in schools decision, 364–365
  Roberts Court and, 404, 424–427
  Scalia and, 414
  school voucher program decision, 215
  seat belt arrest decision, 361

sentencing guidelines decision, 394, 395, 397
  state immunity from citizen suit decision, 131
  Supreme Court appointment of, 68, 283, 327, 424
  Ten Commandments display decision, 222
  Violence Against Women Act decision, 165
  VMI women's admission decision, 283–285
Gitlow v. New York (1925), 153, 180–181, 355
Gobitas, Lillian & William, 184–188
Goldberg, Arthur J.
  contraceptive access decision, 297, 315, 316–317
  public officials libel decision, 197, 200
  reapportionment decision, 238
  right to counsel during interrogations decision, 368, 369
  Supreme Court appointment of, 62
Gold Cause Cases (1933), 10
Gonzales v. Carhart (2007), 153, 295, 324, 328–331
Gonzales v. Oregon (2006), 344
Gonzales v. Raich (2005), 27–29, 129, 168
Good faith exception to exclusionary rule, 363
Gore, Al. *See Bush v. Gore*
Goss v. Board of Education of Knoxville (1963), 267
Gouled v. United States (1921), 354
Graduation ceremonies, prayer at, 219
Graham, Fred P., 39–40, 48–50, 117, 174–177, 269–271, 296–298, 370–371, 383–385
Graham v. Richardson (1971), 286
Grand Central Terminal, preservation of, 310
Grandfather clause and voting rights, 229

Grand jury, 353, 363, 382
Granger Cases (1877), 300
Granholm v. Heald (2005), 142–144
Grant, Ulysses S., 10
Gratz v. Bollinger (2003), 272–275
Gray, Horace, 11
Gray v. Sanders (1963), 237
Great Britain. *See* United Kingdom
Green v. County School Board of New Kent County, Va. (1968), 266, 267
Greenhouse, Linda, 3–4, 25–26, 27–29, 43–44, 65–66, 76–78, 81–84, 93–95, 96–98, 101–102, 118–119, 130–133, 142–147, 157–169, 194–196, 207–209, 211–212, 214–216, 220–222, 240–241, 243–245, 251–252, 273–278, 283–285, 287–289, 312–314, 325–331, 334–344, 345–347, 360–362, 364–367, 372–374, 390–397, 400–402, 405–407, 418–420
Greenhouse gas regulation, 418
Gregg v. Georgia (1976), 384–388, 389
Grier, Robert C., 37, 38
Griffin v. Illinois (1956), 289, 397–398
Griswold, Estelle, 295
Griswold v. Connecticut (1965), 153, 295–298, 314, 315–317, 353, 355
Group homes, equal protection for, 293
Grovey v. Townsend (1935), 230
Grutter v. Bollinger (2003), 272–275
Guantánamo Bay Naval Base, Cuba. *See* Enemy combatants and detainees; Habeas corpus; Military tribunals
Guffey Act, 19, 20
Guinn v. United States (1915), 229
Gulf War, 37
Gun control. *See also* Arms, right to keep and bear; Second Amendment

background checks for purchases, 24, 26, 130, 161–163
handgun ban, 299, 344–347, 405, 410
school zones, firearms in, 7, 24–25, 129, 161–163
taxation on firearms, 30
Gun-Free School Zones Act of 1990, 7, 24–26, 129, 161–183

Habeas corpus
contempt of Congress and, 45
criminal proceedings, 399–402
detainees and, 2–4, 8, 92, 94, 95, 98, 115, 418
exclusionary rule and, 363
Lincoln's suspension of, 1, 56–57, 109
Reconstruction period and, 103–105, 122
Habeas Corpus Act of 1866, 103–105, 122
Hague, Frank, 184
Hague v. Committee for Industrial Organization (1939), 184, 355
Hamdan, Salim Ahmed, 2
Hamdan v. Rumsfeld (2006), 2, 95–98
Hamdi, Yaser, 2, 92–95
Hamdi v. Rumsfeld (2004), 2, 92, 115
Hamilton, Alexander foreign affairs and, 55–56
on judicial power, 106
spending power and, 32
Hammer v. Dagenhart (1918), 15–16, 23
Hampton v. Mow Sun Wong (1976), 287
Hans v. Louisiana (1890), 154
Harding, Warren G.
Supreme Court appointments of, 62
Teapot Dome Scandal and, 79
Hardwick, Michael, 331
Harlan, John Marshall, I
compensation for public use of private property decision, 153
on Congress's authority over interstate commerce, 14

due process decision, 300
income tax decision, 11, 12–13
public accommodation segregation decision, 263
railroad regulation decision, 155
Harlan, John Marshall, II
advocacy of forcible government overthrow decision, 189
contraceptive access decision, 295, 297, 315
divorce filing fee decision, 289
exclusionary rule decision, 350, 351
incorporation doctrine, 354
indictment requirement decision, 353
Miranda decision, 369–370, 371
Pentagon Papers decision, 174–175, 203, 204
prayer in public schools decision, 217
public officials libel decision, 197
reapportionment decision, 236, 237, 238
retirement of, 319
right to counsel decision, 368, 378
sex discrimination decision, 278
Supreme Court appointment of, 62, 188
transcripts for criminal defendants decision, 398
Harper v. Virginia State Board of Elections (1966), 232
Harris, Victor, 362
Harris v. Forklift Systems, Inc. (1993), 285
Harris v. McRae (1980), 323
Harris v. New York (1971), 372
Hatch Act of 1939, 33, 157
Hate crimes, 394
Haver v. Yaker (1870), 42
Hawaii Housing Authority v. Midkiff (1984), 310
Hayes, Rutherford B., 228

Haynsworth, Clement F., Jr., 64, 115
Health maintenance organizations (HMOs), 144
Heart of Atlanta Motel v. United States (1964), 24
Heller; District of Columbia v. (2008), 345
Helvering v. Davis (1937), 32
Henderson v. Wickham (1876), 139
Hepburn v. Griswold (1870), 9, 10
Herbers, John, 233–234
Hernandez v. Texas (1954), 379
Herndon v. Lowry (1937), 181
High-speed vehicular chases by police, 362
Highway funds and minimum drinking age, 33–34, 157
Hill, Anita, 421
Hirabayashi v. United States (1943), 85, 87, 88
HMOs (Health maintenance organizations), 144
Hodgson v. Minnesota (1990), 323, 324
Holmes, Oliver Wendell, Jr.
African American primary voting exclusion decision, 230
child labor decision, 15
foreign instruction in schools decision, 302, 303
freedom of speech decision, 179, 180, 181
migratory bird treaty decision, 44
public school education requirement decision, 305, 306
removal power decision, 68, 69
substantive due process decision, 300
Supreme Court appointment of, 61–62
taking of property decision, 301

Home Building and Loan Association v. Blaisdell (1934), 137–138
Homosexuality. *See* Gay rights
Hoover, Herbert, 62, 115, 116
Hostile work environment and sex discrimination, 285
Hours of work, limitations on, 14–17, 141, 278, 300
House Un-American Activities Committee, 47, 79
Housing, racial segregation in, 253–254, 264
Hoyt, Gwendolyn, 379
Hoyt v. Florida (1961), 278, 379
Hudson v. Michigan (2006), 352, 365
Hughes, Charles Evans
    African Americans exclusion as jurors decision, 356, 359
    assembly right decision, 181
    coerced confession decision, 367
    Court-packing plan and, 112, 113, 114
    flag salute decision, 187
    leadership of, 17, 23–24
    minimum wage decision, 308–309
    Minnesota mortgage moratorium law decision, 137, 138
    NIRA unconstitutionality decision, 17, 76
    NLRA decision, 22
    poultry regulation violations decision, 17, 76
    press gag law decision, 182, 183
    "Scottsboro Boys" decision, 358
    "self-inflicted wounds" speech of, 9, 11
Human Events (publication), 246
Humphrey's Executor v. United States (1935), 70–72
Hunter, David, 134
Hunter, Marjorie, 123–124
Hurtado, Joseph, 353
Hurtado v. California (1884), 353

Huston, Luther A., 30–31, 189–191
Hylton, Daniel, 106
Hylton v. United States (1796), 106

Illinois v. Gates (1983), 363
Immigration. *See also* Aliens
    deportation proceedings and, 76–78
Immunity, presidential, 55, 81–84, 114, 412
Immunity Act of 1954, 47
Impeachment
    Chase, Salmon P., and, 108, 123
    Clinton and, 84
    Douglas and, 123–124
    of federal judges, 50
    Johnson, Andrew and, 68, 103
    Nixon and, 81
    of Supreme Court justices, 123–124
    Warren and, 124
Impoundment of funds by president, 79
Income Tax Cases, 9, 11–13, 29–30
Incorporation doctrine, 153, 180, 300, 354, 355
Indecency and obscenity, 196, 206–209
Independent counsels, 73–75
Independent regulatory agencies, 7, 70–72
Indianapolis v. Edmund (2000), 362
Indian Gaming Regulatory Act of 1988, 130, 165–168
Indictment, requirement for, 353
Individual liberties, protection of, 1, 298. *See also* Liberty, property, and due process
Individuals and states
    Bill of Rights and post–Civil War amendments, 148–151
    equal protection and due process, 147, 151–153
    privacy, right to, 153
Inevitable discovery rule, 363
Information, freedom of, 205

Injuries to employees, liability for, 14
In re. See name of party
Intermediate scrutiny test, 282
Internal Security Act of 1950, 188
International law, use in interpreting U.S. Constitution, 414
Internet and freedom of ideas, 206–209
Interrogation and confession, 367–375
    coerced confessions, 367
    congressional committees, self-incrimination privilege and, 47
    counsel, right to, 367–369
    Fifth Amendment provisions and, 353
    incorporation doctrine, 355
    post-*Miranda* rulings, 127, 352, 367, 372–375
    road to *Miranda,* 352, 354, 367–371
Invasion of privacy lawsuits, 201
Investigative powers of Congress, 45–47, 189
Iran hostage crisis, 101–102
Iredell, James, 134
Issue ads, 250–252

Jackson, Andrew
    Court's judicial power and, 109
    federal vs. state rights and, 135
    Supreme Court appointments of, 61, 108
Jackson, Howell E., 11, 12
Jackson, Robert H.
    flag salute decision, 186, 187
    gambling taxation decision, 31
    school desegregation decision, 265
    steel mills seizure decision, 89–90
    transportation of parochial school children decision, 213
James v. Bowman (1903), 229

Japanese American internment, 1, *85,* 86, 87–88, 126, 264
Jaworski, Leon, 51
Jay, John, 134
Jay Cooke & Company, 45
J.E.B. v. Alabama ex rel. T.B. (1994), 379
Jefferson, Thomas
    Chase impeachment and, 123
    Marbury v. Madison and, 107
    Sedition Act and, 177
    war powers and, 56
Jehovah's Witnesses
    compulsory flag salute and, 184–188, 210
    door-to-door solicitation by, 210
    proselytizing activities, restrictions on, 210
Johnson, Andrew
    Civil Rights Act of 1866 veto and, 260
    impeachment of, 68, 103
    Reconstruction acts, vetoes of, 103
    removal power and, 68
Johnson, Gregory, 194–196
Johnson, Lyndon B.
    civil rights and, 232, 266
    Supreme Court appointments of, 62–64
Johnson v. Louisiana (1972), 379
Johnson v. Transportation Agency, Santa Clara County (1987), 272
Johnson v. Zerbst (1938), 356, 376
Jones, Paula, 82–84
Jones v. Alfred H. Mayer Co. (1968), 266
Jones & Laughlin Steel Corp.; NLRB v. (1937), 21, 22
Journalist's privilege, 205
Judge's sentencing in criminal trials, 382, 394–397
Judicial appointments, 60–68. *See also specific justices and presidents*
    confirmation process, 115–119
Judicial power, 103–127
    confirmation process, 115–119
    Congress vs., 115–124
    Court's beginnings, 106

early developments, 106–108
impeachment, 123–124
Marshall Court, 106–108
president vs., 108–115
public opinion and, 124–127
reversals of rulings of legislature, 120–122
size of Court, changing, 122
Judicial restraint, 105–106
Judiciary Act of 1789, 9, 105, 106, 122, 133, 134
Jurisdiction of Supreme Court, 103–105, 106, 107, 122, 133–134
Jurisdiction-stripping, 122
Jury
grand jury, 353, 363, 382
nonunanimous, 379
racial exclusion in, 356
right to impartial, 264, 353, 376, 379–382
sentencing and, 394–397, 399
six person, 379
Just compensation requirement, 152–153, 299
Justice Department, U.S., 254, 261
Juvenile offenders and capital punishment, 388, 389, 392–394, 412, 417–418

Kahn v. Shevin (1974), 280
Kahriger; United States v. (1953), 30–31
Kansas-Nebraska Act of 1854, 9
Katz v. United States (1967), 363
Kearns, Alexander, 350
Kelo, Susette, *308*, 312
Kelo v. City of New London (2005), *308*, 311–314
Kennedy, Anthony M.
abortion rights decision, 126, 325, 326, 417
affirmative action decision, 273
antisodomy law decision, 334, 335, 336
child rapist capital punishment decision, 394
cigarette smokers' damage suits decision, 145

election of 2000 decision, 242, 243, 244
enemy combatant decision, 3, 93, 404, 418
exclusionary rule decision, 366
flag desecration decision, 194
habeas corpus for detainees decision, 3, 418
independent counsel decision, 74
Indian Gaming Regulatory Act decision, 166
issue ads decision, 252
juvenile offender capital punishment decision, 392, 393, 394
line-item veto decision, 35
medical marijuana decision, 27, 28
mentally retarded capital punishment decision, 391
military commissions decision, 96, 97
Miranda decision, 373
nuclear-waste disposal decision, 161
online indecency decision, 208
partial-birth abortion decision, 328, 330, 331
partisan gerry-mandering decision, 239
peyote use in religious ceremonies decision, 212
physician-assisted suicide decision, 343
prayer at public school graduation ceremonies decision, 219
private developers and eminent domain decision, 313, 314
race-based school assignment decision, 256, 275, 276–278
racial redistricting decision, 234, 239, 240
random drug tests in schools decision, 364

right to die decision, 339
Roberts Court and, 404, 405–407, 414–418, 433
school voucher program decision, 215
seat belt arrest decision, 361
sentencing guidelines decision, 394, 395
sexual orientation discrimination decision, 292
soft money decision, 250
on state immunity for private suits, 168
state immunity from citizen suit decision, 130, 132
Supreme Court appointment of, 66, 323, 414
Ten Commandments display decision, 221
Violence Against Women Act decision, 165
voting record of, 67
wine shipment direct to customers decision, 143
Kennedy, John F., 62
Kennedy v. Louisiana (2008), 389, 394
Keyishian v. Board of Regents (1967), 191
Kilbourn, Hallett, 45
Kimel v. Florida Board of Regents (2000), 168
King, Martin Luther, Jr., 232. *See also New York Times Co. v. Sullivan* (1964)
Kirkpatrick, David D., 251–252
Klopfer v. North Carolina (1967), 355
Knock and announce searches, 365–367, 433
Knowles v. Iowa (1998), 365
Knox v. Lee (1871), 10
Korean War
Congress and, 37
president and, 89–91
steel mills seizure during, 55, 84, 89–91, 114
Korematsu v. United States (1944), 85, 87–88, 264

Kramer v. Union Free School District (1969), 235
Kras; United States v. (1973), 289
Krock, Arthur, 18–19, 21–22, 212
Ku Klux Klan, 191, 229, 260
Ku Klux Klan Act of 1871, 261
Kyllo v. United States (2001), 364

Labor conflicts, 53–60, 125
Labor-Management Relations Act of 1947, 89, 245
Labor unions
campaign donations, 245
Communist party membership, 188
Lamar, Joseph R., 75
Land-use restrictions by governments, 310
Law enforcement powers of president, 53–60, 75–79
Lawrence v. Texas (2003), 334–337
Lawyers, for indigent defendants, 127
L. Cohen Grocery Co.; United States v. (1921), 85
League of United Latin American Citizens v. Perry (2006), 234, 239
Lee v. Weisman (1992), 219
Legal Counsel, Office of, 73
Legal Tender Act of 1862, 9–11
Legal Tender Cases (1870, 1871), 10–11, 42
Legislative veto, 76–78
Lemon v. Kurtzman (1971), 214
Lend-Lease Agreement of 1942, 100
Leon; United States v. (1984), 363
Lethal injections, 389, 394
Lever Food and Fuel Control Act of 1917, 85
Lewis, Anthony, 197–201, 217–219, 268–269, 377–378
Lewis, Neil A., 344, 408–410, 421–426, 431–433
Libel, 196, 197–201
Libertarian National Committee, 250

Liberty, property, and due process, 295–347
    contraceptives, access to, 295–298
    early developments, 299–307
    gay rights, 298, 331–337
    keep and bear arms, right to, 344–347
    in "Lochner Era," 300–308
    medical autonomy, 298, 338–344
    in nineteenth century, 299–300
    privacy rights, 314–344, 355
    property rights, 308–314
Limited pat-down search, 363
Lincoln, Abraham
    Court's judicial power and, 109
    habeas corpus, suspension of, 1, 56–57, 109
    military tribunals of civilians and, 58–59
    slavery and, 124, 259, 260
    Supreme Court appointments of, 61
    war-making powers, exercise by, 37, 56, 109
Line Item Veto Act of 1996, 34–36, 79
Literacy tests, 229, 232, 235, 261, 264
Local government franchising of cable television, 205
Lochner v. New York (1905), 16, 21, 141, 300
"Lochner Era"
    commerce party in, 14–17, 141
    due process in, 300–308
Lockett v. Ohio (1978), 389
Loftus, Joseph A., 90–91
Lopez; United States v. (1995), 24–26, 27, 129, 161
Lottery tickets, prohibition of interstate trafficking in, 14, 134–135
Louisiana ex rel. Francis v. Resweber (1947), 355, 382
Louisiana Purchase, 257
Low-level radioactive waste, 159

Loyalty oaths, 147–148, 188, 191
Lubin v. Parish (1974), 291
Lucas v. South Carolina Coastal Council (1992), 311
Luther v. Borden (1849), 227

Madison, James
    foreign affairs and, 56
    Marbury v. Madison and, 107
    Ninth Amendment, 299
    Sedition Act and, 177
    spending power and, 31–32
    war powers and, 56
Magna Carta, 299
Maher v. Roe (1977), 323, 324
Majority-minority districts, 234, 239–242
Mallory v. United States (1957), 367
Malloy v. Hogan (1964), 355, 368
Manufacturing as commerce, 140
Mapp v. Ohio (1961), 349–352, 355, 362
Marbury, William, 107
Marbury v. Madison (1803), 9, 106–107, 108
Margolick, David, 427–429
Marijuana, 30. *See also* Medical marijuana
Marshall, John
    Bank of the United States state taxation decision, 154
    on Bill of Rights and states, 148
    as Chief Justice, 107–108
    Commerce Clause and, 139
    Congress and Court during term of, 8–9
    Contract Clause decision, 137
    federal vs. state rights and, 134, 135
    Jackson and, 108, 109
    judicial power and, 106–108
    jurisdiction of Supreme Court and, 107
    public opinion and, 124
    review of state laws and, 133
    slavery decision, 257
    Supreme Court appointment of, 61

Marshall, Thurgood, *61*
    abortion rights decision, 321
    campaign finance decision, 248
    capital punishment decision, 383, 384, 385, 386, 387, 388
    children of illegal aliens and public education decision, 287
    executive privilege decision, 54
    flag desecration decision, 194
    FSLA application to states decision, 158
    impartial jury decision, 381
    independent counsel decision, 74
    legislative veto decision, 78
    as NAACP counsel, 264–265, *265*
    Pentagon Papers decision, 175, 176, 202, 203
    peyote use in religious ceremonies decision, 211, 212
    property tax funding of schools decision, 289, 290, 291
    residency requirement to vote decision, 235
    retirement of, 272, 403
    Supreme Court appointment of, 62–64
    Taiwan mutual defense treaty decision, 43
Martin, Denny, 134
Martin v. Hunter's Lessee (1816), 134
Maryland v. Wirtz (1968), 157
Mass Act of 1910, 14–15
Massiah v. United States (1964), 367–368
Matthews, Stanley, 353
Maximum-hour statutes, 14–17, 141, 278, 300
Mayor of New York v. Miln (1837), 139
McCain, John, 249, 250
McCain-Feingold Act of 2002, 249–252
McCardle, William, 103
McCardle, Ex parte, 103–105, 122
McCarran Act of 1950, 188
McCarthy, Eugene L., 246

McCarthy, Joseph R., 79
McCleskey v. Kemp (1987), 388, 389
McConnell, Mitch, 250
McConnell v. Federal Election Commission (2003), 250
McCray v. United States (1904), 30
McCreary County v. American Civil Liberties Union (2005), 220–222
McCulloch v. Maryland (1819), 8–9, 108, 154
McFadden, Robert D., 411–412
McGrain v. Daugherty (1927), 45–47, 79
McKenna, Joseph, 229
McKinley, William, assassination of, 180
McKinley Tariff Act of 1890, 75
McLaurin, George, 254
McLaurin v. Oklahoma State Regents (1950), 254, 255
McLean, John, 259
McNabb v. United States (1943), 367
McReynolds, James C.
    as conservative, 17
    Court-packing plan and, 113
    foreign instruction in schools decision, 301–303
    New Deal legislation and, 20
    public school education requirement decision, 304–305
    removal power decision, 68, 69, 70, 72
    "Scottsboro Boys" decision, 357, 358, 359
    Supreme Court appointment of, 62
Medical autonomy
    physician-assisted suicide, 298, 341–344
    right to die, 338–341
Medical devices, personal injury suits against makers of, 147
Medical marijuana, 14, 27–29, 129, 168
Medicare benefits, aliens and, 286

Meditation or voluntary prayer in public schools, 219

Men, sexual harassment claims by, 285–286

Menorah, displays of. *See* Religious displays

Mentally retarded individuals
  adults, equal protection for, 293
  offenders, capital punishment and, 388, 389, 390–391, 417

Meritor Savings Bank v. Vinson (1986), 285–286

Merryman, John, 56, 109

Merryman, Ex parte (1863), 56–57, 109

Mexican War, 37

Mexico, government of, 99

Meyer v. Nebraska (1923), 153, 301

Michael M. v. Superior Court of Sonoma County (1981), 282

Michigan v. Mosley (1975), 372

Michigan v. Tucker (1974), 372

Michigan Department of State Police v. Sitz (1990), 362

Midwest Oil Co.; United States v. (1915), 75

Miers, Harriet, 404, 430

Migratory Bird Treaty Act of 1918, 44

Military Commission Act of 2006, 2–4, 7, 98, 115

Military commissions, 1, 92, 95, 115

Military draft. *See* Draft law

Military Order No. 1, 92

Military Selective Service Act of 1967, 42

Military tribunals
  civilians during Civil War, 58–59
  enemy combatants and, 1–4, 92–98, 115
  Stevens and, 410
  World War II and, 86–87

Miller, Samuel F.
  Commerce Clause decision, 139–140
  contempt of Congress decision, 45
  military tribunals of civilians decision, 59

railroad regulation decision, 140

Miller, William E., 223–224

Miller v. California (1973), 206

Miller v. Johnson (1995), 242

Miller; United States v. (1939), 345

Milligan, Lambdin, 58

Milligan, Ex parte (1866), 58–59, 103

Milliken v. Bradley (1974), 156, 267, 271

Minersville School District v. Gobitis (1940), 184–188

Minimum wage
  for employees engaged in interstate commerce, 23
  for female workers and children, 16, 17, 21
  property rights, 308–309
  striking down of, 141, 300
  upholding of, 114, 300

Minor v. Happersett (1874), 227, 261, 278

Minority set-asides, 272

Minton, Sherman
  teachers as members of subversive organizations decision, 188
  transcripts for criminal defendants decision, 398

Miranda v. Arizona (1966), 127, *349*, 352, 369–371. *See also* Interrogation and confession

Missouri v. Holland (1920), 44

Missouri v. Jenkins (1990), 156–157, 267

Missouri v. Jenkins (1995), 268, 272

Missouri ex rel. Gaines v. Canada (1938), 254

Missouri Compromise, 9, 257–260

Missouri Women's Suffrage Association, 227

Mitchell v. Helms (2000), 214

M.L.B. v. S.L.J. (1996), 289

Mobile, City of v. Bolden (1980), 234

Molotsky, Irvin, 413–414

Moment of silence in public schools, 219

Monopolies, prohibition of, 14

Monson, Diane, 27, 28

Moore v. Dempsey (1923), 356

Mora v. McNamara (1967), 91

Morehead v. New York (1936), 141, 300

Morgan v. Virginia (1946), 24

Mormon, bigamy conviction of, 209

Morrison, Alexia, 73

Morrison; United States v. (2000), 27, 161

Morrison v. Olson (1987), 73–75

Morse v. Frederick (2007), 177

The Most Democratic Branch (Rosen), 127

Motor vehicles. *See also* Automobile stops by police
  automakers' failure to install air bags, suits against, 147

Mugler v. Kansas (1887), 300

Muller v. Oregon (1908), 17, 278

Municipal economic redevelopment, 310

Murphy, Frank
  counsel for indigent defendants decision, 354
  flag salute decision, 184, 186, 188
  transportation of parochial school children decision, 213

Muslims, 1, 2

Myanmar, sanctions on, 99

Myers, Frank, 68

Myers v. United States (1926), 68–70

NAACP Legal Defense Fund, 382

National Association for the Advancement of Colored People (NAACP), 115, 253, 254, 264

National defense
  Congress and, 8, 36–42, 56
  war powers and president, 55, 56, 84–98

National Firearms Act of 1934, 30, 345

National Industrial

Recovery Act of 1933 (NIRA), 7, 17–19, 76, 86

National Labor Relations Act of 1935, 21–24, 114

National Labor Relations Board, 21

National League of Cities v. Usery (1976), 24, 157

National Recovery Administration (NRA), 17, *19*

National Right to Life Committee, 250–252

National Treasury Employees Union v. Von Raab (1989), 364

Native Americans
  federal jurisdiction and, 135
  gaming, 106
  peyote use in religious ceremonies, 210–212
  right to self-government, 109

Naval war between U.S. and France (1798–1800), 56

Near, Jay, 182

Near v. Minnesota (1931), 181–183

Nebraska, unicameral legislature in, 235

Necessary and Proper Clause, 8

Neely v. Henkel (1901), 99

Negative Commerce Clause, 142

Nelson, Samuel
  Dred Scott decision, 258
  Legal Tender Act decision, 10
  Prize Cases, 38–39

Neutral decision maker requirement for detainees, 2

Nevada Department of Human Resources v. Hibbs (2003), 168

Newberry v. United States (1921), 245

New Deal and Court
  Black Monday, 7, 20, 70, 76
  congressional powers and, 17–25, 32–33
  Court-packing plan and, 62, 114
  Court's reversal of rulings by legislature, 7

Revolution of 1937,
17–20, 183–188
states and Commerce
Clause and, 142
New York v. United States
(1992), 159–161
*New York Times Co. v.
Sullivan* (1964), 196,
197–201, *198*
*New York Times Co. v.
United States* (1971),
173, 173–177, 181,
182, 201–204
Nineteenth Amendment,
17, 226, 227, 278
Ninth Amendment, 296,
299, 315, 355
NIRA. *See* National
Industrial Recovery
Act of 1933
Nix v. Williams (1984), 363
Nixon, Lawrence A., 230
Nixon, Richard M.
Court's judicial power
and, 114
executive privilege,
assertion of, 51–55,
79–80, 114
federal court
appointment of,
410
impeachment of, 81
impoundment of funds
by, 79
law and order and, 372
Pentagon Papers, 201
presidential immunity
and, 81–82
presidential papers
of, 81
Supreme Court
appointments of,
64–66, 115–116, 117,
126, 319, 372
War Powers Act and,
39, 91
*Nixon v. Administrator,
General Services
Administration*
(1977), 81
Nixon v. Condon (1932),
230
Nixon v. Fitzgerald (1982),
81–82
Nixon v. Herndon (1927),
230
Nixon; United States v.
(1974), 51–54, 80–81,
114
Nixon v. United States
(1993), 50
*NLRB v. See name of
opposing party*
No-knock searches,
365–367, 433

*Nollan v. California Coastal
Commission* (1987),
310–311
Norris v. Alabama (1953),
356–359, 379
North Carolina v. Pierce
(1969), 399
*North Carolina State Board
of Education v.
Swann* (1971), 267
NRA. *See* National
Recovery
Administration
Nuclear-waste disposal,
159
Nude dancing, restrictions
on, 194
Nullification Ordinance of
1832, 135

O'Brien, David, 191
O'Brien; United States v.
(1968), 191
Obscenity and indecency,
196, 206–209
O'Connor, Sandra Day,
282
abortion rights
decision, 126,
325–327, 403, 417
affirmative action
decision, 272, 273,
274, 275
antisodomy law
decision, 333, 335,
336
automobile stop
decision, 362
children of illegal
aliens and public
education decision,
288
cigarette smokers'
damage suits
decision, 145
detainee decision, 2,
92, 93, 94, 95
election of 2000
decision, 242, 243,
244
enemy combatant
decision, 92, 93
exclusionary rule
decision, 366
flag desecration
decision, 195
gender-based
classifications
decision, 282
Gun-Free School Zone
Act decision, 162
impartial jury decision,
380, 381
independent counsel
decision, 74

Indian Gaming
Regulatory Act
decision, 166
ineffective assistance
of counsel decision,
378–379
judicial positions of,
403, 404
juvenile offender
capital punishment
decision, 392, 393
legislative veto
decision, 78
line-item veto decision,
35
medical marijuana
decision, 29
mentally retarded
capital punishment
decision, 391
minimum legal age for
drinking decision,
33, 34
Miranda decision, 373
nuclear-waste disposal
decision, 159,
160–161
online indecency
decision, 208
peyote use in religious
ceremonies
decision, 210,
211–212
physician-assisted
suicide decision,
341, 342, 343
private developers and
eminent domain
decision, 313, 314
racial redistricting
decision, 239, 240,
241
random drug tests in
schools decision,
364
Rehnquist's death and,
404
retirement of, 67, 403
right to die decision,
339, 341
school voucher
program decision,
215
seat belt arrest
decision, 360–361
sentencing guidelines
decision, 394, 395
soft money decision,
250
state immunity from
citizen suit decision,
131
Supreme Court
appointment of,
66–67, 282, *282*, 323

Ten Commandments
display decision,
220–221
Violence Against
Women Act
decision, 165
VMI women's admis-
sion decision, 284
voting record of, 67
Oelsner, Lesley, 246–249,
385–388
*Ohio v. Akron Center for
Reproductive Health*
(1990), 323, 324
*Oklahoma v. Civil Service
Commission* (1947),
33, 157
Oliver, In re (1948), 355, 376
Olmstead v. United States
(1928), 363
Olson, Theodore B., 73,
242, 250
Omnibus Crime Control
and Safe Streets Act
of 1968, 363
*Oncale v. Sundowner
Offshore Services,
Inc.* (1998), 285–286
"One person, one vote,"
224, 237–239
Orden v. Perry (2005),
220–222
Oregon, assisted-suicide
statute, 344
Oregon v. Mitchell (1970), 235
Original jurisdiction of
Court, 106, 107
Original meaning, 414
Out-of-state businesses,
prohibition of
discrimination
against, 142–144
Oyama v. California
(1948), 286

PACs (political action
committees), 249
Padilla, Jose, 92–95
Palko v. Connecticut
(1937), 354
*Panama Refining Co. v.
Ryan* (1935), 17, 76
*Papachristou v. City of
Jacksonville* (1972),
362
Paraguay, arms embargo
and, 99–100
Parental notification
for abortions for
minors, 323, 324
*Parents Involved in
Community Schools
v. Seattle School
District No. 1* (2007),
153, 268, 275

Parker, John J., 115, 116
Parker v. Davis (1871), 10
Parochial schools. *See* Schools
Partial-birth abortion, 295, 298, 328–331, 418, 430
Partial-Birth Abortion Ban of 2003, 328
Partisan gerrymandering, 226, 239
Pasadena City Board of Education v. Spangler (1976), 267
Pat-down search, 363
Patent infringement, 168
Patterson v. Alabama (1953), 356–359
Payton v. New York (1980), 362
Pear, Robert, 34–36
Peckham, Rufus W., Jr.
citizen suits against state decision, 154–156
due process and economic rights decision, 152
on privileges and immunities and states, 148
railroad regulation decision, 155, 156
substantive due process decision, 300
Penn Central Transportation Co. v. New York City (1978), 310
Pennsylvania Coal Co. v. Mahon (1922), 300–301
Penry v. Lynaugh (1989), 389
Pension-funding obligations, retroactive, 139
Pentagon Papers, 173–177, 181, 182, 196, 201–204
Penumbra of Bill of Rights, 296
Peremptory challenges, 379
Personal injury lawsuits, federal preemption and, 144–147
Petition, right to, 174, 355
Peyote use in religious ceremonies, 210–212
Pharmacists, price advertising by, 206

Philadelphia v. New Jersey (1978), 144
Phillips v. Martin Marietta Corp. (1971), 279
Phoenix v. Kolodziejski (1970), 235
Phone booths, listening devices in, 363
Physician-assisted suicide, 298, 341–344
Pierce v. Society of Sisters (1925), 153, 304–305
Plain view, use of evidence found in, 365
Planned Parenthood, 318
Planned Parenthood of Southeastern Pennsylvania v. Casey (1992), 324, 325–328
Pledge of Allegiance. *See* Flag salute
Plessy v. Ferguson (1896), 125, 263, 265
Plyler v. Doe (1982), 287–289
Poe v. Ullman (1961), 295
Pointer v. Texas (1965), 355
Police power, 14, 137
Political action committees (PACs), 249
Political ad regulation, 249–252
Political cartoons
Court-packing plan, *103*
"Mr. Dooley," 126
New Deal and Court, *7*
president and Court, *51*
Political participation rights, 223–252. *See also* Fifteenth Amendment; Women
African American voting rights, 226–234, 261, 264, 280
ballot barriers, 229
Bush v. Gore and, 223, 226, 242–245
campaign finance, 245–249
Civil Rights Act and, 232
contested 1876 election and post-Reconstruction voting barriers, 228–229
early developments, 226–229
eighteen, right to vote at, 230, 235

equal vote, right to, 235–245
felons, voting rights of, 235
partisan gerrymandering and racial redistricting, 226, 234, 236, 239–242
poll taxes, 232, 261, 264, 291
post–Civil War expansion of franchise, 226, 227–228
reapportionment, 236–239
"soft money" and political ad regulation, 249–252
spend, right to, 245–252
states and enfranchisement, 235
voting rights, 153, 230–235, 254, 261, 278
Political questions, 99, 227
Pollock v. Farmers' Loan & Trust Co. (1895), 9, 11–13, 29–30
Poll taxes, 232, 261, 264, 291
Polygamy, prohibition on, 209
Poultry, violations of regulations on, 17–19, 76
Powell, Adam Clayton, Jr., 47–50
Powell, Lewis F., Jr.
abortion rights decision, 319, 321, 323
affirmative action decision, 271, 273
antisodomy law decision, 333
campaign finance decision, 248
capital punishment decision, 384, 386
children of illegal aliens and public education decision, 287, 288
confidential source decision, 205
executive privilege decision, 53
impartial jury decision, 379, 380, 381
legislative veto decision, 78

presidential immunity decision, 81
property tax funding of schools decision, 289, 290–291
race-based school assignment decision, 278
Supreme Court appointment of, 64, 319
Taiwan mutual defense treaty decision, 43
Powell v. McCormack (1969), 47–50
Powell v. Texas (1968), 382
Prayer in public schools and equal access, 212, 216–219
Preemption, 144–147
Pregnancy and sex discrimination, 279–280
Pregnancy Discrimination Act of 1978, 279–280
Presentment Clause, 34, 55
President, 51–102. *See also specific presidents*
campaigns, public financing of, 246–249
Court's judicial power and, 108–115
early developments, 53–60
executive powers, 68–79
executive privilege, 79–81
foreign policy, 98–102
immunity of, 55, 81–84, 412
law enforcement, 53–60, 75–79
powers of, 60–102
privilege and immunity, 79–84
removal power, 68–75
Supreme Court appointments and, 60–69
war powers, 55, 56, 84–98
wartime actions, review of, 40
Presidential Records Act of 1978, 81
Press, freedom of, 196–209. *See also* Freedom of ideas
actual malice standard for libel, 201
advertising, 205–206
Bill of Rights, 174

confidential sources and freedom of information, 196, 205
electronic media, 205
First Amendment and, 173
gag law, 181–183
incorporation doctrine, 355
Internet and, 196, 206–209
libel, 197–201
obscenity and indecency, 196, 206–209
Pentagon Papers, 173–177, 181, 182, 201–204
prior restraint, 182
private information made public, 201
war and, 177–179
Price Administration, Office of, 42
Price controls, 42, 85–86
Primary elections, regulation of, 230, 245, 291
Printz v. United States (1997), 130, 161
Prior restraint, 182. *See also* Pentagon Papers
Prison inmates, press interviews of, 205
Privacy, invasion of, 201
Privacy rights, 153, 296, 314–344, 355. *See also* Abortion rights; Contraceptives, access to
Private development, eminent domain for, 312–314
Private individuals, libel standard for, 201
Private property taken for public use, 152–153
Privileges and Immunities Clause, 148, 149, 292, 299
Prize Cases (1863), 37–39, 56
Property ownership requirement to vote, 235
Property rights
eminent domain, *308*, 309–314
rational basis standard, 308–309
Property tax funding of schools, 289–291
Prudential rules, 105

Public accommodations, 24, 151–152, 263
Public demonstrations, 184, 193, 194
Public events, prayer at, 219
Public individuals, libel standard for, 196, 197–201
Publicity Act of 1910, 245
Public opinion and the Court, 124–127, *125*
Burger Court, 126
Civil War to New Deal, 125–126
decision and, 126–127
early views of Court, 124
Warren Court, 126
Public places, right to assemble in, 184
Public schools. *See* Schools
Pulley v. Harris (1984), 388
Pullman strike, 59–69
Pure Food and Drug Act of 1906, 14
Purkett v. Elem (1995), 381

Quinlan, Karen Ann, 338
Quirin, Ex parte (1942), 87

Race-based school assignments, 153, 256, 264, 275–278, 430, 433
Racial equality, 264–278
affirmative action, 271–275
public accommodations, 24, 151–152, 263
race-based school assignments, 153, 256, 264, 275–278, 430, 433
school segregation, 264–271
segregation, 24, 125, 253–254
Racial preferences, 423–424
Racial redistricting, 234, 239–242
Racketeer Influenced and Corrupt Organizations Act of 1970 (RICO), 25–26
Radioactive waste, state governments and, 24
Radio and television stations, regulation of, 205
Raich, Angel, 27, 28, *129*

Railroad regulation, 140, 154–156, 263, 300
Railroad Retirement Act of 1934, 20
Rape victims, publication of name of, 201
Rasul v. Bush (2004), 2, 94, 95, 115
Rational basis standard, 308–309
Reagan, Ronald
Bork nomination and, 118–119
Kennedy appointment by, 3, 116, 414, 415
O'Connor appointment by, 66–67, 282
Rehnquist as Chief Justice under, 66
reshaping of Court by, 64, 129, 323
Scalia appointment by, 404, 413
Reapportionment and redistricting, 153, 223–226, 234, 236–242
Reconstruction Act, 122
Redistricting. *See* Reapportionment and redistricting
Red Lion Broadcasting Co. v. FCC (1969), 205
Reed, Roy, 63–64
Reed, Sally, 280
Reed, Stanley F.
African American primary voting exclusion decision, 230
executive privilege, phrase of, 79
flag salute decision, 186, 188
incorporation doctrine and, 354
school desegregation decision, 265
transcripts for criminal defendants decision, 398
transportation of parochial school children decision, 213
Reed v. County Commissioners of Delaware County, Pa. (1928), 47
Reed v. Reed (1971), 280
Reese; United States v. (1876), 227, 261
Regents of the University of California v. Bakke (1978), 271, 272

Regulatory takings claims, 311
Rehnquist, William H.
abortion rights decision, 319, 320, 321, 325
affirmative action and, 272, 273
antisodomy law decision, 333, 334, 336
automobile stops by police decision, 362
campaign finance decision, 248
capital punishment decision, 383, 384, 386, 387, 388
children of illegal aliens and public education decision, 288
cigarette smokers' damage suits decision, 145
commerce clause and, 14
criminal procedure under, 352
death of, 67, 168–169, 403–404, 407
death of wife of, 344
draft exemption for women decision, 42
election of 2000 decision, 242, 243
on Eleventh Amendment, 165
eminent domain and, 310–314
enemy combatant decision, 93
exclusionary rule and, 360
executive privilege decision, 53
on felons' voting rights, 235
flag desecration decision, 195, 196
Fourth Amendment rules under, 364, 365
freedom of ideas under, 177
FSLA application to states decision, 157
gender-based classifications decision, 282
Gun-Free School Zone Act decision, 24–26, 29, 161–163
habeas corpus decision, 400, 401–402

impartial jury decision, 380
independent counsel decision, 73, 74, 75
Indian Gaming Regulatory Act decision, 166, 167
interstate commerce decision, 24–27
Iran hostage crisis decision, 101
land restrictions by governments decision, 310
leadership of, 7, 67, 168–169
legislative veto decision, 78
line-item veto decision, 35
medical marijuana decision, 14, 28–29, 168
mentally retarded capital punishment decision, 390
minimum legal age for drinking decision, 33–34
Miranda decision, 127, 372–373
nuclear-waste disposal decision, 161
online indecency decision, 208
peyote use in religious ceremonies decision, 212
physician-assisted suicide decision, 341, 342, 343
private developers and eminent domain decision, 313, 314
property tax funding of schools decision, 290
random drug tests in schools decision, 364
right to die decision, 339, 340, 341
school desegregation and, 256
school voucher program decision, 214, 215, 216
seat belt arrest decision, 361
sentencing guidelines decision, 394, 395
sexual harassment decision, 285
soft money decision, 250

state sovereignty and, 14, 129, 159–169
Supreme Court appointment of, 64, 66, 119, 319
Taiwan mutual defense treaty decision, 43
Ten Commandments display decision, 220, 221
Violence Against Women Act decision, 26–27, 29, 161, 163, 165
VMI women's admission decision, 283, 285
Reid v. Covert (1957), 44
Reinhold, Robert, 415–417
Religion, freedom of, 209–222
aid to parochial schools and religious organizations, 177
door-to-door solicitation and, 210
Establishment Clause, 212–222, 355
Free Exercise Clause, 209–212, 355
incorporation doctrine, 355
prayer in public schools and, 212, 216–219
religious displays, 212, 219–222
taxpayer suits limiting federal funds to promote religion, 433
wall of separation and, 212–216
Religious displays, 212, 219–222
Removal power of president, 7, 55, 68–75
Reno v. American Civil Liberties Union (1997), 207–209
Reporter's privilege, 205
Republican Party, 250, 259
Resegregation, 272
Residency requirements, 235, 292
Reston, James, 224–226
Restraint, Supreme Court's rules of, 105
Restrictive covenants, 253–254, 264
Retrial of criminal defendants, 399

Retroactive obligations, 139
Reversals of rulings by Court
by constitutional amendments, 120–122
of legislature, 120–122
Revolution of 1937, 17–20, 183–188
Reynolds v. Sims (1964), 237–239
Reynolds v. United States (1879), 209
Rice v. Santa Fe Elevator Corp. (1947), 144
Richardson v. Ramirez (1974), 235
Richmond; Doe v. (1976), 331
Richmond v. J. A. Croson Co. (1989), 272
Richmond Newspapers, Inc. v. Commonwealth of Virginia (1980), 205
RICO (Racketeer Influenced and Corrupt Organizations Act of 1970), 25–26
"Ride circuit," Supreme Court justices requirement to, 56
Riegel v. Medtronic, Inc. (2008), 147
Right to die, 338–341
Rita v. United States (2007), 397
Roberts, John G., Jr., *403*
abortion rights and, 153, 298, 328
Court of, 403–433
criminal procedure under, 352
criticism of Court action by, 133
freedom of ideas under, 177
habeas corpus for detainees decision, 3, 4, 98
handgun ban decision, 299, 344–347, 405, 410
issue ads decision, 250, 251
judicial restraint and, 105–106
judicial temperament of, 407–410
military commissions decision, 96, 97
partial-birth abortion decision, 328, 330

preemption of personal injury lawsuits and, 147
race-based school assignment decision, 256, 264, 275–278, 430, 433
relationship with Congress during term of, 7
sentencing guidelines decision, 397
state rights and, 133
Supreme Court appointment of, 67, 119, 328, 403–404, 430
unconstitutionality of statues during term of, 7
voting record of, 67
Roberts, Owen J.
AAA taxation decision, 32
flag salute decision, 186, 187, 188
minimum wage for women and children decision, 21
National Labor Relations Act decision, 22
New Deal legislation and, 20
right to counsel decision, 376
Supreme Court appointment of, 115
union assembly in public places decision, 184
Robinson, Joseph T., 113
Robinson v. California (1962), 382
Roe v. Flores-Ortega (2000), 379
Roe v. Wade (1973). *See also* Abortion rights
abortion rights, 153, 319–323, 324
Burger Court and, 126
Court after, 323–337
Kennedy and, 415
privacy and substantive liberty and, 298
protests against, *295*
public opinion and, 127
reaffirmation of, 66
Roberts federal court confirmation hearings and, 407
Scalia and, 414
women's rights movement, 279

Romer v. Evans (1996), 292
Roosevelt, Franklin D. *See also* Court-packing plan; New Deal and Court
  arms embargo and, 99–100
  Court's judicial power and, 112–114
  executive agreements and, 100
  farm relief program of, 32
  on interstate commerce, 19
  Japanese American internment and, 1, *85*, 86, 87–88, 126
  military tribunals and, 86–87
  Supreme Court appointments of, 23, 62, 112, 114
  war powers and, 84
Roosevelt, Theodore, 61–62
Roper v. Simmons (2005), 389
Rosen, Jeffrey, 127
Rosenberg, Julius & Ethel, 123
Ross v. Moffitt (1971), 398–399
Rostker v. Goldberg (1981), 42, 282
Roth v. United States (1957), 206
Routine traffic stops, searches during, 365
Runaway slaves, 135
Runyon v. McCrary (1976), 267
Russia, criticism of U.S. troops sent to, 179
Rutledge, Wiley
  flag salute decision, 186
  transportation of parochial school children decision, 213

Sabbath, refusal to work on, 210
Saboteurs during World War II, 86–87
Saenz v. Roe (1999), 292
St. Patrick's Day Parade, refusal of gay participation in, 334
San Antonio Ind. School Dis. v. Rodriguez (1973), 153, 289–291
Sanford, Edward T.
  freedom of speech decision, 180
  removal power decision, 69

Sanford, John, 257
Saunders, Barry, 229
Sawyer, Charles, 89, 114
Scalia, Antonin
  abortion rights decision, 325–326
  affirmative action decision, 273
  antisodomy law decision, 334
  background checks for gun purchase decision, 130, 161
  cigarette smokers' damage suits decision, 145
  election of 2000 decision, 242, 243, 244
  enemy combatant decision, 3, 4, 92, 98
  exclusionary rule decision, 352, 365, 366
  flag desecration decision, 194
  Ginsburg and, 414
  Gun-Free School Zone Act decision, 162
  habeas corpus for detainees decision, 3, 4, 98
  handgun ban decision, 345–346
  independent counsel decision, 73, 74
  Indian Gaming Regulatory Act decision, 166
  issue ads decision, 252
  juvenile offender capital punishment decision, 392, 393–394
  line-item veto decision, 35
  medical marijuana decision, 28
  mentally retarded capital punishment decision, 390
  military commissions decision, 97
  Miranda decision, 373
  nuclear-waste disposal decision, 161
  online indecency decision, 208
  partial-birth abortion decision, 330
  peyote use in religious ceremonies decision, 210, 211, 212

physician-assisted suicide decision, 343
  private developers and eminent domain decision, 313
  race-based school assignment decision, 276
  racial redistricting decision, 240
  random drug tests in schools decision, 364
  right to die decision, 338–339
  Roberts Court and, 404, 410, 412–414, 433
  school voucher program decision, 215
  seat belt arrest decision, 361
  sentencing guidelines decision, 395
  state immunity from citizen suit decision, 130
  Supreme Court appointment of, 66, 323, 413
  Ten Commandments display decision, 221
  Thomas and, 423
  Violence Against Women Act decision, 165
  VMI women's admission decision, 283
Schaefer v. United States (1920), 179
Schechter Poultry Corp. v. United States (1936), 17–19, 76
Schenck, Carl, 179
Schenck v. United States (1919), 179
Schneckloth v. Bustamonte (1973), 363
School desegregation
  affirmative action, 271–275
  all-white admission policy, 254
  Brown and "massive resistance," *265*, 265–269
  Burger Court and desegregation, 269–271
  challenges to, 264–271
  freedom of choice plans, 266

integration plans, 424
  magnet school plan, 156–157, 272
  major Court decisions (1954–2007), 267
  property taxes and, 156–157
  public opinion and, 126, 264
  race-based school assignments, 153, 256, 275–278, 430, 433
  Rehnquist Court and, 256
  university admissions, 423–424
Schools
  aid to parochial schools, 214
  Amish children and compulsory school attendance, 210
  armband war protests in, 191–193
  attendance requirement, 153
  Bible reading in public schools, 216
  children of illegal aliens and, 287–289
  desegregation. *See* Desegregation
  drug testing in, 364–365
  educational equity reforms, 153
  equal access to public school buildings, 219
  equipment for parochial schools, 214
  Establishment Clause and, 212–216
  federal court jurisdiction and, 156–157
  foreign language instruction in, 153, 301–303
  guns in school zones, 7, 24–25, 129, 161
  prayer in and equal access, 212, 216–219
  property tax funding of, 289–291
  public school education requirement, 153, 304–305
  remedial services for parochial students, 214
  speech, freedom of, 177, 191–193, 194

subsidies of teacher salaries, 214
teachers, members of subversive organizations as, 188
textbooks for parochial schools, 209–210, 214
transportation of parochial school children, 212–213
vouchers, 214–216, 430
wall of separation and parochial schools, 212–216
war protests in, 191–193
Scott, Dred. *See* Dred Scott decision
Scott v. Harris (2001), 362
Scott v. Sanford (1857). *See* Dred Scott decision
Scottsboro Cases (1932), 356–359, 376, 382
Searches and seizures, 360–367
arrests and, 360–362
incorporation doctrine and, 354, 355
no-knock searches, 365–367, 433
searches, 298, 349–352, 354–356, 362–367
Seat belt, arrest for not wearing, 360–362
Second Amendment, 298, 299, 344–347, 405, 410
Second Legal Tender Cases (1871), 10
Second medical opinions, HMOs and, 144
Sedition Act of 1798, 177
Sedition Act of 1917, 178
Selective Draft Law Cases, 40–42
Selective Service. *See* Draft law
Selective Service Act of 1917, 179
Self-incrimination. *See* Interrogation and confession
Selma, Alabama, march on, 232
Seminole Tribe v. Florida (1997), 130, 165–168
Senate
election of senators, 226
subpoena power of, 45–47
treaties and, 42

Seneca Falls conference, 227
Sentencing, 382–397
capital punishment, 382–394
guidelines, 382, 394–397
judge and jury in, 394–397, 399
September 11, 2001, terrorist attacks, 1–2
"Seven Dirty Words," 206
Seventeenth Amendment, 226
Seventh Day Adventist, refusal to work on Sabbath, 210
Sex discrimination, 278–286
FMLA, 168
gender-based classifications, 280–283
sexual harassment, 285–286
women's rights movement, 279–280
Sexual harassment, 285–286
Sexual orientation, discrimination on. *See* Gay rights
Shane, Scott, 431–433
Shapiro, Steven, 407
Shapiro v. Thompson (1969), 292
Shaw v. Reno (1993), 239–242
Shelley, J.D., 253, 254
Shelley v. Kraemer (1948), 253–256
Sherbert v. Verner (1963), 210
Sherman Antitrust Act of 1890, 14, 140
Shiras, George, Jr., 11, 12
"Sick chicken case," 17–18, 76
Sirica, John, 51–54
Sixteenth Amendment, 13, 30, 355
Sixth Amendment. *See also* Counsel, right to; Trials
incorporation doctrine and, 153
provisions of, 353
sentencing guidelines, 395
Waite and Fuller Courts and, 13
Skinner v. Railway Labor Executives' Association (1989), 364

Slaughterhouse Cases (1873), 149, 261, 299
Slavery, 256–257. *See also* Dred Scott decision
abolishment of, 260
ban on importation of slaves, 256
Civil War and, 260
Constitution and, 256
Sleeper cells, 1
Slum clearing, 309–310
Smith v. Allwright (1944), 230–231
Smith Act of 1940, 188–189
Snyder v. Louisiana (2008), 381
Sobriety checkpoints, 362
Socialist Party, 179, 180–181
Social Security Act of 1935, 32, 113
Social Security benefits and gender-based classifications, 282
Sodomy, laws against, 314, 331–337
"Soft money" and political ad regulation, 249–252
Sonzinsky v. United States (1937), 30
Souter, David H.
abortion rights decision, 126, 323, 325, 326, 417
affirmative action decision, 273
antisodomy law decision, 335
cigarette smokers' damage suits decision, 145
detainee decision, 3, 4, 94, 95
election of 2000 decision, 243, 244
Gun-Free School Zone Act decision, 162, 163
habeas corpus for detainees decision, 3, 4, 401
Indian Gaming Regulatory Act decision, 166, 167
issue ads decision, 252
juvenile offender capital punishment decision, 392
line-item veto decision, 35
medical marijuana decision, 28
mentally retarded capital punishment decision, 391

military commissions decision, 97
Miranda decision, 373
nuclear-waste disposal decision, 161
online indecency decision, 208
physician-assisted suicide decision, 343
private developers and eminent domain decision, 313
race-based school assignment decision, 277
racial redistricting decision, 240
random drug tests in schools decision, 364
Roberts Court and, 404, 418–421
school voucher program decision, 215
seat belt arrest decision, 360, 361
sentencing guidelines decision, 394, 395
state immunity from citizen suit decision, 130, 132
Supreme Court appointment of, 66, 323, 418
Ten Commandments display decision, 220, 221, 222
Violence Against Women Act decision, 164, 165
South Carolina v. Katzenbach (1966), 232
South Carolina tariff and nullification theory, 135
South Dakota v. Dole (1987), 33–34, 157
Sovereign immunity, 129, 154
Sovereignty of states, 154–169
"cooperative federalism" and post-New Deal Court, 157–159
dual federalism and early courts, 154–157
Rehnquist Court and revival of state sovereignty, 14, 24, 159–169, 414

Soviet Union, executive agreement with, 100
Spanish-American War, 37, 99
Special prosecutors, 73–75
Speech, freedom of, 183–196
   bad tendency test, 180, 181
   Bill of Rights, 174
   campaign finance and flag burning and, 194–196, 417
   clear and present danger test, 179, 181, 188, 191
   communists and subversives in Cold War, 188
   equal access of religious groups to public buildings, 219
   high school students, 177
   incorporation doctrine and, 153, 355
   revolution of 1937, 184–188
   Sedition Act and, 177
   states and, 179–181
   time, space, and manner restrictions, 193
   Vietnam War era and, 191–196
   war and, 177–179
   Warren Court and, 188–191
Speedy trial, 353, 355
Spending limits for political campaigns, 245–249
Spending power, 29, 31–36
Spinelli v. United States (1969), 363
Spousal consent to abortion, 323, 324
Stanford v. Kentucky (1989), 389
Stansberry, Homer, 103, 105
Stanton, Elizabeth Cady, 227
Stanton v. Baltic Mining Co. (1916), 13
Starr, Kenneth, 84, 250
State laws, unconstitutionality of, 106
States and the Court, 129–169
   Bill of Rights and post–Civil War amendments, 148–151

Commerce Clause, 24, 139–147
Contract Clause, 137–139
criminal trials, review of, 356
early Court clashes and federal supremacy, 133–135
early developments, 133–136
economy and, 137–147
enfranchisement and, 235
equal protection and due process, 151–153
Free Exercise Clause and, 210
free press, 181–183
free speech and, 179–181
Georgia's battle with Court and beyond, 135–136
incorporation doctrine, 153, 180, 300, 354, 355
individual and, 147–153
jury trials and, 379
privacy, right to, 153
sovereignty of states, 14, 24, 154–169, 414
State supreme courts, review of decisions by, 106
Statutory rape and gender-based classifications, 282
Steel mills seizure under presidential war powers, 55, 84, 89–91, 114
Stenberg v. Carhart (2000), 324, 328
Sterilization of habitual criminals, 306–307
Stevens, John Paul
   abortion rights decision, 325
   affirmative action decision, 273
   anti-loitering ordinances decision, 362
   antisodomy law decision, 331, 332, 335
   campaign finance decision, 248
   capital punishment decision, 385, 386, 387, 389

children of illegal aliens and public education decision, 287
cigarette smokers' damage suits decision, 145, 146–147
courthouse accessibility for disabled decision, 168
election of 2000 decision, 243–244
enemy combatant decision, 92
federal court appointment of, 410
flag desecration decision, 195
FSLA application to states decision, 158
Gun-Free School Zone Act decision, 162, 163
habeas corpus for detainees decision, 2, 3, 4, 95, 401
handgun ban decision, 346
indecency decision, 207
independent counsel decision, 74
Indian Gaming Regulatory Act decision, 166, 167
issue ads decision, 252
juvenile offender capital punishment decision, 392
legislative veto decision, 78
line-item veto decision, 34, 35, 36
medical marijuana decision, 27, 28, 168
mentally retarded capital punishment decision, 391
military commissions decision, 95, 96, 97, 98
Miranda decision, 373
nuclear-waste disposal decision, 161
online indecency decision, 207, 208–209
peyote use in religious ceremonies decision, 212
physician-assisted suicide decision, 343, 344

presidential immunity decision, 82, 114
private developers and eminent domain decision, 312–313, 314
race-based school assignment decision, 277
racial redistricting decision, 240
random drug tests in schools decision, 364
Roberts Court and, 404, 410–412
school voucher program decision, 215
seat belt arrest decision, 361
sentencing guidelines decision, 394, 395, 396
soft money decision, 250
state immunity from citizen suit decision, 130–131
student speech decision, 177
Taiwan mutual defense treaty decision, 43
temporary property restrictions decision, 311
Ten Commandments display decision, 222
Violence Against Women Act decision, 165
wine shipment direct to customers decision, 143
Steward Machine Co. v. Davis (1937), 32
Stewart, Potter F.
   abortion rights decision, 321
   Bible reading in public schools decision, 216
   campaign finance decision, 248
   capital punishment decision, 383–384, 385, 386, 387, 388
   Commerce Clause decision, 144
   contraceptive access decision, 296, 315
   Contract Clause decision, 139
   exclusionary rule decision, 350, 351

executive privilege decision, 54

listening devices in public phone booth decision, 363

Pentagon Papers decision, 175, 176, 202, 203–204

prayer in public schools decision, 216, 217, 218

property tax funding of schools decision, 290

public officials libel decision, 197

on racial discrimination, 266

reapportionment decision, 237, 238

right to counsel decision, 368–369, 378

Supreme Court appointment of, 62

Taiwan mutual defense treaty decision, 43

Vietnam War, on Court declining to hear case on, 39–40, 90

Stogner v. California (2003), 147

Stone, Harlan F.
firearm taxation decision, 30
flag salute decision, 184, 185
footnote 4 of *Carolene Products* and, 309
on interstate commerce regulation, 23
Japanese American curfew decision, 87
New Deal legislation and, 20
NLRA decision, 22
price control decision, 86
rational basis standard decision, 309
removal power decision, 69
sterilization of habitual criminals decision, 307
subpoena power of Senate decision, 46, 47
Supreme Court appointment of, 62

Stone v. Mississippi (1879), 137

Stone v. Powell (1976), 363, 400

Stop and frisk, 363

Strauder v. West Virginia (1880), 379

Strickland v. Washington (1984), 378–379

Strict scrutiny standard, 272

Strong, William
appointment of, 10
Legal Tender Act decision, 10

Subpoena power of Congress, 45–47, 89

Substantive due process, 296–307

Suffrage. *See* Political participation rights; Women

Sugar monopoly, 14, 140

Sullivan, L. B., 197, 198

Sunday closing laws, 210

Supremacy Clause, 133. *See also* States and the Court

Supreme Court appointments. *See also specific justices and presidents*
confirmation process, 115–119
president and, 60–69

Surprise justice, 404

Suspect classes, 286–293
aliens, 286–289
other classes, 292–293
residency requirements, 292
sexual orientation, 292–293
wealth-based classifications, 153, 289–291

Sutherland, George
arms embargo decision, 99
coal mining interstate commerce decision, 19–20
as conservative, 17
executive agreement decision, 100
foreign instruction in schools decision, 302
minimum wage for women and children decision, 17
Minnesota mortgage moratorium law decision, 138
New Deal legislation and, 20
removal power decision, 70, 71, 72

"Scottsboro Boys" decision, 357, 358

Strauder v. Charlotte-Mecklenburg County Board of Education (1971), 267, 269–271

Swayne, Noah H., 59

Sweatt, Herman, 254

Sweatt v. Painter (1950), 254, 255

Symbolic speech, 191–193

Syndicalism, 181, 191

Taft, William Howard
appointment to Court of, 62
as Chief Justice, 17, 109
law enforcement power of president decision, 75
minimum wage for women and children decision, 17
removal power decision, 68, 69, 70
resignation and death of, 17, 109
Supreme Court appointments by, 62

Taft-Hartley Act of 1947, 89, 245

Tahoe-Sierra Preservation Council, Inc. v. Regional Planning Agency (2002), 311

Taiwan mutual defense treaty, 43–44

Takahasi v. Fish and Game Commission (1948), 286

Takings Clause, 148, 299, 300, 310

Taney, Roger B.
Commerce Clause and, 139
Contract Clause decision, 137
death of, 259–260
Dred Scott decision, 257, 258, 259–260
dual federalism under, 154
due process decision, 299
Fugitive Slave Act decision, 135
habeas corpus suspension decision, 56–57, 109
leadership of, 61
Missouri Compromise decision, 9
Prize Cases, 39
public opinion and, 124

Supreme Court appointment of, 61
voting rights decision, 227

Tapes, subpoena for Nixon's, 51–54, 79–81, 114

Taxing power, 9, 11–13, 20, 28–31, 106

Taylor, Stuart, Jr., 33–34, 73–75, 331–333, 380–381

Taylor v. Louisiana (1975), 379

Teachers, members of subversive organizations as, 188

Teague v. Lane (1989), 400

Teapot Dome Scandal, 45–47, 79

Television and radio stations, regulation of, 205

Temporary property restrictions, 311

Ten Commandments, display of. *See* Religious displays

Tennessee v. Lane (2004), 168

Tenth Amendment, 44, 154, 157, 168

Tenure limitations for members of Congress, 50

Tenure of Office Act of 1867, 68

Terry v. Ohio (1968), 363

"Test oaths," 147–148

Texas v. Johnson (1989), 194–196

Textbooks for parochial schools, 209–210, 214

Thermal scanner, search by police with, 364

Thirteenth Amendment, 40, 120, 149–151, 260, 261

Thirty-day residency requirement to vote, 235

Thomas, Clarence
abortion rights decision, 126, 323, 325–326
affirmative action decision, 273
antisodomy law decision, 334
cigarette smokers' damage suits decision, 145

detainee decision, 3, 4, 92, 93, 95
election of 2000 decision, 242, 243, 244
exclusionary rule decision, 366
Gun-Free School Zone Act decision, 162
habeas corpus for detainees decision, 3, 4
Indian Gaming Regulatory Act decision, 166
issue ads decision, 252
line-item veto decision, 35
medical marijuana decision, 29
mentally retarded capital punishment decision, 390
military commissions decision, 96, 97
Miranda decision, 373
nuclear-waste disposal decision, 161
online indecency decision, 208
partial-birth abortion decision, 330
physician-assisted suicide decision, 343
private developers and eminent domain decision, 313
race-based school assignment decision, 276, 277
racial redistricting decision, 240
random drug tests in schools decision, 364, 365
Roberts Court and, 404, 421–424, 433
Scalia and, 423
school voucher program decision, 215–216
seat belt arrest decision, 361
sentencing guidelines decision, 394, 395
state immunity from citizen suit decision, 131
Supreme Court appointment of, 67, 119, 323
Ten Commandments display decision, 221

Violence Against Women Act decision, 165
VMI women's admission decision, 283
wine shipment direct to customers decision, 143
Thompson, John, 45
Thompson v. Oklahoma (1988), 389
"Three-fifths Clause," 256
Tilden, Samuel J., 228
Tillman Act of 1907, 245
Time, space, and manner restrictions on speech, 193
Tinker, Mary Beth, *192*
Tinker v. Des Moines Independent Community School District (1969), 191–193, *192*
Tison v. Arizona (1987), 389
Title VII of Civil Rights Act of 1964, 279
Tocqueville, Alexis de, 1
Totality of the circumstances standard, 367, 376
Townsend v. Sain (1963), 399–400
Traffic stops by police, 362, 365
Train v. City of New York (1975), 79
Transcripts for criminal defendants, 289, 398–399
Transportation of parochial school students, 212–213
Transportation workers, drug testing of, 364
Trash, interstate shipment of, 144
Travel, right to, 292
Treason, crime of, 352
Treaties, 36, 42–43, 98, 99. *See also* Foreign affairs
Trials, 376–382. *See also* Counsel, right to
criminal, 376–382
double jeopardy, 353, 354, 355, 399
indictments, 353–354
jury, right to impartial, 376, 379–382
notice of charges, 376
press at, 205
public trials, 355, 376
retrials, 399

speedy trial requirement, 353, 355
transcripts, 289, 398–399
witnesses at, 353, 355
Truman, Harry S.
Court's judicial power and, 112–114
steel mills seizure by, 55, 84, 89–91, 114
Supreme Court appointments of, 62
Truncated hearings for enemy combatants, 1
Turner Broadcasting v. FCC (1997), 205
Turow, Scott, 374–375
Twenty-third Amendment, 235

Ullmann v. United States (1956), 47
Unicameral legislatures, 235
Uniform Code of Military Justice (UCMJ), 1, 95, 115
United Haulers Association, Inc. v. Oneida-Herkimer Solid Waste Management Authority (2007), 144
United Kingdom
Falkland Islands and, 99
Lend-Lease Agreement with, 100
U.S. military courts executive agreement and, 44
Virginia debtors and, 134
United States v. See name of opposing party
United Steelworkers of America v. Weber (1979), 271
University admissions, racial preferences in, 272–275, 423–424
University of Michigan affirmative action cases, 272–275
Unremunerated rights, 296
Urban renewal, 309–310
U.S. Chamber of Commerce, 250
U.S. Term Limits v. Thorton (1995), 50

Vacco v. Quill (1997), 341–344
Valeo, Frank R., 246

Vallandingham, Clement, 177–178
Van Devanter, Willis
as conservative, 17
New Deal legislation and, 20
removal power decision, 69
retirement of, 112, 114
subpoena power of Senate decision, 46
Vare, William S., 47
Vaughn, George, 254
Vermont, franchise in, 227
Vernonia School District No. 47J v. Acton (1995), 364
Veto power
legislative process and, 55
legislative veto, 76–78
line-item veto, 34–36
Vieth v. Jubelirer (2004), 239
Vietnam War
Congress and, 37, 39–41
freedom of speech and, 191–196
president and, 91
Vinson, Frederick M.
death of, 265
freedom of speech decision, 188
restrictive covenants decision, 254, 255–256
steel mills seizure decision, 90–91
Supreme Court appointment of, 62
transportation of parochial school children decision, 213
Violence Against Women Act of 1994, 26–27, 29, 161, 163–165, 430
Virginia; United States v. (1995), 283–285, 414, 427
Virginia Military Institute (VMI), admission of women to, 283–285, 414, 427
Virginia State Board of Pharmacy v. Virginia Citizens Consumer Council (1976), 206
Void, declaration of acts of Congress by Court, 9
Voter registration, 232

Voting rights. *See* African Americans; Political participation rights; Women

Voting Rights Act of 1965, 230, 232–235, 242, 266

Voucher program for schools, 214–216, 430

Vuitch; United States v. (1971), 319

Wabash, St. Louis & Pacific Railway Co. v. Illinois (1886), 140

Waddington, Sarah, 319

Wagner Act of 1935, 21–24

Wainwright v. Sykes (1977), 400

Wainwright v. Will (1985), 381

Waite, Morrison R.
  civil rights statutes and, 13
  Colfax, Louisiana massacre decision, 227
  Contract Clause decision, 137
  women's suffrage decision, 227

Wall of separation and parochial schools, 212–216

Walls, Carlotta, *253*

War. *See also* National defense; *specific conflicts and wars*
  powers, 55, 56, 84–98
  speech, freedom of, 177–179

Warden v. Hayden (1967), 354

Ware v. Hylton (1796), 134

War of 1812, 37, 56

War on terror, 1–4, 84, 92–98, 108

War Powers Act of 1973, 39, 91

Warrants. *See* Arrests; Searches and seizures

Warren, Earl
  capital punishment and, 382
  contraceptive access decision, 297
  criminal procedure under, 127, 133, 352
  death of, 268–269
  draft card burning decision, 191
  exclusionary rule decision, 350, 352, 360, 363

exclusion of member of Congress decision, 48, 49
  impeachment and, 124
  Miranda decision, 369, 370, 371
  prayer in public schools decision, 217
  public officials libel decision, 197
  public opinion and the Court leadership of, 126
  reapportionment decision, 237, 238
  school desegregation decision, 265–266
  speech, freedom of and, 188–191
  stop and frisk decision, 363
  Supreme Court appointment of, 62, 188
  as surprise justice, 403
  Voting Rights Act decision, 232

Washington, George
  executive privilege and, 79
  foreign affairs and, 55–56
  Supreme Court appointments of, 61

Washington v. Glucksberg (1997), 341–344

Washington v. Texas (1967), 355

Washington, County of v. Gunther (1981), 279

Washington, D.C.
  handgun ban decision, 345
  voting rights for, 235

Washington Post, 173, 201

Waste, interstate shipment of, 144

Watergate scandal, 51–55, 73, 79–81, 114, 245

Watkins, John, 47

Watkins v. United States (1957), 47, 189

Watson; United States v. (1976), 360

Waxman, Seth, 250

Wayne, James M., 59

Wealth-based classifications, 153, 289–291

Weaver, Warren, Jr., 52–54, 290–291, 320–322

Webster v. Reproductive Health Services (1989), 323, 324

Weeks v. United States (1914), 354–356

Weisman, Steven R., 66–67

Welfare benefits and medical care, residency requirements and, 292

Wesberry v. Sanders (1964), 239

West Coast Hotel Co. v. Parrish (1937), 21, 308

West Virginia State Board of Education v. Barnette (1943), 186–188

White, Byron R.
  abortion rights decision, 320, 325
  antisodomy law decision, 331, 332, 333
  campaign finance decision, 248
  capital punishment decision, 383–384, 386, 387
  cigarette smokers' damage suits decision, 145
  confidential source decision, 205
  contraceptive access decision, 298, 315
  deadly force use by police officer decision, 362
  executive privilege decision, 54
  flag desecration decision, 195
  FSLA application to states decision, 158
  impartial jury decision, 379, 380, 381
  independent counsel decision, 74
  legislative veto decision, 78
  Miranda decision, 370–371
  nuclear-waste disposal decision, 161
  Pentagon Papers decision, 175, 202, 203–204
  peyote use in religious ceremonies decision, 212
  prayer in public schools decision, 217
  property tax funding of schools decision, 290

public officials libel decision, 197
  racial redistricting decision, 240
  reapportionment decision, 238
  right to counsel decision, 368, 378
  right to die decision, 339
  Supreme Court appointment of, 62

White, Edward D.
  adulterated food seizure decision, 14
  draft law cases, 41
  income tax decision, 11
  taxing power decision, 30

Whites-only policies, 230, 261

Whitney, Anita, 181

Whitney v. California (1927), 181

Whittaker, Charles E., 350

Whitus v. Georgia (1967), 379

Whren v. United States (1996), 365

Wickard v. Filburn (1942), 27

Wiggins v. Smith (2003), 379

Wilkerson v. Utah (1878), 382

Williams v. Florida (1970), 379

Williams v. Illinois (1970), 289

Williams v. Mississippi (1898), 229

Williams v. Suffolk Ins. (1893), 99

Wilson, Woodrow
  Court's judicial power and, 109
  removal power and, 68–70
  Supreme Court appointments of, 62
  war powers and, 84

Wilson v. Arkansas (1995), 365

Wilson v. Blackbird Marsh Co. (1829), 139

Wilson-Gorman Tariff Act of 1894, 9

Wine, direct shipment to customers, 142–144

Wiretapping, 298, 363

Wisconsin v. Yoder (1972), 210

Witherspoon v. Illinois (1968), 381

Witnesses, right to confront, 353, 355
Wolf, Julius, 362
Wolf v. Colorado (1949), 350, 355, 362
Women. *See also* Sex discrimination
  attorneys, licensure as, 278
  draft exemption for, 42, 282
  Equal Protection Clause and, 153
  hours of work, 278
  impartial jury, right to, 379, 381
  interstate transportation for immoral purposes, 15
  minimum wage for, 16, 21

rights movement, 279–280
violence against, 26–27, 29, 161, 430
voting rights and, 17, 226, 227, 254, 261, 278
work hour limitations for, 16–17
Wood, Lewis, 86–87, 88–89, 186–188
Woodson v. North Carolina (1976), 388, 389
Worcester, Samuel, 109, 135
Worcester v. Georgia (1832), 109, 135
Working conditions, regulation of, 15
World War I
  Congress and, 37, 40

president and, 84, 85
protest during, 179
World War II
  Congress and, 37
  Japanese American internment, 1, *85*, 86, 87–88, 126, 264
  president and, 84, 85–89
World Wide Web and freedom of ideas, 206–209

Yakus v. United States (1944), 42, 85–86
Yarbrough, Ex parte (1884), 229
Yarbrough, Jaspar, 229
Yates v. United States (1957), 189

Yazoo River land speculation, 137
Yerger, Edward M., 105
Yick Wo v. Hopkins (1886), 152
Young, Ex parte (1908), 154–156
Young v. American Mini Theatres, Inc. (1976), 206
Youngstown Sheet and Tire Co. v. Sawyer (1952), 89–91, 114

Zeigler, Ron, 51
Zelman v. Simmons-Harris (2002), 214–216
Zones of privacy, 315
Zoning ordinances, 206, 300